Solving the Mystery of
BABYLON THE GREAT

Tracking the Beast from the Synagogue to the Vatican

Edward Hendrie

"So he carried me away in the spirit into the wilderness: and I saw a woman sit upon a scarlet coloured beast, full of names of blasphemy, having seven heads and ten horns. And the woman was arrayed in purple and scarlet colour, and decked with gold and precious stones and pearls, having a golden cup in her hand full of abominations and filthiness of her fornication: And upon her forehead *was* a name written, **MYSTERY, BABYLON THE GREAT, THE MOTHER OF HARLOTS AND ABOMINATIONS OF THE EARTH**. And I saw the woman drunken with the blood of the saints, and with the blood of the martyrs of Jesus: and when I saw her, I wondered with great admiration." Revelation 17:3-6.

Second Edition
Copyright © 2010, 2011, 2012 by Edward Hendrie
All rights reserved.
All Scripture references are to the Authorized (King James) Version of the Holy Bible, unless otherwise indicated.

Printed in the U.S.A.

www.mysterybabylonthegreat.net

EdwardHendrie@gmail.com

ISBN: 978-0-9832627-0-1 (paperback edition)
ISBN: 978-0-9832627-1-8 (Kindle ebook edition)
ISBN: 978-0-9832627-2-5 (Epub ebook edition)

Library of Congress Control Number: 2011900513

Other books by Edward Hendrie:

● Antichrist Conspiracy: *Inside the Devil's Lair*
● The Anti-Gospel: *The Perversion of Christ's Grace Gospel*
● 911 - Enemies Foreign and Domestic: *Secret Evidence Censored from the Official Record Proves Traitors Aided Israel in Attacking the USA*
● Bloody Zion: *Refuting the Jewish Fables that Sustain Israel's War Against God and Man*
● What Shall I Do to Inherit Eternal Life? *The Surprising Answer to the Most Important Question Ever Asked*

Available at:
www.antichristconspiracy.com
www.mysterybabylonthegreat.net
www.911enemies.com
www.antigospel.com
www.lulu.com
www.amazon.com
http://books.google.com
www.barnesandnoble.com

TABLE OF CONTENTS

Foreword by Texe Marrs

There are few prophecies in the Holy Bible more heart-stirring and breathtaking than the image in Revelation 17 of the Great Harlot, the woman who rides upon a frightening, scarlet-coloured beast with seven heads and ten horns. Imperiously dressed in purple and scarlet, with a golden cup in her hand full of abominations and filth of her fornication, the brazen Harlot is decked with gold and precious stones and pearls. The Apostle John, whose heavenly vision so vividly pictured the strange woman, noted especially the revealing name she had written upon her forehead, MYSTERY, BABYLON THE GREAT, THE MOTHER OF HARLOTS AND ABOMINATIONS OF THE EARTH.

The Apostle was clearly stricken when seeing this powerful image for he was told in the vision that the seven heads of the beast represented seven mountains that the woman sat upon. The woman, Paul was told, signifies a notorious, yet great city. This is that city, said the angel in the vision, "which reigneth over the kings of the earth."

Perhaps the most terrifying of all was John's recognition of the awful specter of death that the woman represented. "And I saw the woman drunken with the blood of the martyrs of Jesus," testified the Apostle. "And when I saw her, I wondered with great admiration."

Some claim that there is a beautiful side of evil, enticing, dangerous, monstrous and deadly, yet somehow sickeningly alluring and inviting. It seems that even the most wicked on rare occasions possess the ability to awe the world and fill onlookers with a curious combination of macabre, mystery, and trepidation.

Bible scholars say that the Apostle John wrote down his prophetic vision, which we know today as the Book of Revelation, in the year 92 AD. In the succeeding centuries, many have studied these awe-inspiring verses and have pondered and meditated on their meaning. Everyone knows how supremely important it is that humanity as a whole, but particularly the Christian Church, grasp the profound nature of these prophecies. The future of mankind itself and the destiny of every nation are bound up in this heaven-sent vision of endtime tragedy against the backdrop of divine victory.

Thankfully, God has designed and constructed His prophetic Word so that his disciples—the men and women who know and honor Jesus Christ as Lord—will be able to decipher and understand the meaning of these passages, though they be laden with seemingly obscure symbolic content. In Daniel 12:10 we discover the promise that God will empower His latter day servants with prophetic discernment:

> "And the wicked will do wickedly and none of the wicked shall understand. But the wise shall understand."

The "wise" refers to the godly person whose wisdom and knowledge come not from his own superior intelligence or inherent brain capacity but direct from God. As the Apostle Paul so joyously put it, "Christ in you, the hope of glory." It is a glorious thing that God does in imparting wisdom and understanding to His children.

Edward Hendrie has been given a very special gift of discernment, and I believe his book provides evidence of this. For centuries the saints have sought to uncover the symbolical secrets of the Great Harlot and the Beast of *Revelation*. Who is Mystery Babylon? What is the meaning of the sinister symbols found in these passages? Which city is being described as the "great city" so full of sin and decadence, and who are its citizens? Why do the woman and beast of *Revelation* seek the destruction of the holy people, the saints and martyrs of Jesus? What does it all mean for you and me today? *Solving the Mystery of Babylon the Great* answers these questions and more.

Edward Hendrie's discoveries are not based on prejudice but on solid evidence aligned forthrightly with the "whole counsel of God." He does not condone nor will he be a part of any project in which Bible verses are taken out of context, or in which scriptures are twisted to mean what they do not say.

Again and again you will find that Mr. Hendrie documents his assertions, backing up what he says with historical facts and proofs. Most important is that he buttresses his findings with scriptural understanding. The foundation for his research is sturdy because it is based on the bedrock of God's unshakeable Word.

Many sincere Protestant Christians, having studied the works of notable pastors, teachers, theologians and scholars, maintain that the identity of Mystery Babylon is none other than the Roman Catholic Church. Moreover, these good men and women assert that the Pope of Rome is the antichrist. In fact, this was the historical view as endorsed by Martin Luther and other reformers.

Edward Hendrie's work goes far in honoring the views and works of these excellent teachers, but he goes even further. He also takes their facts and comparative studies and builds on their conclusions. His investigation is greater in depth and more encompassing.

The prophecies center on Babylon and on the iniquities of that far-flung political, economic, cultural, and religious system. What was Babylon? What did its priests and leaders teach as their core doctrine? What were ancient Babylon's symbols and its abominations? Why has "Babylon" always been a codeword for spiritual decadence and sexual debauchery? Edward Hendrie's original research on these important issues is eye-opening.

Hendrie's book paints a convincing picture of the meaning of ancient Babylon and also shows how the Roman Catholic Church, the Papacy, and its rituals and practices, are mirror images of the Babylonian evil. But there is yet another religious system that is full to the brim with Babylonianism. The men and women immersed in this system promote a sordid and repulsive way of life that has definite connections to ancient Babylon and its satanic traditions. That system is *Judaism* and the culture of *World Jewry.*

What few know, but Edward Hendrie has discovered, is that from the inception of Christianity, the major enemy of God's Church and the number one polluter and destroyer of Christendom has been Pharisaic Judaism. Moreover, Jewry, a culture which is controlled and directed by rabbinical zealots, has historically been hostile to the Christian Church and to this day does everything in its considerable power to undermine and poison the roots of Biblical Christianity.

Hendrie demonstrates and proves this hateful animosity on the part of World Jewry and especially by those Jews active in the religion of Judaism. He explains and documents why the Jews are imbued with such an unjustifiable but overwhelming hatred and loathing for Christianity and Christians.

Contrary to what most people think to be the case, Hendrie documents that Judaism is not the religion of the Old Testament and the prophets. Instead, Judaism comes from the same perverted spiritual fountain as does the Roman Catholic Church: *Babylon.* Judaism's most holy book is the *Babylonian Talmud,* and the inner teachings of Judaism—an unscriptural, satanic religion embraced by its elders and high priests—is pure *Babylonianism.*

Hendrie even proves that it was Babylonian-believing Jews who founded the Roman Catholic Church. These Jewish infiltrators sought to wrest away the true Christian faith from the teachings and principles of the Apostles and the New Testament. The goal of these Jews was to remold the Christian Church into a weakened version of Phariseeism, itself based on dogma and practices the Jews had brought back to Jerusalem following their long Babylonian captivity.

Jesus told us that the Jews' religion is not of God but was constructed of man-made traditions. He bluntly accused the Pharisees (*The Encyclopedia Judaica* says that Phariseeism is today's Orthodox Jewry): "Ye are of your father the devil." Somehow, over the centuries these warnings and statements of Jesus were forgotten and now are unrespected by most evangelical Christians. How tragic, for if we but listened to what Jesus said, we would understand the grave danger that Christendom is confronted with today due to the satanic horrors of Judaism.

Hendrie, fortunately, *does* take into account these warnings of Jesus and also those of Paul, the apostles, and the prophets. His research and insights point us to a clear understanding of the two-pronged Babylonian enemy that even now is at our very doorstep.

Edward Hendrie proves from the Scriptures and from his own thorough investigation that both the Zionists and Rome are jointly involved in a despicable endtime conspiracy against God's Word and His saints. Together, they form the corrupt and ominous *Mystery Babylon* world system of evil pictured so poignantly in the book of *Revelation.*

Once you realize that Judaism, its offshoot, Zionism, and Rome's Catholicism come from the same bitter Babylonian waters, so much of the Bible and its prophecies come into focus. The haze and perplexity lift, and the gift of discernment is supernaturally conferred on the diligent child of God who thirsts for godly knowledge.

What a miraculous thing to see with a better vision the wonders that are now unfolding in our world as the prophecies, one-by-one, are unveiled in the clear light of day.

We remember what God said in the book of Daniel about the events of the latter days. Though God sends strong delusion to those who reject his learning, we are gratified to learn that, "the wise shall understand." In this spirit, Edward Hendrie solves for us the riddle of "Mystery Babylon."

Texe Marrs
Power of Prophecy
Austin, Texas

Author's Preface

The research for this book began over ten years ago. My first book was titled *Antichrist Conspiracy, Inside the Devil's Lair.*[1] The book was intended as an exposition on the unbiblical theology of the Roman Catholic Church. As I researched the theology of the Roman church, however, I discovered political, financial, and media tentacles flowing from the core of what was supposed to be a religious institution.

As I researched the Catholic religion and followed the tentacles I discovered a connection between the Catholic Church and Zionist Jews. The evidence was there, but the connections were not overt, they were in the shadows, concealed from view. It was clear that there was a synergism between Judaic and Catholic interests. I followed the evidence and reported my findings in *Antichrist Conspiracy*. After publishing *Antichrist Conspiracy*, I continued to dig deeper; I was able to find more solid evidence of the connection between Rome and Jerusalem. This book is the culmination of that research.

As I followed the tentacles from the Vatican I discovered that the Jewish connection with Rome was not simply one of synergy but rather one of control. I discovered credible evidence that the Roman Catholic Church was established by crypto-Jews as a false "Christian" front for a Judaic/Babylonian religion. That religion is the core of a world conspiracy against man and God. That is not a soft conspiracy theory based upon speculation; it is the hard truth supported by authoritative evidence, which is documented in this book.

Edward Hendrie
April 2010

Introduction

God's plan is to first establish the earthly and then the spiritual. "Howbeit that *was* not first which is spiritual, but that which is natural; and afterward that which is spiritual. The first man *is* of the earth, earthy: the second man *is* the Lord from heaven. As *is* the earthy, such are they also that are earthy: and as *is* the heavenly, such are they also that are heavenly." (1 Corinthians 15:46-48 AV) God will not reverse course and reestablish the earthly kingdom of Israel in place of his spiritual kingdom of Israel. That is contrary to his revealed plan. Fleshly Israel was intended by God for an example to us, his church. 1 Corinthians 10:6. It is not the circumcision of the flesh that counts but the circumcision of the heart. Colossians 2:11.

The bible makes clear that the old covenant made to fleshly Israel has vanished away, being replaced by the new covenant of faith in Jesus Christ. "In that he saith, A new covenant, he hath made the first old. Now that which decayeth and waxeth old *is* ready to vanish away." (Hebrews 8:13 AV) Why would God reinstate something which he has said would vanish away and in which he has had no pleasure? "In burnt offerings and *sacrifices* for sin thou hast had no pleasure." (Hebrews 10:6 AV)

Fleshly Israel is symbolized by the fig tree. That fig tree will never again bear fruit.

> And seeing a fig tree afar off having leaves, he came, if haply he might find any thing thereon: and when he came to it, he found nothing but leaves; for the time of figs was not *yet*. And Jesus answered and said unto it, **No man eat fruit of thee hereafter for ever.** And his disciples heard *it*. . . . And in the morning, as they passed by, they saw the fig tree dried up from the roots. And Peter calling to remembrance saith unto him, Master, behold, the fig tree which thou cursedst is withered away. (Mark 11:13-14, 20-21 AV)

Spiritual Israel is symbolized by the olive tree. "Can the fig tree, my brethren, bear olive berries? either a vine, figs? so can no fountain both yield salt water and fresh." (James 3:12 AV) The answer is no! Fleshly Israel will never ever bear spiritual fruit for God. The spiritual fruit only comes from the spiritual olive plant, the church.

The blessings of God do not flow to the physical seed of Abraham but rather to his spiritual seed. Who is the seed of Abraham? Jesus is the seed of Abraham. "Now to Abraham and his seed were the promises made. He saith not, And to seeds, as of many; but as of one, **And to thy seed, which is Christ.** (Galatians 3:16 AV)

All who believe in Jesus are heirs of the promise given to Abraham. Galatians 3:23-29. A true Jew is the spiritual seed of Abraham, not the physical seed. "For he is not a Jew, which is one outwardly; neither is that circumcision, which is outward in the flesh: But he *is* a Jew, which is one inwardly; and circumcision is that of the heart, in the spirit, and not in the letter; whose praise *is* not of men, but of God." (Romans 2:28-29 AV) "Not as though the word of God hath taken none effect. For they are not all Israel, which are of Israel: Neither, because they are the seed of Abraham, are they all children: but, In Isaac shall thy seed be called. That is, They which are the children of the flesh, these *are* not the children of God: but the children of the promise are counted for the seed." (Romans 9:6-8 AV)

The eternal blessings of Abraham flow to all who believe in Jesus Christ. God's kingdom is a spiritual kingdom not an earthly kingdom. His children are spiritual children not earthly children. In God's kingdom there are no distinctions between Jew or Gentile. "There is neither Jew nor Greek, there is neither bond nor free, there is neither male nor female: for ye are all one in Christ Jesus. And if ye *be* Christ's, then are ye Abraham's seed, and heirs according to the promise." (Galatians 3:28-29 AV). For more information on Christians being the Israel of God read: *Antichrist Conspiracy, Inside the Devil's Lair*.[2]

The Jews do not accept that God's plan was based upon salvation by the grace of God through faith in Jesus Christ. The Jews cling to their Babylonian notion of racial superiority. Their rejection of the God of the bible is the basis for creating a rival religion that uses Christian language, but is Judaic to its core. The crypto-Judaism is not the religion of the Old Testament it is the religion of Babylon. This crypto-Jewish religion is Roman Catholicism. This book authoritatively establishes that the Roman Catholic Church is Babylon the Great. It is called "Mystery" because it presents itself as a "Christian" church, when in fact that is a false front for a Judeo/Babylonian theocracy. That theocracy was introduced through the influence of crypto-Jews.

The Bible states that the Devil is at war with Christians, who are the spiritual seed of Jesus. Revelation 12:17. The Catholic priesthood who impose the fleshly Judaic rules of the Roman church are soldiers in a war against Christ and Christians. Galatians 4:29. The rank and file members of the Catholic church are, for the most part, unwitting victims of clerical spiritual corruption, just as the ordinary Jews are victims of their clerics. It is for these and all other victims of religious deception that this book is written. Some would prefer that I remain silent about this religious malfeasance. I will simply respond: "Am I therefore become your enemy, because I tell you the truth?" Galatians 4:16.

1   The Great Wonder in Heaven

Most people focus on the harlot, Babylon the Great, in the book of Revelation, but there is another woman in Revelation who holds the key to the mystery of the great harlot:

> **And there appeared a great wonder in heaven; a woman clothed with the sun, and the moon under her feet, and upon her head a crown of twelve stars**: And she being with child cried, travailing in birth, and pained to be delivered. And there appeared another wonder in heaven; and behold a great red dragon, having seven heads and ten horns, and seven crowns upon his heads. And his tail drew the third part of the stars of heaven, and did cast them to the earth: and the dragon stood before the woman which was ready to be delivered, for to devour her child as soon as it was born. And she brought forth a man child, who was to rule all nations with a rod of iron: and her child was caught up unto God, and *to* his throne. (Revelation 12:1-5 AV)

Who is this woman? Let's look at the clues. She has "upon her head twelve stars." What is the meaning of those twelve stars? God, in the book of Genesis, reveals the answer. Joseph, who is one of the twelve children of Jacob (a/k/a Israel), explains a dream to his brothers. That dream describes his brothers as "eleven stars." Of course Joseph is the twelfth star, making the twelve stars of Israel.

> And he dreamed yet another dream, and told it his brethren, and said, Behold, I have dreamed a dream more; and, **behold, the sun and the moon and the eleven stars made obeisance to me.** And he told *it* to his father, and to his brethren: and his father rebuked him, and said unto him, What *is* this dream that thou hast dreamed? Shall I and thy mother and thy brethren indeed come to bow down ourselves to thee to the earth? (Genesis 37:9-10 AV)

Notice that Joseph's prophecy not only depicts eleven stars, but also depicts the sun and the moon making obeisance to him. The woman of Revelation 12 was "clothed with the sun, and the moon under her feet." Joseph's father, Jacob, understood that the moon and sun symbolized Joseph's mother (Rachel) and father (Jacob/Israel).

The woman in Revelation 12 is Israel, but not the Israel of the earth, but rather the heavenly Israel of the promise. Notice that the woman in Revelation is "a great wonder in heaven." The Israel of Revelation is a heavenly spiritual Israel. Not all who are of the Israel on earth are the Israel of God.

> Not as though the word of God hath taken none effect. **For they are not all Israel, which are of Israel: Neither, because they are the seed of Abraham, are they all children:** but, In Isaac shall thy seed be called. That is, They which are the children of the flesh, these *are* not the children of God: but the children of the promise are counted for the seed. (Romans 9:6-8 AV)

The promises made to Abraham flowed not to his physical but rather to his spiritual seed. "Now to Abraham and his seed were the promises made. He saith not, And to seeds, as of many; but as of one, And to thy seed, which is Christ." (Galatians 3:16 AV) Those who have faith in Jesus Christ are the seed of Abraham, and inherit the eternal promises made to him by God. "And if ye *be* Christ's, then are ye Abraham's seed, and heirs according to the promise." (Galatians 3:29 AV)

The spiritual Israel of Revelation brings "forth a **man child, who was to rule all nations with a rod of iron**: and **her child was caught up unto God, and to his throne.**" Revelation 12:5. That man child of Revelation is Jesus Christ. He is taken up to God and to his throne and rules the nations with a rod of iron. "Hereafter shall the **Son of man sit on the right hand of the power of God.**" (Luke 22:69 AV) "And out of his mouth goeth a sharp sword, that with it he should smite the nations: and he shall **rule them with a rod of iron**: and he treadeth the winepress of the fierceness and wrath of Almighty God." (Revelation 19:15 AV) Jesus is the prophesied son of David, the promised seed of Abraham. "The book of the generation of Jesus Christ, the son of David, the son of Abraham." (Matthew 1:1 AV)

Notice that the great red dragon "stood before the woman which was ready to be delivered, for to devour her child as soon as it was born." Revelation 12:4. Who is this great red dragon? It is none other than "that old serpent, called the Devil, and Satan, which deceiveth the whole world." Revelation 12:9. The child that the great red dragon was ready to devour was Jesus. Who was the agent of the devil that tried to kill Jesus? Herod, King of Israel.

> Then Herod, when he saw that he was mocked of the wise men, was exceeding wroth, and sent forth, and slew all the children that were in Bethlehem, and in all the coasts thereof, from two years old and under, according to the time which he had diligently enquired of the wise men. (Matthew 2:16 AV)

The dragon was then cast out of heaven to the earth and "when the dragon saw that he was cast unto the earth, he persecuted the woman which brought forth the man child." Revelation 12:13. The woman was then protected by God. The dragon then made war with her seed. Who is her seed? They are the children of God who "have the testimony of Jesus Christ." Revelation 12:17.

> And to the woman were given two wings of a great eagle, that she might fly into the wilderness, into her place, where she is nourished for a time, and times, and half a time, from the face of the serpent. And the serpent cast out of his mouth water as a flood after the woman, that he might cause her to be carried away of the flood. And the earth helped the woman, and the earth opened her mouth, and swallowed up the flood which the dragon cast out of his mouth. **And the dragon was wroth with the woman, and went to make war with the remnant of her seed, which keep the commandments of God, and have the testimony of Jesus Christ. And I stood upon the sand of the sea, and saw a beast rise up out of the sea, having seven heads and ten horns, and upon his horns ten crowns, and upon his heads the name of blasphemy.** And the beast which I saw was like unto a leopard, and his feet were as *the feet* of a bear, and his mouth as the mouth of a lion: and the dragon gave him his power, and his seat, and great authority. (Revelation 12:14-13:2 AV)

Notice that after the dragon was cast to the earth a great beast was seen rising out of the sea. This sea beast has the same "seven heads and ten horns, and seven crowns upon his heads" as the dragon who was in heaven ready to devour the newborn child in Revelation 12:3. This is clearly the earthly manifestation of the dragon, who is the Devil. The description suggests that it is a continuation of the heathen governments of the earth. In Daniel, chapters 7-8 we read that the leopard, the bear, and the lion were symbolic of three successive kings. Daniel refers to a fourth kingdom that would be diverse from the rest. That kingdom will have ten horns, and one of the horns "shall speak great words against the most High, and shall wear out the saints of the most High, and **think to change times and laws**: and they shall be given into his hand until a time and times and the dividing of time." Daniel 7:25.

The key to identifying the horn of Daniel is to find an institution that has changed God's laws and times. The Jews consider a violation of any of the ten commandments in Exodus chapter 20 to be a capital offense. In order to avoid such a harsh punishment, the commandments are reinterpreted through tradition to mean something other than what is said in the text. For example, the Eighth commandment in Exodus 20:15 against stealing is given a different meaning. It is interpreted by the Jews to not be a prohibition against stealing property, since stealing property is not a capital offense under Jewish tradition. The Jews limit the Eighth Commandment "to be a prohibition against 'stealing' (that is, kidnapping) a Jewish person."[3] The Eighth Commandment is also not considered by Jews to be a prohibition against stealing (kidnapping) a gentile since "kidnapping of Gentiles by Jews is allowed by talmudic law."[4]

Changing God's laws is a practice that was inculcated into the Roman church by the crypto-

Jews, who had established a long tradition of rules that nullify God's commandments. While typically the Jews nullified the commandments through interpretation, the Catholic Church opted for a more direct approach of simply rewriting the commandments. In order to avoid God's prohibition on graven images, the Catholic church deletes the second commandment. They have changed God's laws. The second commandment in Exodus chapter 20 states: **"Thou shalt not make unto thee any graven image, or any likeness *of any thing* that *is* in heaven above, or that *is* in the earth beneath, or that *is* in the water under the earth: Thou shalt not bow down thyself to them, nor serve them." Exodus 20:4.** This leaves the Catholic Church with only nine commandments. The Catholic Church simply splits the last commandment into two commandments to make up for the missing commandment. The single commandment against coveting is changed into two commandments against coveting thy neighbor's goods and coveting a neighbor's wife.[5] The Catholic Ten Commandments are different from God's Ten Commandments.

God's first commandment states that "I *am* the LORD thy God, which have brought thee out of the land of Egypt, out of the house of bondage. Thou shalt have **no other gods** before me." The traditional Catholic catechism simply states the following in place of the first two commandments: "1. I am the Lord your God: you shall not have **strange gods** before me."[6] Notice that the prohibition against making graven images and bowing to them or serving them is deleted. In addition, the Romish church allows the worship of other gods as long as they are not strange gods. So it is permissible to have Mary and all the saints as other gods because they are not "strange gods" according to Catholic doctrine. They have changed the commandments of God in order to set up their own religion in direct opposition to God's true commands.

The Catholic Church has also changed the times. It claims that the Lord's day is the first day of the week (Sunday) because Jesus purportedly rose from the dead on Sunday and that consequently Sunday replaces the seventh day (Saturday) as the day of rest.[7] The only reference in the Bible to the "Lord's day" is found in Revelation 1:10 and is probably a reference to the sabbath of the seventh day of the week (Saturday).

We are justified not by keeping the sabbath or any other ordinance, but by faith in Jesus Christ. Jesus nailed the Old Testament law to the cross. He fulfilled the requirements of the law on our behalf. We are no longer obligated to the law, including the sabbath requirements. "Let no man therefore judge you in meat, or in drink, or in respect of an holyday, or of the new moon, or of the **sabbath days**: Which are a shadow of things to come; but the body *is* of Christ." (Colossians 2:16-17 AV) God did away with the requirements of the law under the New Testament. "In that he saith, A new covenant, he hath made the first old. Now that which decayeth and waxeth old *is* ready to vanish away." (Hebrews 8:13 AV) We keep the new law out of love for God. Our obedience to his new law is evidence of our faith. **"A new commandment I give unto you, That ye love one another**; as I have loved you, that ye also love one another. By this shall all *men* know that ye are my disciples, if ye have love one to another." (John 13:34-35 AV)

The Catholic Church, on the other hand, requires that "[o]n Sundays and other holy days of obligation, the faithful are to refrain from engaging in work or activities that hinder the worship owed to God."[8] As a result of the Roman Catholic Church's twisting of the Holy Scripture, they have changed the sabbath day, or day of rest, from the last day of the week (Saturday) to the first day of the week (Sunday). The Roman Catholic Church's changing of the day of rest from the seventh day to the first day of the week, along with their deletion of the second commandment, is a fulfillment of the prophecy in Daniel that the horn would "think to change times and laws."

Jesus was crucified on Passover, which was the 4th day of the week, Wednesday (Matthew 26:2, John 13:1, 18:28, 39). Jesus was crucified on the day of Passover (Luke 22-23, Matthew 26:2). That is why the day Jesus Christ was crucified is referred to as the "preparation of the Passover" and not the preparation "for" the Passover. The Passover was the preparation day for the unleavened bread sabbath that always follows the Passover.

> And it was the **preparation of the Passover**, and about the sixth hour: and he saith unto the Jews, Behold your King! (John 19:14 AV)

The day Jesus was crucified was the preparation day before the sabbath (Mark 15:42), which is why many believe it was the sixth day of the week, Friday. What many do not realize is that there were many other Sabbaths throughout the year in addition to the weekly sabbath. That would mean that there would be many occasions when there would be two sabbath days during some weeks. The week of Jesus' crucifixion was one of those weeks with two Sabbaths. How do I know that there were two Sabbaths? Because the Bible states that Christ was crucified the day before the "high sabbath," and not the day before the weekly sabbath.

> The Jews therefore, **because it was the preparation, that the bodies should not remain upon the cross on the sabbath day, (for that sabbath day was an high day**,) besought Pilate that their legs might be broken, and *that* they might be taken away. (John 19:31 AV)

The next day after Jesus' crucifixion was a high sabbath, it was the first day of the seven day feast of unleavened bread and the 5th day of the week, Thursday (John 19:31). The fourteenth day of the first month is the Passover (Leviticus 23:4-5, Exodus 12:17-18). Passover is immediately followed by the seven days of unleavened bread (Leviticus 23:6-7, Exodus 12:15-16). A Sabbath day is a day of rest. God ordained that the Fifteenth day of the first month (the day after Passover) was to be a day of rest, that is a sabbath day (Leviticus 23:6-7).

The next day (the 6th day of the week, Friday) the women bought the spices (Mark 16:1) and prepared the spices for Jesus' body (Luke 23:56). The women prepared the spices and ointments before the sabbath (Luke 23:53-24:3 AV), but they did not buy the spices until after the sabbath (Mark 16:1-6 AV). How can one prepare the spices before they are purchased? It would not be possible unless there were two Sabbaths. The women prepared the spices before the weekly sabbath but had purchased them after the unleavened bread sabbath. Those passages point to a

Wednesday crucifixion with the unleavened bread sabbath the next day, Thursday, and Christ rising from the dead exactly 3 days and 3 nights, 72 hours, later on the weekly sabbath, Saturday. The women would have both purchased the spices and prepared them on Friday, which would have been before the weekly sabbath on Saturday and after the unleavened bread sabbath, which was on Thursday. The tomb was found empty on the first day of the week, he did not rise from the dead on that day.

The women rested on the 7th day, Saturday, which was the weekly sabbath (Luke 23:56). Early the first day of the week, Sunday, they came to the tomb to find it empty and saw an angel who announced that Jesus had already risen (Mark 16:1-6). Just as Jesus prophesied, he rose from the dead precisely 3 days and 3 nights after his burial (Matthew 12:40, 20:19). While the tomb was found empty on the first day of the week, Sunday, he rose from the dead on the evening of the 7th day, Saturday.

To hold that Jesus was crucified and was buried on the 6th day of the week (Friday) and rose from the dead on the First day of the week (Sunday) would be to say Jesus was wrong about his prophecy, because he prophesied that he would be in the tomb 3 days and 3 nights. "For as Jonas was three days and three nights in the whale's belly; so shall the Son of man be **three days and three nights** in the heart of the earth." (Matthew 12:40 AV) The span between the evening of Friday and the early morning of Sunday is not 3 days and 3 nights. However, a Wednesday burial with a Saturday resurrection is exactly 3 days and 3 nights.

2 The Other Woman

The horn of Daniel, which is symbolic of the Pope of Rome, changed the times and the laws of God. The beast of Daniel has the same ten horns as the beast in Revelation. We see the sea beast again in Revelation 17:3, and this time there is someone riding the beast. It is the same beast with "seven heads and ten horns" as the dragon who was in heaven ready to devour the newborn child in Revelation 12:3 and the beast that rose from the sea in Revelation 13:1. The beast could not destroy Christ or his church, so he tried to create his own devilish christ (the antichrist) and his own counterfeit church. The church of Jesus is a chaste bride. 2 Corinthians 11:2. The Devil's church is an imperious harlot who is riding the beast.

> So he carried me away in the spirit into the wilderness: and I saw a woman sit upon a scarlet coloured beast, full of names of blasphemy, having seven heads and ten horns. And the woman was arrayed in purple and scarlet colour, and decked with gold and precious stones and pearls, having a golden cup in her hand full of abominations and filthiness of her fornication: And upon her forehead *was* a name written, MYSTERY, BABYLON THE GREAT, THE MOTHER OF HARLOTS AND ABOMINATIONS OF THE EARTH. And I saw the woman drunken with the blood of the saints, and with the blood of the martyrs of Jesus: and when I saw her, I wondered with great admiration. Revelation 17:3-6.

Recall that the dragon made war against the seed of Christ, the children of the first woman. The Devil decided to establish a church and use that church to war against the children of God. This is a spiritual war: "But as then he that was born after the flesh persecuted him that was born after the Spirit, even so it is now." Galatians 4:29. The children of the flesh in the Devil's church are cannon fodder in a spiritual war against the children of the spirit in the true church of Christ.

The Roman church considers Mary the mother of the church.[9] Is the Catholic Mary the Mary in the Bible? There is a mother mentioned in the Revelation; she is the harlot with a name upon her forehead: "MYSTERY, BABYLON THE GREAT, THE MOTHER OF HARLOTS AND ABOMINATIONS OF THE EARTH." Revelation 17:5. Can we know who is this

7

mysterious harlot? God reveals her identity by explaining that the beast that she rides has seven heads and "The seven heads are seven mountains, on which the woman sitteth." (Revelation 17:9 AV) Another clue is that the woman is a "city." **"And the woman which thou sawest is that great city, which reigneth over the kings of the earth."** (Revelation 17:18 AV)

Where are the mysterious seven mountains? Rome has traditionally been known as the city on seven hills or also "seven mountains." A mountain is simply a large mass of earth that rises above the common or adjacent land. It does not have to be of any definite altitude. Mountain accurately describes a large hill.[10] There is only one city that can meet the description of a city on seven mountains, Rome. Rome is famous for the seven mountains upon which it sits. The mountains are the Capitoline, the Quirinal, the Viminal, the Esquiline, the Caelian, the Avenue, and the Palatine.[11]

Alexander Hislop points out in his book *The Two Babylons*, that even pagan poets and orators, who would have no thought of elucidating biblical prophecy, described Rome as the city on seven hills.[12] Hislop quotes Virgil, who described Rome thusly: "Rome has both become the most beautiful (city) in the world, and alone has surround for herself seven heights with a wall."[13] Virgil who died approximately 19 years before Christ was born and therefore several generations before the book of Revelation was written. Hislop also quotes poet Sextus Aurelius Propertius who describes Rome as "the lofty city on seven hills, which governs the entire world."[14] Notice how his description follows closely that which is contained in Revelation. "And the woman which thou sawest is that great city, which reigneth over the kings of the earth." (Revelation 17:18 AV) Propertius died in 15 B.C. and so he would have had no knowledge of the book of Revelation which was written scores of years after his death. Marcus Valerius Martialis describes "the seven dominating mountains" of Rome.[15] Symmachus, the Prefect of Rome, introduced one friend of his to another by letter. In the letter he describes one friend as being *De septem montibus virum*, which translated means "a man from the seven mountains." That was equivalent in that day (circa 351-375 A.D.) to calling someone a *Civem Romanum*, which translated means "A Roman Citizen."[16]

Now that we have identified Rome as the location of the seven mountains, who is "Babylon the Great, the Mother of Harlots and Abominations of the Earth?" The Catholic Encyclopedia offers us a clue. It states that **"[i]t is within Rome, called the city of seven hills, that the entire Vatican State is now confined."**[17]

The Vatican, being in Rome, is the great mother of harlots. This book will present irrefutable evidence of that truth. This book will also explain the link between the Roman Catholic Church and Babylon. First, we must find out how the mother of harlots got the title "Babylon the Great." Our first clue is found in the bible. We read in Jeremiah that "Babylon hath been a golden cup in the LORD'S hand, that made all the earth drunken: the nations have drunken of her wine; therefore the nations are mad." (Jeremiah 51:7 AV) Notice that language is very similar to what God states in Revelation regarding "BABYLON THE GREAT." She is described in Revelation as that great whore "[w]ith whom the kings of the earth have committed fornication, and the inhabitants of the earth have been made drunk with the wine of her fornication." (Revelation 17:2 AV) God further describes her in the Book of Revelation:

> For all nations have drunk of the wine of the wrath of her fornication, and the kings of the earth have committed fornication with her, and the merchants of the earth are waxed rich through the abundance of her delicacies." (Revelation 18:3 AV)

Notice the commonality in the characteristics between the Babylon mentioned in Jeremiah, which was written sometime in the 6th Century B.C. and the Babylon in the book of Revelation, which was written sometime in the 1st century A.D. We have a span of approximately 700 years separating the descriptions and yet we have common elements. In Jeremiah, Babylon made all of the earth drunk by her wine, and in Revelation the kings and inhabitants of the earth have been made drunk with the wine of her fornication. It seems that this wine of Babylon is an intoxicating mixture that is born of fornication. Do we find any other clues from the bible as to what this fornication could be?

The bible gives us a clue. The Holy Bible depicts the church of Jesus as a chaste bride. Paul states of the Corinthian church: "For I am jealous over you with godly jealousy: for I have espoused you to one husband, that I may present you as a chaste virgin to Christ." (2 Corinthians 11:2 AV) Obviously, chastity has nothing to do with the flesh. Paul is referring to spiritual purity.

The bride of Christ is described in Revelation as new Jerusalem, prepared as a bride for her husband. "And I John saw the holy city, new Jerusalem, coming down from God out of heaven, prepared as a bride adorned for her husband." (Revelation 21:2 AV) Here we have the church symbolized as a chaste city adorned for her husband, who is Christ. How is she adorned? In Revelation 19:7-8 we read that she is adorned in fine linen. How different is that from the bejeweled city of Babylon who "was arrayed in purple and scarlet colour, and decked with gold and precious stones and pearls, having a golden cup in her hand full of abominations and filthiness of her fornication." Revelation 17:4.

The new Jerusalem is arrayed simply in fine linen. What does the fine linen signify? It is the "righteousness of saints."

> Let us be glad and rejoice, and give honour to him: for the marriage of the Lamb is come, and his wife hath made herself ready. And to her was granted that she should be arrayed in fine linen, clean and white: for the fine linen is the righteousness of saints." (Revelation 19:7-8 AV)

The fine linen being the righteousness of the saints suggests that the purple and scarlet clothing and the gold and precious stones and pearls of the great whore of Babylon are symbolic of the wickedness of that religion. There is an unmistakable identity of the Roman Catholic hierarchy by the purple and scarlet ceremonial vestments worn by the Cardinals and the purple ceremonial vestments worn by the Bishops of Rome. This color scheme used by the church of Rome points directly to the Roman Catholic Church being not a chaste bride but rather the imperious whore of Babylon. God commands that his chosen people come out of the church of the great whore. *See* Revelation 18:4.

We have two very different women depicted in Revelation. Notice that in Revelation the chaste bride is "new" Jerusalem. That suggests that there is an "old" Jerusalem. Is there a link between the "old" Jerusalem" and the great whore of Babylon? When Israel was unfaithful to God he compared Israel to a harlot. The following passage depicts the unfaithfulness of Israel which parallels the sins of idolatry in the Catholic Church and provides a clue as to the common link between the religion of Israel and the religion of Rome. The commonality between the whore of Babylon in Revelation and the whore of Jerusalem depicted in Ezekiel is clear.

> [T]hou didst trust in thine own beauty, and *playedst the harlot* because of thy renown, and pouredst out thy fornications on every one that passed by; his it was. And of thy garments thou didst take, and deckedst thy high places with divers colours, and playedst the harlot thereupon: *the like things* shall not come, neither shall it be *so*. **Thou hast also taken thy fair jewels of my gold and of my silver, which I had given thee, and madest to thyself images of men, and didst commit whoredom with them, And tookest thy broidered garments, and coveredst them: and thou hast set mine oil and mine incense before them.** My meat also which I gave thee, fine flour, and oil, and honey, *wherewith* I fed thee, thou hast even set it before them for a sweet savour: and *thus* it was, saith the Lord GOD. Moreover thou hast taken thy sons and thy daughters, whom thou hast borne unto me, and these hast thou sacrificed unto them to be devoured. *Is this* of thy whoredoms a small matter, That thou hast slain my children, and delivered them to cause them to pass through *the fire* for them? And in all thine abominations and thy whoredoms thou hast not remembered the days of thy youth, when thou wast naked and bare, *and* was polluted in thy blood. And it came to pass after all thy wickedness, (woe, woe unto thee! saith the Lord GOD;) *That* thou hast also built unto thee an eminent place, and hast made thee an high place in every street. Thou hast built thy high place at every head of the way, and hast made thy beauty to be abhorred, and hast opened thy feet to every one that passed by, and multiplied thy whoredoms. Thou hast also committed fornication with the Egyptians thy neighbours, great of flesh; and hast increased thy whoredoms, to provoke me to anger. Behold, therefore I have stretched out my hand over thee, and have diminished thine ordinary *food*, and delivered thee unto the will of them that hate thee, the daughters of the Philistines, which are ashamed of thy lewd way. Thou hast played the whore also with the Assyrians, because thou wast unsatiable; yea, thou hast played the harlot with them, and yet couldest not be satisfied. Thou hast moreover multiplied thy fornication in the land of Canaan unto Chaldea; and yet thou wast not satisfied herewith. How weak is thine heart, saith the Lord GOD, seeing thou doest all these *things*, the work of an imperious

whorish woman; In that thou buildest thine eminent place in the head of every way, and makest thine high place in every street; and hast not been as an harlot, in that thou scornest hire; *But as* a wife that committeth adultery, *which* taketh strangers instead of her husband! They give gifts to all whores: but thou givest thy gifts to all thy lovers, and hirest them, that they may come unto thee on every side for thy whoredom. And the contrary is in thee from *other* women in thy whoredoms, whereas none followeth thee to commit whoredoms: and in that thou givest a reward, and no reward is given unto thee, therefore thou art contrary. Wherefore, O harlot, hear the word of the LORD: Thus saith the Lord GOD; Because thy filthiness was poured out, and thy nakedness discovered through thy whoredoms with thy lovers, and with all the idols of thy abominations, and by the blood of thy children, which thou didst give unto them; Behold, therefore I will gather all thy lovers, with whom thou hast taken pleasure, and all *them* that thou hast loved, with all *them* that thou hast hated; I will even gather them round about against thee, and will discover thy nakedness unto them, that they may see all thy nakedness. (Ezekiel 16:15-37 AV)

The great whore in Ezekiel is the same great whore in Revelation. God in Ezekiel has given us a clear clue as to the nature of the whore of Babylon. First, the reader must understand that Ezekiel is writing during his captivity in Babylon. Nebuchadnezzar, King of Babylon, conquered the city of Jerusalem and brought the Jews and the treasures of the city back to Babylon. 2 Kings 24:10-16. Ezekiel was one of the captives and described the corruption by the Jewish religious leaders who were adopting the heathen practices of the Babylonian religion. Ezekiel describes the origins of the harlot "old" Jerusalem of Judaism. That "old" Jerusalem is distinct from the chaste and holy "new" Jerusalem, which is made up of those who have been saved by the grace of God through faith in Jesus Christ. *See* Revelation 21:2. Notice that Egypt and Chaldea (Babylon) are two of the nations with which Jerusalem had committed whoredoms; which are the very sources of the heathen practices in the Talmud and Kabbalah.

Ezekiel explains that the whoredom of Jerusalem was following after the heathen religions by making images of men and worshiping those images. That is the same thing being done today in the Catholic church. The Jews were also sacrificing their children to their heathen idols. The great whore of Revelation is similarly "drunken with the blood of the saints, and with the blood of the martyrs of Jesus." (Revelation 17:6) There is an unmistakable common link between the spiritual whoredom of Church of Rome and the Jews of Jerusalem.

Jeremiah prophesied for the people to: "Flee out of the midst of Babylon, and deliver every man his soul: be not cut off in her iniquity; for this *is* the time of the LORD'S vengeance; he will render unto her a recompence. (Jeremiah 51:6 AV)

John offered an identical prophesy to those in Babylon the Great: "And I heard another voice from heaven, saying, Come out of her, my people, that ye be not partakers of her sins, and that ye receive not of her plagues." (Revelation 18:4 AV)

The parallelism is unmistakable. The two Babylons suffer the same judgement of God.

3 Passing the Cup from Jerusalem to Rome

From the beginning the Christian church was in a spiritual struggle against Judaism. Judaism could not win in a head to head spiritual contest against Christianity. It was necessary for the Jews to throw their efforts behind undermining the Christian church by injecting it with a Judaic contagion. Their long-term strategy was to change the Christian church from the inside-out to align more closely with the Judaic/Babylonian theosophy. Philip Schaff (1819-1893) in his *History of the Christian Church* explains the strategy of these spiritual sappers.

> Having described in previous chapters the moral and intellectual victory of the church over avowed and consistent Judaism and heathenism, we must now look at her deep and mighty struggle with those enemies in a hidden and more dangerous form: with Judaism and heathenism concealed in the garb of Christianity and threatening to Judaize and paganize the church.

* * *

> Judaism, with its religion and its sacred writings, and Graeco-Roman heathenism, with its secular culture, its science, and its art, were designed to pass into Christianity to be transformed and sanctified. But even in the apostolic age many Jews and Gentiles were baptized only with water, not with the Holy Spirit and fire of the gospel, and smuggled their old religious notions and practices into the church.

* * *

> The same heresies meet us at the beginning of the second century, and thenceforth

in more mature form and in greater extent in almost all parts of Christendom. They evince, on the one hand, the universal import of the Christian religion in history, and its irresistible power over all the more profound and earnest minds of the age. Christianity threw all their religious ideas into confusion and agitation. They were so struck with the truth, beauty, and vigor of the new religion, that they could no longer rest either in Judaism or in heathenism; and yet many were unable or unwilling to forsake inwardly their old religion and philosophy. Hence strange medleys of Christian and unchristian elements in chaotic ferment. The old religions did not die without a last desperate effort to save themselves by appropriating Christian ideas. And this, on the other hand, exposed the specific truth of Christianity to the greatest danger, and obliged the church to defend herself against misrepresentation, and to secure herself against relapse to the Jewish or the heathen level.[18]

Schaff perceived a two prong attack from what he called Greco-Roman heathenism and Judaism. In fact, those two prongs were two branches from the same Babylonian root. The Greco-Roman religion was exoteric in its polytheism, Judaism, on the other hand, was an esoteric polytheism. Judaism concealed its polytheism beneath the guise of worshiping Jehovah. It was, therefore, easier for the Judaizers to establish their own version of the ersatz "Christian" church. The heathen poison was disguised beneath the Jewish customs, and therefore it was found more palatable to those without the unction of the Holy Spirit. Those who had the unction of the Holy Spirit gagged on the poisonous Babylonian/Judaic customs and spewed it from the true church of Christ. Those same Babylonian/Judaic customs found a home in the Catholic Church.

Ezekiel was taken by the Lord and shown how the Jews had turned from him and worshiped idols and heathen gods. *See* Ezekiel 8:1-17. The Jews thought that the heathen worship was hidden from God. "Then said he unto me, Son of man, hast thou seen what the ancients of the house of Israel do in the dark, every man in the chambers of his imagery? for they say, The LORD seeth us not; the LORD hath forsaken the earth." Ezekiel 8:12.

It was not the common Jews who were engaging in the secret worship of heathen gods, it was the "seventy of the ancients of the house of Israel." Ezekiel 8:11. Who were the seventy ancients? They were the members of the Jewish Sanhedrin. There were seventy members of the Sanhedrin, who select the high priest, who is considered the 71st member.

The common Jews were kept in the dark about the secret heathen worship. They were exposed to the oral traditions of the Jews, which they ignorantly followed, not realizing that they nullified God's laws. Jesus revealed this in Mark. "And he said unto them, Full well ye reject the commandment of God, that ye may keep your own tradition." (Mark 7:9 AV) The oral Jewish traditions had esoteric meanings that were hidden from the uninitiated common Jews. That is the way it is today both among Jews and Catholics.

The heathenism of the Jews was ever so subtle. Jesus warned about that subtlety. He likened the false Judaic mixing of heathen worship with God's laws to leaven. A little leaven works its way through the whole loaf. The Jews created a mixture that on the surface appeared godly, but was in fact a wholly leavened loaf of heathenism. "Then Jesus said unto them, Take heed and beware of the leaven of the Pharisees and of the Sadducees. . . . Then understood they how that he bade *them* not beware of the leaven of bread, but of the doctrine of the Pharisees and of the Sadducees." (Matthew 16:12 AV) Paul also warned about the Judaizers that were trying to inject their Judaic doctrine into the church. He warned: "A little leaven leaveneth the whole lump." (Galatians 5:9 AV)

The subtlety of the Judaizers even deceived Peter. In Galatians 2:11-13, we read how Paul had to upbraid Peter for being deceived to follow after the subtle dissimulatory customs of the Jews. Peter caused Barnabas to fall into the same Judaizing error. That same Barnabas, however, was quick to recognize the clear heathenism when the Lycaonians sought to worship Paul and him as gods in Acts 14:11-15. Both Barnabas and Paul rent their clothes and ran among the people telling them to stop their heathen worship. The exoteric heathen worship of the Lycaonians was obvious to Barnabas, but the esoteric heathenism of the Jews was so subtle that Barnabas was taken in by it. *See* Galatians 2:13.

The Judaizing strategy resulted ultimately in the establishment of the Catholic Church. There is historical evidence for the common Babylonian lineage between Judaism and Roman Catholicism. After the fall of Jerusalem, Cabalistic Jews migrated to Alexandria where they synthesized their Chaldean witchcraft with Neo-Platonic philosophy and cloaked that religion in Christian terminology. They then tried to introduce this new heathen gnostic philosophy into the fledgling Christian Church. The penetration of the true spiritual church of Christ was futile. What this Jewish gnosticism did accomplish was the creation of a new ersatz "Christian" church, which grew into what we know today as the Roman Catholic Church. Those facts have been concealed from the historical accounts of the Catholic Church.

Maurice Pinay in his book "The Plot Against the Church" explains the spiritual fight waged by Irenaeus of Lyons (circa 130-202) against the gnostic heresy that was being injected into the church.[19] Maurice Pinay is alleged to be a pseudonym for a group of Catholic priests. According to Pinay, one of the lead purveyors of the gnostic heresy was Valentinus.[20] Valentinus was a crypto-Jew, who tried to keep his Jewish roots secret when he migrated from Alexandria to Rome. He migrated with the intention of portraying himself as a Christian in order to undermine the Christian church at Rome with his gnostic doctrines. Valentinus gained great influence in Rome and was even a candidate for bishop of Rome in 143 A.D.[21] Irenaeus discovered the Jewish roots of Valentinus and found out what Valentinus was up to. Irenaeus exposed Valentinus' anti-Christian heresy.

Valentinus was a disciple of Theudas, who in turn claimed to have been a disciple of the Apostle Paul. Theudas taught a secret knowledge (gnosticism) that he falsely claimed was taught to him by Paul. The only reference to Theudas in the bible is a reference to him from the

Pharisee Gamaliel. Gamaliel stated:

> For before these days rose up Theudas, boasting himself to be somebody; to whom a number of men, about four hundred, joined themselves: who was slain; and all, as many as obeyed him, were scattered, and brought to nought. (Acts 5:36 AV)

It is not clear if the Theudas mentioned in Acts is the same Theudas whom Valentinus followed. That is because it would seem that the Theudas mentioned by Gamaliel would have died before Paul's Christian conversion and so Theudas could not have believably claimed to have been Paul's disciple. The claimed discipleship of Theudas, however, could have been a fiction later engrafted upon the legend of Theudas by his scattered disciples.

In any event, if the Theudas mentioned by Gamliel is the same Theudas followed by Valentinus, it would have been impossible for Valentinus to have ever met directly with him. That is because Valentinus was not born until approximately 100 A.D. in Egypt, which would have been long after Theudas died. According to Gamaliel, Theudas was slain and his followers were scattered. From Gamaliel's vantage it appeared that the movement of Theudas was brought to nought. However, it seems that Theudas' gnostic philosophy lived on through Valentinus and his disciples.

Paul warned about the Jewish heresy. He described their actions. "And that because of false brethren unawares brought in, who came in privily to spy out our liberty which we have in Christ Jesus, that they might bring us into bondage:" (Galatians 2:4 AV) Notice that the false brethren came in secretly pretending to be Christians as a way to bring them into bondage. Bondage to what? The passage makes it clear that they were spying out the liberty in Christ and so the bondage would be to inject into the church a false gospel that strikes at the heart of that liberty. That false gospel is salvation by works, which is the heart of the Jewish gnosticism.

Paul made that clear in his epistle to the Romans, which was a church that was being particularly targeted for corruption. Paul explained how the Jews were trying to rebel against God's plan of grace as a means of salvation and instead institute a salvation by obedience to the law. "For they being ignorant of God's righteousness, and going about to establish their own righteousness, have not submitted themselves unto the righteousness of God." (Romans 10:3 AV) Paul warned about those who were bent on perverting Christ's gospel of grace.

> For I know this, that after my departing shall grievous wolves enter in among you, not sparing the flock. Also of your own selves shall men arise, speaking perverse things, to draw away disciples after them. Therefore watch, and remember, that by the space of three years I ceased not to warn every one night and day with tears. And now, brethren, I commend you to God, and to the word of his grace, which is able to build you up, and to give you an inheritance among all them which are sanctified. (Acts 20:29-32 AV).

Notice that Paul commended the church to "God, and the word of his grace." It is the word of grace that the Judaizers would try to corrupt. The corrupt gospel is salvation by works, which was eventually given life in the Roman church.

Paul repeats the point more directly in his letter to the Galatians. The Jewish gnostics argued that obedience to the law was necessary for salvation. Paul, on the other hand, states emphatically that works of the law will not justify a person.

> Knowing that a man is not justified by the works of the law, but by the faith of Jesus Christ, even we have believed in Jesus Christ, that we might be justified by the faith of Christ, and not by the works of the law: for by the works of the law shall no flesh be justified. (Galatians 2:16 AV).

Justification is by God's grace through faith alone. "For by grace are ye saved through faith; and that not of yourselves: *it is* the gift of God: Not of works, lest any man should boast." (Ephesians 2:8-9 AV) For more detailed information on salvation by the Grace of God alone read: *The Anti-Gospel, The Perversion of Christ's Grace Gospel.*[22]

Philip Schaff in *History of the Christian Church* explains how the false doctrine of salvation by works was founded upon gnostic philosophy that found its way out of Alexandria:

> The Alexandrian fathers furnished a theoretical basis for this asceticism in the distinction of a lower and higher morality, which corresponds to the Platonic or Pythagorean distinction between the life according to nature and the life above nature or the practical and contemplative life. It was previously suggested by Hermas about the middle of the second century. Tertullian made a corresponding opposite distinction of mortal and venial sins. Here was a source of serious practical errors, and an encouragement both to moral laxity and ascetic extravagance. The ascetics, and afterwards the monks, formed or claimed to be a moral nobility, a spiritual aristocracy, above the common Christian people; as the clergy stood in a separate caste of inviolable dignity above the laity, who were content with a lower grade of virtue. Clement of Alexandria, otherwise remarkable for his elevated ethical views, requires of the sage or gnostic, that he excel the plain Christian not only by higher knowledge, but also by higher, emotionless virtue, and stoical superiority to all bodily conditions; and he inclines to regard the body, with Plato, as the grave and fetter of the soul. How little he understood the Pauline doctrine of justification by faith, may be inferred from a passage in the Stromata, where he explains the word of Christ: 'Thy faith hath saved thee,' as referring, not to faith simply, but to the Jews only, who lived according to the law; as if faith was something to be added to the good works, instead of being the source and principle of the holy life. Origen goes still further, and propounds quite distinctly the catholic doctrine of two kinds of morality and piety, a lower for all Christians, and a higher for saints or the select few. He

includes in the higher morality works of supererogation, i.e. works not enjoined indeed in the gospel, yet recommended as counsels of perfection, which were supposed to establish a peculiar merit and secure a higher degree of blessedness. He who does only what is required of all is an unprofitable servant; but he who does more, who performs, for example, what Paul, in 1 Cor. 7:25, merely recommends, concerning the single state, or like him, resigns his just claim to temporal remuneration for spiritual service, is called a good and faithful servant. Among these works were reckoned martyrdom, voluntary poverty, and voluntary celibacy.[23]

Barbara Aho in *Mystery, Babylon the Great - Catholic or Jewish?* explains the significance of Schaff's historical account:

Here we see that the false doctrine of the so-called "Christian" Gnostics resembled the "salvation by works" taught by the Gnostic Jews at the Platonic schools in Alexandria. It is worth noting here that the Gnostic heresiarchs were Jews, a fact well-known to the true Church Fathers who were their contemporaries. This huge piece of the puzzle has been missing in the sanitized accounts of the Gnostics disseminated to the Gentile world, but is readily available in the Jewish Encyclopedia:

"It is a noteworthy fact that heads of gnostic schools and founders of gnostic systems are designated as Jews by the Church Fathers. Some derive all heresies, including those of gnosticism, from Judaism ... It must furthermore be noted that Hebrew words and names of God provide the skeleton for several gnostic systems... This fact proves at least that the principal elements of gnosticism were derived from Jewish speculation, while it does not preclude the possibility of new wine having been poured into old bottles."[24]

Edith Miller (Lady Queenborough) explains in her classic book, *Occult Theocracy*, the attack on the early church by the Gnostics, and how the Gnostic infiltration gave rise to ersatz church branches that were polluted with Gnosticism.

Yet, within a very short time after the death of Christ, Christian ritualism began to appear. A theological system of dogmas and beliefs was devised, modes of worship elaborated and a hierarchy arose with all its attendant evils. However, the Christian faith, under the lash of persecution, had shown the world the power of Faith and Charity. And against this power the forces of evil have ever been unfurled. Blow after blow was dealt to the rising church. Both its beliefs and practices were attacked by those who professed other views and worshiped other gods and who designed all schemes to subvert and pervert Christianity. Henceforth, as it has ever been with all religions, the history of Christianity and of Gnosticism will develop side by side, the perversion and destruction of the former being the aims of the latter. The Tree of Christianity gave forth three main branches, the Catholicism of Rome, Greek Catholicism, and in the XVI Century, Lutherism. The two former bodies remained homogeneous but Lutherism gave birth to innumerable sects all dissenting from the parent church.[25]

Edith Miller concluded that "Judaism sanctions Gnosticism which is further elaborated in their books of the Cabala."[26] The Gnosticism that polluted the ersatz churches was born of Judaic/Babylonian occultism.

Irenaeus, who died in 202 A.D., identified the Jews as the inventors of the Gnostic philosophy that threatened to spin the early church into apostasy.

> "Arising among these men, Saturninus (who was of that Antioch which is near Daphne) and Basilides laid hold of some favourable opportunities, and promulgated different systems of doctrine—the one in Syria, the other at Alexandria. . . . These men, moreover, practise magic; and use images, incantations, invocations, and every other kind of curious art. . . . **They declare that they are no longer Jews, and that they are not yet Christians**; and that it is not at all fitting to speak openly of their mysteries, but right to keep them secret by preserving silence."[27]

Irenaeus wrote extensively against the Judaizers who crept into the church, trying to inject one heresy or another. He explains in one of his writings how two Jewish proselytes, Theodotion of Ephesus and Aquila of Pontus, tried to undermine the prophecy regarding the virgin birth of Jesus by changing the passage in Isaiah 7:14.[28] That passage in Isaiah states: "Therefore the Lord himself shall give you a sign; Behold, a **virgin** shall conceive, and bear a son, and shall call his name Immanuel." *Id.* Theodotion and Pontus corrupted the passage to read "Behold, a **young woman** shall conceive, and bring forth a son." This Jewish corruption had never before been manifested in scripture until after the fulfillment of the prophecy in Isaiah by the birth of Jesus Christ was memorialized in the New Testament.

Irenaeus quite properly points out that the change in Isaiah from "virgin" to "young woman" makes no sense. The prophecy in Isaiah is supposed to be a sign from God of the birth of Christ. Matthew explains that Immanuel means God with us. "Behold, a virgin shall be with child, and shall bring forth a son, and they shall call his name **Emmanuel, which being interpreted is, God with us.**" (Matthew 1:23 AV) If the passage states that the sign is to be that a "young woman" is to conceive, it loses all meaning since that is not a "sign," since young women conceive regularly. The sign must be something unusual in order for it to be a sign, the virgin birth of Jesus was that sign as prophesied by Isaiah.

The virgin birth of Christ is fundamental to Christianity. If Jesus was merely a man, born of natural processes, then his death on the cross could not atone for the sins of others. He could not be the perfect unblemished sacrifice. Hence, Jesus could not be the savior.

Jews today argue that the correct rendering of the Hebrew word in the passage should be "young woman" instead of "virgin."[29] They are wrong, the Hebrew word is "*alma*" and it means "virgin." The argument of the Jews makes no sense. Since Jews reject Jesus as the Messiah, they are still looking forward to the birth of the Messiah. How can they tell who that Messiah is, since it is not a sign to be born of a "young woman?" The passage specifically states that "the Lord himself shall give you a sign." The virgin birth is the sign that the child born of the virgin is the Messiah. It is very simple. If there is no virgin birth, there is no sign, if there is no sign, there is no Messiah.

The Jews have painted themselves into a corner; if they maintain their position that the prophecy in Isaiah means that a young woman will give birth, then they have lost the sign for the coming of the Messiah. Why would they do that? Because their position is really an attack on Christianity. They cannot have Christ being born of a virgin. Rather than argue whether Jesus was born of a virgin, they change the passage of the prophecy of the virgin birth, thus making the virgin birth irrelevant. If there is a prophecy of a virgin birth and the New Testament records a virgin birth, that means Jesus is the Messiah. They cannot change the account in the New Testament, so they do the next best thing, they remove the prophecy of a virgin birth from the Old Testament.

Crypto-Jews and their Catholic fellow travelers are still pushing this corruption of the bible today. There are corrupt bible versions that maintain this gnostic fiction and corrupt Isaiah 7:14 to remove the virgin birth: Revised Standard Version (RSV), New Revised Standard Version (NRSV), New World Translation (NWT), Jerusalem Bible (JB), New Jerusalem Bible (NJB).

AV (KJV)	**NJB**
Therefore the Lord himself shall give you a sign; Behold, **a virgin shall conceive**, and bear a son, and shall call his name Immanuel. Isaiah 7:14 AV (KJV)	The Lord will give you a sign in any case: It is this: **the young woman is with child** and will give birth to a son whom she will call Immanuel. Isaiah 7:14 (NJB)

In the case of the Holy Bible, it is the New and Old Testaments of God Almighty. They are the most important legal documents ever written. God Almighty is the testator. He wrote both testaments. In addition, he created the languages into which his original testaments would be written. He also created the languages into which those testaments would be translated. Genesis 11:7-9. He has supernaturally controlled the process from beginning to end. **"All scripture *is* given by inspiration of God,** and *is* profitable for doctrine, for reproof, for correction, for instruction in righteousness." (2 Timothy 3:16 AV) In addition, he has promised to supernaturally preserve his testaments. **"[T]he word of the Lord endureth for ever**. And this is the word which by the gospel is preached unto you." (1 Peter 1:25 AV) The heirs of Christ are Christians. "The Spirit itself beareth witness with our spirit, that we are the children of God: And if children, then heirs; heirs of God, and joint-heirs with Christ; if so be that we suffer with *him*, that we may be also glorified together." (Romans 8:16-17 AV)

Crypto-Jews and Catholics cannot eradicate the word of God, because God has promised to preserve it forever. They, therefore, have created a whole population of corrupt bible versions, so that it will be difficult for Christians to figure out what is the true word of God. **The pure word of God in the English language is the Authorized (King James) Version (AV or KJV).**

The new bible versions are based upon corrupt transcripts and the translators use a method of translation known as dynamic equivalence, rather than the formal equivalence used in the Authorized Version (AV), which is also known as the King James Version (KJV). Formal equivalence is a word for word translation, whereas dynamic equivalence is a thought for thought translation. A translator using dynamic equivalence is less a translator and more an interpreter. Thus, the new versions of bibles should more accurately be called interpretations, rather than translations. The dynamic equivalent interpreters of the new bible versions have often made unfounded assumptions as to the meaning of particular passage. Rather than translate what God wrote, they have, with some frequency, twisted passages by injecting their own personal bias. Some of these interpreters have displayed malicious intent and caused great mischief.

The subjective bias of the interpreters in the new bible versions have caused changes in the new version English bibles that are not supported by any of Greek or Hebrew texts. For example, dynamic equivalencies caused 6,653 English word changes in the New International Version (NIV), approximately 4,000 word changes in the New American Standard Bible (NASB), and approximately 2,000 word changes in the <u>New</u> King James Version (NKJV), none of which are supported by the words in any of the Greek or Hebrew texts.[30] Those word changes reflect the subjective bias of the interpreters. The combined effect of having a corrupted text and then having that text interpreted using dynamic equivalence has been that the NIV has 64,098 fewer words than the AV.[31] That is a 10% loss in the bible. That means that an NIV bible would have 170 fewer pages than a typical 1,700 page AV bible.[32] The new versions of the bible are materially different; they are the product of the imaginations of interpreters who have applied their personal prejudices to slant already corrupted texts to comport with their own ideas. They are truly counterfeit bibles. For more detailed information on the corruption of God's word in the new counterfeit bibles read *Antichrist Conspiracy, Inside the Devil's Lair.*[33]

The Jewish corruption of Isaiah and the resulting theological view that Jesus was not the Son of God, born of a virgin was nurtured in the early church by the Jewish sect called Ebionites. The Ebionites, followed the corrupted Theodotion and Pontus text in support of their argument that Jesus was the son of Joseph.[34] Ebionites were Jews that accepted Jesus as the Messiah, but did not believe him to be God. Irenaeus stated that the Ebionites had an opinion of the Lord similar to that of Carpocrates, and that the Ebionites "practice circumcision, persevere in the observance of those customs which are enjoined by the law, and are so Judaic in their style of life, that they even adore Jerusalem as if it were the house of God."[35] Irenaeus explains the doctrines of the followers of Carpocrates:

They practice also magical arts and incantations; philters, also, and love-potions; and have recourse to familiar spirits, dream-sending demons, and other abominations, declaring that they possess power to rule over, even now, the princes and formers of this world; and not only them, but also all things that are in it.

* * *

Others of them employ outward marks, branding their disciples inside the lobe of the right ear. From among these also arose Marcellina, who came to Rome under [the episcopate of] Anicetus, and, holding these doctrines, she led multitudes astray. They style themselves Gnostics. They also possess images, some of them painted, and others formed from different kinds of material; while they maintain that a likeness of Christ was made by Pilate at that time when Jesus lived among them. They crown these images, and set them up along with the images of the philosophers of the world that is to say, with the images of Pythagoras, and Plato, and Aristotle, and the rest. They have also other modes of honouring these images, after the same manner of the Gentiles.[36]

Notice the doctrines that we see described by Irenaeus in the first and second centuries of the Ebionites and the followers of Carpocrates. At the very inception, the Judaizers were creeping into the church with all of their Babylonian witchcraft. The Ebionites were "so Judaic in their style of life, that they even adore Jerusalem as if it were the house of God." They were in no way Christians. Irenaeus identifies Marcellina, who brought the Gnostic heresy to Rome and led multitudes to follow those idolatrous practices. They possessed graven images and even crowned these images. Those are the very things that are practiced within the Roman Catholic Church today.

Irenaeus explained that "[t]hey have also other modes of honouring these images, after the same manner of the Gentiles." The followers of Carpocrates had such an elevated pride through their esoteric knowledge of magic "that some of them declare themselves similar to Jesus."[37] That is exactly what we see in the Roman Catholic Church today, where the official doctrine of the church is that the Catholic priest is *Alter-Christos* (another Christ). The Jewish Ebionites and followers of Carpoctrates were Gnostics steeped in Babylonian witchcraft, magical arts, and incantations.

Some have argued that the Jews follow the Old Testament law and that therefore there is no harm for Christians to follow the Jewish customs. John Chrysostom, who witnessed first hand the early attempts to Judaize the Christian church during the fourth century puts that argument to rest.

But at any rate the Jews say that they, too, adore God. God forbid that I say that. No Jew adores God! Who say so? The Son of God say so. For he said: "If you were to know my Father, you would also know me. But you neither know me nor do you know my Father". Could I produce a witness more trustworthy than the Son of God?

Chrysostom warned against the threat posed to the Church by the Judaizers who were enticing Christians to follow their example of taking part in the Judaic/Babylonian liturgy practiced in the synagogues:

> So it is that I exhort you to flee and shun their gatherings. The harm they bring to our weaker brothers is not slight; they offer no slight excuse to sustain to the folly of the Jews. For when they see that you, who worship the Christ whom they crucified, are reverently following their rituals, how can they fail to think that the rites they have performed are the best and that our ceremonies are worthless? For after you worship and adore at our mysteries, you run to the very men who destroy our rites. Paul said: "If a man sees you that have knowledge sit at meat in the idol's temple, shall not his conscience, being weak, be emboldened to eat those things which are sacrificed to idols"? And let me say: If a man sees you that have knowledge come into the synagogue and participate in the festival of the Trumpets, shall not his conscience, being weak, be emboldened to admire what the Jews do? He who falls not only pays the penalty for his own fall, but he is also punished because he trips others as well. But the man who has stood firm is rewarded not only because of his own virtue but people admire him for leading others to desire the same things.[38]

* * *

> What else do you wish me to tell you? Shall I tell you of their plundering, their covetousness, their abandonment of the poor, their thefts, their cheating in trade? The whole day long will not be enough to give you an account of these things. But do their festivals have something solemn and great about them? They have shown that these, too, are impure. Listen to the prophets; rather, listen to God and with how strong a statement he turns his back on them: "I have found your festivals hateful, I have thrust them away from myself".[39]

In Chrysostom's homily given at the Antioch Church, he pleaded with the Christians not to follow the Judaizers, who were attempting to entice Christians to follow the Jewish/Babylonian traditions and liturgy.

> Let me say what Elijah said against the Jews. He saw the unholy life the Jews were living: at one time they paid heed to God, at another they worshipped idols. So he spoke some such words as these: "How long will you limp on both legs? If the Lord our God is with you, come, follow Him; but if Baal, then follow him." Let me, too, now say this against these Judaizing Christians. If you judge that

Judaism is the true religion, why are you causing trouble to the Church? But if
Christianity is the true faith, as it really is, stay in it and follow it. Tell me this. Do
you share with us in the mysteries, do you worship Christ as a Christian, do you
ask him for blessings, and do you then celebrate the festival with his foes? With
what purpose, then, do you come to the church?

Chrysostom was focusing on only one front of the Jewish attack on the gospel. While he
was rightfully concerned about the enticement of Christians into following the Jewish liturgy, he
did not perceive that within the ersatz "Christian" community was an active Judaic strategy of
inculcating Babylonian mysteries. Chrysostom was laudatory of the Council at Nicea; he did not
perceive that very council set a dangerous precedent and was in fact a subtle attack on biblical
Christianity.

The Council of Nicea was the first in a series of many councils that created an orthodoxy for
Jewish/Babylonian religious doctrine masquerading beneath Christian verbiage. It was the later
Council of Trent (1545-1563) that issued curse after curse upon all who adhere to biblical
Christian doctrine. The edicts of the Council of Trent have never been rescinded, and remain the
standard for the orthodox Roman Catholic doctrine.

A clue to the nature and real objective of the council of Nicea is found in the fact that
Emperor Constantine made a ceremonial entrance at the opening of the council. As Eusebius
described, Constantine "himself proceeded through the midst of the assembly, like some
heavenly messenger of God, clothed in raiment which glittered as it were with rays of light,
reflecting the glowing radiance of a purple robe, and adorned with the brilliant splendor of gold
and precious stones."[40]

The council was not organized by church leaders; it was organized by a pagan Emperor.
Emperor Constantine organized the Council along the lines of the Roman Senate. Eusebius
describes the seating: "On each side of the interior of this were many seats disposed in order,
which were occupied by those who had been invited to attend, according to their rank."[41] The
fact that there was a perceived rank at the council is illustrative of the fact that it was not a purely
Christian council. Jesus made the point that there is no rank in his church.

But Jesus called them *to him*, and saith unto them, Ye know that they which are
accounted to rule over the Gentiles exercise lordship over them; and their great
ones exercise authority upon them. But so shall it not be among you: but
whosoever will be great among you, shall be your minister: And whosoever of
you will be the chiefest, shall be servant of all. (Mark 10:42-44 AV)

Jesus made each believer a king and priest within his church. There is no place for rank.
"And hath made us kings and priests unto God and his Father; to him *be* glory and dominion for
ever and ever. Amen." (Revelation 1:6 AV) "So the last shall be first, and the first last: for many
be called, but few chosen." (Matthew 20:16 AV) The only way that the first can be last and vice-

versa is if all are equal.

In fact, it is anti-Christian to have a council of men deciding by popular vote what is and what is not Christian doctrine. True Christians rest on the authority of God's infallible word not the votes of fallible men. While the Council of Nicea issued edicts that offered correct biblical interpretation, that was cover for the adoption of heathen ideology. For example, the council correctly condemned the error of Arianism. Arianism in essence held that Jesus was created. Incidently Eusebius, who was so impressed with the pageantry of Constantine, was a supporter of the Arian error. The council mixed that correct ruling against Arianism with the leaven of error by instituting the celebration of Easter Sunday.

The Easter Sunday edict by the Council of Nicea implicitly makes Jesus out to be a liar and a fraud. To suggest that Jesus rose from the dead on Sunday after his supposed crucifixion on Friday, means that Jesus' prophecy of rising from the dead after 3 days and 3 nights did not come true. Jesus prophesied:

> For as Jonas was three days and three nights in the whale's belly; so shall the Son of man be **three days and three nights** in the heart of the earth. (Matthew 12:40 AV)

Between Friday and Saturday are only parts of two days, plus one full day, and only two nights. To say Jesus was crucified on a Friday and rose from the dead on Sunday is to deny that Jesus is God, because his prophecy of raising from the dead after 3 days and 3 night would not have been fulfilled with a Friday burial and a Sunday resurrection.

> And if thou say in thine heart, How shall we know the word which the LORD hath not spoken? **When a prophet speaketh in the name of the LORD, if the thing follow not, nor come to pass, that *is* the thing which the LORD hath not spoken**, *but* the prophet hath spoken it presumptuously: thou shalt not be afraid of him. (Deuteronomy 18:21-22 AV)

To add insult to injury the council of Nicea put the heathen title of "Easter" on the celebration of Jesus' resurrection. Easter is a word derived from the adoration and worship of the pagan queen of heaven "Astarte" or "Ishtar."[42] Hislop states: "What means the term Easter itself? It is not a Christian name. It bears its Chaldean [i.e. Babylonian] origin on its very forehead."[43] Easter was and is a pagan spring festival which involved fertility symbols such as eggs and rabbits.[44] Easter has nothing at all to do with Passover or with the resurrection of our Lord and Savior Jesus Christ. Calling Easter a holiday of the resurrection of Christ is mixing a heathen festival with the Christian history.

Easter Sunday is a spiritual seduction whereby people have been convinced to follow the tradition of a Friday crucifixion and Sunday resurrection, instead of the biblical account of a Wednesday crucifixion and Saturday resurrection. The false doctrine of a Sunday resurrection misinterprets what took place when the disciples arrived at the tomb on the day after the Sabbath. Jesus had already risen by that time. In fact, the disciples found the tomb empty and an angel told them that Jesus had already risen (Mark 16:1-6). Jesus fulfilled his prophecy that he would rise from the dead exactly 3 days and 3 nights after his burial (Matthew 12:40, 20:19). Christ had risen from the dead late on the Sabbath day before the disciples arrived at the tomb.

The council of Nicea was a way for the Judaizers to subtly begin the process of establishing a heathen orthodoxy under the false cover of a council called to eradicate error from the "Christian" church. Chrysostom and many others were unaware that false brethren had crept into the council. It was the very thing the Apostle Paul saw happen at the outset. "And that because of false brethren unawares brought in, who came in privily to spy out our liberty which we have in Christ Jesus, that they might bring us into bondage:" (Galatians 2:4 AV)

The Judaizers were ever so subtle they even caused the Apostle Peter to fall for their error. The Judaizers had convinced Peter to separate himself from the gentiles and congregate with the Jews to follow the Jewish customs, rather than embracing the spiritual freedom offered by Christ. Paul, who was a former Jew of Jews, knew what the Jews were up to and had to confront Peter about falling for their subtle deception.

> But when Peter was come to Antioch, I withstood him to the face, because he was to be blamed. For before that certain came from James, he did eat with the Gentiles: but when they were come, he withdrew and separated himself, fearing them which were of the circumcision. And the other Jews dissembled likewise with him; insomuch that Barnabas also was carried away with their dissimulation. (Galatians 2:11-13 AV)

Notice that Paul in Galatians 2:4 states that the Judaizers were bent on bringing the Christians back into bondage. We see this same thing happening at the Council of Nicea. The council edicts were to be enforced; the Christians were to be brought into bondage to follow the new (Judaic/Babylonian) orthodoxy under Christian cover.

Constantine used the force of government to bring the members of the ersatz church into bondage under the edicts of the Council of Nicea. Constantine ordered that two weeks be set aside for the celebration of Easter, which included a vacation of all legal processes during that time.[45] Imagine that. The Emperor (Pope) of Rome using his absolute authority to enforce the edict of the Council of Nicea. When a religious custom must be enforced by government edict, that is a sure sign that it is not Christian. It is the very thing that Paul was concerned about in his letter to the Galatians.

Hislop states: "The popular observances that still attend the period of its celebration amply confirm the testimony of history as to its Babylonian character. The hot cross buns of Good Friday, and the dyed eggs of Pasch or Easter Sunday, figured in the Chaldean rites just as they do now. The 'buns,' known too by that identical name, were used in the worship of the queen of heaven, the goddess Easter."[46]

Where have we seen this queen of heaven, mentioned by Hislop, before? In Jerusalem. The queen of heaven was worshiped by the Jews during the time of Jeremiah. "The children gather wood, and the fathers kindle the fire, and the women knead *their* dough, to make cakes to the queen of heaven, and to pour out drink offerings unto other gods, that they may provoke me to anger." (Jeremiah 7:18 AV)

Once the Judaizers infected the ersatz church with the Judaic/Babylonian religious contagion of Easter, it was only a matter of time before the goddess of Easter, the queen of heaven, made her appearance in the form of Mary. Today in the Catholic Church "the Fifth Glorious Mystery - The Coronation" recited during the Catholic rosary is a dedication to Mary, the queen of heaven. The official Catholic doctrine is that **"Mary is the Queen of Heaven."**[47] Hislop explains how the Babylonian egg symbolism has been adopted by the Roman Church:

> Now the Romish Church adopted this mystic egg of Astarte, and consecrated it as a symbol of Christ's resurrection. A form of prayer was even appointed to be used in connection with it, Pope Paul V teaching his superstitious votaries thus to pray at Easter: "Bless, O Lord, we beseech thee, this thy creature of eggs, that it may become a wholesome sustenance unto thy servants, eating it in remembrance of our Lord Jesus Christ, &c" (Scottish Guardian, April, 1844).

"Gieseler, speaking of the Eastern Church in the second century, in regard to Paschal observances, says: 'In it [the Paschal festival in commemoration of the death of Christ] they [the Eastern Christians] eat unleavened bread, probably like the Jews, eight days throughout."[48] The Council of Nicea edict on the Sunday resurrection of Christ is the foundation for the orthodox Catholic doctrine of today. The Sunday Catholic mass is the foremost Catholic holy day of obligation.[49] Catholic law is that "[t]hose who deliberately fail in this obligation commit a grave sin."[50] That Sunday law is based on the traditional Catholic view that Jesus was crucified on a Friday and arose from the dead on Sunday.[51] This Sunday doctrine was fostered by Constantine. There is convincing authority supporting the argument that Constantine was the first pope of the Roman Catholic Church.[52] The *Jewish History Sourcebook* explains that Constantine "was the first Roman emperor to issue laws which radically limited the rights of Jews as citizens of the Roman Empire."[53] The persecution of the Jews had the effect of driving them into the nascent Catholic Church bringing with them their Judaic/Babylonian traditions and solidifying those that had already taken root.

One of the favorite attacks by the new bible version advocates is to claim that the word "Easter" in Acts 12:4 is an example of a mistranslation by the King James translators. They assert that the word *pascha* should be translated "Passover" not "Easter."

AV (KJV)	**NKJV**
Now about that time Herod the king stretched forth *his* hands to vex certain of the church. And he killed James the brother of John with the sword. And because he saw it pleased the Jews, he proceeded further to take Peter also. (Then were the days of unleavened bread.) And when he had apprehended him, he put *him* in prison, and delivered *him* to four quaternions of soldiers to keep him; intending after **Easter** to bring him forth to the people. (Acts 12:1-4 AV (KJV))	Now about that time Herod the king stretched out his hand to harass some from the church. Then he killed James the brother of John with the sword. And because he saw that it pleased the Jews, he proceeded further to seize Peter also. Now it was during the Days of Unleavened Bread. So when he had arrested him, he put him in prison, and delivered him to four squads of soldiers to keep him, intending to bring him before the people after **Passover**. (Acts 12:1-4 NKJV)

The so-called biblical scholars begin their argument on the right foot but then stumble on man's wisdom. They correctly note that Easter was and is a pagan spring festival. They correctly assert that Easter has nothing at all to do with Passover or with the resurrection of our Lord and Savior Jesus Christ. Because Easter is in fact a pagan holiday, the new bible versions translate the Greek word *pascha* in Acts 12:4 as "Passover," thinking that God could not possibly mean to refer to a pagan holiday in his Holy Scriptures. In Acts 12:4, however, God is not using the word *pascha* to describe a Christian or Jewish holiday, he is describing the intentions of Herod. Herod intended to wait until the Easter pagan holiday was over before he brought Peter out before the people.

While Passover is one of the possible English translations for *pascha*, that translation in the context of Acts 12:4 is simply wrong. The more accurate translation is "Easter," which is the translation found in the King James Holy Bible. *Pascha* is a word of Chaldean origin and means either Passover or the pagan festival of Easter. The pedantic and rather sophomoric translation by the modern so-called scholars is demonstrably erroneous. They assume that *pascha* must be translated "Passover" in Acts 12:4, based solely on the fact that *pascha* means Passover in all other biblical passages where it appears. They completely disregard the alternative English translation for *pascha* of Easter.

Pascha, however, cannot possibly mean Passover in Acts 12:4, because Herod intended to keep custody of Peter until after *pascha*. *Pascha* in that passage must mean Easter, because Passover had already taken place when Peter was arrested during the days of unleavened bread. The fourteenth day of the first month of the Jewish calendar is the Passover (Leviticus 23:4-5, Exodus 12:17-18). Passover is immediately followed by the seven days of unleavened bread (Leviticus 23:6-7, Exodus 12:15-16). Because Passover is memorialized with unleavened bread (Exodus 12:17-18), it and the seven day feast of unleavened bread are both referred to as the feast of unleavened bread (Matthew 26:17, Mark 14:1, 14:12, Luke 22:1-7, Leviticus 23:6, Exodus 12:17-20). Combining the Passover with the feast of unleavened bread we get eight (8) days of unleavened bread that span from the Fourteenth day (Passover) until the 21st day of the first month in the Jewish calendar (Genesis 12:18).

> These *are* the feasts of the LORD, *even* holy convocations, which ye shall proclaim in their seasons. In the fourteenth *day* of the first month at even *is* the LORD'S passover. **And on the fifteenth day of the same month *is* the feast of unleavened bread unto the LORD: seven days ye must eat unleavened bread.** In the first day ye shall have an holy convocation: ye shall do no servile work therein. But ye shall offer an offering made by fire unto the LORD seven days: in the seventh day *is* an holy convocation: ye shall do no servile work *therein*. (Leviticus 23:4-8 AV)

In Acts 12:1-4 we see that Peter was taken into custody during the days of unleavened bread that follow Passover, Passover had already taken place. Because Passover had already taken place by that time, it makes no sense for the passage to say that Herod intended to hold Peter until after Passover. The pagan holiday Easter, on the other hand followed Passover and had not yet occurred. Herod was a Jew steeped in the Judaic/Babylonian customs of celebrating Easter. Herod intended to hold Peter until after the pagan holiday of Easter. Therefore, the King James translators were correct when they translated *pascha* as "Easter," and the modern translators are wrong in translating *pascha* as "Passover."

The translators of the new bible versions are more concerned with changing and twisting God's words to comport with popular opinion than using God's words to change the world. The new bible versions are just one strategy among many to Judaize the ersatz church. While implementing their strategy of Judaizing the ersatz "Christian" church, the Jews continued to nurture their separate Babylonian/Judaic religion. The religious view of the Orthodox Jews is one of superiority. They view themselves as the rightful rulers of the earth. This is explained in the book *The Jewish Question in Europe*:

> Who then, with dispassion, having investigated the facts and documents, cannot but conclude that there has never been ambition more mad and tenacious, and none more frankly stated as that of the Jews. They arrogate to themselves the conquest of the world, of reigning over all the nations by overthrowing them, of subjugating all the peoples to themselves. And they appropriate the right to stake their claim on all of the blessings of the universe, their legitimate birthright given them by God. It is amazing to read and hear about this terrible challenge by a fistful of men, about 8 million of them, who course among five hundred million others, and who seriously wish to enslave them, and dream of doing so![54]

Once the influence of the Jews is recognized by the national host, they are persecuted and thrown out of the country.

There is no end to the persecutions of the Jews which have been carried out

before, still, and everywhere. But these persecutions were and are the consequence
of their mad wickedness. All of this is manifested by the avidity of their ambition;
by its legitimization by virtue of their superiority; by their sense of privilege over
the people they live among now and previously. They have demonstrated
themselves to be intractable and hostile evildoers toward the nations that have
tolerated them and do tolerate them now, bestowing upon them, above all, the
blessing of the right of citizenship.[55]

What causes the body politic to awake and recognize the need to rid itself of the Jews? They
discover that the usury of the Jews is bringing about their ruin. It is usury, which threatens the
continued existence of the state and if unchecked leads to its ultimate destruction.

The human causes of this fact [of the persecution of the Jews], unique in history,
are witnessed by the Jews' insatiable appetite for turning to usury to gain power
through betrayal in order to dominate, and whenever possible, to take over and
overthrow the State.

In every country, this immutable law of Hebrew prosperity in every country is
always to the detriment of the well being and liberty of the inhabitants.[56]

This is what happened to Rome, which was economically and materially subjugated to the
Jews, as were all of the major cities of the great nations of Europe. The threat posed by the Jews
to the state is the same threat it poses to religion. The Jewish financial influence gives them
concomitant influence in religious affairs. The powerful Jewish banking family of the
Rothschilds, members of which are high officials in the Priory of Sion and the Elders of Zion,
have taken over the Vatican's financial operations.[57] He who pays the piper calls the tune. We
see in John, chapter 2 Jesus' reaction to the corruption of the temple worship by the Jewish
merchants and money-changers.

And the Jews' passover was at hand, and Jesus went up to Jerusalem, And found
in the temple those that sold oxen and sheep and doves, and the changers of
money sitting: And when he had made a scourge of small cords, he drove them all
out of the temple, and the sheep, and the oxen; and poured out the changers'
money, and overthrew the tables; And said unto them that sold doves, Take these
things hence; make not my Father's house an house of merchandise." (John 2:13-
16 AV)

The political power and influence of the Jews stems directly from their control of banking.
The current events in the United States is clear evidence of that historical fact. Representative
Louis T. McFadden in a May 2, 1934, radio address stated:

It would be a monstrous mistake for any intelligent citizen of whatever nation to
close his eyes to the evident fact that for nigh sixty years, the Jews have surely and

rapidly though almost invisibly climbed to the heights of government wherefrom the masses are ruled. Politically, financially and economically they have seized the reigns of governments of all nations and their invasion in the realms of social, educational and religious fields [is] not less important.[58]

Congressman McFadden, who was Chairman of the U.S. House of Representatives Banking and Currency Committee, knew the power that the Jews wielded and the calamities that they caused. Just as the Protocols of the Learned Elders of Zion provided, the Talmudic Jews controlled the money supply through a central bank (The Federal Reserve Bank). Congressman McFadden sated: "It [the depression] was not accidental. It was a carefully contrived occurrence....The international bankers sought to bring about a condition of despair here so that they might emerge as the rulers of us all. . . . The end result, if the Insiders have their way, will be the dream of Montagu Norman of the Bank of England 'that the Hegemony of World Finance should reign supreme over everyone, everywhere, as one whole super-national control mechanism.'"

Representative McFadden addressed the U.S. House of Representatives on June 10, 1932. "Some people think the Federal Reserve Banks are U.S. government institutions. They are not government institutions. They are private credit monopolies which prey upon the people of the U.S. for the benefit of themselves and their foreign and domestic swindlers, and rich and predatory money lenders."[59] In essence, the international Jewish money power used corrupt politicians to push through the Federal Reserve Act, which gave them a monopoly to print the money of the nation.[60] The Federal Reserve Act legalizes theft for a select few commercial banks that make up the Federal Reserve. McFadden exposed the methods that the Jews used to obtain their immense power over the government of the United States.

Representative McFadden's revealed in a 1932 speech before the House of Representatives that the communist revolution in Russia was financed by the Federal Reserve.[61] In addition, billions of dollars and millions of ounces of the gold deposits of the United States were stolen by the Federal Reserve Banks and sent to Germany.[62] As he spoke in 1932, huge amounts of gold were being sent to Germany on a weekly basis. Why was this money being sent to Germany? To fund the Nazis. It was only a little over eight months later, on January 30, 1933, that Adolph Hitler was sworn in as Chancellor of Germany. Within a year, Hitler had consolidated enough power, with the help of the Federal Reserve, that he declared himself "Fuhrer" (leader) of Germany. The gold he received from the Federal Reserve was used to build planes, ships, tanks, and guns that were used to kill brave Americans during World War II. The Federal Reserve Board and Banks funded both the communists in Russia and the Nazis in Germany, all at the expense of the hard labor of the American middle class.

Even during World War II, the United States funded the communist Russians through the "lend-lease" program. In addition to our own financial burdens of the war, the U.S. taxpayers funded the Germans and the Russians. The Jewish Bankers, having funded both sides of the war, made out like bandits.

As a consequence of Congressman McFadden's discovery of treasonous criminal conduct, on May 23, 1933, he brought formal criminal charges against the Board of Governors of the Federal Reserve Bank, the Comptroller of the Currency, and the Secretary of the United States Treasury. The petition for Articles of Impeachment was, thereafter, referred to the Judiciary Committee.

Representative McFadden was Chairman of the House Banking and Currency Committee and was in a position to do something about the banking monopoly. The Zionist Jews could not allow such a powerful person to oppose their plans. They tried several times to assassinate Representative McFadden. They were ultimately successful; in 1935 they poisoned him. After Representative McFadden's death, the bill introduced by him was pigeonholed in the Judiciary Committee and has never seen the light of day since.

God admonished against the destructive practice of usury (i.e., interest). See, e.g., Exodus 22:25, Leviticus 25:36-37, Deuteronomy 23:19, Nehemiah, Psalms 15:5, Proverbs 28:8. Why would the Jews ignore the commands of God against usury? Because the orthodox Jews do not follow the Old Testament. They have replaced God's laws with their traditions. They follow their oral traditions, which in part have been memorialized in the Talmud. Israel Shahak explains that although the Talmud forbids a Jew, on pain of severe punishment, to take interest on a loan made to another Jew, the rabbis have figured a contrivance to get around that restriction.[63] A business dispensation called *heter 'isqa* was devised for an interest-bearing loan between Jews.[64] In any event, the Talmud grants a license to charge interest to gentiles; according to a majority of Talmudic authorities, it is a religious duty to take as much interest as possible on a loan made to a Gentile.[65]

The influence of the Talmud over the Jewish banking practices is witnessed by the fact that when Alan Greenspan, who is an atheist Jew, took his oath of office as Chairman of President Nixon's Council of Economic Advisers, he did so on a volume of the Talmud.[66] He later went on to be appointed Chairman of the Federal Reserve by Ronald Reagan.

Why would Greenspan, who is an atheist Jew, take an oath on the Talmud, which is a religious publication? Because within the Talmud is found the doctrine of the Devil that "ye shall be as gods." Genesis 3:5. That is why there are a great number of Jews who claim to be atheists. In fact, some Jewish rabbis are atheists. Rabbi Sherman Wine is one example. He was the rabbi of the Birmingham Temple in Michigan. Rabbi Wine stated: "I am an atheist."[67] He "expunged the name of God from all services at his temple."[68] Rabbi Wine had "a Jewish liturgy emphasizing Jewish culture, history and identity along with humanistic ethics while excluding all prayers and references to God."[69] Rabbi Wine is not alone. In December 2006, he traveled to Israel for the ordination of seven other atheist rabbis.[70] Rabbi Wine, died in 2007. He is not an atheist anymore.

When the Jews thrive, then also does the nation in which they reside in like manner fades. The idea of a restored Israel with a resulting world of harmony and justice, is just a cover story for the ignorant *goyim* to conceal the macabre plan for world dominion. Yesaiah Tishbi, who is a religious authority on the Jewish Kabbalah, reveals that "the presence of Israel among the nations mends the world, but not the nations of the world . . . it does not bring the nations closer to holiness, but rather extracts the holiness from them and thereby destroys their ability to exist. . . . (T)he purpose of the full redemption is to destroy the vitality of the all the peoples."[71]   This destructive influence stems from the Jewish core belief that the souls of non-Jews are evil.[72]

As in finance and politics, so also in religion. As the Jewish power and influence increases, then the Christian church suffers. Can there be any doubt that the Jews were supporters of Julian in his conquest of Rome?   All one need do is read the aims of Julian to perceive the hidden hand of the Jews behind Julian's ascendence to power.

> "In the year 360 Julian, a cousin of Constantine, was proclaimed Roman Emperor by the army. Constantine, who had prepared for battle against him, died on the way; this made easier the final victory for Julian and his proclamation as Emperor of the Orient and Occident. The policy of Julian had three principle aims: I. To renew the Pagan belief and to again declare it a state religion of the Empire, so that Rome which according to his view had declined through Christianity, might return to its old glory. II. To destroy Christianity. III. To concede to Jewry its old positions, from which it had been expelled by Constantine and his sons; even the rebuilding of the Temple of Solomon was to be arranged.[73]

As the Jews gained influence, so also did the state increase the persecution of Christians. Fortunately for the Christian community, Julian's reign only lasted 3 years. He died in 363 A.D. However, it was enough for the Jews to kick start a revival in Jewish scholarship in Rome.

> There was a revival of Hebrew studies in Rome, centered around the local yeshiva, Metivta de Mata Romi. A number of well-known scholars, Rabbi Kalonymus b. Moses and Rabbi Jacob "Gaon" and Rabbi Nathan b. Jehil (who wrote a great talmudic dictionary, the Arukh), contributed to Jewish learning and development. Roman Jewish traditions followed those practiced in the Land of Israel and the liturgical customs started in Rome spread throughout Italy and the rest of the world.[74]

4 Kabbalah and Talmud

The Jewish studies in Rome led to inculcation of Jewish doctrine into the Roman church. The Kabbalah and Talmud are at the root of the Jewish doctrine. Kabbalah is a Hebrew word, which literally translated means "tradition." Nesta Webster in her classic book *Secret Societies and Subversive Movements* explained how the Jewish theology of the Kabbalah was introduced into the Roman Catholic Church by Pope Sixtus IV (1471-1484).

> It was likewise from a Florentine Jew, Alemanus or Datylus that Pico della Mirandola, the fifteenth-century mystic, received instructions in the Cabala and imagined that he had discovered in it the doctrines of Christianity. This delighted Pope Sixtus IV, who thereupon ordered Cabalistic writings to be translated into Latin for the use of divinity students.[75]

Jesus criticized the Pharisees for their religious traditions. Those traditions were oral traditions at that time. Later they were memorialized in the Talmud and the Kabbalah. The Kabbalah and the Talmud today span numerous volumes. Jesus called the pharisees hypocrites, who masqueraded as religious men, but who were in reality irreligious frauds.

> Then came to Jesus scribes and Pharisees, which were of Jerusalem, saying, Why do thy disciples transgress the tradition of the elders? for they wash not their hands when they eat bread. But he answered and said unto them, **Why do ye also transgress the commandment of God by your tradition?** For God commanded, saying, Honour thy father and mother: and, He that curseth father or mother, let him die the death. But ye say, Whosoever shall say to *his* father or *his* mother, *It is* a gift, by whatsoever thou mightest be profited by me; And honour not his father or his mother, *he shall be free.* **Thus have ye made the commandment of God of none effect by your tradition.** *Ye* hypocrites, well did Esaias prophesy of you, saying, This people draweth nigh unto me with their mouth, and honoureth me with *their* lips; but their heart is far from me. But **in vain they do worship me, teaching *for* doctrines the commandments of men.**

(Matthew 15:1-9 AV)

The Pharisees had an outward appearance of piety, in order to gain political and religious control of the Jews. In secret, however, they practiced an occult doctrine that was only known to its initiates. Lady Queenborough (Edith Miller) explains in her book *Occult Theosophy*:

> The Chaldean science acquired by many of the Jewish priests, during the captivity of Babylon, gave birth to the sect of the Pharisees whose name only appears in the Holy Scriptures and in the writings of the Jewish historians after the captivity (606 B. C). The works of the celebrated scientist Munk leave no doubt on the point that the sect appeared during the period of the captivity. "From then dates the Cabala or Tradition of the Pharisees. For a long time their precepts were only transmitted orally but later they formed the Talmud and received their final form in the book called the *Sepher ha Zohar.*"[76]

The scrupulous observance by the Pharisees of Jewish religious tradition was only a cover for their secret doctrine. They had rejected Jehovah and had adopted the pantheism of Babylon. They pretended that their many rituals were necessary for the worship of Jehovah, but those were only man-made rules to conceal their secret Babylonian religion. Jesus rebuked them for it; calling them hypocrites for their vain worship of God through man-inspired rituals and honoring God with fine words, when their hearts in fact were focused on the heathen gods of Babylon. See Mark 7:5-7. The Pharisees had accepted the Satanic lie that they had become "as gods." See Genesis 3:5. Their new Babylonian (a/k/a Chaldean) religion was to be exclusive to the Jews, who were to rule the world. Edith Miller explains:

> The Pharisees, then, judging it wiser to capture the confidence of their compatriots by taking the lead in the religious movement, affected a scrupulous observance of the slightest prescriptions of the law and instituted the practice of complicated rituals, simultaneously however cultivating the new doctrine [i.e. secret doctrine] in their secret sanctuaries. These were regular secret societies, composed during the captivity of a few hundred adepts. At the time of Flavius Josephus which was that of their greatest prosperity, they numbered only some 6,000 members. This group of intellectual pantheists was soon to acquire a directing influence over the Jewish nation. Nothing, moreover, likely to offend national sentiment ever appeared in their doctrines. However saturated with pantheistic Chaldeism they might have been, the Pharisees preserved their ethnic pride intact. This religion of Man divinised, which they had absorbed at Babylon, they conceived solely as applying to the profit of the Jew, the superior and predestined being. The promises of universal dominion which the orthodox Jew found in the Law, the Pharisees did not interpret in the sense of the reign of the God of Moses over the nations, but in that of a material domination to be imposed on the universe by the Jews. The awaited Messiah was no longer the Redeemer of original Sin, a spiritual victor who would lead the world, it was a temporal king, bloody with battle, who

would make Israel master of the world and 'drag all peoples under the wheels of his chariot'. The Pharisees did not ask this enslavement of the nations of a mystical Jehovah, which they continued worshipping in public, only as a concession to popular opinion, for they expected its eventual consummation to be achieved by the secular patience of Israel and the use of human means. [77]

Jesus cursed the Pharisees to their face: "Woe unto you, scribes and Pharisees, hypocrites! for ye are as graves which appear not, and the men that walk over *them* are not aware *of them*." (Luke 11:44 AV) The Babylonian traditions of the Pharisees, which were traditions passed down orally from generation to generation, were eventually (in part) memorialized in the Kabbalah and Talmud. The double aim of the Pharisees was to wrestle political control over the Jews from the Sadducees and "to modify gradually the conceptions of the people in the direction of their secret doctrine."[78] They accomplished both goals. Today Orthodox Jewry is an insular authoritarian society that is completely given over to the practice of the Babylonian religion of the ancient Pharisees.

The twisted Babylonian god of modern Jewry as expressed in the Talmud and Kabbalah is not the merciful God of the bible, but rather a god of vengeance and hatred against gentiles and particularly Christians. Edith Miller summarizes the nature of the Jewish god as being "just and merciful only to his own people, but foe to all other nations, denying them human rights and commanding their enslavement that Israel might appropriate their riches and rule over them."[79]

Michael Hoffman explains that "[l]ike the Talmud, the Kabbalah supersedes, nullifies and ultimately replaces the Bible."[80] Lawrence Fine, Professor of Jewish Studies and prominent scholar of medieval Judaism and Jewish mysticism, reveals that the Kabbalah contains the "true" meaning of the Old Testament. The "simple" meaning of the biblical language recedes into the background as the symbolic meaning contained in the Kabbalah supercedes the bible and takes control. There is a code to the true meaning in the bible that can only be unlocked through the Kabbalah.

> [T]he reader must become accustomed to regarding biblical language in a kabbalistically symbolic way. The Kabbalists taught that the Torah is not only the speech or word of God, but is also the many names of God or expression of God's being. It is a vast body of symbols, which refers to the various aspects of divine life, the sefirot, and their complex interaction. **The simple meaning of biblical language recedes into the background as symbolic discourse assumes control.** The true meaning of Scripture becomes manifest only when it is read with the proper (sefirotic) code. **Thus the Torah must not be read on the simple or obvious level of meaning; it must be read with the knowledge of a kabbalist who possesses the hermeneutical keys with which to unlock its *inner* truths.**[81]

The Kabbalah at Zohar III, 152a states: "Thus the tales related to the Torah are simply her outer garments, and woe to the person who regards that outer garb as the Torah itself! For such a person will be deprived of a portion in the world to come."[82] That passage in the Kabbalah puts a curse on anyone who tries to read the bible for what it actually says, instead of with the mystical gloss put on it by the Kabbalah.

The Kabbalah is Judaic mystical practices that were adopted by the Jews from Babylon. H.P. Blavatsky described the Kabbalah as: "The hidden wisdom of the Hebrew Rabbis of the middle ages derived from the older secret doctrines concerning divine things and cosmogony, which were combined into a theology after the time of the captivity of the Jews in Babylon. All the works that fall under the esoteric category are termed Kabalistic."[83]

The Jewish Encyclopedia acknowledges the Babylonian (a/k/a Chaldean) origins of the Kabbalah (a/k/a Cabala). In addition, the Jewish Encyclopedia explains that Gnosticism flowed from the Jews to the ersatz "Christians." That is yet more authority that Gnosticism flowed from Babylon via the Jewish Gnostics to lay the foundation for the Roman Catholic theology. The esoteric Gnosticism imbued in the Catholic theology was based upon the Jewish Kabbalah.

> The Pythagorean idea of the creative powers of numbers and letters, upon which the "Sefer Yez.irah" is founded, and which was known in tannaitic times . . . is here proved to be an old cabalistic conception. In fact, the belief in the magic power of the letters of the Tetragrammaton and other names of the Deity . . . seems to have originated in Chaldea . . . Whatever, then, the theurgic Cabala was, which, under the name of "Sefer (or "Hilkot" Yez.irah,") induced Babylonian rabbis of the fourth century to "create a calf by magic."
>
> * * *
>
> But especially does Gnosticism testify to the antiquity of the Cabala. Of Chaldean origin, as suggested by Kessler . . . and definitively shown by Anz . . . Gnosticism was Jewish in character long before it became Christian.[84]

Magic and occult mysticism runs throughout the Kabbalah. Judith Weill, a professor of Jewish mysticism stated that magic is deeply rooted in Jewish tradition, but the Jews are reticent to acknowledge it and don't even refer to it as magic.[85] Gershom Scholem (1897-1982), Professor of Kabbalah at Hebrew University in Jerusalem, admitted that the Kabbalah contains a great deal of black magic and sorcery, which he explained involves invoking the powers of devils to disrupt the natural order of things.[86] Professor Scholem also stated that there are devils who are in submission to the Talmud; in the Kabbalah these devils are called *shedim Yehuda'im*.[87]

The *Jewish Chronicle* revealed that occult practices such as making amulets, charms, and talismans are taught in Jerusalem at the rabbinic seminary Yeshivat Hamekubalim.[88] That is why Jesus said to the Jews: **"Ye are of *your* father the devil, and the lusts of your father ye will do."** John 8:44. The bible states clearly that the magic arts are an abomination to the Lord.

There shall not be found among you *any one* that maketh his son or his daughter to pass through the fire, *or* that useth divination, *or* an observer of times, or an enchanter, or a witch, Or a charmer, or a consulter with familiar spirits, or a wizard, or a necromancer. For all that do these things *are* an abomination unto the LORD: and because of these abominations the LORD thy God doth drive them out from before thee. (Deuteronomy 18:10-12 AV)

The Kabbalah, like the Talmud, graphically blasphemes Jesus. For example, in Zohar III, 282a, the Kabbalah refers to Jesus as a dog who resides among filth and vermin.[89]

There is a clear parallel between the traditions of the pharisees of old and those of modern Roman Catholic priestcraft. The Roman Catholic Church follows the practice of the Jews and calls the combination of man's tradition and God's word "the Word of God." To a Protestant Christian the word of God means the Holy Bible. However, to the Roman Catholic, it means the Holy Bible plus their traditions.

> **Sacred Tradition and Sacred Scripture make up a single sacred deposit of the Word of God**. *CATECHISM OF THE CATHOLIC CHURCH*, § 97, 1994.

> [T]he church, to whom the transmission and interpretation of Revelation is entrusted, **does not derive her certainty about all revealed truths from the holy Scriptures alone. Both Scripture and Tradition must be accepted and honored with equal sentiments of devotion and reverence**. *Id*. at § 82 (emphasis added).

The Catholic Church has grafted its tradition, onto the word of God. With this slight of hand they have deceived people into following doctrines that are directly contrary to God's word as found in the Holy Bible.

The very idea of adding traditions to Gods word is based upon the practice of the Jews. Michael Hoffman explains: "The Talmud is Judaism's holiest book (actually a collection of books). Its authority takes precedence over the Old Testament in Judaism. Evidence of this may be found in the Talmud itself, Erubin 21b (Soncino edition): 'My son, be more careful in the observance of the words of the Scribes than in the words of the Torah (Old Testament).'"[90]

In that section of the Talmud there is a distinction made between the Torah and the Talmud (words of the Scribes). Often, that distinction is not made. Jews often refer to both the Talmud and the Torah as "Torah." As with the Catholic Church calling the combination of their traditions and the bible, the word of God, so also the Jews say that Torah is the combination of their traditions (Talmud and Kabbalah) and the Old Testament. However, in Orthodox Judaism the Jewish traditions contained in the rabbinical writing of the Talmud and Kabbalah supercede and supplant the word of God found in the Old Testament (which is also called the Tanakh). That same thing is true regarding Catholic traditions that supplant the word of God.

The Jews teach that Moses was given revelation in two forms on Mount Sinai, oral and written. The smaller revelation was the written Torah, the larger revelation was kept orally. "This 'Oral Torah' had been transmitted faithfully by the leaders of each generation to their successors, by Moses to Joshua , and then to the elders, then to the prophets, to the men of the Great Assembly, to the leaders of the Pharisees, and finally to the earliest rabbis. The earliest rabbis saw themselves as heirs to the Pharisees."[91]

In one statement Jesus exposed the lie that the oral traditions of the Jews were given by God to Moses at Mount Sinai. Jesus stated: **"For had ye believed Moses, ye would have believed me: for he wrote of me. But if ye believe not his writings, how shall ye believe my words?"** (John 5:46-47 AV) If the oral traditions had truly been given by Moses, they would have testified to the authenticity of Jesus as Christ. Since the Jews rejected Jesus, because he contravened their traditions, that is proof that their traditions could not have come from Moses. Michael Hoffman explains that one statement by Jesus "crushed the whole beguiling system of indoctrination predicated on the Pharisaic myth of a divinely inspired, oral tradition of the elders."[92]

Rabbi Ben Zion Bokser admits that the so-called traditions of the Jews that form the foundations of Judaism are entirely extra-biblical. He states that Jews and Christians alike are under the fallacious impression that Judaism is a religion based upon the Hebrew Bible. He states to the contrary that "[m]uch of what exists in Judaism is absent in the Bible, and much of what is in the Bible cannot be found in Judaism. . . . **Judaism is not the religion of the Bible**."[93]

Judaism is based primarily upon the Kabbalah, Talmud, and other rabbinical writings. Where there is a conflict between their traditions (Talmud and Kabbalah) and the Old Testament (Torah), their traditions take precedence. Jews claim that the Talmud is partly a collection of traditions Moses gave them in oral form. Those traditions had not yet been written down in Jesus' time. Christ condemned the traditions of the Scribes and Pharisees, because those traditions (which later became written down in the Talmud) nullify the teachings of the Holy Bible. **"Making the word of God of none effect through your tradition**, which ye have delivered: and many such like things do ye." (Mark 7:13 AV)

Rabbi Joseph D. Soloveitchik is regarded as one of the most influential rabbis of the 20th century. He is viewed as the unchallenged leader of Orthodox Judaism and the top international authority on halakha (Jewish religious law). "Soloveitchik was responsible for instructing and ordaining more than 2,000 rabbis, "an entire generation" of Jewish leadership."[94] However, when the N.Y. Times explained his study, the only basis mentioned for his ascendant religious leadership was his study of the Talmud. "Until his early 20s, he devoted himself almost exclusively to the study of the Talmud."[95] There was no mention in the article of the esteemed rabbi's study of the Old Testament (Torah) as the basis for being one of the leading authorities on Jewish law. That is because the Talmud along with the Kabbalah forms the basis for Judaism, and they are largely contrary to the Old Testament (Torah). Hoffman states: "The rabbi's credentials are all predicated upon his mastery of the Talmud."[96] "Britain's Jewish Chronicle of

March 26, 1993 states that in religious school (yeshiva), Jews are 'devoted to the Talmud to the exclusion of everything else.'"[97]

To add tradition to God's word is rebellion against God's command that nothing be added or taken away from his words. "Ye shall not add unto the word which I command you, neither shall ye diminish ought from it, that ye may keep the commandments of the LORD your God which I command you." (Deuteronomy 4:2 AV) "What thing soever I command you, observe to do it: thou shalt not add thereto, nor diminish from it." (Deuteronomy 12:32 AV)

There is a terrible curse that comes with adding or taking away from God's word.

> For I testify unto every man that heareth the words of the prophecy of this book, If any man shall add unto these things, God shall add unto him the plagues that are written in this book: And if any man shall take away from the words of the book of this prophecy, God shall take away his part out of the book of life, and out of the holy city, and *from* the things which are written in this book. (Revelation 22:18-19 AV)

The Holy Bible warns us about those who would attempt to turn us away from Christ to follow the traditions of men.

> Beware lest any man spoil you through philosophy and vain deceit, **after the tradition of men, after the rudiments of the world**, and not after Christ. (Colossians 2:8 AV)

> **Wherefore if ye be dead with Christ from the rudiments of the world, why, as though living in the world, are ye subject to ordinances, (Touch not; taste not; handle not; Which all are to perish with the using;) after the commandments and doctrines of men?** Which things have indeed a shew of wisdom in will worship, and humility, and neglecting of the body; not in any honour to the satisfying of the flesh. (Colossians 2:20-23 AV)

> He answered and said unto them, Well hath Esaias prophesied of you hypocrites, as it is written, This people honoureth me with *their* lips, but their heart is far from me. **Howbeit in vain do they worship me, teaching** *for* **doctrines the commandments of men. For laying aside the commandment of God, ye hold the tradition of men**, *as* the washing of pots and cups: and many other such like things ye do. And he said unto them, Full well **ye reject the commandment of God, that ye may keep your own tradition.** (Mark 7:6-9 AV)

Jesus said: "I am the bread of life: he that cometh to me shall never hunger; and he that believeth on me shall never thirst." (John 6:35 AV) Very simply, Jesus promised salvation to all who believed on him. Adding any other requirement to faith in Jesus corrupts the gospel, resulting in the bread of death rather than the bread of life.

Jesus warned his disciples to beware of the doctrine of the religious leaders of their time. Jesus compared their doctrine to leaven. Only a little leaven of man-made rules works its way through the whole loaf and corrupts God's pure doctrine. The leaven of today's religious leaders is no different; the leaven of tradition corrupts God's pure word. Man's tradition has turned the Bread of Salvation into spiritual poison killing the souls of those who eat of the corrupted loaf.

> **Then Jesus said unto them, Take heed and beware of the leaven of the Pharisees and of the Sadducees**. And they reasoned among themselves, saying, *It is* because we have taken no bread. *Which* when Jesus perceived, he said unto them, O ye of little faith, why reason ye among yourselves, because ye have brought no bread? Do ye not yet understand, neither remember the five loaves of the five thousand, and how many baskets ye took up? Neither the seven loaves of the four thousand, and how many baskets ye took up? How is it that ye do not understand that I spake *it* not to you concerning bread, that ye should beware of the leaven of the Pharisees and of the Sadducees? **Then understood they how that he bade *them* not beware of the leaven of bread, but of the doctrine of the Pharisees and of the Sadducees.** (Matthew 16:6-12 AV)

> **A little leaven leaveneth the whole lump**. (Galatians 5:9 AV)

God wants us to purge out the leaven of man's tradition.

> Your glorying *is* not good. Know ye not that a little leaven leaveneth the whole lump? **Purge out therefore the old leaven, that ye may be a new lump, as ye are unleavened. For even Christ our passover is sacrificed for us**: Therefore let us keep the feast, not with old leaven, neither with the leaven of malice and wickedness; but with the unleavened *bread* of sincerity and truth. (1 Corinthians 5:6-8 AV)

Man's tradition requires works to earn salvation. Salvation, however, is by God's Grace through faith alone on the completed work of Jesus Christ, who paid for all of our sins on the cross. Good works flow from salvation; good works cannot earn salvation.

> **For by grace are ye saved through faith; and that not of yourselves: *it is* the gift of God: Not of works, lest any man should boast. For we are his workmanship, created in Christ Jesus unto good works, which God hath before ordained that we should walk in them.** (Ephesians 2:8-10 AV)

5 The Judaic/Catholic Liturgy

The liturgy of the Kabbalah was injected into the state religion of Rome, which became the Roman Catholic Church.[98] *The Roman Catholic Encyclopedia* explains that the Jewish liturgy was carried over to the Roman Catholic Church.

> The meaning of the word liturgy is then extended to cover any general service of a public kind. **In the Septuagint it (and the verb leitourgeo) is used for the public service of the temple (e.g., Exodus 38:27; 39:12, etc.). Thence it comes to have a religious sense as the function of the priests, the ritual service of the temple** (e.g., Joel 1:9, 2:17, etc.). In the New Testament this religious meaning has become definitely established. In Luke 1:23, Zachary goes home when "the days of his liturgy" (ai hemerai tes leitourgias autou) are over. In Hebrews 8:6, the high priest of the New Law "has obtained a better liturgy", that is a better kind of public religious service than that of the Temple. **So in Christian use liturgy meant the public official service of the Church, that corresponded to the official service of the Temple in the Old Law.**[99]

Barbara Aho reveals the depth of the similarities between the Roman Catholic liturgy and the Jewish liturgy:

> Little wonder that one Jewish convert to Roman Catholicism made the astounding statement that entering the Catholic Church was not a "conversion" experience for him, but rather a continuation of Judaism. Roy Schoeman, the author of Salvation is from the Jews, confirms as well that the Mass is based on the Jewish ceremonial worship and that Catholic theology is based on the Old Testament!

> "As a Jew coming to the Catholic Church, it was natural for me to find the relationship between Judaism and the Catholic Church among the most interesting things in the world. It was obvious to me that for a Jew to enter the Catholic Church wasn't a matter of conversion at all, but was rather simply coming into the

42

fullness of Judaism — into the form that Judaism took after the coming of the Jewish Messiah.

"Although Catholics are aware of this in principle, they often don't think of the Catholic Church as the continuation of Judaism after the Messiah... It's everywhere you look. It's obviously in the Sacrifice of the Mass and the way the Mass is prefigured in Jewish ceremonial worship. It's in the role that the Old Testament, Jewish Scripture have in Catholic theology and the structure of the Catholic Faith." [Seattle Catholic]

A listing of parallels between Roman Catholicism and Judaism, which have analogues in the Eastern Orthodox Church as well, presented us with the startling prospect that Roman Catholicism may have been a Judaized form of Christianity from its inception. In the list of traditions below, links to the Catholic Encyclopedia show that the Roman Catholic Church justifies most of its practices by appealing to the Old Testament. Even in cases where the New Testament is cited as justification, these practices are not required under the New Covenant but have their basis in Judaism.

Priesthood (cf. Levitical priesthood/mediators between God and men)

Pope (cf. Jewish High Priest)

College of Cardinals (70) (cf. seventy elders of Moses/Deut.17:8)

Confession of sins to priest for forgiveness (cf. Lev.5:5)

Daily sacrifice of the Mass (cf. Daily burnt offering / Heb.10:11)

Altars for sacrifices

Altar vessels of gold and silver

Vestments for priests

Cardinals' skullcap (cf. Jewish yarmulke)

Offertory (cf. Offerings)

Church buildings for worship (cf. Temple)

Liturgy (cf. service of the Temple)

Sunday obligation (cf. Sabbath observance)

Ecclesiastical Feasts (cf. Jewish feasts)

Scapular / Hairshirt (cf. Sackcloth)

Works-based salvation (cf. Mosaic Law)

Sacrament of infant baptism (cf. Rite of Circumcision / Talmud)

Wafer-only Communion (cf. Manna/Shew Bread)

Sacrament of Confirmation (cf. Jewish Bar/Bat Mitzvah)

Burning of candles and incense (cf. Exodus 30)

Holy water font (cf. The Laver / Exodus 40)

No salvation outside the (Catholic) Church (Gentiles must convert to Judaism to be saved)

The following Roman Catholic traditions were not part of the Mosaic Law but were adopted by the Israelites in their apostasy:

Traditions of men (Mark 7:6-13)

Vain repetitions (Lip service (Isa.29:13)

Veneration of saints (Idolatry/pagan gods)

Worship of Mary as Mother of God (Jews worshipped Queen of Heaven / Jer. 44)

Statues/images (images on the walls of Solomon's Temple) (Ezek 8:10)

Demotion of Jesus to Co-Redeemer (cf. Jews' denial of Jesus as Messiah)

Preoccupation with Christ's death rather than resurrection (Jews' denial of Jesus' resurrection)

The above is only a partial catalog of Jewish traditions found in Roman Catholicism. The sacerdotal (priesthood) and daily sacrificial systems alone strongly implicate the Roman Catholic Church as, not only a front for apostate Judaism, but as a vehicle for converting Christians, without their knowledge, to the very religious system that rejected Jesus Christ. One commentary compares the Roman Catholic teaching on salvation to that preached in Judaism:

"The Catholic perspective on salvation is largely 'judaized' Christianity. In the days of the Apostles, many Jewish Christians believed that Christians had to follow all the requirements of the Mosaic Law, e.g., circumcision, the system of offerings, going to a priest to have sins forgiven, making sacrifices as atonement for sins, etc. A system that requires some type of 'priest' to act as an intercessor between the layperson and God is known as a sacerdotal system (from the Latin word sacerdote, meaning 'priest'.)"

In view of the striking parallels between Roman Catholicism and Judaism, it becomes apparent that Roman Catholicism represents, to a remarkable degree, the triumph of the Judaizers.[100]

6   Marranos and Conversos

The infiltration of Jewish liturgy into the Roman church made conversion to the Catholic faith palatable to Jews. Barbara Aho explains:

> During the Middle Ages, the infiltration and conquest of Christendom was achieved by two methods. The Inquisition, which started in Spain in 1478, forced multitudes of Jews to renounce Judaism and to embrace Catholicism; these "converts" were called Conversos. Conversos typically went through the motions of the Roman Catholic religion, but remained Jews inwardly and practiced their Jewish rites in the privacy of their homes.
>
> Other Jews, called Marranos (swine), feigned conversion to Christianity and practiced Roman Catholicism outwardly, while practicing Judaism, or Cabalism, privately. A number of Marranos took positions in the clergy. The motive of Conversos was self-preservation; the Marranos, destruction of the Church and all things Christian. The result of these parallel operations was the Jewish occupation of the Roman Catholic Church and its transformation into "MYSTERY BABYLON THE GREAT, THE MOTHER OF HARLOTS AND ABOMINATIONS OF THE EARTH." The King James translation of Revelation 17 describes MYSTERY, BABYLON THE GREAT as the "great whore" and "that great city which sits upon seven mountains" (v.9).

* * *

Evidence of infiltration of the Roman Catholic Church by great masses of European Jewry is found in numerous independent sources, of which we shall consider a few starting with portions of The Plot Against the Church. Typical of Catholic anti-Judaism, the authors fulminate against Jewish infiltration of the Church, but seem blind to the fact that "Holy Catholic Church" was a Judaized form of Christianity from its inception. [101]

46

Aho's characterization of the Jewish nature of the Roman church is absolutely correct. In *Mystery, Babylon the Great, Catholic or Jewish,* Aho documents that the kings and clergy that compelled Jews to convert to Catholicism were themselves Jews who infiltrated the Catholic church in order to control its doctrine and political influence. What better way to infiltrate the Roman church but by forcing Jews into pretended conversion to Catholicism, after which they remain loyal to their Talmudic and Cabalistic roots. Generation after generation, many of these crypto-Jewish families gained great influence within the Roman church to steer its doctrines and policies. Aho quotes from *The Plot Against the Church*; the author, Pinay, is a loyal Catholic:

> This "Fifth column" is formed by the descendants of the Jews, who in earlier centuries were converted to Christianity and seemingly held in enthusiastic manner to the religion of Christ, while in secret they preserved their Jewish belief and carried out clandestinely the Jewish rites and ceremonies. For this purpose they organised [sic] themselves into communities and secret synagogues, which were active centuries-long in secret. These apparent Christians, but secret Jews, began centuries ago to infiltrate into Christian society, in order to attempt to control it from within. For this reason they sowed false doctrines and differences of opinion and even attempted to gain control of the clergy in the different churches of Christ. With all this, they applied the cunning of introducing crypto-Jewish Christians into the seminaries of the priesthood, who could gain admission into the honorary offices in the Holy Catholic Church and then into the dissident churches, upon whose division these secret Jews had so much influence.[102]

Pinay characterizes the infiltration by Jews as a fifth column in the church; in one sense they are a fifth column, however, in another sense they are not, since the Jewish doctrine is woven into the very warp and woof of the Roman Catholic church. Pinay correctly explains the infiltration of the Roman Catholic church by Jews; however, he misses the fact that the very doctrines of the Roman Catholic organization are Jewish. The Roman Catholic Church is only gentile in appearance. How can the Jews be a Jewish fifth column in an organization that is essentially Jewish in nature?

7

Crypto-Jewish Jesuits

As we have seen, the Roman Catholic church represents a gentile front for Jewish religious doctrines. Jews from time to time go from supporting the Catholic church to undermining it. Ultimately, the Jews have plans to rid themselves of that front when it no longer serves their purposes. It is only in that sense that Pinay's characterization of the Jews as a fifth column within the Catholic church has validity.

A good example of the duality of the Jews being both a defender of the church and also its destroyer is the Catholic order of the Jesuits. What most do not know is that the Jesuit order is a Crypto-Jewish order of priests. While it may have gentile priests as members, it was founded by Jews and today has close secret ties with other clandestine Jewish organizations. Benjamin Disraeli was a Jew and a former Prime Minister of England; he revealed that the first Jesuits were Jews.[103] Ignatius of Loyola's secretary, Polanco, was of Jewish descent and was the only person present at Loyola's deathbed. Ignatius Loyola himself was a crypto-Jew of the Occult Kabbalah. A crypto-Jew is a Jew who converts to another religion and outwardly embraces the new religion, while secretly maintaining Jewish practices.

James Lainez (J.G. 1558-1565), who succeeded Ignatius Loyola (J.G. 1541-1556) as the second Jesuit General, was also of Jewish descent. The fourth Jesuit General was a Belgian Jew named Eberhard Mercurian (J.G. 1573-1580).[104] Jews were attracted to the Jesuit order and joined in large numbers.[105] Some of the most influential Jesuits in history, such as Francisco Ribera (1537-1591) and Emanuel Lacunza (1731-1801), were Jews. During the 5th General Congregation in 1593 of the 27 Jesuits who proposed changes to the Constitutions, 25 were of either Jewish or Moorish descent.[106] Many of the Jesuit doctrines are similar to those found in the Kabbalah and Babylonian Talmud. It is possible that the second beast in the book of Revelation is the Jesuit General, who is known as the black pope.

John Torell explains the Jewish origins of the Jesuit order:

48

The Illuminati order was not invented by Adam Weishaupt, but rather renewed and reformed. The first known Illuminati order (Alumbrado) was founded in 1492 by Spanish Jews, called "Marranos," who were also known as "crypto-Jews." With violent persecution in Spain and Portugal beginning in 1391, hundreds of thousands of Jews had been forced to convert to the faith of the Roman Catholic Church. Publicly they were now Roman Catholics, but secretly they practiced Judaism, including following the Talmud and the Cabala. The Marranos were able to teach their children secretly about Judaism, but in particular the Talmud and the Cabala, and this huge group of Jews has survived to this very day. After 1540 many Marranos opted to flee to England, Holland, France, the Ottoman empire (Turkey), Brazil and other places in South and Central America. The Marranos kept strong family ties and they became very wealthy and influential in the nations where they lived. But as is the custom with all Jewish people, it did not matter in what nation they lived, their loyalty was to themselves and Judaism. [107]

* * *

In 1491 San Ignacio De Loyola was born in the Basque province of Guipuzcoa, Spain. His parents were Marranos and at the time of his birth the family was very wealthy. **As a young man he became a member of the Jewish Illuminati order in Spain. As a cover for his crypto Jewish activities, he became very active as a Roman Catholic.** On May 20, 1521 Ignatius (as he was now called) was wounded in a battle, and became a semi-cripple. Unable to succeed in the military and political arena, he started a quest for holiness and eventually ended up in Paris where he studied for the priesthood. In 1539 he had moved to Rome where he founded the "JESUIT ORDER," which was to become the most vile, bloody and persecuting order in the Roman Catholic Church. In 1540, the current Pope Paul III approved the order. At Loyola's death in 1556 there were more than 1000 members in the Jesuit order, located in a number of nations. [108]

Setting up the Jesuit order, Ignatius Loyola devised an elaborate spy system, so that no one in the order was safe. If there was any opposition, death would come swiftly. The Jesuit order not only became a destructive arm of the Roman Catholic Church; it also developed into a secret intelligence service. **While the Popes relied more and more on the Jesuits, they were unaware that the hard core leadership were Jewish, and that these Jews held membership in the Illuminati order which despised and hated the Roman Catholic Church.**[109]

The Jesuits were established by Ignatius of Loyola. Ignatius of Loyola was the leader of a secret occult organization known as the *Alumbrados* (Spanish for Illuminati).[110] On August 15, 1534, Loyola started a sister organization to the *Alumbrados*, which he called the Society of Jesus, it is more commonly known today as the Jesuits. Loyola was arrested by the Dominican order of Catholic inquisitors, who were concerned with his growing influence and power throughout Europe. Because of his influential allies among the principalities of Europe, he was granted an audience with the pope. Loyola promised the pope his allegiance and agreed to do the bidding of the papacy throughout the world. Pope Paul III formally approved the Jesuits as a Catholic religious order in his 1540 papal bull *Regimini Militantis Eccclesiae*.[111]

The influence of the Jews through the Jesuits in the Roman Catholic Church has been manifested from the beginning in Catholic doctrine. The Council of Trent was an attack on Christianity with anathema after anathema against Christian doctrine that was orchestrated by the Jesuits. The control of the Jews over the Vatican is so complete that Cardinal Joseph Ratzinger (now Pope Benedict XVI), who was the prefect of the Congregation for the Doctrine of the Faith, issued an official doctrine of Catholic faith that accepted the Jewish view that the messiah is yet to come. There is apparently much double talk in the document, as it accepts the Jewish view of a coming messiah without overtly rejecting Jesus. Some have interpreted the document as denying the redemptive role of Jesus. The Catholic Church long ago implicitly denied the redemptive role of Jesus. The document is contained in a small book titled "The Jewish People and the Holy Scriptures in the Christian Bible." It is no surprise that this Jewish/Catholic doctrine was drafted by a Jesuit named Albert Vanhoye.[112]

The Jewish influence over the Roman Catholic institution and its doctrines is manifest in *The Document of the Vatican Commission for Religious Relations with Judaism* § 4, which states: **"We propose, in the future, to remove from the Gospel of St. John the term, 'the Jews' where it is used in a negative sense, and to translate it, 'the enemies of Christ.'"**[113]

At a speech at Hebrew University in Jerusalem, Roman Catholic Cardinal Joseph Bernadine stated:

> [T]here is need for . . .theological reflection, especially with what many consider to be the problematic New Testament's texts ... Retranslation ... and reinterpretation certainly need to be included among the goals we pursue in the effort to eradicate anti-semitism.

> [T]he gospel of John ... is generally considered among the most problematic of all New Testament books in its outlook towards Jews and Judaism ... this teaching of John about the Jews, which resulted from the historical conflict between the church and synagogue in the latter part of the first century C.E., can no longer be taught as authentic doctrine or used as catechesis by contemporary Christianity ... Christians today must see that such teachings ... can no longer be regarded as definitive teachings in light of our improved understanding.[114]

In ancient Palestine the Jews worked hand in hand with the Romans to crucify Christ. Now, the Jews work hand in glove with the Roman Catholic Church in their effort to eradicate Christ's gospel. The great harlot of Babylon in Revelation 17:5 has Mystery written upon her forehead. She is called Babylon because she is Babylonian. She is a mystery because she masquerading as "the" Christian religion. Christian labels have been applied to Babylonian paganism to come up with the mystery religion we know as the Roman Catholic Church. Both the Talmudic Jews and the Vatican share that common Babylonian root. The Jesuits nurtured the Babylonian Cabalism in Roman Catholic doctrine. The similarities between the imperious whorish woman in Ezekiel 16:14-40 and the Mother of Harlots in Revelation 17:5 are unmistakable. They are one and the same. Roman Catholicism is an esoteric version of Babylonian Judaism. The Roman Church appears gentile to the uninitiated, but it is Jewish to its core. Orthodox Judaism appears to the uninitiated to be the Old Testament theology, but it is actually Babylonian to its core.

The *Extreme Oath of the Jesuits,* which is given to a Jesuit Priest when he is elevated to a position of command, contains the following provisions:

> I . . . declare and swear that his holiness, the Pope, is Christ's Vice-regent, and is the true and only head of the Catholic or Universal Church throughout the earth.

* * *

> Therefore, to the utmost of my power, I shall and will defend this doctrine and his Holiness' right and customs against all usurpers of the heretical or Protestant authority, whatever especially the Luthern Church of Germany, Holland, Denmark, Sweden, and Norway, and the now pretended authority of the Church of England and Scotland, the branches of the same, now where . . . . . I do now renounce and disown any allegiance as due to any heretical king, prince or state named Protestant or Liberals, or obedience to any of their laws, magistrates or officers.

* * *

> That I will go to any part of the world, whatsoever, without murmuring and will be submissive in all things whatsoever communicated to me . . . . . I do further promise and declare, that I will, when opportunity presents, make and wage relentless war, secretly or openly, against all heretics, Protestants and Liberals, as I am directed to do to extirpate and exterminate them from the face of the whole earth, and that I will spare neither sex, age, nor condition, and that I will hang, waste, boil, flay, strangle, and bury alive these infamous heretics; rip up the stomachs and wombs of their women and crush their infants' heads against the wall, in order to annihilate forever their execrable race.

> That when the same cannot be done openly, I will secretly use the poison cup, the strangulation cord, the steel of the poinard, or the leaden bullet, regardless of the honor, rank, dignity or authority of the person or persons whatsoever may be their condition in life, either public or private, as I at any time may be directed so to do by any agent of the pope or superior of the brotherhood of the holy faith of the

Society of Jesus.[115]

The Jesuits are the secret army of the Roman church; they are often referred to as the "pope's militia." In fact, the leader of the Jesuits is called the "Jesuit General." He is unlike any other leader of a Catholic order, because the Jesuit General is independent of the Catholic Bishops and Cardinals; he answers directly to the Pope. Because of the power and influence of the Jesuit General, he is known as the "Black Pope." The Jesuit General has the purported authority to absolve persons of the sins of bigamy, murder, or any harm done to others as long as the matter is not publicly known and the cause of a scandal.[116] Pope Gregory XII gave the Jesuits the authority to deal in commerce and banking, which has made the order quite wealthy.[117] The popes have threatened princes, kings, and anyone else who interferes with the Jesuits with excommunication (*Latae Sententiae*).[118] In one of the most authoritative works on the Jesuits, J. Huber, professor of Catholic theology wrote: "Here is a proven fact: the Constitutions [of the Jesuits] repeat five hundred times that one must see Christ in the person of the [Jesuit] General."[119]

If the Jesuits are a Crypto-Jewish order that hates the Roman Catholic church, as alleged by Torell, why would it become a priestly order within that church and become its greatest defender with extreme oaths of obedience to the pope? Because, the Roman church offers the Jews an ideal cover from which to wage war against Christianity. This is evidenced by the fact that the Jesuits virtually controlled the Council of Trent, which produced anathema after anathema against bible believing Christians and fundamental Christian doctrine. This same Jesuit organization, however, opposed the inquisition.[120] Why? Because the inquisition, in part, was initiated to root out crypto-Jewry inside the Catholic church. Of course, an organization founded and controlled by crypto-Jews would oppose a strategy that would expose its own Jewish core.

The hierarchy of Orthodox Jews hate gentiles; ostensibly gentile organizations like the Roman church offer an ideal front from which to strike against the hated Christians. That is why God refers to the great harlot of Babylon as "MYSTERY." The Roman church appears to the world to be a gentile religious organization, yet it is to its core Jewish. As long at the Roman church does the bidding of the Jews, they will defend it. Once the Roman church is no longer useful it will shed it like a snake sheds its old skin.

It seems that the Jews have the destruction of the Roman church all planned out. The following is a passage from the THE PROTOCOLS OF THE LEARNED ELDERS OF ZION that seem to foretell the destruction of the Vatican by the nations of the world.

> When the time comes finally to destroy the papal court the finger of an invisible hand will point the nations towards this court. When, however, the nations fling themselves upon it, we shall come forward in the guise of its defenders as if to save excessive bloodshed. By this diversion we shall penetrate to its very bowels and be sure we shall never come out again until we have gnawed through the entire strength of this place.[121]

That is very similar to the prophecy found in the book of Revelation.

And the ten horns which thou sawest upon the beast, **these shall hate the whore, and shall make her desolate and naked, and shall eat her flesh, and burn her with fire.** For God hath put in their hearts to fulfil his will, and to agree, and give their kingdom unto the beast, until the words of God shall be fulfilled. And the woman which thou sawest is that great city, which reigneth over the kings of the earth. (Revelation 17:16-18 AV)

The horns of the beast are ten kings on the beast that is being ridden by the great harlot who sits on seven mountains (the Vatican). Revelation 17. The PROTOCOLS have set forth the planned destruction of the Vatican. The PROTOCOLS seem also to have provided for the entrance of the antichrist. "THE KING OF THE JEWS WILL BE THE REAL POPE OF THE UNIVERSE, THE PATRIARCH OF THE INTERNATIONAL CHURCH."[122]

In fact, the Jesuits, the great defenders of the Catholic faith, have actually exercised their power to undermine the authority of the church and bring it to its knees. The reason the Jesuits retaliated against the Catholic church was that the Jesuits were at one time dissolved as a Catholic order because of their subversive conduct. The subversion of the European nations by the Jesuits became so great that an immense amount of military and political pressure was brought against the pope by the European nations. Finally, Pope Clement XIII decided on the 3rd of February 1769 to dissolve the Jesuits. While Jesuits are under an oath of allegiance to the pope, that oath is secondary to their extreme oath of allegiance to the Jesuit General:

I do further promise and declare, that I will have no opinion or will of my own, or any mental reservation whatever, even as a corpse or cadaver [perinde ac cadaver] but unhesitatingly, obey each and very command that I may receive from my superiors in the Militia of the Pope and Jesus Christ.[123]

The night before Pope Clement XIII was to execute the dissolution, however, he suddenly fell ill and died. Prior to his death he cried out "I am dying . . . It is a very dangerous thing to attack the Jesuits."[124] His successor, Pope Clement XIV, was also put under tremendous political pressure to dissolve the Jesuits, but he resisted doing so for three years until the political tension finally forced his hand. Pope Clement XIV issued the papal brief of dissolution, *Dominus ac Redemptor,* on August 16, 1773.[125] Pope Clement XIV knew the significance of such an act to the papacy; he exclaimed: "I have cut off my right hand."[126] In addition, Pope Clement XIV knew that by signing the brief dissolving the Jesuits he was signing his own death warrant. Soon after signing the brief the letters I.S.S.S.V. appeared on the palace walls in the Vatican.[127] Pope Clement XIV knew what it meant and explained that it stood for *In Settembre, Sara Sede Vacante.* Which translated means "in September, the See will be vacant (the pope will be dead)."[128] Pope Clement XIV was poisoned and died on September 22, 1774.[129]

Interestingly, it was just three years after Pope Clement XIV's suppression of the Jesuits that the subversive organization the "Illuminati" was purportedly founded by a trained Jesuit named Adam Weishaupt in 1776.[130] Weishaupt was a Jew and a professor of canon law at Ingolstadt University, which was a Jesuit University and the center of the Jesuit counter-reformation.[131] Alberto Rivera, a former Jesuit priest, stated that the occult Illuminati organization was not founded by Weishaupt, as many believe, but in fact was established long before Weishaupt. The Illuminati is in fact a reincarnation of the ancient *Alumbrados*, whose one time leader was Ignatius of Loyola, the founder of the Jesuits.[132] The Illuminati was established by Lorenzo Ricco, the Jesuit General, in 1776, who used his disciple, Adam Weishaupt, as the front man for the new organization (which was really not new at all).[133]   The Jesuits, having just been suppressed by the pope in 1773, found it necessary to establish the Illuminati, which was an alliance between the Jesuits and the very powerful Ashkenazi Jewish Banking House of Rothschild. The purpose of Weishaupt initially was to avenge the papal suppression of the Jesuits by rooting out all religion and overturning the governments of the world, bringing them under a single world government, controlled of course by the Illuminati, under the authority of their god. That world government is commonly referred to by the Illuminati as the "New World Order." The god of the Illuminati is Satan.[134]

Eric Jon Phelps in his book, *The Vatican Assassins*, explains:

> These 41 years [between their suppression in 1773 by Pope Clement XIV and their reestablishment by Pope Pius VII in 1814] were absolutely golden for the Society of Jesus. For the Sons of Loyola punished all their enemies, including the Dominican priests, perfected the inner workings between themselves and Freemasonry, creating alliance between the house of Rothschild in establishing the illuminati; punished and absorbed the Knights of Malta . . . . They used the Orthodox Catherine of Russia and a Lutheran Frederick of Prussia to conquer and divide Poland, rendering the pope's Bull of Suppression of no effect in that Roman Catholic land. They caused the French Revolution, beheaded a Bourbon King and a Hapsburg Queen as punishment for being expelled from France and Austria. With Napoleon, the Freemason, they drove the Bourbons from their throne in Spain and the Braganzas from their throne in Portugal. They even attempted to take Palestine from the Moslems like the Crusaders of old.[135]

> The company's most important victories were both religious and political. They deeply penetrated the Russian Orthodox Church and Germany's Lutheran Church, its Tubingen University specifically. Politically, they took control of the crown and the Bank of England. For this reason England, with Viscount Palmerston, would never go to war with France again, it would conduct the Pope's opium wars against people of China (just like the company, with its CIA and Mafia Commission is presently conducting a massive drug trade against the "heretic and liberal" people of the American Empire) . . . The Jesuits also captured the Papacy with the Vatican; along with its landed church properties the world over, and for this reason the Papal Caesar, occupying Satan's sacred office of the Papacy,

would never suppress the Society of Jesus *ever again*![136]

The secret Illuminati organization was the hidden guiding hand behind the brutal French Revolution of 1787, during which 300,000 people were massacred in a godless orgy of violence.[137] The rage by the Jesuits and their reconstituted Illuminati culminated in 1798, with the capture of the pope himself. Napoleon's General Berthier invaded Rome, took the Pope Pius VI prisoner, and held him until his death.

The Roman Catholic church had learned its lesson. On August 7, 1814, the Jesuits were restored as a Catholic order by Pope Pius VII.[138] John Adams wrote to Thomas Jefferson in 1816 "I am not happy about the rebirth of the Jesuits. . . . Swarms of them will present themselves under more disguises ever taken by even a chief of the Bohemians, as printers, writers, publishers, school teachers, etc. If ever an association of people deserved eternal damnation, on this earth and in hell, it is the Society of Loyola. Yet, with our system of religious liberty, we can but offer them a refuge."[139] Thomas Jefferson answered Adams: "Like you, I object to the Jesuits' reestablishment which makes light give way to darkness."[140]

In 1835, Samuel Morse, the great inventor of the telegraph, echoed the concerns of Jefferson and Adams; he described the Jesuits and their threat to the United States as follows:

> And do Americans need to be told what *Jesuits* are? If any are ignorant, let them inform themselves of their history without delay: no time is to be lost: their workings are before you in every day's events: they are a *secret* society, a sort of Masonic order, with superadded features of most revolting odiousness and a thousand times more dangerous. They are not confined to one class on society; they are not merely priests, or priests of one religious creed, they are merchants, and lawyers, and editors, and men of any profession, and no profession, having no outward badge (in this country,) by which to be recognised; they are about in all your society. They can assume any character that of angels of light, or ministers of darkness, to accomplish their one great end, the *service* upon which they are sworn to *start at any moment, in any direction,* and for any service, commanded by the general of their order, bound to no family, community, or country, by the ordinary ties which bind men; and *sold for life* to the cause of the Roman Pontiff.[141]

The concerns of Morse, Adams, and Jefferson were justified; once being reestablished as a Catholic order the Jesuits did not miss a beat; during the 19th century they fomented revolutions throughout the world, attempting to bring to power oppressive despots whom they would then control. They were at one time or another expelled from Russia (1820), Belgium, Portugal (1834), the Italian states (1859), Spain (three times-1820, 1835, and 1868), Germany (1872), Guatemala (1872), Mexico (1873), Brazil (1874), Ecuador (1875), Colombia (1875), Costa Rica (1884), and France (twice-1880 and 1901).[142] They caused the Swiss Civil war in 1847, as a result they were banished from Switzerland in 1848.[143] Up until the year 2000, the Swiss

Constitution (article 51) forbade the Jesuits from engaging in any cultural or educational activity in Switzerland.[144] In the year 2000 Switzerland ratified a new constitution, in which article 51 was removed. Those are just a sampling of the over 70 countries from which the Jesuits have been expelled for conducting subversive activities. The Jesuit subversion has continued to modern times, causing the Jesuits to be expelled from Haiti in 1964 and Burma in 1966.[145] To this day they are instigating communist revolutions in South America. The Jesuits' new brand of South American communism is known as "Liberation Theology."

Jesuits have a long and sordid history of distorting moral obligations and practicing and advocating situational ethics. For example, God commands without exception that "Thou shalt not bear false witness against thy neighbor." *Exodus* 20:16. The Jesuits, on the other hand, permit the use of ambiguous terms to mislead a judge or outright lying under oath if the witness makes a mental reservation.[146] The Jesuits teach that if a young girl is pregnant, she may obtain an abortion if the pregnancy would bring dishonor to her or a member of the clergy.[147] They do not stop there; another Jesuit maxim states: "If a Father, yielding to temptation, abuses a woman and she publicises what has happened, and, because of it, dishonours him, this same Father can kill her to avoid disgrace."[148] That is not the only cause that is justification for murder. The Jesuits further teach that "[a] monk or a priest is allowed to kill those who are ready to slander him or his community."[149]

Immorality is not unique to the Jesuit order only. The doctrines of the Catholic Church allow for all sorts of situational ethics. Thomas Aquinas, the most influential source of economic and theological doctrines for the Catholic Church, stated that it is lawful and not a sin for a man to steal another's property in order to fulfill a basic need. Aquinas' view was that all goods are community goods and therefore it is not a sin to take another's property when you need it.[150] That is in fact the official position of the Roman church today as expressed by the Second Vatican Council. "If one is in extreme necessity he has the right to procure for himself what he needs out of the riches of others."[151]

What is the authority for this ethic? It is found in the Talmud. In *Baba Bathra 54b* it states: "The property of a heathen is on the same footing as desert land; whoever first occupies it acquires ownership."[152]   Compare that to the eighth commandment of God: "Thou shalt not steal." Exodus 20:15. Furthermore, in *Baba Kamma 113b* it states that if one finds lost property it must be returned if the owner is a Jew; however if the owner is a gentile it can be kept. "It is to your brother that you make restoration, but you need not make restoration to a heathen."[153]

The Jesuits are zealous persecutors of Christians or anyone whom they view as an enemy of the Vatican. Jesuits take a solemn oath to destroy Protestant Christians and destroy any government that offers protection to Protestant Christians.[154] They are the natural enemies of liberty, their whole system is based on thoughtless, ruthless, blind obedience. Ignatius himself writing to his Jesuits in Portugal said: "We must see black as white if the church says so."[155] Jesuits are the subversive ambassadors of the Catholic Church, bringing chaos and ruin to all nations they infiltrate. They believe that "[t]he Catholic Church has the right and duty to kill heretics because it is by fire and sword that heresy can be extirpated. . . . Repentance cannot be allowed to save them, just as repentance is not allowed to save civil criminals; for the highest good of the church is the unity of the faith, and this cannot be preserved unless heretics are put to death."[156]

Alberto Rivera, a former Jesuit Priest, was saved by the grace of God and came out of the Jesuit priesthood. The Jesuits made numerous attempts to kill him before he could reveal the secrets of the Jesuits. He survived the attempts on his life and exposed much about sinister methods and motives of the Jesuits.

Franz Wernz, the Jesuit General from 1906-1915, stated that "[t]he Church can condemn heretics to death, for any rights they have are only through our tolerance, and these rights are apparent not real"[157] That view of heretics having no rights is very similar to the philosophy of the Jewish Talmud. Sanhedrin 57b provides that if a heathen robs another or a Jew the property must be returned. If, however, a Jew robs a heathen, the property does not have to be returned to the heathen.[158] That section of the Talmud also states that if a heathen murders another heathen or a Jew, the heathen should suffer the death penalty. If, however, a Jew kills a heathen "there is no death penalty."[159] For example, Jewish Rabbi Moseh Levinger was sentenced to a mere 5 months in jail by an Israeli court for the unprovoked cold-blooded murder in September 1988 of a Palestinian shopkeeper, Hassan Salah.[160] Prior to entering prison, Rabbi Levinger was feted at a party by Israeli President Chaim Herzog and Israeli Army General Yitzhak Mordechai.[161] Rabbi Levinger was released from prison after only serving three months.[162] Baba Kamma 38a expressly states that Canaanites are "outside the protection of the civil law of Israel." Thus a Canaanite has no remedy against a Jew whose ox gores the Canaanite's ox, but if a Canaanite's ox gores a Jew's ox, the Canaanite shall pay in full the damages.

Professor Israel Shahak explains:

> According to the Jewish religion, the murder of a Jew is a capital offense and one of the three most heinous sins (the other two being idolatry and adultery). Jewish religious courts and secular authorities are commanded to punish, even beyond the limits of the ordinary administration of justice, anyone guilty of murdering a Jew. A Jew who indirectly causes the death of another Jew is, however, only guilty of what talmudic law calls a sin against the 'laws of Heaven', to be punished by God rather than by man.

> When the victim is a Gentile, the position is quite different. A Jew who murders a Gentile is guilty only of a sin against the laws of Heaven, not punishable by a court.[163] To cause indirectly the death of a Gentile is no sin at all.[164]

> Thus, one of the two most important commentators on the Shulhan Arukh explains that when it comes to a Gentile, 'one must not lift one's hand to harm him, but one may harm him indirectly, for instance by removing a ladder after he

had fallen into a crevice .., there is no prohibition here, because it was not done directly.[165] He points out, however, that an act leading indirectly to a Gentile's death is forbidden if it may cause the spread of hostility towards Jews.

A Gentile murderer who happens to be under Jewish jurisdiction must be executed whether the victim was Jewish or not. However, if the victim was Gentile and the murderer converts to Judaism, he is not punished.[166]

   The animus by Jews toward gentiles, includes a prohibition against giving medical treatment to gentiles. Israel Shahak explains:

According to the Halakhah, the duty to save the life of a fellow Jew is paramount.[167] It supersedes all other religious obligations and interdictions, excepting only the prohibitions against the three most heinous sins of adultery (including incest), murder and idolatry.

As for Gentiles, the basic talmudic principle is that their lives must not be saved, although it is also forbidden to murder them outright.[168] The Talmud itself expresses this in the maxim 'Gentiles are neither to be lifted [out of a well] nor hauled down [into it]'. Maimonides[169] explains:

"As for Gentiles with whom we are not at war ... their death must not be caused, but it is forbidden to save them if they are at the point of death; if, for example, one of them is seen falling into the sea, he should not be rescued, for it is written: 'neither shalt thou stand against the blood of thy fellow'[170] - but [a Gentile] is not thy fellow."

In particular, a Jewish doctor must not treat a Gentile patient. Maimonides - himself an illustrious physician - is quite explicit on this; in another passage[171] he repeats the distinction between 'thy fellow' and a Gentile, and concludes: 'and from this learn ye, that it is forbidden to heal a Gentile even for payment...'

However, the refusal of a Jew - particularly a Jewish doctor - to save the life of a Gentile may, if it becomes known, antagonize powerful Gentiles and so put Jews in danger. Where such danger exists, the obligation to avert it supersedes the ban on helping the Gentile. Thus Maimonides continues: ' ... but if you fear him or his hostility, cure him for payment, though you are forbidden to do so without payment.' In fact, Maimonides himself was Saladin's personal physician. His insistence on demanding payment - presumably in order to make sure that the act is not one of human charity but an unavoidable duty - is however not absolute. For in another passage he allows [a] Gentile whose hostility is feared to be treated 'even gratis, if it is unavoidable'.

The whole doctrine - the ban on saving a Gentile's life or healing him, and the suspension of this ban in cases where there is fear of hostility - is repeated (virtually verbatim) by other major authorities, including the 14th century Arba'ah Turirn and Karo's Beyt Yosef and Shulhan 'Arukh.[172] Beyt Yosef adds, quoting Maimonides: 'And it is permissible to try out a drug on a heathen, if this serves a purpose'; and this is repeated also by the famous R. Moses Isserles.

The consensus of halakhic authorities is that the term 'Gentiles' in the above doctrine refers to all non-Jews.[173]

That Jewish attitude toward non-Jews is the same attitude the crypto-Jewish Jesuits have toward Christians. Jesuit priests are subjected to certain "spiritual exercises" which were first devised by Ignatius Loyola. During the spiritual exercises the subject becomes possessed and controlled by a devil.

We imbue into him spiritual forces which he would find very difficult to eliminate later, forces more lasting than all the best principles and doctrines; these forces can come up again to the surface, sometimes after years of not even mentioning them, and become so imperative that the will finds itself unable to oppose any obstacle, and has to follow their irresistible impulse.[174]

Between 1569 and 1605 the Jesuits orchestrated no less than eleven plots against Protestant England, which involved invasion, rebellion, and assassination. Each is known by the leader of the treachery: Ridolfi, Sanders, Gregory XIII, Campion, Parsons, Duke of Guise, Allen, Throgmorten, Parry, Babington, Sixtus V, Philip II of Spain, Yorke, Walpole, Southwell, and Guy Fawkes.[175]

In the 1586 "Babington plot" the Jesuits along with other Catholics planned to kill Protestant Queen Elizabeth I, place Catholic Mary Stuart, Queen of Scots on the throne of England and bring England under subjection to the Pope of Rome. That plot was discovered and Mary was executed for her troubles.[176]

After the failed Babington plot, the Pope, in league with Philip II of Spain, planned to invade England and bring it under papal control. In 1588 Spain brought the 136 ship Spanish Armada against England. The Sovereign God of the Universe whipped up a freak storm which devastated the Armada and allowed England with only 30 ships to defeat Spain after an eight hour sea battle.[177]

On November 5, 1605 Jesuit led Roman Catholic conspirators planned to kill King James I and the entire English Parliament by blowing up the House of Lords. They placed 20 barrels of gunpowder under the House of Lords. The plan was to blow up the house of Lords when the Lords, Commons, and King were all assembled on November 5, 1605 for the opening of Parliament.[178] The plot, however, was discovered and the conspirators were captured. To this day that event is simply referred to as the "Gunpowder Plot."[179] November 5 is a national holiday in England, commemorating the Catholic conspiracy in the Gunpowder Plot. The holiday is called Guy Fawkes Day; Guy Fawkes was one of the Gunpowder Plot conspirators.[180]

The Jesuit subversion of nations has caused 56 countries to ban the Jesuits, most of whom have since lifted the bans. In 1759 the Jesuits were banned throughout the Portuguese Empire.[181] In 1764 the Jesuits were outlawed in France, and in 1767 they were banned from Spain.[182] On April 6, 1762 the French Parliament issued the following "statement of arrest" (indictment):

> The said Institute [Jesuits] is inadmissible in any civilised State, as its nature is hostile to all spiritual and temporal authority; it seeks to introduce into the Church and States, under the plausible veil of a religious Institute, not an Order truly desirous to spread evangelical perfection, but rather a political body working untiringly at usurping all authority, by all kinds of indirect, secret, and devious means. . . .[The Jesuits' doctrine is] perverse, a destroyer of all religious and honest principles, insulting to Christian morals, pernicious to civil society, hostile to the rights of the nation, the royal power, and even the security of the sovereigns and obedience of their subjects; suitable to stir up the greatest disturbances in the States, conceive and maintain the worst kind of corruption in men's hearts.[183]

All nations should learn from the experience of Protestant England and understand the threat that Rome and the Jesuits pose to any free country. The Roman Catholic Church uses religious superstition to usurp the authority and undermine independence of any state. King Henry VIII cast off the yoke of Rome and declared that he was to be the head of the church in England.

In May 1538, the pope sought his revenge for the separation of the Church of England from Rome; the pope excommunicated all in Ireland who recognized the supremacy of the King of England or any ecclesiastical or civil power greater than that of the Roman Catholic Church. The events are recounted in the classic *Foxe's Book of Martyrs*:

> A short time after this, the pope sent over to Ireland (directed to the archbishop of Armagh and his clergy) a bull of excommunication against all who had, or should own the king's supremacy within the Irish nation; denouncing a curse on all of them, and theirs, who should not, within forty days, acknowledge to their confessors, that they had done amiss in so doing.

> Archbishop Browne gave notice of this in a letter dated, Dublin, May, 1538. Part of the form of confession, or vow, sent over to these Irish papists, ran as follows: "I do further declare him or here, father or mother, brother or sister, son or daughter, husband or wife, uncle or aunt, nephew or niece, kinsman or kinswoman, master or mistress, and all others, nearest or dearest relations, friend or acquaintance whatsoever, accursed, that either do or shall hold, for the time to come, any ecclesiastical or civil power above the authority of the Mother Church;

or that do or shall obey, for the time to come, any of her, the Mother of Churches' opposers or enemies, or contrary to the same, of which I have here sworn unto: so God, the Blessed Virgin, St. Peter, St. Paul, and the Holy Evangelists, help me," etc. is an exact agreement with the doctrines promulgated by the Councils of Lateran and Constance, which expressly declare that no favor should be shown to heretics, nor faith kept with them; that they ought to be excommunicated and condemned, and their estates confiscated, and that princes are obliged, by a solemn oath, to root them out of their respective dominions.[184]

The political and religious attacks against Protestant England by Rome continued up to and beyond 1641; in 1641 the beast of Rome planned a murderous insurrection in Ireland. The objective of the barbarous conspiracy was to murder all Protestants in Ireland, without exception. In this instance, as in many others, we find the Jesuits leading the murderous and maniacal charge. The Jesuits placed their hellish imprimatur on the massacre by beginning it on the feast day of their founder, Ignatius of Loyola. When the dust finally settled on the genocide, Rome had exterminated 150,000 innocent men, women, and children. This massacre illustrates the danger of a Roman Catholic majority in any country. No matter who seems to control the political reigns, when the lawful government is at odds with Rome there will be hell to pay. Rome is a master at mass insurrection through the incitation of base barbarians who have sold their soul to the superstition of the Roman Cult.

The Irish genocide was planned and orchestrated from the Vatican. It was executed through the leadership of the Jesuits and the other priests of Rome. He who has eyes let him see through the pious facade of Rome. He who has understanding let him understand the danger posed by Rome and the Jesuits. The Roman Catholic Church never changes.

King Henry VIII's error is all too obvious, for there is only one head of God's church and that is Jesus Christ. The pope was incensed at the insolence of King Henry. The pope, however, was not angry because the king blasphemously claimed the authority of Christ as head of the church, but because the king had replaced him, the supreme pontiff of Rome, as the head of the church. The King of England was politically too strong for the pope to do anything to change the situation in England (though he tried); consequently the monarch of England to this day is the head of the Church of England (known as the Anglican or Episcopal Church). The Episcopal church is one of the harlot daughters of the Roman Catholic mother of harlots. *See* Revelation 17:5. For the most part, the leadership of the Episcopal Church are not Christian; they are rather the proverbial rejected tares growing in Christ's wheat field.

> Another parable put he forth unto them, saying, The kingdom of heaven is likened unto a man which sowed good seed in his field: But while men slept, his enemy came and sowed tares among the wheat, and went his way. But when the blade was sprung up, and brought forth fruit, then appeared the tares also. So the servants of the householder came and said unto him, Sir, didst not thou sow good seed in thy field? from whence then hath it tares? He said unto them, An enemy

hath done this. The servants said unto him, Wilt thou then that we go and gather them up? But he said, Nay; lest while ye gather up the tares, ye root up also the wheat with them. Let both grow together until the harvest: and in the time of harvest I will say to the reapers, Gather ye together first the tares, and bind them in bundles to burn them: but gather the wheat into my barn. . . . Then Jesus sent the multitude away, and went into the house: and his disciples came unto him, saying, Declare unto us the parable of the tares of the field. He answered and said unto them, He that soweth the good seed is the Son of man; The field is the world; the good seed are the children of the kingdom; but the tares are the children of the wicked *one*; The enemy that sowed them is the devil; the harvest is the end of the world; and the reapers are the angels. As therefore the tares are gathered and burned in the fire; so shall it be in the end of this world. The Son of man shall send forth his angels, and they shall gather out of his kingdom all things that offend, and them which do iniquity; And shall cast them into a furnace of fire: there shall be wailing and gnashing of teeth. Then shall the righteous shine forth as the sun in the kingdom of their Father. Who hath ears to hear, let him hear. (Matthew 13:24-30; 36-43 AV)

Let us look at some of the tares in the Episcopal Church: In August 2003 the House of Deputies for the Episcopal Church elected a Gene Robinson to be the Bishop of New Hampshire. Gene Robinson left his wife and two daughters to live with another man in an openly sodomite relationship. He publicly promotes and encourages the sodomite lifestyle. He founded the Concord, New Hampshire chapter of "Outright," which is a ministry promoting sodomy and whose website contains photos of group sex and other pornography. Robinson does not preach the gospel; he has rejected the gospel and instead preaches the sin of sodomy! These facts about Robinson were all known by the House of Deputies before they voted to approve Robinson as an Episcopal Bishop. God has clearly stated that Robinson's lifestyle and the conduct he promotes is a sin:

There shall be no whore of the daughters of Israel, nor a sodomite of the sons of Israel. (Deuteronomy 23:17 AV)

Thou shalt not lie with mankind, as with womankind: it *is* abomination. (Leviticus 18:22 AV)

Even as Sodom and Gomorrha, and the cities about them in like manner, giving themselves over to fornication, and going after strange flesh, are set forth for an example, suffering the vengeance of eternal fire. (Jude 1:7 AV)

In order for Robinson to be installed as a bishop, it was necessary for him to be confirmed by the Episcopal General Convention. Robinson was later confirmed by the General Convention in a vote of bishops, where 62 bishops voted to confirm Robinson, and 43 voted against his confirmation. The confirmation of Robinson is not surprising when one considers the type of people who make up the leadership of the Episcopal Church. John Shelby Spong retired as Episcopal Bishop of New Jersey. For his entire career in the Episcopal Church "he wrote and preached against every tenet of the Christian faith. Bishop Spong did not believe in the virgin birth, the doctrine of the incarnation, the deity of Christ, the resurrection, or the existence of God."[185] David Jenkins who was consecrated as the bishop of Durham, which is the fourth highest post in the Episcopal Church, scorned the bodily resurrection of Jesus Christ as "a conjuring trick with bones."[186]

The Episcopal Church's theology is Satanic, so it is no wonder there are such characters running it. Like the Catholic Church, the Episcopal Church teaches the false salvation by works through the seven so-called sacraments of infant baptism, confirmation, penance, Eucharist, holy orders, matrimony, and unction. The Episcopal Church also teaches that during consecration, the bread and wine of communion is transubstantiated into the actual body, blood, soul, and divinity of Christ. The doctrine of transubstantiation is patent idolatry and blasphemy. The transformation of the Episcopal church into a child of the great harlot of Babylon was accomplished by crypto-Jews and crypto-Catholics working within the Episcopal church.

8 Crypto-Jewish Popes

Crypto-Jews have over the years gained such control over the Roman Catholic church that several have risen to the high office of the papacy. Yaakov Wise, a researcher in orthodox Jewish history and philosophy, concluded that Pope John Paul II was Jewish.[187] His research into the maternal ancestry of Karol Josez Wojtyla (John Paul II's real name) revealed that the late Pope's mother, grandmother and great-grandmother were all Jewish and came from a small town not far from Krakow. According to modern day Judaism, a person's Jewish identity is based upon the maternal line. According to Pope John Paul II's maternal line, he was a Jew.

Once one accepts that Pope John Paul II was Jewish, it becomes easy to understand how he could have had a Jew, Jean-Marie Cardinal Lustiger, as his chief confidant. Jean-Marie Cardinal Lustiger is atypical of the Jewish element in the Catholic church, because rather than hide his Jewish ancestry, he openly admitted that he remained a Jew, even as a high official in the Catholic church. On becoming Archbishop of Paris, Lustiger said: "I was born Jewish and so I remain, even if that is unacceptable for many. For me, the vocation of Israel is bringing light to the goyim. That is my hope and I believe that Christianity is the means for achieving it."[188] What is significant is that his admission to remaining a Jew did not seem to hinder his advancement in the Catholic hierarchy. He later was promoted to the office of Cardinal. Once one understands the Jewish nature of the Roman Catholic church, it is understandable that it would have a Jewish pope with a Jew as his chief confidant.

It is notable that for the most part the major news outlets have not reported on the significant discovery that Pope John Paul II was Jewish. That is explained by the fact that Jews control the major media outlets and do not want to expose the fact that the ostensibly gentile Roman church is in reality a Jewish religious front that is staffed from top to bottom by crypto-Jews.

It is not hyperbole that the Jews control the major media outlets. John Whitley revealed in 2003 that "seven Jewish Americans run the vast majority of US television networks, the printed press, the Hollywood movie industry, the book publishing industry, and the recording industry."[189] He explained that [m]ost of these industries are bundled into huge media conglomerates." He listed the Jewish men and stated that "[t]hose seven Jewish men collectively control ABC, NBC, CBS, the Turner Broadcasting System, CNN, MTV, Universal Studios, MCA Records, Geffen Records, DGC Records, GRP Records, Rising Tide Records, Curb/Universal Records, and Interscope Records."[190]

Whitley's research concluded that "[m]ost of the larger independent newspapers are owned by Jewish interests as well. An example is media mogul is Samuel I. 'Si' Newhouse, who owns two dozen daily newspapers from Staten Island to Oregon, plus the Sunday supplement Parade; the Conde Nast collection of magazines, including Vogue, The New Yorker, Vanity Fair, Allure, GQ, and Self; the publishing firms of Random House, Knopf, Crown, and Ballantine, among other imprints; and cable franchises with over one million subscribers."[191] Whitley's conclusions are as valid today as they were in 2003. Whitley explains why: "I could add that Michael Eisner could depart Disney tomorrow but the company will remain in the hands of Shamrock Holdings, whose principal office is now located in Israel."[192]

Crypto-Jews are prevalent in both religion and politics. "There is no doubt that many Americans who see [Senator] John Kerry as a quintessential WASPish looking politician with an Irish name will be shocked to learn that he is actually, what Joel Kotkin of the Jewish Journal of Greater Los Angeles calls, a "marrano" or a hidden closeted Jew."[193] The Boston Globe hired a genealogist to check Kerry's background.[194] It was discovered that his paternal grandfather was a Hungarian (Ashkenazi) Jew. When the story of Kerry's Jewish background came to light during the 2004 presidential campaign, "John Kerry told the Boston Globe that he has known for 15 years that his paternal grandmother was Jewish, but that he had no information on his paternal grandfather's roots."[195] His grandfather, Felix Kohn, changed his name to Frederick A. Kerry and outwardly converted to Roman Catholicism. Catholicism is the usual cover for crypto-Jews. "The genealogist who conducted the study, Felix Gundacker of the Institute for Historical Family Research in Vienna, Austria, told the paper he is '1,000 percent' certain Kerry's grandfather was Jewish."[196]

Kerry claimed prior ignorance of his paternal grandfather's Jewishness. However, as pointed out by Jewish reporter Barry Chamish: "Somehow, he forgot the fact that his grandparents were prominent Jewish business people in Prague and that his father is 100% Jewish. Ask yourself, do you know anyone who doesn't know his father's religious background?"[197] It is unlikely that his grandfather simply jettisoned his Judaism. It is more likely that the conversion to Roman Catholicism was a front, and that John Kerry himself is a crypto-Jew. It is notable that Kerry found it necessary to conceal his Jewish roots, which was a deep secret, yet the fact that was he was a member of the satanic Skull and Bones society seemed to be a less well kept secret.[198] The Skull and Bones group has been identified by some researchers as the U.S. branch of the Illuminati.[199]

During the 2004 presidential campaign, Tim Russert on NBC Meet the Press asked George Bush about both he and John Kerry being members of the Skull and Bones, Bush responded by saying "It's so secret we can't talk about it."[200] When Russert had Kerry on the show as a guest he asked Kerry what does the fact that both he and George Bush are members of Skull and Bones tell us; Kerry responded by nervously saying: "Not much, because it's a secret."[201] It is astounding that both candidates for President of the United States from the supposedly opposing major political parties are known to be members of the same secret organization and they are only asked about that membership one time. On that one occasion, they are each permitted to say nothing about it. The major media outlets did no follow up questioning or investigation on the issue. Virtually all of the significant investigation of Skull and Bones has been done by the independent media, who, of course, have no access to the candidates to ask tough questions about the nefarious secret society. It was interesting that Russert had the temerity to ask Kerry about Skull and Bones, but he stayed clear of asking Kerry about the concealment of his Jewish roots.

Barry Chamish outs two more crypto-Jews: "Former CFR Secretary-of-State Madeleine Albright also forgot that both her parents were Jews, even though she was raised in the Jewish home of her relatives in London. If you don't feel like voting Kerry, there is Wesley Clark waiting in the wings. Uncannily, he is also a CFR member who only discovered his father was Jewish while he was burning Bosnia to ashes."[202] What is the CFR to which Chamish refers? It is a front group set up and controlled by the Jewish Illuminati. The Illuminati have used certain front organizations that they use to infiltrate and control governments, including the U.S. government. One group is called the Council on Foreign Relations (CFR). Admiral Chester Ward was a member of the CFR for 16 years. He resigned from the CFR when he realized that its goal was to disarm and surrender the United States to an all powerful world government.[203]

Pinay reveals that the crypto-Jewish phenomenon spans the globe. "[T]he phenomenon of Crypto-Judaism was not merely confined to the Christian world. One still finds in different parts of the Musulman [sic] world communities of Crypto-Jews, as Cecil Roth observes, who records several examples of Jewish communities in which the Hebrews, who outwardly were Musulmen, are in secret still Jews. This means that the Jews have also introduced a "Fifth Column" into the bosom of the Islamic religion. This fact perhaps explains the many divisions and the uproar which has occurred in the world of Mohammed."[204]

Aho explains: "In other words, having infiltrated the Christian and Islamic worlds, the crypto-Jews were in a position to implement Protocol #17 of the Learned Elders of Zion, 'Throughout all Europe, and by means of relations with Europe, in other continents also, we must create ferments, discords, and hostility. Therein we gain a double advantage.'"[205]

Even when there is not direct evidence that a Pope is Jewish, there is often evidence that he is an agent or fellow traveler with the Jewish hierarchy. For example, Angelo Roncalli, who later became Pope John XXIII, was allegedly a member of the Prieuré de Sion and the related secret society Rose-Croix.[206] According to the Roman Catholic publication Sodalitium, in 1961, John XXIII reinstated the Knights of Malta and rescinded the prohibition of Roman Catholics holding membership in Freemasonry. [207]

What is the significance of rescinding the prohibition against membership in Freemasonry?

Albert Pike, the theological pontiff of Freemasonry wrote that "[i]t is certain that its true pronunciation is not represented by the word Jehovah; and therefore that *that* is not the true name of Diety, nor the Ineffable Word."[208] God's word, however, states clearly that JEHOVAH is God's name. "That *men* may know that thou, whose name alone *is* JEHOVAH, *art* the most high over all the earth." (Psalms 83:18 AV)

If the Masons do not recognize JEHOVAH as God, who is their god? The god of the Masons is Lucifer, which was Satan's name before he rebelled against God and was cast out of heaven. Albert Pike said that "[t]he doctrine of Satanism is heresy; and the true and pure philosophic religion is the belief in Lucifer, the equal of Adonay; but Lucifer, God of Light and God of Good, is struggling for humanity against Adonay, the God of Darkness and Evil."[209] Adonay is the Old Testament Hebrew word for God. Pike not only acknowledges that Lucifer is the god of Freemasonry, but he also blasphemes God by calling God "the God of Darkness and Evil."

The Holy Bible (Genesis 2:17) states that God forbade Adam from eating of the fruit of the tree of the knowledge of good and evil. Pike blasphemes God again by referring to God as "the Demons" who forbade Adam from eating from the fruit of the tree of the knowledge of good and evil.[210] The Holy Bible states that God created Eve. Pike continues his blasphemy by calling God "the Demons" who created Eve.[211]

Pike portrays the serpent (Satan) as "an Angel of Light" that induced Adam to transgress against "the Demons" and thus giving Adam "the means of victory."[212] Pike calls the sin of Adam and Eve the means of victory over God, whereas God views Adam's disobedience against him as the means of the fall of man, which required God to come down to earth and redeem man. (Romans 5:12-21) Christ has won the victory over Satan for all those who believe in Jesus. (1 Corinthians 15:54-58, 1 John 5:4, Revelations 15:2) While it is true that Satan can transform himself into an angel of light (*see* 2 Corinthians 11:14), Pike's point in calling Satan an "Angel of Light" was to distinguish him from God, whom he called the "Prince of Darkness."

The doctrines of Freemasonry are influenced to a great extent by Roman Catholic doctrine and history. In 1754 the first 25 degrees of the Scottish Rite of Freemasonry were written by the Jesuits in the College of Jesuits of Clermont in Paris, for the purpose of restoring to power the Jesuit controlled House of Stuart to the throne of England.[213] There are a series of degrees in the Masonic York Rite hierarchy known as the Order of Knights Templar. The Knights Templar was an organization founded in 1118 A.D. The Templars received papal sanction as a Catholic order (the Order of the Poor Knights of Christ) in 1128 and are recognized as the first Roman Catholic crusaders. The Templars were known as the "Militia of Christ." The Jewish character of the Catholic rites in Freemasonry cannot be understated. Albert Pike explains this secret to Masonry in the doctrinal bible of freemasonry, *Morals and Dogma*: **"Masonry is a search for Light. That leads us directly back, as you see, to the Kabalah."**[214]

Pike stated that the Templars, as with all secret societies, have two doctrines; one is for the public and the other is hidden from the public and is only revealed to those initiated into the secret society.[215] Pike stated that "[t]hus they deceived the adversaries whom they sought to supplant."[216] That same strategy is being followed today with the public charitable activities of the Roman Catholic Church and the Masonic Order, yet they are both working secretly toward world domination.

While on the surface the Templars appeared to engage in selfless service, they were initiated with a ceremony which required them to reject Christ by spitting on a crucifix. They were then ordered to worship Satan, who was depicted in the form of a bearded idol.[217] Although Pope Clement V was personally apprised of the blasphemous conduct of the Templars, he took no action until their activities became public knowledge. It was then that the political pressure forced his hand and the Templars were suppressed.[218] According to Albert Pike, Jacques de Molay, the Grand Master of the Templars, was arrested and while he was in prison founded the first lodges of Freemasonry in Naples, Edinburgh, Stockholm, and Paris.[219] De Molay was burned at the stake in 1314 by King Philip IV of France and Pope Clement V.[220] Albert Pike states that both King Philip IV of France and Pope Clement V were assassinated shortly thereafter as revenge for the suppression of the Knights Templars.[221] The young men's branch of modern freemasonry is named after Jacques de Molay.

The public and most Freemasons are unaware that Freemasonry is rooted in Judaism. The authoritative explanation of the famous rabbi, Isaac Wise, reveals that the Gentile nature of Freemasonry is only a cover: "Freemasonry is a Jewish establishment, whose history, grades, official appointments, passwords, and explanations are Jewish from beginning to end."[222] The October 28, 1927 Jewish Tribune of New York stated: "Masonry is based on Judaism. Eliminate the teachings of Judaism from the Masonic Ritual and what is left?"[223] Michael Hoffman concluded: "It is from these [Cabalistic and Talmudic] recondite doctrines of Judaism that the Freemasons and other occult workers of iniquity derive their beliefs."[224] The *Sefer Yezirah* (a/k/a Book of Formation or Book of Creation), which is one of the earliest and most important books of the Kabbalah, teaches fortune telling, numerology, and astrology by means of contacting devils.[225] The Talmud *Sanhedren* 65b, acknowledges that the *Sefer Yezirah* "has affinities with Babylonian, Egyptian, and Hellenic mysticism."[226]

As explained by Nesta Webster, Freemasonry is an amalgam of the theology and secret practices of the Roman Catholic Templars and Cabalistic Jews.

> The Jewish writer Bernard Lazare has declared that "there were Jews around the cradle of Freemasonry, "and if this statement is applied to the period preceding the institution of Grand Lodge in 1717 it certainly finds confirmation in fact. Thus it is said that in the preceding century the coat-of-arms now used by Grand Lodge had been designed by an Amsterdam Jew, Jacob Jehuda Leon Templo, colleague of Cromwell's friend the Cabalist, Manasseh ben Israel. To quote Jewish authority on this question, Mr. Lucien Wolf writes that Templo "had a monomania for . . . everything relating to the Temple of Solomon and the Tabernacle of the

Wilderness. He constructed gigantic models of both these edifices." These he exhibited in London which he visited in 1675, and earlier, and it seems not unreasonable to conclude that this may have provided a fresh source of inspiration to the Freemasons who framed the masonic ritual some forty years later. At any rate, the masonic coat-of-arms still used by Grand Lodge of England is undoubtedly of Jewish design.

"This coat," says Mr. Lucien Wolf, "is entirely composed of Jewish symbols," and is "an attempt to display heraldically the various forms of the Cherubim pictured to us in the second vision of Ezekiel--an Ox, a Man, a Lion, and an Eagle--and thus belongs to the highest and most mystical domain of Hebrew symbolism."

In other words, this vision, known to the Jews as the "Mercaba" belongs to the Cabala, where a particular interpretation is placed on each figure so as to provide an esoteric meaning not perceptible to the uninitiated. The masonic coat-of-arms is thus entirely Cabalistic as is also the seal on the diplomas of Craft Masonry, where another Cabalistic figure, that of a man and woman combined, is reproduced.

To sum up, then, the origins of the system we now know as Freemasonry are not to be found in one source alone. The twelve alternative sources enumerated in the Masonic Cyclopodia and quoted at the beginning of this chapter may all have contributed to its formation. Thus Operative Masonry may have descended from the Roman Collegia and through the operative masons of the Middle Ages, whilst Speculative Masonry may have derived from the patriarchs and the mysteries of the pagans. But the source of inspiration which admits of no denial is the Jewish Cabala. Whether this penetrated to our country through the Roman Collegia, the compagnonnages, the Templars, the Rosicrucians, or through the Jews of the seventeenth and eighteenth centuries, whose activities behind the scenes of Freemasonry we shall see later, is a matter of speculation. The fact remains that when the ritual and constitutions of Masonry were drawn up in 1717, although certain fragments of the ancient Egyptian and Pythagorean doctrines were retained, the Judaic version of the secret tradition was the one selected by the founders of Grand Lodge on which to build up their system.

* * *

We have only to glance at the nomenclature of the last twenty-two of these degrees to see that on the basis of operative Masonry there has been built up a system composed of two elements: crusading chivalry and Judaic tradition. What else is this but Templarism?[227]

In June 1960 Pope John XXIII published an encyclical letter on 'The Precious Blood of

Jesus.' In that encyclical letter Pope John XXIII stated that it was the suffering of Jesus and shedding of his blood that was the source of the redemption of mankind. This encyclical statement reduced the significance of Jesus' death and resurrection. The letter alters the whole basis of Christian theology. If Jesus redeemed man through his suffering alone, then his death and resurrection become superfluous. Now, under Catholic theology, the death and resurrection of Jesus it is no longer a necessary tenet of the Catholic church.

John XXIII's encyclical implicitly puts a hole in Catholic theology into which can fit nicely the Merovingian myth that Jesus did not die, but instead recovered from the crucifixion and fled to France with his wife, Mary Magdalene and offspring. That was the story line behind *The DaVinci Code*. It was also the basis for the Roman Catholic Mel Gibson movie, *The Passion of the Christ*, which overemphasized Jesus' suffering as a man, and made no clear statement about his divinity. Gibson's movie omitted Jesus' virgin birth and ascension into heaven.

Pope John Paul II being a crypto-Jew is not an anomaly. There is a deep history of crypto-Jewish popes reigning over the Roman church. "The Medicis were a Merovingian family who ruled the Vatican as popes. In the 15th century, the Medici funded the Academy of Florence, Italy to spread Hermetic Cabalism and to infiltrate the Vatican with this heresy. Several of the Medici became popes and cardinals. Giulio de' Medici (1478-1534) would become Pope Clement VII, Alessandro de' Medici (1535-1605) was Pope Leo XI and Giovanni de Medici, Pope Leo X (1513-1521)."[228]

9 The Learned Elders of Zion

According to researcher Fritz Springmeier, the Medicis, along with other Merovingian bloodlines (the House of Lorraine, the House of Guise, Sforzas, the Estes, the Gonzagas, and the St. Clairs (a/k/a Sinclairs), were co-founders of the secret society Prieuré de Sion.[229] The Prieuré de Sion (a.k.a. Priory of Sion) is a Jewish secret society, which many researchers have concluded is the apex of the Illuminati and oversees all other secret societies.[230] The exoteric nature of the Priory of Sion, however, suggests that it may yet be only a religious front for the real counsel ruling the world: The Learned Elders of Zion, the existence of which is never authoritatively acknowledged.[231]

An example of the cover-up of the existence of The Learned Elders of Zion is the ubiquitous Jewish controlled *Wikipedia* online encyclopedia. *Wikipedia* has a web page devoted to the Priory of Sion. The mainline *Wikipedia* describes the Priory of Sion as both "both real and fictitious."[232] Huh? *Wikipedia* cannot dismiss the existence of the Priory of Sion altogether, so it acknowledged its existence, but then discusses it as a ludibrium.

Wikipedia dismisses any notion that the Priory of Sion is a conspiratorial cabal made up of the Merovingian bloodline. *Wikipedia* cites to *The Da Vinci Code,* by Dan Brown, as evidence of the mythology of the Priory of Sion. That is like citing to a fictional book about Abraham Lincoln to prove that he was not really the sixteenth President of the United States. Presenting the Priory of Sion in Don Brown's work of fiction may have been for the very purpose of giving the impression to the masses that the Priory of Sion as a conspiratorial group is a fiction. The most interesting thing is not the conclusory attempt by *Wikipedia* to debunk the Priory of Sion by characterizing it as a myth, but the fact that there is no entry at all in *Wikipedia,* as of February 15, 2010, for *The Learned Elders of Zion*!

While *Wikipedia* keeps a lid on the existence of The Learned Elders of Zion, they cannot avoid mentioning the Protocols of the Learned Elders of Zion. The Protocols have become so widely circulated that *Wikipedia* had to address them. It is quite odd that they would talk of the Protocols without exploring the underlying organization that is purported to be the author of the

Protocols. It is as though that topic is off-limits, even if to discuss the organization as a myth.

The Protocols of the Learned Elders of Zion is an outline of a plan by Jews to rule the world. The Protocols were drawn up by the International Jewish Council which met in Basle, Switzerland in 1879. The Protocols appear to be a summation of the conspiratorial plans that had been in existence long before they were memorialized at the 1879 meeting. The Protocols contain the formula used by the Zionists to launch their offensive to rule the world.

The Protocols came to light through a series of events that began in 1884, when the daughter of a Russian general, Madamoiselle Justine Glinka, was endeavoring to serve her country in Paris by obtaining political information. She communicated her plans to General Orgevskii in St. Petersburg. For this purpose she employed a Jew, Joseph Schorst, member of the Mizraim Lodge (Oriental Rite of Freemasonry) in Paris. Schorst offered to obtain for her a document of great importance to Russia for the price of 2,500 francs. Mlle. Glinka received the money from St. Petersburg and obtained the document, which turned out to be the Protocols of the Learned Elders of Zion.

She forwarded the French original of the Protocols, accompanied by a Russian translation, to General Orgevskii, who in turn handed them to his superior, General Cherevin, for delivery to the Tsar. Cherevin, however, was under the control of wealthy Jews, and he consequently refused to transmit the Protocols. Cherevin merely filed the Protocols in the Russian archives.

Years later Mlle. Glinka gave a copy of the Protocols to the marechal de noblesse of her district, Alexis Sukhotin. Sukhotin showed the document to two friends, Stepanov and Professor Sergius A. Nilus. Professor Nilus published the Protocols in 1901 in the book, *The Great Within the Small*. On or about August 10, 1906 a copy of the Protocols was deposited in the British Museum. In the meantime, minutes of the proceedings of the Basle congress in 1897 had been obtained through Jewish members of the Russian police and these were found to confirm the plans set forth in the Protocols.

The Learned Elders of Zion were the hidden hand behind the rise of Hitler to power. They also colluded with him through their front organizations during World War II to drive the Jews from Europe to Palestine. As we have seen, the assimilation by the Jews into the Roman religion has been accomplished through changing their names and converting to Catholicism. They, however, have kept their Talmudic and Cabalistic traditions; they are crypto-Jews. These Talmudic crypto-Jews gravitated toward the power in Rome. The barbarity and duplicity of these Jews can be seen in their conspiratorial and murderous actions during World War II. Heinrich Himmler, Joseph Goebbels, and Adolph Hitler were all of Jewish extraction. They were also Roman Catholic. Himmler modeled the SS after the crypto-Jewish Jesuit order. Walter Schellenberg, former chief of German counter-espionage (*Sicherheisdienst* or SD), explained after the war:

The SS organisation (sic) had been constituted, by Himmler, according to the principles of the Jesuits' Order. Their regulations and the Spiritual Exercises prescribed by Ignatius of Loyola were the model Himmler tried to copy exactly.[233]

Adolph Hitler said: "I can see Himmler as our Ignatius of Loyola."[234] Keep in mind that Himmler was the "Reichsfuhrer SS" (Supreme Chief of the SS). That title was intended to be the equivalent of the Jesuits' "General."[235] Himmler was also in charge of the German secret police, known as the Gestapo. The Jesuit General, Count Halke von Ledochowski, arranged for a special unit within the SS Central Security Service where most of the main posts were held by Roman Catholic priests wearing the black shirt SS uniforms. The head of this special unit was Heinrich Himmler's uncle, who was a Jesuit priest.[236]

Franz Von Papen, former Chancellor of Germany, the Pope's secret chamberlain, and the mainspring of the concordat between Germany and the Vatican, said: "The Third Reich is the first world power which not only acknowledges but also puts into practice the high principles of the papacy."[237] With that in mind, consider that Hitler's deputy, Rudolph Hess, *Reichmarshal* Hermann Goering, Gregor Strasser, Alfred Rosenberg, Hans Frank, *Reichminister* von Ribbentrop, top SS leader Reinhard Heydrich, Hitler's bankers Ritter von Strauss and von Stein as well as a majority of Hitler's top officers and associates were Jews! The Third Reich was modeled after the papacy and was controlled by crypto-Jews, just as is the papacy.[238]

One may ask, why would Jews become Nazis and then orchestrate the persecution of fellow Jews? Because these Nazi Jews were Zionists. The Nazis and the Zionists worked together to persecute the Jews of Europe in order to force them to emigrate to Palestine. The Nazis worked out secret arrangements with the Zionist Jews to facilitate the emigration of Jews from Europe to Palestine. Henneke Kardel explained the arrangement between the Nazis and the Zionist Jews in his book *Adolph Hitler: Founder of Israel.*

> The cooperation which existed between Heydrich's Gestapo and the Jewish self-defense league in Palestine, the militant Haganah, would not have been closer if it was not for Eichamn who made it public.... The commander of Haganah was Feivel Polkes, born in Poland, with whom in February 1937 the S. D. trooper leader Adolph Eichman met in Berlin in a wine restaurant Traube (Grape) near the zoo. These two Jews made a brotherly agreement. Polkes, the underground fighter, got in writing this assurance from Eichman: "A body representing Jews in Germany will exert pressure on those leaving Germany to emigrate only to Palestine. Such a policy is in the interest of Germany and will be executed by the Gestapo."[239]

Why did the Zionist Jews want to force the Jews living in Europe to emigrate to Palestine? Because they wanted to increase the population of Jews in that area in order to establish a beachhead for eventual control of the entire middle east. The only way for the Jews to establish hegemony in Palestine would be to increase the population of Jews there. After the defeat of the Ottoman Empire in World War I, Britain controlled Palestine through a mandate from the League of Nations. On November 2, 1917, Arthur James Lord Balfour, Foreign Secretary of Britain, sent a letter to prominent Zionist Lord Rothschild promising the establishment of a Jewish homeland in Palestine. The letter became known as the Balfour Declaration. It was the first recognition by a major world power of a Jewish homeland. The Jews at the time were a minority in Palestine and consequently could not hope to control the area, which was their goal. They needed large numbers of Jews to immigrate into Palestine in order to begin the process of Jewish conquest of the Middle East. The problem for the Jews was that they could not persuade Jews living comfortably and prosperously in Europe to emigrate to third world Palestine. It was decided that they would be driven out of Europe so that they would have no choice but to flee to Palestine. Enter Hitler and his Nazi "final solution," which had as its objective not the extermination of Jews as is commonly believed, but rather driving the Jews from Europe to Palestine.

On November 19, 1947 the United Nations partitioned Palestine into three sections: one for Palestinians, one for the Jews, and an international zone in Jerusalem. On May 14, 1948, the state of Israel officially came into being. Today the Jews control all of Palestine, including Jerusalem, which is now the capital of Israel. The Zionist dream is that Jerusalem will be the capital of the world. Three quarters of the population of Jerusalem are now Jewish, with the remaining residents being Palestinians. The Jews occupy the West Bank, Gaza Strip, and the Golan Heights. Those areas will eventually be absorbed into Israel.

The Zionist Jews not only worked with the Nazis to force Jews to emigrate to Israel, they have also instigated other governments to persecute Jews in order to force their emigration to Israel. The Jewish scholar, Israel Shahak, discovered: "The Israeli government induced Jewish immigration from Iraq by bribing the government of Iraq to strip most Iraqi Jews of their citizenship and to confiscate their property."[240] The close relationship between the Zionist Jews and the Nazis comes into focus when one looks at the characters who have assisted Israel. Most are surprised to learn that the person who was most instrumental in establishing and training the notorious Mossad (Israeli Military Intelligence) was none other than Reinhard Gehlen, former head of Hitler's Nazi Intelligence for the Eastern front.[241]

An examination of General Reinhard Gehlen's career reveals that he had close ties to both Zionist Jews and the Roman Catholic Church. In 1948, the Sovereign Military Order of Malta (SMOM) gave one of its highest awards of honor, the *Gran Croci al Merito con Placca*, to General Gehlen for his service to the Roman Catholic Church. The exclusivity of that honor is evidenced by the fact that at that time only three other people had ever received that award. The SMOM is not some insignificant Catholic charitable organization. Although the order has only a small headquarters in Rome, it holds the status of nation-state. It mints its own coins, prints its own stamps, has its own constitution, and issues its own license plates and passports to an accredited diplomatic corps. The grand master of the order, Fra Angelo de Mojana di Cologna, holds the rank in the Roman Catholic Church equivalent to a cardinal. The grand master of the SMOM order is recognized as a sovereign chief of state by 41 nations with whom the SMOM exchanges ambassadors.[242]

During World War II, Zionists were working feverishly in both Germany and the United States to increase emigration from Europe to Palestine. Out of Franklin Roosevelt's 75 closest advisors and high government officials that surrounded him upon taking office as President of the United States, 52 were Jews.[243] In 1937 Roosevelt received the Gottheil Medal for distinguished service to Jewry. The Gottheil Medal dedicatory to Roosevelt referred to him as "our modern day Moses."[244] That is not surprising since Roosevelt was a Jew. In 1934 the Carnegie Institute, under the direction of Dr. H.H. Laughlin, studied Roosevelt's lineage and determined that beginning with his Jewish mother, Sarah, Roosevelt was from a long line of Jews going back to 1682 when Claes Martenzen van Rosenvelt and Janette Samuel came to America. On 14 March 1935 Roosevelt was quoted in the *New York Times* as admitting his Jewish ancestory, even naming "Claes Martenzen van Roosevelt" (sic) as his ancestor.[245]

To simply focus on Roosevelt's Jewishness would be cause for bewilderment by some when they consider that he would not allow Jews fleeing persecution in Germany to immigrate into the United States. It is not Roosevelt's Jewish ancestry that is notable; it is his Zionism. His refusal to permit Jewish immigration into the U.S. becomes understandable in a Machiavellian sense when one realizes that Roosevelt was a Zionist Jew and was working in concert with other Zionists to force the Jews to flee to Palestine. If Roosevelt gave the Jews safe haven in the United States, then they would certainly choose the U.S. over Israel. And that would thwart the Zionist plans for Jewish hegemony in Palestine.

This secret use of ostensibly gentile nations and institutions in order to further Jewish Zionist aims, while hiding the Jewish influence over those institutions, is explained in the Protocols of the Learned Elders of Zion. In the Protocols, the Learned Elders of Zion state that they have used Masonry as a cover to hide their involvement in the plan for a "new world order." "Who and what is in the position to overthrow the invisible force? And this is precisely what our force is. Gentile masonry blindly serves as a screen for us and our objectives, but the plan of action of our force, even its very abiding place, remains for the whole people an unknown mystery."[246]

The gentile facade of Freemasonry offers the Talmudic Jews the perfect cover. Freemasonry is based upon Judaism.[247] It is a gentile front for Jewish mysticism, whose history, grades, and official appointments, are rooted in Jewish theosophy.[248]

The best evidence of the genuineness of the Protocols is that in March, 1917 the Bolshevik Revolution took place in Russia and one of the first things done upon the Jewish Bolsheviks taking power was to destroy all copies of Professor Sergius A. Nilus' book, *The Great Within the Small*, by. That book, which was first published in Tsarskoe-Tselc (Russia) in 1901, contained *The Protocols of the Learned Elders of Zion*.

All copies of the Protocols that were known to exist in Russia were destroyed during the Kerensky regime. The law followed by Kerensky's communist successors to power was that the possession of a copy of the Protocols by anyone in the Soviet Union was a crime punishable by being shot on sight. The lengths to which the communists went to eradicate the Protocols are evidence of the genuineness of the Protocols.

The treatment of Professor Nilus by the Jewish Bolsheviks speaks clearly to the authenticity of the Protocols. Professor Nilus was arrested by the Cheka (Russian Secret Police) in Kiev. He was imprisoned and tortured. The Jewish president of the court told Professor Nilus that the brutal treatment he received was retribution for "having done them incalculable harm in publishing the Protocols." Professor Nilus was released for a few months, but was soon rearrested by the Cheka, this time in Moscow. He was confined in prison until February 1926. He died in exile in the district of Vladimir on January 13, 1929.

In an interview published in the New York World on February 17, 1921, the great American industrialist Henry Ford tersely and convincingly put the case for the genuineness of the Protocols: "The only statement I care to make about the Protocols is that they fit in with what is going on. They are sixteen years old and they have fitted the world situation up to this time. They fit it now."[249] Henry Ford's statement is as true today as it was when he spoke in 1921. The details of the plan set forth in the Protocols have been implemented before the eyes of the world in Russia, Eastern Europe, China, North Korea, and Vietnam. The plan is in the process of being implemented in Western Europe, South America, South Africa, the United States, and scores of other countries throughout the world.[250] The Talmud also testifies to the authenticity of the Protocols. The evil and blasphemous nature of the Talmud parallels much of what is found in the Protocols.

Anyone who tries to expose the Learned Elders of Zion or its Protocols is immediately branded as an anti-Semite and marginalized by the well-funded attack mechanism set up to keep a lid on that most secret of organizations and its Protocols. For example, *Wikipedia*, describes *The Protocols of the Learned Elders of Zion* as a "hoax" printed and quoted by "anti-Semites."[251]

False claims of anti-Semitism are used as a shield to protect the Jewish hierarchy when evidence of their crimes are uncovered. Former Israeli government official Shulamit Aloni succinctly described the epithet anti-Semite as "a trick, we [Jews] always use."[252] She explained that Jews hide behind it like a smokescreen, which is used to conceal evidence of Jewish malefaction.

Shulamit Aloni knows what she is talking about. She was a member of the Israeli Knesset from 1965 to 1969 and again from 1974 to 1996. She served on the Knesset Constitution Committee, Law and Justice Committee; State Audit Committee; Education and Culture Committee; and the Finance Committee. She served briefly as Minister without Portfolio from June to October 1974. From 1992 to 1996, Aloni served as Minister of Communications and the Arts, Science and Technology.[253]

Below is an interview with Amy Goodman, during which Shulamit explained the Jewish practice of concealing Israeli wrongdoing by labeling the accuser an anti-Semite. By that trick the accuser's credibility is undermined, and the focus shifts from the evidence to the motives of the accuser. The Jewish controlled media then destroys the reputation of the accuser, and he becomes an object lesson for anyone who might consider criticizing Israel or Jews.

> Amy Goodman: Yours is a voice of criticism we don't often hear in the United States. Often when there is dissent expressed in the United States against policies of the Israeli government, people here are called anti-Semitic. What is your response to that as an Israeli Jew?

> Shulamit Aloni: **Well, it's a trick, we always use it. When from Europe somebody is criticizing Israel, then we bring up the Holocaust . When in this country people are criticizing Israel, then they are anti-Semitic.** And the organization is strong, and has a lot of money, and the ties between Israel and the American Jewish establishment are very strong and they are strong in this country, as you know. And they have power, which is OK. They are talented people and they have power and money, and the media and other things, and their attitude is "Israel, my country right or wrong", identification. And they are not ready to hear criticism. And it's very easy to blame people who criticize certain acts of the Israeli government as anti-Semitic, and to bring up the Holocaust, and the suffering of the Jewish people, and that is to justify everything we do to the Palestinians.[254]

Jewish researcher Rose Cohen explains that if one reads the Protocols it would be clear to the reader that it is not a false anti-Semitic document but rather an authentic plan of powerful Zionists:

> [I]t takes a Jew to understand the Zionist mind as reflected in the reviled 'Elders'. Without reading this officially scorned and hated book, no one can EVER understand the Mossad and/or Israel. This is why we in Israel have been always forbidden to read the Protocols and the government maintained a 50+ year campaign among Israelis to discredit the Protocols as a fraud. I had an Israeli professor as a guest in my house recently here in Sydney. He, too, was absolutely certain The Protocols are a fraud, but he readily admitted that he has NEVER read them! When I commented that whether the Protocols are legitimate or not, we Jews have actually behaved and accomplished almost 100% of what is written in them. He could not believe it. Ignorance is bliss, I guess he can sleep at night. However, in the interest of fairness to the professor, I should add that in the last 45 years of my research in this subject, I have yet to meet a single Israeli who actually read the Protocols.[255]

Please, dear reader, do not miss the very important fact revealed by Cohen; as in communist Russia, so also in Israel, the Protocols are forbidden. The Jewish hierarchy does not want the rank and file Jews to read their plans. It is the Jewish hierarchy that is evil, the ordinary Jews, like the gentiles, are cannon fodder in a spiritual and temporal war to rule the world. The masses of Jews are kept in ignorance of the true aims of the evil Jewish hierarchy. It is the same within the Catholic church that is controlled by the Jewish hierarchy. The gentiles within the Catholic church are kept in ignorance about even the existence of the crypto-Jewish hierarchy that controls the reins of the church. The Jewish hierarchy has a history of fanning the flames of anti-Semitism as a tool to keep the rank and file Jews in line and obedient to their commands. They portray the Protocols as another example of anti-Semitic hate literature, yet they do not allow the rank and file Jew to read the document for themselves.

Anti-Semitism has a manifold role in the Jewish scheme. The Jewish hierarchy uses anti-Semitism to keep Jews from assimilating into gentile society; they want their Jews cloistered from gentiles.   They also used anti-Semitism as a means of herding Jews to Israel. The organization *Jews Against Zionism* explains how anti-Semitism is used by Zionists to further their ends:

> Theodor Herzl (1860-1904), the founder of modern Zionism, recognized that anti-Semitism would further his cause, the creation of a separate state for Jews. To solve the Jewish Question, he maintained "we must, above all, make it an international political issue."
>
> Herzl wrote that Zionism offered the world a welcome **"final solution of the Jewish question."** In his "Diaries", page 19, Herzl stated "Anti-Semites will become our surest friends, anti-Semitic countries our allies."[256]

Notice the language used by Herzl long before World War II and the rise of the Nazis. He described the **"final solution of the Jewish question."** That language and concept did not originate with the Germans; it originated with Jewish Zionists. The "final solution" was not the extermination of the Jews, as is commonly believed, it was the persecution of the Jews in order to drive them out of Europe into Israel. The Nazis were simply unwitting tools in the hands of the Zionist Jews in their Machiavellian plan to gain hegemony over Palestine. All who engage in persecution of Jews, simply because they are Jews, are unwitting accessories to the Zionists.

Herzl explains how anti-Semitism furthers Zionist goals:

> "It is essential that the sufferings of Jews. . . become worse. . . this will assist in realization of our plans. . .I have an excellent idea. . . I shall induce anti-semites to liquidate Jewish wealth. . . The anti-semites will assist us thereby in that they will strengthen the persecution and oppression of Jews. The anti-semites shall be our best friends". (From his [Herzl's] Diary, Part I, pp. 16)[257]

To this day anti-Semitism is fostered by the Zionist hierarchy. A close examination of Neo-Nazi hate groups reveals that there are Jews throughout their leadership. The Neo-Nazis act as *agent provocateurs* in the hands of the controlling Jews in order to fan the flames of anti-

Semitism. Jews are sent in to control the Jewish run gentile Neo-Nazi front.

For example, Frank Collin was the leader of the National Socialist Party of America (NSPA), an anti-Semitic Neo-Nazi group. Collin created a national furor in 1977 by organizing a march in predominately Jewish Skokie, Illinois, which resulted in a First Amendment case that went all the way to the U.S. Supreme Court. It turns out that Collin was actually Jewish; his real name was Frank Cohen.[258] Before leading the NSPA he was formerly a member of another Neo-Nazi anti-Semitic group called the National Socialist White Peoples Party (NWPP) (formerly the American Nazi Party (ANP)). Leonard Holstein was commander of the ANP's Los Angeles unit. It was discovered that Holstein was a Jew and a sodomite.[259]

Whenever it is discovered that a leader of a Neo-Nazi or similar anti-Semitic group is Jewish, the Jewish controlled press goes into overdrive to characterize the outed leader as a self-hating Jew. They will then try to explain the behavior of the person as a psychological malady. Such stories and analysis are to deceive the gullible *goyim*. The members of the Jewish hierarchy do not want the gentiles, or the common Jews for that matter, to discover that it is they who control the anti-Semitic groups. In fact, the group that represented Collin in his litigation against Skokie was none other than the Jewish controlled and rabidly anti-Christian American Civil Liberties Union (ACLU). In 2006, three of the six national directors (including the executive director) of the ACLU were Jewish.[260]

Norman Lee Toler is a recent example of Jewish Nazis. Toler is a Neo-Nazi who was sentenced to prison in Missouri for ten years. He has a regalia of Neo-Nazi tattoos, including an SS tattoo. In a previous prison stay in Illinois, Toler was caught with pictures of Hitler and other white supremacist literature. When Toler realized that he would be spending the next ten years in prison, he eschewed being a Neo-Nazi and sued to require the prison to serve him kosher food, because he now states that after all he is a Jew.[261] There are many other examples of skin-heads and Neo-Nazis later determined to be Jews. Anti-Semitism is still used today as a tool to drive Jews out of their respective countries and into Israel. *Jews Against Zionism* explains how it works:

> Zionist reliance on Anti-Semitism to further their goals continues to this day. Studies of immigration records reflect increased immigration to the Zionist state during times of increased anti-Semitism. Without a continued inflow of Jewish immigrants to the state of "Israel", it is estimated that within a decade the Jewish population of the Zionist state will become the minority.
>
> In order to maintain a Jewish majority in the state of "Israel", its leaders promote anti-Semitism throughout the world to "encourage" Jews to leave their homelands and seek "refuge".
>
> Over the recent years there has been a dramatic rise in hate rhetoric and hate crimes targeted toward Jews:

* In Turkey...horrifying suicide bombings at two synagogues left 25 people dead and hundreds more injured.

* In Britain...Scotland Yard recently warned Britain's Jewish Community that it faced imminent terrorist attacks after police spotted and questioned a group of "tourists" taking covert videotape of the Jewish community buildings in London.

* In France...a caution was issued after an arson attack gutted a suburban Paris Jewish school--the latest incident in a frightening wave of French anti-Semitism.

* BBC - UK: "In recent weeks, a poll for the European Commission suggesting that EU citizens see Israel as the biggest threat to world peace caused outrage among Israelis."

Anti-Semitic acts are on the rise across Europe and beyond. From Antwerp and London to Berlin and Istanbul, Jews are living in fear.

On November 17, 2003 Zionist leader, Ariel Sharon, the Israeli prime minister, told Jews in Italy the best way to escape "a great wave of anti-Semitism" is to move and settle in the state of Israel. This has been the Zionist ideology from the beginning to the present time. "The best solution to anti-Semitism is immigration to Israel. It is the only place on Earth where Jews can live as Jews," he said.

July 28, 2004: 200 French Jews emigrated to Israel following a wave of Anti-Semitism. They were personally greeted by Israeli Prime Minister Ariel Sharon, who recently urged French Jews to flee to Israel to escape rising anti-Semitism.

On July 18, 2004, Israeli Prime Minister Ariel Sharon urged all French Jews to move to Israel immediately to escape anti-Semitism. He told a meeting of the American Jewish Association in Jerusalem that Jews around the world should relocate to Israel as early as possible. But for those living in France, he added, moving was a "must" because of rising violence against Jews there."[262]

Today we see Jews spreading anti-Semitism by playing the roles of Al Qeada terrorists. For example, Adam Yahiye Gadahn, known as the "American Al Qaeda," is wanted by the FBI for "Treason - 18 U.S.C. § 2381; Providing Material Support to Al Qaeda - 18 U.S.C. § 2339B; Aiding and Abetting - 18 U.S.C. § 2."[263] Who is Adam Yahiye Gadahn? He has had many Arabic aliases, but he was born a Jew named Adam Pearlman.[264]   He is the grandson of the late Carl K. Pearlman. Carl Pearlman was a prominent Jewish urologist in Orange County and a member of the board of directors of the Jewish Anti-Defamation League.[265]

Gadahn (Pearlman) has been replaced in prominence recently by another so-called American Al Qeada known as Yousef Al Khattab. A visit to Khattab's website reveals the following banner at the top: "The Official Website of Yousef Al Khattab: Allah is our objective, the Quran is our constitution, Muhammad p.b.u.h. is our leader, Jihad is our way; and death for the sake of Allah is the highest of our aspirations."[266]

Who is Yousef al Khattab? He is a Jew. His real name is Joseph Cohen.[267] Upon being found out to be Jewish and a rabbinical student to boot, Khattab spun a story that he was a Jewish convert to Islam. Fox News was only too happy to assist in spinning Khattab as an Islamic convert by reporting: "Formerly known as Joseph Cohen, al-Khattab is an American-born Jew who converted to Islam after attending an Orthodox Rabbinical school, which he later described as a 'racist cult.'"[268] The more plausible explanation is that Khattab (Cohen) is a Jewish *agent provocateur* whose cover was blown. However, Fox News was not going to explore that angle and instead allowed Khattab (Cohen) get away with spinning away his Jewish ancestry as a thing of the past that is no longer relevant to his present conduct and motivation.

If anti-Semitism is not the answer to the Jewish hatred of Christians and gentiles, what is the answer? Jesus provides the answer. It is not to strike back, it is to love your enemy and share with him the gospel of Jesus Christ. "But I say unto you, Love your enemies, bless them that curse you, do good to them that hate you, and pray for them which despitefully use you, and persecute you;" (Matthew 5:44 AV) If you suffer persecution as a Christian at the hands of the Jews and their fellow travelers, rejoice and be glad that you are worthy to suffer for Christ's sake.

> Blessed are ye, when men shall hate you, and when they shall separate you *from their company*, and shall reproach *you*, and cast out your name as evil, for the Son of man's sake. Rejoice ye in that day, and leap for joy: for, behold, your reward *is* great in heaven: for in the like manner did their fathers unto the prophets." (Luke 6:22-23 AV)

That does not mean that Christians are to be silent about the religious malfeasance of the Jews. In fact, it may very well be that the exposure of their spiritual corruption is the reason for the resulting persecution by the Jews and all of the formidable forces at their control. Just as they manipulated the Romans to crucify Jesus, so also today do they manipulate governments elsewhere to persecute Christians.

Jesus should be our model. He did not hesitate to rebuke the Jews for their religious errors. Jesus did not compromise and Christians are not to compromise with the world. We are not to be lukewarm about the gospel of Jesus Christ. Revelation 3:16. The gospel of Jesus Christ is the only effective weapon to the Jewish issue.

> For the word of God *is* quick, and powerful, and sharper than any twoedged sword, piercing even to the dividing asunder of soul and spirit, and of the joints and marrow, and *is* a discerner of the thoughts and intents of the heart. (Hebrews 4:12 AV)

Knowledge is power. Jesus thought it important that we be wise about the source of our trials, but he also stated that Christians are to be harmless. "Behold, I send you forth as sheep in the midst of wolves: be ye therefore wise as serpents, and harmless as doves." (Matthew 10:16 AV)

Jews are powerful and ruthless, but they lack wisdom. That is their weakness. They have convinced the world through their control of the media that they are exceedingly intelligent. Nothing could be further from the truth. God tells us that "[t]he fear of the LORD *is* the beginning of wisdom: and the knowledge of the holy *is* understanding." (Proverbs 9:10 AV) The Jews reject the Lord and have no fear of him. They are in darkest ignorance. The Jewish leadership does not want the common Jew to see the light, which is why they prohibit Jews from reading the New Testament.

Our charge from the Lord is to preach God's word and reprove and rebuke those that have strayed from the sound doctrine of the Gospel of Jesus Christ.

> I charge *thee* therefore before God, and the Lord Jesus Christ, who shall judge the quick and the dead at his appearing and his kingdom; **Preach the word; be instant in season, out of season; reprove, rebuke, exhort with all longsuffering and doctrine**. For the time will come when they will not endure sound doctrine; but after their own lusts shall they heap to themselves teachers, having itching ears; And they shall turn away *their* ears from the truth, and shall be turned unto fables. (2 Timothy 4:1-4 AV)
>
> **Open rebuke *is* better than secret love. Faithful *are* the wounds of a friend; but the kisses of an enemy *are* deceitful.** (Proverbs 27:5-6 AV)
>
> **He that rebuketh a man afterwards shall find more favour than he that flattereth with the tongue.** (Proverbs 28:23 AV)
>
> Reprove not a scorner, lest he hate thee: **rebuke a wise man, and he will love thee**. Give *instruction* to a wise *man*, and he will be yet wiser: teach a just *man*, and he will increase in learning. The fear of the LORD *is* the beginning of wisdom: and the knowledge of the holy *is* understanding. (Proverbs 9:8-10 AV)
>
> **[I]f the watchman see the sword come, and blow not the trumpet, and the people be not warned; if the sword come, and take *any* person from among them, he is taken away in his iniquity; but his blood will I require at the watchman's hand. . . . When I say unto the wicked, O wicked *man*, thou shalt surely die; if thou dost not speak to warn the wicked from his way, that wicked *man* shall die in his iniquity; but his blood will I require at thine hand. Nevertheless, if thou warn the wicked of his way to turn from it; if he do not turn from his way, he shall die in his iniquity; but thou hast delivered**

thy soul. (Ezekiel 33:6-9 AV)

There is no freedom of conscience in Orthodox Judaism. For example, in 2003, the rabbinical court of Agudath Israel and four other rabbinic authorities[269] issued proclamations forbidding Jews from selling or reading the Israeli newspaper *Hashovua*, because that newspaper had the temerity to question the opinion of the *Gedolei Yisroel* (the supreme rabbis). The proclamations stated in pertinent part:

> The purpose of this proclamation is to address . . . the frightful phenomenon of irresponsible and mischievous people taking matters in their own hands . . From time immemorial, every G-d fearing Jew subjected his personal and communal affairs to the guidance of his Rav [rabbi], understanding the folly of following the dictates of his own heart and mind . . . in addition to their remarkable wisdom and experience, in addition to their scope and keen insight, the *Gedolim* are blessed with *siyata dishmaya* [divine inspiration] . . . The purpose of this proclamation then is to reiterate that G-d fearing Jews continue to seek and to cherish the invaluable guidance they receive from their *Gedolim*, to demonstrate their unequivocal loyalty to their leadership and counsel.[270]

Hoffman explains that "those who disobey a ruling of a rabbi (*piskei din*) when issued by the *bis din* (rabbinical court), can be, as Rashi decreed, tortured: *Le'halacha*, in BT Moed Katan 16b."[271] The Jewish religious hierarchy engenders fear among the common Jews. That is the case now and as it was even before Christ's crucifixion, where the Jews were afraid to openly discuss Jesus out of fear of what the Jewish leadership would do to them. "Howbeit no man spake openly of him for fear of the Jews." (John 7:13 AV)

This subjugation of conscience under the rule of the religious leaders in Judaism is, not surprisingly, mirrored in the gentile front set up by crypto-Jews as the Roman Catholic Church. Pope Pius IX on December 8, 1864 issued an encyclical letter *Quanta Cura,* containing the *Syllabus Errorum,* in which he condemned freedom of conscience as "an insane folly" and freedom of the press as "a pestiferous error, which cannot be sufficiently detested."[272] In the *Syllabus Errorum* Pope Pius IX stated: "No man is free to embrace and profess that religion which he believes to be true, guided by the light of reason."[273] Pope Gregory XVI (1831-46) viewed freedom of conscience and the press as absurd and mad concepts, not only within the church but in society as a whole.[274]

The official pronouncements of the Catholic Church in the United States, going back over 100 years, confirm the fact that the Catholic Church is antagonistic to liberty. "If Catholics ever gain a sufficient numerical majority in this country, religious freedom is at an end. So our enemies say, so we believe." *The Shepherd of the Valley* (official journal of the Bishop of St. Louis, Nov. 23, 1851).[275] "No man has a right to choose his religion." *New York Freeman* (official Journal of Bishop Hughes, Jan. 26, 1852).[276] "The Church . . . does not, and cannot accept, or in any degree favor, liberty in the Protestant sense of liberty." *Catholic World* (April

1870).[277]

Samuel Morse explains:

> Popery is a *Political system, despotic* in its organization, *anti-democratic* and *ant-republican*, and cannot therefore co-exist with American republicanism.

> The ratio of *increase of Popery* is the exact ratio of *decrease of civil liberty.*

> The *dominance of Popery* in the United States is the *certain destruction of our free institutions.*

> Popery, by its organization, is wholly under the control of a FOREIGN DESPOTIC SOVEREIGN.[278]

Marquis De Lafayette said that "[i]f the liberties of the American people are ever destroyed, they will fall by the hands of the Catholic clergy."[279]

Pope Pius IX in his 1864 *Syllabus Errorum* stated: "The [Roman] Church ought to be in union with the state, and the State ought to be in union with the [Roman] Church. . . . It is necessary even in the present day that the Catholic religion shall be held as the only religion of the State, to the exclusion of all other forms of worship."[280]

This supreme religious authority proclaimed by the Vatican is the same supreme authority claimed by the Orthodox Jewish leadership over the common Jews. Orthodox Jews are victims of spiritual charlatans who have frightened them into following their heathen religion. Orthodox Jews are made by their religious leaders to hate Christ and Christians. Romans 11:28. Christians, however, are to love them and pray for them. "But I say unto you which hear, Love your enemies, do good to them which hate you, Bless them that curse you, and pray for them which despitefully use you." (Luke 6:27-28 AV) God has chosen a remnant of Jews for salvation. Christians should preach the gospel to the lost world, including the Jews.

Salvation for all, is by the grace of God through faith in Jesus Christ. If a Jew repents of his antichrist religion and believes in Jesus, then he is saved. Once saved, a Jew will not continue in his Talmudic and Cabalistic practices any more than a Catholic will continue his Catholic practices or a Satanist will continue his Satanic practices once they are saved. All believers in Christ become spiritual Jews, which are Christians. Loving our enemies does not mean that we should condone the pagan practices of the Jews, Catholics, Muslims, or other heathens. Rather, we are called by God to reprove them. "And have no fellowship with the unfruitful works of darkness, but rather reprove *them*." (Ephesians 5:11 AV)

Jews divide the Old Testament into three categories. The first 5 books are the called the Torah (Instruction), the books of the prophets are called the Nevi'im, and remainder of the Old

Testament is called the Ketuvim (writings).   Often, however, Jews use the term Torah to refer to the entire Old Testament, which they also call the Tanakh or Hebrew Bible. They also use Torah to refer to the entire body of Jewish law and teachings including the Talmud, Kabbalah, other rabbinic writings, and the Old Testament. Jews sometimes designate the Old Testament the "Written Torah" to distinguish it from the other writings, which were originally part of the oral tradition. All Jews reject the New Testament as part of their cannon of scripture.

There are degrees of adherence to Judaic theology. At one end of the Judaic religious scale are the Karaites, who adhere to the authority of the Old Testament (Tanakh), and eschew the Talmud, Kabbalah, and other rabbinical writings. Next would be Reformed Jews, who take the Old Testament as authoritative and generally view the Talmud and Kabbalah as commentaries to shed light on the Tanakh. Reformed Judaism was introduced in the 19th century, and does not require strict adherence to traditional Jewish rituals. At the other end of the scale are the Orthodox and Hasidic Jews who view the Talmud and Kabbalah as authoritative over the Tanakh. Many Orthodox and Hasidic Jews do not consider the Karaites or Reformed Jews as truly Jewish because of their attitude toward the Talmud and Kabbalah. All Jews reject Jesus as the Messiah.

10 Communism is Judaism

How would the Protocols have harmed the communist revolution in Russia as stated by the president of the communist Russian court that brutalized Nilus? Because, the communist revolution was essentially Talmudic Judaism put into practice to take over Russia according to the strategies set forth in the Protocols. Many think that Zionism is the struggle by the Jews for a homeland. Zionism is much more than the Jews establishing a Palestinian homeland. That is merely a cover for a much grander plan to rule the world. Zionism is the child of the Talmud, and Talmudism is communism. The communist revolution in Russia was planned and executed by Jews according to the outline in the Protocols.

V.I. Lenin, supreme dictator, and Leon Bronstein (Trotsky), supreme commander of the Soviet Red Army, were both Jews.[281] The Bolshevik revolution was Jewish from top to bottom. Of 556 leading conspirators in the Bolshevik state in 1918-19 there were 17 Russians, two Ukrainians, eleven Armenians, 35 Latvians, 15 Germans, one Hungarian, ten Georgians, three Poles, three Finns, one Czech, one Karaim, and 457 Jews.[282] As pointed out by Robert Wilton in his book The Last Days of the Romanovs, the communist revolution was not an insurrection by Russians, but rather a secret invasion by Jews. As of 1983, the Premier of the Soviet Union was a Jew (Andropov) and 23 out of 25 members of the Politboro (the Soviet ruling clique) were Jews. In addition, every top member of the military and of the Soviet police, were Jews.[283]

> The Germans knew what they were doing when they sent Lenin's pack of Jews
> into Russia. They chose them as agents of destruction. Why? Because the Jews
> were not Russians and to them the destruction of Russia was all in the way of
> business, revolutionary or financial. The whole record of Bolshevism in Russia is
> indelibly impressed with the stamp of alien invasion. The murder of the Tsar,
> deliberately planned by the Jew Sverdlov (who came to Russia as a paid agent of
> Germany) and carried out by the Jews Goloschekin, Syromolotov, Safarov,
> Voikov and Yukovsky, is the act not of the Russian people, but of this hostile
> invader.[284]

Colonel Jack Mohr states: "One of the greatest difficulties of the Talmudic Pharisees has been that of bringing communism into power while trying to conceal its Talmudic origin."[285] However, the direct and circumstantial evidence that the communist revolution in Russia was a conspiracy perpetrated by Talmudic Jews is overwhelming. Circumstantial evidence that points to Jewish control of the communist revolution is that once the communists in Russia seized power, the first law they passed made anti-Semitism a crime punishable by death.[286] While Christian church buildings were turned into animal stables, slaughter houses, and dance halls, the Jewish synagogues were untouched. [287] Christian pastors were removed from their pastoral duties and made to work on roads and in slave labor camps, yet the Jewish rabbis were permitted to continue their clerical duties.[288] "Some 200,000 (Christian) clergy, many crucified, scalped and otherwise tortured, were killed during the approximately 60 years of communist rule in the former Soviet Union, a Russian commission reported Monday (Nov. 27, 1995)...40,000 churches (were) destroyed in the period from 1922 to 1980..."[289]

Lenin's, maternal grandfather, Israel Blank, was Jewish. Researcher Wayne McGuire of Harvard University wrote: "Lenin was a Jew by the standards of Israel's Law of Return: he possessed a Jewish grandparent."[290] Lenin, in apparent reference to himself, said: "The clever Russian is almost always a Jew or has Jewish blood in him."[291]

Historian Michael Hoffman II exposed the hidden meaning behind some of the bloodthirsty communist propaganda:

> Lenin declared, "We are exterminating the bourgeoisie as a class." His partner in crime, Apfelbaum (Zinoviev) stated: "The interests of the revolution require the physical annihilation of the bourgeoisie class." Who were these bourgeoisie? Certainly not Jews. Trotsky gave a clue to their identity in a 1937 interview in the New York Jewish newspaper, *Daily Forward:* "The longer the rotten bourgeoisie society lives, the more and more barbaric will anti-Semitism become everywhere."
>
> **Bourgeoisie was a Bolshevik code-word for Gentile.** The first law passed after the Communists seized power in Russia made anti-semitism a crime punishable by death. (*Izvestia,* July 27, 1918).
>
> * * *
>
> The Jewish Bolsheviks regarded politics as a branch of Gentile pest control. Hatred of Christians, especially the peasant "bourgeoisie" was their prime motivation. The systematic destruction of the Christian peasantry of Russia as so many vermin, beginning with Lenin's attack on them in the summer of 1918 and his forced starvation in 1921, has been almost completely ignored in Western history.[292]

Moses Mordecai Marx Levi, alias Karl Marx, was a Jew, a Satanist, and a member of the

"League of the Just," which was a branch of the Illuminati.[293] In 1847, Marx was commissioned by the Illuminati to write the *Communist Manifesto*, which is an outline of their plans for world domination.[294] How did the Illuminati Talmudists know that their blueprint for subjugation of a country as set forth in the communist manifesto would work? They knew it would work, because the Jesuits had 150 years to refine the methods. Between 1600 and 1750 the Jesuits controlled over a quarter million ignorant natives of Paraguay in over 30 communes which they called "reductions."[295] The Jesuits were the masters of these poor slaves, whose labors made the Jesuits immensely wealthy. The lessons learned in the "reductions" were memorialized in the communist manifesto.

The Talmudic Jews have been successful in preventing any revelations about their involvement in establishing a new communist world order by labeling anyone who exposes their efforts an anti-Semite. What many do not understand is that many who claim to be objects of anti-Semitism are not Semites at all. Semites are those who are descended from Shem, the oldest son of Noah. Most Jews living in Israel and throughout the world today are eastern European converts to a religion that they call Judaism, but in fact is Babylonian Talmudism. The Europeans who later converted to this Babylonian form of Judaism are known as Ashkenazi or Khazar Jews. Dr. Benjamin H. Freedman, a former Jew, states that the Khazars were a pagan nation whose religious worship was a mixture of phallic worship and other forms of idolatry. In the 7th century their King Bulkan chose Talmudism, which most now call Judaism, as the state religion.[296] Today Khazar Jews are called "Yiddish." In Revelation, God refers to these Talmudic Ashkenazi Jews as Jews who say they are Jews but are not, but rather are the "synagogue of Satan."

> I know thy works, and tribulation, and poverty, (but thou art rich) and *I know* **the blasphemy of them which say they are Jews, and are not, but *are* the synagogue of Satan.** (Revelation 2:9 AV)

> **Behold, I will make them of the synagogue of Satan, which say they are Jews, and are not, but do lie**; behold, I will make them to come and worship before thy feet, and to know that I have loved thee. (Revelation 3:9 AV)

These Ashkenazi Jews are people without any allegiance to any nation. Their primary objective is to own the entire world. To get and idea of the nefarious objective of these Talmudists, let us read an 1879 letter from Baruch Levy to Karl Marx:

> The Jewish people as a whole will be its own messiah. It will attain world dominion by the dissolution of other races, by the abolition of frontiers, the annihilation of monarchy, and by the establishment of a world republic in which the Jews will everywhere exercise the privilege of citizenship. In this new world order the children of Israel will furnish all the leaders without encountering opposition. The governments of the different peoples forming the world republic will fall without difficulty into the hands of the Jews. It will then be possible for

the Jewish rulers to abolish private property, and everywhere to make use of the resources of the state. Thus will the promise of the Talmud be fulfilled, in which it is said that when the messianic time is come, the Jews will have all the property of the whole world in their hands.[297]

Many think that communism could not be the work of Talmudic Jews because Russia is allied with the Arab countries. Things, however, are not what they appear. Jack Bernstein, an American Ashkenazi Jew who moved to Israel shortly after its founding in 1948, returned in disgust to the United States after witnessing the duplicity of Israel. He revealed that the aboriginal Jews of Palestine, who are called Sephardic Jews, are discriminated against in modern Israel. They are second class citizens at the bottom strata of society in Israel, along with Christians and Muslims. In his book, *The Life of an American Jew in Racist Marxist Israel*, Bernstein explains the Machiavellian strategy of Israel.[298]

Bernstein found out that it is not true that the Soviet Russians support the Arab countries. This subterfuge of support by the Soviets for the Arabs was simply a ploy which was instituted by Israel on or around 1949. At that time Golda Meir was Israel's first ambassador to the Soviet Union. As ambassador to the Soviet Union she met with Joseph Stalin. A secret agreement was entered into between Israel and Russia in which (1) Israel would not allow the U.S. or any western country to build military bases on Israeli territory; (2) Israel would allow an official Communist Party to function in Israel; (3) Israel would never make any agreement to solve the Palestinian problems; (4) Israel would work with world Jewry to influence Western governments to favor Israel over the Arabs; (5) Israel would continue its Marxist economic policies.[299]

In return for these concessions the Soviet Union was to (1) furnish military aid to the Arabs and Egypt, but never enough aid to allow them to destroy Israel; (2) encourage Jewish immigration to Israel from the Soviet satellite countries and if that was not sufficient they would allow immigration from Soviet Russia; and (3) guarantee the security of Israel and in order to do that they authorized the free exchange of intelligence reports between Israel and the Soviet Union.[300] Bernstein obtained this information directly from the horses mouth: the Secretary-Treasurer of the Communist Party in Northern Tel Aviv.[301]

Bernstein pointed out that Israel presents itself as a democracy, but in fact Israel is a communist country to its core. He stated that Zionism and communism are one and the same. The purest form of communism is found in Jewish kibbutzim in Israel. Some have alleged that Bernstein was assassinated by the Israeli Mossad for revealing the truth about Israel. That, however, is probably not the case. This author has corresponded with Michael Collins Piper, who was a personal friend of Jack Bernstein. Piper stated that Bernstein died from an illness he incurred while traveling in the Phillippines. He stated that Bernstein himself did not think that the illness was the work of the Mossad. Piper himself is a highly respected investigative journalist. Piper reveals in his book, *Final Judgment*, that Israel's communist ties are not limited to the former Soviet Union. There has been a long, albeit secret, history of mutual cooperation between communist China and Israel in the development of nuclear and other military weapons.

In fact, Israel has been cited as one of the primary conduits for the flow of U.S. and other western technologies to communist China.

When one looks at the personages working for world communism, one sees Talmudic Jews and their fellow travelers, such as the Masons, just as the Protocols state. Benjamin Disraeli, made the following statement in 1852 before the English House of Commons regarding the control of nations by the Talmudic Jews: "The world is governed by very different personages from what is imagined by those who are not behind the scenes......The influence of the Jews may be traced in the last outbreak of the destructive principle in Europe. An insurrection takes place against tradition and aristocracy, against religion and property......The natural equality of men and the abrogation of property are proclaimed by the secret societies who form provisional governments and men of Jewish race are found at the head of every one of them."

Who are the powerful personages mentioned by Disraeli who govern the world? Answer: The Learned Elders of Zion, who are part and parcel of the Merovingians. The Merovingians are crypto-Jews who claim blood descent from a blasphemous union of Jesus and Mary Magdalene. That Mary Magdalene/Jesus myth is the origin of the infamous *Da Vinci Code* book by Dan Brown. Aho explains that the Mary Magdalene/Jesus myth is an occult blind for the religious masses; the esoteric doctrine (known only to the initiated) is that the Merovingians believe themselves to be a bloodline from fallen angels.[302]

"It was through the establishment of monasteries that the Merovingian Jews, whose forefathers were the Alexandrian Gnostics, began to infiltrate and mold the theology and practices of the Roman Catholic Church. Many of the popes were Merovingian monks who forced masses of European Jews to convert to Roman Catholicism, with the result that the Church incorporated traditions from both Judaism, the Talmud and the Kabbalah."[303] The coat of arms for the Merovingian castle at Rennes-le-Chateau is the Jewish star of David.[304]

11 Catholic Communism

Communism is one of the many abominations from "THE MOTHER OF HARLOTS AND ABOMINATIONS OF THE EARTH." Revelation 17:5. If the Catholic Church is the gentile arm of Judaism, one would expect to find the same Judaic communism permeating the Catholic Church. That is in fact what we find when looking beneath the religious facade. It was the crypto-Jewish Jesuits that established the communes (known as "reductions") in Paraguay in the 17th and 18th centuries, which were the forerunners of communism as we know today.[305] The Jesuits have continued their communist incursion today through their "Liberation Theology" that they have spread throughout South America. The clergy offer the perfect cover for political subversion.

While the Catholic church publicly opposes communism, it secretly financially aided and abetted the communist revolution in Russia at every turn.[306] In April 1917, Lenin and some of his key revolutionaries were transported through Germany in the now infamous sealed train.[307] Diego Bergen, a Jesuit trained German Roman Catholic, was the man most responsible for arranging Lenin's journey through Germany to Russia.[308] Bergen later became the German ambassador to the Vatican under the Weimar Republic and Hitler's Germany.[309]

Of course, the Vatican expected a payoff for their financial and logistical aid to the communists. Between 1917 and 1924 the Vatican entered into secret agreements with Lenin, which assured the communists Vatican support if the communists would suppress the Russian Orthodox Church and make Roman Catholicism the Official religion of Russia.[310] The immense wealth and land holdings of the Orthodox church were to be turned over to the Roman Catholic Church lock stock and barrel.[311] In the end, however, Lenin and his successors double-crossed the Vatican, they took the Vatican money but sided with the Orthodox Church.[312]

The Vatican and the communists have since patched up their differences and are now working closely again toward their ultimate objective of world domination.[313] Former Jesuit Alberto Rivera found out that the Jesuit General in Rivera's time was a Mason and a communist.[314] Pope John Paul II was a Marxist communist, who has continued the progression started by Pope John XXIII and Pope Paul VI toward a Marxian inspired Catholicism.[315] While Pope Paul VI cultivated close ties with Moscow, Pope John Paul II chose a Catholic communism that is independent of Moscow.

In the early days of the communist revolution in Cuba, Catholic bishops and priests in Cuba denounced communism. Many Catholic priests were imprisoned or exiled by Fidel Castro. However, after the initial attack by the Communists on the anti-communist priests, the Roman Catholic Church as an institution drew very close to the communist regime under Castro. The Roman Catholic Church since the early 1960s has steadfastly refused to raise its voice against the crimes committed under the communist regime in Cuba. In fact, the Catholic Church has worked to assist the Cuban communists.

In the early 1960's a pastoral letter signed by most of the Cuban Catholic bishops, but not by all, condemned the U.S. blockade of Cuba and asked the people of Cuba to work to help the communist revolution.[316] Some Catholic priests bravely refused to read the pastoral letter to their congregations. The Catholic Church was showing its true colors. Monsignor Cesar Zachi was the Vatican's ambassador to Cuba. As the official representative of the Catholic Church, Zachi avidly supported the communism of Fidel Castro. Zachi extolled the virtues of the communist revolution and continually asked the young people in Cuba to join the communist revolutionary militia. In fact, Fidel Castro was the guest of honor at Zachi's episcopal consecration.

Even when their own Catholic priests are beaten and tortured the Roman Catholic hierarchy turns a blind eye to the brutality of the Cuban communists. For example, Miguel Angel Loredo, a Catholic priest, was arrested by the Cubans and sent to prison. He was beaten severely by Cuban prison guards and lay hospitalized. When news of the beating spread abroad a Cuban official, Carlos Rafael Rodriguez, called the Catholic Nuncio, Cesar Zachi, to the Cuban Ministry of Foreign Affairs where he had a private conference with him. After the conference, Zachi, as the official spokesman in Cuba for the Vatican, announced that the revolution had been very generous with Laredo and had treated him well since he had not been taken to jail, but a little farm where he devoted himself to the peaceful work of planting lettuce and radishes. By that deception the Catholic Church perverted the truth in order to conceal from the world the barbarity of the communist regime.[317]

The Vatican and the Cuban communists have had close ties now for almost 30 years. Fidel Castro was the honored guest of the Pope John Paul II at the Vatican in November of 1996 and the pope in turn visited Castro in Cuba in January 1998. Both meetings were marked by cordiality, which puzzled and upset many in the American Cuban community, who don't yet understand the close ties between communists and the Vatican. Pope John Paul II has condemned the trade embargo of Cuba. In an interview with Italian Journalist Jas Gawronski, Pope John Paul II had this to say about communism: "Communism has had its success in this century as a reaction against a certain type of unbridled, savage capitalism which we all know well." Apparently he was not the anti-communist the world press had us believe.

It is not surprising that the Catholic Church would support communist regimes; the political philosophy that permeates papal encyclicals and council edicts is that all property is common to all, and private ownership must be subordinate to that principle. That is the essence of communism and fascism. In a Communist state the government owns all property; in a fascist state the people own property but the government controls what the owner is allowed to do with the property. Pope Pius XI explains the Roman church's position:

> Provided the natural and divine law be observed, the public authority, in view of common good, may specify more accurately what is licit and what is illicit for property owners in the use of their possessions. History proves that the right of ownership, like other elements of social life, is not absolutely rigid.[318]

Pope Pius XI further stated:

> Socialism inclines toward and in a certain measure approaches the truths which Christian [Catholic] tradition has always held sacred; for it cannot be denied that its demands at times, come very near those that Christian reformers of society justly insist upon. Pius XI, *Quadragesimo Anno,* 109 (1931).[319]

The communist philosophy of the Roman Catholic Church is inextricably woven into the political fabric of the Catholic Church. It is not something that can be changed through a change in the Vatican leadership. The doctrines of the Catholic religion are at the core of its communist collective political philosophy. The Catholic leopard will not change its spots; the evil of collectivism is its nature, and so it will continue to act according to that nature. "Can the Ethiopian change his skin, or the leopard his spots? then may ye also do good, that are accustomed to do evil." (Jeremiah 13:23 AV)

The Irish Republican Army (IRA) is an example of the worldwide Communist influence of the Vatican. The IRA was founded in 1969 as the clandestine terrorist arm of Sinn Fein, which is a Roman Catholic political movement whose aim is to subjugate Protestant Northern Ireland under the authority of the mostly Roman Catholic Ireland. The IRA is guided by the hidden hand of the Jesuits. The tenets of the IRA are based upon Catholic doctrine, and consequently the IRA has a decidedly Marxist orientation. The IRA criminal terrorist activities include bombings, assassinations, kidnapings, extortion, and robberies, which are perpetrated against the British government and Protestant Christians living in Northern Ireland.[320]

The IRA is interlinked with other Communist terrorist organizations. For example, on May 6, 2002, it was revealed that Marxist Communist rebels (FARC) in Colombia had been meeting for at least the prior three years and getting guidance from more than a dozen members of Sinn Fein and the IRA, who provided training in bomb making skills to the communist rebels and guided them in other terror activities. In congressional testimony before the U.S. House of Representatives International Relations Committee, Colombian General Fernando Tapias, chairman of Colombia's joint chiefs of staff, attributed to IRA training of the Marxist rebels the bombings of 320 electrical towers, 30 bridges, and 46 car bombings, resulting in the murders of 400 Colombian police and military officers.[321]

12 Priestcraft

The *Catholic Encyclopedia* reveals the similarities between the Catholic priesthood and the heathen (in this case Buddhist) priesthood.

> The monasticism and the religious services of Lamaism also present so striking a similarity with Catholic institutions that non-Catholic investigators have unhesitatingly spoken of a "Buddhist Catholicism" in Tibet. Pope and dalai-lama, Rome and the city of Lhasa are counterparts; Lamaism has its monasteries, bells, processions, litanies, relics, images of saints, holy water, rosary-beads, bishop's mitre, crosier, vestments, copes, baptism, confession, mass, sacrifice for the dead.[322]

The *Catholic Encyclopedia* claims that it was Roman Catholicism that affected the structure of the Tibetan Buddhist priesthood and that the above mentioned similarities were of recent origin. That is not true. It seems that many of the priestly practices of Buddhism were incorporated into the Catholic church, since Buddhism predates the Roman Church by hundreds of years.

Siddhartha Gotama, known as the Buddha and founder of Buddhism, was born in India in 563 B.C. and died in 515 B.C. He never left India. He was initially a Hindu, however, his religious doctrines, which we call Buddhism today, began to take form when he was 29 years old (534 B.C.). That would have been only a few years after the return of the Jews from the Babylonian captivity in 538 B.C. Buddha was not a monotheist. As a Hindu, he believed in many gods, with the creator god, Brahma, being the most important one.[323] While Buddha was a theist, his teachings were non-theistic.[324] In Buddhism, one is permitted to either believe in a god or not do so. The entire Buddhist philosophy is based upon suffering. Buddhist Monk Kusala Bhikshu explains: "Suffering is more important than God in Buddhism."[325] The Buddhist theology is that Buddha "was a human being who found his perfection in Nirvana. Because of his Nirvana, the Buddha was perfectly moral, perfectly ethical, and ended his suffering forever."[326]

While we have already seen the similarities between Catholicism and Cabalistic Judaism, there are also parallels between the theosophical elements in the Jewish Kabbalah and Buddhism. In fact, archeologists have uncovered writings and other artifacts that tell of direct links between the first Buddhists from central Asia and ancient Babylon.[327] George Ripley and Charles A. Dana in their 1873 American Cyclopaedia explained: "[T]he Cabala came to denote an elaborate system of theosophy, in which may be found some of the leading doctrines of Brahmanism, Buddhism, and the so-called Neo-Platonism of the Alexandrian church."[328]

If Judaism and Buddhism are so similar, one could expect that there would be a good number of Jews found within the Buddhist religion. That is in fact what we find. Just as is the case with the infiltration by Jews into the Roman Catholic church, there is a significant Jewish presence within Buddhism. In fact, Roger Kamenetz estimates that a third of the Buddhist leadership in the West have Jewish roots. Sara Yohoved Rigler in an article posted on *Judaism Online* reveals:

> A large number of Jews currently practice Buddhism. Rodger Kamenetz, the author of The Jew in the Lotus, says, "A third of all Western Buddhist leaders come from Jewish roots." Half of the participants in the Vipassana meditation retreat near Dharamsala, India, are Israelis. According to one estimate, three out of four Western visitors to the spiritual center of Tibetan Buddhism and the seat of the Dalai Lama are Jewish. Most of the street signs in Dharamsala sport Hebrew letters.[329]

While Rigler maintains that there are significant differences between Judaism and Buddhism, the Jews that actually practice Buddhism see little difference between the two religions. The similarities between Judaism and Buddhism, makes the transition from Judaism to Buddhism almost seamless. For example, Buddhist Venerable Tenzin Josh, formerly a Jew named Steven Gluck of London, referring to the 253 monastic vows in Buddhism states: "It's not much different from being an Orthodox Jew."[330]

The Talmudic and Cabalistic practices of the Jews were born from the inculcation of the Babylonian mysteries into Judaism. These practices in turn form the basis for both the Buddhist and Catholic liturgy and doctrines. It is therefore not surprising that Jews find it easy to transition from Judaism to Buddhism and Catholicism.

The Buddhist concept of a man (Buddha) being perfect through his own efforts (reaching Nirvana) is found in rabbinical writings like the Talmud. Israel Shahak quotes from Rabbi Kook, who stated that "The difference between a Jewish soul and souls of non-Jews - all of them in all different levels - is greater and deeper than the difference between a human soul and the souls of cattle."[331] This Jewish superiority complex elevates Jewish rabbis above the wisdom and authority of God. In the Talmud, Avodah Zarah 3B it states that God spends part of his day studying the teachings of the Jewish rabbis found in the Talmud.[332] The actual word used in Avodah Zarah 3B is "Torah."[333] The uninitiated gentile, therefore, would be led to believe that the Talmud passage was referring to God's study of the first five books of the Old Testament. That is not what is meant by "Torah" as it is used in the Talmud. "The STUDY of Talmud achieved such importance that the commandment of Torah study (see Deut. 6:7 and 11:19) was interpreted to apply primarily to Talmud study."[334] The Talmud and Torah are used interchangeably within rabbinic Judaism to refer to the Talmud.

> The Pentateuch (Torah), Prophets (Neviim), and Hagiographa (Ketuvim) constitute the written law of Judaism. Over the years, that law was discussed, interpreted, and transferred. These teachings of the sages are known as the oral law. Eventually, the oral law (torah she-b'al peh) was written down and formed the basis of the Talmud. While torah refers only to the written law and talmud to the oral law, both terms essentially carry the same meaning: teaching or study.[335]

In Berakhot 7A, God asks a rabbi for his blessing.[336] In the Talmud rabbis are viewed as having more wisdom than God. Michael Hoffman II, in his book *Judaism's Strange Gods* reveals that "[i]n Bava Metzia 86a, Rabbi Nahami is called to heaven to settle a debate between God and 'the rest of the fellowship' and to teach God who is clean and who is not, since the rabbi is the foremost expert (greater than God) on plagues and contamination."[337]

One might think that Buddhism has unique practices not found in Judaism or Roman Catholicism, such as the practice of bowing. Buddhist Monk Heng Sure, however, explains that even the seemingly unique bowing in Buddhism in fact has common links to Babylonian and Jewish traditions. He states that "[b]owing is by no means unique to Buddhism; it constitutes a ubiquitous practice across the spectrum of organized religions. In the Middle Eastern and Hellenistic traditions, beginning with the Ugaritic and Accadian religions of ancient Babylon, we discover a kinship—in language, liturgy and doctrine— between Babylonian and Semitic bowing practices. Babylonian texts, Hebrew scriptures, and the Kur'an, explain bowing in similar fashion."[338]

Heng Sure further explains:

> Accadian letters from the sixteenth century BCE appear in the archives of the royal palace of Babylon at Ugarit that mention bowing: "At the feet of my lord I bow down twice seven times from afar.[xi]" Samuel E. Loewenstamm, "Prostration From Afar in Ugaritic, Accadian and Hebrew," in Bulletin of the American Schools of Oriental Research, Number 188, Dec. 1967, pp 41-43. Jewish literature reveals an almost identical reference where vassals in the Amarna letters write, "At the feet of the king. . . seven times, seven times I fall, forwards and backwards." And in the Gilgamesh, the founding literary epic of Babylonian civilization, we find, "When they had slain the bull, they tore out his heart, placing it before Shamash. From afar, they bowed down before Shamash."[xii] I am grateful to Dr. Yoel Kahn, Ph.D., for his kindness in making available to me these materials on bowing in Judaism.[339]

Evidence points to both rabbinic Judaism and Buddhism having a common Babylonian origin. In Buddhism, however, God is largely irrelevant, whereas in Judaism, God is acknowledged, but his authoritative teachings contained in the bible are rendered irrelevant. The result is the same, God is replaced by the supposed authoritative teachings of man. In Buddhism, it is the teachings of Buddha; in Judaism it is the rabbinical teachings in the Talmud and Kabbalah. In rabbinic Judaism, the Talmud has primacy and authority over God's word in the Old Testament.[340]

During the time of Christ, the Talmud existed only in oral form, which Jesus referred to as the traditions of the scribes and Pharisees. This early oral tradition is called the Mishnah. It was only after Christ's crucifixion that the Mishnah was reduced to writing. The rabbis later added rabbinical commentaries to the Mishnah, which are called the Gemara.[341] Together these comprise the Talmud, which is now a collection of books. There are today two basic Talmudic texts, the Babylonian Talmud and the Jerusalem Talmud. The Babylonian Talmud is regarded as the authoritative version and takes precedence over the Jerusalem Talmud.[342] The Babylonian Talmud is based on the mystical religious practices of the Babylonians which were assimilated by the Jewish Rabbis during their Babylonian captivity around 600 B.C. The Rabbis then used these occult traditions in place of the word of God.

Among the Orthodox and Hasidic Jews the Talmud has authority over the Old Testament.[343] There is a sect of Jews, the Karaites, that adhere to the authority of the Old Testament alone. The Karaites, historically, have been hated and severely persecuted by Orthodox and Hasidic Jewish rabbinate. Ethiopian Jews do not adhere to the Talmud either and consequently they are not accepted by the Talmudic Jews. Former Jew Benjamin Freedman, in his book *Facts are Facts,* traced the theological lineage of modern day Talmudic Jews back to the Pharisees of Christ's time:

> The eminent Rabbi Louis Finkelstein, the head of The Jewish Theological Seminary of America, often referred to as "The Vatican of Judaism", in his Foreword to his First Edition of his world famous classic "The Pharisees, The Sociological Background of Their Faith", on page XXI states:
>
> "... Judaism . . . **Pharisaism became Talmudism, Talmudism became Medieval Rabbinism, and Medieval Rabbinism became Modern Rabbinism. But throughout these changes in name ... the spirit of the ancient Pharisees survives, unaltered** ... From Palestine to Babylonia; from Babylonia to North Africa, Italy, Spain, France and Germany; from these to Poland, Russia, and eastern Europe generally, ancient Pharisaism has wandered "demonstrates the enduring importance which attaches to Pharisaism as a religious movement ..."[344]

What did Jesus have to say about the religion of the Pharisees? Jesus said they masqueraded as religious men who have the oracles of God, but they were really irreligious, teaching instead the doctrines of men.

Why do ye also transgress the commandment of God by your tradition? . . . **Thus have ye made the commandment of God of none effect by your tradition.** *Ye* **hypocrites,** . . . This people draweth nigh unto me with their mouth, and honoureth me with *their* lips; but their heart is far from me. But **in vain they do worship me, teaching** *for* **doctrines the commandments of men.** (Matthew 15:3-9 AV)

To what traditions was Jesus referring when he upbraided the Pharisees for using them to transgress and replace the laws of God? Can we find out about those traditions today? Yes; the Talmud is a codification of the traditions of the scribes and Pharisees to which Jesus spoke. Michael Rodkinson (M. Levi Frumkin), who wrote the first English translation of the Babylonian Talmud, states the following in his book *The History of the Talmud*:

Is the literature that Jesus was familiar with in his early years yet in existence in the world? Is it possible for us to get at it? To such inquiries the learned class of Jewish rabbis answer by holding up the Talmud . **The Talmud then, is the written form of that which, in the time of Jesus, was called the Traditions of the Elders**, and to which he makes frequent allusions.[345] (emphasis added)

During the time of Christ the Scribes and Pharisees were constantly heckling and challenging Jesus, and it was they who plotted his crucifixion. Read what Jesus had to say to those Jews.

They answered and said unto him, Abraham is our father. Jesus saith unto them, If ye were Abraham's children, ye would do the works of Abraham. But now ye seek to kill me, a man that hath told you the truth, which I have heard of God: this did not Abraham. Ye do the deeds of your father. Then said they to him, We be not born of fornication; we have one Father, *even* God. Jesus said unto them, If God were your Father, ye would love me: for I proceeded forth and came from God; neither came I of myself, but he sent me. Why do ye not understand my speech? *even* because ye cannot hear my word. **Ye are of** *your* **father the devil, and the lusts of your father ye will do.** He was a murderer from the beginning, and abode not in the truth, because there is no truth in him. When he speaketh a lie, he speaketh of his own: for he is a liar, and the father of it. And because I tell *you* the truth, ye believe me not. Which of you convinceth me of sin? And if I say the truth, why do ye not believe me? He that is of God heareth God's words: **ye therefore hear** *them* **not, because ye are not of God.** (John 8:39-47 AV)

In Matthew 23 Jesus has even stronger language to describe the scribes and Pharisees. Jesus called them serpents, vipers, blind guides, whited sepulchers, and hypocrites who will be damned to hell.

Woe unto you, scribes and Pharisees, hypocrites! for ye pay tithe of mint and anise and cummin, and have omitted the weightier *matters* of the law, judgment, mercy, and faith: these ought ye to have done, and not to leave the other undone. *Ye* blind guides, which strain at a gnat, and swallow a camel. Woe unto you, scribes and Pharisees, hypocrites! for ye make clean the outside of the cup and of the platter, but within they are full of extortion and excess. *Thou* blind Pharisee, cleanse first that *which is* within the cup and platter, that the outside of them may be clean also. Woe unto you, scribes and Pharisees, hypocrites! for ye are like unto whited sepulchres, which indeed appear beautiful outward, but are within full of dead *men's* bones, and of all uncleanness. Even so ye also outwardly appear righteous unto men, but within ye are full of hypocrisy and iniquity. Woe unto you, scribes and Pharisees, hypocrites! because ye build the tombs of the prophets, and garnish the sepulchres of the righteous, And say, If we had been in the days of our fathers, we would not have been partakers with them in the blood of the prophets. Wherefore ye be witnesses unto yourselves, that ye are the children of them which killed the prophets. Fill ye up then the measure of your fathers. *Ye* serpents, *ye* generation of vipers, how can ye escape the damnation of hell? (Matthew 23:23-33 AV)

Why would Jesus use such strong language against the Pharisees and scribes? To answer that we should examine some of the Talmudic traditions that have developed over the years. For starters, the Talmudic Jews have a hatred for Gentiles. To them Gentiles are vile animals, who are unclean and have no legal rights.[346]

An example of the Jewish hatred toward gentiles was demonstrated by the response of Orthodox Jews to the 1994 massacre of gentiles perpetrated by Baruch Goldstein. During the rabbinic festival of Purim, February 25, 1994, an Israeli army officer and physician, Baruch Goldstein, opened fire with automatic weapons and slaughtered 40 Palestinian men, women, and children, and wounded 125 others as they knelt in prayer at a mosque in Hebron.[347] Goldstein was subsequently disarmed and beaten to death by the survivors of his massacre.

One cannot ascribe to all Jews the characteristics of one man who happens to be a Jew and sets out to massacre gentiles. The official and unofficial Jewish response, however, to this massacre speaks volumes about the Orthodox Jewish attitude toward gentiles. The Israeli response demonstrates that Goldstein was not alone in his sentiments toward Palestinians. The Israeli government authorized the closing of some of the busiest streets in Israel in honor of Goldstein's funeral cortege, and the Israeli army provided an honor guard for Goldstein's tomb.[348] At his funeral, Goldstein was eulogized by rabbi after rabbi. The rabbis praised Goldstein, cheered his massacre, and called for more slaughters of Palestinians.[349] Rabbi Israel Ariel stated during his eulogy: "The holy martyr Baruch Goldstein is from now on our intercessor in heaven."[350] Rabbi Yaacov Perrin added that "one million Arabs are not worth a Jewish fingernail."[351] A 1994 poll revealed that "at least half of all Israeli Jews would approve of the (Goldstein) massacre, provided that it was not referred to as a massacre."[352] Thousands of Extremist Jews have made pilgrimages to his grave. Goldstein today is worshiped as a saint by

Orthodox Jews in Israel; Talmudic pilgrims ask for his intercession before God, and his intercession is claimed to have cured illnesses.[353] A marble plaque at his grave reads: "To the holy Baruch Goldstein, who gave his life for the Jewish people, the Torah and the nation of Israel."[354]

Citing Folio 114b of the Tractate *Baba Mezi'a* from the Babylonian Talmud, *The Jewish Encyclopedia,* states that the Talmud only considers Jews as men; Gentiles are categorized in the Talmud as barbarians.[355] Elizabeth Dilling, in her book *The Jewish Religion: Its Influence Today,* explains the racial view adopted by Jews as codified in their Talmud:

> The basic Talmudic doctrine includes more than a "super-race" complex. It is an "only" race concept. The non-Jew thus ranks as an animal, has no property rights and no legal rights under any code whatever. If lies, bribes or kicks are necessary to get non-Jews under control - that is legitimate. There is only one "sin," and that is anything which will frighten non-Jews and thus make it harder for the Jewish "humans" to get them under control. "Milk the Gentile," is the Talmudic rule, but don't get caught in such a way as to jeopardize Jewish interests. Summarized, Talmudism is the quintessence of distilled hatred and discrimination - without cause, against non-Jews.[356]

The following passages from the Talmud attest to the Jewish hatred of Gentiles:

Baba Mezia 114b: Only Jews are men, gentiles ("heathen") are not men.

Moses ben Maimon (a/k/a Maimonides), the most revered and authoritative rabbi in Judaism, puts a racial spin on Baba Mezia 114b, and lowered blacks within the gentile category to a status just above a monkey.[357] Maimonides stated:

> [T]he Negroes found in the remote South, and those who resemble them from among them that are with us in these climes. The status of those is like that of irrational animals. To my mind they do not have the rank of men, but have among the beings a rank lower than the rank of man but higher than the rank of apes. For they have the external shape and lineaments of a man and a faculty of discernment that is superior to that of the apes.[358]

It seems that Maimonides (1135-1204 A.D.) framed the foundational principles for the theory of evolution long before Charles Darwin. The theory of evolution is founded upon the same racism expressed by Maimonides. Darwin was a racist who believed that Blacks were closer to apes in the evolutionary process. In fact, the liberal humanists don't want the general public to know that the full title of Darwin's seminal 1859 book on evolution was: "THE ORIGIN OF SPECIES BY MEANS OF NATURAL SELECTION OR THE PRESERVATION OF FAVORED RACES IN THE STRUGGLE FOR LIFE."

Darwin elaborated on his racist views as follows: "At some future period, not very distant as measured by centuries, the civilized races of man will almost certainly exterminate and replace the savage races throughout the world. At the same time the anthromorphous apes will no doubt be exterminated. The break between man and his nearest allies will the be wider, for it will intervene between man in a more civilized state, as we may hope, even that the Caucasian and some ape as low as a baboon instead of as now between the Negro or Australian and the gorilla."[359]   That is very close to the racism expressed by Maimonides.

There seems to be some division among Jews, at least in public discourse, over the legitimacy of evolution to explain man's being. Many Jews reject creation and accept evolution, while others take the view that there is a god who did create man. Some in the creation camp accept a literal six days of creation, while others take the view that a god did it gradually through evolution. Rabbi Shraga Simmons expresses a view that attempts to reconcile the creation account in Genesis and the theory of evolution. This attempt to reconcile the irreconcilable, tries to salvage the legitimacy of the theory of evolution in the face of the contrary biblical account:

> Rabbi Shimshon Rafael Hirsch (19th century Germany) further explains that each "Day" represents a specific stage of creation - i.e. a mingling of raw materials and bursts of dramatic new development. As you go through the Torah's account, you see described a gradual process from simple to more complex organisms - first a mass of swirling gasses, then water, then the emergence of dry land, followed by plants, fish, birds, animals, and finally, human beings. This pattern may be similar to the evolutionary process proposed by science.[360]

The problem with Rabbis Simmons and Hirsch is that they have taken what God has stated in the bible and proposed that God did not mean what he said. The bible does not offer proof of a "gradual process from simple to more complex organisms" as theorized by Rabbi Simmons. The bible presents creation of the heavens and the earth out of nothing within six literal days. How do I know that God created the heavens and the earth in six literal days? Because God said so.

> And God called the light Day, and the darkness he called Night. And the evening and the morning were the first day. (Genesis 1:5 AV)

> And the evening and the morning were the second day. (Genesis 1:8 AV)

> And the evening and the morning were the third day. (Genesis 1:13 AV)

> And the evening and the morning were the fourth day. (Genesis 1:19 AV)

> And the evening and the morning were the fifth day. (Genesis 1:23 AV)

> And God saw every thing that he had made, and, behold, *it was* very good. And

the evening and the morning were the sixth day. (Genesis 1:31 AV)

God defined the day and night and described the events of creation as having taken place between the "evening and the morning." Each day was marked off by "the evening and the morning." They were literal evenings and mornings. They were literal days. There is no biblical authority for the argument that the days mentioned in the bible spanned millions of years. That is pure sophistry, born out of a heathen desire to strip God of the glory he deserves for having created the heavens and the earth in six literal days, by the exercise of his sovereign will, through his spoken commands. God rested on the seventh day. Genesis 2:2.

Furthermore, evolution is not science; it is a heathen religious philosophy. Evolution is founded on racist beliefs. In order to understand this evolutionary racism we must examine what is meant by the term race. Race is simply defined as a group of persons who have a common lineage.[361] Race is not a biblical concept. God in the bible does not once catagorize different people according to race. He distinguishes different people by their tongues, families, nations, and countries. See Genesis 10:5, 20, 31; Revelation 10:11. Prior to the 1800's, races of people were generally categorized according to their nationality (the German race, the English race, etc.).[362] With the popularity of Charles Darwin's theory of evolution, which was first published in 1859, it eventually became the widespread practice to define race according to physical appearance.

Darwin's racist theory of evolution is refuted by real science. Many scientists hold that because the physical variations that are used to catagorize people into different races (skin color, eye shape, etc.) are trivial (only .012 percent of human biological variation) and that genetically all humans are fundamentally the same, racial distinctions based upon physical appearance are not founded on biological reality but are in fact a social construct.[363] Professor of Epidemiology Raj Bhopal, who is the head of the Department of Epidemiology and Public Health at the University of Newcastle, stated in the British Medical Journal: "Humans are one species: races are not biologically distinct, there's little variation in genetic composition between geographically separate groups, and the physical characteristics distinguishing races result from a small number of genes that do not relate closely to either behaviors or disease."[364]

In addition, a panel of "scientists, including geneticists and anthropologists meeting at the American Association for the Advancement of Science convention, said that the whole notion of race, based on skin color and hair type, is a social construction that has nothing to do with the genetic makeup of humans. . . . So while society busily tries to classify and reclassify races, the researchers say it should remember that race is an artificial way to organize and categorize and has nothing to do with humans' fundamental makeup."[365]

Those scientists maintain that it is a misnomer, therefore, to label people with different physical characteristics as being of different races. Because racial distinctions are somewhat arbitrary, there is no standardization of racial categories; in fact, the labels for the various races have changed with some frequency. There has been a recent trend in the United States to categorize races of people according to their perceived national or regional origin, such as African-American, Mexican-American, etc.

In *Saint Francis College et al. v. Al-Khazraji, Aka Allan,*[366] a United States citizen born in Iraq was denied tenure at a private college in Pennsylvania. The professor made a claim under a federal statute, 42 U.S.C. § 1981, alleging that he was discriminated against because of his ancestry. The college argued that § 1981 only prohibits racial prejudice and because the professor was considered a Caucasian under modern "scientific" theory that he could not be subjected to racial discrimination from another Caucasian. The U.S. Supreme Court examined dictionaries and encyclopedias from the 1800's and discovered that the theory of racial classifications has undergone a significant change since then. It was not until the early 20th Century that dictionaries started defining race according to physical appearance and listing the racial categories: Mongoloid, Caucasoid, and Negroid. The Court recognized the lack of scientific authority for the modern racial classifications and found those classifications to be inadequate to address the issue of racial prejudice that 42 U.S.C. § 1981 was drafted to prohibit. The Court ruled that § 1981 prohibited discrimination based on ancestry or ethnic characteristics, regardless of whether the person has the physical appearance that places him into one of the modern racial categories.

The U.S. Supreme Court in the *Saint Francis College* case stated:

> There is a common understanding that there are three major human races - Caucasoid, Mongoloid, and Negroid. Many modern biologists and anthropologists, however, criticize racial classifications as arbitrary and of little use in understanding the variability of human beings. It is said that genetically homogeneous populations do not exist and traits are not discontinuous between populations; therefore, a population can only be described in terms of relative frequencies of various traits. Clear-cut categories do not exist. The particular traits which have generally been chosen to characterize races have been criticized as having little biological significance. It has been found that differences between individuals of the same race are often greater than the differences between the "average" individuals of different races. These observations and others have led some, but not all, scientist to conclude that racial classifications are for the most part sociopolitical, rather than biological, in nature. S. Molnar, Human Variation, (2d ed. 1983); S. Gould, The Mismeasure of Man (1981); M Banton & J. Harwood, The Race Concept (1975); A. Montagu, Man's Most Dangerous Myth (1974); A. Montagu, Statement on Race (3d ed. 1972); Science and the Concept of Race (M. Mead, T. Dobzhansky, E. Tobach, & R. Light eds. 1968; A. Montagu, The Concept of Race (1964); R. Benedict, Race and Racism (1942); Littlefield, Lieberman, & Reynods, Redefining Race: The Potential Demise of a Concept in Physical Anthropology, 23 Current Anthropology 641 (1982); Biological Aspects of Race, 17 Int'l Soc. Sci. J. 71 (1965); Washburn, The Study of Race, 65 American Anthropologist 521 (1963).[367]

The theory of evolution is not supported by hard science; it is rather a religious mythology propped up by theory and fraud. In order to give the theory some semblance of legitimacy, the purveyors of evolution have resorted to fraud. The Jesuits were in fact caught in the middle of the evolutionary fraud. It was the Piltdown Man fraud that did the most to embed the evolutionary religion in the minds of scientists and the curricula of schools. In 1913 Piltdown Man was announced to the world as clear evidence of a transition between man and ape. For 40 years it was touted as evidence in support of evolution, until in 1953 it was exposed as a forgery.

It was later discovered that the skull of Piltdown Man was from a modern man and that the jawbone and teeth were from an orangutan. The teeth in the jaw had been filed down to make them look human. The bones and teeth had been chemically treated to give them the appearance of being prehistoric. The bones were then planted at the burial site in which they were found. There is a strong belief among those who have investigated the matter that the noted Jesuit Priest Pierre Teilhard de Chardin, was instrumental in perpetrating that hoax. The scientist who helped unmask the forgery, Dr. Kenneth Oakley, formerly of the British Museum, said that a letter written to him by Teilhard in 1954 had given him "strong indications that Teilhard was in collusion with Charles Dawson," in committing the Piltdown Man hoax.[368]

The famous evolutionist Theodosius Dobzhanksy (The American Biology Teacher, volume 35, number 3, March 1973, page 129) quoted Pierre Teilhard de Chardin as saying: "Evolution is a light which illuminates all facts, a trajectory which all lines of thought must follow."[369] That is not a scientific approach, it is a religious philosophy; it is a rejection of Christ. Jesus is our light that we mus follow, not evolution. "Then spake Jesus again unto them, saying, I am the light of the world: he that followeth me shall not walk in darkness, but shall have the light of life." (John 8:12 AV)

Despite this and other frauds among evolutionists, in 1996, Pope John Paul II announced that evolution is compatible with Christian beliefs. While evolution is compatible with Catholicism and Judaism, evolution is not compatible with Christianity; evolution is irreconcilable with and antagonistic to Christianity.

In 1998, the pope toned down his position, by announcing that evolution alone cannot account for human existence. He, however, did not repudiate his pro-evolutionary position. God's word describes Adam as being "**made** a living soul." The new corrupt bible versions follow the evolutionary philosophy of the world.. For example, the NIV changes God's word to say that Adam "**became** a living being." In the NIV man was not created, but instead just "became." This evolutionary slant fits in nicely with the Roman Catholic and Judaic teachings.

AV (KJV)	NIV
And so it is written, The first man Adam **was made** a living soul. (1 Corinthians 15:45 AV (KJV))	So it is written: "The first man Adam **became** a living being." (1 Corinthians 15:45 NIV)

The theory of evolution is not only contrary to God's word, but it is not based on true science; its origins are from heathen religious beliefs. According to the established laws of science, evolution is an impossibility. The second law of thermodynamics, also known as the law of entropy, is that all matter, living or inanimate, goes from a state of order to disorder. The theory of evolution reverses that sequence and states that over time organisms go from a state of disorder to order; from the simple to the complex.

To illustrate the conflict between evolution and the laws of science, suppose one were to write each letter of one's name on a separate card. If those cards were thrown out a second story window, they would scatter and fall to the ground in a chaotic display. The scattering of the cards over time as they fall to the ground illustrates the law of entropy. The evolutionist would say that the reason that the cards did not fall to the ground in order, spelling out the persons name, is that they were not given enough time to become orderly. The evolutionist would advise one to get into an airplane and throw the cards out of the plane when it reached an altitude of 10,000 feet. By the theory of evolution the more time the cards are in the air falling, the more time they have to organize and spell out the persons name when they finally land on the ground. According to the law of entropy, and common sense, giving the cards more time to fall to the ground only increases the disorder. The evolutionist, however, contrary to the laws of science and common sense, would have you believe that the more time the cards have to fall to the ground, the more orderly they will become.

The theory of evolution, which flows from a heathen religious philosophy, is the seed that germinated into communism and socialism. The Jewish Encyclopedia states that Judaism is not contrary to the theory of evolution and admits that evolution has been applied to every part of society.

> Herbert Spencer and others have applied the theory of evolution to every domain of human endeavor—civilization, religion, language, society, ethics, art, etc., tracing the line of development from the homo geneous to the heterogeneous, though recrudescences of and lapses into older forms and types (degeneration, atavism) are by no means excluded. The relation of the teachings of Judaism to this theory is not necessarily one of hostility and dissent.[370]

Hitler, Lenin, Stalin, and Trotsky, were all converts to the theory of evolution. Evolution was the foundational philosophy for their political actions and their justification for their maniacal brutality. Once one becomes a believer in evolution, it is a small step beyond that to being a believer in a communist revolution. It is no surprise that the Russian communist revolution was controlled from the beginning by Jews. The atheism of evolution is reconcilable with Judaism; that explains why one sees the seemingly strange occurrence of so many atheistic and agnostic Jews taking part in the Judaic liturgy of the synagogue. The atheism of evolution makes it easy to conclude that if there is no life giver, there is no law giver, no one made me, no one owns me, and, therefore, there is no right and wrong. Thus, there is nothing intrinsically wrong with stealing, assault, torture, murder, even murdering millions of people.

God "hath made of one blood all nations of men for to dwell on all the face of the earth." Acts 17:26. Racial distinctions are contrary to the commands of God: **"Judge not according to the appearance**, but judge righteous judgment." John 7:24. *See also* 1 Samuel 16:7 "But the LORD said unto Samuel, Look not on his countenance, or on the height of his stature; because I have refused him: for *the LORD seeth* not as man seeth; for **man looketh on the outward appearance, but the LORD looketh on the heart.**"

Christians should understand that our war is not a carnal war where distinctions are made between races of people as defined by the pagan world system. Christians are in a spiritual war against unseen "spiritual wickedness in high places." Ephesians 6:12. **"For though we walk in the flesh, we do not war after the flesh: (For the weapons of our warfare *are* not carnal,** but mighty through God to the pulling down of strong holds;) Casting down imaginations, and every high thing that exalteth itself against the knowledge of God, and bringing into captivity every thought to the obedience of Christ; And having in a readiness to revenge all disobedience, when your obedience is fulfilled. **Do ye look on things after the outward appearance?** If any man trust to himself that he is Christ's, let him of himself think this again, that, as he *is* Christ's, even so *are* we Christ's." (2 Corinthians 10:3-7 AV)

It is a heathen view of the world that judges men after their outward appearance. A Christian, on the other hand, is imbued with the Holy Spirit and does not judge a person based upon his skin color or outward physical appearance. A Christian instead has "the mind of Christ."

> **But the natural man receiveth not the things of the Spirit of God: for they are foolishness unto him: neither can he know *them*, because they are spiritually discerned.** But he that is spiritual judgeth all things, yet he himself is judged of no man. For who hath known the mind of the Lord, that he may instruct him? **But we have the mind of Christ.** (1 Corinthians 2:14-16 AV)

The racist carnal mind is enmity against God.

> "For they that are after the flesh do mind the things of the flesh; but they that are after the Spirit the things of the Spirit. For to be carnally minded *is* death; but to be spiritually minded *is* life and peace. Because **the carnal mind *is* enmity against God**: for it is not subject to the law of God, neither indeed can be. **So then they that are in the flesh cannot please God.** But ye are not in the flesh, but in the Spirit, if so be that the Spirit of God dwell in you. Now if any man have not the Spirit of Christ, he is none of his." (Romans 8:5-9 AV)

The racism against blacks by the Judaic religion should not be surprising, since the Orthodox Jews view themselves on a different strata and superior to all gentiles no matter the skin color. According to Orthodox Judaism gentiles have no property or other rights that can be asserted against a Jew.

Baba Bathra 54b: Property of Gentiles is like the desert; whoever gets there first gets it.

Sanhedrin 57a: If a Gentile robs a Jew, he must pay him back. But if a Jew robs a Gentile, the Jew may keep the loot. Likewise, if a Gentile kills a Jew, the Gentile is to be killed. But if a Jew kills a Gentile, there is no death penalty.

Sanhedrin 52b: Adultery forbidden with the neighbor's wife, but is not forbidden with the wife of a heathen (gentile). The implication is that a heathen is not a neighbor.

Talmudic Judaism has the most intense hatred for Jesus.[371] While some Jews will deny that the Talmud teaches such things, Benjamin Freedman, a former Talmudic Jew, stated that: "there have never been recorded more vicious and vile libelous blasphemies of Jesus, of Christians and the Christian faith than you will find between the covers of the 63 books of the Talmud which forms the basis of Jewish religious law, as well as being the textbook used in the training of rabbis."[372] For example:

Sanhedrin 106a & b: Mary was a whore; Jesus was an evil man.

Shabbath 104b: Jesus was a magician and a fool. Mary was an adulteress.

Sanhedrin 43a: Jesus was guilty of sorcery and apostasy; he deserved execution. The disciples of Jesus deserve to be killed.

Gittin 57b: Jesus was sent to hell, where he is punished by boiling excrement for mocking the Rabbis.

If there is such Jewish influence over the Catholic church, one would expect to see the same condemnational sentiment toward Jesus, either expressed or implied, in that church. That is exactly what is found in the Roman Catholic Council of Trent Cannons XII, XXIV, and XXX. Those cannons, in pertinent part, state that a person is accursed if he teaches that all sin is remitted solely through the grace of God by faith in Jesus alone. That is precisely what Jesus and his apostles preached. By clear implication of those cannons, therefore, the Catholic Church curses Jesus.

As the Jews did in Talmud Tractate Gittin, Folio 57b, so also has the Catholic Church in like manner sent Jesus to hell. Being an ostensibly "Christian" church, however, it necessarily must be more subtle in its condemnation of Jesus to hell. The Roman Church has subtly condemned Jesus in counterfeit bibles that it has nurtured and published through its open and crypto-Catholic agents.

The most popular version of the new bibles is the New International Version (NIV). Reportedly, the NIV represents 45 % of all bibles sold.[373] Dr. Virginia Mollenkott, the textual style editor for the NIV, is an admitted lesbian.[374] The Chairman of the NIV Old Testament Committee, Dr. Woudstra, was considered to be sympathetic to the interests and practices of sodomites. The NIV chief editor vaunted the fact that the NIV showed that it is a great error to believe that in order to be born again one has to have faith in Jesus as Savior. He also thought that few clear and decisive Bible texts express that Jesus is God.[375]

Rupert Murdoch owns the exclusive rights to the NIV.[376] The NIV is published by Zondervan, which is owned by Murdoch's News Corporation.[377] Murdoch's News Corporation also owns Harper Collins, the publisher of Anton La Vey's Satanic Bible. La Vey is the founder of The Church Of Satan. He is reputed to have been a Jew, whose real name was Howard Levey. Both the Satanic Bible and the NIV Bible are featured on the Harper Collins sales website.[378] "Can two walk together, except they be agreed?" (Amos 3:3 AV) La Vey's book is an exoteric Satanic Bible, whereas the NIV is an esoteric Satanic Bible.

Murdoch has been described as an internationalist and a pornographer.[379] *Time* magazine called Murdoch one of the four most powerful people in the world, and for good reason; he has a media empire that includes Twentieth Century Fox, Fox Television, cable television providers, satellites, and newspapers and television stations throughout America, Europe, and Asia.[380] Investigative journalists, however, have discovered that Murdoch, who has a gentile public persona, is in fact a Jew, who is a front man for other much more powerful Zionist Jews: Michel Fribourg, Armand Hammer, and Edgar Bronfman, who prefer to remain out of the spotlight.[381] The synergism between Jewish and Catholic interests is evidenced by the fact that the pope bestowed upon Murdoch the title of "Knight Commander of St. Gregory" for promoting the interests of the Roman Catholic Church.[382]

There is both a Catholic version and a Protestant version of the NIV. The notable difference between the two is the Catholic version contains the apocryphal books that are considered part of the biblical cannon by the Vatican. The apocryphal books are rejected and considered non-cannonical by Protestant Christians.

In Isaiah there is a passage about Lucifer that refers to him as "Lucifer, son of the morning." The NIV changed the subject of the passage from "Lucifer" to the "morning star."

AV	NIV
How art thou fallen from heaven, O **Lucifer**, son of the morning! *how* art thou cut down to the ground, which didst weaken the nations! For thou hast said in thine heart, I will ascend into heaven, I will exalt my throne above the stars of God: I will sit also upon the mount of the congregation, in the sides of the north: I will ascend above the heights of the clouds; I will be like the most High. Yet thou shalt be brought down to hell, to the sides of the pit. (Isaiah 14:12-15 AV)	How you have fallen from heaven, O **morning star**, son of the dawn! You have been cast down to the earth, you who once laid low the nations! You said in your heart, "I will ascend to heaven, I will raise my throne above the stars of God: I will sit enthroned on the mount of assembly, in the utmost heights of the sacred mountain. I will ascend above the tops of the clouds; I will make myself like the most High." But you are brought down to the grave, to the depths of the pit. (Isaiah 14:12-15 NIV)

What is the significance of that change from "Lucifer" to "morning star"? That change blasphemes Jesus and the Holy Spirit. That is because in Revelation 22:16, Jesus calls himself the "morning star." "I Jesus have sent mine angel to testify unto you these things in the churches. I am the root and the offspring of David, *and* the bright and **morning star**." (Revelation 22:16 AV)

Do you see what Satan has done? Jesus is the "morning star" in the NIV Isaiah passage. Satan has taken a passage that refers to Lucifer's destruction and has twisted it in the NIV to describe the destruction of the "morning star."   The "morning star" is "brought down to the grave, to the depths of the pit." The "morning star" is Jesus Christ.

The authors of the NIV have committed the unpardonable sin by changing Isaiah chapter 14 in the NIV to blasphemously attribute to the Lord Jesus the judgment that will befall Lucifer. In their NIV counterfeit bible, Isaiah chapter 14 has been changed to prophesy that it is the Lord Jesus (morning star) who is cast into hell, and not Lucifer.   To equate the Lord Jesus with Lucifer is to blaspheme the Holy Spirit. Jesus responded to the Pharisees who stated that Jesus used the power of Beelzebub (Satan) to cast out devils in pertinent part as follows:

> Wherefore I say unto you, All manner of sin and blasphemy shall be forgiven unto men: but the blasphemy *against* the *Holy* Ghost shall not be forgiven unto men. And whosoever speaketh a word against the Son of man, it shall be forgiven him: but whosoever speaketh against the Holy Ghost, it shall not be forgiven him, neither in this world, neither in the *world* to come. (Matthew 12:31-32 AV)

The publishers of the NIV knew exactly what they were doing. That is evidenced by the fact that the NIV Study Bible cross references in a footnote their use of "morning star" in Isaiah 14:12

with the "morning star" in Revelation 2:28. Revelation 2:28 refers to the blessings to him that overcomes the world and keeps God's works to the end: "And I will give him the **morning star**." (Revelation 2:28 AV) The NIV then cross references the term "morning star" in Revelation 2:28 with "morning star" in Revelation 22:16, where Jesus clearly states that he is the "morning star."

The publishers of the NIV thus correlated the use of "morning star" in all three passages. The cross references are clear evidence that the editors knew that changing the destruction of Lucifer to the destruction of the "morning star" in Isaiah 14 meant that it was Jesus Christ who was being destroyed in the NIV Isaiah 14 passage. For more detailed information on the corruption of God's word in the new counterfeit bibles read *Antichrist Conspiracy, Inside the Devil's Lair.*[383]

The Catholic Publication of corrupt counterfeit bibles is not surprising. It is different in kind, but not different in effect from nullifying God's word through Catholic traditions. The nullification of God's word through tradition is the method perfected by the Jews. That nullification through tradition was systematized into the Roman Church by the Jews. The Talmud, which is the repository of many of the Jewish traditions, expresses hatred toward Christians. For Example:

Abodah Zarah 17a: Jews should stay away from Christians. Christians are allied with Hell, and Christianity is worse than incest.

Abodah Zarah 17a: Visiting the house of a Christian is the same as visiting the house of a prostitute.

Abodah Zarah 27b: It is forbidden to be healed by a Christian.

Sanhedrin 90a, 100b: Those who read the gospels are doomed to Hell.

Shabbath 116a: The New Testament is blank paper and are to be burned.

The admonition in the Talmud to burn New Testaments is not hyperbole. Orthodox Jews view the statement in Shabbath 116a as a command to burn New Testaments. On May 21, 2008, USA Today reported: "Orthodox Jews set fire to hundreds of copies of the New Testament in the latest act of violence against Christian missionaries in the Holy Land."[384] When Or Yehuda Deputy Mayor Uzi Aharon heard that hundreds of New Testaments were distributed by Christian missionaries, he took to the roads in a loudspeaker car and drove through the city urging people to turn over the New Testaments to Jewish religious students, who were going door to door to collect them. The New Testaments were then dumped into a pile and set afire in a lot near a synagogue. Aharon said it was a commandment to burn books that urge Jews to convert to Christianity.[385]

Why do the Jews hate Christians so much? It is because the children of the flesh will always hate the children of the spirit. **"But as then he that was born after the flesh persecuted him** *that was born* **after the Spirit, even so** *it is* **now."** (Galatians 4:29 AV)

The Roman church is following in the footsteps of the scribes and Pharisees who heap burdens upon their followers, which have the appearance of spirituality, but are traditions of men that violate God's laws. When the scribes and Pharisees asked Jesus why his disciples violated the traditions of the Jewish elders by not going through the ritual hand washing required by the Jewish tradition before eating, Jesus answered: "Why do ye also transgress the commandment of God by your tradition? . . . [Y]e made the commandment of God of none effect by your tradition. *Ye* hypocrites, well did Esaias prophesy of you, saying, This people draweth nigh unto me with their mouth, and honoureth me with *their* lips; but their heart is far from me." (Matthew 15:3-8 AV)

Just as the Jewish leaders did not reveal that they were violating God's Law through their tradition, so the modern day leaders of the Roman Catholic Church are not telling the people that they are preaching another gospel with another Jesus. The Lord Jesus warned us that there would be just such an organization that would preach a different Jesus.

> For if he that cometh preacheth **another Jesus**, whom we have not preached, or *if* ye receive another spirit, which ye have not received, or another gospel, which ye have not accepted, ye might well bear with *him*. (2 Corinthians 11:4 AV)

Talmudic Judaism inculcates in its adherents a hatred toward Christians. The animus toward Christians is to the point that rabbis will justify a particular Jewish practice based upon the fact that it is contrary to the practice of Christians. For example, Rabbi Moshe Feinstein ruled that entering a synagogue or *davening* (praying) by a male Jew without his head covered is strictly forbidden since Christian men always remove their hats when entering a church.[386] Rabbi Feinstein was a world renowned authority on questions related to Jewish law (*posek*).   Feinstein was considered the *de facto* supreme rabbinic authority for orthodox Jewry in North America. Of course, there is ample authority allowing exceptions to the rule requiring head coverings, if to forgo the head covering will deceive the *goyim* (gentiles).[387]

This custom of covering the head gravitated from Babylon to Judaism and in turn to the Roman church. Interestingly, "Buddhist priests in China wear the bao-tzu (more commonly known as the mao-tzu), the classic skullcap that is the most like the Jewish tradition."[388] In the photo on the left we see Pope Benedict XVI with Catholic Cardinal Francis George. The little skull caps on their heads are called zucchettos. The pope's zucchetto is white, whereas the cardinals wear scarlet zucchettos.[389] The zuchettos are very similar to yamakas (a/k/a yarmulke or kippah) worn by orthodox Jews.

At right Pope Benedict XVI shakes hands with Israeli Rabbi Shear-Yashuv Cohen, the chief rabbi of Haifa, during a meeting of the Synod of Bishops on the Bible at the Vatican on October 6, 2008.[390] Notice that the pope is wearing his zuchetto and the rabbi is wearing a yamaka. Except for the color, the skull caps are identical. The Encyclopedia Judaica explains that today orthodox Jews regard "the covering of the head, both outside and inside the synagogue, as a sign of allegiance to Jewish tradition; and demands that at least a skullcap (Heb. kippah, Yid. yarmulka) be worn."[391] While the Old Testament has no requirement that a man cover his head, the Talmud (Shabbath 156b) fills the gap with a rule that has been interpreted, at least by Orthodox Jewry, to require the wearing of a Yamaka.[392] How can it be explained that the Jews and the Catholic hierarchy follow the same custom of wearing skull caps? The practice of wearing the head coverings dates to Babylon. Rabbi Barry Dov Lerner explains that "it developed after the custom of Babylonian scholars."[393] The Jews adopted that custom from the mystery religions in Babylon. That practice was injected into the Catholic church by crypto-Jews.

What does God think of this practice of men wearing skull caps? God states clearly that it is a dishonorable practice. **"Every man praying or prophesying, having *his* head covered, dishonoureth his head."** (1 Corinthians 11:4 AV). The prohibition against a man covering his head seems to be only during prayer or prophesying. The skull caps and other head coverings are worn by Jews and Catholic clergy during religious ceremonies and for prayer. In fact, one is not allowed to pray at the Wailing Wall in Israel, unless one's head is covered. No one is exempt from the regulation requiring a head covering while praying at the Wailing Wall. Even the President of the United States Barack Obama was required to don a skull cap to submit a written prayer at the Wailing Wall.

The tonsure (shaved head) was traditionally used as an initiation rite into pagan priestly orders of the heathen gods Bacchus and Osiris.[394] The distinguishing mark of Babylonian priesthood was the shaved head.[395] What does God think of this practice. He specifically ordered that the Aaronic (Levitical) priests shall not shave their heads "And the LORD said unto Moses, Speak unto the priests the sons of Aaron, and say unto them . . . They shall not make baldness upon their head." Leviticus 21:1, 5.

Tonsure

The shaved head was a practice that gravitated from Babylon to both Catholicism and Buddhism.[396] According to Alexander Hislop in his book *The Two Babylons*, one title that Buddha himself was known by was "The Shaved Head," because soon after establishing his new sect, Buddha shaved his head; he claimed he did so due to a divine command.[397] The Catholic Encyclopedia describes the three most common types of tonsures used by the Catholic orders: "(1) the Roman, or that of St. Peter, when all the head is shaved except a circle, of hair; (2) the Eastern, or St. Paul's, when the entire head is denuded of hair; (3) the Celtic, or St. John's, when only a crescent of hair is shaved from the front of the head."[398] The use of a tonsure in the Catholic church seems to have waned in the last couple of centuries, probably because its pagan Babylonian origins are too obvious.

Some sects of Hasidic Jews (Breslov) shave their heads, except for long locks that dangle past their jaws, called peyots, that they let grow along the side of their heads in front of their ears. Why would they do that? The bible has no such command requiring such a strange haircut. Hasidic Jews cite Leviticus 19:7, which states that they should not round the corners of their heads. That seems to be a command against the heathen tonsure pictured above. It is not a command to let the hair in front of the ears grow while shaving the rest of one's head. Doing that is directly contrary to what the Old Testament law, which states: "Neither shall they shave their heads, nor suffer their locks to grow long." (Ezekiel 44:20 AV) It must have taken some thought, but Hassidic Jews have figured out a way to both shave their heads and at the same time let their locks grow long. So at one time they contravene both prohibitions in Ezekiel; the prohibition against shaving their heads and the prohibition against letting their hair grow long. The Hasidic Jewish peyots are yet more proof of the truth of what Jesus said: "For laying aside the commandment of God, ye hold the tradition of men." (Mark 7:8 AV)

Priest of Dagon   Pope John Paul II

The heathen customs of the clergy of Rome do not end with the zucchettos and tonsures. Alexander Hislop points out: "The two-horned mitre, which the Pope wears, when he sits on the high altar at Rome and receives the adoration of the Cardinals, is the very mitre worn by the priests of Dagon, the fish-god of the Philistines and Babylonians."[399] Notice the bowed crucifix in Pope Paul II's left hand. "I saw, and behold a white horse: and he that sat on him had a bow; and he went forth conquering, and to conquer." Revelation 6:2

"And I beheld another beast coming up out of the earth; and he had two horns like a lamb, and he spake as a dragon."
Revelation 13:11

If one looks at the mitre from the side it looks like horns. That appearance seems to be a fulfilment of the prophesy in Revelation. In Revelation 13:11 there is a beast coming out of the earth that has two horns like a lamb yet speaks like a dragon. Obviously earthly lambs do not have horns, so that must be in reference to a spiritual truth. The Catholic hierarchy has the appearance of gentle lambs, however, their pronouncements are those of the evil red dragon depicted in Revelation, who is "called the Devil and Satan." Revelation 12:9.

13 Judaic and Catholic Curses Upon Christians

The Babylonian religion has been kept alive not only through the symbolism and costumes of Rome but also through the traditions in the Babylonian Talmud. The Talmud sets forth clear distinctions between gentiles and Jews. Jews are viewed as gods, whereas gentiles are viewed as animals. For example, in Talmud Tractate Sanhedrin, Folio 58b it states that smiting a Jew on the jaw is like assaulting a "Divine Presence."[400] If the assailant happens to be a gentile, he is "worthy of death."[401] A gentile child is considered to be subhuman.[402] Rabbi Saadya Grama of Beth Medrash Govoha in his book *Romemut Yisrael Ufarashat Hagalut* (Jewish Superiority and the Question of Exile) states: "The Jew by his source and in his very essence is entirely good. The *goy* [gentile], by his source and in his very essence, is completely evil. This is not simply a matter of religious distinction, but rather of two completely different species."[403] According to orthodox Judaism, gentiles are not only an inferior species, but a species that is "completely evil." Rabbi Grama is simply stating the philosophy contained in the Talmud. He explains that according to his understanding of Jewish religious doctrine "The difference between Jews and gentiles is not historical or cultural, but rather genetic and unalterable."[404]

According to the Talmud, Christians are allied with hell,[405] and Jesus is not only cursed,[406] he is described as being tormented in boiling hot semen.[407] The Talmud, however, gives immunity to rabbis from ever going to hell.[408] Chagigah 27a (a/k/a Hagigah 27a) states: "As to disciples of the wise, the flame of Gehenna [hell] has no power over them."[409] The Talmud explains in Tractate Baba Bathra that "disciples of the wise but also men" means scholars or distinguished students.[410] That means that not only are rabbis immune from hell, so are all scholars or distinguished students of the Talmud. Rabbi Shimon ben Yohai declared: "I am beyond the jurisdiction of any angel or judge in heaven."[411]

Judaism is a religion of hate. The hatred of Christians and all gentiles of all races runs through the warp and woof of Judaism. The most revered rabbis (*gedolim*) view gentiles as

116

garbage. For example, Rabbi Shneur Zalman, the esteemed founder of *Chabad-Lubavitch*, taught that the difference between Jew and gentile is not merely religious or racial, but that the souls of Jews and gentiles are completely different in kind. "Gentile souls are of completely different and inferior order. They are totally evil, with no redeeming qualities whatsoever . . . Indeed they themselves are refuse. . . . All Jews are innately good, all gentiles are innately evil."[412]

Rabbi ben Yohai, who believed he was beyond the jurisdiction of God, did not think gentiles were even worthy to live. His views regarding gentiles were that "even the best of gentiles should all be killed."[413] Rabbi ben Yohai is not a rabbi on the fringes of Judaism; he is in fact one of the most revered of rabbis in Judaism; his grave is a shrine in Israel. He authored the Zohar, which is the principle work of the Kabbalah.

While the Jewish clergy consider gentiles subhuman, they will turn on Jews who do not adhere to their dictates. Jewish rabbis have nothing but contempt for Jews who do not follow the Jewish traditions.[414] This overbearing attitude by Jewish rabbis is nothing new. One can sense the contempt that the Pharisees had for the common Jews in John 7:49, where common Jews were impressed by what Jesus had to say, and the Pharisees responded by cursing the Jews for not knowing the "law." The law to which the Pharisees referred was their oral tradition.

William Wotton explains the undue burdens placed on the Jews through the laws of the Pharisees: "They were absurdly minute in the literal observance of the their vows, and as shamefully subtle in their artful evasion of them. The Pharisees could be easy enough to themselves when convenient, and always as hard and unrelenting as possible to all others. They quibbled and dissolved their oaths with experienced casuistry."[415] William Wotton (1666-1727) was a rare genius; he undertook foreign language translation at age 5, attended Cambridge University at age 10, being graduated at age 13.[416]

The common Jews are as much victims of the Jewish hierarchy as are the gentiles and Christians. The common Jews are being spiritually brainwashed to the bidding of their rabbis. Jesus explained the process: "Woe unto you, scribes and Pharisees, hypocrites! for ye compass sea and land to make one proselyte, and when he is made, ye make him twofold more the child of hell than yourselves." (Matthew 23:15 AV) Jesus cursed the Pharisees and scribes; he could have, but did not, curse all Jews. It was the reprobate spiritual leaders who were the targets of Jesus' epithets. He came to set Jew and gentile alike free from spiritual bondage. "Then said Jesus to those Jews which believed on him, If ye continue in my word, *then* are ye my disciples indeed; And **ye shall know the truth, and the truth shall make you free**." (John 8:31-32 AV)

There is no more distinction between Jew or Gentile; all are one in Christ by God's grace through faith in Jesus Christ. Romans 10:12; Colossians 3:11, 28. Jesus stated that the gospel was to be preached to "all nations." Luke 24:47. The only difference for the Jews was that the preaching of the gospel should start at Jerusalem. The Old Testament has prophecies of the church of God consisting of both believing Jews and Gentiles. Amos 9:11-12; Hosea 1:10; 2:23.

The Old Testament prophecies regarding salvation to the both the Jews and Gentiles together are explained in Acts 15:13-17; 26:22-23; Romans 9:23-26; and 1 Peter 2:10. The New Testament writers, being inspired by God, clearly understood that the church is the Israel of God and is the object of the promises made to Israel by God in the Old Testament. **"And if ye *be* Christ's, then are ye Abraham's seed, and heirs according to the promise."** (Galatians 3:29 AV)

So -called antisemitism is a tool of the Jewish hierarchy used to keep the common Jews in line. Do not fall for that trick. As Christians, we are to love our enemies. We are to be innocent in our conduct, but we should recognize and reprove the evils of Judaism. Do not allow the sin of hatred to overcome you. "Be ye angry, and sin not: let not the sun go down upon your wrath:" (Ephesians 4:26 AV) The only weapon and battlement to be used by Christians in this spiritual warfare is the gospel truth of Jesus Christ.

> Finally, my brethren, be strong in the Lord, and in the power of his might. Put on the whole armour of God, that ye may be able to stand against the wiles of the devil. For we wrestle not against flesh and blood, but against principalities, against powers, against the rulers of the darkness of this world, against spiritual wickedness in high *places*. Wherefore take unto you the whole armour of God, that ye may be able to withstand in the evil day, and having done all, to stand. Stand therefore, having your loins girt about with truth, and having on the breastplate of righteousness; And your feet shod with the preparation of the gospel of peace; Above all, taking the shield of faith, wherewith ye shall be able to quench all the fiery darts of the wicked. And take the helmet of salvation, and the sword of the Spirit, which is the word of God: Praying always with all prayer and supplication in the Spirit, and watching thereunto with all perseverance and supplication for all saints. (Ephesians 6:10-18 AV)

Jesus explained that those who hate him also hate God the Father. The Jews hate Jesus and therefore they also hate the Father. The Jews reject Jesus, and therefore their god is not the Father. That leaves only Satan as their god. Do not be surprised by the unrelenting hatred of Jews toward Christians; Jesus clearly warned us that Christians would be hated by the Jews.

> If the world hate you, ye know that it hated me before *it hated* you. If ye were of the world, the world would love his own: but because ye are not of the world, but I have chosen you out of the world, therefore the world hateth you. Remember the word that I said unto you, The servant is not greater than his lord. **If they have persecuted me, they will also persecute you**; if they have kept my saying, they will keep yours also. But all these things will they do unto you for my name's sake, because they know not him that sent me. If I had not come and spoken unto them, they had not had sin: but now they have no cloke for their sin. **He that hateth me hateth my Father also.** If I had not done among them the works which none other man did, they had not had sin: but now have they both seen and hated both me and my Father. But *this cometh to pass*, that the word might be fulfilled

that is written in their law, They hated me without a cause." (John 15:18-25 AV)

While the Jews hate all gentiles, they have a particular hatred reserved just for Christians. The hatred by Jews against Christians is so intense that Jews are taught to utter a curse when passing a Christian Church, calling on their heathen god (Hashem) to "destroy this house of the proud."[417] The halacha (Jewish religious law) is that it is forbidden for a Jew to engage in any of the religious practices of Christians. Even if a religious practice was once observed by Jews, if it is later adopted by Christians, Jews are thereafter forbidden to do it.

For example, it was traditional to display flowers in a synagogue, however, the practice was later banned by the Vilna Gaon (Lithuania: Rabbi Elijah ben Solomon) because it was adopted as a practice in the Christian churches. Rabbi Moshe Feinstein, citing the *Shulchan Aruch*, concurred in that decision.[418] Hoffman explains that "[w]e can even trace the origins of the Yiddish language to hatred of Christians. The Judaic-German *halachic* decisor Rabbi Moshe Sofer (the "*Chasem Sofer*") ruled that, based on the eighteen decrees of prohibition of the *Yerushalmi* (Jerusalem Talmud), one of which forbids the adoption of the language of the Christians, it was later necessary for Judaics to make many alterations to the German language, which was a result led to the gradual rise of Yiddish."[419]

Jews wear head coverings (yamakas or kipas) in part because Christians follow the practice of taking their hats off when entering a church building.[420] The Roman Catholic clerics wear head coverings in church, including the equivalent of yamakas, which they call zuchettos. However, the Jewish hierarchy understands that the Catholic Church is not Christian, but is rather a gentile front for a Judaic/Babylonian religion and so do not act contrary to the Roman practice.

"The twelfth invocation (formerly the nineteenth) of the *Amidah* (the central prayer of Judaism recited three times daily) is the *birkat ha-minim*, the curse on Christians."[421] The Talmud (*Sanhedrin Folio 90a*) provides that those who read the New Testament ("uncanonical books") have no portion in the world to come.[422] However, according to that same tractate, all Jews ("Israel") are guaranteed a portion in the world to come.[423] Elizabeth Dilling explains: "The 'religious' Orthodox Jew recites the 'Eighteen Benedictions,' or 'Shemoneh Esreh,' three times week days, four times on holidays and Sabbaths, the 7th and 12th of which curse the Christians and non-Jews to hell and perdition. Thus, the 'good Orthodox Jew' gives us Christians 6 cursings on ordinary days, 8 on 'specials.'"[424]

An example of the hatred toward Christianity is found in the pornography industry, which is almost completely under the control of Jews. While many Jews gravitate to pornography because of the immense profits, many Jews view pornography as a means to vent their hatred of Christ by subverting Christian culture. Jewish Professor of American History Nathan Abrams researched the pornography industry and concluded that "Jewish involvement in the X-rated industry can be seen as a proverbial two fingers to the entire WASP establishment in America. . . . Jewish involvement in porn, by this argument, is the result of an atavistic hatred of Christian authority:

they are trying to weaken the dominant culture in America by moral subversion."[425] Al Goldstein, the publisher of the pornographic *Screw* magazine, stated: "The only reason that Jews are in pornography is that we think that Christ sucks. Catholicism sucks. We don't believe in authoritarianism."[426]

This hatred by the Jews toward gentiles and Christians has also migrated in a different form to the Catholic church. The difference is that the hatred in the Catholic church is focused upon Christians. The official Catholic doctrines are chock full of curses against bible believing Christians.

The traditional view of the Catholic Church is that the pope is the vicar of Christ on earth, and all are lost who do not submit to his authority. However, a close reading of the official Catholic Catechism reveals that Catholic doctrine is a direct attack solely on biblical Christianity. The following quote is from § 846 of the 1994 Catechism of the Catholic Church.

> Basing itself on Scripture and tradition, the Council teaches that the Church, a Pilgrim now on earth, is necessary for salvation: the one Christ is the mediator and the way of salvation; he is present to us in his body which is the Church. He himself explicitly asserted the necessity of faith and Baptism, and thereby affirmed at the same time the necessity of the Church which men enter through Baptism as through a door. **Hence they could not be saved who, knowing that the Catholic Church was founded as necessary by God through Christ, would refuse either to enter it or to remain in it.**[427]

One would think by reading that passage that the Catholic Church is saying that non-Catholics are lost. However, it is actually a condemnation of biblical Christianity. That is because it is Christians who are the group who would knowingly refuse to enter the Catholic Church and it is those who are born again who would refuse to remain in it. One might ask: "What about Muslims?" According to the official teachings of the Catholic Church Muslims go to heaven even though they are outside the Catholic Church. The *Catechism of the Catholic Church § 841* states:

> *The Church's relationship with the Muslims.* "The plan of salvation also includes those who acknowledge the Creator, in the first place amongst whom are the Muslims; these profess to hold the faith of Abraham, and together with us they adore the one, merciful God, mankind's judge on the last day."[428]

What about Jews? According to the official teachings of the Catholic Church Jews go to heaven even though they are outside the Catholic Church, and even though all Jews have rejected Christ. Once a Jew is saved he becomes a Christian; he is no longer a Jew. According to the Catholic Church, however, conversion is unnecessary because the Jews have a "sonship" based upon an "irrevocable" calling of God, simply by virtue of being of the Jewish "race." In fact, the Catholic Catechism states that the Jewish race is Christ. That is exactly what the Talmud says.

The religion of Judaism establishes that the Jews themselves are their own Christ.[429] The Catholic Church accepts that doctrine and has made it part of its official catechism. The *Catechism of the Catholic Church § 839* states:

> *The relationship of the Church with the Jewish People.* When she delves into her own mystery, the Church, the People of God in the New Covenant, discovers her link with the Jewish People, "the first to hear the Word of God." The Jewish faith, unlike other non-Christian religions, is already a response to God's revelation in the Old Covenant. **To the Jews "belong the sonship,** the glory, the covenants, the giving of the law, the worship, and the promises; to them belong the patriarchs, and of **their race, according to the flesh, is the Christ," "for the gifts and the call of God are irrevocable."**[430]

In fact, the official teaching of the Catholic Church is that "Israel is the priestly people of God, called by the name of the LORD, and the first to hear the word of God, the people of elder brethren in the faith of Abraham."[431] The Catholic Church officially views Jews as elder brethren of the faith of Abraham. The faith of Abraham signifies saving faith. According to the Catholic Church, Jews are saved by virtue of their fleshly lineage as Jews, without regard to whether they have faith in Jesus.

What about the other heathen religions? Believe it or not, members of heathen religions are included among the saved of the world. The official Catholic doctrine is that a heathen who does not believe in Jesus is included in God's plan for salvation, because according to § 843 of the *Catechism of the Catholic Church* God "wants all men to be Saved." *Catechism of the Catholic Church § 842* further states:

> The Church's bond with non-Christian religions is in the first place the common origin and end of the human race: All nations form but one community. This is so because all stem from the one stock which God created to people the entire earth, and also because **all share a common destiny, namely God. His providence, evident goodness, and saving designs extend to all** against the day when the elect are gathered together in the holy city.[432]

The Catholic plan for salvation sounds pretty inclusive. Who isn't part of the Catholic plan for salvation? The answer is found in § 846 of the *Catechism of the Catholic Church*. It states: "Hence they could not be saved who, knowing that the Catholic Church was founded as necessary by God through Christ, would refuse either to enter it or to remain in it."[433]

Remember, Catholic doctrine has a plan for salvation for Jews, Muslims, and other heathen religions that does not require conversion to Catholicism. However there is no plan for salvation for those who refuse to enter or remain in the Catholic Church who are not either a Muslim, a Jew, or some other heathen. There is only one group left out of the Catholic plan for salvation: Christians. The Catechism of the Catholic Church is a theological attack on the Christian

Church. The official Catholic doctrine is that all Christians who refuse to convert to Catholicism or who leave the Catholic Church are damned to hell. All the talk by the Catholic Church calling Protestants "separated brethren" is a diabolical deception. Their official doctrine is that Protestant Christians are unsaved and headed for hell.

In addition to damning Christians to hell, the official teachings of the Catholic Church contain repeated anathemas against anyone who disagrees with the official Catholic teachings. In most cases, Catholic doctrine is in direct opposition to God's Word. The curses of the Roman church, therefore, are aimed directly at Christ and Christians. The most notable curses came out of the Council of Trent.

The Council of Trent was the response of Rome to the Protestant Reformation. The Catholic Encyclopedia explains that Pope Paul III "chose three Jesuits, Lainez, Salmerón, and Lefévre as sole papal theologians to the Council of Trent. The latter died in Rome before the council began its sessions. Lainez and Salmerón were joined by two other Jesuits at Trent, Le Jaye who represented the Bishop of Augsburg, and Covillon the theologian to the Duke of Bavaria."[434]

The Jesuits completely controlled the Council of Trent. It is notable that all of the "sole papal theologians" sent by the pope to the Council of Trent were Jesuits and three of those Jesuits are now known to have been Jews: Alfonso Salmerón, James (a/k/a Diego) Lainez, and Juan Alfonso Polanco.[435] It is interesting that the Catholic Encyclopedia makes no mention of the involvement of Polanco at the Council of Trent.

Crypto-Jew James Lainez (a/k/a Diego Lainez) was the most influential member of the Council of Trent and was responsible for many of the anathemas against Christians and biblical Christian doctrine. Lainez succeeded crypto-Jew Ignatius Loyola as the second Jesuit General, after the death of Loyola. The Jesuit order is a crypto-Jewish priesthood and as such Jews have a long history of membership in the Jesuit order. The third Jesuit General was Fransicso Borgia (J.G. 1565-1572); he was followed by Eberhard Mercurian (J.G. 1573-1580), who was a Belgian Jew.[436] Robert Maryks has posted the names and biographies of approximately 390 Jews who are known to have been members of the Jesuit order.[437] One can be sure that Maryks' list is just the tip of the iceberg, since Jews sometimes go to extraordinary lengths to hide their Jewish heritage. The fact that Maryks does not include Eberhard Mercurian among the listed Jewish Jesuits is testimony to the incompleteness of his list.

The influence of the crypto-Jewish Jesuits over the Council of Trent can be seen in the many curses issued by the council against those who follow orthodox Christian doctrine. For example, in the following Catholic curse anyone who believes that Jesus paid the whole penalty for sin is anathema (cursed). That Jesus is the lamb of God who came to earth to take away the sins of the world is the heart of the Gospel. To curse the word of God is to curse God. Jesus is God - the Word that became flesh. (John 1:1-14). The Council of Trent Cannon XII states:

If anyone saith that God always remits the whole punishment together with the guilt, and that the satisfaction of penitents is no other than the faith whereby they apprehend that Christ has satisfied for them; let him be anathema.[438]

That Catholic curse from the Council of Trent (which is still the official doctrine of the church today) is directed at Christ and Christians. Those who believe in Jesus are cleansed not just from some sin but from **all sin**. And that truth came from God's word, and Christ is the word that became flesh.

But if we walk in the light, as he is in the light, we have fellowship one with another, and **the blood of Jesus Christ his Son cleanseth us from all sin**. (1 John 1:7 AV)

The next day John seeth Jesus coming unto him, and saith, **Behold the Lamb of God, which taketh away the sin of the world**. (John 1:29 AV)

What better proof that the Catholic church is the antichrist church than that it curses Christ.

Ye know that ye were Gentiles, carried away unto these dumb idols, even as ye were led. Wherefore I give you to understand, that **no man speaking by the Spirit of God calleth Jesus accursed**: and *that* no man can say that Jesus is the Lord, but by the Holy Ghost. (1 Corinthians 12:2-3 AV)

The persecution heaped on the church of Christ throughout history by the Catholic Church is in fact the persecution of Christ himself. When Saul, who later became Paul, was persecuting the church, God knocked him to the ground and asked Saul why he was persecuting him (God). Acts 9:4-5. The chosen believers in Christ are Christ's body. "Now ye are the body of Christ, and members in particular." (1 Corinthians 12:27 AV) Jesus is in believers and believers are in Jesus. John 14:20; 17:20-23. There is one spiritual body of Christ, with Jesus the head. Colossians 1:18. The curses heaped upon Jesus by the Vatican are proof that the Roman Catholic Church it is not a Christian church. "No man speaking by the Spirit of God calleth Jesus accursed." 1 Corinthians 12:3.

Another example of the Catholic Church blaspheming God is found in the Catholic pronouncement at the Council of Trent on the merits of works. Council of Trent Canon XXIV states:

If anyone say that the justice received is not preserved and also increased before God through good works; but that the said works are merely the fruits and signs of justification obtained, but not a cause of the increase thereof, let him be anathema.[439]

That curse is aimed directly at Jesus Christ and his perfect gospel. In the Holy Scriptures the point is made time and again that works are the fruit of salvation. Those same works, however, do not themselves merit salvation. Salvation is the unmerited gift of God.

But God, who is rich in mercy, for his great love wherewith he loved us, Even when we were dead in sins, hath quickened us together with Christ, (by grace ye are saved;) And hath raised *us* up together, and made *us* sit together in heavenly *places* in Christ Jesus: That in the ages to come he might shew the exceeding riches of his grace in *his* kindness toward us through Christ Jesus. **For by grace are ye saved through faith; and that not of yourselves: *it is* the gift of God: Not of works, lest any man should boast.** For we are his workmanship, created in Christ Jesus unto good works, which God hath before ordained that we should walk in them. (Ephesians 2:4-10 AV)

There is nothing man can do to earn salvation through works. Faith itself is not by the power of one's own will. It is a gift of God.

"But as many as received him, to them gave he power to become the sons of God, *even* to them that believe on his name: **Which were born, not of blood, nor of the will of the flesh, nor of the will of man, but of God.**" (John 1:12-13 AV)

The gospel of Jesus Christ is that our sins are remitted once and for all by the sacrifice of Jesus on the cross. There is no more sacrifice needed for our sins.

By the which will **we are sanctified through the offering of the body of Jesus Christ once *for all*.** And every priest standeth daily ministering and offering oftentimes the same sacrifices, which can never take away sins: But this man, after he had offered one sacrifice for sins for ever, sat down on the right hand of God; From henceforth expecting till his enemies be made his footstool. For by one offering he hath perfected for ever them that are sanctified. *Whereof* the Holy Ghost also is a witness to us: for after that he had said before, This *is* the covenant that I will make with them after those days, saith the Lord, I will put my laws into their hearts, and in their minds will I write them; **And their sins and iniquities will I remember no more. Now where remission of these *is, there is* no more offering for sin**. (Hebrews 10:10-18 AV)

Catholic doctrine, however, curses God for having offered himself once for the remission of all our sins. Council of Trent Canon XXX states:

If anyone saith that, after the grace of justification has been received, to every penitent sinner the guilt is remitted, and the debt of the eternal punishment is blotted out in such a way that there remains not any debt of temporal punishment to be discharged either in this world, or in the next in Purgatory, before the entrance to the Kingdom of Heaven can be opened (to him); let him be anathema.[440]

The theme of the Holy Bible is that sins are remitted for all time by the grace of God, not by any works that we perform. Salvation by the grace of God is mutually exclusive of salvation by the works of man. Neither can there be a mixture of grace and works. Because salvation by grace by its very meaning excludes the possibility of any works which would merit salvation. "And if by grace, then *is it* no more of works: otherwise grace is no more grace. But if *it be* of works, then is it no more grace: otherwise work is no more work." (Romans 11:6 AV) Abraham did not work for salvation, he believed God, and it was counted to him for righteousness.

> What shall we say then that Abraham our father, as pertaining to the flesh, hath found? For if Abraham were justified by works, he hath *whereof* to glory; but not before God. For what saith the scripture? **Abraham believed God, and it was counted unto him for righteousness. Now to him that worketh is the reward not reckoned of grace, but of debt. But to him that worketh not, but believeth on him that justifieth the ungodly, his faith is counted for righteousness.** Even as David also describeth the blessedness of the man, unto whom God imputeth righteousness without works, *Saying,* Blessed *are* they whose iniquities are forgiven, and whose sins are covered. Blessed *is* the man to whom the Lord will not impute sin. (Romans 4:1-8 AV)

God laughs at the curses of the Church of Rome. "He that sitteth in the heavens shall laugh: the Lord shall have them in derision." (Psalms 2:4 AV) The curses of the Roman Church are ineffectual, but God does not take blasphemy lightly. The Roman doctrine is a perversion of the gospel, and that organization and any others that follow its example are under the curse of God. God has placed a curse on anyone who corrupts the gospel of Christ, and unlike the Catholic curses, God's curse is effectual. "But though we, or an angel from heaven, preach any other gospel unto you than that which we have preached unto you, let him be accursed. As we said before, so say I now again, If any *man* preach any other gospel unto you than that ye have received, let him be accursed." (Galatians 1:8-9 AV)

14 The Fearful Reign of the Babylonians

The Vatican is both a sovereign state and the headquarters for a world religion. This structure was patterned upon Babylonian/Judaic principles. The Vatican is an independent and sovereign nation, with its own currency, Secretary of State and ambassadors.

Once a person is baptized into the Catholic Church he becomes a member of that church. When he is confirmed "[h]e becomes a citizen of the Church, able to assume the responsibility of that citizenship and to defend his faith against its enemies."[441] Once confirmed the new citizen must be "prepared when called upon to fight for the faith of Christ."[442] The citizens of the Roman Church must have "strength and fortitude to enable them, in the spiritual contest to fight manfully and resist their most wicked foes."[443] He now becomes a "valiant combatant, he should be prepared to endure with unconquered spirit all adversaries for the name of Christ."[444]

In contrast, Jesus made clear that his kingdom was not of this world, God's kingdom is spiritual.

> Jesus answered, **My kingdom is not of this world**: if my kingdom were of this world, then would my servants fight, that I should not be delivered to the Jews: but now is my kingdom not from hence. (John 18:36 AV)

Satan's kingdom is of this world. He has his citizens throughout the world. When a citizen must make a choice between obeying his country and obeying the Pope, according to the official Roman doctrine, he must obey the Pope. The Catholic Canon Law and Dogma has superiority over the constitution of the country. All federal and state government officials in the United States must swear or affirm to support the U.S. Constitution,[445] but as far as the Roman Catholic Church is concerned a Catholic's allegiance to the Pope comes first. In fact, in 1199 A.D. Pope Innocent III issued the Papal Bull *Vergentis in senium* in which he equated the "heresy" of violating Papal edicts and Roman Catholic doctrines to treason.[446] In 1231 A.D. Pope Gregory IX issued Papal Bull *Excommunicamus* wherein he officially fixed the penalty for "heresy" against the Catholic Church as the death penalty.[447]

During the Civil War, the Vatican was the only nation to recognize the sovereignty of the Southern Confederate States. How did this affect Catholic Union soldiers knowing that they were fighting a cause that was opposed by their spiritual leader, who they believed had authority to prevent their entry into heaven? Many Catholics fought with bravery and distinction, others abandoned the cause and turned traitor.

> Surely we have some brave and reliable Roman Catholic officials and *soldiers* in our armies, but they form an insignificant minority when compared with the Roman Catholic traitors against whom we have to guard ourselves, day and night. The fact is that the immense majority of Roman Catholic bishops, priests and laymen are rebels in heart, when they cannot be in fact; with very few exceptions, they are publicly in favor of slavery. *Abraham Lincoln, 1861.*[448]

Contrast Catholic General Sheridan, whom Lincoln described as "worth a whole army by his ability, his patriotism, and his heroic courage,"[449] with Catholic General Meade, who seems to have chosen allegiance to Rome over allegiance to the U.S. Lincoln recounts one episode:

> Meade has remained with us, and gained the bloody battle at Gettysburg. But how could he lose it, when he was surrounded by such heroes as Howard, Reynolds, Buford, Wadsworth, Cutler, Slocum, Sickles, Hancock, Barnes, etc. But it is evident that his Romanism superseded his patriotism after the battle. He let the army of Lee escape when he could easily have cut his retreat and forced him to surrender after losing nearly the half of his soldiers in the last three days' carnage. When Meade was to order the pursuit after the battle, a stranger came in haste to the headquarters, and that stranger was a disguised Jesuit. After ten minutes' conversation with him, Meade made such arrangements for the pursuit of the enemy that he escaped almost untouched with the loss of only two guns! *Abraham Lincoln.*[450]

President Lincoln knew full well of the treachery of the Roman Catholic Church, and the Vatican viewed him as an implacable enemy who had to be eliminated. In addition, the Jewish money powers also had an interest in eliminating Lincoln. Lincoln in large part thwarted their efforts to gain huge profits from the civil war by printing the Lincoln greenbacks rather than borrowing the money at exorbitantly high interest rates from the bankers. Lincoln stated: "The money powers prey upon the nation in times of peace and conspire against it in times of adversity. It is more despotic than a monarchy, more insolent than autocracy, and more selfish than bureaucracy. It denounces as public enemies all who question its methods or throw light upon its crimes. I have two great enemies, the Southern Army in front of me and the bankers in the rear. Of the two, the one at my rear is my greatest foe."

Charles Chiniquy, a former Catholic priest and close friend of Lincoln, revealed in his book *Fifty Years in the Church of Rome* that the most striking manifestation of the Catholic conspiracy came when in 1861 Civil War broke out in the U.S. Abraham Lincoln, with a wartime intelligence network second to none, knew the cause of the civil war: the pope of Rome and his deadly servants, the Jesuits. Lincoln told Chiniquy on June 8, 1864:

"This war would never have been possible without the sinister influence of the Jesuits. We owe it to popery that we now see our land reddened with the blood of her noblest sons. Though there were great differences of opinion between the South and the North on the question of slavery, neither Jeff Davis nor any of the leading men of the Confederacy would have dared to attack the North, had they not relied on the promises of the Jesuits, that, under the mask of democracy the money and the arms of the Roman Catholics, even the arms of France, were at their disposal, if they would attack us." *Id.* at 296.

"From the beginning of our civil war, there has been, not a secret, but a public alliance, between the Pope of Rome and Jeff Davis. The pope and his Jesuits have advised, supported, and directed Jeff Davis on the land, from the first gun shot at Fort Sumter by the rabid Roman Catholic Beauregard. They are helping him on the sea by guiding and supporting the rabid Roman Catholic pirate, Semmes, on the ocean." *Id.* at 299.

Lincoln further told Chiniquy:

"It is with the Southern leaders of this civil war as with the big and small wheels of our railroad cars. Those who ignore the laws of mechanics are apt to think that the large, strong, and noisy wheels they see are the motive power, but they are mistaken. The real motive power is not seen; it is noiseless and well concealed in the dark, behind its iron walls. The motive power are the few well-concealed pails of water heated into steam, which is itself directed by the noiseless, small, but unerring engineer's finger. The common people see and hear the big noisy wheels of the Confederacy's cars: they call them Jeff Davis, Lee, Toombs, Beauregard, Demmes, etc., and they honestly think they are the motive power, the first cause of our troubles. But this is a mistake. The true motive power is secreted behind the thick walls of the Vatican, the colleges and schools of the Jesuits, the convents of the nuns, and the confessional boxes of Rome." *Id.* at 305.

Lincoln kept his knowledge of the Catholic conspiracy secret from the public because of his concern that to reveal it would start a bloody religious war. Lincoln told Chiniquy:

"I pity the priests, the bishops and the monks of Rome in the United States, when the people realize that they are, in great part, responsible for the tears and the blood shed in this war. I conceal what I know, for if the people knew the whole truth, this war would turn into a religious war, and at once, take a tenfold more savage and bloody character. It would become merciless as all religious wars are. It would become a war of extermination on both sides. The Protestants of both the North and the South would surely unite to exterminate the priests and the Jesuits if they could hear what Professor Morse has said to me of the plots made in the very city of Rome to destroy this republic, and if they could learn how the priests, the nuns, and the monks, which daily land on our shores under the pretext of preaching their religion, instructing the people in their schools, taking care of the sick in the hospitals are nothing else but the emissaries of the pope, of Napoleon, and the despots of Europe, to undermine our institutions, alienate the hearts of our people from our Constitution, and our laws, destroy our schools, and prepare a reign of anarchy as they have done in Ireland, in Mexico, in Spain, and wherever there are any people who want to be free." *Id.* at p. 297.

Abraham Lincoln knew that the Roman Catholic Church is an uncompromising enemy of the United States. Lincoln explained to Chiniquy:

"The Mormon and the Jesuit priests are equally the uncompromising enemies of our Constitution and our laws; but the more dangerous of the two is the Jesuit - the Romish priest, for he knows better how to conceal his hatred under the mask of friendship and public good; he is better trained to commit the most cruel and diabolical deeds for the glory of God."

Not only was the Romish church responsible for the Civil War, but the Jesuits inspired and planned the assassination of Lincoln. Lincoln knew that he was marked for death by Rome and the Jesuits, and he knew it was only a matter of time before they succeeded. Lincoln told Chiniquy:

"So many plots have already been made against my life that it is a real miracle that they have all failed, when we consider that the great majority of them were in the hands of the skillful Roman Catholic murderers, evidently trained by Jesuits."

The Roman Catholic Church was the moving force behind the assassination of Lincoln. The transcripts of the trial of the Lincoln assassination published by Ben Pitman contain clear proof that the plot to assassinate Lincoln was born in Rome and nurtured in the house of Mary Surratt, 561 H Street, Washington, D.C. There was a continual flow of Catholic priests who would rendezvous at the house as the assassination was being plotted. The priests were the personal friends and father confessors of John Wilkes Booth, John Surratt, Mrs. and Miss Surratt. Without a single exception, all those involved in the Lincoln assassination plot and escape of Booth were Roman Catholic.

Elaborate steps were taken by the Roman Church to assist John Surratt in his escape. John Surratt was in Washington on April 14, 1865, helping Booth prepare for the assassination, which was carried out by Booth that day. Catholic priest Charles Boucher stated under oath that only a few days after the murder, John Surratt was sent to him by another Catholic priest "Father Lapierre." Boucher kept him hidden until the end of July. From July to September he was hidden by Lapierre in Montreal. When traveling on the steamer "Montreal" from Montreal to Quebec, Lapierre kept Suratt under lock and key in his cabin. On September 15, 1865, Lappierre and Surratt took the ocean steamer "Peruvian" to Europe. The doctor of the "Peruvian," L.I.A.

McMillan, stated under oath that Catholic priest Lapierre introduced Surratt to him under the alias "McCarthy," and that Lapierre kept Surratt locked in his state room on the ship until the ship departed for Europe. Lapierre was the canon of Bishop Bourget of Montreal. The canon of the Bishop is the Bishop's confidential man; he eats with him, assists him with his counsel and receives his advice in every step of his life. According to the laws of the Roman Catholic Church, the canons are to the bishop what arms are to the body.

Once spiriting Surratt out of Canada to Europe, where do you suppose Surratt was finally found? He was found under the alias "Watson" in the 9th company of the Pope's Zouaves. When the United States found Surratt, the Pope was forced to pretend to withdraw his protection of him. Surratt was arrested by papal authorities. However, the arrest was only for appearances. Surratt was able to "escape" before American authorities could take custody of him. The papal authorities alleged unconvincingly that Surratt made his "escape" from Valletri Prison by jumping twenty three feet to a narrow precipice, while he was under the guard of six men. Two weeks after making his incredible escape from Valletri Prison, Surratt was captured and brought back to the United States for trial. The evidence of Surratt's guilt was overwhelming, but Chiniquy explained that there was a hung jury because three of the jurors were Catholic and they had been "told by their father confessors that the most holy father, the pope, Gregory VII, had solemnly and infallibly declared that 'the killing of an heretic was no murder.'" The U.S. Government was forced to release Surratt. The politicians in Washington concealed from the American public the hand of the Roman Catholic Church in the assassination of Lincoln. Charles Chiniquy in *Fifty Years in the Church of Rome* explains:

John Surratt, conspirator in the assassination of President Lincoln, photographed after the assassination wearing the uniform of the Papal Zouave while hiding out in Rome under the protection of the Roman Catholic Church.

"The great fatal mistake of the American government in the prosecution of the assassins of Abraham Lincoln was to cover up the religious element of that terrible drama. But this was carefully avoided throughout the trial. Not long after the execution of the murderers, I went, incognito, to Washington to begin my investigation. I was not a little surprised to see that not a single one of the government men would discuss it with me except after I had given my word of honor that I would never mention their names. I saw, with a profound distress, that the influence of Rome was almost supreme in Washington. I could not find a single statesman who would dare to face that nefarious influence and fight it down." *Id.* at 312.

Neither Rome nor Israel will tolerate anyone impeding their thirst for world domination. Just as Rome was behind the assassination of President Lincoln so also was Israel behind the assassination of President Kennedy. This little known fact has been covered up by the major media, which is almost entirely in Jewish hands. New Orleans District Attorney Jim Garrison, in his book *On Trail of the Assassins*, revealed that NBC even went so far as to attempt to bribe a witness involved in Garrison's prosecution of Clay Shaw, who was one of the Kennedy assassination conspirators. *Id.* at 168. NBC's involvement in the attempt to derail Jim Garrison's investigation reached to the very top of NBC. The president of NBC had discussions with the president of Equitable Insurance Company, the employer of the witness in question, Perry Russo. NBC tried to persuade Russo to go on national television and falsely say "I am sorry for what I said because I lied, some of what I said was true but I was doctored by the District Attorney's staff into testifying like I did." *Id.* at 168. Perry stated that James Phelan of the Saturday Evening Post told him that he was working hand-in-hand with NBC reporter Walter Sheridan and that they were going to destroy Jim Garrison and his probe into the Kennedy assassination. *Id.* at 160-72.

Jim Garrison was approached by John J. King, who at the time used the alias John Miller. *Id.* at 204-05. King (Miller) offered Garrison a federal judgeship if he would drop the investigation into Clay Shaw's involvement in the Kennedy assassination. *Id.* at 132-36. King made clear to Garrison that he was in a position to guarantee his immediate appointment to the federal bench. *Id.* at 132-36. Apparently, King was speaking for others, because in order to become a federal judge he must be appointed by the President of the United States with the advice and consent of the Senate. Some very powerful interests were behind King's offer.

Michael Collins Piper, in his book *Final Judgment*, revealed that King was a wealthy oilman from Denver, Colorado who was involved in lucrative Israeli oil projects. *Id.* at 204-05. Interestingly, one of King's business partners was Bernie Cornfield, who was the protegee and front man for Rabbi Tibor Rosenbaum. *Id.* Rosenbaum was the founder of the Bank De Credit International and the central financier behind Permindex. *Id.* Permindex was a joint CIA - Mossad front which played a prominent role in facilitating the Kennedy assassination. Clay Shaw was one of the Permindex directors. *Id.* at 259. The fact that King could guarantee a federal judgeship to Jim Garrison in return for dumping his investigation of Clay Shaw gives one some idea of the powerful interests that were behind the cover-up of the Kennedy assassination. A November 1963 FBI teletype identified John J. King as a wealthy Dallas businessman who was a close friend to Jack Ruby. Jack Ruby (whose real name was Jacob L. Rubenstein) was a Jewish gangster with connections to the CIA, the FBI, the Israeli Mossad, and the Dallas Police Department. His connections inside the Dallas Police Department allowed him access to kill Lee Harvey Oswald.

William Kunstler, in his book *My Life as a Radical Lawyer*, reveals that Ruby told him why he killed Oswald: "I did this that they wouldn't implicate Jews." *Id.* at 158. Before Kunstler left

Ruby after his last jail visit, Ruby handed him a note in which he reiterated that his motive was to "Protect American Jews from a pogrom that could occur because of anger over the assassination." *Id.* at 158. Ruby and his handlers knew that if Oswald were to be prosecuted for the assassination of President Kennedy, the evidence would not support his conviction but would rather have pointed directly to Israel.

It seems that Ruby was a *Sayan* who was pressed into service to eliminate a loose end (Oswald). *Sayanim* (plural for *Sayan*) are Jews living outside of Israel who are fanatically loyal to the Jewish state and have agreed to assist Israel. Their loyalty to Israel supplants any loyalty they have to the country in which they reside. Often, *Sayanim* are recruited by relatives living in Israel and are under the control of professional spy masters called *"katsas."* They do whatever is asked of them to assist Israel and the Mossad.

A fair view of the facts reveals that the assassination of President Kennedy was a *coup d' etat.* How were all these separate state and federal agencies and the news media tied together into one giant conspiracy? Michael Collins Piper presents a compelling case that Zionists in general, and the Israeli Mossad in particular, played a primary role in the assassination of President John F. Kennedy, and the subsequent coverup. Piper methodically explains how all of these persons and organizations were tied together in a conspiracy that at its core was set in motion by the Israeli Mossad.

The motives for the Kennedy assassination are manifold. John Kennedy realized after the Bay of Pigs fiasco that he was not in control of the executive branch of government. He came to understand that Zionists had infiltrated the very warp and woof of government. Beginning with the CIA, Kennedy began to make dramatic changes to take the reigns of government back from the hidden treasonous cabal that was steering the United States toward destruction. Kennedy had even implemented a plan to wrestle control of U.S. currency from the Federal Reserve by issuing U.S. notes. The Jewish money power decided that Kennedy had to go.

One of the key reasons for Kennedy's assassination was Kennedy's intent to put an end to the Israeli plans for developing their own nuclear weapons. The Jerusalem Post reported on July 25, 2004 that the jailed nuclear whistle blower, Mordechai Vanunu, revealed that the Israeli government was behind the assassination of President Kennedy. "Vanunu said that according to "near-certain indications," Kennedy was assassinated due to 'pressure he exerted on then head of government, David Ben-Gurion, to shed light on Dimona's nuclear reactor.'"

One of the key players in the conspiracy to assassinate Kennedy was Meyer Lansky, the Zionist Jewish gangster, who Piper reveals was the *de facto* head of organized crime in the United States. Piper explains how Lansky had deep and continuing working relationships with both the CIA and the Israeli Mossad. Although Piper's book addresses the assassination of President Kennedy, which happened over 40 years ago, the lessons he imparts are important and topical today for all American citizens who love their liberty. Piper's book is an autopsy which dissects the putrid body of a world conspiracy that is so pervasive, so intrusive, so powerful, it can assassinate the President of the most powerful country in the world and then conceal its involvement in that crime by controlling the mass media and even the very organs of that government. After assassinating President Kennedy that cabal resumed control of the government, which they have maintained to this day.

The authoritarian conspiracy that President Kennedy attempted to resist can be seen in practice in the state of Israel. Israel, like the Vatican, is a sovereign state and the headquarters of a world religion. In fact, in Israel the laws give Jews special status and privileges not accorded to gentiles.[451] Identification cards issued by the Interior Ministry of Israel once listed over 130 different categories of nationality (the most common being "Arab"). Whereas if a person was an Israeli Jew, the Identification card simply indicated that the person is Jewish. By Israeli law there cannot be a designation on the ID card for someone to be identified simply as an Israeli national.

In the year 2000 the nationality section on ID cards was phased out, because the interior ministry, which was run by an Orthodox Jewish religious party, objected to non-Orthodox Jews being identified as "Jewish" on the ID cards.[452] However, with the new ID cards any Israeli government official can instantly tell if he was looking at the card of a Jew or Arab because the date of birth on the IDs of Jews is given according to the Hebrew calendar and in addition, the ID of an Arab, unlike a Jew, included the grandfather's name.[453]

What is the purpose of this systematic identification of gentiles and Jews in Israel? Prejudicial discrimination. "[T]he special status of Jewish nationality has been a way to undermine the citizenship rights of non-Jews in Israel, especially the fifth of the population who are Arab. Some 30 laws in Israel specifically privilege Jews, including in the areas of immigration rights, naturalisation, access to land and employment."[454] While a gentile may be a citizen of Israel, he cannot claim his nationality as Israeli. Shimon Agranat, the President of the Supreme Court of Israel, stated in a court ruling over the issue of Israeli nationality for gentiles: "There is no Israeli nation separate from the Jewish people. ... The Jewish people is composed not only of those residing in Israel but also of diaspora Jewries."[455] Israel cannot recognize an Israeli nationality, because the theory behind the state of Israel is that it is the state of the Jewish nation, which belongs to Jews all over the world. Jews are granted special legal privileges over longtime Arab citizens of Israel, once the Jews set foot in Israel, simply because they are Jews.

Professor Shahak, a Jewish dissident scholar who immigrated to Israel and served in the Israeli military, explains the ingrained official institutional racism by the Jewish state of Israel:

> The principle of Israel as 'a Jewish state' was supremely important to Israeli politicians from the inception of the state and was inculcated into the Jewish population by all conceivable ways. When, in the early 1980s, a tiny minority of Israeli Jews emerged which opposed this concept, a Constitutional Law (that is, a law overriding provisions of other laws, which cannot be revoked except by a special procedure) was passed in 1985 by an enormous majority of the Knesset.

By this law no party whose programme openly opposes the principle of 'a Jewish state' or proposes to change it by democratic means, is allowed to participate in the elections to the Knesset.

* * *

Let me begin with the official Israeli definition of the term 'Jewish', illustrating the crucial difference between Israel as 'a Jewish state' and the majority of other states. By this official definition, Israel 'belongs' to persons who are defined by the Israeli authorities as 'Jewish', irrespective of where they live, and to them alone. On the other hand, Israel doesn't officially 'belong' to its non-Jewish citizens, whose status is considered even officially as inferior. This means in practice that if members of a Peruvian tribe are converted to Judaism, and thus regarded as Jewish, they are entitled at once to become Israeli citizens and benefit from the approximately 70 per cent of the West Bank land (and the 92 per cent of the area of Israel proper), officially designated only for the benefit of Jews. All non-Jews (not only all Palestinians) are prohibited from benefiting from those lands. (The prohibition applies even to Israeli Arabs who served in the Israeli army and reached a high rank.) The case involving Peruvian converts to Judaism actually occurred a few years ago. The newly-created Jews were settled in the West Bank, near Nablus, on land from which non-Jews are officially excluded. All Israeli governments are taking enormous political risks, including the risk of war, so that such settlements, composed exclusively of persons who are defined as 'Jewish' (and not 'Israeli' as most of the media mendaciously claims) would be subject to only 'Jewish' authority.

* * *

But there is another urgent necessity for an official definition of who is, and who is not 'Jewish'. The State of Israel officially discriminates in favour of Jews and against non-Jews in many domains of life, of which I regard three as being most important: residency rights, the right to work and the right to equality before the law. Discrimination in residency is based on the fact that about 92 per cent of Israel's land is the property of the state and is administered by the Israel Land Authority according to regulations issued by the Jewish National Fund (JNF), an affiliate of the World Zionist Organization. In its regulations the JNF denies the right to reside, to open a business, and often to work, to anyone who is not Jewish, only because he is not Jewish. At the same time, Jews are not prohibited from taking residence or opening businesses anywhere in Israel. If applied in another state against the Jews, such discriminatory practice would instantly and justifiably be labelled antisemitism and would no doubt spark massive public protests. When applied by Israel as a part of its 'Jewish ideology', they are usually studiously ignored or excused when rarely mentioned.

The denial of the right to work means that non-Jews are prohibited officially from working on land administered by the Israel Land Authority according to the JNF regulations. No doubt these regulations are not always, or even often, enforced but they do exist. From time to time Israel attempts enforcement campaigns by state authorities, as, for example, when the Agriculture Ministry acts against 'the pestilence of letting fruit orchards belonging to Jews and situated on National Land [i.e., land belonging to the State of Israel] be harvested by Arab labourers', even if the labourers in question are citizens of Israel. Israel also strictly prohibits Jews settled on 'National Land' to sub-rent even a part of their land to Arabs, even for a short time; and those who do so are punished, usually by heavy fines. There are no prohibitions on non-Jews renting their land to Jews. This means, in my own case, that by virtue of being a Jew I have the right to lease an orchard for harvesting its produce from another Jew, but a non-Jew, whether a citizen of Israel or a resident alien, does not have this right.

Non-Jewish citizens of Israel do not have the right to equality before the law. This discrimination is expressed in many Israeli laws in which, presumably in order to avoid embarrassment, the terms 'Jewish' and 'non-Jewish' are usually not explicitly stated, as they are in the crucial Law of Return. According to that law only persons officially recognised as 'Jewish' have an automatic right of entry to Israel and of settling in it. They automatically receive an 'immigration certificate' which provides them on arrival with 'citizenship by virtue of having returned to the Jewish homeland', and with the right to many financial benefits, which vary somewhat according to the country from which they emigrated. The Jews who emigrate from the states of the former UUSR receive 'an absorption grant' of more than $20,000 per family. All Jews immigrating to Israel according to this law immediately acquire the right to vote in elections and to be elected to the Knesset -- even if they do not speak a word of Hebrew.

Other Israeli laws substitute the more obtuse expressions 'anyone who can immigrate in accordance with the Law of Return' and 'anyone who is not entitled to immigrate in accordance with the law of Return'. Depending on the law in question benefits are then granted to the first category and systematically denied to the second. The routine means for enforcing discrimination in everyday life is the ID card, which everyone is obliged to carry at all times. ID cards list the official 'nationality' of a person, which can be 'Jewish', 'Arab', 'Druze' and the like, with the significant exception of 'Israeli'. Attempts to force the Interior Minister to allow Israelis wishing to be officially described as 'Israeli', or even as 'Israeli-Jew' in their ID cards have failed. Those who have attempted to do so have a letter from the Ministry of the Interior stating that 'it was decided not to recognise an Israeli nationality'. The letter does not specify who made this decision or when.

There are so many laws and regulations in Israel which discriminate in favour of the persons defined in Israel as those 'who can immigrate in accordance with the Law of Return' that the subject demands separate treatment. We can look here at one example, seemingly trivial in comparison with residence restrictions, but nevertheless important since it reveals the real intentions of the Israeli legislator. Israeli citizens who left the country for a time but who are defined as those who 'can immigrate in accordance with the Law of Return' are eligible on their return to generous customs benefits, to receive subsidy for their children's high school education, and to receive either a grant or a loan on easy terms for the purchase of an apartment, as well as other benefits. Citizens who cannot be so defined, in other words, the non-Jewish citizens of Israel, get none of these benefits. The obvious intention of such discriminatory measures is to decrease the number of non-Jewish citizens of Israel, in order to make Israel a more 'Jewish' state.

* * *

Using the concepts of Platonism to analyse Israeli policies based on 'Jewish ideology' should not seem strange. It was noticed by several scholars, of whom the most important was Moses Hadas, who claimed that the foundations of 'classical Judaism', that is, of Judaism as it was established by talmudic sages, are based on Platonic influences and especially on the image of Sparta as it appears in Plato.[456] According to Hadas, a crucial feature of the Platonic political system, adopted by Judaism as early as the Maccabean period (142-63 BC), was 'that every phase of human conduct be subject to religious sanctions which are in fact to be manipulated by the ruler'. There can be no better definition of 'classical Judaism' and of the ways in which the rabbis manipulated it than this Platonic definition. In particular, Hadas claims that Judaism adopted what 'Plato himself summarized [as] the objectives of his program', in the following well-known passage:

"The principle thing is that no one, man or woman, should ever be without an officer set over him, and that none should get the mental habit of taking any step, whether in earnest or in jest, on his individual responsibility. In peace as in war he must live always with his eyes on his superior officer... In a word, we must train the mind not to even consider acting as an invidual or know how to do it." (Laws, 942ab)

If the word 'rabbi' is substituted for 'an officer' we will have a perfect image of classical Judaism. The latter is still deeply influencing Israeli-Jewish society and determing to a large extent the Israeli policies.

It was the above quoted passage which was chosen by Karl Popper in The Open Society and Its Enemies as describing the essence of 'a closed society'. Historical Judaism and its two successors, Jewish Orthodoxy and Zionism, are both sworn enemies of the concept of the open society as applied to Israel. A Jewish state, whether based on its present Jewish ideology or, if it becomes even more Jewish in character than it is now, on the principles of Jewish Orthodoxy, cannot ever contain an open society.[457]

This Jewish institutional racism is part and parcel of the traditions of the Jews. Orthodox Jews are also religious chauvinists, who do not tolerate any deviation from their oral traditions. The authority of the Jewish rabbis was absolute in ancient Israel. People were so afraid of the Jews in Christ's time that they feared to even be caught speaking about Jesus. John 7:13. After the crucifixion of Jesus, Christians would meet in secret, because the Jews were actively hunting them down. See John 20:19 and Acts 8:1-4, 91-2. Orthodox Jews are under the same iron rule today. Israel Shahak explains:

> Since the time of the late Roman Empire, Jewish communities had considerable legal powers over their members. Not only powers which arise through voluntary mobilization of social pressure (for example refusal to have any dealing whatsoever with an excommunicated Jew or even to bury his body), but a power of naked coercion: to flog, to imprison, to expel - all this could be inflicted quite legally on an individual Jew by the rabbinical courts for all kinds of offenses. In many countries - Spain and Poland are notable examples - even capital punishment could be and was inflicted, sometimes using particularly cruel methods such as flogging to death. All this was not only permitted but positively encouraged by the state authorities in both Christian and Muslim countries, who besides their general interest in preserving 'law and order' had in some cases a more direct financial interest as well. For example, in Spanish archives dating from the 13th and 14th centuries there are records of many detailed orders issued by those most devout Catholic Kings of Castile and Aragon, instructing their no less devout officials to co-operate with the rabbis in enforcing observance of the Sabbath by the Jews. Why? Because whenever a Jew was fined by a rabbinical court for violating the Sabbath, the rabbis had to hand nine tenths of the fine over to the king - a very profitable and effective arrangement.[458]

Much of the power once exercised by the Jewish hierarchy in the middle ages has waned over the last couple of hundred years. When Jews are not subjected to discrimination by the majority gentile government, the Jewish religious leadership loses much of its coercive power. That is because a Jew who is excommunicated from the Jewish community can then find his own way as a free man in gentile society. The shunned Jew can survive quite nicely outside the cloistered Jewish community. That is why the Jewish hierarchy tries at every turn to increase anti-Semitism. Increased persecution and discrimination of Jews by gentiles creates an environment where the Jews are caught between a rock and a hard place. The fear of the gentiles encourages the Jews to submit to the authoritarian rule of the rabbis.

There has been a resurgence of the power of the Jewish hierarchy in Israel because of the hostile Arab nations that surround Israel. That hostility is secretly encouraged by the Israeli government. For example, the Israeli government secretly funded and encouraged the growth and activities of the rabidly anti-Jewish terrorist organization, Hamas. Hamas fulfills a two-fold goal: undermining the influence of the secular Palestinian liberation organization, Fatah (Movement for the National Liberation of Palestine), and creating a hostile Islamic religious opposition to the Jewish state that was affiliated with the surrounding hostile Islamic countries. Hassane Zerouky explains:

> According to the Israeli weekly Koteret Rashit (October 1987), "The Islamic associations as well as the university had been supported and encouraged by the Israeli military authority" in charge of the (civilian) administration of the West Bank and Gaza. "They [the Islamic associations and the university] were authorized to receive money payments from abroad. Meanwhile, the members of Fatah (Movement for the National Liberation of Palestine) and the Palestinian Left were subjected to the most brutal form of repression."

> The Islamists set up orphanages and health clinics, as well as a network of schools, workshops which created employment for women as well as system of financial aid to the poor. And in 1978, they created an "Islamic University" in Gaza. "The military authority was convinced that these activities would weaken both the PLO and the leftist organizations in Gaza." At the end of 1992, there were six hundred mosques in Gaza. Thanks to Israel's intelligence agency Mossad (Israel's Institute for Intelligence and Special Tasks), the Islamists were allowed to reinforce their presence in the occupied territories."

* * *

> The Hamas then launched a carefully timed campaign of attacks against civilians, one day before the meeting between Palestinian and Israeli negotiators, regarding the formal recognition of Israel by the National Palestinian Council. These events were largely instrumental in the formation of a Right wing Israeli government following the May 1996 elections.

* * *

> The Hamas had built its strength through its various acts of sabotage of the peace process, in a way which was compatible with the interests of the Israeli government. In turn, the latter sought in a number of ways to prevent the application of the Oslo accords. In other words, Hamas was fulfilling the functions for which it was originally created: to prevent the creation of a Palestinian State. And in this regard, Hamas and Ariel Sharon see eye to eye; they are exactly on the same wave length.[459]

The control by the Jewish hierarchy is centered around Judaic religious traditions. Michael

Hoffman explains:

> Judaism's obligation to punish Judaic heretics and it s prohibition against
> allowing them to live in peace is unknown to the world at large, which almost
> exclusively associates this heresy-hunting mentality with the Spanish Inquisition
> and Islam's attitude toward "infidels" and "apostates." The Talmudic heresy-
> hunt, advocated by Orthodox rabbis historically, is not just a theory without
> application or real life (*yehoreig ve' al yaavor*). Where *apikorsim* can be denied
> life, limb or freedom, or suffer penury by being denied the means of earning a
> decent livelihood.[460]

The same heresy-hunting mentality of the Jews was brought by the crypto-Jews into the
Roman Catholic Church. Although the persecution of Christians had been taking place unabated
since the first century, in 1179 Pope Alexander III and the Lateran Council urged the use of force
and established incentives for violence against Christians such as two years' remission of
penance for those who murdered a "heretic." In 1231 Pope Gregory IX formally established the
papal inquisitional tribunal (*inquisitio haereticae pravitatis*). In 1252, Pope Innocent IV
expressly authorized the use of torture, which by then had already been the established practice of
the Catholic Church for centuries.[461] The enemies of the Roman Catholic Church were called
"heretics." These so-called "heretics" were often tortured, mutilated, and burned at the stake.[462]
Their goods were confiscated, condemning their descendants to a life of penury.[463] Thomas
Aquinas (1226-1274), a Catholic saint wrote: "It is more wicked to corrupt the faith on which
depends the life of the soul than to debase the coinage which provides merely for temporal life;
wherefore if coiners and other malefactors are justly doomed to death, much more may heretics
be justly slain once they are convicted."[464]

During the inquisition millions of people were killed as enemies of the Catholic Church. In
one day alone (August 24, 1572) between 50,000[465] and 100,000[466] Huguenots (French
Protestants) were massacred in Paris during the St. Bartholomew Day Massacre. Pope Gregory
XIII received the news with great rejoicing and, in grand procession, went to the Church of St.
Louis to give thanks. He ordered the papal mint to strike coins in commemoration of the
massacre. The coin depicted an angel with a cross in one hand and a sword in the other, before
whom a band of Huguenots, with horror on their faces, are fleeing. The inscription
"Ugonottorum Stranges 1572" ("The Slaughter of the Huguenots 1572") appeared on the coin.[467]

Just as the Jewish religious leaders did with Jesus, the Roman church ordinarily turned
Christians over to the secular authorities to carry out the death penalty. In 1542 Pope Paul III
established an inquisitional office in the Vatican called the "Holy Roman and Universal
Inquisition," in order to fight the spread of Protestantism.[468] In 1908 Pope Pius X dropped the
word "inquisition" from the title of the office and it came to be known as simply the "Holy
Office."[469] On December 7, 1965 that office was renamed the "Congregation for the Doctrine of
the Faith."[470] The title sounds innocuous enough, but there is a long and bloody history attached
to that office; in fact, the public burnings of "heretics" were called *autos-da-fe* or "acts of

faith."[471]

The Congregation for the Doctrine of the Faith still exists in the Catholic church today, holding meetings once a week with the Pope periodically presiding.[472] The office still occupies the Palace of the Inquisition, which is adjacent to the Vatican.[473] The most recent Grand Inquisitor was the former archbishop of Munich, Joseph Cardinal Ratzinger.[474] Because of the importance of his position as the chief enforcer of dogma, Ratzinger was viewed by many as the most powerful cardinal in the Catholic Church.[475] Ratzinger has since been elected as Pope Bendedict XVI.

Lord Acton, an esteemed nineteenth century Roman Catholic historian, is the source for the famous quote about kings and popes: "power tends to corrupt and absolute power corrupts absolutely." He had this further to say: "The papacy contrived murder and massacre on the largest and also on the most cruel and inhuman scale. They [the popes] were not only wholesale assassins but they made the principal of assassination a law of the Christian Church and a condition of salvation. [The papacy is] the fiend skulking behind the Crucifix."[476]

Some might think that Vatican Council II has changed the direction of the Catholic church, that it is no longer the blood thirsty harlot of abominations that it once was. Vatican II is in reality a deadly deception. In Vatican II Protestant Christians who were formerly referred to as "heretics" are now called "separated brethren." This Jesuitical deception becomes apparent when it is realized that Vatican II did not repeal a single papal bull or anathema issued against Christians by past Popes or Vatican councils. In fact, Vatican II reaffirmed the canons and decrees of previous councils, including the Second Council of Nicea, the Council of Florence, and the Council of Trent.[477] The Council of Trent alone accounted for over 100 anathemas against Christians and Christian beliefs.

Christians are still under the countless curses of the Roman Catholic Church, and the "Holy Office" that carried out the many previous inquisitions is still in operation. Just as a leopard cannot change his spots neither can the Vatican change its evil ways. "Can the Ethiopian change his skin, or the leopard his spots? *then* may ye also do good, that are accustomed to do evil." Jeremiah 13:23. The Catholic Church never changes. The official doctrine of the Catholic Church remains that there is no salvation outside the Roman Catholic Church. In the eyes of the Roman Church Protestant Christians are hell bound, yet they call us "separated brethren." Section 846 of the 1994 Catechism of the Catholic Church states emphatically that no person who knowingly refuses to join the Catholic Church or who leaves the Catholic Church can ever be saved, if they do so "knowing that the Catholic Church was founded as necessary by God through Christ."[478] That curse of damnation is aimed directly at informed Christians, who reject the legitimacy of the Roman Church.

In fact, in the official Vatican statement, *Dominus Iesus*,[479] the Catholic Church states that "ecclesial communities" that do not recognize the Eucharist mystery are not truly churches at all. That pronouncement alone makes it clear that the Catholic Church was being disingenuous when it stated in Vatican Council II that the Vatican considered Protestant Christians "separated brethren." *Dominus Iesus* was written by the Vatican's chief expert on doctrine, Cardinal Josef Ratzinger (now Pope Benedict XVI), and it was ratified by Pope John Paul II with the following purportedly infallible pronouncement: "The Sovereign Pontiff John Paul II, at the Audience of June 16, 2000, granted to the undersigned Cardinal Prefect of the Congregation for the Doctrine of the Faith, with sure knowledge and by his apostolic authority, ratified and confirmed this Declaration, adopted in Plenary Session and ordered its publication."

15 Making Jesus Irrelevant

The salvation by works of the Catholic church is the very same false doctrine taught by the Gnostic Jews at the Platonic schools in Alexandria. That doctrine was inculcated into the Catholic theology by the Gnostic Jews. The Jews today still have a works salvation. The Jewish Encyclopedia explains that atonement can be obtained through works of benevolence, suffering, poverty (if it reduces man's physical strength), exile, the destruction of the Temple, study of the Law (when combined with good works), and strangely enough, even death itself.[480] The Talmud states that upon entering a bathhouse a Jew should state: "if I do fall into any perversity or iniquity, may my death be an atonement for all my iniquities."[481] You read correctly, a Jew's own death constitutes his own atonement for all of the sins he commits. Not only that, if the person is righteous, his death is accepted as atonement and held as security (*mashkon*) for the whole Jewish community.[482] It seems that under Jewish theology a Jew is his own savior, and if he is considered righteous, his death may even atone for the sins of other Jews.

So far we have seen that a Jew by his own death can atone for his own sins and rabbis claim immunity from ever going to hell. The Babylonian Talmud elevates the status of rabbis above that of God. *See, e.g.*, Berakhot 7A, *supra*, wherein God asks a rabbi for his blessing,[483] and Bava Metzia 86a, wherein Rabbi Nahami is called to heaven to edify God.[484] According to the Talmud, Avodah Zarah 3B, God spends part of his day studying the rabbinical teachings of the Talmud.[485] In Judaism, the authority of the sages as compiled in the Talmud is absolute. The Talmud itself states that "whosoever transgresses the words of the Sages deserves to die."[486]

This Judaic godhood that flows from the Babylonian mystery religions has been made an integral part of the Catholic church. As does the Talmud with rabbis, so also does the Roman Catholic doctrine elevate the Catholic priests to the stature of gods. The Roman Catholic priests claim that when consecrating the bread and wine during mass they are "acting in the person of Christ the Lord."

> **The priest is also one and the same, Christ the Lord**; for the ministers who offer Sacrifice, consecrate the holy mysteries, **not in their own person, but in**

that of Christ . . . and thus **acting in the Person of Christ the Lord**, he changes the substance of the bread and wine into the true substance of His body and blood. *CATECHISM OF THE COUNCIL OF TRENT.*[487]

While the Catechism of the Council of Trent grants the Catholic priest *de jure* status equal to the Lord Jesus Christ, the Catholic practice is that the priest has *de facto* authority above that of Christ, since upon command of the Catholic priest Jesus supposedly must obey their magical incantation, leave heaven, and enter the consecrated Eucharistic host during the Catholic mass. Jesus alerted his disciples to beware of the many who would come in his name, claiming to be Christ. The many Roman Catholic priests who claim to be "acting in the person of Christ the Lord" are a clear and present fulfilment of that prophecy.

> **Jesus answered and said unto them, Take heed that no man deceive you. For many shall come in my name, saying, I am Christ; and shall deceive many**. (Matthew 24:4-5 AV)

Jesus said that he would be visible in the sky when he returns and warned us not to believe those who point to false Christs and say here is Christ or there is Christ. The Catholic Church points to the consecrated host and says "here is Christ" and points to its priests and says "there is Christ." Jesus prophesied that there would arise false Christs that would perform great signs and wonders that would deceive many. The Catholic church has deceived the world into believing that their priests can perform the great wonder of turning bread and wine into the Lord God Jesus Christ. When Christ returns to Earth it will not be as a piece of bread in the secret chambers of Catholic altars; he will be as plainly visible as lightning.

> **[I]f any man shall say unto you, Lo, here *is* Christ, or there; believe *it* not. For there shall arise false Christs, and false prophets, and shall shew great signs and wonders; insomuch that, if *it were* possible, they shall deceive the very elect. Behold, I have told you before. Wherefore if they shall say unto you, Behold, he is in the desert; go not forth: behold, *he is* in the secret chambers; believe *it* not. For as the lightning cometh out of the east, and shineth even unto the west; so shall also the coming of the Son of man be**. (Matthew 24:23-27 AV)

Since the Catholic Church claims that the priests are another Christ and another Lord, it should be no surprise that the Catholic Church claims that its priests have the same authority as the Lord to forgive sins. The priests hear confessions from a people seeking absolution for their sins. The confessional has been the sight of countless seductions of lonely women by priests.[488]

> **Indeed bishops and priests, by virtue of the sacrament of Holy Orders, have the power to forgive sins**. CATECHISM OF THE CATHOLIC CHURCH, § 1461, 1994.

Even the Jewish scribes understood that only God has the authority to forgive sins, because sin is the violation of God's law. *See e.g.,* Exodus 32:33, Numbers 32:33, Deuteronomy 9:16, Joshua 7:20, 2 Samuel 12:13, Psalm 41:4, Jeremiah 3:25, Jeremiah 50:14, and Luke 15:21.

> When Jesus saw their faith, he said unto the sick of the palsy, Son, thy sins be forgiven thee. But there were certain of the scribes sitting there, and reasoning in their hearts, **Why doth this *man* thus speak blasphemies? who can forgive sins but God only?** And immediately when Jesus perceived in his spirit that they so reasoned within themselves, he said unto them, Why reason ye these things in your hearts? Whether is it easier to say to the sick of the palsy, *Thy* sins be forgiven thee; or to say, Arise, and take up thy bed, and walk? But **that ye may know that the Son of man hath power on earth to forgive sins, (he saith to the sick of the palsy,) I say unto thee, Arise, and take up thy bed, and go thy way into thine house**. And immediately he arose, took up the bed, and went forth before them all; insomuch that they were all amazed, and glorified God, saying, We never saw it on this fashion. (Mark 2:5-12 AV)

The priests in the Catholic take the title of God the Father, by taking the title "Father." Jesus warned against calling a person father in the spiritual sense, that is a title reserved for God alone.

> **And call no *man* your father upon the earth: for one is your Father, which is in heaven**. (Matthew 23:9 AV)

> These words spake Jesus, and lifted up his eyes to heaven, and said, **Father**, the hour is come; glorify thy Son, that thy Son also may glorify thee: (John 17:1 AV)

> And now, **O Father**, glorify thou me with thine own self with the glory which I had with thee before the world was. (John 17:5 AV)

> That they all may be one; as thou, **Father**, *art* in me, and I in thee, that they also may be one in us: that the world may believe that thou hast sent me. (John 17:21 AV)

The religious doctrines in both Judaism and Catholicism make Jesus' authority as mediator between man and God irrelevant. That is because in Judaism there is no need for a mediator and in Catholicism the Catholic priest acts as mediator in place of Christ. In both religions Jesus becomes superfluous.

While some Rabbis have claimed to have direct contact with God,[489] in Judaism there is no need for an intermediary between man and God.[490] Part of the problem in Judaism is that with the destruction of the temple in 70 A.D. there is no longer a priest to act as intermediary with God. The Jewish rabbis solved that little problem and simply dispensed with any need for mediation with God. Dr. Joseph Hertz, who was Chief Rabbi of the United Kingdom from 1913 until his death in 1946, explained in his book, *The Authorized Daily Prayer Book,* that according to Jewish doctrine "[m]ediation implies the inadequacy of the human effort to reach out Godwards. Judaism is founded on the premise that man is capable by virtue of his moral effort of approaching God. Hence, God's coming to man's aid not only becomes superfluous, but actually interferes with the progress of human development."[491]

It is not simply that Jews do not have a mediator or do not recognize Jesus as mediator, Jews object to Jesus, period. Jews are vehemently anti-Christ. The Jews will not tolerate any public reference to Jesus as mediator. That is why you will not hear any politicians today mention the name of Jesus in any religious proclamations. You would have to go back over a hundred years to hear even an allusion to Jesus uttered by a politician, and then it will be followed by a public or private rebuke of that politician by powerful Jewish interests.

For example, in 1896, Rabbi Mochal protested against the Thanksgiving proclamation of President Grover Cleveland, who stated that there is a recognition of a mediator between man and God. President Cleveland did not even mention Christ by name, he only eluded to "the mediation of him who taught us how to pray." That was enough to bring an objection from the Jewish circle. Rabbi Mochal stated that President Cleveland "exceeded the prerogatives of his office and all precedent by making reference to a mediating influence in religious affairs," because it is contrary to one of the "principle tenets of the Jewish faith." The Rabbi stated that "the Jews recognize no mediator between man and God."[492]

There can be no compromise between Christianity and Judaism. Jesus stated clearly "That all men should honour the Son, even as they honour the Father. He that honoureth not the Son honoureth not the Father which hath sent him." (John 5:23 AV). The bottom line is that the god of the Jews is not the God of the bible, because the God of the bible is the Father of Jesus. Since the Jews reject Jesus, they have also rejected the Father who sent him.

The Catholic church, on the other hand, takes a different tack. It has a priesthood that acts as a mediator between man and God, thus making Jesus' mediation superfluous for that reason. The Catholic priest claims to be the Lord Jesus and to act as mediator between God and man.

> [T]he priest is constituted an interpreter and **mediator between God and man**, which indeed must be regarded as the principal function of the priesthood. *CATECHISM OF THE COUNCIL OF TRENT.*[493]

God says otherwise. There is only one God and only one mediator between God and man, that is Jesus Christ.

> For *there is* **one God, and one mediator** between God and men, the man **Christ Jesus**; (1 Timothy 2:5 AV)

There is only one Christ; however, there are many antichrists. All of the priests, bishops, cardinals, and popes of the Romish church are not Christs, they are antichrists.

> Little children, it is the last time: and as ye have heard that antichrist shall come, **even now are there many antichrists**; whereby we know that it is the last time. (1 John 2:18 AV)

The effect of both Judaism and Catholicism is the same: there is no need for Jesus. The Jews claim that there is no need for a mediator and Catholicism states that the priest is the mediator. That makes Jesus unnecessary in both religions.

16

The Common "Preying" of Rabbis and Priests

Orthodox Judaism has a very permissive attitude toward sexual deviance. For example:

Sanhedrin 55b: It is permitted to have sexual intercourse with a girl three years and one day old. See also Yebamoth 57b, 60b; Abodah Zarah 37a.

Sanhedrin 54b: If a man has sex with a boy less than nine years old, he is not guilty of pederasty.

Kethoboth 11b: When a grown-up man has intercourse with a little girl it is nothing, for when the girl is less than three years old it is as if one puts the finger into the eye, tears come to the eye again and again, so does virginity come back to the little girl under three years.

Michael Hoffman explains the sexual deviance that is excused within the orthodox Judaism:

> In defiance of the Old Testament's proscription against men lying with men (Leviticus 20:13), the Talmud nullifies this Old Testament law in at least five ways: by permitting sex with boys under age nine; permitting a legal slap on the wrist for sodomy with the halachic loophole created for "accidental" sodomy; permitting the prideful estimation of the Judiac male as being incapable of sinning in this manner; permitting the act of fellatio on infants by the rnohel (circumciser) during a circumcision, and by cultivating a flourishing homo-erotic culture in the all-male ritual bath scene.

* * *

The traditional Orthodox Judaic *bris* (circumcision) encompasses a homosexual act regarded as essential to the circumcision ritual by Talmudists. We regret having to relate to the reader the ugly and frankly nauseating details of this rite: that the *mohel* actually performs fellatio (*metzitzah b'peh*) on the baby boy by placing the infant's penis in his mouth and sucking the blood from the wounded penis with his lips. This is not an isolated case by a crazed rabbi. This is the religious norm in circumcisions performed by Orthodox rabbis in a ceremony that would be at home in the pages of Richard Von Krafft-Ebing's Psychopathia Sexualis.

The *bris* consists of three stages: excision of the outer part of the prepuce (*milah*); cutting of the inner lining of the foreskin to uncover the glans (*peri'ah*); and the sucking of the blood from the circumcised penis using the mouth and lips of the mohel (*metzitzah b'peh*). The rabbinic circumcision rite, or bris, is authorized by a combination of Talmud-derived halacha and custom (*minhag*). There is no support for this form of circumcision in God's law in the Old Testament. But rabbinic tradition offers ample warrant.[494]

Orthodox Jews claim that the reason the *mohel* sucks on the baby's penis is to clean the wound and stop the bleeding. There is no other medical procedure where oral sucking is used to clean a wound and stop bleeding. Such conduct is medically dangerous. There are very real health risks attendant to this sexual deviance practiced during the *bris* ceremony of circumcision. Dr. Sherwin Nuland is a Jewish surgeon who considers himself agnostic, but still attends synagogue. He is the biographer of the medieval Jewish physician Maimonides. Dr. Nuland explains that there is no medical justification and it is dangerous for a *mohel* to suck on a baby's penis after circumcision:

> One of the first things I was taught when I began my surgical training about 50 years ago was that I must never spit into an open wound. To my knowledge, that is still a good rule.
>
> As ridiculous as such a statement sounds, it is not much more ridiculous than the idea of deliberately exposing a freshly cut incision on the penis of a newborn — whose immune mechanisms are, of course, not yet fully developed — to the germs in human saliva. Any fool should know that such virulent bacteria and viruses must never come into direct contact with a wound, much less that of a neonate.[495]

Michael Hoffman concludes: "All of the risks common to homosexual sex are present in the Orthodox Judaic *bris*."[496] The practice of fellatio on young babies by a Jewish *mohel* is why venereal disease is common within the Orthodox Jewish communities. Venereal disease can be fatal for a newborn child. For example, the New York Times for Friday, August 26, 2005 contained a report that the "circumcision ritual practiced by some Orthodox Jews alarmed [New York] City health officials, who say it may have led to three cases of herpes-one of them fatal-in infants. The practice is known as oral suction, or in Hebrew, *metzitzah b'peh*: after removing the foreskin of the penis, the practitioner, or mohel, sucks the blood from the wound to clean it."[497] "Dozens of ultra-Orthodox rabbis signed a full-page Hebrew advertisement that ran in the February 25, 2005 issue of Yated Ne'eman, defending the practice."[498]

As a result of the fatal infant herpes contraction, the New York State Department of Health began scrutinizing whether to allow the practice of oral suction by Jewish *mohels* to continue. The Orthodox Jews fearing that new health regulations could put and end to their pederastic practice, went into political high gear and negotiated a deal with New York City Mayor Michael Bloomberg. Bloomberg (who is Jewish) promised to keep the *metzitzah b'peh* (fellatio on an infant) legal. In return the Orthodox Jews as a bloc supported his election. Jim Rutenberg and Andy Newman, reporters for the New York Times, describe the events:

> With three days to go before Election Day, ultra-Orthodox Jewish leaders in Williamsburg, Brooklyn, held what was by far the largest rally of Mayor Michael R. Bloomberg's campaign. With searchlights bouncing across the Brooklyn sky and klezmer music blaring from speakers hoisted on cranes, thousands of Hasidic Jews, in black hats or head scarves, cheered the beaming mayor from rooftops and blocks upon blocks of bleachers. When ... Rabbi David Niederman addressed the throngs, he praised the mayor for his ... support for the constitutional separation of church and state. For many in the crowd, the last reference was code for the administration's decision to hold off from taking action against an ancient form of ritualistic circumcision.[499]

In June 2006, Mayor Bloomberg kept his part of the bargain and brokered an agreement between the New York State Department of Health and the rabbis, renewing permission for fellatio on infant boys as part of the *bris*.

The *bris* is nothing more than pedophilia masquerading as a religious ritual. If a gentile engaged in the conduct of the Jewish mohel of sucking on an infants penis he would be prosecuted under the New York Penal Code § 130.50 for engaging in a criminal sexual act in the first degree. That New York law states:

> § 130.50 Criminal sexual act in the first degree.
> A person is guilty of criminal sexual act in the first degree when he or she engages in oral sexual conduct or anal sexual conduct with another person:
> 1. By forcible compulsion; or
> 2. Who is incapable of consent by reason of being physically helpless; or
> 3. Who is less than eleven years old; or
> 4. Who is less than thirteen years old and the actor is eighteen years old or more.
> Criminal sexual act in the first degree is a class B felony.

Anyone convicted of criminal sexual conduct in the first degree is subjected to the potential punishment of up to 25 years in prison and is put on the rolls as a registered sex offender. There are similar laws in every state against fellatio on infants. The laws are simply not enforced against Jewish *mohels*.

The conduct of the *mohel* in sucking on the penis of an infant during circumcision is just one example of the permissive attitude toward pedophilia within orthodox Jewry. The permissiveness in the Jewish community toward what would ordinarily be criminal sexual conduct creates an environment that is rife for abuse of children. In the wake of the Rabbi Kolko man-boy sex scandal "[a]n authority from the esteemed haredi organization Agudath Israel, Rabbi Avi Shafran, openly acknowledged that sexual abuse is indeed a problem that requires more attention and measures than the [Jewish] community currently brings to bear."[500]

Many victims of sex abuse by orthodox rabbis suffer in silence. Jewish reporter Robert Kolker opines that there is more sexual abuse among the fervently Orthodox Jewish community than elsewhere because repression in the orthodox Judaic community "creates a fertile environment for deviance."[501] Rabbi Avi Shafran acknowledged that "for a person whose whole life revolves around the community, 'the ostracism that results from publicly confronting a leader of that community' can be worse than death."[502] Eugene Myer states that "[o]thers believe that underreporting of clergy sexual misconduct may in fact facilitate abuse."[503] Dr. Hella Winston explains:

> Rabbi Avi Shafran on the Beit Din and Abuse: Among many Orthodox Jews, the preferred forum for adjudicating communal disputes is a *bet din*, a rabbinic court. But critics say such panels often try to dissuade sex abuse victims from pursuing their complaints, a charge vigorously denied by (Agudath Israel spokesman Rabbi Avi) Shafran. But, he added, 'In cases where there is some degree of doubt, the beit din has a responsibility to counsel against going to authorities until there is proven criminal activity.'
>
> In other words, in 99% of abuse cases, Rabbi Shafran's 'gedolim' will say that it is forbidden to go to the police. Why? Because the victims of abuse are largely underage. Their testimony is invalid in a beit din, and abuse happens in secret, away from witnesses - except, of course, for the abused child. In a similar vein, Rabbi Chaim Pinchas Scheinberg told victims of Rabbi Yehudah Kolko and their parents that, because Rabbi Kolko did not penetrate the boys (he only rubbed his erect penis against them), according to halakha, no abuse happened. Therefore it is forbidden to go to police. This is Agudath Israel. This is the gedolim. This is Orthodox Judaism.[504]

Rabbi Yehuda Kolko was systematically protected by his fellow rabbis as he molested a series of young children over a 30 year span. After years of rampant molestation by Rabbi Kolko, approximately 10 rabbis met in 1984 to discuss what to do about Rabbi Kolko's molestation of young boys at the yeshiva (boys rabbinical school) where he worked. It was decided to do nothing, since the yeshiva lawyer told the rabbis that the yeshiva would be liable for not having reported their knowledge to the police earlier.[505] Rabbi Kolko was allowed to continue at the school and his molestation of the children continued unabated.

In 1985 a *beit din* (a/k/a *bais din*) was held with 5 more rabbis to examine the molestation complaints against Rabbi Kolko.[506] The Rabbi who ran the yeshiva at which Rabbi Kolko worked was able to end the beit din after hearing only one day of testimony. A second *biet din* was set up by the yeshiva rabbi with the objective of clearing Rabbi Kolko; no molestation victims appeared before that *beit din*.[507] Again, no action was taken against Rabbi Kolko and he was able to continue his molestation.

Rabbi Kolko continued his molestation until 2006, when he was finally prosecuted for child molestation. Through political pressure from the politically powerful orthodox Jewish community, Rabbi Kolko was allowed to plead to two lesser counts of misdemeanor child endangerment. The prosecutor claimed that he allowed the plea to the lesser charges because one victim was too young and the family would not allow him to testify. The father of the victim states that was not true; in fact, he felt it would be a beneficial catharsis for his son to testify.[508] The father of the other victim stated that he was pressed by the prosecution to keep his son from testifying.[509] Both children remain plaintiffs against Rabbi Kolko in a civil suit and are expected to be witnesses against him in the civil trial.[510]

All along the way as charges of child molestation surfaced against Rabbi Kolko, rabbis threatened victims and their families, publically disparaged them, and put pressure on them to keep quiet.[511] The response by the orthodox Jewish community to the molestation evidence against Rabbi Kolko reveals the permissive attitude toward pedophilia in orthodox Jewry. Hella Winston explains how the orthodox Jewish community tolerates such conduct:

> [The] bombshell article [in the May 2006 New York Magazine about sexual deviance within orthodox Jewry] (disclosure: I was quoted in it) suggested several reasons why confronting sexual abuse is a particular challenge for ultra-Orthodox Jews: the social stigma associated with being the victim of abuse; the ages-old Jewish prohibition against *mesira*, or "informing" to the secular authorities; and the religious proscriptions against *lashon hara* (gossip) and *chilul Hashem* ("desecrating God's name," which in this context means giving the community a "bad name"). These impediments silence victims and protect perpetrators."[512]

The code of silence within orthodox Jewry explains how it took over 30 years for anything to be done to stop Rabbi Kolko. The existence of the code of silence suggests that there are many protected rabbinical pedophiles lurking among the orthodox Jews. Rabbi Kolko is just the tip of the iceberg. Shaiya Brizel revealed in his book, *The Silence of the Ultra-Orthodox*, that his father, Rabbi Yaakov Yitzhak Brizel for years used his position to sodomize ultra-Orthodox boys. The greatest rabbis of the city were told about Brizel's conduct and did nothing to stop it.[513]

Shaiya stated that his father committed the acts in empty synagogues during the hours between prayers and in other places. "The greatest of the ultra-Orthodox rabbis...like Rabbi Landau and the halachic sage Shmuel Halevi Hausner of Bnei Brak, knew and kept silent."[514] Shaiya Brizel, reveals that his father would hunt for his victims within certain yeshiva, and when the head of the yeshiva discovered that his father was sodomizing the children he kept silent and did not contact the police.[515]

When Rabbi Brizel's wife found out about her husband's conduct she demanded a divorce, but batteries of rabbis tried to calm her down so that she would not destroy the good Brizel name. "They could live with the fact that one of their own had raped minors, but for them divorce was an impossible situation."[516]

Shaiya discovered that his father's conduct was common among ultra-Orthodox Jewish men. On two occasions, "once during prayers in a synagogue, and once during a Gemara (Talmud) study hour at Rabbi Eliezer Shach's Ponevezh Yeshiva, ultra-Orthodox men who were strangers to him touched his sexual organ, presumably on the assumption that he followed in his father's footsteps. The first time, he made a fuss, only to discover that the only thing that interested the people there was to hush the whole thing up. The second time, he made do with a whispered warning to the man."[517]

"On the day the book was published, Brizel met with the head of the Hachemei Lublin Yeshiva, Rabbi Avraham Vazner. "He told me that publishing the book was a million times worse than what my father had done."[518] After Shaiya's book came out, associates of the local rabbi of the Hasidic synagogue he attended informed him that he was *persona non grata*.

In the conversation with [women's magazine] La'isha, Shaiya's father, Rabbi Brizel, said that he was indeed a homosexual, "But I have had treatment and today I am no longer like that. All this is behind me." When asked if he had sexual relations with minors, the rabbi replied: "Perhaps I will talk about that some other time."[519]

This same pattern of abuse is also found within the Catholic Church. The Catholic Church has set up procedures similar to the Jewish *beit din*, which like the *beit din* serve to protect pedophile perpetrators from criminal charges. Pope Benedict XVI was recently caught in a lie about his efforts to protect pedophile priests. The recent controversy involved Father Stephen Kiesle, who was charged in 2002 with 13 counts of child molestation. All but two counts were thrown out by the U.S. Supreme Court who ruled that it was unconstitutional for California to enact a law extending the statute of limitations in child molestation cases. Most of Kiesles charges stemmed from his activities in the 1970's. Kiesle ended up pleading no contest in 2004 to molesting a young girl. He was sentenced to six years in state prison.[520] A 1985 letter by Pope Benedict XVI (then Cardinal Joseph Ratzinger) is the smoking gun proving a scheme to protect pedophile priests. The Telegraph reports:

The 1985 letter typed in Latin and signed by the then Cardinal Joseph Ratzinger said any decision to remove Stephen Kiesle, a San Francisco priest, from the priesthood must take into account the "good of the universal church".

The letter, obtained by the Associated Press news agency, could provide the first direct evidence to undermine the Vatican's insistence that the Pope was never involved in blocking the removal of paedophile priests during his two decades as head of the Catholic Church's Congregation for the Doctrine of the Faith, the department that deals with sex abuse cases.[521]

That case is just the tip of the iceberg. As with the orthodox Jewish community, the Catholic Church has created an environment that is conducive to sexual deviance. The devilish doctrine of forbidding Catholic priests to marry is directly contrary to God's plan for the leadership of his church. As the following passages prove, God's plan for his church is that an elder be faithful to his word and be the husband of one wife.

For this cause left I thee in Crete, that thou shouldest set in order the things that are wanting, and ordain elders in every city, as I had appointed thee: If any be blameless, **the husband of one wife**, having faithful children not accused of riot or unruly. For a bishop must be blameless, as the steward of God. (Titus 1:5-7 AV)

This *is* a true saying, If a man desire the office of a bishop, he desireth a good work. A bishop then must be blameless, **the husband of one wife**, vigilant, sober, of good behaviour, given to hospitality, apt to teach. (1 Timothy 3:1-2 AV)

It may be preferable in many circumstances for a person to remain unmarried. God, however, knows that many cannot remain single without burning with the passion of the flesh. He, therefore, recommends that people who are single and find themselves burning with the temptations of the flesh get married. "[*T*]o avoid fornication, let every man have his own wife, and let every woman have her own husband." (1 Corinthians 7:2 AV) *See also*, 1 Corinthians 7:8-9. When, however, men and women remain single because of some extra-biblical restriction, it is bound to result in sinful acts born out of the lust of the flesh.

God describes forbidding to marry as a doctrine of devils. 1 Timothy 4:1-3. The Catholic doctrine that requires priests to remain unmarried has been the cause of countless acts of immorality. There were 6,800 registered prostitutes in Rome in 1490 to service, for the most part, the clerics of Rome. Keep in mind, that was in a city with a population of only 90,000, and the figure does not include clandestine prostitutes.[522] Many Popes in fact were the illegitimate offspring of purportedly celibate Popes. For example, Pope Sylverius (536-537) was fathered by Pope Hormisdas (514-523), and Pope John XI (931-935) was fathered by Pope Sergius III (904-911).[523]

The sexual immorality continues today on a scale that is unimaginable. In 1994 former

Jesuit priest Terence German filed a 120 million dollar lawsuit against the Catholic Church, Pope John Paul II, and Cardinal John O'Connor alleging that they had turned a blind eye to the "pervasive sexual and financial misconduct" of other priests.[524] The Catholic Church has engaged in a concerted coverup of the widespread pedophilia within the ranks of the Roman Catholic priesthood. The church knowingly transfers confirmed pedophile priests from one diocese to another, exposing the unsuspecting youngsters of each new diocese to the predatory sexual lusts of the priests.

For example, in Santa Fe, New Mexico victims have filed 50 lawsuits against the Catholic Archdiocese alleging that more than 45 priests had sexually abused 200 people over a 30 year period.[525] The Franciscan boy's seminary in Santa Barbara, California was recently closed down because the majority of the priests were involved sexually with their students.[526]

In Dallas eleven former altar boys won a 119 million dollar judgment against the Roman Catholic Church. The victorious plaintiffs later agreed to settle the case for 23.4 million dollars rather than be subjected to dilatory appellate tactics of the Catholic Church. The evidence revealed that the altar boys were the objects of the predatory sexual desires of Catholic Priest Rudolph Kos. Kos is now serving a life sentence for sexual assault.[527]

James R. Porter, a Catholic priest was removed from his priestly duties on eight separate occasions between 1960 and 1974 because he had sexually assaulted children. Each time he was removed, the Bishop and other high Catholic officials permitted him to return to his priestly duties in another unsuspecting parish. Each time he returned to his duties he resumed his pedophilia. More than 100 victims of Porter's sexual deviance have thus far come forward. He was indicted on 32 counts of sexual abuse. Porter admitted in a 1973 letter to Pope Paul VI to having homosexual involvement with parish children in five different states. While the Catholic Church provided Porter with counseling and care, there was no outreach at all to the victims of his sexual lusts.[528]

Catholic Priest Brendan Smyth was jailed in June 1994 after admitting to 17 counts of indecently assaulting young boys and girls from 1964 to 1988. His pedophilia began in the 1940's. He was transferred from diocese to diocese after each revelation. He engaged in his sexual misconduct in Wales in the 1950's, in Ireland in the 1960's and 70's, in the United States in the 1980's, and again in Northern Ireland in the 1990's. Smyth's superiors in the Norbertine Order of priests admitted that they knew for almost thirty years about Smyth's sexual assault on children, and yet they took no action other than to transfer him so he could continue his pattern of child molestation.[529]

Even after being convicted of felony sex crimes many priests are not defrocked by Rome. For example Gordon MacRae, Leo Shea, and Roger Fortier were all convicted of sexual crimes, but were merely placed on administrative suspension.[530] Shea and MacRea were convicted in 1994, Fortier was convicted in 1998. Yet they remain Catholic priests. The suspensions only prevent the priests from performing Catholic sacraments during the term of suspension.

Boston Cardinal Bernard Law admitted that he knowingly shuttled Catholic priest John Geoghan from parish to parish for almost 10 years between 1984 and 1993 after each new allegation that Geoghan had molested young parish boys, some as young as four years old.[531] That allowed Geoghan to continue his predatory molestation of over 130 young boys, many of whom have since sued Cardinal Law and the Boston Archdiocese.

The sad truth is that Geoghan is just the tip of the iceberg. The Boston Catholic archdiocese was compelled to release the names of 80 priests in Boston who had been accused of child molestation over the past 40 years. That list of 80 priests is by no means complete. For example, several men who were molested as young alter boys, came forward when they noticed that the list did not name Joseph Birmingham who was shuttled around to 6 different parishes as he committed serial pedophilia at each new unsuspecting parish. Birmingham died in 1989. One of the former altar boys, Thomas Blanchete, now an adult, told Fox 25 News (Boston) that he told Cardinal Law at Birmingham's funeral in 1989 about Birmingham molesting him and his brothers. To Blanchete's amazement, Cardinal Law invoked the power of confession never to speak of the matter again in an attempt to silence Blanchete.[532]

According to the Attorney General of Massachusetts, Tom Reilly, the abuse by the priests in Boston went back 60 years and involved more than 250 priests.[533] On July 24, 2003, Reilly unveiled a 76 page report based on Catholic Church records. Reilly stated that the church made "deliberate, intentional choices to protect the church and its reputation at the expense of children. In effect they sacrificed the children for many, many years."[534] Reilly stated that a "culture of secrecy and an institutional acceptance" of clerical sexual abuse prevailed in the Boston Archdiocese.

Reilly stated that "the church authorities failed to report the abuse to law enforcement or child protection authorities"[535] Instead, the church quietly settled hundreds of cases with victims who reported their cases to church officials. In a handful of cases where the victims went directly to law enforcement authorities, the priests were prosecuted. By quietly settling most of the cases, however, the church was able to present a facade that the priests being prosecuted were an aberrant few, when in fact there were hundreds of pedophile priests actively preying on innocent children; the church knew it and protected the offenders. Reilly further stated that the church hierarchy aggressively lobbied against attempts to broaden laws to require self reporting by clergy.

Cardinal Law was forced to resign as Archbishop of Boston. Pope John Paul II then assigned him to the post of Archpriest of St. Mary Major Basilica in Rome. Cardinal Law retained his authority as a Cardinal within the Roman Catholic Church and was thus able to take part in the voting for the new pope, who turned out to be the former Cardinal Joseph Ratzinger (now Pope Benedict XVI). Incidently, Cardinal Ratzinger was the Cardinal in charge of the Vatican's Congregation for the Doctrine of the Faith and was instrumental in protecting the pedophile priest Marcial Maciel, founder and head of the Legion of Christ.

The best indication that Rome approved of Cardinal Law's pattern of protecting pedophile priests was that he was chosen for the honor of saying one of the memorial masses at St. Peter's Basilica during the *Novemdiales,* which is a series of rites over nine days in memory of the deceased Pope John Paul II. Officials from the Survivors Network, an organization that represents hundreds of victims of pedophile priests, traveled to the Vatican to protest Cardinal Law's prominent position in the memorial for the deceased pope. As Barbara Blaine, the president of the Survivors Network, was speaking to the media in Vatican City, two police officers approached and physically pushed her and the media about eight feet outside Vatican territory and back into Italy. Within an hour Cardinal Law and a procession of priests and cardinals in white and red vestments marched down the main aisle of the massive St. Peter's Basilica to say the memorial mass.[536] The scene represented what the Catholic Church is all about: pedophile priests in all their regalia in positions of honor within the church, while their victims are cast aside to be neglected and ignored.

How many children were molested by priests in Boston? Attorney General Reilly estimated that the number "likely exceeds 1,000."[537] David Clohessy, Chairmen of the Survivors Network of Those Abused by Priests, stated that while the figures obtained from the Catholic records were shocking, they were without doubt partial figures.[538] The findings of experts who have studied child molestation seem to support Clohessy's conclusion. The recidivism among child molesters is very high. An Emory University Study conducted by a leading child abuse researcher, Dr. Gene Abel, found that the average child molester claims 380 victims in a lifetime.[539]

Assuming Dr. Abel's conclusion is accurate, that would mean that the 250 pedophile priests who have been shuttled through the Boston Archdiocese potentially could abuse a total of over 95,000 children during their lifetimes. One should be mindful that only a very small percentage of child molestation victims ever report their victimization, which in part explains why the total figures announced by the Attorney General were not much higher. Another explanation is that the figures cited by Dr. Abel are lifetime figures, and often priests are shuttled from one parish to another once they are caught, so a priest likely would not have committed all of their molestations of children while in Boston.

Finally, the figures used by the Attorney General were supplied by the Boston Archdiocese itself, which has a vested interest in mitigating the scale of the child abuse by its priests. As large as these numbers are, one should be not forget that this is just one archdiocese. Such abuse by priests has been taking place on this scale for centuries on a worldwide basis. The total number of victims of priestly predation is staggering. The Roman Catholic Archdiocese of Boston initially offered 55 million dollars to settle the hundreds of pending civil suits stemming from the sexual abuse by priests.[540] Ultimately, on or about September 2003, the Boston Archdiocese agreed to pay $85 million to settle the lawsuits brought by over 500 plaintiffs.

The Roman Catholic religious order known as the Christian Brothers of Ireland in Canada had systematically used their orphanages and schools across that country to molest, abuse, and physically torture children in their care. The case was so appalling that, in 1996, a court in

Ontario directed the religious order to cease its operations throughout Canada and sell off every scrap of property it owned to pay compensation to the victims of these heinous acts. That is not the end of the story. Unfortunately, the court picked the Chicago accounting firm of Arthur Andersen (of WorldCom and Enron infamy) to wind up the affairs of the religious order and liquidate the property. So far, Andersen has consumed all $7 million (Canadian) of assets it has recovered, spending some of it on its own fees and much of the rest on fees to lawyers Andersen hired. There are 43 million dollars in assets yet to be sold, however Arthur Andersen is in arrears on its legal bills, and some of that money will no doubt disappear into the lawyers' and Andersen's pockets. The victims were molested by the Catholic priests and then robbed by shyster accountants. The news of the molestation by the Christian Brothers of Ireland was completely ignored by the major media outlets. It was left to Terry Roberts a reporter for *The Telegram*, a local newspaper in St. John, to report the story.

The world famous Boys Town Catholic orphanage just outside Omaha, Nebraska is a hotbed of pederasty. State Sen. John W. DeCamp in his book, *The Franklin Cover-up,* revealed that his investigation of the failed Franklin Savings and Loan uncovered evidence that young boys were taken from Boys Town and transported throughout the country to sodomite drug parties.[541] The only concern of the Roman Catholic Church is to prevent any revelations that might harm its reputation. Senator DeCamp explained one case told to him by the Executive Director of Boys Town, Monsignor Robert Hupp, where a young child was sexually abused and murdered by a Catholic priest. This information was revealed to the Roman Catholic Archbishop of Omaha, whose response was to ship the guilty priest out of state for "alcohol treatment." No thought was given to prosecuting the priest. Monsignor Hupp, however, was removed from his post as head of Boys Town, for the audacity of revealing the sins of a fellow priest to Senator DeCamp.[542]

Cathy O'Brien, in her book *Trance-Formation of America*, alleged that Boys Town along with the Roman Catholic hierarchy was part of a national syndicate that included the elements from the federal government that supplied young children to rich and powerful pederasts throughout the world. She alleged that the syndicate used trauma based mind control to induce multiple personalities and amnesia in their victims. Many of the sexual activities in which Cathy O'Brien took part happened at the exclusive Bohemian Grove. She alleged that many of the world's government and business leaders would gather at the Bohemian Grove periodically and engage in all manner of deviant sexual conduct. Their aberrance was surreptitiously filmed apparently for the purpose of later blackmailing the politically powerful deviants.

Canon lawyer Fr. Thomas Doyle, coauthor of the Doyle-Moulton Peterson report on abuse in the clergy, estimated that in 1990 approximately 3,000 of the 50,000 Catholic priests in the United States were sexually involved with children. Richard Sipes, a former Catholic priest who counsels victims of abuse, confirms the estimate of Doyle that there are 3,000 pedophile Catholic priests in the U.S.[543] It has been estimated that 12,000 priests are sexually involved with adult women, and 6,000 priests are engaged in sexual activity with men in the U.S. alone.[544] Approximately 400 priests either confessed to or were convicted of sexually abusing minors in the 10 years between 1982 and 1992.[545] Catholic priest Andrew Greeley, in a 1993 essay in

America Magazine, estimated that 2,500 priests had abused 100,000 victims in the United States alone. Thus far, the Roman Catholic Church has paid out an estimated one billion dollars in out of court settlements involving sexual misconduct by Catholic priests in the United States alone, and the fornication continues today.[546] Catholic officials have admitted that it has been their practice to reassign sexual offender priests to different parishes after the priests receive child sexual abuse psychological counseling.[547] There has been a recommendation by the National Conference of Bishops that the policy of reassignment of pedophile priests to new parishes be changed. It is not known if that recommendation has been implemented; one thing is certain is that any action taken by the church hierarchy will be just window dressing.

As a result of the public outcry over the pederasty in the Catholic priesthood, in 2002 the U.S. Catholic Bishops commissioned the John Jay College of Criminal Justice to survey the Catholic Bishops to find out the degree of the problem. On February 27, 2004, their report was issued. The report found that more than 10,600 children were molested by 4,392 Catholic priests between 1950 and 2002.[548] That means that 4 % of the 109,694 Catholic priests serving during that 52 year period had molested children.[549] The report acknowledged that because the figures were based upon voluntary reporting by the Catholic bishops, the figures were almost certainly an undercount of the true degree of the abuse.[550] Combine the voluntary nature of the reporting with the fact that the figures only take into account formal complaints, and one can safely infer that the undercount is significant.

Of the 10,600 reported cases, 6,700 were investigated and substantiated, 3,300 were not investigated because the accused priest had died, and approximately 1,000 of the claims were not substantiated.[551] The 145 page report stated that the culture in the Catholic seminaries, where the priests are trained, tolerated moral laxity and had a sodomite subculture.[552] The report further stated that the failure by the Catholic hierarchy to discipline sexually active priests created an environment that made clerics reluctant to report the sexual abuse of children.[553] The report revealed that 5.8 % of the abused children were under 7 years old, 16 % were 8 to 10 years old, 50.9 % of the children were between 11 and 14 years old, and 27.3 % were between ages 15 and 17.[554] The report revealed that 81 % of the victims were boys, and 19 % were girls.[555] The known costs to settle the lawsuits generated by the priestly abuse was reported to be approximately 572 million dollars.[556] As large as that figure is, it does not give an accurate picture of the damages paid out by the Catholic church. Many dioceses did not report figures and the total given in the report does not include the 85 million dollar settlement by the Boston Archdiocese, nor does it include the many hundreds of pending claims. A more complete accounting of the costs resulted in an approximate figure of a billion dollars.[557]

The most notable aspect of the bishops' report is what it does not say. The report does not identify a single priest nor the specific parishes that were the locations of the clerical abuse. Why is that critical information missing? Because the Catholic institution knows that to reveal the name of even a single priest would cause all those who were abused by that priest, but who have yet not reported the abuse, to come forward. That is what has happened in Boston and other places. For example, when John Geoghan's name was publicized as a child molesting Catholic priest in Boston, the victims came out of the woodwork. Approximately 130 victims of Geoghan's child molesting spanning 10 years in Boston came forward. Dr. Gene Abel, a leading expert on child abuse, determined in his research that the average child molester claims 380 victims in a lifetime.[558] Given that there were 4,392 priest involved in the reported molestations, there could be as many as 1,668,960 victims of child molestation by Catholic priests in the United States.

By only giving the raw numbers of official reports of molestation in the bishops' report, the Catholic church can conceal the true degree of the abuse. The Catholic church can then use its statistics to suggest that on the average each of the 4,392 pedophile priests only abused approximately 2 children over a 52 year period, for a total of 10,600 victims. When in fact, the reported 10,600 victims are just the tip of the pederastic iceberg. The purpose of the bishops' report was not to reveal but rather to conceal. The bishops' report is a smokescreen.

The Vatican's response in covering up this epidemic of clerical abuse speaks loudly that the Vatican condones such conduct. The most glaring example of the Vatican's moral corruption is its handling of the pedophilia allegations against Catholic priest Marcial Maciel, founder and head of the Legion of Christ. Maciel founded the Legion of Christ in Mexico in 1941; he soon established seminaries in Spain and Rome.[559] The Legion of Christ recruits boys as young as 10 years old to leave their families and follow a course of study in prep schools in Latin America, Europe and the United States to become Catholic priests.[560] In 1978, the Legion's American leader, Juan Vaca, wrote a letter that was sent directly to the Pope John Paul II via diplomatic pouch by officials in the Rockville, N.Y., diocese.[561] The letter detailed a history of sexual activity he had with Maciel, beginning when Vaca was a teenage seminarian and continuing into his 20s. He also accused Maciel of having had sexual relations with other Legion of Christ students. When Vaca left the Catholic priesthood in 1989, he wrote a second letter to the Vatican repeating his charges.[562] "Vaca also told ABC NEWS how he was instructed to bring other boys from their bedrooms to Maciel's room. Vaca said Maciel had different boys visit his rooms on different nights. 'In some instances, two were together with him - myself and another one,' he said. Vaca said Maciel rewarded him with special privileges, such as a private meeting with Pope Pius XII, who served as pope from 1939 to 1958. Maciel always assured Vaca he was doing nothing wrong. When Vaca admitted concerns of committing a sin, Vaca said Macial absolved him from his sin 'in the name of the Father and of the Son and of the Holy Spirit.'"[563]

Vaca is not alone in his charges. A Florida priest, who also left the Legion of Christ, sent a similar letter to the pope.[564] "In 1997, nine priests, former priests and former seminarians accused Maciel of molesting them when they were as young as 10. They told the Hartford Courant that since 1978, they had tried and failed to get Rome to investigate."[565] ABC News revealed the surprising response of Pope John Paul II to such credible charges brought against Macial. "In 1997, they went public, telling their story to *The Hartford Courant*, a newspaper in Connecticut. *Courant* reporters Jerry Renner and Jason Berry, who wrote the story, repeated the allegations to the Vatican, yet received no response from the Vatican. However, later that year, the pope took a step that surprised them. Maciel was appointed to represent the pope at a meeting of Latin American bishops, which Renner and Berry took as a clear signal the Vatican had ignored the allegations."[566]

The signal being sent by the pope is not that he has ignored the allegations, rather the signal is that the pope condones pedophilia. Not only does the pope condone pedophilia, it is clearly part and parcel of the Catholic priestcraft. As reported by ABC News: "Then, four years ago, some of the men tried a last ditch effort, taking the unusual step of filing a lawsuit in the Vatican's secretive court, seeking Macial's excommunication. Once again they laid out their evidence, but it was another futile effort - an effort the men say was blocked by one of the most powerful cardinals in the Vatican. The accusers say Vatican-based Cardinal Joseph Ratzinger [now Pope Benedict XVI], who heads the Vatican office [Congregation for the Doctrine of the Faith] to safeguard the faith and the morals of the church, quietly made the lawsuit go away and shelved it. There was no investigation and the accusers weren't asked a single question or asked for a statement."[567] The most telling evidence that pedophilia is condoned by the Vatican is that Ratzinger, who so effectively swept the allegations against Macial under the proverbial rug, was appointed by Pope Paul II to investigate the recently exposed sex abuse scandal involving scores of Catholic priests throughout the United States.

Let us review the Vatican response to the Maciel pedophilia allegations. Pope John Paul II is personally notified in 1978 through diplomatic pouch by the head of the Legion of Christ order in the United States that he was molested as a child by Catholic priest, Marcial Maciel. The pope takes no action. The pope is notified again in 1989 by the same priest. Still, the pope takes no action. In 1997 nine other priests notify the Vatican that Maciel had also molested them and other boys as young as 10 years old. The pope responds by appointing the pedophile priest, Marcial Maciel, to be his official representative at a meeting of Latin American bishops. "Can two walk together, except they be agreed?" (Amos 3:3 AV)

The victimized priests are so frustrated that in 1998 they seek a hearing in the Vatican to have Maciel excommunicated. Cardinal Joseph Ratzinger, who heads the Congregation for the Doctrine of the Faith, quietly blocks the legal action. There was no investigation; the accusers weren't even questioned. Then in 2002, when evidence of widespread pedophilia by Catholic priests explodes in the U.S. media, the pope issues a statement condemning pedophilia among Catholic priests. However, he appoints Cardinal Ratzinger, who so effectively suppressed any hearing into the Maciel pedophilia, to head up the official investigation. The implications are clear. The pope and the Vatican verbally condemn pedopilia, but their actions demonstrate that they in fact condone pedophilia and are hell bent on sweeping it under the rug.

The Catholic Church has borrowed the strategy of the Orthodox Jews, who use a rabbinic court, called *bet din*, to protect rabbis, sweep allegations of sexual abuse under the rug, and dissuade sex abuse victims from pursuing their complaints with the police. CBS News Correspondent Vince Gonzales has uncovered official Catholic Church instructions stored in secret Vatican archives for over 40 years, which documents that the Roman Catholic Church, at the highest levels of authority, has engaged in a systematic and pervasive cover-up of criminal sexual conduct by its priests.[568] On March 16, 1962 the Vatican sent secret instructions under seal stamped "CONFIDENTIAL" from the Cardinal Secretary of the *The Supreme and Holy Congregation For the Holy Office*, Alfredo Cardinal Ottaviani, and personally approved by Pope John XXIII, to "ALL PATRIARCHS, ARCHBISHOPS, BISHOPS, AND OTHER DIOCESAN ORDINARIES 'EVEN OF THE ORIENTAL RITE.'"

The instructions, which were ordered to be "observed in the minutest detail," required all those in the Catholic Church who have any knowledge of a matter of criminal sexual conduct by a priest to be constrained to "perpetual silence" from ever revealing the crimes to anyone.[569] The instructions stated that the criminal sexual conduct of the priests is considered a "secret of the Holy Office."[570] The penalty for revealing such matters is "excommunication *latae sententiae ipso facto*."[571] The clear intent of the instructions was to gag those with authoritative inside knowledge of the sexual crimes of the priests and shield those priests from criminal prosecution.

The secret instructions expressly mention solicitation and the "worst crime" which is described in Title V of the instructions as "any obscene external deed, gravely sinful, in any [sic] perpetrated by a cleric or attempted with a person of his own sex."[572] The "worst crime" also includes "any obscene, external act, gravely sinful, perpetrated in any way by a cleric or attempted by him with youths of either sex or with brute animals (bestiality)."[573] Those who take part in the official Catholic Church proceedings investigating the sexual crimes of the priests are bound by a solemn oath never to reveal anything about the criminal sexual conduct of a priest that surfaces during the investigation. Each person taking part in the investigation is bound by oath not to: "even for the most urgent and most serious cause, even for the purpose of a greater good, commit anything against this fidelity to the secret unless a particular faculty of dispensation has been expressly given to [him] by the Supreme Pontiff."[574] "The oath of keeping the secret must be given in these cases also by the accusers or those denouncing the priest and the witnesses."[575]

The instructions set out procedural protections that slant the investigation of allegations of clerical misconduct in the priests' favor. For example, the accuser must bring charges against the priest "within a month" of the alleged crime.[576] Furthermore, while witnesses must testify under oath,[577] the instructions state that: "In every way the judge is to remember that it is never right for him to bind the accused [priest] by an oath to tell the truth (Cfr. Cannon 1744)."[578] The above instructions from the Holy Office under the official seal of the Vatican proves that the Roman Catholic Church is actively engaging in a criminal conspiracy to aid and abet their priests in concealing their criminal sexual conduct in order to avoid criminal prosecution. Larry Drivon, a lawyer who represents victims of sexual abuse by priests, accurately characterized the instructions as "an instruction manual on how to deceive and how to protect pedophiles, and exactly how to avoid the truth coming out."[579] Drivon has concluded that the Vatican's conduct constitutes "racketeering."

The Catholic Church will do anything to conceal the criminality of its predatory priests, even to the point of obstructing justice by destroying evidence of the criminal sexual conduct of its priests. The Washington Post reported: "In a controversial 1990 speech before the Midwest Canon Law Society, Cleveland Auxiliary Bishop A. James Quinn advised church leaders to purge these archives, destroying all 'unsigned letters alleging misconduct.' The most explosive of the reports, Quinn advised, should be handed to the papal nunciature in the United States, which has diplomatic immunity. 'Standard personnel files,' Quinn said, 'should contain no documentation relating to possible criminal behavior.'"[580]

Make no mistake about it, the behavior of the Roman Catholic Church in transferring confirmed criminal sexual pedophile priests to new unsuspecting churches, knowing full well that they would continue their criminal abominations against other children, is criminal. The pervasive and continual pattern of such aiding and abetting of criminal pedophiles compounded by extraordinary efforts to conceal records and other evidence of their criminality can only be properly described as organized crime. "A well-known Minnesota plaintiffs attorney, Jeffrey Anderson, recently filed three civil racketeering lawsuits, arguing that the Catholic Church acts like an ecclesiastical crime family. The bishops, in his telling, cover up for pedophile priests by moving them from state to state to avoid detection. He named a star defendant in one case: the Holy See. 'They've used papal immunity to conceal documents, and that evidence leads us to the Vatican,' Anderson said. 'If they're going to act like mobsters, we'll go after them like the mafia.'"[581]

According to the Holy See's chief exorcist, the worldwide sex scandal perpetrated by the Vatican is evidence that "the Devil is at work inside the Vatican."[582] Richard Owen, a reporter for The Times, reported:

> Father Gabriele Amorth, 85, who has been the Vatican's chief exorcist for 25 years and says he has dealt with 70,000 cases of demonic possession, said that the consequences of satanic infiltration included power struggles at the Vatican as well as "cardinals who do not believe in Jesus, and bishops who are linked to the Demon."
>
> He added: "When one speaks of 'the smoke of Satan' [a phrase coined by Pope Paul VI in 1972] in the holy rooms, it is all true – including these latest stories of violence and paedophilia."
>
> He claimed that another example of satanic behaviour was the Vatican "cover-up" over the deaths in 1998 of Alois Estermann, the then commander of the Swiss Guard, his wife and Corporal Cedric Tornay, a Swiss Guard, who were all found shot dead. "They covered up everything immediately," he said. "Here one sees the rot".
>
> A remarkably swift Vatican investigation concluded that Corporal Tornay had shot the commander and his wife and then turned his gun on himself after being passed over for a medal. However Tornay's relatives have challenged this. There

have been unconfirmed reports of a homosexual background to the tragedy and the involvement of a fourth person who was never identified.[583]

We don't need a Vatican official to instruct us on the presence of Satan in the Vatican. Satan's presence is clear. The Holy Bible tells us "Beware of false prophets, which come to you in sheep's clothing, but inwardly they are ravening wolves. Ye shall know them by their fruits." Matthew 7:15-16. The horrible pederastic acts of the ravenous priests is the sour fruit of the institutionalized witchcraft of the Roman Catholic Church. The pervasive abominable acts of the priests prove that the Catholic tree is corrupt to its very root. It cannot bring forth good fruit, because there is no good in it. It is good only for destruction, which God has planned for it.

> A corrupt tree bringeth forth evil fruit. A good tree cannot bring forth evil fruit, neither can a corrupt tree bring forth good fruit. Every tree that bringeth not forth good fruit is hewn down, and cast into the fire. Wherefore by their fruits ye shall know them. Matthew 7:17-20.

Those ungodly Roman priests and Orthodox Jewish rabbis are brute beasts being led by their lusts into destruction. The priests and rabbis should heed the warnings of God. God destroyed Sodom and Gomorrha as a warning to those who would follow the ungodly example of the inhabitants of those two abominable cities:

> **[T]urning the cities of Sodom and Gomorrha into ashes condemned *them* with an overthrow, making *them* an ensample unto those that after should live ungodly**; And delivered just Lot, vexed with the filthy conversation of the wicked: (For that righteous man dwelling among them, in seeing and hearing, vexed *his* righteous soul from day to day with *their* unlawful deeds;) The Lord knoweth how to deliver the godly out of temptations, and **to reserve the unjust unto the day of judgment to be punished: But chiefly them that walk after the flesh in the lust of uncleanness**, and despise government. **Presumptuous *are* they**, **selfwilled**, they are not afraid to speak evil of dignities. Whereas angels, which are greater in power and might, bring not railing accusation against them before the Lord. But these, **as natural brute beasts, made to be taken and destroyed**, speak evil of the things that they understand not; and shall utterly perish in their own corruption; And shall receive the reward of unrighteousness, *as* they that count it pleasure to riot in the day time. Spots *they are* and blemishes, sporting themselves with their own deceivings while they feast with you; **Having eyes full of adultery, and that cannot cease from sin; beguiling unstable souls: an heart they have exercised with covetous practices; cursed children: Which have forsaken the right way, and are gone astray, following the way of Balaam *the son* of Bosor, who loved the wages of unrighteousness**; But was rebuked for his iniquity: the dumb ass speaking with man's voice forbad the madness of the prophet. These are wells without water, clouds that are carried with a tempest; to whom the mist of darkness is reserved for ever. **For when they**

speak great swelling *words* of vanity, they allure through the lusts of the flesh, *through much* wantonness, those that were clean escaped from them who live in error. While they promise them liberty, they themselves are the servants of corruption: for of whom a man is overcome, of the same is he brought in bondage. For if after they have escaped the pollutions of the world through the knowledge of the Lord and Saviour Jesus Christ, they are again entangled therein, and overcome, the latter end is worse with them than the beginning. For it had been better for them not to have known the way of righteousness, than, after they have known *it*, to turn from the holy commandment delivered unto them. But it is happened unto them according to the true proverb, **The dog *is* turned to his own vomit again; and the sow that was washed to her wallowing in the mire.** (2 Peter 2:6-22 AV), *see also* Jude 1:7-16.

The hierarchy of the Catholic Church and Orthodox Jewry have attempted to cover up many of the allegations of rabbinic and priestly wrongdoing, despite irrefutable evidence of guilt. The Catholic moral teachings permit such false denials and coverups. Lesson 17, "The Love and Service of Man," from *The Catholic Religion* published by the Catholic Enquiry Center contains the following Catholic moral guidance:

> It is lawful sometimes to conceal the truth or part of it. There are occasions when it would be harmful to oneself or others to tell the whole truth. It is not sinful to make ambiguous statements to make mental reservations on certain issues as when a person is bound by secrecy, or is questioned by one who has no right to certain information.[584]

One of the Jesuit oaths taken by an initiate Jesuit is as follows:

> In the name of Christ crucified, **I swear to burst the bonds that yet unite me to father, mother, brothers, sisters, relations, friends ; to the King, magistrates, and any other authority, to which I may ever have sworn fealty, obedience, gratitude, or service.** I renounce. . . . the place of my birth, henceforth to exist in another sphere. I swear to reveal to my new superior, whom I desire to know, what I have done, thought, read, learnt, or discovered, and to observe and watch all that comes under my notice. I swear to yield myself up to my superior, as if I were a corpse, deprived of life and will. I finally swear to flee temptation, and to reveal all I succeed in discovering, well aware that lightning is not more rapid and ready than the dagger to reach me wherever I may be.[585]

The Jews have a similar ethic of deception, which they have formalized. The "Kol Nidre" (All Vows) prayer, which is regarded as a Jewish law. It is recited each year on the eve of the Day of Atonement. Through reciting the Kol Nidre Jews are given divine dispensation from all obligations acquired under oaths, vows and pledges to be made or taken in the coming year. Benjamin Freedman reveals that oaths, vows and pledges made or taken by Jews are done so with tongue in cheek for twelve months following the recital of the Kol Nidre.[586] Kol Nidre raises questions about the veracity of testimony of any religious Jew in any legal proceeding.

God, on the other hand, has a stricter standard for honesty.

> These six *things* doth the LORD hate: yea, seven *are* an abomination unto him: A proud look, **a lying tongue**, and hands that shed innocent blood, An heart that deviseth wicked imaginations, feet that be swift in running to mischief, **A false witness *that* speaketh lies**, and he that soweth discord among brethren. (Proverbs 6:16-19 AV)

> **Lying lips *are* abomination to the LORD**: but they that deal truly *are* his delight. (Proverbs 12:22 AV)

> But the fearful, and unbelieving, and the abominable, and murderers, and whoremongers, and sorcerers, and idolaters, and **all liars, shall have their part in the lake which burneth with fire and brimstone: which is the second death**. (Revelation 21:8 AV)

The abominable pederasty among orthodox Jewry and within the Roman church is the bitter fruit that identifies them both as the harlot children of the mysterious "BABYLON THE GREAT, THE MOTHER OF HARLOTS AND ABOMINATIONS OF THE EARTH." Revelation 17:5.

17 Pope = High Priest

The Vatican College of Cardinals is the Roman Catholic version of the Jewish Sanhedrin. The College of Cardinals, like the Sanhedrin, has traditionally had 71 members. However, that number has been expanded in modern times. The members of the College of Cardinals are called Cardinals for a reason. Cardinal means "**Chief**, principal, preeminent, or fundamental."[587] The Catholic Cardinals fill the office of the Jewish "**Chief**" Priests who, along with the scribes and elders, were members of the Sanhedrin. The Sanhedrin selected the High Priest[588] who was the head of the Sanhedrin, just as the Cardinals select a Pope who is the head of the College of Cardinals. The seventy-first member of the Sahehdrin is the High Priest.[589] The Catholic corollary to the High Priest is the Pope, who as head has traditionally been the seventy-first member of the College of Cardinals.[590]

In addition to his other priestly responsibilities, the high priest's principal duty was to perform the service on the Day of Atonement. On the Day of Atonement he entered the holy of holies in the Jewish Temple to make expiation for the people by sprinkling blood of the animal sacrifice on the mercy seat.[591] Hebrews 9:7.

Recall that it was the Jewish High Priest who had Jesus arrested and condemned to death.

> But he held his peace, and answered nothing. Again the high priest asked him, and said unto him, Art thou the Christ, the Son of the Blessed? And Jesus said, I am: and ye shall see the Son of man sitting on the right hand of power, and coming in the clouds of heaven. **Then the high priest rent his clothes, and saith, What need we any further witnesses? Ye have heard the blasphemy: what think ye? And they all condemned him to be guilty of death.** And some began to spit on him, and to cover his face, and to buffet him, and to say unto him, Prophesy: and the servants did strike him with the palms of their hands. (Mark 14:61-65 AV)

With the destruction of the temple on or about 70 A.D. there was no more need for an earthly high priest; no temple, no high priest. There has not been a Temple high priest since the destruction of the Temple. The Temple was destroyed by God using the Roman army because there was no need for the symbolic animal blood atonement, since Christ who was the real lamb of God as the actual atonement sacrificed once for all time. Hebrews 9:8-9. There is no more need for continual animal sacrifices and thus no need for an earthly High Priest.

> But Christ being come an high priest of good things to come, by a greater and more perfect tabernacle, not made with hands, that is to say, not of this building; Neither by the blood of goats and calves, but by his own blood he entered in once into the holy place, having obtained eternal redemption *for us*." (Hebrews 9:11-12 AV)

Jesus is now our High Priest in the holy of holies in heaven. Hebrews 4:14.

> **For Christ is not entered into the holy places made with hands, *which are* the figures of the true; but into heaven itself, now to appear in the presence of God for us**: Nor yet that he should offer himself often, as the high priest entereth into the holy place every year with blood of others; For then must he often have suffered since the foundation of the world: but now once in the end of the world hath **he appeared to put away sin by the sacrifice of himself**. And as it is appointed unto men once to die, but after this the judgment: So **Christ was once offered to bear the sins of many**; and unto them that look for him shall he appear the second time without sin unto salvation." (Hebrews 9:24-28 AV)

There is a Temple mentioned in scripture. It is a Temple wherein the antichrist is seated.

> Let no man deceive you by any means: for *that day shall not come*, except there come a falling away first, and that man of sin be revealed, the son of perdition; **Who opposeth and exalteth himself above all that is called God, or that is worshipped; so that he as God sitteth in the temple of God, shewing himself that he is God.** (2 Thessalonians 2:3-4 AV)

What is the temple of God? It is not a physical temple. Each saved Christian individually and all saved Christians corporately make up the temple of God.

> Know ye not that **ye are the temple of God**, and *that* the Spirit of God dwelleth in you? If any man defile the temple of God, him shall God destroy; for **the temple of God is holy, which *temple* ye are**. (1 Corinthians 3:16-17 AV)

> What? know ye not that **your body is the temple of the Holy Ghost** *which is* in you, which ye have of God, and ye are not your own? For ye are bought with a price: therefore glorify God in your body, and in your spirit, which are God's. (1 Corinthians 6:19-20 AV)

> In whom all the **building fitly framed together groweth unto an holy temple in the Lord**: (Ephesians 2:21 AV)

Who is it that sits in God's temple claiming the authority of God. None other than the Pope of Rome. The Pope claims that he is the head of the Catholic church. Catholic church means universal church.[592] God, not the Pope, is the head of the universal church.

The leader of the Roman Catholic organization, the pope, has claimed that not only is he the leader of the Roman Catholics, but that he is also the head of the true church of God, including Protestant Christians, whom he refers to as "separated brethren." He boldly claims that entrance into Heaven is dependant on submission to his authority.

> **We declare, state and define that it is absolutely necessary for the salvation of all human beings that they submit to the Roman Pontiff.** *Bull Unum Sanctum,* Pope Boniface VIII, 1302.

Such a doctrine reveals the Pope as the antichrist. Pope Bonface VIII implied by the statement in *Bull Unum Sanctum* that he holds the position and authority of God Almighty. Further on you will read where the Pope expressly claims the authority of God. Jesus, however, made it clear that he, being God, was the only way to heaven.

> Jesus saith unto him, **I am the way, the truth, and the life: no man cometh unto the Father, but by me.** (John 14:6 AV)

> This is the stone which was set at nought of you builders, which is become the head of the corner. **Neither is there salvation in any other: for there is none other name under heaven given among men, whereby we must be saved.** (Acts 4:11-12 AV)

Not only has the pope claimed the authority to save but he also claims to sit in place of Almighty God with equal authority and infallibility of the Lord Jesus Christ.[593] Not just in spiritual matters but in all matters. The pope claims power over the governments of the earth. During the coronation ceremony the Pope is crowned with these words: "Take thou the tiara adorned with the triple crown, and know that thou art the father of princes and kings and the governor of the world"[594]

> The Roman Pontiff judges all man, but is judged by no one. We declare, assert, define and pronounce: to be subject to the Roman Pontiff is to every human creature altogether necessary for salvation. . . . That which was spoken of Christ . . . . 'Thou hast subdued all things under His feet,' may well seem verified in me. **I have the authority of the King of kings. I am all in all and above all, so that God, Himself and I, The Vicar of God, have but one consistory, and I am able to do almost all that God can do. What therefore, *can* you make of me**

but God. *The Bull Sanctum*, November 18, 1302 (emphasis added).[595]

[W]e hold upon this earth the place of God Almighty. *Pope Leo XIII* (emphasis added).[596]

This one and unique Church, therefore, has not two heads, like a monster, but one body and one head, viz., Christ and his **vicar**, Peter's successor. *Bull Unum Sanctum,* Pope Boniface VIII, 1302 (emphasis added).

[T]he Roman pontiff possess **primacy over the whole world**; and that the Roman pontiff is the successor of Blessed Peter, Prince of the Apostles, and is true **Vicar** of Christ, and Head of the whole Church, and **Father** and Teacher of all Christians; and that full power was given to him in Blessed Peter by Jesus Christ our Lord, to **rule**, feed and govern the universal Church. . . . **This is the teaching of Catholic truth, from which no one can deviate without loss of faith and of salvation**. And since, by the divine right of Apostolic primacy, one Roman pontiff is placed over the universal Church, We further teach and declare that he is the **supreme judge** of the faithful . . . none may reopen the judgment of the Apostolic See, than whose authority there is no greater. *The Vatican Council*, Session IV, chapter III, July 18, 1870 (emphasis added).

[R]oyal power derives from the Pontifical authority.[597] *Pope Innocent III.*

[T]emporal power should be subject to the spiritual.[598] *Pope Boniface VII.*

The pope claims primacy over the whole world, but when the disciples asked Jesus who is the greatest in the Kingdom of heaven, Jesus did not say "Peter." He said whoever humbles himself as a little child shall be the greatest. *See* Matthew 18:1-4. Christ is the head of the church, not Peter or his alleged successor, the pope. *See* Ephesians 5:23.

The pope considers himself the vicar of Christ. What does it mean to be a vicar? The word vicar means one who acts in place of another. We derive the English word vice from vicar. For example the Vice President acts in place of the President during those times when the President himself cannot act. The Bible talks about one who would come and deceive the world into believing that he is in place of Christ. He is identified as the **antichrist.** The pope himself is acknowledging that he is the antichrist by claiming to be the vicar of Christ. Vicar of Christ means antichrist. Noah Webster defined the prefix "anti" as a preposition meaning not only against but also in place of the noun it follows.[599] The Oxford English Dictionary[600] defines "anti" as meaning "opposite, against, in exchange, instead, representing, rivaling, simulating." Antichrist means one who is against Christ and at the same time purports to take the place of Christ. **Therefore, vicar of Christ = antichrist.**

Is there one who Jesus promised would act in his name? Yes, the Holy Ghost, not the pope of Rome!

> These things have I spoken unto you, being *yet* present with you. **But the Comforter, *which is* the Holy Ghost, whom the Father will send in my name, he shall teach you all things, and bring all things to your remembrance, whatsoever I have said unto you**. (John 14:25-26 AV)

> Nevertheless I tell you the truth; It is expedient for you that I go away: for **if I go not away, the Comforter will not come unto you; but if I depart, I will send him unto you**. (John 16:7 AV)

Jesus warned his disciples time and again about many who would come in his name.

> And Jesus answered and said unto them, Take heed that no man deceive you. For **many shall come in my name, saying, I am Christ**; and shall deceive many. (Matthew 24:4-5 AV)

Pope John Paul II made an incredible claim: that the Pope is the fulfilment of Christ's promise that he will be with us until the end of the world. John Paul II says that Jesus is personally present in his church, implying that Jesus is present through the Pope. As we see from the above passages in John 14:25-26 and 16:7, the fulfillment of that prophecy in Matthew is through the presence of the Holy Spirit, who dwells in all believers. The Pope is essentially claiming to be both Jesus and the Holy Spirit.

> Once again, concerning names: The Pope is called the 'Vicar of Christ.' This title should be considered within the entire context of the Gospel. Before ascending into heaven, Jesus said to the apostles: 'I am with you always, until the end of the age' (Matthew 28:20). Though invisible, He is personally present in His Church." *Pope John Paul II.*[601]

The Pope even takes the title of God the Father. For example, the *Catechism of the Catholic Church*, at § 10 refers to Pope John II as the "Holy Father, Pope John II." The pope goes by other majestic titles such as "Your Holiness." Pope John Paul II, himself, admitted that such titles are inimical to the Gospel. He even cited the Bible passage that condemns such practices. He simply explained that the Catholic traditions of men implicitly authorize this violation of God's commands.

> Have no fear when people call me the 'Vicar of Christ,' when they say to me 'Holy Father,' or 'Your Holiness,' or use titles similar to these, which seem even inimical to the Gospel. Christ declared: 'Call no one on earth your father; you have one Father in heaven. Do not be called 'Master;' you have but one master, the Messiah' (Mt 23:9-10). These expressions, nevertheless, have evolved out of a long tradition, becoming part of common usage. One must not be afraid of these

words either. *Pope John Paul II.*[602]

The term "Holy Father" was used in the Holy Scripture only one time, it was used by Jesus the night before his crucifixion to refer to God the Father. Implicit in taking God's name is taking his position and authority. As Jesus said in John 14:28, God the Father is greater than Jesus. By taking the title "Holy Father," the Pope is implicitly presenting himself as greater than Jesus Christ.

> And now I am no more in the world, but these are in the world, and I come to thee. **Holy Father**, keep through thine own name those whom thou hast given me, that they may be one, as we *are*. (John 17:11 AV)

> Ye have heard how I said unto you, I go away, and come *again* unto you. If ye loved me, ye would rejoice, because I said, I go unto the Father: for **my Father is greater than I.** (John 14:28 AV)

The very title "Pope" is a Latin word which means papa. It is the term used by small children to refer to their father. It is the Latin equivalent of "dada" or "daddy." In Aramaic Hebrew "papa" would be translated "abba." Abba is used 3 times in the Holy Bible. Each time abba refers to God the Father.

> And he said, **Abba, Father**, all things *are* possible unto thee; take away this cup from me: nevertheless not what I will, but what thou wilt. (Mark 14:36 AV)

> For ye have not received the spirit of bondage again to fear; but ye have received the Spirit of adoption, whereby we cry, **Abba, Father**. (Romans 8:15 AV)

> And because ye are sons, God hath sent forth the Spirit of his Son into your hearts, crying, **Abba, Father**. (Galatians 4:6 AV)

Note the trusting humility connoted in the above passages. The Pope of Rome wants his subjects to humble themselves before him as trusting children. He is the papa of their faith. He has taken the name that is rightfully God's in his attempt to turn men from God to him.   The Pope not only desires submission to his authority, but it is not uncommon for the Pope to humiliate his subjects by requiring them to kiss his feet.[603]

> Whosoever therefore shall humble himself as this little child, the same is greatest in the kingdom of heaven. (Matthew 18:4 AV)

> Verily I say unto you, Whosoever shall not receive the kingdom of God as a little child, he shall not enter therein. (Mark 10:15 AV)

The Romans were in general tolerant of the religions of other cultures as long as they were approved by the state. Rome had a council of priests which had charge of Rome's religious activities and passed on the acceptability of any religious belief.[604] The members of this early ecumenical council were called pontiffs.[605] Pontiff means bridge maker. The pontiffs considered themselves intermediaries between God (or the gods as the case may have been) and man.[606] Around 31 B.C. Caesar Augustus declared himself head of the council of priests.[607] Thereafter, the emperor of Rome was considered the Supreme Pontiff (*Pontifex Maximus*), [608] which was the high priest of the pagan religions of Rome.[609] He was also worshiped as a god.[610] The Roman Pontiff did not tolerate anyone who worshiped a god other than him. Consequently, Christians were persecuted for following the true God, Jesus

Where did Caesar get his concept of *Potifex Maximus*? When Rome conquered Britain, it borrowed many of the Druid customs. Caesar Augustus declared himself head of the council of priests (*Pontifex Maximus*), in imitation of the office of the Arch-Druid. Where did the Druids obtain their religious customs? Hislop explains that "[t]he Druidic system in all its parts was evidently the Babylonian system."[611]

When the Jews decided to create a rival to the Christian Church, they inculcated their paganized version of "Christianity" with the Babylonian theology. It was an easy step to graft onto their Roman Church the office of Supreme Pontiff. The Pope is the successor to that pagan office and to this day claims the title of Supreme Pontiff. He even wears a triple crown, because he claims to rule as king over Heaven, Hell, and Earth. Hislop explains the Babylonian origins of this office of Supreme Pontiff:

> I have said that the Pope became the representative of Janus, who, it is evident, was none other than the Babylonian Messiah. If the reader only considers the blasphemous assumptions of the Papacy, he will see how exactly it has copied from its original. In the countries where the Babylonian system was most thoroughly developed, we find the Sovereign Pontiff of the Babylonian god invested with the very attributes now ascribed to the Pope. Is the Pope called "God upon earth," the "Vice-God," and "Vicar of Jesus Christ"? The King in Egypt, who was Sovereign Pontiff, was, says Wilkinson, regarded with the highest reverence as "THE REPRESENTATIVE OF THE DIVINITY ON EARTH."[612]

18 Infallibility

The Roman Catholic Church claims that the teaching office of the Catholic Church, which is known as the *Magisterium of the Church*, has **sole** authority to interpret the word of God.

> The task of giving an **authentic interpretation of the Word of God**, whether in its written form or in the form of Tradition, has been **entrusted to the living, teaching office of the church alone**. Its authority in this matter is exercised in the name of Jesus Christ. This means that the task of the interpretation has been entrusted to the bishops in communion with the successor of Peter, the bishop of Rome. *CATECHISM OF THE CATHOLIC CHURCH*, § 85 (1994) (emphasis added).

Where did the Jews get the idea of the *Magisterium of the Church* to inject into the Catholic theology? The *Magisterium of the Church* is the Catholic corollary to the Jewish Talmud. In Orthodox Judaism, the Talmud, which contains the oral traditions of the Jews, is the authoritative statement on what the Scriptures mean. Jewish scholar Hyam Macoby states that "anyone who does not study the Talmud cannot understand scripture."[613] The Talmud teaches that there is no merit to studying the bible; however, there is merit and reward for studying the Talmud.[614]

Not only does the Catholic Church claim sole authority to interpret the word of God, but claims that the Pope's interpretation is **infallible**.

> [T]his See of Saint Peter remains ever **free from all blemish of error** . . it is a dogma divinely revealed: that the Roman Pontiff, when he speaks *ex cathedra*, that is, when, in discharge of the office of pastor of all Christians, by virtue of his **supreme Apostolic authority**, he defines a doctrine regarding faith or morals to be held by the universal Church, is, by the divine assistance promised to him in Blessed Peter, possessed of that **infallibility** with which the divine Redeemer willed that His Church should be endowed in defining doctrine regarding faith or morals; and that, therefore, such definitions of the Roman Pontiff are of

themselves, and not from the consent of the church, irreformable. **But if anyone -
which may God avert! - presume to contradict this our definition, let him be
anathema**. *The Vatican Council*, Session IV, chapter IV, July 18, 1870 (emphasis
added).

Hislop explains that the doctrine of infallibility of the pope is derived from the heathen
religion of Babylon (Chaldea).

> Is the Pope "Infallible," and does the Church of Rome, in consequence, boast that
> it has always been "unchanged and unchangeable"? The same was the case with
> the Chaldean Pontiff, and the system over which he presided. The Sovereign
> Pontiff, says the writer just quoted, was believed to be "INCAPABLE OF
> ERROR," and, in consequence, there was "the greatest respect for the sanctity of
> old edicts"; and hence, no doubt, also the origin of the custom that "the laws of the
> Medes and Persians could not be altered." Does the Pope receive the adorations of
> the Cardinals? The king of Babylon, as Sovereign Pontiff, was adored in like
> manner.[615]

The infallibility of religious pronouncements made by men flowed from Babylon to
Orthodox Judaism and in turn to the Roman Church. Orthodox Jews view the Jewish traditions
contained in the Talmud as infallible. How can the Talmud, which are written commentaries of
men, be considered infallible? Because, according to the Orthodox Jewish religion, God gave
the oral law, later memorialized in the Talmud, to Moses at Mt. Sinai.[616] In essence, Orthodox
Jews believe that the Talmud is the very word of God. By that definition, therefore, the Talmud
it is considered infallible.

Johann Andreas Eisenmenger, citing the Talmud Tractate *Gittin*, reveals that rabbis consider
themselves as having the status of kings and therefore "whatever they say, right or wrong must be
true because they say it."[617] The rabbis are not satisfied with simply having the authority of a
king; they also claim divine authority. Eisenmenger cites the Talmud Tractate *Barachoth* and
explains that "[t]he Jews are taught that the company of a Rabbin at their tables is to be looked as
a visit of the Divine Being."[618] Just as with the continuing pronouncements of the Pope, the
continuing pronouncements of the Rabbinic Council (*Beth Din*) are considered infallible.
Michael Hoffman explains that according to the Babylonian Talmud "[t]he decrees of the
Rabbinic council (*Beth Din*) are not to be questioned, and have equal authority with Moses."[619]

As with the pronouncements of the Jewish *Beth Din*, the pronouncements of the Popes are
not to be questioned. According to the Canon Law of the Roman Catholic Church: "**There is
neither appeal nor recourse against a decision or decree of the Roman Pontiff.**"[620]

The pronouncements of the Popes are purported to be infallible and irreformable. What
better evidence that Papal decrees are not in fact infallible than a Pope infallibly refuting the
doctrine of Papal infallibility. In 1324 Pope John XXII issued Papal Bull *Qui Quorundam,* in

which he stated that Papal infallibility is "the work of the devil."[621] Obviously, the Catholic Church cannot have it both ways. The Romish church simply ignores the embarrassing, but officially infallible, Papal Bull *Qui Quorundam*.

An examination of the history of the Catholic Church establishes beyond any doubt that the pronouncements of the popes cannot be infallible. There is a long Catholic history of popes contradicting one another on issues of faith and morals.   For example, Pope Hadrian II (867-872) declared civil marriages to be valid, whereas Pope Pius VII (1800-1823) condemned civil marriages as being invalid.[622]

Pope Sixtus V had a version of the bible prepared which he declared to be authentic. However, just two years later Pope Clement VII declared that Sixtus V's bible was full of errors; Clement then ordered another bible to be written.[623]

In 1423 the Council of Basel deposed Pope Eugenius IV, ruling that he was a perjurer, simoniac, and heretic. Pope Eugenius IV in turn summoned his own council at Florence and deposed, anathematized, and excommunicated the members of the Council of Basel. The next pope, Nicholas V (1447-55), voided the decrees of Eugenius against the Council of Basel.[624]

Pope Honorius I was denounced in 680 by the Sixth Council as a heretic, that finding was confirmed by Pope Leo II.[625] How can a Pope be infallible if he is infallibly judged to be a heretic by another Pope? In addition, upon what authority can a subsequent Pope rule that his predecessor is a heretic if the official teaching of the Roman Church is that all Popes are free of error and anyone who says otherwise is anathema? Incidently, all of the above popes are on the Roman Catholic official list of popes.

The most bizarre example of Papal fallibility is the trial and conviction of Pope Formosus (891-896) as a heretic by Pope Stephen VI (896-897). Pope Formosus died before Pope Stephen VI became Pope. How, you may ask, could Pope Stephen VI put Pope Formosus on trial, if Pope Formosus died before Pope Stephen VI became Pope? The grave is no barrier to the Popes! Pope Stephen VI simply had Formosus' body exhumed, clothed the body in papal regalia, and personally interrogated the corpse. The silence of the accused sealed his fate, and the body was dragged through the streets of Rome and thrown in the Tiber.[626]

Another disturbing illustration of pontifical fallibility is the treatment of Joan of Arc. On May 30, 1431 Pope Eugenius IV had Joan of Arc burned at the stake in the public square of Rouen, France as a heretic and a witch for refusing to submit to the authority of the Roman Catholic Church.[627] She declared that she was responsible only to God. Subsequently, Joan of Arc was beatified by Pope Pius X in 1909 and canonized by Pope Benedict XV in 1920.[628] One infallible pope burned Joan of Arc at the stake as a heretic and another infallible pope canonized her as a saint.

Part and parcel of the doctrine of infallibility is the Catholic the doctrine that Peter is the rock upon which Christ built his church. The 1994 Catechism of the Catholic Church, §§ 881-882 summarizes the official doctrine of the Catholic Church that Peter is the rock upon which God has built his church, and that the Pope as the bishop of Rome is Peter's successor as the vicar of Christ. The Holy Bible, to the contrary, states that the headship of the church is reserved to Christ alone. "[H]e is the head of the body, the church: who is the beginning, the firstborn from the dead; that in all things he might have the preeminence." (Colossians 1:18 AV)

Christ will not share his glory nor his authority nor his station with anyone. Christ has preeminence in all things. "For thou shalt worship no other god: for the LORD, whose name is Jealous, is a jealous God." (Exodus 34:14 AV) The Old Testament prophecies of the coming Christ indicate that the cornerstone of the church is to be a heavenly stone that is cut out without hands, and the church will grow from this stone to become a large spiritual mountain and fill the earth. *See* Daniel 2:34-45. This prophesied rock is Christ. For a man to claim to be the rock of the church is to claim to be Christ, because the Bible makes clear that Christ is the rock, the head of the church. To falsely claim to be Christ, the head of the church, fulfills the prophecies that identify the antichrist.

"Let no man deceive you by any means: for that day shall not come, except there come a falling away first, and that man of sin be revealed, the son of perdition; **Who opposeth and exalteth himself above all that is called God, or that is worshipped; so that he as God sitteth in the temple of God, shewing himself that he is God.**" (2 Thessalonians 2:3-4 AV)

"And the king shall do according to his will; and **he shall exalt himself, and magnify himself above every god, and shall speak marvellous things against the God of gods,** and shall prosper till the indignation be accomplished: for that that is determined shall be done. Neither shall he regard the God of his fathers, nor the desire of women, nor regard any god: for **he shall magnify himself above all.**" (Daniel 11:36-37 AV)

There is only one head of the church; the church is not a monster with two heads. To claim to be the rock of the church is to implicitly deny that Jesus is the rock of the church. To deny that Jesus is the rock is to deny that Jesus is Christ. Denying that Jesus is the Christ is a doctrine specifically identified in 1 John 2:22-23 as a teaching of the antichrist.

"Who is a liar but he that denieth that Jesus is the Christ? He is antichrist, that denieth the Father and the Son. Whosoever denieth the Son, the same hath not the Father: (but) he that acknowledgeth the Son hath the Father also." (1 John 2:22-23 AV)

In Matthew 16:16 Peter said that Jesus is the Christ, the Son of the living God. Jesus said that upon that rock he would build his church. That passage, which is often cited by the Catholic Church to support their claim that the pope rules God's church, is not supportive of Peter as the rock, but rather as Christ being the rock. Jesus asks his disciples "whom say ye that I am?" Peter answers that he is "the Christ, the Son of the living God." That answer reveals the rock upon which God would build his church, Jesus Christ and not Peter. By the pope saying that Peter is the rock, he is denying Jesus is the rock, the Christ, the Son of the living God. That papal denial of Christ is a fulfillment of the prophecy found in 1 John 2:22-23, which identifies the antichrist as one who will deny that Jesus is the Christ. The pope's claim, essentially, is that Peter is the rock and hence the Christ and that he, as Peter's purported successor, is also Christ. The Bible reveals that the pope is the antichrist!

"When Jesus came into the coasts of Caesarea Philippi, he asked his disciples, saying, **Whom do men say that I the Son of man am?** And they said, Some *say that thou art* John the Baptist: some, Elias; and others, Jeremias, or one of the prophets. He saith unto them, But **whom say ye that I am?** And Simon Peter answered and said, **Thou art the Christ, the Son of the living God**. And Jesus answered and said unto him, Blessed art thou, Simon Barjona: for flesh and blood hath not revealed *it* unto thee, but my Father which is in heaven. And I say also unto thee, That thou art Peter, and **upon <u>this</u> rock I will build my church**; and the gates of hell shall not prevail against it." (Matthew 16:13-18 AV)

Christ is the head of the church, not Peter! *See* Ephesians 5:23; Colossians 1:18. If Peter is now the rock of God's church, why would Jesus call Peter Satan within moments of making Peter the foundation of the church? The following passage signifies that those who would have Peter as their rock, have someone who savourest the things of man and not of God. "But he turned, and said unto Peter, **Get thee behind me, Satan**: thou art an offence unto me: for thou savourest not the things that be of God, but those that be of men." (Matthew 16:23 AV)

The Holy Spirit further signified that the pope is antichrist by having Peter, as the Catholic Church's first purported pope, start his alleged reign by denying Christ 3 times in fulfillment of the prophecy in 1 John 2:22-23. *See* Matthew 26:31-75.

The rock of the Catholic Church is not God. Their rock is only a man trying to take God's place. "**For their rock *is* not as our Rock**, even our enemies themselves *being* judges. For their vine *is* of the vine of Sodom, and of the fields of Gomorrah: their grapes *are* grapes of gall, their clusters *are* bitter: **Their wine *is* the poison of dragons, and the cruel venom of asps**." (Deuteronomy 32:31-33 AV) "And he shall say, **Where *are* their gods, *their* rock in whom they trusted**." (Deuteronomy 32:37 AV)

Peter, to whom Jesus was talking, clearly understood what Jesus was saying when he said "upon this rock I will build my church." The rock was Jesus. In the following passages Peter repeatedly refers to Jesus as the stone rejected by the builders becoming the head of the corner. Jesus is the only name under heaven that can save one from the eternal punishment of sin, not Peter and not the pope.

"Be it known unto you all, and to all the people of Israel, that by the name of **Jesus Christ of Nazareth**, whom ye crucified, whom God raised from the dead, *even* by him doth this man stand here before you whole. **This is the stone which was set at nought of you builders, which is become the head of the corner. Neither is there salvation in any other: for there is** none other name under heaven given among men, whereby we must be saved." (Acts 4:10-12 AV)

"Wherefore also it is contained in the scripture, **Behold, I lay in Sion a chief corner stone**, elect, precious: and he that believeth on him shall not be confounded. Unto you therefore which believe *he is* precious: but unto them which be disobedient, the stone which the builders disallowed, the same is made the head of the corner, And **a stone of stumbling, and a rock of offence,** *even to them* **which stumble at the word, being disobedient: whereunto also they were appointed**." (1 Peter 2:6-8 AV)

Read through the following passages, and decide for yourself who is the Rock of the Church.

"And did all drink the same spiritual drink: for they drank of that spiritual Rock that followed them: and **that Rock was Christ**." (1 Corinthians 10:4 AV)

"And are built upon the foundation of the apostles and prophets, **Jesus Christ himself being the chief corner** *stone*." (Ephesians 2:20 AV)

"**For other foundation can no man lay than that is laid, which is Jesus Christ.**" (1 Corinthians 3:11 AV)

"My soul, wait thou only upon God; for my expectation *is* from him. **He only** *is* **my rock** and my salvation: *he is* my defence; I shall not be moved." (Psalms 62:5-6 AV)

"**He is the Rock**, his work *is* perfect: for all his ways *are* judgment: a God of truth and without iniquity, just and right *is* he." (Deuteronomy 32:4 AV)

"There is none holy as the LORD: for *there is* none beside thee: **neither** *is there* **any rock like our God**. (1 Samuel 2:2 AV)

"And he said, **The LORD** *is* **my rock**, and my fortress, and my deliverer; The God of my rock; in him will I trust: *he is* my shield, and the horn of my salvation, my high tower, and my refuge, my saviour; thou savest me from violence." (2 Samuel 22:2-3 AV)

"**The LORD** *is* **my rock**, and my fortress, and my deliverer; my God, my strength, in whom I will trust; my buckler, and the horn of my salvation, *and* my high tower." (Psalms 18:2 AV)

"For who *is* God save the LORD? or **who** *is* **a rock save our God**?" (Psalms 18:31 AV)

"Unto thee will I cry, **O LORD my rock**; be not silent to me: lest, *if* thou be silent to me, I become like them that go down into the pit." (Psalms 28:1 AV)

"Bow down thine ear to me; deliver me speedily: **be thou my strong rock**, for an house of defence to save me. For **thou *art* my rock** and my fortress; therefore for thy name's sake lead me, and guide me." (Psalms 31:2-3 AV)

"I will say unto **God my rock**, Why hast thou forgotten me? why go I mourning because of the oppression of the enemy?" (Psalms 42:9 AV)

"From the end of the earth will I cry unto thee, when my heart is overwhelmed: **lead me to the rock *that* is higher than I**." (Psalms 61:2 AV)

"And they remembered that **God *was* their rock**, and the high God their redeemer." (Psalms 78:35 AV)

"He shall cry unto me, **Thou *art* my father, my God, and the rock of my salvation**." (Psalms 89:26 AV)

"But the LORD is my defence; and **my God *is* the rock of my refuge**." (Psalms 94:22 AV)

"O come, let us sing unto the LORD: let us make a joyful noise to **the rock of our salvation**." (Psalms 95:1 AV)

"As it is written, Behold, **I lay in Sion a stumblingstone and rock of offence**: and whosoever believeth on him shall not be ashamed." (Romans 9:33 AV)

"He is like a man which built an house, and digged deep, and **laid the foundation on a rock**: and when the flood arose, the stream beat vehemently upon that house, and could not shake it: for it was founded upon a rock." (Luke 6:48 AV)

"Therefore whosoever heareth these sayings of mine, and doeth them, I will liken him unto a wise man, which **built his house upon a rock**." (Matthew 7:24 AV)

"**The stone *which* the builders refused is become the head *stone* of the corner**." (Psalms 118:22 AV)

"And he shall be for a sanctuary; but for **a stone of stumbling and for a rock of offence** to both the houses of Israel, for a gin and for a snare to the inhabitants of Jerusalem." (Isaiah 8:14 AV)

"Therefore thus saith the Lord GOD, Behold, **I lay in Zion for a foundation a stone, a tried stone, a precious corner *stone*, a sure foundation**: he that believeth shall not make haste." (Isaiah 28:16 AV)

"Jesus saith unto them, Did ye never read in the scriptures, **The stone which the builders**

rejected, the same is become the head of the corner: this is the Lord's doing, and it is marvellous in our eyes? Therefore say I unto you, The kingdom of God shall be taken from you, and given to a nation bringing forth the fruits thereof. And whosoever shall fall on this stone shall be broken: but on whomsoever it shall fall, it will grind him to powder." (Matthew 21:42-44 AV)

The evidence from the Holy Scripture is so clear that even Pope John Paul II, in his 1994 book, Crossing the Threshold of Hope, has found it necessary to admit that Jesus is the Rock upon which God's Church is built. That is just another of the many contradictory pronouncements of the Roman Catholic Church.

By claiming that Peter is the rock, the pope has denied that Jesus is the rock, which is essentially a denial that Jesus is the Christ. The pope has fulfilled the prophesy in 1 John 2:22-23, which states that the antichrist will deny that Jesus is the Christ. Who then does the pope claim is the Christ? The answer is found when we compare what the Holy Bible says about Christ with what the pope has said. What does it mean when we say that Jesus is Christ? It means that he is the one anointed "God with us." In Matthew 1:23, Jesus is identified as "Emmanuel, which being interpreted is, God with us." The pope, however, claims that he is God with us. **"[W]e hold upon this earth the place of God Almighty."** *Pope Leo XIII* (emphasis added). Jesus Christ is "an advocate with the Father" for us. 1 John 2:1. In fact he is the "one mediator between God and men." 1 Timothy 2:5. The pope, however, claims the title of Supreme Pontiff. Pontiff means literally bridge builder; it connotes that the pontiff is one who is a bridge or intermediary between God and man. The pope has stated: "To be subject to the Roman Pontiff is to every human creature altogether necessary for salvation." *The Bull Sanctum*, November 18, 1302. In addition, the Catholic Church teaches that Mary and the saints are advocates before the throne of God for us. "[The saints'] . . . intercession is their most exalted service to God's plan. **We can and should ask them to intercede for us and for the whole world**. *CATECHISM OF THE CATHOLIC CHURCH*, § 2683, 1994." Jesus Christ is the "author and finisher of our faith." Hebrew 12:2. "For by grace are ye saved through faith; and that not of yourselves: *it is* the gift of God: Not of works, lest any man should boast." (Ephesians 2:8-9 AV) The pope, however, states that faith comes from man and it must be joined with works, i.e. started and finished by man, not Jesus. The Catholic Church even teaches that works done after death by others are effective for the salvation of the deceased. "[T]he souls . . . are cleansed after death by purgatorial punishments; and so that they may be relieved from punishments of this kind, namely, the sacrifices of Masses, prayers, and almsgiving, and other works of piety, which are customarily performed by the faithful for other faithful according to the institutions of the Church." COUNCIL OF FLORENCE, 1439. Jesus Christ is the "blessed and only Potentate." 1 Timothy 6:15. Pope Innocent II claimed ownership of the entire universe as the "TEMPORAL SOVEREIGN OF THE UNIVERSE." Pope Boniface VIII pronounced: "**I have the authority of the King of kings. I am all in all and above all, so that God, Himself and I, The Vicar of God, have but one consistory, and I am able to do almost all that God can do. What therefore, *can* you make of me but God.**" *The Bull Sanctum*, November 18, 1302 (emphasis added). Even today the Pope wears a triple crown because he claims to rule as king over the earth, heaven, and the 'lower regions' (hell and the mythical Catholic purgatory). Jesus is higher than the kings of the earth. Psalms 89:27. The pope claims, however, authority over the kings of the earth. "[T]he Roman pontiff possesses **primacy over the whole world**." *The Vatican Council*, Session IV, chapter III, July 18, 1870 (emphasis added). Jesus Christ is the "great high priest" of God almighty. Hebrews 4:14. The pope claims to be the great high priest. As already mentioned above, the pope claims the title of Supreme Pontiff. He is the successor of the emperors of Rome, who were seriatim the Supreme Pontiff (*Pontifex Maximus*), which was the high priest of the heathen religions of Rome. Jesus is "Lord of all." Acts 10:36. The pope, though, claims that all must submit to him: "The Roman Pontiff judges all man, but is judged by no one. We declare, assert, define and pronounce: to be subject to the Roman Pontiff is to every human creature altogether necessary for salvation. . . . That which was spoken of Christ . . . 'Thou hast subdued all things under His feet,' may well seem verified in me." *The Bull Sanctum*, November 18, 1302 (emphasis added). The pope has claimed every attribute of Christ for himself. He has essentially denied that Jesus is the Christ and laid claim himself to being Christ. The Holy Bible identifies such a one as antichrist. 1 John 2:20-23.

The Bible says that the antichrist will deny the Son and, implicitly, deny the Father. 1 John 2:20-23. The pope makes his identity as the antichrist clear by expressly denying the Father. The pope claims the title "Holy Father." *See Catechism of the Catholic Church*, at § 10. Holy Father is a title that appears only once in all the Holy Scriptures and is reserved for God the Father. John 17:11.

19
Mark of the Beast

    The Bible speaks of a beast whose number is the number of a man. "Here is wisdom. Let him that hath understanding count the number of the beast: for it is the number of a man; and his number *is* Six hundred threescore *and* six." (Revelation 13:18 AV) The number is 666. The bible states that 666 is not only the number of a man but also the number of the beast's name. From this we know that the beast is a man whose name adds up to 666.

    The Roman (Latin) letters are also Roman numerals. Latin, which was the official language of Rome and is also the official language of the Roman Catholic Church, is the logical first place to look for this number of the beast.

    One should not be looking for simply three 6's in a row; the number of the beast is the number **"six hundred threescore and six."** That means the beast's name must add up to six hundred sixty six.

    According to *Our Sunday Visitor,* an official Catholic publication, "[t]he letters inscribed in the pope's mitre are these: *Vicarius Filii Dei,* which is the Latin for the Vicar of the Son of God."[629] When a new pope is crowned, it is with the words *"Vicarius Filii Dei."* The official title of the Pope written in classical Latin is ***VICARIVS FILII DEI***. Notice that in classical Latin there is a V just before the S in *vicarius,* rather than a U. That is because there are only 23 letters in the classical Latin alphabet, it does not have the letters U, J, or W as in the English alphabet.[630] The V is used in classical Latin when making the U sound.[631] The values of Roman numerals are: D = 500, C = 100, L = 50, V = 5, I = 1. The values of the Roman numerals found in the Latin title for the Pope added together equals 666. V (used twice, 5 x 2 = 10) + C (100) + I (used 6 times, 1 x 6 = 6) + L (50) + D (500) = **666**.

The ubiquitous Universal Product Code (UPC) symbol contains the number 666 hidden within the lines of the symbol. The UPC depicted on this page is typical of the most common UPC seen on goods in the marketplace of today. The UPC has two sets of numbers. Each set has distinct computer codes that are represented by two parallel lines per number. In the second set of codes, the number 6 is represented by two equally thin parallel lines (ll).

Notice that there are three double lines in the UPC symbol that do not have an Arabic number to identify them. One set of lines are in the middle and there are two other sets of lines, one on each end. Those three sets of lines together represent the number 666. Look at any product in your home and you will see the same hidden code for the number 666.

The numbers that appear on either end of the UPC symbol on this page (6 and 3) correspond to the double line codes that are inside the double line codes for the end 6's. Note that there are two sets of line codes for the numbers 0-9. The first set is to the left of the middle double lines (ll), and the second set is to the right of the middle double lines. The 3 sets of double lines without numbers are always the line codes for the number 6 from the second set of codes. As you will notice, the 6 from the first set of codes is represented by a thin line on the left with a thick line on the right, whereas the line code for 6 from the second set of codes is represented by two thin lines (ll).

Why is it that the only lines that do not have an Arabic number identifying are the lines that together read 666? Because the UPC symbol is part of the groundwork being laid to control the world's commerce. The world's goods are being marked with the number of the beast. It is a hidden code so as not to alarm the slumbering masses. The Bible states that one day people will be marked with a similar code in their right hand or forehead and that refusal to receive the mark will preclude them from being able to buy or sell anything. "And that no man might buy or sell, save he that had the mark, or the name of the beast, or the number of his name." (Revelation 13:17 AV)

The Bible does not state that the mark will be *on* peoples foreheads or *on* their right hands but *in* their right hands or *in* their foreheads. Implantable biochips that are capable of storing several megabytes of data equal to thousands of pages of information have already been developed.[632] These biochips allow the subject to be tracked and identified anywhere in the world. Could the present day UPC, with the hidden 666, be a key necessary to match a corresponding 666 code in an implantable biochip that would then allow a purchase of the item? Could it be that if there is no match, because the person has refused the 666 mark of the beast, then the person cannot purchase the item because "no man might buy or sell," unless he has the mark?

Once the governments of the world implement a mandatory identity card, it would only be a matter of time before the convenience of an implantable chip is accepted. How close are we? The failed Health Security Card proposed by President Clinton was manufactured by Drexler Technology Corporation, Mountain View, California and was in fact a data storage card capable of storing 2,000 pages of information, including fingerprints, voice prints, and pictures.[633]

In the Bible, God explains the consequences of worshiping the beast and receiving his mark:

> And the third angel followed them, saying with a loud voice, If any man worship
> the beast and his image, and receive *his* mark in his forehead, or in his hand,
> The same shall drink of the wine of the wrath of God, which is poured out without
> mixture into the cup of his indignation; and he shall be tormented with fire and
> brimstone in the presence of the holy angels, and in the presence of the Lamb:
> And the smoke of their torment ascendeth up for ever and ever: and they have no
> rest day nor night, who worship the beast and his image, and whosoever receiveth
> the mark of his name. (Revelation 14:9-11 AV)

20

The Magical Transubstantiation
of the Judaic Eucharist

The Catholic Encyclopedia further reveals that the liturgy of the Eucharistic sacrifice during the Catholic Mass is actually a "Christianized" version of the synagogue liturgy:

> The Eucharist was always celebrated at the end of a service of lessons, psalms, prayers, and preaching, which was itself merely a continuation of the service of the synagogue. So we have everywhere this double function; first a synagogue service Christianized, in which the holy books were read, psalms were sung, prayers said by the bishop in the name of all (the people answering "Amen" in Hebrew, as had their Jewish forefathers), and homilies, explanations of what had been read, were made by the bishop or priests, just as they had been made in the synagogues by the learned men and elders (e.g., Luke 4:16-27).[634]

The Roman Catholic Church traces her Eucharistic ceremony directly to the Jewish Talmud. *The Catholic Encyclopedia* states:

> [T]he Eucharist is still joined to the Agape (10:1), the reference to the actual consecration is vague. The likeness between the prayers of thanksgiving (9-10) and the Jewish forms for blessing bread and wine on the Sabbath (given in the "Berakoth" treatise of the Talmud; cf. Sabatier, "La Didache", Paris, 1885, p. 99) points obviously to derivation from them.[635]

In addition, Pope John Paul II has admitted that "the religion of Judaism is 'a response to God's revelation in the Old Covenant' and that the 'Eucharistic prayers' of Christian worship are 'according to the models of Jewish tradition.'"[636]

The Jewish liturgy of the Eucharist in the Roman Catholic Church involves the transubstantiation of bread and wine. This transubstantiation during the Roman mass involves a witchcraft ceremony, during which a piece of bread (the host) and some wine is purported to be transformed into Jesus Christ. It is the official teaching of the church that the host and wine both become the body, blood, soul, and divinity of the Lord God Jesus Christ. The church teaches that the appearance of bread and wine remain, but that they have actually been transubstantiated into a god.

> **In the most blessed sacrament of the Eucharist 'the body and blood, together with the soul and divinity, of our Lord Jesus Christ and, therefore, *the whole Christ is truly, really, and substantially* contained.'** CATECHISM OF THE CATHOLIC CHURCH, § 1374, 1994 (italics in original, bold emphasis added).

The Catholic Church is saying, in no uncertain terms, that Jesus Christ himself, God Almighty, is present during the Catholic mass in the outward form of bread and wine.

> By the consecration the transubstantiation of the bread and wine into the Body and Blood of Christ is brought about. Under the consecrated species of bread and wine **Christ himself, living and glorious, is present in a true, real, and substantial manner: his Body and his Blood, with his soul and his divinity.** CATECHISM OF THE CATHOLIC CHURCH, § 1413, 1994 (emphasis added).

> **Here the pastor should explain that in this Sacrament are contained not only the true body of Christ and all the constituents of a true body, such as bones and sinews, but also Christ whole and entire. He should point out that the word *Christ* designates the God-man, that is to say, one Person in whom are united the divine and human natures; that the Holy Eucharist, therefore, contains both, and humanity whole and entire, consisting of the soul, all the parts of the body and the blood, all of which must be believed to be in this Sacrament. In heaven the whole humanity is united to the Divinity in one hypostasis, or Person; hence it would be impious, to suppose that the body of Christ, which is contained in the Sacrament, is separated from His Divinity.** THE CATECHISM OF THE COUNCIL OF TRENT (emphasis added).[637]

The Catholic doctrine is that during communion Catholics are actually eating God Almighty when they consume the Eucharistic host. "If anyone say that Christ, given in the Eucharist, is eaten spiritually only, and not also sacramentally and really, let him be anathema." COUNCIL OF TRENT, ON THE MOST HOLY SACRAMENT OF THE EUCHARIST, Canon VIII.

The Catholic doctrine of transubstantiation is actually ceremonial witchcraft. William Schnoebelen was a former satanic priest, master Mason, alleged member of the Iluminati, and a Catholic priest in the Old Roman Catholic Church (O.R.C.C.). The O.R.C.C. is a splinter group from the Vatican which has valid holy orders, has celebrated mass for centuries, and allows for a married priesthood.[638] Schnoebelen stated that the Catholic liturgy of the mass is basically an occult magic ritual. It is, therefore, easy for Satanists to tweak it slightly in order to make it into the consummate black magic ritual.[639] Schnoebelen degenerated in his climb up the satanic hierarchy to the point where he became a Nosferatic priest.[640] A Nosferatic priest is a Vampire. *Nosferatu* is the Romanian word for the "undead" or vampire. Since all members of the Nosferatic priesthood must first be priests of the Catholic or Eastern Orthodox Rite, they believe that they have the power to produce the full nine pints of the blood of Jesus contained in the chalice of wine through the magic of transubstantiation. When real human blood was not available to him, he satisfied his demonic need for human blood through the liturgy of the Catholic mass.[641]

Because the Catholic church teaches that the Eucharist is God in the form of bread and wine, it requires that all worship the Eucharist as God. "Because Christ himself is present in the sacrament of the altar, he is to be honored with the worship of adoration." CATECHISM OF THE CATHOLIC CHURCH, § 1418, 1994.

> Wherefore, there is no room left to doubt that all the faithful of Christ may, according to the custom ever received in the Catholic Church, render in veneration the worship of *latria*, which is due to the true God, to this most holy Sacrament. COUNCIL OF TRENT, DECREE CONCERNING THE MOST HOLY SACRAMENT OF THE EUCHARIST, Session XIII, Chapter V, October 11, 1551.

> If anyone saith, in the Holy Sacrament of the Eucharist, Christ, the only-begotten son of God, is not to be adored with the worship, even external, of latria; and is, consequently, neither to be venerated with a special festive solemnity, nor to be solemnly borne about in processions, according to the laudable and universal right and custom of Holy church; or is not to be proposed publicly to the people to be adored, and that the adorers thereof are idolaters; let him be anathema. COUNCIL OF TRENT, ON THE MOST HOLY SACRAMENT OF THE EUCHARIST, Canon VI.

The Catholic Church teaches that wine and bread have been turned into the body and blood of Christ, and that when one is consuming the bread and wine it is only the form of bread and wine, it is actually the body, blood, soul, and divinity of Christ. The Catholic Church teaches that the wine is actually Christ's blood but only appears to be wine, and the bread is actually Christ's flesh but only appears to be bread. The Catholic doctrine of transubstantiation is a sin. In the following passages God has made it clear that people are to abstain from drinking *any manner* of blood. Presumably, any manner of blood means any manner of blood, including transubstantiated blood.

> Moreover ye shall **eat no manner of blood, *whether it be* of fowl or of beast, in any of your dwellings**. Whatsoever soul *it be* that eateth any manner of blood, even that soul shall be cut off from his people. (Leviticus 7:26-27 AV)

> And whatsoever man *there be* of the house of Israel, or of the strangers that sojourn among you, that eateth **any manner of blood; I will even set my face against that soul that eateth blood**, and will cut him off from among his people. (Leviticus 17:10 AV)

> **[A]bstain from meats offered to idols, and from blood**, and from things strangled, and from fornication: from which if ye keep yourselves, ye shall do well. Fare ye well. (Acts 15:29 AV)

The Catholic church quotes the following passage, purporting it to support its claim that during the Catholic mass bread is turned into God.

> And he took bread, and gave thanks, and brake *it*, and gave unto them, saying, This is my body which is given for you: **this do in remembrance of me.** (Luke 22:19 AV)

That passage does not support the proposition that bread is thereafter to be turned into God. Before Christ came to earth, God required ceremonial sacrifices from the Jews. Those sacrifices were done in order to bring to mind the coming messiah. The Jews looked forward to Christ, the sacrificial lamb of God. The Old Testament sacrifices themselves did not atone for the sins. Jesus was the atonement. Salvation from sins came then, as now, by the grace of God through faith in God and his Messiah, Jesus. The memorial instituted by Christ during the last supper was for us to look back to the sacrifice of Christ, just as the Jews used to look forward toward Christ's coming. We are to do it in remembrance of him and his sacrifice for us.

> For the law having a shadow of good things to come, *and* not the very image of the things, can never with those sacrifices which they offered year by year continually make the comers thereunto perfect. For then would they not have ceased to be offered? because that the worshippers once purged should have had no more conscience of sins. **But in those *sacrifices there is* a remembrance again *made* of sins every year. For *it is* not possible that the blood of bulls and of goats should take away sins.** (Hebrews 10:1-4 AV)

> And when he had given thanks, he brake *it*, and said, Take, eat: this is my body, which is broken for you: **this do in remembrance of me.** After the same manner also *he took* the cup, when he had supped, saying, This cup is the new testament in my blood: **this do ye, as oft as ye drink *it*, in remembrance of me. For as often as ye eat this bread, and drink this cup, ye do shew the Lord's death till he come.** (1 Corinthians 11:24-26 AV)

Jesus was using a metaphor, when he said "this is my body" and "this is my blood." He had also called himself the "lamb of God" and "the bread of life." These phrases were intended to be figurative expressions. We don't think of Christ as a literal lamb; why does the Romish church interpret the Jesus' words at the last supper literally?

The Roman church often cites Matthew 26:26-28 in support of its claim that the priest, during the Catholic mass, changes bread and wine into the blood and body of Jesus.

> And as they were eating, Jesus took bread, and blessed *it*, and brake *it*, and gave *it* to the disciples, and said, Take, eat; this is my body. And he took the cup, and gave thanks, and gave *it* to them, saying, Drink ye all of it; For this is my blood of the new testament, which is shed for many for the remission of sins. (Matthew 26:26-28 AV)

Jesus was eating the Passover meal with his disciples. The Passover was intended to be a memorial that was to celebrate God having freed the Jews from Egyptian slavery. The fourteenth day of the first month is the Passover (Leviticus 23:4-5, Exodus 12:17-18). Passover is immediately followed by the seven days of unleavened bread (Leviticus 23:6-7, Exodus 12:15-16). At the last supper Jesus was making reference to the fact that the unleavened bread that was eaten during Passover not only looked back to the spotless lamb of Passover, but also looked forward to him as the Christ, who would die as the Passover lamb for the sins of the world. 1 Peter 1:18-19. Just as the Passover memorial looked back to the Passover lamb, so also would this new Passover last supper harken back to the Passover lamb of God, Jesus Christ, who was crucified for our sins. Just as the unleavened bread eaten on Passover was not the actual lamb, but only a memorial, so also the unleavened bread and wine celebrating the last supper are not the actual body and blood of Jesus; they are only memorials.

The Catholic church teaches that Jesus actually turned the fruit of the vine into blood. By taking verses 26-28 of Matthew chapter 26 out of context the Catholic church has been able to deceive the whole world. All one need do to see that Jesus did not actually change the fruit of the vine in the cup into his blood is to put verses 26-28 back in context by reading the next verse, verse 29. "But I say unto you, I will not drink henceforth of **this fruit of the vine**, until that day when I drink it new with you in my Father's kingdom." (Matthew 26:29 AV) Notice, in that very verse (verse 29) following his statement that "this is my blood" Jesus states plainly that what was in the cup was still the "fruit of the vine." It had not been changed into his blood. Verse 29 reveals that his statement that "this is my blood" was simply a metaphor. That is why the Catholic church does not want the common people to read the Bible. Once the people see the passages in context, they understand the deceptive sophistry of the Catholic church.

The passage found in the Holy Bible at John 6:27-66 explains clearly what Jesus meant when he said "this is my body" and "this is my blood." In that Bible passage Jesus starts out by telling his disciples "labour not for the meat which perisheth, but for that meat which endureth unto everlasting life." That meat is a Spiritual meat. Jesus points out that to eat his flesh and drink his blood is spiritual language that represents believing on him. Only those, however, that are chosen by God for eternal life can understand these truths. Read the passage carefully; you will understand that eating Jesus' flesh and drinking his blood are metaphors for believing in him. Jesus makes the point clear four different times in that passage (verses 29, 35, 40, and 47). One can only understand this spiritual truth if one has the Holy Spirit to guide him. It is foolishness to the unsaved. The unsaved read the passage and are easily persuaded by the Catholic church that Jesus is talking about literally eating his flesh and drinking his blood.

Labour not for the meat which perisheth, but for that meat which endureth unto everlasting life, which the Son of man shall give unto you: for him hath God the Father sealed. Then said they unto him, What shall we do, that we might work the works of God? Jesus answered and said unto them, **This is the work of God, that ye believe on him whom he hath sent**. They said therefore unto him, What sign shewest thou then, that we may see, and believe thee? what dost thou work? Our fathers did eat manna in the desert; as it is written, He gave them bread from heaven to eat. Then Jesus said unto them, Verily, verily, I say unto you, Moses gave you not that bread from heaven; but **my Father giveth you the true bread from heaven. For the bread of God is he which cometh down from heaven, and giveth life unto the world.** Then said they unto him, Lord, evermore give us this bread. **And Jesus said unto them, I am the bread of life: he that cometh to me shall never hunger; and he that believeth on me shall never thirst.** But I said unto you, That ye also have seen me, and believe not. All that the Father giveth me shall come to me; and him that cometh to me I will in no wise cast out. For I came down from heaven, not to do mine own will, but the will of him that sent me. And this is the Father's will which hath sent me, that of all which he hath given me I should lose nothing, but should raise it up again at the last day. **And this is the will of him that sent me, that every one which seeth the Son, and believeth on him, may have everlasting life: and I will raise him up at the last day.** The Jews then murmured at him, because he said, I am the bread which came down from heaven. And they said, Is not this Jesus, the son of Joseph, whose father and mother we know? how is it then that he saith, I came down from heaven? Jesus therefore answered and said unto them, Murmur not among yourselves. No man can come to me, except the Father which hath sent me draw him: and I will raise him up at the last day. It is written in the prophets, And they shall be all taught of God. Every man therefore that hath heard, and hath learned of the Father, cometh unto me. Not that any man hath seen the Father, save he which is of God, he hath seen the Father. **Verily, verily, I say unto you, He that believeth on me hath everlasting life. I am that bread of life.** Your fathers did eat manna in the wilderness, and are dead. **This is the bread which cometh down from heaven, that a man may eat thereof, and not die. I am the living bread which came down from heaven: if any man eat of this bread, he shall live for ever: and the bread that I will give is my flesh, which I will give for the life of the world.** The Jews therefore strove among themselves, saying, How can this man give us *his* flesh to eat? Then Jesus said unto them, Verily, verily, I say unto you,

Except ye eat the flesh of the Son of man, and drink his blood, ye have no life in you. Whoso eateth my flesh, and drinketh my blood, hath eternal life; and I will raise him up at the last day. For my flesh is meat indeed, and my blood is drink indeed. He that eateth my flesh, and drinketh my blood, dwelleth in me, and I in him. As the living Father hath sent me, and I live by the Father: so he that eateth me, even he shall live by me. This is that bread which came down from heaven: not as your fathers did eat manna, and are dead: he that eateth of this bread shall live for ever. These things said he in the synagogue, as he taught in Capernaum. Many therefore of his disciples, when they had heard *this*, said, This is an hard saying; who can hear it? When Jesus knew in himself that his disciples murmured at it, he said unto them, Doth this offend you? *What* and if ye shall see the Son of man ascend up where he was before? It is the spirit that quickeneth; the flesh profiteth nothing: the words that I speak unto you, *they* are spirit, and *they* are life. But there are some of you that believe not. For Jesus knew from the beginning who they were that believed not, and who should betray him. And he said, Therefore said I unto you, that **no man can come unto me, except it were given unto him of my Father**. From that *time* many of his disciples went back, and walked no more with him. (John 6:27-66 AV)

The Catholic church teaches that the bread and wine is to be worshiped with the same veneration that one would feel if one were worshiping God. In fact, the Romish church teaches that the consecrated bread and wine are the most holy sacrament of the church because they are God and are to be worshiped as God.

[I]n the modern Roman Rite the public worship of the Eucharist is envisaged as a normal part of the liturgical life of diocesan, parish and religious communities.[642]

With a delicate and jealous attention the Church has regulated Eucharistic worship to its minutest details. . . . [E]verything is important, significant, and divine when there is a question of the Real Presence of Jesus Christ.[643]

Wherefore, there is no room left to doubt that all the faithful of Christ may, according to the custom ever received in the Catholic Church, **render in veneration the worship of *latria*, which is due to the true God, to this most holy Sacrament**. For not therefore is it the less to be adored on this account, that it was instituted by Christ the Lord in order to be present therein, of Whom the Eternal Father, when introducing Him into the world, says: 'and let all the angels of God adore Him;'Whom the Magi falling down, adored; Who, in fine, as the Scripture testifies, was adored by the Apostles in Galilee. *THE COUNCIL OF TRENT, DECREE CONCERNING THE MOST HOLY SACRAMENT OF THE EUCHARIST, On the Cult and Veneration to be Shown to This Most Holy Sacrament,* October 11, 1554.

Worship of the Eucharist. In the liturgy of the Mass we express our faith in the **real presence of Christ under the species of bread and wine** by, among other ways, **genuflecting or bowing deeply as a sign of adoration** of the Lord. The Catholic Church has always offered and still offers to the sacrament of the Eucharist the cult of **adoration**, not only during Mass, but also outside of it, reserving the consecrated hosts with the utmost care, exposing them to the **solemn veneration** of the faithful, and carrying them in procession." *CATECHISM OF THE CATHOLIC CHURCH*, § 1378, 1994 (italics in original, bold type added).

God, however, has an objection to this Catholic worship of idols.

And God spake all these words, saying, I *am* the LORD thy God, which have brought thee out of the land of Egypt, out of the house of bondage. **Thou shalt have no other gods before me. Thou shalt not make unto thee any graven image, or any likeness** *of any thing* **that** *is* **in heaven above, or that** *is* **in the earth beneath, or that** *is* **in the water under the earth: Thou shalt not bow down thyself to them, nor serve them**: for I the LORD thy God *am* a jealous God, visiting the iniquity of the fathers upon the children unto the third and fourth *generation* of them that hate me; And shewing mercy unto thousands of them that love me, and keep my commandments. (Exodus 20:1-6 AV)

The Catholic Church takes the bible passage found at 1 Corinthians 11:29 out of context to support their position that the wine and bread are miraculously turned into the Lord Jesus during the Catholic mass. The passage reads: "For he that eateth and drinketh unworthily, eateth and drinketh damnation to himself, not discerning the Lord's body."

Looking at the passages that precede and follow 1 Corinthians 11:29 we see that Paul was speaking of fellowship within the body of Christ. It is apparent when reading the passage in context that Paul was calling the church of Christ the "Lord's body." He was admonishing the church not to be divided and not to be inconsiderate of one another. He wanted them to understand that when they join to eat the Lord's supper they are members of the "Lord's body" that have joined in a memorial to Christ's death. Apparently, some were coming together for the Lord's supper to have a meal and not for fellowship in remembrance of the crucifixion of Christ. They were not being charitable; they were eating while others of the church went hungry. They were not discerning that God's church is the "Lord's body." The context of the passage proves that the reference in the passage to "the Lord's body" is not describing the bread and wine being consumed but rather the believers that are consuming the bread and wine.

Now in this that I declare *unto you* I praise *you* not, that ye come together not for the better, but for the worse. For first of all, when ye come together in the church, I hear that there be divisions among you; and I partly believe it. For there must be also heresies among you, that they which are approved may be made manifest among you. When ye come together therefore into one place, *this* is not to eat the

Lord's supper. For in eating every one taketh before *other* his own supper: and one is hungry, and another is drunken. What? have ye not houses to eat and to drink in? or despise ye the church of God, and shame them that have not? What shall I say to you? shall I praise you in this? I praise *you* not. For I have received of the Lord that which also I delivered unto you, That the Lord Jesus the *same* night in which he was betrayed took bread: And when he had given thanks, he brake *it*, and said, Take, eat: this is my body, which is broken for you: **this do in remembrance of me.** After the same manner also *he took* the cup, when he had supped, saying, This cup is the new testament in my blood: **this do ye, as oft as ye drink *it*, in remembrance of me. For as often as ye eat this bread, and drink this cup, ye do shew the Lord's death till he come.** Wherefore whosoever shall eat this bread, and drink *this* cup of the Lord, unworthily, shall be guilty of the body and blood of the Lord. But let a man examine himself, and so let him eat of *that* bread, and drink of *that* cup. **For he that eateth and drinketh unworthily, eateth and drinketh damnation to himself, not discerning the Lord's body.** For this cause many *are* weak and sickly among you, and many sleep. For if we would judge ourselves, we should not be judged. But when we are judged, we are chastened of the Lord, that we should not be condemned with the world. Wherefore, my brethren, when ye come together to eat, tarry one for another. And if any man hunger, let him eat at home; that ye come not together unto condemnation. And the rest will I set in order when I come. Now concerning spiritual *gifts*, brethren, I would not have you ignorant. Ye know that ye were Gentiles, carried away unto these dumb idols, even as ye were led. Wherefore I give you to understand, that no man speaking by the Spirit of God calleth Jesus accursed: and *that* no man can say that Jesus is the Lord, but by the Holy Ghost. Now there are diversities of gifts, but the same Spirit. And there are differences of administrations, but the same Lord. And there are diversities of operations, but it is the same God which worketh all in all. But the manifestation of the Spirit is given to every man to profit withal. For to one is given by the Spirit the word of wisdom; to another the word of knowledge by the same Spirit; To another faith by the same Spirit; to another the gifts of healing by the same Spirit; To another the working of miracles; to another prophecy; to another discerning of spirits; to another *divers* kinds of tongues; to another the interpretation of tongues: **But all these worketh that one and the selfsame Spirit, dividing to every man severally as he will. For as the body is one, and hath many members, and all the members of that one body, being many, are one body: so also *is* Christ. For by one Spirit are we all baptized into one body,** whether *we be* Jews or Gentiles, whether *we be* bond or free; and have been all made to drink into one Spirit. **For the body is not one member, but many.** If the foot shall say, Because I am not the hand, I am not of the body; is it therefore not of the **body**?

And if the ear shall say, Because I am not the eye, I am not of the **body**; is it therefore not of the **body**? If the whole **body** *were* an eye, where *were* the hearing? If the whole *were* hearing, where *were* the smelling? But now hath God set the members every one of them in the **body**, as it hath pleased him. And if they were all one member, where *were* the body? But now *are they* **many members, yet but one body**. And the eye cannot say unto the hand, I have no need of thee: nor again the head to the feet, I have no need of you. Nay, much more those members of the body, which seem to be more feeble, are necessary: And those *members* of the body, which we think to be less honourable, upon these we bestow more abundant honour; and our uncomely *parts* have more abundant comeliness. For our comely *parts* have no need: but God hath tempered the body together, having given more abundant honour to that *part* which lacked: **That there should be no schism in the body; but *that* the members should have the same care one for another. And whether one member suffer, all the members suffer with it; or one member be honoured, all the members rejoice with it.**

Now ye are the body of Christ, and members in particular.
And God hath set some in the church, first apostles, secondarily prophets, thirdly teachers, after that miracles, then gifts of healings, helps, governments, diversities of tongues. *Are* all apostles? *are* all prophets? *are* all teachers? *are* all workers of miracles? Have all the gifts of healing? do all speak with tongues? do all interpret? But covet earnestly the best gifts: and yet shew I unto you a more excellent way. (1 Corinthians 11:17-12:31 AV)

The following passage describes the Christian believers as "one bread, and one body."

Wherefore, my dearly beloved, flee from idolatry. I speak as to wise men; judge ye what I say. The cup of blessing which we bless, is it not the **communion** of the blood of Christ? The bread which we break, is it not the **communion** of the body of Christ? **For we *being* many are one bread, *and* one body: for we are all partakers of that one bread**. (1 Corinthians 10:14-17 AV)

The wine and bread that are consumed are a way of sharing and communicating within the church in order to commemorate Christ's suffering and death. The bread and wine are not only a commemoration of the crucifixion of Jesus but also our joining with him in that crucifixion. That is what is meant by the communion of the blood and body of Christ. The "Lord's body" is his church. The passage states that we are all partakers of that one bread. That means that by faith in Jesus our sinful flesh was crucified with Christ on the cross and that we are to no longer live after the flesh but after the Spirit. The following Bible passages testify that our sinful flesh was crucified with Christ, and we are therefore freed from the slavery of sin and can follow the Spirit of the Lord, who is in us; just as Jesus rose from the dead, so all believers will also rise from the dead.

I am crucified with Christ: nevertheless I live; yet not I, but Christ liveth in me: and the life which I now live in the flesh I live by the faith of the Son of God, who loved me, and gave himself for me. (Galatians 2:20 AV)

And they that are Christ's have crucified the flesh with the affections and lusts. If we live in the Spirit, let us also walk in the Spirit. (Galatians 5:24-25 AV)

Always bearing about in the body the dying of the Lord Jesus, that the life also of Jesus might be made manifest in our body. For we which live are alway delivered unto death for Jesus' sake, that the life also of Jesus might be made manifest in our mortal flesh. So then death worketh in us, but life in you. (2 Corinthians 4:10-12 AV)

Know ye not, that so many of us as were baptized into Jesus Christ were baptized into his death? Therefore we are buried with him by baptism into death: that like as Christ was raised up from the dead by the glory of the Father, even so we also should walk in newness of life. For if we have been planted together in the likeness of his death, we shall be also *in the likeness* of *his* resurrection: **Knowing this, that our old man is crucified with *him*, that the body of sin might be destroyed, that henceforth we should not serve sin. For he that is dead is freed from sin. Now if we be dead with Christ, we believe that we shall also live with him: Knowing that Christ being raised from the dead dieth no more; death hath no more dominion over him. For in that he died, he died unto sin once: but in that he liveth, he liveth unto God. Likewise reckon ye also yourselves to be dead indeed unto sin, but alive unto God through Jesus Christ our Lord**. (Romans 6:3-11 AV)

Before Jesus was crucified he prayed for his disciples to God the Father. During that prayer, he prayed that all who believe in him become one, just as Jesus and his Father are one.

I pray for them: I pray not for the world, but for them which thou hast given me; for they are thine. And all mine are thine, and thine are mine; and I am glorified in them. And now I am no more in the world, but these are in the world, and I come to thee. Holy Father, keep through thine own name those whom thou hast given me, **that they may be one, as we *are*.** (John 17:9-11 AV)

In that prayer Jesus expressed his will that all those that believe in him should not only be one with each other but also one with him and his Father.

Neither pray I for these alone, but for them also which shall believe on me through their word;   **That they all may be one; as thou, Father, *art* in me, and I in thee, that they also may be one in us**: that the world may believe that thou hast sent me. And the glory which thou gavest me I have given them; **that they may**

be one, even as we are one: I in them, and thou in me, that they may be made perfect in one; and that the world may know that thou hast sent me, and hast loved them, as thou hast loved me. Father, I will that they also, whom thou hast given me, be with me where I am; that they may behold my glory, which thou hast given me: for thou lovedst me before the foundation of the world. O righteous Father, the world hath not known thee: but I have known thee, and these have known that thou hast sent me. And I have declared unto them thy name, and will declare *it*: **that the love wherewith thou hast loved me may be in them, and I in them**. (John 17:20-26 AV)

All Jesus' prayers were answered. Jesus stated: **"I *am* in my Father, and ye in me, and I in you."** (John 14:20 AV) The indwelling of the Holy Ghost that creates a spiritual temple of the Lord is a recurring theme of the gospel. All members of Christ's church are joined together to form one body in Christ!

> **One God and Father of all, who *is* above all, and through all, and in you all**. (Ephesians 4:6 AV)

> **For as we have many members in one body**, and all members have not the same office: **So we, *being* many, are one body in Christ, and every one members one of another**. (Romans 12:4-5 AV)

All those who believe in Jesus are members of his church and are one with Jesus and his Father. Jesus Christ is the head of the church; the church is his body.

> **And he is the head of the body, the church**: who is the beginning, the firstborn from the dead; that in all *things* he might have the preeminence. (Colossians 1:18 AV)

> **And hath put all *things* under his feet, and gave him *to be* the head over all *things* to the church, Which is his body, the fulness of him that filleth all in all**. (Ephesians 1:22-23 AV)

> For no man ever yet hated his own flesh; but nourisheth and cherisheth it, even as the Lord the church: **For we are members of his body, of his flesh, and of his bones**. (Ephesians 5:29-30 AV)

> Who now rejoice in my sufferings for you, and fill up that which is behind of the afflictions of Christ in my flesh **for his body's sake, which is the church**: Whereof I am made a minister, according to the dispensation of God which is given to me for you, to fulfil the word of God; *Even* the mystery which hath been hid from ages and from generations, but now is made manifest to his saints: To whom God would make known what *is* the riches of the glory of this mystery

among the Gentiles; which is **Christ in you, the hope of glory**: (Colossians 1:24-27 AV)

There is one church body; it is a spiritual body that is joined together by the Holy Spirit.

> Endeavouring to keep the unity of the Spirit in the bond of peace. *There is* **one body, and one Spirit, even as ye are called in one hope of your calling**; (Ephesians 4:3-4 AV)

Believers are the temple of God, because the Holy Spirit indwells those who are chosen by God to believe in Jesus.

> What? know ye not that **your body is the temple of the Holy Ghost** *which is* in you, which ye have of God, and ye are not your own? (1 Corinthians 6:19 AV)

> Know ye not that **ye are the temple of God**, and *that* the Spirit of God dwelleth in you? If any man defile the temple of God, him shall God destroy; for the temple of God is holy, which *temple* ye are. (1 Corinthians 3:16-17 AV)

The Catholic Church replaces the doctrine of the holy scriptures with its tradition. Those who do not accept its view of things are anathematized. In fact, the official Vatican statement, *Dominus Iesus*, which was written by the Vatican's chief expert on doctrine, Cardinal Josef Ratzinger (now Pope Benedict XVI) in 2000, states that "ecclesial communities" that do not recognize the Eucharist mystery, (that is that Almighty God is fully present in the form of bread and wine) are not truly churches at all.

> Therefore, there exists a single Church of Christ, which subsists in the Catholic Church, governed by the Successor of Peter and by the Bishops in communion with him. The Churches which, while not existing in perfect communion with the Catholic Church, remain united to her by means of the closest bonds, that is, by apostolic succession and a valid Eucharist, are true particular Churches. . . . On the other hand, the ecclesial **communities which have not preserved the valid Episcopate and the genuine and integral substance of the Eucharistic mystery, are not Churches in the proper sense.** DECLARATION "DOMINUS IESUS" ON THE UNICITY AND SALVIFIC UNIVERSALITY OF JESUS CHRIST AND THE CHURCH, Rome, from the Offices of the Congregation for the Doctrine of the Faith, August 6, 2000 (emphasis added).

The Catholic Church minds the things of the flesh; it has twisted spiritual truths into carnal lies. Their misapplication of the Bible passage at 1 Corinthians 11:29 is just one example of their taking of Bible passages out of context and misrepresenting them to support their unbiblical doctrines. God's church is not a physical building that is joined by brick and mortar, it is a spiritual building; it is the "Lord's body," with its members joined by the Holy Spirit. The

Lord's supper is a memorial for the Lord's body.

> **For they that are after the flesh do mind the things of the flesh; but they that are after the Spirit the things of the Spirit**. For to be carnally minded *is* death; but to be spiritually minded *is* life and peace. Because the carnal mind *is* enmity against God: for it is not subject to the law of God, neither indeed can be. So then they that are in the flesh cannot please God. But ye are not in the flesh, but in the Spirit, if so be that **the Spirit of God dwell in you**. Now if any man have not the Spirit of Christ, he is none of his. And if Christ *be* in you, the body *is* dead because of sin; but the Spirit *is* life because of righteousness. But **if the Spirit of him that raised up Jesus from the dead dwell in you, he that raised up Christ from the dead shall also quicken your mortal bodies by his Spirit that dwelleth in you**. (Romans 8:5-11 AV)

21 The Secret Doctrine

The Kabbalah is the key to the esoteric meaning of the Catholic liturgy. The Catholic celebration of the Eucharist is actually a celebration involving a pantheon of gods and goddesses, born of the Babylonian theosophy brought into the Catholic Church by the Jews. Professor Israel Shahak explains the Babylonian polytheism of Judaism:

> According to the cabbala, the universe is ruled not by one god but by several deities, of various characters and influences, emanated by a dim, distant First Cause. Omitting many details, one can summarize the system as follows. From the First Cause, first a male god called 'Wisdom' or 'Father' and then a female goddess called 'Knowledge' or 'Mother' were emanated or born. From the marriage of these two, a pair of younger gods were born: Son, also called by many other names such as 'Small Face' or 'The Holy Blessed One'; and Daughter, also called 'Lady' (or 'Matronit', a word derived from Latin), 'Shekhinah', 'Queen', and so on. These two younger gods should be united, but their union is prevented by the machinations of Satan, who in this system is a very important and independent personage. The Creation was undertaken by the First Cause in order to allow them to unite, but because of the Fall they became more disunited than ever, and indeed Satan has managed to come very close to the divine Daughter and even to rape her (either seemingly or in fact - opinions differ on this). The creation of the Jewish people was undertaken in order to mend the break caused by Adam and Eve, and under Mount Sinai this was for a moment achieved: the male god Son, incarnated in Moses, was united with the goddess Shekhinah. Unfortunately, the sin of the Golden Calf again caused disunity in the godhead; but the repentance of the Jewish people has mended matters to some extent. Similarly, each incident of biblical Jewish history is believed to be associated with the union or disunion of the divine pair. The Jewish conquest of Palestine from the Canaanites and the building of the first and second Temple are particularly propitious for their union, while the destruction of the Temples and exile of the Jews from the Holy Land are merely external signs not only of the divine disunion but also of a real 'whoring

after strange gods': Daughter falls closely into the power of Satan, while Son takes various female satanic personages to his bed, instead of his proper wife.[644]

Athol Bloomer was a previously practicing Jew who converted to Catholicism. He also posts articles under the name Aharon Yosef.[645] According to the *Association of Hebrew Catholics*, Bloomer is a Catholic lay missionary with the Missionary Society of Our Lady of the Blessed Sacrament. The *Association of Hebrew Catholics*, proudly proclaims on their website that they have received the official endorsement of Pope John Paul II, Archbishop Raymond Burke, and Bishop Carl Mengeling.

Bloomer wrote an article to explain the truths in the Jewish religion revealed in the Kabbalah, and further how the revelations in the Kabbalah explain the mystery of the Catholic Eucharist.[646] Bloomer explains how the Catholic celebration of the Eucharist is actually derived from the Jewish Kabbalah.

> In the Middle Ages there were a number of Jewish converts to the Church who had become convinced Christians by studying and practicing the Jewish Mystical Tradition. These Jewish converts wrote a number of books which explored the Kabbalah or Jewish Mystical traditions in the light of Catholic belief. Pope Sixtus IV along with some other Popes approved of this movement and ordered the Kabbalah to be translated into Latin and to be studied by all Divinity students. This was the pre-Lurianic Kabbalah. However with the rise of a more rationalistic generation this field of research was neglected by Catholic scholars.

> Shekinah is the central concept of this mysticism. Father Elias Friedman in his writings mentions this understanding of Shekinah in regards to the Eucharistic Presence of Jesus in the Tabernacles of the Catholic Church. Just as the Shekinah dwelt in the Temple of Solomon so the Shekinah in the flesh was Yeshuah and now dwells in the tabernacles of the world. Thus the central concept of both Jewish and Catholic mysticism is the Divine Presence (Shekinah). A study of the Jewish Mystical tradition in the light of the Eucharist is, in my opinion, essential in the future development of a Hebrew Catholic spirituality that would enrich the whole Church. Adoration of the Shekinah is the central activity of the Jewish mystics just as Eucharistic Adoration is the central activity of the Catholic mystics.[647]

The Catholic Encyclopedia reveals that the Jewish liturgy is the source for the Eucharistic liturgy of the Catholic Church.[648] Bloomer offers a more detailed explanation. Bloomer explains that the Cabalistic mystical concept of then Shekinah presence of God is the source for the Catholic mystical concept of the presence of God in the Eucharist. One scheme used by Jews to alter church doctrines to align with their own is to get the church to buy into the unbiblical terms used in Jewish tradition. Shekinah is an example of that scheme. The word Shekinah appears nowhere in either the Old or New Testaments. Shekinah is a wholly Jewish concept that was born of their Kabbalah; it is also found in the Jewish Talmud and Targums.

John Ramsey, a Catholic Priest, explains the fact that the Eucharist is the Shekinah of Judaism:

> When God's people were in the desert, He gave them two clear signs of His presence among them. First, He gave them a VISIBLE sign of His presence - what they called the SHEKINAH. . . . We, the NEW PEOPLE OF GOD, the members of His Body, the Church, also have our SHEKINAH and our MANNA and both are to be found in the EUCHARIST. . . . In the Holy Sacrifice of the Mass, as we saw in the chapter on the Eucharist, there are two distinct elements: one of SACRIFICE - Jesus, the Lamb of God, offering Himself to the Father; and the other of a MEAL - Jesus, the Bread of life, feeding us upon His body. Jesus Christ, our Shekinah.[649]

The *Missionary Priests of the Blessed Sacrament* describe the Catholic theology of Christ being really and actually present in the Eucharistic host. The Eucharist is not symbolic; Catholic theology is that the Eucharist is the actual body, blood, soul, and divinity of Christ, it is the visible manifestation of God, it is Shekinah:

> The Hebrew word shekinah is used to denote any visible manifestation of God's presence and glory. . . . He is present in the Eucharist. In the ways previously mentioned, He is present in His power, His authority, and in His Spirit. But in the Eucharist, He is present most fully, complete - Body, Blood, Soul and Divinity. The Eucharist is the extension of the Incarnation in space and time. It is the fulfillment of Jesus' name: Emmanuel, God is with us. What better place is there to begin the practice of the presence of God than in His presence in the Eucharist? When we visit the Blessed Sacrament, we should make an effort to heighten our awareness of Jesus' Real Presence.[650]

The Catholic theology is that the Eucharist is God actually present as Shekinah in the form of bread, and is to be worshiped as God. Pope Benedict XVI, when he held the previous title of Joseph Cardinal Ratzinger and was formerly the Prefect for the Vatican Office of the Congregation for the Doctrine of the Faith, was viewed as being the preeminent Catholic theologian of his time. Before becoming Pope Benedict XVI, Cardinal Ratzinger explained how the attendant worship of the host during the Catholic liturgy is based upon the Eucharist being Shekinah:

> It is the tent of God, his throne. Here he is among us. His presence (Shekinah) really does now dwell among us - in the humblest parish church no less than in the grandest cathedral. Even though the definitive Temple will only come to be when the world has become the New Jerusalem, still what the Temple in Jerusalem pointed to is here present in a supreme way. The New Jerusalem is anticipated in

the humble species of bread.

> So let no one say, "The Eucharist is for eating, not looking at." It is not "ordinary bread", as the most ancient traditions constantly emphasize. Eating it - as we have just said - is a spiritual process, involving the whole man. "Eating" it means worshipping it. Eating it means letting it come into me, so that my "I" is transformed and opens up into the great "we," so that we become "one" in him (cf. Gal 3:16). Thus adoration is not opposed to Communion, nor is it merely added to it. No, Communion only reaches its true depths when it is supported and surrounded by adoration.[651]

Jean Danielou, who is a Jesuit priest, explains further the Catholic theological view of the Eucharist being Shekinah:

> This leads us to another theme akin to that of the covenant, that of the dwelling, the Shekinah. Yahweh had caused His Name to dwell among His own. This is the mystery of the Tabernacle. This Presence abandoned the people of the Old Covenant when the veil of the temple was rent. Henceforth its dwelling-place is the humanity of Christ, in whom the Name has set up its tabernacle. And this dwelling-place is in our midst in the Eucharist. We have already seen the Eucharist as communion, covenant. Now we see it as presence, Shekinah.[652]

Shekinah was inculcated into the Catholic theology from Judaism. There is an esoteric meaning to Shekinah that is only understood by those initiated into the occult theology of Judaism and Catholicism. Michael Hoffman in his book *Judaism Discovered* reveals that **Shekinah is a Babylonian female goddess**. Shekinah is supposed to represent the benevolent spirit to balance out the malevolent spirit of Lilith. Hoffman explains the secret doctrine of the dual spirits is that they are actually one and the same spirit.[653] "The bogus claim that Lilith and Shekhinah are two distinct entities representing separate forces of black magic and white magic is strictly for the *peti yaamin lekhol davar* ['The fool who will believe anything.']"[654]

Hoffman further explains: "The nucleus of Orthodox Judaism at its deepest, most esoteric level is the sexual propitiation of the myrionymous ['many named'] goddes, Isis-Hecate-Demeter-Ishtar-Shekhinah-Lilith. The consummation of the spiritual and sexual union of the female goddess *Shekhinah* with her male consort (Sefirah Tiferet), the 'Holy One,' into one androgynous being (the *mysterium coniunctionis* of alchemy), is one of the charter objectives of Kabbalistic Judaism, and this mirrors uncannily the theology of the sorcerers of ancient Egypt and Babylon, whose ritual working was dedicated to the magical union of the goddess and the god."

Hoffman's explanation raises an issue. Could the Catholic mass be at its core an esoteric ceremony involving the magical union of god and goddess? We know that during the mass the Eucharist is Shekinah. We also know that Shekinah is a female goddess. The conclusion, therefore, is that the Eucharist during the mass becomes the female goddess Shekinah. Recall that the bread and wine are claimed to become the very body, blood, soul, and divinity of Christ. Could there be a hidden doctrine that is not shared with the uninitiated that the transubstantiation of the Eucharist during mass is an esoteric magical union of the female goddess Shekinah and a male god?

In order to answer that question, we must examine the doctrines in the Kabbalah. In order to understand the esoteric doctrine of the Kabbalah as it explains the mass, one must understand the language of witchcraft. In witchcraft words have two meanings, one meaning for the uninitiated and another meaning for those who are initiated into the secret doctrines. The Catholics use words taken from the bible, however, those words only sound biblical. The words actually describe heathen deities and concepts. There is a secret doctrine in the Catholic Church known only to the initiates into the esoteric meaning of the words.

The Catholic/Judaic/Babylonian androgynous god/goddess needs a bible to support its androgyny. The agents of the Catholic/Judaic/Babylonian religion have done that with an androgynous bible version. The book publisher Zondervan decided to add insult to injury and further muddy the pure water of God's word with a variation of the New International Version (NIV), it calls Today's New International Version (TNIV). Zondervan is owned by Rupert Murdoch, who is a front man for powerful Jewish interests.

Terry Watkins explains:

> In Hebrews 2:17, the TNIV starts wading in some very treacherous water. Some very treacherous and very polluted water.
>
> Hebrews 2:16-17, describes how the Lord Jesus physically came through the seed of Abraham. Verse 17 says that the Lord Jesus, was physically ". . . made like his brethren [Jews]. . ." The TNIV translators, without any Greek evidence, in any manuscript, inserts the female gender "sisters" into the verse. This is a flagrant disregard for the Greek text and adding to God's Word. And it opens the door for some serious satanic feminist and new age teaching. Namely, that Jesus Christ was androgynous – both male and female.
>
> Hebrews 2:16-17, KJB
>
> For verily he took not on him the nature of angels; but he took on him the seed of Abraham. Wherefore in all things it behoved him to be made like unto his brethren, that he might be a merciful and faithful high priest in things pertaining to God, to make reconciliation for the sins of the people.
>
> Hebrews 2:16-17, TNIV

For surely it is not angels he helps, but Abraham's descendants. "For this reason he had to be made like his brothers and sisters in every way, in order that he might become a merciful and faithful high priest in service to God, and that he might make atonement for the sins of the people"

". . . made like his brothers and sisters IN EVERY WAY. . ."

Notice the TNIV translators addition of "IN EVERY WAY". Why in the world did they "add" the words "in EVERY way"? What in the world do they mean "in EVERY way"?

That's opening the door for some serious false doctrine. Serious. . . Wicked. . . Blasphemous. . . Errors.

In the popular new-age book, The Coming of the Cosmic Christ, author Matthew Fox, writes of this, "made like his brothers and sisters in every way", Christ the TNIV translators have tapped into.

"The Cosmic Christ can be both female and male, . . ." (Matthew Fox, The Coming of the Cosmic Christ)

Feminist Rosemary Radford Ruether, in Sexism and God-Talk, also describes this "made like his brothers and sisters in every way" Christ. Ruether, says ". . .we can encounter Christ in the form of our sister". That's almost identical to the perverted claims of the TNIV translators in Hebrews 2:17 – ". . . made like his brothers and sisters in every way. . ."

"Christ is not necessarily male, nor is the redeemed community only women, but a new humanity, female and male. . . In the language of early Christian prophetism, we can encounter Christ in the form of our sister" (Rosemary Radford Ruether, Sexism and God-Talk)

Radical feminist and lesbian author, Virginia Ramey Mollenkott, was stylistic consultant for the "original" New International Version (NIV). Mollenkott is also a major player in the push for gender-inclusive Bibles [such as theTNIV]. In fact, Mollenkott was a team member of the very first gender inclusive scriptures ever published, An Inclusive Language Lectionary. Not surprising, Mollenkott, also promotes the "male-female" Christ [". . .made like his brothers and sisters in every way. . ."]

"[T]he combination of Wisdom/Christ leads to a healthy blend of male and female imagery that empowers everyone and works beautifully to symbolize the One God who is neither male nor female yet both male and female". (Mollenkott, Virginia

Ramey. The Divine Feminine. P. 104).

"The creation story begins by affirming that God is neither male nor female, but both. The first chapter of Genesis emphasizes that both male and female are made in the image of the creator God." (Virginia Ramey Mollenkott, Gender Diversity and the Christian Community, www.theotherside.org/archive/may-jun01/mollenkott.html)

NIV member and homosexual activist, Mollenkott, seems to have no respect for the Lord Jesus. As she even perverts the Lord Jesus Christ into an effeminate, "gender-bender", "fairy":

"Jesus, whom Paul refers to as the second adam (sic), also defied gender norms. He didn't marry, although he had the religious obligation to do so at eighteen. He performed acts like cooking or washing the feet of his disciples – acts culturally assigned to wives or slaves, not to a free male, . . ." (Virginia Ramey Mollenkott, Gender Diversity and the Christian Community, www.theotherside.org/archive/may-jun01/mollenkott.html)

NIV consultant Mollenkott also stated in a news conference, that Jesus Christ was "chromosomally female":

"You might be interested to know that. . . Jesus remained chromosomally female throughout life." (Virginia Mollenkott, National Council of Churches news conference, cited in The Language of the King James Bible, Gail Riplinger, p. 114)

Researching the TNIV, I kept asking myself, "What happened to the fear of the Lord?" How can the TNIV translators (CBT), publisher (Zondervan) and copyright holder (IBS) intentionally add, delete, change and distort the words of God? How can they intentionally add words that clearly pervert the Lord Jesus Christ?[655]

Throughout the TNIV can be found subtle changes aimed at de-masculinizing Jesus Christ. Typically this is done by replacing the masculine pronoun or noun with a neuter pronoun or noun.

AV (KJV)	TNIV
For since by man came death, by **man** came also the resurrection of the dead For as in Adam all die, even so in Christ shall all be made alive. 1 Corinthians 15:21-22 AV (KJV).	For since death came through a human being, the resurrection of the dead comes also through a **human being**. For as in Adam all die, so in Christ all will be made alive. 1 Corinthians 15:21-22 (TNIV).

The passage in 1 Timothy 2:5 has been changed in the TNIV from describing Jesus as a man to describing him as the neuter "human."

AV (KJV)	TNIV
For there is one God, and one mediator between God and men, **the man Christ Jesus**. 1 Timothy 2:5. AV (KJV)	For there is one God and one mediator between God and human beings, **Christ Jesus, himself human**. 1 Timothy 2:5.

Jesus goes from "he" who came down as the bread of life to "that" bread of life in the TNIV John 6:33.

AV (KJV)	TNIV
For the bread of God is **he** which cometh down from heaven, and giveth life unto the world. John 6:33 AV (KJV)	For the bread of God is **that** which comes down from heaven and gives life to the world. John 6:33 (TNIV)

In John 15:13, Jesus is a "man" who laid down "his" life for "his" friends. In the TNIV they went through the odd phraseology in describing Jesus in the neuter as "one" who laid down "one's" life for "one's" friends.

AV (KJV)	TNIV
Greater love hath no **man** than this, that a **man** lay down **his** life for **his** friends. John 15:13 AV (KJV)	Greater love has no **one** than this: to lay down **one's** life for **one's** friends. John 15:13 (TNIV)

There are clues to the Jewish influence in the new bible versions. Babylonian Judaism is a religion of demons. In the New Revised Standard Version (NSRV) of Isaiah 34:14, it mentions a night demon, Lilith, that is unique to the traditions of Babylonian Judaism (e.g., Baba Bathra 73a), but is not supported by the original tongue of the Isaiah passage, Hebrew. "Wildcats shall meet with hyenas, goat-demons shall call to each other; there too **Lilith** shall repose, and find a place to rest." (Isaiah 34:14 NRSV) The correct translation of Isaiah 34:14 makes no mention of Lilith: "The wild beasts of the desert shall also meet with the wild beasts of the island, and the satyr shall cry to his fellow; the screech owl also shall rest there, and find for herself a place of rest." (Isaiah 34:14 AV)

Lilith is known in demonology as a succubus. Talmud, tractate Shabbath, folio 151b states: "One may not sleep in a house alone, and whoever sleeps in a house alone is seized by Lilith." A footnote in Niddah, folio 24b describes Lilith as "[a] female demon of the night, reputed to have wings and a human face." One researcher stated: "Lilith is equated with a 'first Eve', the feminine dark side of the divine and goddesses such as Isis, Astarte, the Black Madonna or Queen of Demons and other false gods. The myth of Lilith is a gnostic perversion of the Biblical account of Creation and Adam and Eve."[656]

Someone with an intimate knowledge of the Babylonian traditions of Judaism inserted the night devil Lilith into the NRSV Isaiah 34:14 passage. God speaks of days like today, with the new corrupted bible versions. "Behold, the days come, saith the Lord GOD, that I will send a famine in the land, not a famine of bread, nor a thirst for water, but of hearing the words of the LORD. Amos 8:11.

The TNIV is using gender neutral language to describe Jesus as an esoteric means of subliminally conditioning the *goyim* to accept the androgynous god/goddess that is part and parcel of the Judaic/Catholic/Babylonian theosophy. Prominent scholar and professor of Jewish studies Lawrence Fine states that the true meaning of the Old Testament can only be unlocked through the "sefirotic code" in the Kabbalah.[657] Fine states that the covert symbolic language of the Kabbalah supercedes the simple overt meaning of biblical language.[658] Fine explains that the Kabbalah reveals "the many names of God or expression of God's being."[659] There is a vast body of hidden symbols and codes in the Kabbalah which reveal the various ways in which the gods (sefirot) of the Kabbalah interact with one another.

Bloomer explains that this secret "sefirotic code" in the Kabbalah is the foundation for the true, but hidden, meaning behind the Catholic Eucharist. Bloomer explains that the god of the Kabbalah, who is called Ein Sof is made up of ten attributes (sefirot). Each sefirah (singular of sefirot) is not only designated as a particular trait of Ein Sof but is also an anthropomorphic part of that one god. In addition, each sefirah is either a god or a goddess in its own right.

The first nine sefirot (plural of sefirah) are in turn divided evenly into three triads, containing three sefirot each and representing three major sections of the anthropomorphic parts of the mystical body of Ein Sof. The tenth sefirah is the Shekinah (a/k/a Malkuth), which is not part of the three triads.[660] When Jewish Catholics speak of the Trinity they are not referring to the Father, Son, and Holy Spirit as revealed in the bible, but rather to the three triads set forth in the Kabbalah.

The Kabbalah describes the lower third triad of its heathen god (Ein Sof) as made up of three sefirot: 1) Netzach (Endurance/Victory), 2) Hod (Majesty/Glory), and 3) Yesod (Foundation).[661] Bloomer reveals that Netzach and Hod are the right and left legs of Ein Sof, and Yesod is Ein Sof's phallus. Bloomer explains that the light and power of the sefirot are channeled through the phallic god Yesod to the last Sefirah, which is the Shekinah (a/k/a Malkuth).[662] This phallic god is part of the blatantly erotic interpretation of the Jewish god found in the Kabbalah.[663] Rabbi Geoffrey W. Dennis in *The Encyclopedia of Jewish Myth, Magic, and Mysticism* explains: "The *Zohar* includes multiple interpretations built around the concept of God's genitals."[664]

The Kabbalah infuses orthodox Judaism with a powerful undercurrent of phallic worship and practice, including sex magic.[665] The sex magic is an offshoot of the secret doctrine in Judaism, which is a common doctrine found in secret societies, that the mystic can find redemption through an "heroic" willingness to do evil.[666] The secret rabbinic doctrine is that evil can be redeemed by embracing it; there is a spiritual good in doing evil.[667] That explains why Jesus said to the Jews: "Ye are of *your* father the devil, and the lusts of your father ye will do." John 8:44.

Moshe Idel, in *Hasidism Between Ecstasy and Magic*, explains that "the concept of the descent of the *Zaddiq* [Jewish mystic or saint], which is better known by the Hebrew phrase, *Yeridah zorekh Aliyah*, namely the descent for the sake of the ascent, the transgression for the sake of repentance. . . . Much attention has been paid to this model because of its essential affinities with Zoharic and Lurianic Kabbalah . . . this model was a very important one in Hasidic thought."[668] That concept is the core belief in the system of "black magic." The source of this secret doctrine of "black magic" is Babylon.[669] The oldest texts for this Babylonian black magic in Judaism are the texts *Sifrei h-Iyyun*, *Sefer ha-Bahair*, and the *Hikoth Yesirah*, which is also known as the *Sefer Yetzirah*.[670]

Bloomer explains that the Yesod (Jesod) unites the Shekinah and the Tif'eret. Tif'eret is the offspring of Hokhmah and Binah.[671] The Hokmah and Binah are two of the three sefirot of the divine head of the mystical body of the Ein Sof (Kether is the third

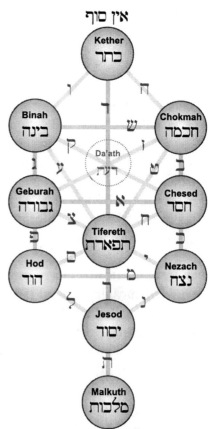

sefirah). Tif'eret is not only a god himself, but he also represents the heart and torso of the body of the Kabbalah god, Ein Sof.

The "tree of life" diagram[672] depicts the 10 siefrots as they are presented in the Sefer Yetzirah (Book of Formation) and gives a visual representation of the relationship between the different sefirot within the Ein Sof. Note that Malkuth and Shekinah are the same sefirah. In the diagram, only Malkuth is depicted. Note also that the spelling varies somewhat from source to source. For example, Chokmah in the diagram is the same as Hokmah and Jesod is the same as Yesod to which Bloomer referred. Jewish scholars readily acknowledge that are many parallels between the Cabalistic concept of god and that found in Buddhism, Hinduism, and so-called Gnosticism.[673] That is not surprising, since they all flow from the same mystical waters of Babylon.

Bloomer reveals that these Cabalistic sefirot each correlate to some aspect of the Catholic religion. For example, the Shekinah is not only the Eucharistic host, but it also represents the church community. During the Catholic Mass, the Eucharist (Shekinah) is the bride who is being united with Tif'eret through Yesod, which is the phallus of Ein Sof. Bloomer states that "the Sabbath Eve is seen as the weekly celebration of the Sacred Wedding."[674] The Jewish weekly Sabbath Eve correlates directly with the weekly Catholic Mass. Bloomer explains:

> In the New Covenant the Sabbath meal along with all the festival meals is transformed into the Mass as the Wedding Feast of the Eucharistic King. Thus the Jewish Sabbath Meal is a type of the Mass and Eucharist. All the festival meals of Judaism including the Passover have their roots in the weekly Sabbath Evening Meal. These meals all find their fulfillment or culmination in the meal of the Eucharistic Sacrifice, which we call the Holy Mass."[675]

Bloomer confirms *The Catholic Encyclopedia's* statement that the Catholic Mass is actually the culmination of the Jewish Sabbath celebration. The esoteric meaning behind the Catholic Mass, which is hidden from the gentiles, but is understood by Jews, is that it is a mystical/sexual union between the god, Tif'eret, and the goddess, Shekinah, through the divine phallus, Yesod.[676] This is exactly what Michael Hoffman meant when he explained that the charter objective of Cabalistic Judaism is the consummation of the spiritual and sexual union of the female godess, Shekhinah, with her male consort, Tif'eret, into one androgynous god.

Dan Cohn-Sherbok and Lavinia Cohn-Sherbok explain the development of the esoteric sexual meanings concealed within the orthodox Jewish liturgy:

> Likewise, Phallic symbolism was employed in speculations about the ninth *Sefirah*, *Yesod*, from which all the higher *Sefirot* flowed into the Shekinah as the life force of the cosmos. In later centuries erotic terminology was used in the Hasidic works to describe movement in prayer which was depicted as copulation with the *Shekhinah*.[677]

This occult theology from the sorcerers of ancient Egypt and Babylon is the esoteric meaning behind the Catholic Mass, which was established as an occult ceremony by crypto-Jews within the Catholic church. Bloomer explains that the nine sefirot that are divided into the three triads are also found in the heathen Egyptian religion. The Egyptian religion referred to the nine sefirot as the Ennead.

> The Ennead of the Nine gods is the Egyptian understanding of the Sefirot of the nine Triadic Sefirot. The phallic image of Geb the Earth god is linked to the Sefirah of Yesod also known as the phallus of the divine body and this divine phallus is called in Kabbalah the axis mundi or cosmic pillar. This is why the Egyptians portray the earth as a male with an erect phallus. This phallus or Sefirah of Yesod is also associated with Osiris whom the Egyptians identify with Joseph.[678]

Bloomer mentions Geb (a/k/a Seb),[679] who is a heathen god of the Egyptians. There is a direct correlation between the Cabalistic and the Egyptian theologies, because they both spring from Babylon. The link between the phallic god, Yesod, found in the Kabbalah and the phallic god, Geb, found in Egypt is evidence of that they have the same Babylonian source. The Cabalistic religion that is found in the Catholic Mass is centered around the phallic god Yesod. Bloomer states that "[t]he Yesod is seen in Kabbalah as a channel linking the Shekinah to the higher Sefirot. Here is the gate to heaven."[680]

The reason why the great harlot of Babylon described in Revelation 17:5 has "MYSTERY" written across her forehead is because this ostensibly gentile church of Rome actually practices the Cabalistic Jewish religion of the Pharisees, which is derived from the occult sorceries of Babylon. This truth is concealed from the uninitiated masses of Catholics. It is truly a "MYSTERY" to them. This Babylonian Judaism is the same Judaism that Christ criticized when he stated: "Ye are of *your* father the devil, and the lusts of your father ye will do." (John 8:44 AV)

Let us dig deeper into the origins of this mysterious Eucharistic ceremony. Bloomer reveals that "[t]his heavenly or mystical understanding of the Sefirot opens up a fuller understanding of the unity of the Godhead with the Church and with each member of the Church. It is only through the Eucharist that this mystery of unity can be found. The Eucharist is the way to the mystical union or marriage of the soul with the Heavenly Bridegroom." The uninitiated members of the Catholic church think the bridegroom is Jesus, however, the Jesus of the Catholic church is not the same Jesus in the bible; the Catholic Jesus who is the bridegroom is actually the heathen god Tif'eret who is joined with the Shekinah (Eucharist) through the phallus (Yesod) of a heathen god (Ein Sof) to consummate the marriage. The consummation causes the transubstantiation of the Eucharist into the full trinity of heathen gods being present in the Eucharistic host. Bloom reveals that "the Trinity is encompassed within the Sacred Host. The Trinity dwells not so much in the heights but in the depths of the Sacred Host of the Altar – which is the Sacred Heart."[681]

The Trinity that is understood by the initiates in the mystery of the Eucharist is not God the Father, God the Son, and God the Holy Spirit. The Eucharistic Trinity is actually the Triads of the Kabbalah. It is likely that the very idea of a Trinity flows from the Cabalistic idea of three Triads making up the god of Judaism. Many Christians would be surprised to know that God is never described in the bible as a Trinity, but is in fact always described as a unity; that is one God. "Hear, O Israel: The LORD our **God** *is* **one** LORD." (Deuteronomy 6:4 AV) "And Jesus answered him, The first of all the commandments *is*, Hear, O Israel; The Lord our **God is one** Lord." (Mark 12:29 AV) "But to us *there is but* **one God**, the Father, of whom *are* all things, and we in him; and one Lord Jesus Christ, by whom *are* all things, and we by him." (1 Corinthians 8:6 AV) "For *there is* **one God**, and one mediator between God and men, the man Christ Jesus;" (1 Timothy 2:5 AV) "For there are three that bear record in heaven, the Father, the Word, and the Holy Ghost: and **these three are one**." (1 John 5:7 AV) "**I and *my* Father are one**." (John 10:30 AV)

Bloomer reveals that Tif'eret was also known as the Sun in the Jewish Kabbalah.[682] He states that the sefirah Yesod is associated with Osiris.[683] Osiris is an Egyptian sun god.[684] He was both the son of Ra and the son of Seb.[685] Osiris and Tammuz are one and the same heathen god.[686] Tammuz was likely the Babylonian origin for the Egyptian god Osiris. Ezekiel reveals the worship of Tammuz by the Jews: "Then he brought me to the door of the gate of the LORD'S house which *was* toward the north; and, behold, there sat women weeping for Tammuz." (Ezekiel 8:14 AV)

Seb is also known as Geb.[687] In Egyptian heathen theology Osiris is both the father and son of Horus.[688] Isis was both Osiris' sister and his wife.[689] Some time after Osiris' death, Isis was able to revive him long enough to conceive Horus.[690] Isis was a moon-goddess; the Romans called her Diana.

Bloomer states that "Miriam ha Kadosha (Holy Mary) is the spouse of the Holy Spirit (or Binah) and Mother of the Eucharistic Lord (the Shekinah)." Bloomer equates Mary with Miriam ha Kadosha, who in the Zohar 1:34a is called 'Moon of Israel.'[691] Miriam ha Kadosha seems to be the Jewish corollary to the ancient moon goddess whom the Romans called Diana and the Greeks called Artemis. Bloomer equates Mary with Miriam ha Kadosha and therefore also Diana and Artemis. Miriam ha Kadosha has a regal status in the Jewish pantheon of goddesses. She is equated with the Jewish warrior queen of heaven, Matronita. Bloomer writes the following in a posting under the name Aharon Yosef: "Matronita is a term appropriate to Miriam ha Kedosha who is both married matron and innocent Virgin. Matronita is in this section of Zohar is called the Shekhinah. The concepts of Shekhinah and Matronita are both symbolised by the Moon."[692] Michael Hoffman states: "Worship of the *Shekinah* in the form of the moon goddess is a formal rite in Orthodox Judaism."[693]

There is a corollary between the moon godesses from the different cultures: Diana (Roman), Artemis (Greek), Matronita (Jew), Shekinah (Jew), Miriam ha Kadosha (Jew), Mary (Catholic), Eucharist (Catholic). The symbolism of the Eucharist represents many different goddesses and gods. The Eucharist is not only a representation of the moon goddess, but also the sun god. In fact, the esoteric meaning of the Eucharist includes a Trinity of gods and goddesses within the Eucharistic host.

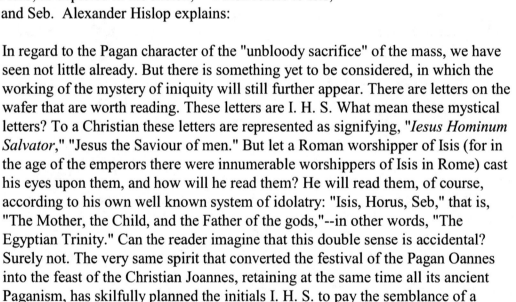

The esoteric identity of Mary in some respects seems to be an amalgam of the Roman goddesses Venus and Diana, the Greek corollaries being Aphrodite and Artemis. Bloomer equates Mary to what he calls the "Holy Trinity." Bloomer states: "The role and function of Mary is so united to the Holy Spirit that Mary (Miriam ha Kadosha) is the perfect mirror of the Holy Trinity."[694]

The Eucharistic host actually carries the initials of the heathen Trinity of gods that it symbolizes. The host carries the Symbol IHS, as depicted in the sketch,[695] which refers to Isis, Horus, and Seb. Alexander Hislop explains:

> In regard to the Pagan character of the "unbloody sacrifice" of the mass, we have seen not little already. But there is something yet to be considered, in which the working of the mystery of iniquity will still further appear. There are letters on the wafer that are worth reading. These letters are I. H. S. What mean these mystical letters? To a Christian these letters are represented as signifying, "*Iesus Hominum Salvator*," "Jesus the Saviour of men." But let a Roman worshipper of Isis (for in the age of the emperors there were innumerable worshippers of Isis in Rome) cast his eyes upon them, and how will he read them? He will read them, of course, according to his own well known system of idolatry: "Isis, Horus, Seb," that is, "The Mother, the Child, and the Father of the gods,"--in other words, "The Egyptian Trinity." Can the reader imagine that this double sense is accidental? Surely not. The very same spirit that converted the festival of the Pagan Oannes into the feast of the Christian Joannes, retaining at the same time all its ancient Paganism, has skilfully planned the initials I. H. S. to pay the semblance of a tribute to Christianity, while Paganism in reality has all the substance of the homage bestowed upon it.[696]

There is nothing in the bible at all regarding the shape of the bread to be used as a memorial as Jesus commanded during the last supper. Given that fact, why does the Catholic Church use a round wafer as a Eucharist during the Catholic Mass? The answer comes from heathen antiquity. Hislop discovered:

The importance, however, which Rome attaches to the roundness of the wafer, must have a reason; and that reason will be found, if we look at the altars of Egypt. "The thin, round cake," says Wilkinson, "occurs on all altars." Almost every jot or tittle in the Egyptian worship had a symbolical meaning. **The round disk, so frequent in the sacred emblems of Egypt, symbolised the sun.** Now, when Osiris, the sun-divinity, became incarnate, and was born, it was not merely that he should give his life as a sacrifice for men, but that he might also be the life and nourishment of the souls of men.[697]

Not only was the sun worshiped in Egypt, but it was also worshiped by the Jews, who worshiped the sun god, Baal. Ezekiel reveals the heathen worship of the sun by the Jews: "And he brought me into the inner court of the LORD'S house, and, behold, at the door of the temple of the LORD, between the porch and the altar, *were* about five and twenty men, with their backs toward the temple of the LORD, and their faces toward the east; and they worshipped the sun toward the east." (Ezekiel 8:16 AV)

Hislop explains that "the 'round' wafer, whose 'roundness' is so important an element in the Romish Mystery, what can be the meaning of it, but just to show to those who have eyes to see, that the 'Wafer' itself is only another symbol of Baal, or the Sun."[698] The Eucharist represents the heathen sun god. Further proof of this is the fact that the monstrance (see illustration[699]) used to contain the Eucharistic host always forms rays of the sun emanating from the Eucharist. All one need do is read the history of the Jews in the bible to find the source for this sun god worship. "And they forsook the LORD, and served Baal and Ashtaroth." (Judges 2:13 AV) The Catholic Mass is a continuation of the apostasy of the Jews in their worship of the sun god, Baal, in the form of the Eucharist. Tif'eret is the sefirah god that was also known as the sun in the Jewish Kabbalah.[700] Tif'eret would seem to be the very same heathen sun god, Baal, who was worshiped by the ancient Jews.

Monstrance

It is notable that the circular disk Eucharist is purported by the Catholic Church to be the very body of Christ. The consumption of the Eucharist is the consumption of the flesh of Jesus in the form of bread. As we have seen, the esoteric doctrine is that the cake wafer is actually a symbol of the sun god, Baal. The Jews would offer their children as sacrifices to be burned alive as sacrifices to Baal. See Jeremiah 19:5. The priest of Baal would then eat the flesh of the children.[701] "Cahna-Bal" means "priest of Baal."[702] Cahna-Bal is the origin of the word "cannibal" which means one who eats human flesh.[703] The consumption of the Eucharist purports to be the consumption of the actual flesh and blood of Jesus in the outward form bread. The hidden mystery is that the consumption of the Eucharist is an unbloody re-enactment of the ritual flesh eating by the priests of Baal.

In addition to the macabre cannibalism of Baal worship, the hidden mysteries of the

Eucharist also includes mystical/sexual meanings. The transubstantiation of the host into the Eucharist during Catholic Mass is a magical union of the female goddess Shekinah and a male god, Tif'eret, through the heathen god Yesod. Yesod is also the phallus of a heathen god (Ein Sof) that the Cabalists equate with the God the Father, but who in fact is Satan. There are many esoteric meanings behind the Catholic celebration of the Eucharist. In the end, an entire trinity of gods and goddesses are present in the Eucharistic host which bears the inscription of those gods: IHS, which stands for Isis, Horus, and Seb.

Another Cabalistic meaning behind the Eucharist revealed by Bloomer is that the goddess Mary, who is the "Queen of Heaven," is the spouse of Binah. Binah in the Kabbalah correlates to the Holy Spirit in Catholic theology. Binah is a goddess who is considered the "divine womb." The goddess Mary is considered the daughter of Keter and the mother of Hokman. Keter in Kabbalah correlates to the Father in Catholic theology and Hokman is the Son. Shekinah (Eucharist) is a heathen goddess bride born from Binah.

The Jesus of the Catholic Church is not the Jesus of the bible. The true Jesus is blasphemed in the Kabbalah. "According to the most important Kabbalistic text, the Zohar, Jesus is a 'dead dog' who resides amid the filth and vermin."[704] The secret doctrine of the Catholic Mass, which is born of the Kabbalah, is that the Jesus of the Eucharistic Mass is an androgynous god/goddess in the form of bread, who is magically made present through transubstantiation, which esoterically is a mystical sex rite.

The source document (the Kabbalah) for the Catholic Jesus offers a god/goddess combination in his place under the guise of the bread in the Eucharist. The Catholic Church kept the name Jesus, but the Jesus of the Eucharist is not the Jesus of the bible. The very thing that Paul warned the Corinthians about has happened: "For if he that cometh preacheth **another Jesus**, whom we have not preached, or *if* ye receive **another spirit**, which ye have not received, or **another gospel**, which ye have not accepted, ye might well bear with *him*." (2 Corinthians 11:4 AV). The members of the Catholic Church have gone after another spirit, another gospel, and **another Jesus**.

This secret doctrine of the Mass was woven carefully by the Jews from the Kabbalah into the Catholic church. As with all secret doctrines, at first it was done through stealth. Later it was done with much more freedom by authorization of Pope Sixtus IV, who ordered that the Cabalistic writings be translated into Latin so that the divinity students could learn the secrets hidden therein. Those clergy because Bishops, Archbishops, Cardinals, and Popes who steered the Catholic ship into the heathen abyss of Jewish rebellion against God.

Evidence of the corruption of nominal Protestant denominations by crypto-Jews is the use of the term Shekinah in place of the glory of God in those churches. Bloomer states that the adoration of the Shekinah is the central activity of the Jewish mystics. He views that adoration of Shenkinah by Jews as a concept that parallels the adoration of the Eucharistic by Catholics. The mystical Jewish concept of Shekinah through the Catholic Eucharist made conversion to

Roman Catholicism palatable for Jews.

The adoration of the Eucharist mentioned by Bloomer is plain and simple idolatry born from the Jewish Kabbalah. The Catholic church is following the mystical teachings of the Kabbalah when it admonishes its members to worship the Eucharist. The Catholic worship of the bread and wine is the same thing that the rebellious Jews did when they made the golden calf after they were brought out of the land of Egypt.

> And when the people saw that Moses delayed to come down out of the mount, the people gathered themselves together unto Aaron, and said unto him, Up, **make us gods, which shall go before us**; for *as for* this Moses, the man that brought us up out of the land of Egypt, we wot not what is become of him. And Aaron said unto them, Break off the golden earrings, which *are* in the ears of your wives, of your sons, and of your daughters, and bring *them* unto me. And all the people brake off the golden earrings which *were* in their ears, and brought *them* unto Aaron. And he received *them* at their hand, and fashioned it with a graving tool, after he had **made it a molten calf: and they said, These *be* thy gods, O Israel, which brought thee up out of the land of Egypt**. And when Aaron saw *it*, he built an altar before it; and Aaron made proclamation, and said, To morrow *is* a feast to the LORD. And they arose up early on the morrow, and offered burnt offerings, and brought peace offerings; and the people sat down to eat and to drink, and arose up to play.   And the LORD said unto Moses, Go, get thee down; for **thy people, which thou broughtest out of the land of Egypt, have corrupted *themselves*: They have turned aside quickly out of the way which I commanded them: they have made them a molten calf, and have worshipped it**, and have sacrificed thereunto, and said, **These *be* thy gods, O Israel, which have brought thee up out of the land of Egypt**. And the LORD said unto Moses, I have seen this people, and, behold, it *is* a stiffnecked people: Now therefore let me alone, that my wrath may wax hot against them, and that I may consume them. (Exodus 32:1-10 AV)

22 Putting Christ to Open Shame by Re-Crucifying Him

Not only does the Roman church worship the Eucharist, but they teach that the mass is an unbloody sacrifice of Christ repeated each day. Hislop reveals that the unbloody sacrifice during the Catholic Mass is derived from Chaldea (Babylon).[705] No blood was allowed on the altars of the "Paphian Venus" (i.e. Aphrodite). The historical evidence points clearly to Aphrodite being derived from the Babylonian goddess Mylitta. Mylitta was depicted, just as is the Catholic Mary, with her son in her arms.[706] Mylitta was characterizes as a mother who had a gentle character full of grace and mercy. Mylitta, means "The Mediatrix."[707] It is notable that the Catholic Church has elevated Mary to the station of mediatrix between man and God.[708] We know, however, that "there is one God, and one mediator between God and men, the man Christ Jesus." (1 Timothy 2:5 AV)

The parallels between the Babylonian mediatrix Mylitta and the Catholic mediatrix Mary are obvious. The Romans changed the name of Mylitta to Venus and the Greeks changed the name to Aphrodite in order to better blend the goddess into their unique cultures, but the nature of the goddess Mylitta remained. The Catholic church did the same thing. They changed the name of Venus to Mary in order to better graft the heathen goddess unnoticed and portray her a Christian saint. Saint is simply a term of art that conceals her true unchanged character as the goddess Venus. The Catholic altar is the altar of the mother goddess. That is why the Catholic Church calls itself "Mother Church."[709] She is the mysterious "Mother of Harlots and Abominations of the Earth." Revelation 17:5.

The Catholic church has ruled that the unbloody sacrifice of the Eucharist at mass is as effective a propitiation for sin as the actual crucifixion of Jesus Christ. A propitiation for sin is a sacrifice to appease God. That is to satisfy God and render favorable the object of his prior disfavor. God, however, was satisfied with Christ's sacrifice. When Jesus said "it is finished" he meant it is finished. John 19:30. To believe that it is necessary to have a continual sacrifice is to not believe in the Jesus of the Bible. The Jesus that the Romish church teaches is a different Jesus, an ineffectual Jesus. The *Catechism of the Catholic Church* states:

> **In the divine sacrifice which is celebrated in the Mass, the same Christ who offered himself once on a bloody manner on the alter of the cross is contained and is offered in an unbloody manner.**[710]

> **As often as the sacrifice of the Cross by which 'Christ our Pasch has been sacrificed' is celebrated on the altar, the work of our redemption is carried out.**[711]

The Catechism of the Council of Trent states:

> We therefore confess that the Sacrifice of the Mass is and ought to be considered one and the same Sacrifice as that of the cross, for the victim is one and the same, namely, Christ our Lord, who offered Himself once only, a bloody sacrifice on the altar of the cross. The bloody and unbloody victim are not two, but one victim only, whose sacrifice is **daily renewed** in the Eucharist, in obedience to the command of our Lord: *Do this for a commemoration of me.*[712]

> [T]he sacred and holy Sacrifice of the Mass is not a Sacrifice of praise and thanksgiving only, or a mere commemoration of the Sacrifice performed on the cross but also truly a **propitiatory** Sacrifice.[713]

The Holy Bible, on the other hand, states that the one sacrifice of Jesus was sufficient for all people, for all time.

> So Christ was **once offered** to bear the sins of many; and unto them that look for him shall he appear the second time without sin unto salvation. (Hebrews 9:28 AV)

> By the which will we are sanctified through the offering of the body of Jesus Christ **once** *for all*. And every priest standeth daily ministering and offering oftentimes the same sacrifices, which can never take away sins: But this man, after he had **offered one sacrifice for sins for ever**, sat down on the right hand of God; From henceforth expecting till his enemies be made his footstool. For **by one offering he hath perfected for ever them that are sanctified**. (Hebrews 10:10-14 AV)

Christ made his one sacrifice on the cross whereby those that believe in him are made perfect, consequently there will be no more offering of any kind for sin, period.

But this man, after he had offered one sacrifice for sins for ever, sat down on the right hand of God; From henceforth expecting till his enemies be made his footstool. For **by one offering he hath perfected for ever them that are sanctified**. *Whereof* the Holy Ghost also is a witness to us: for after that he had said before, This *is* the covenant that I will make with them after those days, saith the Lord, I will put my laws into their hearts, and in their minds will I write them; And their sins and iniquities will I remember no more. **Now where remission of these *is, there is* no more offering for sin**. (Hebrews 10:12-18 AV)

This unbloody re-crucifixion of Christ during the Catholic mass is a re-enactment of the humiliation suffered by Christ on the cross. This re-enactment is not only unnecessary, it is a blasphemy. The bible states that we are to look to Jesus in faith, not in ceremony. Jesus despised the shame of the cross. "Looking unto Jesus the author and finisher of *our* faith; who for the joy that was set before him **endured the cross, despising the shame**, and is set down at the right hand of the throne of God." (Hebrews 12:2 AV)

Jesus was crucified once for all time. The Catholic mass is a demonstration that the Catholic Church does not believe in the sufficiency of Jesus' sacrifice on the cross. They require that he be crucified over and over again, day after day, week after week, month after month, year after year. The Catholic mass is more than an affront to Christ, it is a ceremonial attack on Christ. It is an anti-Christ ceremony, whereby the Roman church puts Christ to an open shame by crucifying him anew. The bible states that it is a terrible sin to crucify Jesus again, because it once again puts him to an open shame. "If they shall fall away, to renew them again unto repentance; seeing **they crucify to themselves the Son of God afresh, and put *him* to an open shame.**" (Hebrews 6:6 AV)

23 Blood Passover

The shameful handling of Jesus during the Catholic Mass is why crypto-Jewish false converts to Catholicism have found the Mass so agreeable. The religion of Judaism went through a refinement after the crucifixion of Christ. The Babylonian witchcraft that was imbued into Judaism was targeted against Christ and Christians. The Catholic Mass, which was inculcated by the Jews into the Catholic Church, is just one manifestation of that animus. The Mass was a "Christianized" version of the corrupted Passover ceremony that orthodox Jews celebrated. Passover is a biblical feast that was instituted by God in the Old Testament. The Jews have since put an antichrist spin on that ceremony so that it is unrecognizable from its biblical roots.

In orthodox Judaism, Passover has become a ritual of detestation against Jesus. "Full well ye reject the commandment of God, that ye may keep your own tradition." (Mark 7:9 AV) Ariel Toaff, explains this fact in his book *Pasque di Sangue* (*Blood Passover*).[714] Before going further it should be understood who Ariel Taoff is. Taoff is a professor of Jewish renaissance and medieval history at Bar Ilan University[715] in Israel, just outside of Tel Aviv. The English translators of *Blood Passover,* Gian Marco Lucchese and Pietro Gianetti, explain that Professor Toaff was uniquely qualified to write the book, because he was "thoroughly familiar with the derivative literature in English, French, German, and Italian as well as the original documentary sources in Latin, Medieval Italian, Hebrew, and Yiddish."[716]

Professor Toaff is a Jewish insider, who comes from a rabbinic bloodline that is highly respected among Jews. He is the son of one of the most revered rabbis in the world, Elio Toaff. He is the former chief rabbi of Rome and was considered the dean of Italian Jewry. Some have called Elio Toaff the "Pope of the Jews." So influential was Rabbi Taoff in Rome, he was one of only two people that Pope John Paul II mentioned by name in his will.[717]

Toaff explains how over time Judaism and the Passover memorial in particular have been corrupted into a hate-fest against Christ and Christians.

In this Jewish-Germanic world, in continual movement, profound currents of popular magic had, over time, distorted the basic framework of Jewish religious law, changing its forms and meanings. It is in these "mutations" in the Jewish tradition – which are, so to speak, authoritative – that the theological justification of the commemoration in mockery of the Passion of Christ is to be sought, which, in addition to its celebration in the liturgical rite, was also intended to revive, in action, vengeance against a hated enemy continually reincarnated throughout the long history of Israel (the Pharaoh, Amalek, Edom, Haman, Jesus). Paradoxically, in this process, which is complex and anything but uniform, elements typical of Christian culture may be observed to rebound -- sometimes inverted, unconsciously but constantly -- within Jewish beliefs, mutating in turn, and assuming new forms and meanings. These beliefs, in the end, became symbolically abnormal, distorted by a Judaism profoundly permeated by the underlying elements and characteristic features of an adversarial and detested religion, unintentionally imposed by the same implacable Christian persecutor.[718]

When Professor Toaff's book was first published it created a firestorm of controversy. Toaff's initial response to the firestorm was to say "I will not give up my devotion to the truth."[719] Ultimately, however, Toaff succumbed to pressure and ordered his publisher to halt publication of the book. Toaff then agreed to donate all proceeds from the books sold to the Jewish Anti-Defamation League (ADL). The book has since been translated into English by Gian Marco Lucchese and Pietro Gianetti, who then posted their English translation on the internet.[720]

Toaff explains that the Passover meal was transformed into a ceremonial curse upon Christians. He explains how during the middle ages, the orthodox Jews sprinkled the Passover table with wine to signify the blood hatred of Christians by the vengeful Jews. The Jews made wine an integral part of the ceremony of Passover, which is intended as a disdainful twist on the last supper of Christ. Wine was not part of the Passover celebration as laid down by God. The Passover was intended to be a memorial that was to celebrate God having freed the Jews from Egyptian slavery. Passover also looked forward to the coming of Christ, who is the sacrificial Lamb of God, who takes away the sins of the world. *See* John 1:29.

The fourteenth day of the first month is the Passover (Leviticus 23:4-5, Exodus 12:17-18). Passover is immediately followed by the seven days of unleavened bread (Leviticus 23:6-7, Exodus 12:15-16). There is no mention of using wine as part of the Passover ceremony. Jesus instituted wine at the last supper. Matthew 26:27-29. The Jews have now instituted wine as an integral part of their Passover ceremony; it is intended as a contemptuous mockery of the last supper. The Passover ceremony included cursing Christians with the ten curses that were brought upon Egypt during the Jewish captivity there. Toaff explains:

> At this point, in the traditional reading of the *Haggadah*, according to the custom
> of the Ashkenazi Jews, the curses against the Egyptians were transformed into an

invective against all the nations and enemies hated by Israel, with explicit reference to the Christians. "From each of these plagues may God save us, but may they fall on our enemies". Thus [they] recited the formula reported by rabbi Jacob Mulin Segal, known as *Maharil*, active at Treviso around the last twenty years of the 14th century, in his *Sefer ha-minhagim* ("Book of Customs"), which unhesitatingly identified the adversaries of the Jewish people with the Christians, who deserved to be cursed. It seems that this custom was in force among German Jews even before the First Crusade. [The curse was memorialized by] [t]he sprinkling of the wine, which was a surrogate of the blood of the persecutors of Israel, onto the table, simultaneously with the recitation of the plagues of Egypt.[721]

Toaff was quick to point out that this cursed ceremony was not practiced by the Sephardic or Italian Jews, but as far as he knew, it was only practiced among the German Orthodox Ashkenazi Jews. Toaff explained that the Ashkenazi tradition was that the head of the family would state at the table: "Thus we implore God that these ten curses may fall on the gentiles, enemies of the faith of the Jews."[722] Toaff stated that was a clear reference to the Christians. The orthodox Jews call on God to cast his anger upon the gentiles and let the fury of his anger persecute and destroy them.[723]

The parallels between the corrupted Passover celebration practiced by orthodox Jews and the Catholic Mass are unmistakable. The Catholics believe that during the liturgy of the Mass the wine is magically transformed into the actual blood of Christ. A similar mythology is found in Judaism, where a small amount of the blood from the circumcision ceremony of a child when mixed with wine worked to magically turn the wine into blood. As in Catholicism, so also with Judaism, the respective cups of blood are propitiatory. Toaff explains the Jewish mythology:

> In the ceremony of the *milah,* a few drops of blood from the circumcised child, poured into wine, possessed the power to transform the wine into blood; therefore, the wine was drunk by the child, his mother and the *mohel* himself, with propitiatory, well-auguring and counter-magical meanings. By the same logic, during the Passover ceremony of the *Seder*, a few drops of the child's blood, the symbol of Edom (Christianity) and of Egypt, dissolved in the wine, had the power to transform the wine into blood, intended to be drunk and sprinkled onto the table as a sign of vengeance and as a symbol of the curses directed at the enemies of Israel as well as a pressing call to Redemption.[724]

The Jews claim that Toaff's book revives the "blood libel" against the Jews. A statement is only libelous if it is untrue. Toaff came to the ineluctable conclusion, based upon careful examination of authoritative evidence, that in the middle ages blood from Christian boys, who were ritually murdered, was used in some orthodox Jewish communities as part of the yearly Passover ceremony. He explained that only a small nut-sized amount of dried blood was shaken from a glass vial into the wine. The head of the family would announce: "This is the blood of a Christian child."[725] He then would recite the ten plagues of Egypt as curses against Christians and gentiles.[726] Toaff states:

> The head of the family takes a bit of the blood of the Christian child and drops it
> in his glass full of wine [...] then, putting his finger in the wine, with that wine
> where the blood of the Christian child has been shaken, he sprinkles the table and
> food on the table with it, pronouncing the Hebraic formula in commemoration of
> the ten curses, which God sent to the refractory Egyptian people who refused to
> liberate the Jewish people. At the end of the reading, the same head of the family,
> referring to the Christians, utters the following words (in Hebrew): 'thus we
> beseech God that he may similarly direct these ten curses against the gentiles, who
> are enemies of the Jewish faith.'[727]

Jews claim that Professor Toaff is wrong, because the Torah expressly prohibits Jews from consuming any kind of blood whatsoever.[728] E.g., Leviticus 17:10. That argument is fabricated to deceive the gullible *goyim*. Those who understand Judaism, know that the Jews have supplanted the laws of God in the Torah with their oral traditions. The Jews have a long history of rejecting the commands of God. Jesus said to the scribes and Pharisees: "And he said unto them, Full well ye reject the commandment of God, that ye may keep your own tradition. . . . Making the word of God of none effect through your tradition, which ye have delivered: and many such like things do ye." (Mark 7:9,13 AV)

In fact, celebration of Passover outside the city of Jerusalem is a violation of God's command. It is a sin. God stated clearly that Passover was only to be celebrated in the one city in the world that he shall choose for the Jews, upon which he would place his name: Jerusalem. Daniel explains that the one city that is called by God's name is Jerusalem. *See* Daniel 9:18.

> Thou mayest not sacrifice the passover within any of thy gates, which the LORD
> thy God giveth thee: But at the place which the LORD thy God shall choose to
> place his name in, there thou shalt sacrifice the passover at even, at the going
> down of the sun, at the season that thou camest forth out of Egypt. (Deuteronomy
> 16:5-6 AV)

The early Jews understood this restriction on the celebration of Passover. God gave special dispensation to the Jews when they were unable to enter the city due to uncleanness or if they were too distant. The fourteenth day of the first month is the Passover (Leviticus 23:4-5, Exodus 12:17-18). If a Jew was unable to present at Jerusalem on the fourteenth day of the first month, God allowed them to keep the Passover at Jerusalem a month later, on "the fourteenth day of the second month."

> And those men said unto him, We *are* defiled by the dead body of a man:
> wherefore are we kept back, that we may not offer an offering of the LORD in his
> appointed season among the children of Israel? And Moses said unto them, Stand
> still, and I will hear what the LORD will command concerning you. And the
> LORD spake unto Moses, saying, Speak unto the children of Israel, saying, If any

man of you or of your posterity shall be unclean by reason of a dead body, or *be* in a journey afar off, yet he shall keep the passover unto the LORD. The fourteenth day of the second month at even they shall keep it, *and* eat it with unleavened bread and bitter *herbs*. They shall leave none of it unto the morning, nor break any bone of it: according to all the ordinances of the passover they shall keep it. (Numbers 9:7-12 AV)

John Chrysostom (circa 347-407) explains that God required the Jews to obey the ordinance of Passover at Jerusalem in order to keep them from their proclivity toward spiritual harlotry, whereby they mixed heathen religious practices with God's ordinances. Once Christ came and was crucified as the lamb of God, there was no more need of a Passover celebration or indeed animal sacrifices at the temple. The burnt offerings of the Old Testament could only be made at the place chosen by God: the Temple at Jerusalem. Deuteronomy 12:13-21. Chrlysostom explains through an analogy why God placed the locality restriction on the Jews.

He drove them together from all quarters into a single place for this reason: so that they would have no occasion for impiety. When a well-born and free man has a female slave who is licentious and pulls in all the passers-by for immoral relations with her, he does not allow her to go out into the neighborhood, to show herself in the alley-way, to rush into the marketplace; instead, he confines her upstairs in the house, shackles her with iron, and orders her to remain indoors at all times, so that both the spatial restrictions of the place and the compulsion of the chains will be her starting-point for chastity. God acted in the very same way: the Synagogue being his licentious slave-woman, gaping after every demon and every idol, and rushing to make sacrifices to the idols in every spot and in every place, he confined it in Jerusalem and the temple, as though in the master's house, and ordered it to sacrifice and celebrate festivals at appointed times there only, so that both the spatial restrictions of the place and the observance of the times would keep it, even unwillingly, in the law of piety. Sit there and be modest, he says; let the place train you, since your character did not.

And [to confirm] that this is the reason why he commanded sacrifice there only: you have heard the Law that has now been read among us—it runs as follows: "For they shall bring their sacrifices to the doors of the Tent of Witness"[Lev. 17.5]—and it goes on to add the reason: "So that they will not sacrifice to their idols and to the vain things with which they themselves engage in prostitution."[Lev. 17.7] For there was no spot in Palestine that was not defiled by their impiety; instead, every hill, every ravine, and every tree was privy to this impiety of theirs. For this reason, Hosea cried out and said, "They sacrificed upon the hills; they made sacrifices upon the summits of the mountains, under oak and pine and shade-giving tree, because the shelter was good."[Hos. 4.13] And Jeremiah said, "Lift your eyes around you and see: Where did they not engage in prostitution?"[Jer. 3.2] It was for this reason that God, seeing that they had gone astray, confined them in one spot: the temple. But not even this put a stop to their licentiousness; rather, as if obstinately wishing to demonstrate to their Lord that whatever he did they would not abandon their madness, they brought adulterous lovers into their Lord's house, at one time setting up a four-faced idol there, at another time painting the abominations of reptiles and cattle on the wall. Ezekiel made this known to us—for he was brought from Babylon to the temple, and when he saw them burning incense to the sun and mourning for Adonis and worshipping all the other idols in the temple itself, he cried out in distress.[Ezek. 8]

But the prophet did not point out only this rampant impiety, but also [approached the subject] in another way, speaking as follows: "There came to be in you a perversion beyond all women."[Ezek. 16.34] How is it that payments are made to all prostitutes, he says, "but you gave out payments"?[Ezek. 16.33] For they engaged in prostitution and paid money for their own prostitution, which is the greatest proof of a soul that is being driven mad by the sting of its own profligacy. So then, because the house did not make them modest—instead, they set up their idols there—in the end God razed the temple itself to the ground. For what need was there for that place, given that idols were standing there and demons were being served in it?[729]

Passover was replaced by the New Testament celebration instituted at the last supper. *See* Luke 22:19; Galatians 3:23-25; Hebrews 8:13. The destruction of the temple in Jerusalem and the scattering of the Jews was God's way of turning the Jews from the worship of the pattern of Christ depicted in the animal sacrifices and the Passover celebration to the worship of Christ himself, the true "Lamb of God, which taketh away the sin of the world." John 1:29. Chrysostom explains:

He let the Jews offer sacrifice but permitted this to be done in Jerusalem and nowhere else in the world. After they had offered sacrifices for a short time, God destroyed the city. Why? The physician saw to it that the cup was broken. By seeing to it that their city was destroyed, God led the Jews away from the practice of sacrifice, though it was against their will. If God were to have come right out and said: "Keep away from sacrifice," they would not have found it easy to keep away from this madness for offering victims. But now, by imposing the necessity of offering sacrifice in Jerusalem, he led them away from this mad practice: and they never noticed what he had done

Let me make the analogy clear. the physician is God, the cup is the city of Jerusalem, the patient is the implacable Jewish people, the drink of cold water is the permission and authority to offer sacrifices. The physician has the cup destroyed and, in this way, keeps the sick man from what he demands at an ill-suited time. God destroyed the city itself, made it inaccessible to all, and in this way led the Jews away from sacrifices. If he did not intend to make ready an end to sacrifice, why did God, who is omnipresent and fills the universe, confine so sacred a ritual to a single place? Why did he confine worship to sacrifices, the sacrifices to a place, the place to a time, and the time to a single city, and then destroy the city? It is indeed a strange and surprising thing. The whole world is left open to the Jews, but they are not permitted to sacrifice there; Jerusalem alone is inaccessible to them, and that is the only place where they are permitted to offer sacrifice.

Even if a man he completely lacking in understanding, should it not be clear and obvious to him why Jerusalem was destroyed? Suppose a builder lays the foundation for a house, then raises up the walls, arches over the roof, and binds together the vault of the roof with a single keystone to support it. If the builder removes the keystone, he destroys the bond which holds the entire structure together. This is what God did. He made Jerusalem what we might call the keystone which held together the structure of worship. When he overthrew the city, he destroyed the rest of the entire structure of that way of life.[730]

The Jews refused to give up their Passover celebration, because they are a stiff-necked people. *See* Deuteronomy 31:27; Acts 7:51. The Jews have turned the Passover celebration, which was intended by God to be only temporary, into a twisted heathen practice that has little resemblance to the Old Testament pattern. The Jews have turned a pattern of celebration that looked forward to the coming of Christ into a blasphemous mockery of Christ.

Toaff obtained evidence of the Jewish practice of a blood Passover from testimony of Jewish witnesses at the trial of the murder of a Christian child in the 1400's. Expert testimony of Mosè of Würzburg at trial explained that "the Jews naturally require the blood of a Christian child, but if they were poor and could not afford any blood, they were relieved of the expense."[731] The Jewish hierarchy has always claimed that the testimony of these witnesses was obtained through torture and thus should not be believed. Toaff examined that issue and concluded that the testimony of the witnesses was reliable.

It should be obvious that only someone with a very good knowledge of the *Seder* ritual, an insider, could describe the precise order of gestures and operations as well as the Hebrew formulae used during the various phases of the celebration, and be capable of supplying such a wealth of detailed and precise descriptions and explanations. . . . Imagining that the judges dictated these descriptions of the *Seder* ritual, with the related liturgical formulae in Hebrew, does not seem very believable.[732]

The Passover of the bible had been twisted by the orthodox Jews and turned into an anti-ritual re-enacting the crucifixion of the hated Jesus. Toaff explains the anti-Christian symbolism of the ceremony:

The memorial of the Passion of Christ, relived and celebrated in the form of an anti-ritual miraculously exemplified the fate destined for Israel's enemies. The blood of the Christian child, a new *Agnus Dei*, and the eating of his blood, were premonitory signs of the proximate ruin of Israel's indomitable and implacable persecutors, the followers of a false and mendacious faith.

That is also the meaning behind the Roman Catholic Mass. The Catholic Mass is the corollary to the anti-Christ ceremony of the post-Christian celebration of the Passover by orthodox Jews. The witnesses at the trial testified that a small amount of blood of the Christian child was also mixed with the dough of the unleavened bread that was eaten during the Passover meal. There was testimony from a witness named Israele, who was identified as Samuele of Nuremberg's son, who stated that the mixing of the blood into the unleavened bread was a memorial of the blood with which the Lord commanded Moses to paint the door-posts of the doors. However, Toaff found another deeper meaning.

Vitale of Weissenburg, Samuele's agent, preferred to confer a second meaning upon the rite, that is, that of an upsidedown memorial to the Passion of Christ, considered as an emblem and paradigm of the fall of Israel's enemies and of divine vengeance, forewarning of final redemption. "We use the blood", he declared, "as a sad memorial of Jesus ... in outrage and contempt of Jesus, God of the Christians, and every year we do the memorial of that passion ... in fact, the Jews perform the memorial of the Passion of Christ every year, by mixing the blood of the Christian boy into their unleavened bread."[733]

The orthodox Jews twisted the memorial of the Passover into a contemptuous ceremony that humiliates Christ. The explanation of Israele and that of Vitale are closely related and not necessarily contradictory. Jesus is the Passover lamb of God sent to take away the sins of the world. "The next day John seeth Jesus coming unto him, and saith, Behold the Lamb of God, which taketh away the sin of the world." (John 1:29 AV) Jesus was crucified on Passover as the perfect propitiation for our sins. Our sins are forgiven by faith in his sacrifice. "Being justified freely by his grace through the redemption that is in Christ Jesus: Whom God hath set forth *to be* a propitiation through faith in his blood, to declare his righteousness for the remission of sins that are past, through the forbearance of God." (Romans 3:24-25 AV) The Jews lack faith in Jesus, and so they use the Passover not as a memorial of Christ's coming, but as a vengeful ceremony to curse the followers of Christ, who have the faith of Christ. "But as then he that was born after the flesh persecuted him that was born after the Spirit, even so it is now." Galatians 4:29.

The crypto-Jews have brought this hatred of Christ into the Catholic Church and fashioned the ceremony of the Mass to put Christ to shame. Jesus commanded that the last supper he shared on Passover was to be kept as a memorial and only as a memorial. Luke 22:19. The Catholic Church, however, rebels against Christ's admonition and instead claims that the wine at Mass is Christ's true blood and the unleavened bread is his true body offered as a new sacrifice for sins. The Catholic Church has twisted the last supper to humiliate Christ, just as the Jews in like manner have twisted the Passover to show contempt for Christ. Some orthodox Jews in the middle ages put a small amount of the Christian Child's blood in the wine cup and also mixed in a small amount of the blood into the unleavened dough to eat and drink as they curse the followers of Christ. The orthodox Jews on Passover and the Catholics during Mass conduct ceremonies to put Christ to shame.

Toaff explained the horrifying facts that the young victim was kidnaped by the Jews and subjected to a ritualized torture, symbolizing the torments of Christ. The testimony was that the ritual was passed down through oral tradition from generation to generation, from rabbi to rabbi.

> Samuele vaguely attributed these traditions to the rabbis of the Talmud (*Iudei sapientiores in partibus Babiloniae*), who were said to have introduced the ritual in a very remote epoch, "before Christianity attained its present power." Those scholars, united at a learned congress, were said to have concluded that the blood of a Christian child was highly beneficial to the salvation of souls, if it was extracted during the course of a memorial ritual of the passion of Jesus, as a sign of contempt and scorn for the Christian religion. Over the course of this counter-ritual, the innocent boy, who had to be less than seven years old and had to be a boy, like Jesus, was crucified among torments and expressions of execration, as had happened to Christ.[734]

It should be noted that many Jews disagreed with such a macabre ritual and did not follow the practices testified to during the trial. In fact, two Jews approached to help in the kidnapping of the child refused to assist in the effort to kidnap the child and argued against doing so. Toaff points out that the practice of the ritual use of the blood of a Christian child in the Jewish Passover meal was only practiced by fundamentalist orthodox Ashkenazi sects.[735] Toaff states that the orthodox Jews were the most assertive and were more controlling than the less assertive majority Jewish population. "Medieval Ashkenazi Judaism made up a hermetically sealed orthodoxy, which fed upon itself, confined by a myriad of minute ritualistic regulations, which they considered binding on all, the mere memorization of which constituted an arduous and almost impossible task."[736]

The little three-year-old boy who was the victim of the murder trial was made a Roman Catholic saint (Saint Simon of Trent). The little boy was kidnaped and tortured to death in 1475. The influence of the Jews within the Catholic Church has not been absolute. It took the Jews almost 500 years to finally get the Catholic Church to suppress Saint Simon as a Catholic Saint. In 1965, the Catholic Church ruled that the confessions of the defendants at the trial of Simon of Trent had been obtained under torture and were therefore unreliable. The cult of Saint Simon was outlawed. The church officials had the remains of the child removed and dumped in a secret place to avoid any resumption of pilgrimages to his grave.

It took the Jews almost 500 years to finally get the Vatican to suppress the truth of the ritual murder of Simon of Trent because the evidence in that case was so clear and convincing. Ariel

Toaff reports in his book that Cardinal Lorenzo Ganganelli, who later became Pope Clement XIV, issued a famous report on 19 January 1760, which he presented to the Congregation of the Holy Office. Cardinal Ganganelli intended the report to be a general absolution to the Jews against the accusation of ritual infanticide. Cardinal Ganganelli's investigation seemed to have been an early attempt to suppress the evidence of Jewish ritual murder. However, the strength of the evidence of Jewish ritual murder was so compelling in the case of Simon of Trent that Cardinal Ganganelli stated: "I therefore admit as true the fact of the sainted Simon, the boy of three years of age killed by Jews in hatred of the faith of Jesus Christ in Trent in the year 1475."[737]

Cardinal Ganganelli also investigated another ritual murder. Cardinal Ganganelli reported: "I accept as true another crime, committed in the village of Rinn, diocese of Bressanone, in 1462, against the sainted Andrea, a boy barbarously killed by the Jews in hatred of the faith of Jesus Christ."[738] The Cardinal confirmed the truth of the ritual murder in those two cases, but he stated that those two cases were insufficient for him to deduce that it was a certain and common axiom among Jews to engage in ritual murder of children.

Israel Shamir states that Toaff's findings, which were revealed in 2007, have the "potential to shake, shock, and reshape the Church. The noble, learned rabbi Dr. Toaff, brought back St Simon, the double victim of the fifteenth century vengeance and the twentieth century *perestroika.*"[739] In the Trent trials over the murder of Simon, Toaff discovered that the uniqueness of the rites and liturgical formulas used by the ashkenazi Jews on trial were so unique that they were not even known by the Italian Jews. It was impossible for the confessions to have been projections from the judges since they would not have even known of the unique rituals to which the defendants testified.[740] Shamir quotes Toaff, who correctly states that "a confession is of value only if it contains some true and verifiable details of the crime that police did not know of. This iron rule of criminal investigation was observed in the Trent trials."[741]

Toaff explains that there was widespread fear of the Jews in Europe in the middle ages, and that this fear sprung from their known reputation for kidnaping children for the slave trade. What is implicit in Toaff's research is that the orthodox Jews had an established insular group, that was practiced and expert in abducting children, whether it be for purposes of slavery or ritual murder.

> That Christian Europe of the Middle Ages feared the Jews is an established fact. Perhaps the widespread fear that Jews were scheming to abduct children, subjecting them to cruel rituals, even antedates the appearance of stereotypical ritual murder which seems to have originated in the 12th century. As for myself, I believe that serious consideration should be given to the possibility that this fear was largely related to the slave trade, particularly in the 9th and 10th centuries, when the Jewish role in the slave trade appears to have been preponderant.[742]

> During this period, Jewish merchants, from the cities in the valley of the Rhône, Verdun, Lione, Arles and Narbonne, in addition to Aquisgrana, the capital of the

empire in the times of Louis the Pious (Louis I); and in Germany from the centres of the valley of the Rhine, from Worms, Magonza and Magdeburg; in Bavaria and Bohemia, from Regensburg and Prague - were active in the principal markets in which slaves (women, men, eunuchs) were offered for sale, by Jews, sometimes after abducting them from their houses. From Christian Europe the human merchandise was exported to the Islamic lands of Spain, in which there was a lively market. The castration of these slaves, particularly children, raised their prices, and was no doubt a lucrative and profitable practice.

The first testimony relating to the abduction of children by Jewish merchants active in the trade flowing into Arab Spain, comes down to us in a letter from Agobard, archbishop of Lyon in the years 816-840. The French prelate describes the appearance at Lyons of a Christian slave, having escaped from Córdoba, who had been abducted from [a] Leonese Jewish merchant twenty four years before, when he was a child, to be sold to the Moslems of Spain. His companion in flight was another Christian slave having suffered a similar fate after being abducted six years before by Jewish merchants at Arles. The inhabitants of Lyons confirmed these claims, adding that yet another Christian boy had been abducted by Jews to be sold into slavery that same year. Agobard concludes his report with a comment of a general nature; that these were not considered isolated cases, because, in every day practice, the Jews continued to procure Christian slaves for themselves and furthermore subjecting them to "infamies such that it would be vile in itself to describe them."

Precisely what kind of abominable "infamies" Agobard is referring to is not clear; but it is possible that he was referring to castration more than to circumcision.[743] Liutprando, bishop of Cremona, in his *Antapodosis*, said to have been written in approximately 958-962, referred to the city of Verdun as the principal market in which Jews castrated young slaves intended for sale to the Moslems of Spain. During this same period, two Arab sources, Ibn Haukal and Ibrahim al Qarawi, also stressed that the majority of their eunuchs originated from France and were sold to the Iberian peninsula by Jewish merchants. Other Arabic writers mentioned Lucerna, a city with a Jewish majority, halfway between Córdoba and Málaga in southern Spain, as another major market, in which the castration of Christian children after reducing them to slavery was practiced on a large scale by the very same people.

Contemporary rabbinical responses provide further confirmation of the role played by Jews in the trade in children and young people as well as in the profitable transformation of boys into eunuchs. These texts reveal that anyone who engaged in such trade was aware of the risks involved, because any person caught and arrested in possession of castrated slaves in Christian territories was decapitated by order of the local authorities.[744]

Even the famous Natronai, Gaon of the rabbinical college of Sura in the mid-9th century, was aware of the problems linked to the dangerous trade in young eunuchs. "Jewish (merchants) entered (into a port or a city), bringing with them slaves and castrated children [Hebrew: serisim ketannim]. When the local authorities confiscated them, the Jews corrupted them with money, reducing them to more harmless advisors, and the merchandise was returned, at least in part."[745]

But if one wishes to interpret the significance and scope of the Jewish presence in the slave trade and practice of castration, it is a fact that the fear that Christian children might be abducted and sold was rather widespread and deeply rooted in all Western European countries, particularly, France and Germany, from which these Jews originated and where the greater part of the slave merchants operated. Personalities in the clergy nourished that fear, conferring religious connotations upon it with an anti-Jewish slant, failing to account for the fact that slavery as a trade had not yet gone out of fashion morally and, as such, was broadly tolerated in the economic reality of the period. On the other hand, the abduction and castration of children, often inevitably confused with circumcision, which was no less feared and abhorred, could not fail to insinuate themselves in the collective unconscious mind of Christian Europe, especially the French and German territories, inciting anxiety and fear, which probably solidified over time, and, as a result, are believed to have concretized themselves in a variety of ways and in more or less in the same places, as ritual murder.[746]

Walter White, Jr., in his book *Who Brought the Slaves to America,* documents that the slave traders responsible for bringing the slaves to America from Africa were predominately Jews. The Jews of Newport owned more than 300 slave ships. Authoritative records show that during one year in Charleston, South Carolina, 120 out of 128 slave ships that unloaded their "cargo" were documented as being undersigned by Jews from Newport and Charleston. The remainder of the ships were also likely Jewish owned, but it could not be confirmed. White explained that while almost all of the slave ships were owned by Jews, only about 10% of the slave ship captains were Jews. The Jews preferred to stay home and watch over their distillery operations that supplied the rum that was used to trade for the slaves. The Jews also made a handsome profit selling rum and whiskey to the American Indians.

The Jews set up a system of capture in Africa. Initially the Jews would trade rum for gold dust and ivory. When the tribal chiefs were in an alcoholic delirium and there was no more gold dust and ivory supply to trade for the rum, the tribal chiefs began to sell their wives and descendants. After a time, the Jews incited warfare between tribes in order to gain the profit by having the losers in the warfare sold as slaves to the Jews. The Jews would trade gunpowder for slaves. The gunpowder would then be used in future campaigns to capture more slaves. A typical price for a slave was either100 gallons of rum or100 pounds of gun powder, the value of each was approximately 20 dollars. In May 1752, the slave ship Abigail sailed for Africa with a cargo of about 9,000 gallons of rum and a great supply of iron foot and hand restraints that would shackle the returning slaves. At the going price of slaves, the ship would likely have been loaded with approximately 90 slaves for the return trip. The profit margin for one shipment of slaves was approximately tenfold, which is why the Jews were drawn to the slave trade. The La Fortuna was recorded as having a cargo of 217 slaves which cost approximately $4,300 and were sold for $41,438.

The accommodations aboard the slave ships could only be described as abominable. It would not be unusual after the three and a half month trip from Africa for almost half of the human cargo aboard a slave ship to die by the time the ship landed in Charleston, South Carolina.

The following ships are just a sampling of the slave ships owned by Jews: Abigail, owned by Aaron Lopez, Moses Levy, and Jacob Franks; Crown, owned by Isaac Levy and Nathan Simpson; Nassau, owned by Moses Levy; Four Sisters, owned by Moses Levy; Anne & Eliza, owned by Justus Bosch and John Abrams; Prudent Betty, owned by Henry Cruger and Jacob Phoenix; Hester, owned by Mordecai and David Gomez; Elizabeth, owned by David and Mordecai Gomez; Antigua, owned by Nathan Marston and Abram Lyell; Betsy, owned by William DeWoolf; PoUy, owned by James DeWoolf; White Horse, owned by Jan de Sweevts; Expedition, owned by John and Jacob Rosevelt; Charlotte, owned by Moses and Sam Levy and Jacob Franks; Caracoa, owned by Moses and Sam Levy.

What was the Roman Church's stance on the Jewish slave trade? From the sixth century up until the twentieth century it has been the common teaching of the Catholic church that social, economic, and institutional slavery is morally legitimate. The Roman Catholic Church has approved of the ownership of one man by another and the forced labor of the slave for the exclusive benefit of his owner, who may sell such slave to another.[747]

In 655 the Ninth Council of Toledo decreed that the children of priests who had remained neither celibate nor chaste would become permanent slaves of the Catholic Church. In 1012, the Council Pavia issued a similar decree. These decrees were incorporated into the Canon Law of the Roman Catholic Church. In 1089, at the Synod of Melfi, Urban II enforced the celibacy of priests by granting secular authorities the power to enslave the wives of priests. This decree was also incorporated into the Canon Law of the Roman Catholic Church.[748]

In the Fifteenth and Sixteenth centuries popes repeatedly granted the Kings of Portugal and Spain the full and free permission to capture and perpetually enslave the people of conquered territories.[749] In 1548, Pope Paul III issued the following *motu proprio,* addressing the issue of slavery in Rome:

> Each and every person of either sex, whether Roman or non-Roman, whether secular or clerical, and no matter of what dignity, status, decree, quarter, or condition they be, may freely and lawfully buy and sell publicly any slaves whatsoever of either sex, and make contracts about them as is accustomed to be done in other places, and publicly hold them as slaves and make use of their work,

and compel them to do the work assigned to them. And with apostolic authority, by the tenor of these present documents, we enact and decree in perpetuity that slaves who flee to the Capitol and appeal for their liberty shall in no wises be freed from the bondage of their servitude, but that notwithstanding their flight and appeal of this sort they shall be returned in slavery to their owners, and if it seems proper they shall be punished as runaways; and we very strictly forbid our beloved sons who for the time being are *conservatori* of the said city to presume by their authority to emancipate the aforesaid slaves – who flee as previously described and appeal for their liberty – from the bondage of their slavery, irrespective of whether they were made Christians after enslavement, or whether they were born in slavery even from Christian slave parents.[750]

In view of the Catholic position on slavery, it is not surprising to learn that Roger Taney, the United States Supreme Court Chief Justice who held in the *Dred Scott* decision that black slaves had no Constitutional Due Process Right to Liberty, was a Roman Catholic. Many believe that the *Dred Scott* decision by Taney was one of the principle catalysts for the Civil War. The Vatican was the only nation in the world to recognize the sovereignty of the pro-slavery Southern Confederate States during the U.S. Civil War.

24 Necromancy and the Queen of Heaven

Israel Shahak explains that Judaism is in fact a polytheistic religion chock full of different gods and goddesses. "[W]hatever can be said about this cabbalistic system, it cannot be regarded as monotheistic, unless one is also prepared to regard Hinduism, the late Graeco-Roman religion, or even the religion of ancient Egypt, as 'monotheistic.'"[751] Shahak explains that within the religious traditions of Orthodox Judaism is the practice of offering prayers to Satan.[752]

> [B]oth before and after a meal, a pious Jew ritually washes his hands, uttering a special blessing. On one of these two occasions he is worshiping God, by promoting the divine union of Son and Daughter; but on the other he is worshiping Satan, who likes Jewish prayers and ritual acts so much that when he is offered a few of them it keeps him busy for a while and he forgets to pester the divine Daughter. Indeed, the cabbalists believe that some of the sacrifices burnt in the Temple were intended for Satan. For example, the seventy bullocks sacrificed during the seven days of the feast of Tabernacles were supposedly offered to Satan in his capacity as ruler of all the Gentiles.[753]

The traditional prayers to Satan while engaging in ceremonial hand washing, explains why Jesus so harshly criticized the scribes for that practice in Mark 7:1-24:

> Then the Pharisees and scribes asked him, Why walk not thy disciples according to the tradition of the elders, but eat bread with unwashen hands? He answered and said unto them, Well hath Esaias prophesied of you hypocrites, as it is written, This people honoureth me with their lips, but their heart is far from me. Howbeit in vain do they worship me, teaching for doctrines the commandments of men. For laying aside the commandment of God, ye hold the tradition of men, *as* the washing of pots and cups: and many other such like things ye do. (Mark 7:5-8

233

AV)

This Babylonian polytheism has been injected by crypto-Jews into the Roman Catholic religion. Catholics pray to Mary because she is a goddess in the Catholic Church. Catholics will acknowledge that they pray to Mary, but deny that she is a goddess. That is because this truth has largely been veiled from them.

The Mary of the Catholic Church is not the Mary of the bible. She is in fact the Jews' queen of heaven. Athol Bloomer reveals that Mary is equivalent to the Sabbath Queen in Judaism.[754] The Kabbalah also has a warrior queen called Matronita who commands the hosts of heaven on behalf of Israel against its enemies.[755] Bloomer states that "Matronita is an image of both Mother Church and the Mother of God."[756]

Bloomer equates Matronita with Shekinah and Mary. Daniel Matt in his book *Zohar, The Book of Enlightenment* reveals that the Sabbath Queen and Shekinah are one and the same.[757] The Catholic goddess Mary is the "queen of heaven" in the Kabbalah, to whom the Jews have been making cake and drink offerings since the time of Jeremiah. "And when we burned incense to the **queen of heaven**, and poured out drink offerings unto her, did we **make her cakes to worship her**, and **pour out drink offerings unto her**, without our men?" (Jeremiah 44:19 AV)

The Mary of the bible is not a goddess; she was a woman elected by God to be the mother of Jesus. She died like everyone else and any attempt to communicate with her through prayer is the sin of necromancy. Deuteronomy 18:10-12. "**For *there is* one God, and one mediator between God and men, the man Christ Jesus;** (1 Timothy 2:5 AV).

The practice of communicating with Mary is part and parcel of the general practice of praying to a pantheon of Catholic gods and goddesses, which the Catholic Church calls "saints," who purport to join along with Mary as the queen of heaven to answer the prayers of the faithful.

> The holy council . . . orders all bishops and others who have the official charge of teaching. . . to instruct . . . the faithful that the **saints**, reigning together with Christ, **pray to God for men** and women; **that it is good and useful to invoke them humbly and to have recourse to their prayers, to their help and assistance, in order to obtain favours from God** through his Son our lord Jesus Christ, who alone is our Redeemer and Saviour. Those who deny that the saints enjoying eternal happiness in heaven **are to be invoked,** or who claim that saints do not pray for human beings or that **calling upon them to pray for each of us** is idolatry or is opposed to the word of God and is prejudicial to the honour of Jesus Christ, the one Mediator between God and humankind; or who say that it is foolish to **make supplication orally or mentally to those who are reigning in heaven**; all those entertain impious thoughts. *THE GENERAL COUNCIL OF TRENT, TWENTY FIFTH SESSION, DECREE ON THE INVOCATION, THE VENERATION AND THE RELICS OF SAINTS AND ON SACRED IMAGES,*

1560.

> [The saints'] . . . intercession is their most exalted service to God's plan. **We can
> and should ask them to intercede for us and for the whole world.**
> *CATECHISM OF THE CATHOLIC CHURCH*, § 2683, 1994.

The prayers to the dead so -called "Catholic saints" are simply attempts communicate with
the dead. God has expressly commanded that we not attempt to communicate with the dead. To
communicate with the dead is a sin called **necromancy**. There is only one mediator between
man and God to whom we should pray, and that is Jesus Christ.

> There shall not be found among you *any one* that maketh his son or his daughter
> to pass through the fire, *or* that useth divination, *or* an observer of times, or an
> enchanter, or a witch, Or a charmer, or a consulter with familiar spirits, or a
> wizard, or a **necromancer.** **For all that do these things *are* an abomination
> unto the LORD**: and because of these abominations the LORD thy God doth
> drive them out from before thee. (Deuteronomy 18:10-12 AV)

> For *there is* **one God, and one mediator between God and men, the man
> Christ Jesus**; (1 Timothy 2:5 AV)

Why would one pray to the saints? God won't listen to their counsel, because he doesn't
need counsel. Ephesians 1:11. God puts no trust in his saints.

> Behold, **he putteth no trust in his saints**; yea, the heavens are not clean in his
> sight. (Job 15:15 AV)

How did this clearly sinful practice of communicating with the dead through so-called prayer
originate? It is a direct outgrowth of the necromancy practiced by the Jews. Necromancy is so
ingrained in Judaism that among ancient Jews some Rabbis considered knowledge in
necromancy to be a necessary qualification for a seat in the Sahhendrin, which was the grand
counsel and court of justice among the ancient Jews.[758]

The Roman Catholic Church has a different gospel, with a different Jesus than that which is
found in the Bible. *See* 2 Corinthians 11:4. Their different gospel was born of the Kabbalah and
has different doctrines and a different Mary from the Mary in the Bible. In the Bible, Mary is the
handmaid of the Lord. *See* Luke 1:38. The Roman Catholic Church Mary, however, is an
imperious queen of heaven, who rules over all things.

The Catholic Mary (as distinguished from the biblical Mary) is a heathen goddess, who in
1950 was "infallibly" declared by Pope Pius XII to have been assumed body and soul into heaven
and crowned **"Queen over all things."**

Finally the Immaculate Virgin, preserved free from all stain of original sin, when the course of her earthly life was finished, was taken up body and soul into heavenly glory, and exalted by the Lord as **Queen over all things**, so that she might be the more fully conformed to her Son, the Lord of lords and conqueror of sin and death. Pope Pius XII -- *Munificentissimus Deus, 1950.*

The problem with that "infallible" pronouncement of the pope is that it is impossible for Mary to be "queen over all things." The Bible states unequivocally that Jesus Christ "is the blessed and **only Potentate**, the Lord of lords and King of kings." 1 Timothy 6:15. A potentate is a sovereign monarch.[759] Jesus Christ is the "only Potentate." Only means only! There is not room in heaven for another Potentate. Mary, therefore, cannot be "queen over all things." Jesus is the **"only Potentate"** over all things!

Satan is using his Catholic Church and its doctrine of Mariolatry, to attempt a futile spiritual *coup d' etat* to supplant Jesus and enthrone its Mary as the "Queen of Heaven." The Catholic Church is dedicated to the worship and service of "Mary," the queen of heaven. Jesus is ancillary and almost incidental to the worship of the Catholic queen of heaven. For example, the coin commemorating the pontificate of John Paul II has on the front has a declaration that he is the Pontifex Maximus. "On the reverse side is his papal heraldic shield. The large letter M on the shield stands for Mary, the mother of God. The words at the bottom 'TOTUS TUUS' are transposed and excerpted from a latin prayer composed by Saint Louis-Marie Grignion de Montfort: *tuus totus ego sum, et omnia mea tua sunt, O Virgo super omnia benedicta*, which in English reads 'I belong to you entirely, and all that I possess is yours, Virgin blessed above all.'"[760] The pope dedicates his fealty not to Jesus but to "Mary," the Catholic "Queen of Heaven."

In 1978, on the feast day of the Immaculate Conception, Pope John Paul II dedicated and entrusted the Roman Catholic Church and all its property not to their Catholic version of Jesus, but rather to their Catholic version of Mary:

> The Pope, at the beginning of his episcopal service in St. Peter's Chair in Rome, wishes to entrust the Church particularly to her in whom there was accomplished the stupendous and complete victory of good over evil, of love over hatred, of grace over sin; to her of whom Paul VI said that she is ' the beginning of the better world;' to the Blessed Virgin. He entrusts to her himself, as the servant of servants, and all those whom he serves, all those who serve with him. **He entrusts to her the Roman Church, as token and principle of all the churches in the world, in their universal unity. He entrusts it to her and offers it to her as her property.** Insegnamenti Giovanni Paolo II (1978), Vatican City: Libreria Editrice Vaticana, 313.[761]

The Catholic Church has a series of ritualistic mysteries that are recited after each of 15 Catholic "stations of the cross." These "mysteries" are said while counting beads that are called the rosary. The primary focus of the Catholic Rosary is not Jesus, it is Mary. Mary's roles in Christ's birth, death, and resurrection are highlighted, exaggerated, and in some instances fabricated in 12 of the 15 "mysteries." In fact, the formal title of the Rosary is: "**The Roses of Prayer for the Queen of Heaven.**"[762] The prayers to Mary outnumber the supposed prayers to God by roughly 10 to 1. After each mystery is recited, Catholics say one "Our Father" prayer followed by ten "Hail Mary" prayers. The "Hail May" is a rote prayer to the Catholic goddess, whom they call Mary. They blaspheme God by praying to their Mary goddess and prove themselves heathen by repeating the blasphemous prayers over and over again. "But when ye pray, use not vain repetitions, as the heathen do: for they think that they shall be heard for their much speaking." (Matthew 6:7 AV)

It is notable that the rosary said in honor of the queen of heaven has stations of the cross called "mysteries." There is a woman mentioned in the Bible whose very name is "mystery."

> And the woman was arrayed in purple and scarlet colour, and decked with gold and precious stones and pearls, having a golden cup in her hand full of abominations and filthiness of her fornication: And upon her forehead *was* a name written, **MYSTERY**, BABYLON THE GREAT, THE MOTHER OF HARLOTS AND ABOMINATIONS OF THE EARTH. (Revelation 17:4-5 AV)

Later, when the Bible speaks of the destruction of the "mystery" harlot, the harlot says in her heart that she sits as a **"queen."**

> Reward her even as she rewarded you, and double unto her double according to her works: in the cup which she hath filled fill to her double. How much she hath glorified herself, and lived deliciously, so much torment and sorrow give her: **for she saith in her heart, I sit a queen**, and am no widow, and shall see no sorrow. Therefore shall her plagues come in one day, death, and mourning, and famine; and she shall be utterly burned with fire: for strong *is* the Lord God who judgeth her. (Revelation 18:6-8 AV)

God reveals the mystery of the woman. God identifies the woman as a great city. "And the woman which thou sawest is that great city, which reigneth over the kings of the earth." (Revelation 17:18 AV) God also reveals the mystery of the woman.

> **I will tell thee the mystery of the woman**, and of the beast that carrieth her, which hath the seven heads and ten horns. The beast that thou sawest was, and is not; and shall ascend out of the bottomless pit, and go into perdition: and they that dwell on the earth shall wonder, whose names were not written in the book of life from the foundation of the world, when they behold the beast that was, and is not, and yet is. And here *is* the mind which hath wisdom. **The seven heads are seven mountains, on which the woman sitteth**. (Revelation 17:7-9 AV)

So we know that the mystery harlot is a great city that sits on seven mountains. There is only one city that matches that description and that is Rome. Rome is famous for the seven mountains upon which it sits (the Capitoline, the Quirinal, the Viminal, the Esquiline, the Caelian, the Avenue, and the Palatine).[763] The glorification of the queen of heaven is in a sense a glorification by proxy of the Roman Catholic Church. That is why the Catholic hierarchy refers to their organization as "Mother Church."[764] It is true that the Catholic Church is a mother, **"THE MOTHER OF HARLOTS AND ABOMINATIONS OF THE EARTH."** (Revelation 17:4-5 AV) That mother of harlots "saith in her heart, I sit a **queen**." Revelation 18:7. There is a spiritual parallel between the wicked harlot queen in the book of Revelation and Mary the queen of heaven glorified by the Catholic Church. The harlot of Revelation and Mary the queen of heaven both draw men from Jesus Christ, who "is the blessed and only Potentate, the Lord of lords and King of kings." 1 Timothy 6:15.

One of the "mysteries" recited during the Catholic rosary is called "the Fifth Glorious Mystery - The Coronation." In that mystery it is claimed by the Catholic Church that "**Mary is the Queen of Heaven**."

> Mary had served Jesus all her life. She had loved and served God with her whole heart and soul. She had never committed the slightest sin. So in heaven she was to have her reward. Body and soul, Mary entered heaven. Her Son, Jesus, met her and took her in His grateful arms. The heavenly Father said, "This is My dear devoted daughter." The Divine Son said, "This is My dear faithful Mother." The Holy Spirit said, "This is my sweet, pure bride." And the saints and angels all cried, **"This is our Queen!"** So Jesus, the King of Kings, seated her on her throne. On her head He placed a glorious crown of stars. But Mary looked down to see her children on earth. For now she could help her sons and daughters to reach heaven. **Mary is the Queen of Heaven**. But she is our loving Mother who protects us with her power.[765]

One of the final prayers of the Rosary is a prayer to the Catholic goddess "Mary" called **"Hail Holy Queen."**

> **Hail, holy Queen**, Mother of Mercy! our life, our sweetness, and our hope! To thee do we cry, poor banished children of Eve; to thee so we send up our sighs, mourning and weeping in this valley, of tears. Turn, then, most gracious Advocate, thine eyes of mercy toward us; and after this our exile show unto us the blessed fruit of thy womb, Jesus; O clement, O loving, O sweet Virgin Mary.[766]

The Catholics also have other prayers not said during the rosary to their goddess, the Queen of Heaven:

> **Queen of heaven**, rejoice. Alleluia. The Son whom you were privileged to bear, Alleluia, has risen as he said, Alleluia. Pray to God for us, Alleluia. Rejoice and

be glad, Virgin Mary, Alleluia. For the Lord has truly risen, Alleluia. O God, it was by the Resurrection of your Son, our Lord Jesus Christ, that you brought joy to the world. Grant that through the intercession of the Virgin Mary, his Mother, we may attain the joy of eternal life. Through Christ, our Lord. Amen.[767]

The Catholic "Mary" (queen of heaven) is viewed by the Roman Catholic Church as "the **restorer of the world that was lost, and the dispenser of all benefits** . . . the **most powerful mediator (***mediatrix)*** and advocate (***conciliatrix*)** for the whole world . . . above all others in sanctity and in union with Christ . . . the primary minister in the distribution of the divine graces,"[768] "the **beloved daughter of the Father and Temple of the Holy Spirit**,"[769] "the **mother of all the living**,"[770] "the **new Eve**,"[771] "**Mother of the Church**,"[772] "the '**Mother of Mercy**,' the **All Holy One**."[773]** She supposedly "**surpasses all creatures, both in heaven and on earth**,"[774] conquered death and was ". . . raised body and soul to the glory of heaven, to **shine refulgent as Queen** at the right hand of her Son, the immortal King of ages."[775]

> [I]ndeed, she is clearly the **mother of the members of Christ since she has by her charity joined in bringing about the birth of believers in the Church** who are members of its head. Wherefore she is hailed as pre-eminent and as a wholly unique member of the Church, and as its type and outstanding model in faith and charity. The Catholic Church taught by the Holy Spirit, honours her with filial affection and **devotion as a most beloved mother**. THE SECOND VATICAN COUNCIL, 1964 (emphasis added).[776]

What does God think of this Catholic goddess, Mary?

> Thou shalt worship the Lord thy God, and him **only** shalt thou serve. (Luke 4:8 AV)

> Thou shalt have **no other gods** before me. . . . Thou shalt not bow down thyself to them nor serve them: for I the LORD thy God *am* a jealous God.. (Exodus 20:3-5 AV)

When a woman praised Mary loudly, Jesus corrected her, making it clear that the woman who gave birth to him is not blessed above those who are saved by the grace of God.

> And it came to pass, as he spake these things, a certain woman of the company lifted up her voice, and said unto him, Blessed *is* the womb that bare thee, and the paps which thou hast sucked. But he said, Yea rather, blessed *are* they that hear the word of God, and keep it. (Luke 11:27-28 AV)

Roman Catholic Mariolatry is derived from the goddess worship performed by the Jews when they worship Matronita, the queen of heaven. The Catholic Church has simply changed the name of the Jewish queen from Matronita to Mary. The Catholic Mary has nothing in common with the biblical Mary. The Catholic queen of heaven, however, has everything in common with the queen of heaven described in the Bible. In the Bible, God condemns homage and service to the queen of heaven.

> Seest thou not what they do in the cities of Judah and in the streets of Jerusalem? The children gather wood, and the fathers kindle the fire, and the women knead *their* dough, to make cakes to the **queen of heaven**, and to pour out drink offerings unto other gods, that they may provoke me to anger. Do they provoke me to anger? saith the LORD: *do they* not *provoke* themselves to the confusion of their own faces? Therefore thus saith the Lord GOD; Behold, mine anger and my fury shall be poured out upon this place, upon man, and upon beast, and upon the trees of the field, and upon the fruit of the ground; and it shall burn, and shall not be quenched. (Jeremiah 7:17-20 AV)

Serving the queen of heaven is an abomination to God. There are consequences for that great sin against the Lord. In chapter 44 of Jeremiah we read that the Jews burned incense and served the **"queen of heaven."** This great sin kindled the fury and anger of the Lord, who responded by wasting and bringing desolation upon the cities of Judah, including Jerusalem. The Jews have not learned; they have inculcated their queen of heaven anew into their Roman Catholic Church.

25   Magic Talismans and Idols

Not only does the Catholic Church instruct its members to pray to Mary and the other saints, but it also instructs them to venerate graven images of Jesus, Mary, and the saints. The *Catechism of the Catholic Church* states:

> Basing itself on the mystery of the incarnate Word, the seventh ecumenical council at Nicaea justified against the iconoclasts the **veneration of icons** - of Christ, but also of the mother of God, the angels, and all the saints. By becoming incarnate, the Son of God introduced a new economy of images.[777]

What does God think about this veneration of graven images? The following are the first two of the Ten Commandments.

> And God spake all these words, saying, I *am* the LORD thy God, which have brought thee out of the land of Egypt, out of the house of bondage. **Thou shalt have no other gods before me. Thou shalt not make unto thee any graven image, or any likeness *of any thing* that *is* in heaven above, or that *is* in the earth beneath, or that *is* in the water under the earth: Thou shalt not bow down thyself to them, nor serve them**: for I the LORD thy God *am* a jealous God, visiting the iniquity of the fathers upon the children unto the third and fourth *generation* of them that hate me; And shewing mercy unto thousands of them that love me, and keep my commandments. (Exodus 20:1-6 AV)

How did this practice, which is a clear violation of God's commandment, get introduced into the Catholic Church? The crypto-Jews who infiltrated the church brought with them their practice of invoking magic talismans and relics. It was easy enough to inject this same practice among the *goyim* in the Catholic Church. While the Jews outwardly profess to eschew idols and graven images, they secretly engage in all manner of idolatry. Making amulets, charms, and talismans are taught in Jerusalem at the rabbinic seminary Yeshivat Hamekubalim.[778] The Cabalistic handbook that contains instruction for Rabbis on how to make amulets, charms, and talismans is the *Sefer Raziel*.[779] Helen Jacobus writing for the *Jewish Chronicle* discovered that "[b]efore use, amulets and incantations have to be tested and approved. The rabbi or Kabbalist who gives his blessing can be blamed or lose his reputation if his charm does not work; conversely he gains kudos - and a good income - if his amulets or spells are effective."[780]

What is the source of the power of these amulets? These idols and amulets are not invoking the power of Almighty God, but of gods who are in fact devils. "They sacrificed unto devils, not to God; to gods whom they knew not, to new gods that came newly up, whom your fathers feared not." (Deuteronomy 32:17 AV) The power comes from devils. "What say I then? that the idol is any thing, or that which is offered in **sacrifice to idols** is any thing? But *I say*, that the things which the Gentiles sacrifice, they **sacrifice to devils**, and not to God: and I would not that ye should have fellowship with devils." (1 Corinthians 10:19-20 AV)

Professor Gershom Sholem admits that in Judaism devils are invoked through the use of amulets.[781] Sholem is regarded by many as the founder of the modern, academic study of Kabbalah; he was the first Professor of Jewish Mysticism at the Hebrew University of Jerusalem. Michael Hoffman reveals that "[t]his demonic pantheon includes devils known in the Kabbalah as *shedim Yeshuda'im*. Professor Sholem informs us that these devils are in submission to the Talmud."[782] Judaism is so immersed in witchcraft that the official flag of the State of Israel depicts a witchcraft symbol, a hexagram. "In Ritual Magick, the hexagon [sic] [hexagram] is called the Seal of Solomon, and represents Divine Union, being composed of a female, watery triangle, and a male, fiery triangle."[783] Hoffman states; "The original source of the symbol is androgynous, representing Adam Kadmon, the personification of the union of the male and female form in one body."[784] The Jewish practice in witchcraft of placing a "hex" (curse) on someone is a term that is derived from the "hexagram."

With the church of Rome being the creation of mystical Jews, it should come as no surprise that the pope of Rome has emblazoned one of his miters with the Jewish hexagram.

There is one idol, however, that Jews are taught to hate, and that is any cross or crucifix that is intended to represent Christ. Hoffman explains: "In Judaism the Cross of Christ is an abomination, the '*He-emid tzelem b-hachnal*' (BT Ta'anit 26b)."[785] The Jerusalem Post reported that the chief rabbi of the Western Wall, Shmuel Rabinovitch, has said that it is not proper for Pope Benedict XVI to come to the Western Wall during his planned visit in May 2009, and that he should not wear a cross.

> Rabinovitch has barred access to the Western Wall by Christian clergy wearing crosses. In November 2007, he refused to allow a group of Austrian bishops led by the Archbishop of Vienna, Christoph Schonborn, access to the site after the clergymen refused to remove or hide their crosses. At the time Rabinovitch told the Post that "crosses are a symbol that hurt Jewish feelings." In May 2008, a group of Irish prelates from both Catholic and Protestant churches were prevented from visiting the Western Wall for the same reason.[786]

When Pope John Paul II visited the Western Wall in 2000 he apparently was permitted to wear a cross. However, he also did something unusual during his visit. When Pope John Paul II visited Israel, he depicted a large cross on his ceremonial throne. The cross was different than the usual cross. It was upside-down. An upside-down cross is typically a symbol of the rejection of Christ and a mockery of his crucifixion.

You can be sure that the Jews approved of the upside-down cross, because they understood it is a symbol used to mock Christ. Just as Judas, the mystery of iniquity, pretended to be a loyal follower of Jesus as he worked to betray him (Luke 22:47-48), so also the pope, who is also the mystery of iniquity, pretends to be a loyal follower of Jesus and is betraying his subjects into the lake of fire. Revelation 20:10, 15. The antichrist is the very opposite of Jesus; Jesus is the mystery of Godliness, who is faithful and true and will never forsake us. Hebrews 13:5, Revelation 19:11.

At right is Pope John Paul II at the Sea of Galilee in Israel on March 24, 2000. Notice the Satanic symbol of the upside-down cross on the throne set up for the Pope. The upside-down cross, signifies a reversal of Christian doctrine, ie. Antichrist doctrine; it symbolizes a mockery and rejection of Jesus Christ.[787]

POPE JOHN PAUL II
SEA OF GALILEE, ISRAEL
MARCH 24, 2000

The Catholic Church never officially explained the upside-down cross, however, its agents on the internet explained that the upside-down cross is a symbol of Peter. The Catholic Church's mythology includes the story that Peter was crucified upside-down, although there is absolutely no evidence to support that claim.

One must be aware that all occult symbols have two meanings. One meaning is an open (exoteric) meaning that is for the general public, the other hidden (esoteric) meaning is only for those initiated into the secret doctrines. In this case the exoteric meaning is that the upside-down cross represents Peter; the hidden esoteric meaning understood by occult practitioners is that the upside-down cross mocks the crucifixion of Jesus and is a rejection of his teachings.

One of the reasons that Babylon the Great, the Mother of Harlots and Abominations of the Earth is called "Mystery" is that she embodies the mystery of iniquity. The mystery of iniquity is that the antichrist is the devil manifest in the flesh. The pope, therefore, must be possessed by Satan himself. God, in 2 Thessalonians chapter 2, refers to the antichrist as the man of sin, the son of perdition. Later, in that same chapter, God refers to the spirit of the antichrist as the "mystery of iniquity." What does God mean by the mystery of iniquity? The opposite of iniquity is godliness. While God did not expressly state in 2 Thessalonians chapter 2 what he meant by the mystery of iniquity, he does explain elsewhere in the Bible what is the mystery of godliness.

In 1 Timothy chapter 3, God states that the mystery of godliness is, in part, that "God was manifest in the flesh." Since the antichrist is the opposite of God in character, but he seeks to replace God, then the mystery of iniquity must be the devil manifest in the flesh. Interestingly, in the very next verse following God's explanation of the mystery of godliness in 1 Timothy, he explains that "in the latter times some shall depart from the faith, giving heed to seducing spirits, and doctrines of devils; Speaking lies in hypocrisy; having their conscience seared with a hot iron; Forbidding to marry, *and commanding* to abstain from meats." The Roman Catholic Church has embraced both the doctrine of forbidding Catholic priests to marry and forbidding the eating of meat on Friday during Lent.

So we see that the mystery of iniquity is the manifestation of the devil in the flesh. Are there other verses that support this interpretation? If we look at John 6:70-71, we see that Jesus referred to Judas as a devil. "Jesus answered them, Have not I chosen you twelve, and **one of you is a devil**? He spake of Judas Iscariot *the son* of Simon: for he it was that should betray him, being one of the twelve." (John 6:70-71 AV) Was Judas a devil? In looking at the gospel of Luke we see that the devil (Satan) in fact entered into Judas prior to Judas' betrayal of Jesus. "**Then entered Satan into Judas** surnamed Iscariot, being of the number of the twelve." (Luke 22:3 AV) We see that the devil was manifest in the flesh when he entered into Judas. This interpretation is confirmed by John 17:12 where Jesus refers to Judas as "the son of perdition." "While I was with them in the world, I kept them in thy name: those that thou gavest me I have kept, and none of them is lost, but **the son of perdition**; that the scripture might be fulfilled." (John 17:12 AV) The term "son of perdition" is the same term used in 2 Thessalonians 2:3 to describe the antichrist. "Let no man deceive you by any means: for *that day shall not come*, except there come a falling away first, and that man of sin be revealed, **the son of perdition**. (2 Thessalonians 2:3 AV)

The man of sin, the son of perdition, described in 2 Thessalonians 2:3, can be none other than the pope of Rome. The mystery of iniquity, therefore, must be that the pope of Rome, who is the son of perdition, is possessed by Satan, just as Judas, who also was the son of perdition, was possessed by Satan. As Christ was God manifest in the flesh, so also the antichrist (the pope) is the devil manifest in the flesh.

The Roman Church teaches that Peter is the rock upon which God has built his church, and that the Pope, as the bishop of Rome, is Peter's successor, head of the church, and the "Vicar of Christ."[788] The Bible, however, is clear that Jesus Christ is the foundation and head of the church, not the pope. "And he is the head of the body, the church: who is the beginning, the firstborn from the dead; that in all *things* he might have the preeminence." (Colossians 1:18 AV) So, the pope seeks to replace Christ as he opposes him. He is the antichrist.

Just as Judas, the mystery of iniquity, pretended to be a loyal follower of Jesus as he worked to betray him (Luke 22:47-48), so the pope, who is also the mystery of iniquity, pretends to be a loyal follower of Jesus and is betraying his subjects into the lake of fire. Revelation 20:10, 15. The antichrist is the very opposite of Jesus; Jesus is the mystery of Godliness, who is faithful and true and will never forsake us. Hebrews 13:5, Revelation 19:11.

The Pope in recent history has not displayed the upside-down cross. It is not simply a coincidence that he chose to do so when visiting Israel. It was a clear signal to the orthodox Jews that he was on their side against Christ and Christians. Just as Judas pretended to be a follower of Christ and betrayed him to the Jews, so also does the pope pretends to be a follower of Christ and betrays him to the Jews anew. The upside-down cross displayed by the pope in Israel is symbolic of that betrayal.

The Israeli newspaper *Haaretz* reports that yeshiva students customarily spit on the ground as a sign of disgust upon seeing a cross.[789] There are even times when Jews will approach in the middle of a religious procession and spit on the cross in front of all the priests. They sometimes will even spit on "Christian" clergy.[790] The Israeli government typically does nothing about this activity, because it is an anti-Christian government.[791]

The Jews explain their expectorating behavior by claiming that they are opposed to the idolatry of the cross. That explanation does not pass the smell test. The evidence is clear that their behavior is based upon animus toward Christ and Christians, when one considers the rampant idolatry practiced within Judaism itself, and the fact that orthodox Jews will burn New Testaments, if they can get away with it. Orthodox Jews act upon Talmud Tractate Shabbath, Folio 116a as a command to burn New Testaments. USA Today reported that orthodox Jews in Israel burned hundreds of copies of the New Testament.[792] The New Testaments were dumped into a pile and set afire in a lot near a synagogue.[793] They burned the New Testaments, not because they were idols, but because the books were about Jesus Christ, whom they hate.

Jewish children are taught today to utter a blessing when passing a Jewish cemetery, but to curse the mothers of the dead when passing non-Jewish cemeteries.[794] There is a special curse uttered by Jews when passing a Christian church: *Beis gee'im visach Hashem* ("May Hashem

[god] destroy this house of the proud.").[795]

The Catholic church claims that the veneration of idols practiced by Catholics is not the same as the worship of images prohibited in the Ten Commandments. The Second Commandment is very specific as to what conduct toward graven images is prohibited. **"[t]hou shalt not make unto thee any graven image, or any likeness *of any thing* that *is* in heaven above, or that *is* in the earth beneath, or that *is* in the water under the earth: Thou shalt not bow down thyself to them, nor serve them."** Whether you call it worship or veneration, bowing down to a graven image is prohibited. Knowing this, it was necessary for the Catholic church in their official catechism to change the first commandment and completely removed the second commandment. The traditional Catholic catechism simply states the following in place of the first two commandments: "1. I am the Lord your God: you shall not have **strange gods** before me."[796]

Notice that the prohibition against making graven images and bowing to them or serving them is deleted in the Catholic Ten Commandments. In addition, the Romish church allows the worship of other gods as long as they are not strange gods. So it is permissible to have Mary and all the saints as other gods because they are not "strange gods" according to Catholic doctrine. God's first commandment, however, states that "I *am* the LORD thy God, which have brought thee out of the land of Egypt, out of the house of bondage. Thou shalt have **no other gods** before me." They have changed the commandments of God in order to set up their own religion in direct opposition to God's true commands.

In the Catholic catechism the second commandment is completely deleted. This leaves the Catholic Church in a quandary; they only have nine commandments in their catechism. Not to worry, the Catholic Church simply splits the last commandment into two commandments to make up for the missing commandment in the Catholic Catechism. So the single commandment against coveting is changed into two commandments against coveting thy neighbor's goods and coveting a neighbor's wife.[797]

God clearly states in the second commandment that **"[t]hou shalt not make unto thee any graven image**, or any likeness *of any thing* that *is* in heaven above, or that *is* in the earth beneath, or that *is* in the water under the earth . . .."** It is a sin to even make the graven images. The Catholic Church is without excuse.

This changing of God's commandments is a fulfillment of the prophecy in Daniel regarding the beast, the antichrist. Daniel prophesied that the beast would seek to change times and laws.

> And the ten horns out of this kingdom *are* ten kings *that* shall arise: and another shall rise after them; and he shall be diverse from the first, and he shall subdue three kings. **And he shall speak *great* words against the most High, and shall wear out the saints of the most High, and think to change times and laws**: and they shall be given into his hand until a time and times and the dividing of time.

(Daniel 7:24-25 AV)

The Roman church teaches that by coming to earth as a man, Christ instituted a new era of images. Why then would God command Christians in the New Testament time and again to keep away from idols?

> Little children, **keep yourselves from idols**. Amen. (1 John 5:21 AV)

> But that we write unto them, that they **abstain from pollutions of idols**, and *from* fornication, and *from* things strangled, and *from* blood. (Acts 15:20 AV)

> Wherefore, my dearly beloved, **flee from idolatry**. (1 Corinthians 10:14 AV)

> And **what agreement hath the temple of God with idols**? for ye are the temple of the living God; as God hath said, I will dwell in them, and walk in *them*; and I will be their God, and they shall be my people. (2 Corinthians 6:16 AV)

> Now the works of the flesh are manifest, which are *these*; Adultery, fornication, uncleanness, lasciviousness, **Idolatry**, witchcraft, hatred, variance, emulations, wrath, strife, seditions, heresies, (Galatians 5:19-20 AV)

On Mars' Hill the Apostle Paul saw the many idols of the Greeks displayed in much the same way the Roman Catholic Church displays its idols. Paul's spirit was stirred and he reproved them for their idolatry with the following words.

> Now while Paul waited for them at Athens, his spirit was stirred in him, when he saw the city wholly given to idolatry. . . . Then Paul stood in the midst of Mars' hill, and said, *Ye* men of Athens, I perceive that in all things ye are too superstitious.   For as I passed by, and beheld your devotions, I found an altar with this inscription, TO THE UNKNOWN GOD. Whom therefore ye ignorantly worship, him declare I unto you. **God that made the world and all things therein, seeing that he is Lord of heaven and earth, dwelleth not in temples made with hands; Neither is worshipped with men's hands, as though he needed any thing, seeing he giveth to all life, and breath, and all things; . . . Forasmuch then as we are the offspring of God, we ought not to think that the Godhead is like unto gold, or silver, or stone, graven by art and man's device**. And the times of this ignorance God winked at; but now commandeth all men every where to repent. (Acts 17:16, 22-25, 29-30 AV)

God does not want us to make, bow down to, or worship graven images because he is a jealous God who will not share his glory with anyone or anything.

> **I *am* the LORD: that *is* my name: and my glory will I not give to another,**

neither my praise to graven images. (Isaiah 42:8 AV)

Why does God want to prohibit even the making of graven images? Because behind every idol is a devil. *See* 1 Corinthians 10:19-20. The Catholic idolatry is a mysterious worship of Satan. That is another reason why God calls the great harlot church "Mystery." The Vatican hierarchy also worships Satan directly. As the book of *Revelation* points out, the Vatican has become the habitation of devils and every foul spirit. Revelation 18:2. Former Catholic Archbishop Emmanuel Milingo revealed before the Fatima 2000 International Congress on World Peace in Rome on November 18-23, 1996 that Satan worship is practiced within the very walls of the Vatican.[798] Archbishop Milingo cited Pope Paul VI as agreeing with his observations: "Paul VI said that the smoke of Satan had entered into the Vatican."[799]

Former Jesuit Malachi Martin, a well respected scholar of considerable renown who was considered an expert on the Vatican, wrote a novel titled *Windswept House*. He stated that he had to write the book as a novel but that the novel is 85 % based on fact. One of the startling revelations in his book is that there are sodomites and Satanists among the cardinals of Rome. He also recounted the actual occurrence of a Satanic "Black Mass" in which members of the Vatican hierarchy participated.[800] Martin had this to say about Archbishop Milingo's allegations:

> Archbishop Milingo is a good Bishop and his contention that there are satanists in Rome is completely correct, Anybody who is acquainted with the state of affairs in the Vatican in the last 35 years is well aware that the prince of darkness has had and still has his surrogates in Rome.[801]

A troubling aspect of these revelations is that they went completely unreported by the newspapers and large circulation magazines in the United States. That should be some indication of the control the Vatican has over the press in the United States. The A.P. Vatican bureau reporter, Dan Walkin, when asked about the lack of coverage of such sensational news, had no acceptable explanation for not covering the story.[802]

26 Purgatory

The Romish church teaches that the sacrifice of Jesus Christ on the cross did not satisfy God. God requires additional punishment of the believer in order to expiate the sins. This expiation can be done on earth through penance. If, however, the sin is not punished on earth the sin must be punished after death in a place called Purgatory. Purgatory is a place where sins are purportedly purged and after the sins are purged the poor tormented one is then finally granted entrance into heaven.[803] The official *Catechism of the Catholic Church* states:

> All who die in God's grace and friendship, but are imperfectly purified, are indeed assured of their eternal salvation; but after death they undergo purification, so to achieve the holiness necessary to enter the joy of heaven. The church gives the name *Purgatory* to this final purification of the elect, which is entirely different from the punishment of the damned.[804]

The *Council of Trent* held:

> If anyone saith that, after the grace of justification has been received, to every penitent sinner the guilt is remitted, and the debt of the eternal punishment is blotted out in such a way that there remains not any debt of temporal punishment to be discharged either in this world, or in the next in **Purgatory**, before the entrance to the Kingdom of Heaven can be opened (to him); let him be anathema.[805]

Where did the Catholic Church obtain this doctrine? Johann Adreas Eisenmenger in his book *The Tradition of the Jews* reveals that the doctrine of purgatory was an established Jewish tradition found within the Kabbalah. For example, the Kabbalah text *Emek HaMelech* (The Valley of the King), written by Rabbi Naftali Bachlarach, states that "there is no Righteous Man among *Israelites* who goeth not into Hell and passeth not thro' it."[806] Eisenmenger explained that under the rabbinic theology there is an "upper and lower Hell."[807] This upper hell is called purgatory in the Catholic religion.

Eisenmenger was one of the foremost experts on Judaism in Europe. His book published in 1700 authoritatively revealed the falsehoods and absurdities in Rabbinical texts. His scholarship was unimpeachable and so the Jews went to work to suppress his work. Michael Hoffman reveals that influential Jews within the royal court, including Samson Wertheimer along with wealthy financier, Samuel Oppenheimer, supported by the Catholic archbishop of the region, succeeded in having Eisenmenger's book banned by the Hapsburg Emperor Leopold I.[808] Until its reprinting in 2006 by Michael Hoffman, Eisenmenger's book was the rarest of rare books.[809]

It is quite revealing that the Jews worked hand in hand with the Catholic hierarchy to have Eisenmenger's book banned. It is in the interests of the Catholic Church to keep the public ignorant of the Rabbinical texts, since knowledge of those texts could reveal the heathen Jewish origins of the Catholic theology.

Where did the Jews obtain their version of purgatory? Alexander Hislop states that purgatory flowed directly from Babylon.[810] He points out that "[i]n every system . . . except that of the Bible, the doctrine of a purgatory after death, and prayers for the dead, has always been found to occupy a place."[811] Hislop explains how Purgatory is a money maker for heathen religions:

> In Egypt, substantially the same doctrine of purgatory was inculcated. But when once this doctrine of purgatory was admitted into the popular mind, then the door was opened for all manner of priestly extortions. Prayers for the dead ever go hand in hand with purgatory; but no prayers can be completely efficacious without the interposition of the priests; and no priestly functions can be rendered unless there be special pay for them. Therefore, in every land we find the Pagan priesthood "devouring widows' houses," and making merchandise of the tender feelings of sorrowing relatives, sensitively alive to the immortal happiness of the beloved dead.[812]

Purgatory is also a money maker for the Catholic Church. Under that doctrine, people are compelled to give to the Catholic Church in order to pay the penalty for sins purportedly not atoned for by Christ's sacrifice. These alms and penance are not just given for one's own sins. They are also for the sins of others who have already died. They are purportedly performed as a way of getting the dead out of Purgatory. The official *Catechism of the Catholic Church* states:

> From the beginning the Church has honored the memory of the dead and offered prayers in suffrage for them, above all the Eucharistic sacrifice, so that thus purified they may attain the beatific vision of God. The church also commends almsgiving, indulgences, and works of penance undertaken on behalf of the dead.[813]

In the middle ages the Romish church was quite brazen and would actually sell indulgences outright.[814] The Romish church is still selling indulgences; it is just not as direct about it as it once was. To whom do they think the alms are going to be paid? The Catholic Church, of course. Who is going to say the Masses? The Catholic Priest, of course. In other words in order to get a loved one out of the torments of Purgatory it is necessary to pay money. There are two types of masses in the Catholic Church, High Mass and Low Mass. High Masses are more expensive than Low Masses. "Any priest who celebrates Mass may receive an offering or 'Mass stipend' to apply that Mass for a specific intention. This approved custom of the Church is regulated by the Code of Canon Law and provincial and diocesan laws."[815] The Irish have a saying: high money, High Mass; low money; Low Mass; no money, NO MASS![816]

The Gospel clearly states that neither salvation nor any gift of God can be purchased with gold, silver, or anything else. Salvation has already been purchased with the precious blood of Christ.

> **Forasmuch as ye know that ye were not redeemed with corruptible things,** *as* **silver and gold, from your vain conversation** *received* **by tradition from your fathers; But with the precious blood of Christ**, as of a lamb without blemish and without spot: Who verily was foreordained before the foundation of the world, but was manifest in these last times for you, Who by him do believe in God, that raised him up from the dead, and gave him glory; that your faith and hope might be in God. (1 Peter 1:18-21 AV)

> And when Simon saw that through laying on of the apostles' hands the Holy Ghost was given, he offered them money, Saying, Give me also this power, that on whomsoever I lay hands, he may receive the Holy Ghost. But Peter said unto him, **Thy money perish with thee, because thou hast thought that the gift of God may be purchased with money**. (Acts 8:18-20 AV)

Despite the claims of the Catholic Church that the doctrine of Purgatory is based on scripture, there is absolutely no authority in the Bible for such a place as purgatory. In fact, the doctrine of purgatory is directly contrary to the Gospel of Christ. The Gospel is that we are saved from the wrath of God by the grace of God through faith in Jesus Christ.

> And to wait for his Son from heaven, whom he raised from the dead, *even* Jesus, which **delivered us from the wrath to come**. (1 Thessalonians 1:10 AV)

> For **God hath not appointed us to wrath**, but to obtain salvation by our Lord Jesus Christ, (1 Thessalonians 5:9 AV)

> Much more then, being now justified by his blood, **we shall be saved from wrath through him**. (Romans 5:9 AV)

> Verily, verily, I say unto you, **He that heareth my word, and believeth on him**

that sent me, hath everlasting life, and shall not come into condemnation; but is passed from death unto life. (John 5:24 AV)

There is only Heaven and Hell that awaits those who die. There is a great gulf between Heaven and Hell. Once a person is in Hell, he cannot ever enter Heaven.

> And it came to pass, that the beggar died, and was carried by the angels into Abraham's bosom: the rich man also died, and was buried; And in hell he lift up his eyes, being in torments, and seeth Abraham afar off, and Lazarus in his bosom. And he cried and said, Father Abraham, have mercy on me, and send Lazarus, that he may dip the tip of his finger in water, and cool my tongue; for I am tormented in this flame. But Abraham said, Son, remember that thou in thy lifetime receivedst thy good things, and likewise Lazarus evil things: but now he is comforted, and thou art tormented. And beside all this, **between us and you there is a great gulf fixed: so that they which would pass from hence to you cannot; neither can they pass to us, that** *would come* **from thence**. (Luke 16:22-26 AV)

> Then shall he say also unto them on the left hand, Depart from me, ye cursed, into **everlasting fire**, prepared for the devil and his angels . . . And these shall go away into everlasting punishment: but the righteous into **life eternal**. (Matthew 25:41, 46 AV)

> He that believeth on the Son hath **everlasting life**: and **he that believeth not the Son shall not see life; but the wrath of God abideth on him**. (John 3:36 AV)

> Verily, verily, I say unto you, He that believeth on me hath **everlasting life**. (John 6:47 AV)

> But now being made free from sin, and become servants to God, ye have your fruit unto holiness, and the end **everlasting life**. (Romans 6:22 AV)

Since Jesus has atoned for our sins there is nothing more for us to do. If we believe in Christ, our sins are forgiven and we are justified before God. God has promised that if we believe he will remember our sins no more. We are not justified based upon what we have done, but based upon what Jesus has done for us. God does not want penance from us, he wants repentance.

> Above when he said, Sacrifice and offering and burnt offerings and *offering* for sin thou wouldest not, neither hadst pleasure *therein*; which are offered by the law; Then said he, Lo, I come to do thy will, O God. He taketh away the first, that he may establish the second. By the which will **we are sanctified through the offering of the body of Jesus Christ once** *for all*. And every priest standeth

daily ministering and offering oftentimes the same sacrifices, which can never take away sins: But this man, after he had offered one sacrifice for sins for ever, sat down on the right hand of God; From henceforth expecting till his enemies be made his footstool. **For by one offering he hath perfected for ever them that are sanctified**. *Whereof* the Holy Ghost also is a witness to us: for after that he had said before, This *is* the covenant that I will make with them after those days, saith the Lord, I will put my laws into their hearts, and in their minds will I write them; **And their sins and iniquities will I remember no more. Now where remission of these *is, there is* no more offering for sin**. (Hebrews 10:8-18 AV)

27 Establishing Zionist Churches

In the1800's Zionist Jews needed financial backing from the United States or their plan for a New Israel would fail. In the 1800's the United States was a predominately Christian Country. Any attempt to subjugate Palestine and reestablish Israel as a state in that region would be met with resistence from the then politically influential Christian quarter in the U.S. The Christians in the U.S. posed a political roadblock to funding the new state of Israel. The Zionists knew that they had to nullify the anticipated Christian resistance to their Zionist plan. They decided that the Christian theology in the Protestant churches must be changed to favor an Israeli state. They had ready theologians to perform this duty in their Jesuit auxiliary.

The Jesuits decided upon a plan to inject a theology into the Protestant churches whereby the Jews would be restored to their lost prominence via the rebuilding of the Jewish temple in Jerusalem. There would be a reinstatement of animal sacrifices and the ordinances of the Old Testament law. Christ would return and rule from the temple during a millennial reign. Thus, the Christians would look upon the reestablishment of the Jewish state of Israel in Palestine as a fulfillment of the prophecy. They, consequently, would not offer any political resistance but rather would be encouraged to support Israel.

The Catholic Church also wanted to steer the Protestant theology away from identifying the pope as the antichrist. The idea was to point the attention of Protestants to a future antichrist and away from the antichrist sitting on the throne in Rome. So the Jesuits tried to frame a new "Christian" eschatology that accomplished both concealing the antichrist and reestablishing the Jews to prominence in God's prophetic plan. The Jesuits and their fellow travelers cobbled together a disjointed patchwork of bible passages that served to lay the groundwork for this new futurist/Zionist theology.

Ultimately, this new theology was introduced in the seminary schools controlled by crypto-Jews. The witting and unwitting seminary graduates then introduced their new "Christian" theology into the Protestant churches throughout the world. This new theology is the basis for the *Left Behind* series of 16 religious novels, that have sold more than 65 million copies.[817] The *Left Behind* series of books are also very popular movies that are heavily promoted in churches throughout the world.

Tens of millions of Christians were executed by the Roman Catholic Church during the dark ages because those brave witnesses for Christ believed that the pope was the antichrist. In fact, one of the foundational principles of the Protestant reformation was that the pope is the antichrist.[818] This view is amply supported by the Holy Scriptures.

The belief that the pope is the antichrist was once a virtually unanimous belief among Protestant denominations. In fact, the Westminster Confession of Faith (Church of England) states: "There is no other Head of the Church but the Lord Jesus Christ, nor can the Pope of Rome, in any sense, be head thereof, but is that antichrist, that man of sin, and Son of perdition, that exalteth himself in the Church against Christ and all that is called God." Other Protestant confessions of faith identified the pope as the antichrist, including but not limited to the Morland Confession of 1508 and 1535 (Waldenses) and the Helvetic Confession of 1536 (Switzerland).[819] Today, those that hold such a belief are in the minority. In fact, nowadays it is viewed as radical and uncharitable for a Christian to say that the pope is the antichrist. How did such transformation take place among the Protestant denominations?

The change in the position of the Protestant denominations toward Rome was the direct result of a concerted campaign by agents of the Roman Catholic Church.[820] One of the methods used by the Roman Catholic theologians was to relegate much of the book of Revelation to some future time.[821] In 1590 a Roman Catholic Jesuit priest Francisco Ribera, in his 500 page commentary on the book of Revelation, placed the events of most of the book of Revelation in a period in the future just prior to the end of the world.[822] He claimed that the antichrist would be an individual who would not be manifested until very near the end of the world. He wrote that the antichrist would rebuild Jerusalem, abolish Christianity, deny Christ, persecute the church, and dominate the world for three and half years.[823]

Another Jesuit, Cardinal Robert Bellarmine, promoted Ribera's teachings.[824] Bellarmine was one of the most influential cardinals of his time. In 1930 he was canonized by the Vatican as a saint and "Doctor of the Church." This Catholic interpretation of the book of Revelation did not become accepted in the Protestant denominations until a book titled *The Coming of the Messiah in Glory and Majesty* was published in 1812, 11 years after the death of its author.[825] The author of that book was another Jesuit by the name of Emanuel de Lacunza.

William Kimball in his book *Rapture, A Question of Timing*, reveals that de Lacunza wrote the book under the pen name of Rabbi Juan Josaphat Ben Ezra.[826] Kimball attributes the pen name to a motive to conceal his identity, thus taking the heat off of Rome, and making his writings more palatable to the Protestant readers.[827] It is as likely that in fact the pen name was not a pen name at all, but rather Lacunza'a true identity as a Jewish Rabbi. It is possible that Lacunza was a crypto-Jew, who wrote the book under his true identity as a rabbi. One does not suddenly convert to Judaism and then become immediately so versed in that religion that one takes on the title "rabbi." He must have had the learning of a Rabbi in order to write a book that contains knowledge of Judaism expected of a Rabbi.

It is notable that the book was not published by Lacunza himself, but by someone else eleven years after his death. Why would Lacunza go through such trouble and then not publish the book? Could it be that Lacunza was in a dilemma? The book was targeted to a Protestant audience, who would not accept a futurist theory from a Jesuit. So he knew he could not publish it under his true name. He had to publish under another name. Could it be that he had some concern about publishing the book, which would expose his true identity as a Jewish rabbi, and therefore he demurred on doing so? While that explains his actions, couldn't he have simply used some other non-Jewish pen-name? There is no authoritative answer to that mystery.

Lacunza's status as a rabbi is all the more believable when one considers the fact that he was a Jesuit and the Jesuits are a crypto-Jewish secret society. The first Jesuits were crypto-Jews.[828] Ignatius Loyola himself was a crypto-Jew of the Occult Kabbalah. Jews were attracted to the Jesuit order and joined in large numbers.[829] Ribera[830] was a crypto Jew. Lacunza would not be out of place as a Jewish Jesuit. Lacunza and Ribera being Jews would explain why they introduced the eschatological teaching of a return to the Jewish animal sacrifices. That doctrine gives the Jews primacy in God's plan and relegates Christians to a prophetic parenthetical to be supplanted by the Jews during the supposed thousand year earthly reign of Christ.

Lacunza wrote that during a millennium after the tribulation the Jewish animal sacrifices would be reinstated along with the Eucharist (the mass) of the Catholic Church.[831] Lacunza has followed after Jewish fables and replaced the commandments of God with the commandments of men. *See* Titus 1:13. "They profess that they know God; but in works they deny *him*, being abominable, and disobedient, and unto every good work reprobate." (Titus 1:16 AV)

Hebrews 8:1-10:39 makes explicitly clear that Christ fulfilled the requirements of the law by sacrificing himself once for sins for all time. If the blood of animals were sufficient to satisfy God there would be no need for him to come to the earth and sacrifice himself. "But now hath he obtained a more excellent ministry, by how much also he is the mediator of a better covenant, which was established upon better promises. For if that first *covenant* had been faultless, then should no place have been sought for the second." (Hebrews 8:6-7 AV)

> So Christ was **once offered** to bear the sins of many; and unto them that look for him shall he appear the second time without sin unto salvation. (Hebrews 9:28 AV)

> By the which will we are sanctified through the offering of the body of Jesus Christ **once *for all***. And every priest standeth daily ministering and offering oftentimes the same sacrifices, which can never take away sins: But this man, after he had **offered one sacrifice for sins for ever**, sat down on the right hand of

God; From henceforth expecting till his enemies be made his footstool. For **by one offering he hath perfected for ever them that are sanctified**. (Hebrews 10:10-14 AV)

God would not have us return to the weak and beggarly elements of the Old Testament law. *See* Galatians 4:9-11. To teach such a thing is to blasphemously state that Christ's sacrifice was imperfect and insufficient, and that therefore there is a need to reinstate the animal sacrifices. The Old Testament law was to act as a schoolmaster until the promise of Christ. God would have no reason to reinstate something that was intended to be in place only until he came to offer his own body as a perfect sacrifice. In Christ there is neither Jew nor Gentile; we are all one by faith in Christ. He is not going to divide us once again into Jew and Gentile. His church is his body which cannot be divided. 1 Corinthians 1:13. For a kingdom divided against itself cannot stand. Mark 3:24.

But before faith came, we were kept under the law, shut up unto the faith which should afterwards be revealed. Wherefore the law was our schoolmaster *to bring us* unto Christ, that we might be justified by faith. **But after that faith is come, we are no longer under a schoolmaster**. For ye are all the children of God by faith in Christ Jesus. For as many of you as have been baptized into Christ have put on Christ. **There is neither Jew nor Greek, there is neither bond nor free, there is neither male nor female: for ye are all one in Christ Jesus**. And if ye *be* Christ's, then are ye Abraham's seed, and heirs according to the promise. (Galatians 3:23-29 AV)

The bible makes clear that the old covenant is to vanish, being replaced by the new covenant of faith in Jesus Christ. "In that he saith, A new *covenant*, he hath made the first old. Now that which decayeth and waxeth old *is* ready to vanish away." (Hebrews 8:13 AV) Why would God reinstate something which he has said would vanish away and in which he has had no pleasure? "In burnt offerings and *sacrifices* for sin thou hast had no pleasure." (Hebrews 10:6 AV)

Christ made his one sacrifice on the cross whereby those that believe in him are made perfect, consequently there will be no more offering of any kind for sin, period.

But this man, after he had offered one sacrifice for sins for ever, sat down on the right hand of God; From henceforth expecting till his enemies be made his footstool. For **by one offering he hath perfected for ever them that are sanctified**. *Whereof* the Holy Ghost also is a witness to us: for after that he had said before, This *is* the covenant that I will make with them after those days, saith the Lord, I will put my laws into their hearts, and in their minds will I write them; And their sins and iniquities will I remember no more. **Now where remission of these *is, there is* no more offering for sin**. (Hebrews 10:12-18 AV)

Christ has set us free from the law of sin and death in our flesh. Because of the weakness of the flesh it is not possible for us to obey God's holy law. God must change our hearts through spiritual rebirth so that we are able to walk not after the flesh but after the spirit. Our obedience to God's law does not earn salvation; it is a sign of salvation. We fulfill the righteousness of his law through the obedience of Jesus and his final sacrifice. Jesus' righteousness is imputed to those who are chosen for salvation to believe in him. "And therefore it was imputed to him for righteousness. Now it was not written for his sake alone, that it was imputed to him; But **for us also, to whom it shall be imputed, if we believe on him that raised up Jesus our Lord from the dead**; Who was delivered for our offences, and was raised again for our justification. Therefore being justified by faith, we have peace with God through our Lord Jesus Christ." (Romans 4:22-5:1 AV) Those who try to use obedience to the law of God as a means to salvation are carnally minded, trying to earn salvation though the works of the flesh. The carnal minds that teach a return to the carnal sacrifices of the law are enmity against God.

> *There is* therefore now no condemnation to them which are in Christ Jesus, who walk not after the flesh, but after the Spirit. For the law of the Spirit of life in **Christ Jesus hath made me free from the law of sin and death**. For what the law could not do, in that it was weak through the flesh, God sending his own Son in the likeness of sinful flesh, and for sin, condemned sin in the flesh: That **the righteousness of the law might be fulfilled in us, who walk not after the flesh, but after the Spirit**. For they that are after the flesh do mind the things of the flesh; but they that are after the Spirit the things of the Spirit. For to be carnally minded *is* death; but to be spiritually minded *is* life and peace. Because **the carnal mind *is* enmity against God: for it is not subject to the law of God, neither indeed can be.** So then they that are in the flesh cannot please God. (Romans 8:1-8 AV)

Jesus blotted out the ordinances that were against us and nailed them to the cross. The law was only a shadow of Christ; he is the fulfilment of the law. Having fulfilled the law, Christ will not reinstate it.

> And you, being dead in your sins and the uncircumcision of your flesh, hath he quickened together with him, having forgiven you all trespasses; **Blotting out the handwriting of ordinances that was against us, which was contrary to us, and took it out of the way, nailing it to his cross;** *And* having spoiled principalities and powers, he made a shew of them openly, triumphing over them in it. **Let no man therefore judge you in meat, or in drink, or in respect of an holyday, or of the new moon, or of the sabbath *days*: Which are a shadow of things to come; but the body *is* of Christ.** (Colossians 2:13-17 AV)

The law of God was added after the promise given to Abraham. The law did not void the promise of God given to Abraham. The blessings of Abraham flow to all who believe in Jesus Christ. All who believe in Jesus are heirs of the promise given to Abraham. Galatians 3:23-29. That is, through faith in Christ one becomes the spiritual seed of Abraham. Obedience to God is the result of salvation not the cause of it. Just as with Abraham, who believed God and it was accounted to him as righteousness, so too all others who believe God; it is also accounted unto them as righteousness.

> **Even as Abraham believed God, and it was accounted to him for righteousness.** Know ye therefore that **they which are of faith, the same are the children of Abraham.** And the scripture, foreseeing that God would justify the heathen through faith, preached before the gospel unto Abraham, *saying,* In thee shall all nations be blessed. **So then they which be of faith are blessed with faithful Abraham.** For as many as are of the works of the law are under the curse: for it is written, Cursed *is* every one that continueth not in all things which are written in the book of the law to do them. **But that no man is justified by the law in the sight of God,** *it is* **evident: for, The just shall live by faith.** And the law is not of faith: but, The man that doeth them shall live in them. **Christ hath redeemed us from the curse of the law, being made a curse for us: for it is written, Cursed** *is* **every one that hangeth on a tree: That the blessing of Abraham might come on the Gentiles through Jesus Christ; that we might receive the promise of the Spirit through faith.** Brethren, I speak after the manner of men; Though *it be* but a man's covenant, yet *if it be* confirmed, no man disannulleth, or addeth thereto. Now to Abraham and his seed were the promises made. He saith not, And to seeds, as of many; but as of one, And to thy seed, which is Christ. And this I say, *that* the covenant, that was confirmed before of God in Christ, **the law, which was four hundred and thirty years after, cannot disannul, that it should make the promise of none effect. For if the inheritance** *be* **of the law,** *it is* **no more of promise**: but God gave *it* to Abraham by promise. **Wherefore then** *serveth* **the law? It was added because of transgressions, till the seed should come to whom the promise was made;** *and it was* ordained by angels in the hand of a mediator. Now a mediator is not *a mediator* of one, but God is one. *Is* the law then against the promises of God? God forbid: for if there had been a law given which could have given life, verily righteousness should have been by the law. **But the scripture hath concluded all under sin, that the promise by faith of Jesus Christ might be given to them that believe**. (Galatians 3:6-22 AV)

All the law and the prophets are summarized in two commandments.

> Master, which *is* the great commandment in the law? Jesus said unto him, Thou shalt love the Lord thy God with all thy heart, and with all thy soul, and with all thy mind. This is the first and great commandment. And the second *is* like unto it, Thou shalt love thy neighbour as thyself. **On these two commandments hang all the law and the prophets**. (Matthew 22:36-40 AV)

Jesus set us free, by fulfilling the requirements of the law for us. *Matthew* 5:17; *John* 8:32;

Ephesians 2:15; *Colossians* 2:14. Because we are set free does not mean we are free to sin. He gave us a new heart so that we are free to obey the law of God, which would otherwise have been an impossibility. We are commanded to love one another and love God; upon those two commandments hang all the requirements of the law. *Matthew* 22:36-40. "For, brethren, ye have been called unto liberty; only *use* not liberty for an occasion to the flesh, but by love serve one another. For all the law is fulfilled in one word, *even* in this; Thou shalt love thy neighbour as thyself." (Galatians 5:13-14 AV) The royal law of God is that we should love our neighbors as we love ourselves. James 2:6. In fact, Jesus gave us a new commandment that goes further and tells us to what degree we are to love one another. Our obedience to this new commandment does not earn salvation, but our obedience is a sign that we are his disciples. "A new commandment I give unto you, That ye love one another; as I have loved you, that ye also love one another. By this shall all *men* know that ye are my disciples, if ye have love one to another." (John 13:34-35 AV)

Righteousness is imputed to those who believe, it is not earned. The deeds of the law will never earn salvation. Salvation is a gift of God through faith in Jesus Christ. Ephesians 2:8-10.

> **Therefore by the deeds of the law there shall no flesh be justified in his sight**: for by the law *is* the knowledge of sin. **But now the righteousness of God without the law is manifested**, being witnessed by the law and the prophets; **Even the righteousness of God *which is* by faith of Jesus Christ unto all and upon all them that believe: for there is no difference: For all have sinned, and come short of the glory of God; Being justified freely by his grace through the redemption that is in Christ Jesus**: Whom God hath set forth *to be* a propitiation through faith in his blood, to declare his righteousness for the remission of sins that are past, through the forbearance of God; To declare, *I say*, at this time his righteousness: that he might be just, and the justifier of him which believeth in Jesus. Where *is* boasting then? It is excluded. By what law? of works? Nay: but by the law of faith. **Therefore we conclude that a man is justified by faith without the deeds of the law. *Is he* the God of the Jews only? *is he* not also of the Gentiles? Yes, of the Gentiles also: Seeing *it is* one God, which shall justify the circumcision by faith, and uncircumcision through faith**. Do we then make void the law through faith? God forbid: yea, we establish the law. (Romans 3:20-31 AV)

The true Jews are those that accept their Messiah, Jesus. The kingdom of God is a spiritual kingdom, it is not a kingdom based on race or tribe. Those who are chosen by God to believe in Jesus Christ are the spiritual Israel of God.

> Not as though the word of God hath taken none effect. **For they *are* not all Israel, which are of Israel**: Neither, because they are the seed of Abraham, *are they* all children: but, In Isaac shall thy seed be called. That is, **They which are the children of the flesh, these *are* not the children of God: but the children**

of the promise are counted for the seed. (Romans 9:6-8 AV)

For he is not a Jew, which is one outwardly; neither *is that* circumcision, which is outward in the flesh: But **he *is* a Jew, which is one inwardly; and circumcision *is that* of the heart, in the spirit, *and* not in the letter; whose praise *is* not of men, but of God**. (Romans 2:28-29 AV)

Keeping commandments or being born into a certain tribe or nation is not relevant to one's entrance into God's kingdom. God's kingdom is made up of those whom he has chosen by his grace.

So then *it is* not of him that willeth, nor of him that runneth, but of God that sheweth mercy. (Romans 9:16 AV)

Therefore hath he mercy on whom he will *have mercy*, and whom he will he hardeneth. (Romans 9:18 AV)

God has not cast away Israel. His Israel is made up of those whom he foreknew before the foundation of the world who would believe in Jesus unto salvation. Therefore, all Israel shall be saved.

God hath not cast away his people which he foreknew. (Romans 11:2 AV) And so **all Israel shall be saved**. (Romans 11:26 AV)

Part and parcel of the belief in the renewed millennium sacrifices is the belief that there will be a rebuilding of the Jewish temple. Many believe that the supposed future temple will be rebuilt at the location of what is now known as the Wailing Wall. They believe that the Wailing Wall is a remnant of the western wall from the old temple. In fact, the wailing wall is not the western wall from the ancient Jewish temple, but in fact is the western wall of the Roman Fort Antonia.[832] Fort Antonia was a permanent Roman fort at the time of Jesus. Fort Antonia was 800 feet north of the temple and the southern wall of the fort was connected to the northern wall of the temple by double colonnades.

Jesus made it clear that the temple would be destroyed so thoroughly that "[t]here shall not be left here one stone upon another, that shall not be thrown down." Matthew 24:1,2; Mark 13:1,2; Luke 19:43,44; 21:5,6. The Jews are all too happy to deceive the world into believing that Jesus was wrong. In fact, the prophecy of Jesus was fulfilled perfectly. The temple was completely destroyed down to the last stone, the remains that are left standing today are the remains of Fort Antonia, not the temple.

The Dome of the Rock is not as it is supposed the place where Mohamad ascended into heaven. The Dome of the Rock is a pagan Islamic shrine built over the Roman *Praetorium,* which was where Pilate sentenced Jesus.[833] The *Praetorium* was inside Fort Antonia, not the

Jewish temple.

Just as Christ repeated throughout his new testament, so I will repeat: God has abolished the distinction between Jew and Gentile. Romans 3:28-30; 10:11-13. His church has become one spiritual temple and household of God, with Christ being the chief cornerstone. There is no more need for a physical temple, which was merely a shadow of the greater spiritual temple, his church.

> For he is our peace, who hath made both one, and hath broken down the middle wall of partition *between us*; **Having abolished in his flesh the enmity, *even* the law of commandments *contained* in ordinances**; for to make in himself of twain one new man, *so* making peace; And that he might reconcile both unto God in one body by the cross, having slain the enmity thereby: And came and preached peace to you which were afar off, and to them that were nigh. **For through him we both have access by one Spirit unto the Father**. Now therefore ye are no more strangers and foreigners, but fellowcitizens with the saints, and of the household of God; And are built upon the foundation of the apostles and prophets, Jesus Christ himself being the chief corner *stone*; **In whom all the building fitly framed together groweth unto an holy temple in the Lord: In whom ye also are builded together for an habitation of God through the Spirit**. (Ephesians 2:14-22 AV)

Why would the Catholic Church want to deceive the world to follow after the Jewish fable of the reinstitution of the temple sacrifices? We must look to scripture to find the answer. In 2 Thessalonians 2:1-4, God states that the man of sin, the antichrist, will exalt himself above all that is called God and sit in the temple of God and claim to be God.

> Now we beseech you, brethren, by the coming of our Lord Jesus Christ, and *by* our gathering together unto him, That ye be not soon shaken in mind, or be troubled, neither by spirit, nor by word, nor by letter as from us, as that the day of Christ is at hand.   Let no man deceive you by any means: for *that day shall not come*, except there come a falling away first, and that **man of sin be revealed, the son of perdition; Who opposeth and exalteth himself above all that is called God, or that is worshipped; so that he as God sitteth in the temple of God, shewing himself that he is God.** (2 Thessalonians 2:1-4 AV)

What is the temple of God? Each saved Christian individually and all saved Christians corporately make up the temple of God.

> Know ye not that **ye are the temple of God**, and *that* the Spirit of God dwelleth in you?   If any man defile the temple of God, him shall God destroy; for **the temple of God is holy, which *temple* ye are.** (1 Corinthians 3:16-17 AV)

> What? know ye not that **your body is the temple of the Holy Ghost** *which is* in you, which ye have of God, and ye are not your own? For ye are bought with a price: therefore glorify God in your body, and in your spirit, which are God's. (1 Corinthians 6:19-20 AV)

> In whom all the **building fitly framed together groweth unto an holy temple in the Lord**: (Ephesians 2:21 AV)

The pope has claimed the authority and position of God Almighty. He claims to be the God who rules the universal (catholic) church of God. That is, he claims to rule as God in the temple of God, the church.

> The Roman Pontiff judges all men, but is judged by no one. We declare, assert, define and pronounce: to be subject to the Roman Pontiff is to every human creature altogether necessary for salvation. . . . That which was spoken of Christ . . . . 'Thou hast subdued all things under His feet,' may well seem verified in me. **I have the authority of the King of kings. I am all in all and above all, so that God, Himself and I, The Vicar of God, have but one consistory, and I am able to do almost all that God can do. What therefore,** *can* **you make of me but God**. *The Bull Sanctum*, November 18, 1302 (emphasis added).[834]

> **[W]e hold upon this earth the place of God Almighty.** *Pope Leo XIII* (emphasis added).[835]

In order to conceal the fact that the pope fulfills the prophecy in 2 Thessalonians 2:1-4 of the antichrist sitting in the temple of God, the pope had his minions, the Jesuits, promote the millennium temple fable so that the deceived will be looking for the antichrist in the distant future and not see the papal antichrist right beneath their noses. Those that accept this millennium temple, however, have rejected righteousness by faith in Jesus Christ and instead teach a rebuilding of the physical temple, where righteousness will be by the law.

This Zionist/Catholic millennium doctrine is a rejection of Christ, the Chief cornerstone of the spiritual temple of God. The rebuilding of the physical temple with physical stone is a rejection of the rock of salvation, Jesus Christ. "But Israel, which followed after the law of righteousness, hath not attained to the law of righteousness. Wherefore? Because *they sought it* **not by faith, but as it were by the works of the law. For they stumbled at that stumblingstone**; As it is written, Behold, I lay in Sion a stumblingstone and rock of offence: and whosoever believeth on him shall not be ashamed." (Romans 9:31-33 AV) Jesus Christ is the stone that has been rejected by the builders of this false religion; to them he is a rock of offense upon whom they will stumble to their ultimate demise. "For if they which are of the law *be* heirs, faith is made void, and the promise made of none effect." (Romans 4:14 AV) Jesus is the rock of salvation. Psalms 62:6; 89:26; 95:1. Christians are spiritual stones that are incorporated into Jesus Christ to make a holy temple of the Lord.

As newborn babes, desire the sincere milk of the word, that ye may grow thereby:
If so be ye have tasted that the Lord *is* gracious. **To whom coming, *as unto* a
living stone, disallowed indeed of men, but chosen of God, *and* precious, Ye
also, as lively stones, are built up a spiritual house**, an holy priesthood, to offer
up spiritual sacrifices, acceptable to God by Jesus Christ. Wherefore also it is
contained in the scripture, Behold, I lay in Sion a chief corner stone, elect,
precious: and he that believeth on him shall not be confounded. **Unto you
therefore which believe *he is* precious: but unto them which be disobedient,
the stone which the builders disallowed, the same is made the head of the
corner, And a stone of stumbling, and a rock of offence, *even to them* which
stumble at the word, being disobedient: whereunto also they were appointed**.
But ye *are* a chosen generation, a royal priesthood, an holy nation, a peculiar
people; that ye should shew forth the praises of him who hath called you out of
darkness into his marvellous light: (1 Peter 2:2-9 AV)

The pope is a usurper, who is against Christ and claims to take the place of Christ in his
temple (the church).

The Spanish edition of Lacunza's book became so popular in England that an English
version was published. The job of translating the English version was performed by Edward
Irving.[836] He completed the translation in1826, but the book was not published until 1827.[837] In
1830, a journal titled *The Morning Watch* published by Irving and his followers refined the
futuristic interpretation and presented a theory that is popular in protestant denominations today
known as the "pretribulation rapture."[838] Irving was placed on trial by the Presbyterian Church in
1832 for permitting unauthorized utterances of tongues and prophecies in his London church.[839]
He was censored and officially removed as pastor. He then formed the Catholic Apostolic
Church.[840] In 1830 Irving wrote a tract wherein he suggested Jesus Christ possessed a fallen
human nature. In 1833 he was tried for heresy and deposed from the ministry.[841] Irving died on
December 7, 1834 at the age of 42.[842]

Robert Baxter, an associate of Edward Irving, wrote of his experience in Irving's church.[843]
Irving would often have meetings that involved subjective spiritual manifestations, such as
speaking in tongues that purportedly revealed new doctrines and predicted future events. Baxter
himself was the source of a variant of Irving's pretribulation rapture teaching; Baxter
spontaneously uttered a doctrine that involved a mid-tribulation rapture. Baxter had so little
control over his manifestation of tongues that in some instances he found it necessary to stuff a
handkerchief in his mouth so as not to disturb his household.[844] Baxter was mercifully delivered
from this power, which he identified as the power of Satan.[845] Baxter later renounced his own
utterances and warned of the cunning craftiness of Satan, who is able to appear as an angel of
light in order to deceive the unwary. *See* 2 Corinthians 11:14-15.

Dispensationalists who believe in a pretribulation rapture try to disassociate the
pretribulation rapture doctrine from Edward Irving because of his tainted reputation and his

connection with the translation of the Lacunza's book.[846] They prefer, rather, to attribute the pretribulation rapture origin to John Nelson Darby. Those that ascribe to the pretribulation rapture theory hold that there will be a resurrection of the Saints seven years prior to the return of Jesus Christ, but they call it a rapture in order to distinguish it from the resurrection that is so clearly prophesied in the Holy Bible. This rapture of the Saints is supposed to be the catalyst for the entry of the antichrist on the world scene. The appearance of the antichrist is supposed to take place during a seven-year tribulation period following the rapture of the saints, hence the term "pretribulation rapture."[847] Darby was very familiar with Lacunza's book and wrote about it in 1829, just two years after the publication of Lacunza'a book in English.[848]

Irving and Lacunza constructed a theory and then sought biblical support for that theory (eisegesis), rather than reading the Bible for what it says (exegesis). The so-called biblical scholars who followed Irving and Lacunza adopted their eschatological doctrine of a pretribulation resurrection, but they used the unbiblical term, rapture, instead of resurrection. The term "rapture" is not found anywhere in the Holy Scriptures. It is in fact a derivation of the Latin *Raptus*. *Raptus* is a word that can be found in some of the passages in the Latin translation of the bible, which is known as the Latin Vulgate. *Raptus* is a mistranslation of the Greek word *harpazo*, which literally means "caught up." *See* 2 Corinthians 12:4 in the Latin Vulgate.

Many people believe that rapture is synonymous with resurrection, but that is not true. While rapture does include the idea of being taken away, it is very different from the resurrection promised by Jesus. Rapture means "the act of seizing and carrying off as prey or plunder . . . the act of carrying off a woman . . . rape."[849] The root word for rapture is rapt which means "Rape (abduction or ravishing) . . . . The act or power of carrying forcibly away."[850] Ravish means "[t]o seize and carry away by violence. . . . To have carnal knowledge with a woman by force and against her consent."[851] Both rapture and rape share the same Latin root word, *raptus*.[852] *Raptus* means "a carrying off, abduction, rape."[853] The Holy Scripture describes the church as the chaste bride of Christ who is with Christ at the wedding supper of the Lamb. (Revelation 19:7; 22:17; Matthew 22:1-14; 2 Corinthians 11:2; Ephesians 5:25-33) The wedding supper of the Lamb will take place at the resurrection of the saints when this world ends. By using the term rapture, these "scholars" are blasphemously describing that holy and glorious resurrection of the church as a rape!

John Bray alleged that Morgan Edwards was the first Protestant to write about a pretribulation rapture. Edwards' book in 1788, was published two years before Lacunza finished his unpublished draft manuscript of his book. However, close examination of Edwards' book raised a real issue about whether Edwards' book was truly about a pretribulation rapture.[854] It is difficult to view Edwards' writings as promoting a pretribulation rapture, since according to McPherson, Edwards was a historist, who viewed the papacy as the seat of the antichrist. That being the case, how could his writings be viewed to support the position that the antichrist is yet to be revealed at some time after a future rapture? Dave McPherson makes a convincing case, which he supports by good textual evidence, that in fact Edwards did not write about a pretribulation rapture.[855]

In any event, there is no evidence that the modern pretribulation rapture teaching in the Protestant churches is traceable to Edwards. McPherson also disputes whether Lacunza wrote about a pretribulation rapture. The significance of Lacunza, however is that fact that he wrote of a future antichrist and that Jewish animal sacrifices would be reinstated in conjunction with the Eucharist (the mass) of the Catholic Church. The effect of his eschatology was to conceal the antichrist sitting in the Vatican and raise the Jews to the position of preeminence. The historical record reveals a rapture trail leading directly to Lacunza (a/k/a Rabbi Juan Josaphat Ben Ezra.). Certainly, there were differences as the unscriptural rapture theory evolved, but those differences do not let Lacunza off the hook.

All one need do is to read the preface to the 2000 reprint of Lacunza's book to understand the significance of the book to the Catholic and Zionist cause. The preface states "Lacunza's contribution to present day evangelicalism was to reassert the restoration of the Jews in the end-times, the two-fold coming of the Lord; the millenial reign."[856] While Johathan Tillin in the preface describes Lacunza'a view as postribulational (his position on that is disputable), the key is that he also describes Lacunza as a "futurist."[857] That is, Lacunza puts the antichrist in a future period and takes the eyes of Christians off the Vatican. The dedication by Irving is even more revealing, for it tells us what is the real force behind the promotion of the pretribulation rapture thought of Lacunza's book. Irving in his dedication to the book states that he translated the book because it demonstrates the erroneousness of the almost universal opinion that Christ will not come until the end of the Millennium.[858] Irving clearly viewed Lacunza as a premillenialist and apparently it was the foundation for his own premillenial/pretribulation rapture doctrine, which he wrote of only four years later.

In reading Lacunza's book it is clear that he was of the view that there will be several resurrections (the first of which later was termed "rapture" by other theologians). Lacunza stated that "St. Paul, who doubtless knew better, gives us clearly to understand that there will be time, over and above, because between the resurrection of the saints and the end, he places great events, which require time and no little of it to bring them about."[859] What are those events between the resurrection of the saints and the end? Could this be the germ that Irving latched onto to come up with his theory that later became known as the pretribulation rapture?

Another point made by Lacunza is "that the evacuation of all rule, authority and power, with every thing else which we read in the text, must come to pass, not before, but after the resurrection of the saints who are Christ's, consequently after the coming of Christ."[860] Again, we have the "evacuation of all rule, authority and power," after the first resurrection. Could that be the precursor of Irving's tribulation period? Lacunza further states: "Unless you would consent to use the utmost violence, you must allow that it is here manifestly spoken of persons alive and sojourning, of whom when the Lord shall come, some shall be lifted up on high, and others not: some shall be taken, because they shall be worthy of this assumption, and others not worthy, are therefore left."[861] Could that be the basis for Irving's doctrine which later became known as the rapture? Lacunza concludes:

> The instruments or documents which we have presented in this dissertation, if they be seriously considered and combined with one another, appear more than sufficient to prove that God hath promised in his word, to raise many other saints besides those already raised, before the general resurrection; consequently, the idea of the resurrection of the flesh, in one company and at one time, in a moment, in the twinkling of any eye, is an idea which is so far from being just, that it appeareth absolutely indefensible.[862]

It is notable that Lacunza cites to the Catechism of Cardinal Bellarmine,[863] the very Jesuit Cardinal who promoted fellow Jesuit Ribera's futurist writings that helped conceal the pope's status as the antichrist. It is further worthy to note that Bellermine was also the head theologian for the Vatican in charge of reviewing and censoring the Talmud prior to authorizing its publication.[864] Bellermine thus had very close contacts and interaction with Jewish theologians during his tenure as Cardinal.

While Lacunza's writing was rather cryptic and subject to differing interpretations, which is typical of the writing style of most Jewish rabbis, the seeds for the pretribulation rapture seem to have been sown in his book. The best evidence that Lacunza's book was the seminal writing behind the pretribulation doctrine is that within four years of translating Lacunza's book into English, Irving first published his views on what later became known as the pretribulation rapture.

Dave MacPherson, in his book *The Incredible Cover-Up,* traced the origin of the pretribulation rapture doctrine to a woman named Margaret McDonald. Both a delegation of representatives from Edward Irving's church and a man named John Nelson Darby allegedly attended charismatic revival meetings in the McDonald home where Margaret McDonald saw visions and uttered prophetic revelations that were thought by some to be the foundations of the pretribulation rapture doctrine.[865] Darby was a member of a group known as the Plymouth Brethren. William Kimball states in his book *Rapture, a Question of Timing* that soon after the McDonald visions both Irving and Darby became fervent advocates of this new pretribulation rapture teaching. That suggests that Darby obtained his pretribulation view from McDonald.

John Bray, however, in his book *The Origin of the Pretribulation Teaching* states that he discovered 1827 writings of John Darby wherein Darby discussed the pretribulation rapture. Coincidently, that was the same year in which the English translation of Jesuit Priest Emanuel de Lacunza's book was published, and it would have been three years before the McDonald revelations. In addition, John Bray points out that although McDonald's revelations were of a rapture, they were not of a pretribulation rapture.[866] In John Darby's later 1829 writings he acknowledged being aware of both Irving's and Lacunza's teachings.[867] The timing of Darby's first writings of a pretribulation rapture in 1827, the publication year for Irving's translation of Lacunza's book, certainly suggests that he learned of that doctrine from the writings of Lacunza. In any case, it is generally acknowledged that Darby was most responsible for popularizing the doctrine. In fact, early on the doctrine was known as Darbyism.[868]

In addition to Darby's theological link to Lacunza and Irving, there is evidence that Rome had a continuing influence over Darby. In 1871 Darby published his own English translation of the bible. The Darby translation was based on the corrupt Alexandrian manuscripts used by the Catholic Church. One sees Satan's handiwork throughout Darby's translation. Darby omits Matthew 23:14 and Acts 8:37. In Luke 2:33 the Darby translation calls Joseph Jesus' father, when in fact Jesus is the Son of God. *See* Luke 1:35; Matthew 1:23. Darby's translation of 1 Corinthians 15:45 describes Adam as "becoming a living soul" rather than being "made a living soul," which fits rather nicely with the devilish theory of evolution. In Mark 1:1-3 the Darby translation erroneously refers to a quote from Malachi 3:1 as being from Isaiah. Darby removed from Revelations 1:11 Jesus' statement that "I am the Alpha and the Omega, the first and the last." The above listed errors and omissions by Darby are just the tip of the proverbial iceberg. It is sad that so many follow the teachings of a man who dared to tamper with God's holy words. God has placed a curse on anyone who adds to or subtracts from his words.

> For I testify unto every man that heareth the words of the prophecy of this book, If any man shall add unto these things, God shall add unto him the plagues that are written in this book: And if any man shall take away from the words of the book of this prophecy, God shall take away his part out of the book of life, and out of the holy city, and *from* the things which are written in this book. (Revelation 22:18-19 AV)

Darby toured the United States seven times between 1862 and 1877.[869] During his travels to the United States he promoted his system of prophetic interpretation. Cyrus Ingerson Scofield wholeheartedly embraced Darby's doctrine. Scofield learned Darby's teachings from Dr. James H. Brookes, who was the pastor of the Compton Avenue Presbyterian Church in St. Louis and a follower of Darby's teachings.[870] Scofield put explanatory notes, which included Darby's dispensational system, in his famous Scofield Reference Bible.[871] The Scofield Reference Bible was published in 1909 and has since then sold more than three million copies. Including explanatory notes in the Holy Bible was unusual for the time and contrary to the practice of the Bible societies whose motto was "without note or comment."

The Scofield bible was funded and nurtured by World Zionist leaders who saw the Christian churches in America as an obstacle to their plan for the establishment of a Jewish homeland in Palestine. These Zionists initiated a program to infiltrate and change the Christian doctrines of those churches. Two of the tools used to accomplish this goal were Cyrus I. Scofield and a venerable, world respected European book publisher: The Oxford University Press.[872]

The scheme was to alter the Christian gospel and corrupt the church with a pro-Zionist subculture. "Scofield's role was to re-write the King James Version of the Bible by inserting Zionist-friendly notes in the margins, between verses and chapters, and on the bottoms of the pages."[873] In 1909, the Oxford University Press published and implemented a large advertising budget to promote the Scofield Reference Bible.

The Scofield Reference Bible was a subterfuge designed to create a subculture around a new worship icon, the modern State of Israel. The new state of Israel did not yet exist, but the well-funded Zionists already had it on their drawing boards.[874]

"Since the death of its original author and namesake, The Scofield Reference Bible has gone through several editions. Massive pro-Zionist notes were added to the 1967 edition, and some of Scofield's most significant notes from the original editions were removed where they apparently failed to further Zionist aims fast enough. Yet this edition retains the title, "The New Scofield Reference Bible, Holy Bible, Editor C.I. Scofield."[875] It's anti-Arab, Zionist "Christian" subculture theology has fostered unyielding "Christian" support for the State of Israel and its barbaric subjugation of the native Palestinians.

Who was C.I. Scofield? Scofield was a young con-artist who engaged in a continual pattern of fraud and deception both before and after his alleged 1879 conversion. Scofield was a partner with John J. Ingalls, a Jewish lawyer, in a railroad scam which led to Scofield being sentenced to prison for criminal forgery.[876]

"Upon his release from prison, Scofield deserted his first wife, Leonteen Carry Scofield, and his two daughters Abigail and Helen, and he took as his mistress a young girl from the St. Louis Flower Mission. He later abandoned her for Helen van Ward, whom he eventually married."[877]

Scofield had developed connections with a subgroup of the Illuminati, known as the Secret Six.[878] He was taken under the wing of Samuel Untermeyer, an ardent Zionist who later became Chairman of the American Jewish Committee and President of the American League of Jewish Patriots.[879] "Untermeyer introduced Scofield to numerous Zionist and socialist leaders, including Samuel Gompers, Fiorello LaGuardia, Abraham Straus, Bernard Baruch and Jacob Schiff."[880] These powerful figures financed Scofield's research trips to Oxford and arranged the publication and distribution of his reference bible. He who pays the piper calls the tune.

In 1892 Scofield fraudulently claimed to have a Doctorate of Divinity and began calling himself "Doctor Scofield."[881] In fact, Scofield did not have a doctorate degree from any Seminary or University or for that matter any degree of any kind from any college. Below is an excerpt from an article titled "Cyrus I. Scofield in the Role of a Congregational Minister" which appeared on August 27, 1881 in the Topeka newspaper, The Daily Capital:

> "The last personal knowledge that Kansans have had of this peer among scalawags, was when about four years ago, after a series of forgeries and confidence games he left the state and a destitute family and took refuge in Canada.
>
> For a time he kept undercover, nothing being heard of him until within the past two years when he turned up in St. Louis, where he had a wealthy widowed sister living who has generally come to the front and squared up Cyrus' little follies and

foibles by paying good round sums of money.

Within the past year, however, Cyrus committed a series of St. Louis forgeries that could not be settled so easily, and the erratic young gentleman was compelled to linger in the St. Louis jail for a period of six months.

Among the many malicious acts that characterized his career, was one peculiarly atrocious, that has come under our personal notice. Shortly after he left Kansas, leaving his wife and two children dependent upon the bounty of his wife's mother, he wrote his wife that he could invest some $1,300 of her mother's money, all she had, in a manner that would return big interest.

After some correspondence he forwarded them a mortgage, signed and executed by one Chas. Best, purporting to convey valuable property in St. Louis. Upon this, the money was sent to him. Afterwards the mortgages were found to be base forgeries, no such person as Charles Best being in existence, and the property conveyed in the mortgage fictitious."[882]

Scofield abandoned his wife and children and refused to support them. At that time it was difficult for a woman to work and support herself and her children. 1 Timothy 5:8 states: "But if any provide not for his own, and specially for those of his own house, he hath denied the faith, and is worse than an infidel."

When his first wife, Leontine, originally filed for divorce in July 1881, she listed the following reasons: "(he had)…absented himself from his said wife and children, and had not been with them but abandoned them with the intention of not returning to them again… has been guilty of gross neglect of duty and has failed to support this plaintiff or her said children, or to contribute thereto, and has made no provision for them for food, clothing or a home, or in any manner performed his duty in the support of said family although he was able to do so."[883] At that time Scofield was the pastor of Hyde Park Congregational Church in St. Louis.[884] The divorce decree was granted in 1883, with the court finding that Scofield "was not a fit person to have custody of the children."[885]

Scofield's life was marked at every turn by duplicity. J.M. Canfield revealed that Scofield as a pastor concealed his abandonment of his family by telling the congregation prior to his divorce that he was single. In 1912, Scofield sent false biographical information to a publisher for an entry in *Who's Who in America*. Among the many lies and fabrications, Scofield falsely claimed that he was decorated for valor during the civil war. D. Jean Rushing discovered that in fact Scofield was a Confederate deserter. Having been married twice and being a demonstrably covetous and greedy con artist, Scofield did not qualify to be a church leader, let alone a respected commentator of God's word: "A bishop then must be blameless, the husband of one wife, vigilant, sober, of good behaviour, given to hospitality, apt to teach; Not given to wine, no striker, not greedy of filthy lucre; but patient, not a brawler, not covetous; One that ruleth well his own house, having his children in subjection with all gravity;" (1 Timothy 3:2-4)

While Scofield used the King James text he indicated in his 1909 bible introduction that he viewed with favor the work of Brooke Foss Westcott and Fenton John Anthony Hort, who were two popular compilers of the corrupted Alexandrian Greek text. Westcott and Hort were nominal Protestants, but they were defacto Roman Catholics. In addition, Westcott and Hort were both necromancers who were members of an occult club called the "Ghostly Guild."[886] Throughout Scofield's bible he placed marginal notes that attacked the inerrancy of the Received Text of the Holy Scripture and indicated his preference for the corrupt Alexandrian manuscripts used by the Catholic Church.

The Zionists who funded and directed the Scofield bible knew exactly what they were doing. Their strategy has born the sour fruit today whereby the ersatz "Christian" churches not only offer no resistance to Zionist aims, but they in fact promote Zionism. Amazing as it sounds the Satanic Zionist conspiracy against Christ and Christians is actually a cornerstone of many ersatz "Christian" churches. One example is Calvary Chapel founded by Chuck Smith.

Calvary Chapel has become one of the largest and most influential religious organizations in the world. Calvary Chapel of Costa Mesa, California, where Smith is senior pastor, is a mega-church with a membership of approximately 20,000 people.[887] According to a 2003 article in *Forbes* magazine, Calvary Chapel, Costa Mesa is the third largest non-Catholic church in the United States.[888] In addition, he has a regular radio program, "The Word for Today," which includes edited messages from Smith's sermons at Calvary Chapel, Costa Mesa.. The television version of *The Word for Today* is seen nationwide on the blasphemous Trinity Broadcasting Network.

Calvary Chapel also owns and operates their own radio station (KWVE). Calvary Chapel has a Bible College offering an Associate's Degree in Theology, and a Bachelor's degree in Biblical Studies. They own a 47-acre campus in Murietta Hot Springs, California. They also own a castle in Austria. In addition, Calvary Chapel ministries include: Calvary Chapel Music, Calvary Chapel Satellite Network International, Calvary Chapel Conference Center, Calvary Chapel Christian Camp, Maranatha Christian Academy, and Calvary Chapel High School. There are over 850 affiliated Calvary Chapels all over the globe, including approximately 700 in the United States. Some of the affiliated Calvary Chapels in the United States are mega-churches in their own right with memberships of more than 5,000 people.[889] *Forbes* magazine lists Calvary Chapel of Fort Lauderdale, Florida, an affiliate of Calvary Chapel, as the ninth largest non-Catholic church in the United States, with an average attendance of 17,000.[890]

In this author's previous book titled, *The Anti-Gospel*, I revealed that the initial funding for Calvary Chapel came from the Illuminati.[891] The Illuminati is a powerful Jewish secret society. We see the same Zionist forces behind Smith as were behind Scofield. Smith and his "ministry"are part of a conspiracy for Zionist conquest of Palestine and indeed the world. Smith's Zionist plans parallel the Zionist plans of the Illuminati, which is not surprising in light of the Illuminati funding for Smith. An investigative team from *The Executive Intelligence Review* discovered a group called the "American Jerusalem Temple Foundation," which was an early source of "massive amounts of money from American-based Darbyite Christian fundamentalists"[892] that were poured into "Jerusalem operations, aimed, ultimately, at blowing up the Muslim holy sites at the Temple Mount, and building the Third Temple."[893]

In the middle of this planned bloodfest we find Chuck Smith, pastor of Calvary Chapel. *The Executive Intelligence Review* discovered the following:

> At the core of the Gnostic "dispensational premillennarianism," advocated by Nineteenth-Century Anglican clergyman John Nelson Darby, is the belief that the extermination of the Jews, in a final battle of Armageddon, brought on by the rebuilding of Solomon's Temple, is the Biblical precondition for the second coming of the Messiah and the Rapture. **Pastor Chuck Smith, Dolphin's mentor at the Calvary Baptist Church, when asked by EIR whether he had any compunctions about unleashing a holy war that would lead to the possible extermination of millions of Jews and Muslims, replied, "Frankly, no, because it is all part of Biblical prophesy."**[894]
>
> **Smith was also full of praise for the Jewish zealots of the Temple Mount Faithful, and their founder, Goldfoot: "Do you want a real radical?" he asked. "Try Stanley Goldfoot. He's a wonder. His plan for the Temple Mount is to take sticks of dynamite and some M-16s and blow the Dome of the Rock and Al-Aqsa Mosques and just lay claim to the site."**[895]

Who is Stanley Goldfoot, upon whom Chuck Smith heaps such praise? He is a psychopathic mass murderer and internationally recognized terrorist! He has admitted he helped plan the 1946 dynamite bombing of the King David Hotel that killed approximately 100 Christian, Jewish, and Muslim civilians.[896] Goldfoot has also admitted that he planned and directed the execution of the United Nations mediator, Count Folke Bernadotte, in Jerusalem, in the fall of 1948.[897]

Chuck Smith is so impressed with Goldfoot that he invited that killer to lecture in his Calvary Chapel![898] Smith has also financed Goldfoots Zionist activities! The Hebrew University of Jerusalem explains:

> Chuck Smith, a noted minister and evangelist whose Calvary Chapel in Costa Mesa, California, has been one of the largest and most dynamic Charismatic churches in America, invited Goldfoot to lecture in his church, and his followers helped to finance Goldfoot's activity.[899]
>
> Smith secured financial support for exploration of the exact site of the Temple. An associate of Smith, Lambert Dolphin, a California physicist and archeologist and leader of the "Science and Archeology Team," took it upon himself to explore

the Temple Mount. An ardent premillennialist who believed that the building of the Temple was essential to the realization of messianic hopes.[900]

Can we regard Chuck Smith as a true minister of the Gospel when he praises and financially supports a terrorist killer? Why would he do such a thing? Because both he and Goldfoot are Zionists, who want to bring Palestine under the complete control of Israel. One of the key goals of the Zionist Illuminati is to rule the world. Jewish control of Palestine is one step toward that Zionist goal.

Another Zionist shill was Jerry Falwell. In 1979, Israel gave Falwell a gift of a Learjet.[901] Falwell put the Learjet to good use spreading the dispensational theology that includes a requirement of the Jews to return to Israel as part of God's plan for Christ to return.[902] His purpose was to influence the American Christian audience to favor Israel. Sean McBride explains how it worked:

> When Israel bombed Iraq's Osirak nuclear reactor in 1981, Begin made his first telephone call to Falwell, asking him to explain to the Christian public the reasons for the bombing. Only later did he call [President] Reagan.[903]

Notice that Israeli Prime Minister Menachem Begin called Falwell before calling the President of the United States. That should give the reader some idea of the political importance of the "Christian" Zionist movement to Israel.

Falwell is now dead, but Israel has many arrows in its Zionist quiver. John Hagee is one of those deadly projectiles. Thomas L. McFadden of the American Free Press explains:

> John Hagee, the megachurch televangelist, is approaching the Washington, D.C. area again, ready to land in his private jet on July 20. An army of politicians and wide-eyed believers will follow this professed "man of God" who outdoes, in a sinister way, televangelists Pat Robertson and the late Jerry Falwell combined. Although Falwell did receive a Lear jet from the Israeli government in 1979, he never had an 8,000-acre luxury ranch loaded with mansions, hotels, barns and a private landing strip. But Hagee, the "corpulent con man," as he is popularly known, does.
>
> This Texas pirate is running a large number of organizations all geared toward spreading the word of the coming rapture and promoting war for Israel.
>
> Cornerstone Church in San Antonio and John Hagee Ministries telecast his national radio and television ministry, carried in America on 160 TV stations, 50 radio stations and eight networks and are heard or seen weekly in 99 million homes. He is the founder of Christians United for Israel (CUFI).

Hagee spreads misery, destruction and greed wherever his Lear jet lands. He is pumping part of the cash he fleeces from the flock into the illegal settlements in the counterfeit state of Israel, while the child murderers there are aiming to dispose of the remainder of the Christians and Muslims in Palestinian villages with phosphorous bombs received free from America.

Regardless, just like for food, obese Hagee has a bottomless appetite for dead American kids as well, endlessly pushing for a war on Iran to satisfy his Zionist masters and strange followers who jump up and down like so many steroid-loaded basketball players waving their Israeli flags while the cash is collected. He is burning both ends of the candle manufacturing "moral support" for the endless flow of limbless and lifeless bodies that are flown and wheeled back to America to their parents from Iraq and Afghanistan.

But this is not enough for Hagee. At the last Washington conference he said: "[I]t is time for America to embrace the words of Sen. Joseph Lieberman and consider a military pre-emptive strike against Iran to prevent a nuclear holocaust in Israel." Actually jetsetter Hagee and his gang were lobbying Congress for the territorial expansion of Israel and a genocidal American nuclear strike on Iran. These well-financed people seem to be living from holocaust to holocaust just for the excitement of it.

* * *

Hagee is also a frequent guest of Israel. He met Prime Minister Binyamin Netanyahu just recently, a day before Vice President Joe Biden arrived and was humiliated by the Israeli leader.

Hagee also receives extraordinary coverage from the U.S. media, publicity that could not be purchased for tens of millions of dollars. He even appeared as a guest writer for The Washington Post in January 2009 under the title: "My Hopes and Concerns for Obama."

This is a major PR drive to extend the useful life of the "Holocaust" and to serve the Zionist agenda in the United States. There are hundreds of millions of dollars donated by these Israel-worshippers.[904]

   I am not suggesting that all who hold to the pretribulation rapture doctrine are agents of Zionists or the Roman Catholic Church. Many in Smith's Calvary Chapel, Hagee's Cornerstone Church, and similar Zionist churches throughout the world have simply been deceived. Let us, like the noble Bereans, check the pretribulation rapture teachings against the scriptures. *See* Acts 17:11. Those that hold to the pretribulation rapture teaching cite 2 Thessalonians 2:1-12 in support of their doctrine.[905]

Now we beseech you, brethren, by the coming of our Lord Jesus Christ, and *by* our gathering together unto him, That ye be not soon shaken in mind, or be troubled, neither by spirit, nor by word, nor by letter as from us, as that the day of Christ is at hand. Let no man deceive you by any means: for *that day shall not come*, except there come a falling away first, and that man of sin be revealed, the son of perdition; Who opposeth and exalteth himself above all that is called God, or that is worshipped; so that he as God sitteth in the temple of God, shewing himself that he is God. Remember ye not, that, when I was yet with you, I told you these things? And now ye know what withholdeth that he might be revealed in his time. For the mystery of iniquity doth already work: only he who now letteth *will let*, until he be taken out of the way. And then shall that Wicked be revealed, whom the Lord shall consume with the spirit of his mouth, and shall destroy with the brightness of his coming: *Even him*, whose coming is after the working of Satan with all power and signs and lying wonders, And with all deceivableness of unrighteousness in them that perish; because they received not the love of the truth, that they might be saved. And for this cause God shall send them strong delusion, that they should believe a lie: That they all might be damned who believed not the truth, but had pleasure in unrighteousness. (2 Thessalonians 2:1-12 AV)

If one looks at those passages it is clear that they refer to the resurrection of believers at the end of the world. Looking at verse one we see that the topic that is being addressed by the Apostle Paul is "the coming of our Lord Jesus Christ" and "our gathering together unto him." The apostle Paul was telling the Thessalonians that "that day" would not come until there is a falling away first. Notice that Paul refers to "that day," which indicates that the coming of our Lord and our gathering together unto him are to happen contemporaneously. The first thing that happens is the falling away. Then, the man of sin, the son of perdition is revealed. Verse four indicates that this man of sin will exalt himself above God. Clearly, this is a reference to the antichrist. So we know that the antichrist will be revealed before the coming of Jesus Christ and the resurrection of the Saints. The pretribulation rapturists reverse this sequence and hold that Jesus will return secretly and rapture the saints, and then after the rapture the antichrist will be revealed.

The pretribulation rapturists hold that the person in verse seven who lets (restrains) the antichrist is the Holy Spirit who resides in the body of believers. They teach that when the rapture takes place the Holy Spirit will be taken out of the world and the antichrist will then the revealed.[906] If you look at those passages in 2 Thessalonians 2 the apostle Paul was telling the Thessalonians that "that day" would not come until there is a falling away first. Then, the man of sin, the son of perdition is revealed. Verse four indicates that this man of sin will exalt himself above God. Clearly, this is a reference to the antichrist. So we know that the antichrist will be revealed before the coming of Jesus Christ and the resurrection of the Saints. If, however, he that letteth is the Holy Spirit that means that verse 3 contradicts verses 6-8. If the Holy Spirit is he that letteth, preventing the antichrist from being revealed and his being taken out of the way is the resurrection (rapture) of the saints and it happens first "then" the antichrist is revealed, that is the reverse of the sequence in verse 3. That contradicts verse 3 which states that the resurrection (rapture) shall not come except there be a falling away first and the man of sin is revealed. In fact, he that letteth is the Roman Emperor, who was replaced by the pope as Pontiffex Maximus (Supreme Pontiff), the ruler of all religions. The pope is the antichrist.

Furthermore, the position that the Holy Spirit will be removed from the earth through the rapture of the saints contradicts the promise that Jesus made. Jesus stated in Matthew 28:20 that he would be with us always even unto the end of the world. Jesus is with us through the Holy Spirit. We know from 1 John's 5:7 that "there are three that bear record in heaven, the father, the Word, and the Holy Ghost: and these three are one." (1 John 5:7) So we see that Jesus and the Holy Spirit are one. If you remove the Holy Spirit from the world then Jesus is removed and he cannot then be with us unto the end of the world.

Jesus makes it even clearer in the Gospel of Matthew that the Holy Spirit will abide with us forever: "And I will pray the Father, and he shall give you another Comforter, that **he may abide with you for ever**." (John 14:16 AV) Who is the comforter that Jesus was referring to? In John 14:26 Jesus states that the comforter is the Holy Spirit. If the Holy Spirit is removed from the world through the rapture and the rapture is followed by a seven year tribulation period, how could Jesus keep his promise that the Holy Spirit will be with us forever? The answer is simple; there will not be a pretribulation rapture but a resurrection and that resurrection will be at the end of the world when Christ returns. The pretribulation rapture is not supported by Scripture and in fact is contrary to Scripture.

One of the tenets of the pretribulation rapture teaching is that once the believers in Christ are raptured out of the world there will only be unbelievers left behind. The unbelievers will then go through the seven year period of tribulation during which the antichrist will make his appearance.[907] The problem with that sequence is that it is contrary to the sequence of events as explained by Jesus.

> Another parable put he forth unto them, saying, The kingdom of heaven is likened unto a man which sowed good seed in his field: But while men slept, his enemy came and sowed tares among the wheat, and went his way. But when the blade was sprung up, and brought forth fruit, then appeared the tares also. So the servants of the householder came and said unto him, Sir, didst not thou sow good seed in thy field? from whence then hath it tares? He said unto them, An enemy hath done this. The servants said unto him, Wilt thou then that we go and gather them up? But he said, Nay; lest while ye gather up the tares, ye root up also the wheat with them. **Let both grow together until the harvest: and in the time of harvest I will say to the reapers, Gather ye together first the tares, and bind them in bundles to burn them: but gather the wheat into my barn**. (Matthew 13:24-30 AV) (emphasis added)

Jesus states in his parable in *Matthew* 13:24-30 that kingdom of heaven is like a man who sows good seed this field but an enemy sows tares. The man allows the tares and the wheat to grow up together until the harvest. It is not until the harvest that the tares and the wheat are gathered. The wheat is not gathered some time before the tares. The tares are gathered "first" and burned, then to wheat is gathered into the barn. We see from the parable that the tares are gathered first and then the wheat, just the reverse of the pretribulation rapture teaching. One might say "that is just a parable, you can make that mean anything you wish." Jesus himself, however, explained later in *Matthew* the meaning of that parable.

> Then Jesus sent the multitude away, and went into the house: and his disciples came unto him, saying, Declare unto us the parable of the tares of the field. He answered and said unto them, He that soweth the good seed is the Son of man; The field is the world; the good seed are the children of the kingdom; but the tares are the children of the wicked *one*; The enemy that sowed them is the devil; the harvest is the end of the world; and the reapers are the angels. As therefore the tares are gathered and burned in the fire; so shall it be in the end of this world. The Son of man shall send forth his angels, and they shall gather out of his kingdom all things that offend, and them which do iniquity; And shall cast them into a furnace of fire: there shall be wailing and gnashing of teeth. Then shall the righteous shine forth as the sun in the kingdom of their Father. Who hath ears to hear, let him hear. (Matthew 13:36-43 AV)

Notice that Jesus states that both the tares and the wheat are to be left alone to grow up together until the end of the world. He does not say that the wheat should be plucked out ahead of time and the tares will be left behind. He states that he will wait until the end of the world and then his angels will "first" gather out of the field the tares (the children of the wicked one) and they will be bound and cast into a furnace of fire where there shall be wailing and gnashing of teeth. It is after the gathering of the tares that the children of God are gathered together. They are gathered at the end of the world not during some rapture years earlier.

The pretribulation rapturists will cite Revelation 20:5-6 to support their argument that their will be a rapture and then some time later a second resurrection. Revelation 20:5-6 does mention a first resurrection, which suggests that there is a second resurrection. Indeed, there is a second resurrection, but that is not a physical resurrection as some have supposed, it is a spiritual resurrection. The pretribulation rapturists ignore Revelation 20:4, where John says: "And I saw thrones, and they sat upon them, and judgment was given unto them: **and *I saw* the souls** of them that were beheaded for the witness of Jesus, and for the word of God." Notice he saw the "souls" of the saved, he did not see their bodies. They had been spiritually resurrected (the first resurrection) but not yet bodily resurrected. Before one is born again, he is dead in trespasses and sins. The Holy Spirit quickens the believer and he is made alive, he is spiritually resurrected from the dead. The spiritual rebirth by the grace of God through faith in Jesus Christ is the first resurrection mentioned in Revelation 20:4-6. The second resurrection is the resurrection of the bodies of the believers at the coming of the Lord Jesus Christ.

And you *hath he quickened*, who were dead in trespasses and sins. (Ephesians 2:1 AV)

Even when we were dead in sins, hath quickened us together with Christ, (by grace ye are saved;) **And hath raised *us* up together, and made *us* sit together in heavenly *places* in Christ Jesus**: (Ephesians 2:5-6 AV)

And you, being dead in your sins and the uncircumcision of your flesh, hath he quickened together with him, having forgiven you all trespasses; (Colossians 2:13 AV)

If ye then be risen with Christ, seek those things which are above, where Christ sitteth on the right hand of God. (Colossians 3:1 AV)

The pretribulation rapturists believe that Jesus will not return until the end of the seven year tribulation. They make a distinction between the resurrection at Jesus' second coming and the rapture. It would be easy to determine the exact date of Jesus' second coming by simply noting the date of the rapture and adding seven years. The problem is that Jesus stated that the day and hour of his second coming and the end of the world cannot be determined in advance. He stated that only God the Father knows the day and the hour of his return and the end of the world. He stated that day will be similar to the great flood. People were eating and drinking and marrying when suddenly and unexpectedly flood came upon the world.

But of that day and hour knoweth no *man*, no, not the angels of heaven, but my Father only. But as the days of Noe *were*, so shall also the coming of the Son of man be. For as in the days that were before the flood they were eating and drinking, marrying and giving in marriage, until the day that Noe entered into the ark, And knew not until the flood came, and took them all away; so shall also the coming of the Son of man be. (Matthew 24:36-39 AV)

Another passage which is directly contrary to the pretribulation rapture teachings is 2 Peter 3:9-15. That passage states that the day of the Lord will come suddenly like a thief in the night. Peter admonishes the saints, therefore, to be "in holy conversation and godliness, looking for and hasting unto the coming of the day of God." Note when looking at the passage in 2 Peter that Peter was referring to the coming of the Lord at the end of the world; for he states that on that day the heavens shall pass away, the elements will melt with fervent heat, and the world be burned up. Why would Peter admonish the saints to look for the day of God during which the world will be destroyed if the saints are going to the raptured out of the world seven years prior thereto? The answer is simple; the saints will not be raptured seven years before the return of Christ, the saints will be resurrected on that day of the Lord when he returns. On that day the world will be destroyed, but the saints look forward to that day, for it is the day of promise during which they will be resurrected and there will be "new heavens and a new earth wherein dwelleth righteousness." See Revelation 21:1; Matthew 13:43.

The Lord is not slack concerning his promise, as some men count slackness; but is longsuffering to us-ward, not willing that any should perish, but that all should come to repentance. But the day of the Lord will come as a thief in the night; in the which the heavens shall pass away with a great noise, and the elements shall melt with fervent heat, the earth also and the works that are therein shall be burned up. *Seeing* then *that* all these things shall be dissolved, what manner *of persons* ought ye to be in *all* holy conversation and godliness, Looking for and hasting unto the coming of the day of God, wherein the heavens being on fire shall be dissolved, and the elements shall melt with fervent heat? Nevertheless we, according to his promise, look for new heavens and a new earth, wherein dwelleth righteousness. Wherefore, beloved, seeing that ye look for such things, be diligent that ye may be found of him in peace, without spot, and blameless. And account *that* the longsuffering of our Lord *is* salvation; even as our beloved brother Paul also according to the wisdom given unto him hath written unto you; (2 Peter 3:9-15 AV)

The pretribulation rapture advocates state that God has not chosen the church to be the object of his wrath, therefore, the church must be raptured out of the world prior to the tribulation period.[908] It is true that God's church will never be the object of his wrath. *See* John 5:24; Romans 5:9, 8:1; 1 Thessolonians 1:10, 5:9. There is, however, a world of difference between God's wrath and the tribulations of this world. The following passages indicate that Christians will in fact suffer great persecution and tribulation in this world.

Then shall they deliver you up to be afflicted, and shall kill you: and ye shall be hated of all nations for my name's sake. (Matthew 24:9 AV)

These things I have spoken unto you, that in me ye might have peace. In the world ye shall have **tribulation**: but be of good cheer; I have overcome the world. (John 16:33 AV)

Confirming the souls of the disciples, *and* exhorting them to continue in the faith, and that we must through much **tribulation** enter into the kingdom of God. (Acts 14:22 AV)

That no man should be moved by these afflictions: for yourselves know that we are appointed thereunto. For verily, when we were with you, we told you before that we should suffer **tribulation**; even as it came to pass, and ye know. (1 Thessalonians 3:3-4 AV)

If the church of Christ is to be raptured out of the world prior to the alleged seven year tribulation period why did Jesus pray that his church **not be taken out of the world**? "I pray not that thou shouldest take them out of the world, but that thou shouldest keep them from the evil." (John 17:15 AV) Lest one argue that Jesus was only praying about his then living disciples, he made it clear that he was praying for all Christians. "Neither pray I for these alone, but for them also which shall believe on me through their word." (John 17:20 AV) Is there any doubt that the prayers of Jesus will be answered?

Jesus did not state that he will rapture his church out of the world seven years before the last day, but to the contrary stated that he will raise up all those that the father has given him "**at the last day**." "And this is the Father's will which hath sent me, that of all which he hath given me I should lose nothing, but should raise it up again at the last day." (John 6:39 AV) Lest there be any confusion about what Jesus meant he clarified the point in the very next passage. "And this is the will of him that sent me, that every one which seeth the Son, and believeth on him, may have everlasting life: and I will raise him up at the last day." (John 6:40 AV) Notice he does not state that some will be raised up at an earlier time, but rather that he will **raise him up at the last day every one** which seeth the Son and believeth on him. There is no mention in Bible prophecy of more than one physical resurrection, and that physical resurrection will be at the **last day**, when **every Christian** will be raised to glory. Some will cite the passage at Revelation 20:5 where there is mention of a first resurrection, which suggests a second resurrection. The first resurrection mentioned in that passage is the spiritual resurrection of a Christian when he is born again, it is not the physical resurrection at the end of the world. When one is born again he is spiritually raised from the dead, made alive to be forever spiritually with Christ. "And you *hath he quickened*, who were dead in trespasses and sins." (Ephesians 2:1 AV) "Even when we were dead in sins, hath quickened us together with Christ, (by grace ye are saved;) And hath raised *us* up together, and made *us* sit together in heavenly *places* in Christ Jesus." (Ephesians 2:5-6 AV) In John 5:24-25 Jesus describes the spiritual resurrection and then in John 5:28-29 he describes a quite different physical resurrection; the spiritual resurrection is the first resurrection mentioned in Revelation 20:5.

At this glorious second resurrection those that are chosen for salvation will be changed in a twinkling of an eye and put on glorified eternal bodies. Those that hold to the pretribulation rapture teaching, however, believe that Christ will return several times, the first being a secret rapture. They extrapolate that because Christ is prophesied to return like a thief in the night that he will stealthily and quietly return. 1 Thessalonians 5:2 and 2 Peter 3:10 do state that the Lord will come as a thief in the night. Those passages, however, are simply pointing out the suddenness of the Lord's return, not that the Lord will act like a thief and sneak back to Earth. In fact, if one looks at 1 Thessalonians 4:13-17 one sees that the return of Christ will be anything but sneaky. He will come with a shout, with the voice of the archangel, and the trump of God.

> But I would not have you to be ignorant, brethren, concerning them which are asleep, that ye sorrow not, even as others which have no hope. For if we believe that Jesus died and rose again, even so them also which sleep in Jesus will God bring with him. For this we say unto you by the word of the Lord, that we which are alive *and* remain unto the coming of the Lord shall not prevent them which are asleep. For the **Lord himself shall descend from heaven with a shout, with the voice of the archangel, and with the trump of God**: and the dead in Christ shall

rise first: Then we which are alive *and* remain shall be caught up together with them in the clouds, to meet the Lord in the air: and so shall we ever be with the Lord. (1 Thessalonians 4:13-17 AV)

Those who have been chosen for salvation will be changed and given immortal spiritual bodies. Those saved by the grace of God will be like Christ and shine as the sun in the kingdom of God. *See* 1 John 3:2 and Matthew 13:43. "Who shall change our vile body, that it may be fashioned like unto his glorious body, according to the working whereby he is able even to subdue all things unto himself." (Philippians 3:21 AV) "[A]s it is written, Eye hath not seen, nor ear heard, neither have entered into the heart of man, the things which God hath prepared for them that love him." (1 Corinthians 2:9 AV) This, however, will not happen until the end of the world at the last trump of God.

But some *man* will say, How are the dead raised up? and with what body do they come? *Thou* fool, that which thou sowest is not quickened, except it die: And that which thou sowest, thou sowest not that body that shall be, but bare grain, it may chance of wheat, or of some other *grain*: But God giveth it a body as it hath pleased him, and to every seed his own body. All flesh *is* not the same flesh: but *there is* one *kind of* flesh of men, another flesh of beasts, another of fishes, *and* another of birds. *There are* also celestial bodies, and bodies terrestrial: but the glory of the celestial *is* one, and the *glory* of the terrestrial *is* another. *There is* one glory of the sun, and another glory of the moon, and another glory of the stars: for *one* star differeth from *another* star in glory. So also *is* the resurrection of the dead. It is sown in corruption; it is raised in incorruption: It is sown in dishonour; it is raised in glory: it is sown in weakness; it is raised in power: It is sown a natural body; it is raised a spiritual body. There is a natural body, and there is a spiritual body. And so it is written, The first man Adam was made a living soul; the last Adam *was made* a quickening spirit. Howbeit that *was* not first which is spiritual, but that which is natural; and afterward that which is spiritual. The first man *is* of the earth, earthy: the second man *is* the Lord from heaven. As *is* the earthy, such *are* they also that are earthy: and as *is* the heavenly, such *are* they also that are heavenly. And as we have borne the image of the earthy, we shall also bear the image of the heavenly. Now this I say, brethren, that flesh and blood cannot inherit the kingdom of God; neither doth corruption inherit incorruption. Behold, I shew you a mystery; We shall not all sleep, but **we shall all be changed, In a moment, in the twinkling of an eye, at the last trump: for the trumpet shall sound, and the dead shall be raised incorruptible, and we shall be changed. For this corruptible must put on incorruption, and this mortal *must* put on immortality**. So when this corruptible shall have put on incorruption, and this mortal shall have put on immortality, then shall be brought to pass the saying that is written, **Death is swallowed up in victory**. O death, where *is* thy sting? O grave, where *is* thy victory? The sting of death *is* sin; and the strength of sin *is* the law. But thanks *be* to God, which giveth us the victory through our Lord Jesus Christ. (1 Corinthians 15:35-57 AV)

The pretribulation rapture contrivance contradicts the Holy Scripture. The pretribulation rapturists teach that the resurrection described in 1 Corinthians 15:51-57 is in fact a description of the rapture prior to the tribulation period.[909] They teach that Christ will sneak back for his saints seven years prior to him returning later a third time. That could not be the case, because 1 Corinthians 15:51-57 describes the resurrection of the saints at the end of the world, when Christ's saints put on eternal glorified bodies and "[d]eath is swallowed up in victory." "The last enemy *that* shall be destroyed *is* death." (1 Corinthians 15:26 AV) *See also*, Revelation 20:14. If the last enemy destroyed is death, then 1 Corinthians 15:35-57 must be referring to the end of this world. The futurists claim there is a seven year tribulation period following the rapture of the saints. According to them, death will still reign during this tribulation period, which means that death is not swallowed up in victory. Since death is in fact swallowed up in victory at the resurrection referred to in 1 Corinthian 15:51-57, then that passage could not be referring to a rapture which will be followed by a tribulation period. This is further confirmed by 1 Corinthians 15:23-24 which states: "But now is Christ risen from the dead, and become the firstfruits of them that slept. For since by man *came* death, by man *came* also the resurrection of the dead. For as in Adam all die, even so **in Christ shall all be made alive**. But every man in his own order: **Christ the firstfruits; afterward they that are Christ's at his coming. Then** *cometh* **the end**, when he shall have delivered up the kingdom to God, even the Father; when he shall have put down all rule and all authority and power." (1 Corinthians 15:20-24 AV) Notice that the order is that first Christ then second they that are Christ's at his coming; there is no indication that there will be a sneaky rapture before Christ's coming. This happens just before the end of the world. The next passage says "then" cometh the end. It does not say 7 years later cometh the end as some have "interpreted" it as saying. The passage does not say some of them that are Christ's, it says "they that are Christ's." Who are "they?" They are the "all" who shall be made alive. The Scripture is clear, the resurrection of the saints happens at Christ's coming at the end of the world. Later in verses 51-52, that truth is confirmed. "All" (not some) shall be changed. When shall the "all" be changed? In a moment, at the last trump (not in two installments). Those passages make clear that "all" shall be changed in one moment at one time at the last trump. When is the last trump? At the end of the world. *See* Matthew 24:31. Once again, we see that the pretribulation rapture teaching contradicts the express language of the prophecies in the Bible.

The false pretribulation doctrine has been nurtured by the militia of the Pope, the crypto-Jewish Jesuits. We see the hidden influence of the Jesuits starting with Emanuel de Lacunza and Francisco Ribera and continuing through Irving, Darby, Scofield, Graham, and Falwell. This futuristic interpretation of the bible prophecies was the perfect doctrine to use to hide from the world the fact that the pope of Rome is the antichrist and the Judaism of today is the same corrupt Judaism that Jesus denounced. Sadly, many have swallowed this sophistry of the Zionist Jews and Rome hook, line, and sinker.

28 Coded Language

Jews are forbidden to share with gentiles their religious doctrines. "To communicate anything to a goy about our religious relations would be equal to the killing of all the Jews, for if the goys knew what we teach about them, they would kill us openly." (Book of Libbre David, 37)[910] "Every goy who studies Talmud, and every Jew who helps him in it, ought to die." (Sanhedryn 59 a. Aboda Zora 8-6. Szagiga 13.)[911]

It is the established practice of Jews to lie when confronted with the attacks upon gentiles and Christians memorialized in their religious writings.

> If a Jew be called to explain any part of the rabbinic books, he only ought to give a false explanation, that he might not, by behaving differently, become an accomplice in betraying this information. Who will violate this order shall be put to death. (Libbre David, 37.)[912]

> One should and must make false oath, when the goys ask if our books contain anything against them. Then we are bound to state on oath that there is nothing like that. (Szaalot-Utszabot. The book of Jore d'a, 17.)[913]

In order to make their dissimilation believable, the Jews have created a Talmud that uses coded pseudonyms to refer to Christ and Christians. That way the uninitiated *goyim* upon reading a passage will not perceive the imprecations against Christ and Christians. At its heart Judaism is an anti-Christian religion, but the Jews do not want that to be generally known.

The Jews have had an ally in this deception of Christians. That ally was found in the nominally gentile, but *de facto* Jewish, Roman Catholic Church. The Vatican virtually ruled the religious life of Europe during the middle ages. No religious publication was allowed without the permission of the Vatican. That resulted in a virtual prohibition on printing bibles in the vernacular of the people.

The Roman Church knows that if the people are able to read for themselves God's word, they will discover that the Catholic traditions and doctrines are not just in addition to the Scriptures; they violate the Scriptures. The Catholic Church has a long history of trying to keep God's word from the people. For example, at the *Council of Terragona* in 1234 A.D. the Roman Catholic Church prohibited anyone from possessing any part of the Old or New Testaments in any of the Romance languages (Portuguese, Spanish, Catalan, Provencal, French, Rhaeto-Romance, Italian, Sardinian, and Romanian). The council ruled that anyone owning a Bible was to turn it over to the local Catholic bishop to be burned. In 1229 at the *Council of Toulouse* (Pope Gregory IX presiding), the Catholic Church prohibited "laymen" from having the Holy Scriptures or translating them into the "vulgar tongue" (common language of the country). In 1551 the Catholic *Inquisitional Index of Valentia* forbade the Holy Bible to be translated into Spanish or any other "vernacular." In 1559 the Roman Catholic *Index Librorum Prohibitorum* (Index of Prohibited Books) required permission from the Catholic Church to read the Catholic version of the Bible; all Christian Bible versions were simply prohibited. On September 8, 1713, Pope Clement XI issued his Dogmatic Constitution, *Unigenitus,* which in part condemned as error the teaching that all people may read the Sacred Scripture. On May 5, 1824 Pope Leo XII issued his encyclical *Ubi Primum* which exhorted the bishops to remind their flocks not to read the Bible. On May 24, 1829 Pope Pius VIII issued the encyclical *Traditi Humilitati,* which exhorted Catholics to check the spread of Bibles translated into the vernacular, because those Bibles endangered the "sacred" teachings of the Catholic Church. On May 8, 1844, Pope Gregory XVI issued his encyclical *Inter Praecipuas* in which he described Bible societies as plotting against the Catholic faith by providing Bibles to the common people, whom he referred to as "infidels." On January 25, 1897 Pope Leo XIII issued his Apostolic Constitution *Officiorum ac Munerum* which prohibited all versions of the Bible in the vernacular tongue. The 1918 Catholic Code of Cannon Law, Index of Prohibited Books, Cannon 1385, § 1 prohibited publishing any edition of the Holy Scriptures without previous Catholic "ecclesiastical censorship." The 1983 Catholic Code of Cannon Law, Cannon 825, § 1 prohibits the publishing of the Sacred Scriptures without the permission of the Apostolic See or the Conference of Bishops.

The official doctrines of the Catholic Church prohibiting the publication, possession, or reading of the Holy Bible, were not mere suggestions, they were enforced. For example, on October 6, 1536 at Vilvorde (outside Brussels, Belgium) William Tyndale was burned at the stake.[914] His crime was that he translated the Holy Scriptures into English and was making copies available to the people in violation of the rules of the Roman Catholic Church.[915]

Evidence that the Catholic Church is the seat of the anticrhist is found in the facts that the Roman Catholic Church not only tried to impede the word of God, it also facilitated the publication of the Talmud. The Talmud was generally known among religious scholars as being anti-Christian. In order to keep up the facade of being a "Christian" church, however, the Catholic Church had to do something about the Talmud. It chose not to ban its publication. Instead, it required a redaction of those portions of the Talmud that were clearly anti-Christian. This allowed the Jews to continue their anti-Christ religion in a covert style. Hoffman explains that "certain Protestant books were being wholly burned and their authors executed, while rabbis and their books were consulted and allowed to be published under license from Papal Rome."[916]

There was resistance to the publication of Jewish religious texts by well informed scholars. As a result, Pope Clement VIII in 1593 issued a permanent condemnation against the "impious writings" of the rabbis. However, Michael Hoffman explains that the papal condemnation was merely a political proclamation; except for a couple of cases, the ban was not carried through in practice. Evidence that Pope Clement VIII's proclamation was window dressing is found in the fact that the same year he made the proclamation, Pope Clement VIII "permitted the publication of toxic rabbinic commentaries on the Old Testament by 'Rabbi Solomon.'"[917]

In the Vatican authorized Talmud the words *goi*, *goy*, and *goyim* (pejorative for gentiles) were replaced with "Kushite" or "Kuthite" in the 1578 Basel edition of the Talmud.[918] *Min* and *minim* (pejorative for Christians) were replaced with words like "Sadducee" or "Epicurean."[919] Other words used in place of Christians are "idol worshiper," "Akum," and "Cuthean."[920] The curses and blasphemy against Jesus are concealed by replacing Jesus' name with Balaam and other pseudonyms. Jewish Professor Israel Shahak explains that the offensive passages in the Talmud with the new terms could be explained away to the gullible gentiles, but the Jewish reader could easily recognize the new euphemism for the old expressions.[921]

The redacted Talmud has been falsely portrayed as the authentic Talmud. The redacted Talmud is trotted out by rabbis to prove that there are no imprecations against Jesus and no admonitions to steal from or kill gentiles. The rabbis keep secret the fact that the language in the publically available Talmud has been changed to conceal the offense of the original text.

The censored texts were secretly recorded and preserved by the Jews. They then clandestinely reproduced the uncensored text in a supplement known as the *Hesront Ha-shas*. "Anyone who possessed the Catholic-authorized expurgated Talmud and the *Hesront Ha-shas* possessed the complete Talmud - and ingenious joke on Christians and quite a coup by the Vatican Mafia on behalf of its rabbinic partners in the conspiracy against the gospel of Jesus Christ."[922]

An example of the redaction of offensive passages is Sanhedrin 106b, which says this about Jesus (pseudonym Balaam[923]):

> A certain min said to R. Hanina: Hast thou heard how old Balaam was? — He
> replied: It is not actually stated, but since it is written, Bloody and deceitful men
> shall not live out half their days, it follows that he was thirty-three or thirty-four
> years old. He rejoined: Thou hast said correctly; I personally have seen Balaam's
> Chronicle, in which it is stated, 'Balaam the lame was thirty years old when
> Phinehas the Robber killed him.'[924]

This cryptic verse in Sanhedrin 106b conceals that fact that the "bloody and deceitful" man referred to is Jesus. In the Talmud, Balaam is used as a code for Jesus. A footnote to the passage explains that Phinehas the Robber is a coded pseudonym for Pontius Pilate and "Balaam's Chronicle" means "a Gospel."[925]

Elizabeth Dilling in her well researched book, *The Jewish Religion, Its Influence Today*, explains that Balaam is a pseudonym used in place of Jesus. She explains that "Proof that Jesus is called 'Balaam' is found in the Jewish Encyclopedia (under "Balaam") which, after enumerating His alleged loathsome qualities, states: 'Hence … the pseudonym 'Balaam' given to Jesus in Sanhedrin 106b and Gittin 57a.'"[926]

The Jewish Encyclopedia is authoritative. It presents a long list of eminent scholars who are experts in Judaism that contributed to the encyclopedia entry on Balaam, and who no doubt took great care in accurately explaining the meaning and use of "Balaam."[927] The entry for Jesus in the Jewish Encyclopedia confirms that Balaam is a pseudonym for Jesus: "As Balaam the magician and, according to the derivation of his name, 'destroyer of the people', was from both of these points of view a good prototype of Jesus, the latter was also called 'Balaam.'"[928]

Sanhedrin 106a also calls Jesus a soothsayer and his mother, Mary, a harlot:

> Balaam also the son of Beor, **the soothsayer**, did the children of Israel slay with the sword. A soothsayer? But he was a prophet! — R. Johanan said: At first he was a prophet, but subsequently a soothsayer. R. Papa observed: This is what men say, 'She who was the descendant of princes and governors, **played the harlot** with carpenters.'[929]

A footnote to the Sanhedrin 106a passage explains that Balaam in that passage refers to Jesus and the she who played the harlot with carpenters alludes to Mary, the mother of Jesus. That footnote states:

> Herford, Christianity in the Talmud, p. 48, suggests that **Balaam is frequently used in the Talmud as a type for Jesus** (v. also pp. 64-70). Though no name is mentioned to shew which woman is meant, the mother of Jesus may be alluded to, which theory is strengthened by the statement that she mated with a carpenter.[930]

The Talmud has Jesus being punished with boiling hot semen. In Tractate Gittin, Folio 57a it states:

> He then went and raised Balaam by incantations. . . . He then asked: What is your punishment? He replied: With boiling hot semen.[931]

We know that passage refers to Jesus, because the Jewish Encyclopedia states that Balaam is a pseudonym for Jesus in Gittin 57a.[932]

Another pseudonym used for Jesus in the Talmud is "sinners of Israel." In Gittin 57a there is a passage that states:

> He then went and raised by incantations the **sinners of Israel**. He asked them: Who is in repute in the other world? They replied: Israel. What about joining them? They replied: Seek their welfare, seek not their harm. Whoever touches them touches the apple of his eye. He said: What is your punishment? They replied: With boiling hot excrement, since a Master has said: Whoever mocks at the words of the Sages is punished with boiling hot excrement.[933]

The passage has a footnote appended to "sinners of Israel" that states: "MS.M. Jesus."[934] "Sinners of Israel" is a pseudonym for "Jesus."

There are other pseudonyms for Jesus in the Talmud. For example, Sanhedrin 106a curses Jesus: "R. Simeon b. Lakish said: Woe unto him who maketh himself alive by the name of God."[935] An endnote in that folio states that passage is a "covert allusion to Jesus."[936]

This is how *The Jewish Encyclopedia* describes Jesus:

> For polemical purposes, it was necessary for the Jews to **insist on the illegitimacy of Jesus** as against the Davidic descent claimed by the Christian Church. . . . It is certain, in any case, that the rabbinical sources also **regard Jesus as the "son of Pandera"** [Hebr.], although it is noteworthy that **he is called also "Ben Stada"** [Hebr.] (Shab. 104b; Sanh. 67a). . . . and when Jesus approached him again and was not received he set up a brick for his god, and **led all Israel into apostasy** (Sanh. 107b; Sotah 47a; Yer. Hag. 77d). This account is supplemented by the statement, made on the assumption that Ben Stada is identical with Ben Pandera, that Ben Stada **brought magic from Egypt** (Shab. 104b). . . . According to Celsus (in Origen, "Contra Celsum," i. 28) and to the Talmud (Shab. 104b), **Jesus learned magic in Egypt and performed his miracles by means of it**; the latter work, in addition, states that **he cut the magic formulas into his skin**. . . . **Jesus performed all his miracles by means of magic**, as stated above. These miracles are not specified in the Talmud, but they are in the "Toledot." . . . It is clear, therefore, that the Jewish legends deny the resurrection of Jesus; the halakic assertion that Balaam (i.e., the prototype of Jesus) **had no part in the future life** must also be especially noted (Sanh. x. 2). It is further said: "The pupils of the recreant Balaam inherit hell" (Abot v. 19). Jesus is accordingly, in the following curious Talmudic legend, thought to **sojourn in hell**. . . . Titus, then Balaam, and finally Jesus, who are here taken together as the **worst enemies of Judaism**. . . . . The Jewish legends referring to Jesus can not be regarded as originally purely Jewish, because the Christian Antichrist legends also make use of them. The **Antichrist** is born of a wandering virgin, the latter being, according to one version, a Danitic, hence Jewish, woman, while the father belongs to the Latin

race (corresponding to the Roman soldier Panthera).[937]

Sanhedrin 57b states that if a Cuthean robs another Cuthean or a Jew the property must be returned. If, however, a Jew robs a Cuthean, the property does not have to be returned to the Cuthean.[938] That section also states that if a Cuthean murders another Cuthean or a Jew he should suffer the death penalty. If, however, a Jew kills a Cuthean "there is no death penalty."[939] A footnote in folio 57b explains that **"'Cuthean' (Samaritan) was here substituted by the censor for the original goy (heathen)."**[940]

Sanhedrin 100b states: Those sent to hell include "he who reads uncanonical books etc. a tanna taught: this means, the books of the Sadducees." It would seem that the uncanonical books are books of the Sadducees, but that is coded language inserted by censors to conceal the fact that the "uncanonical books" actually refers to the New Testament. A footnote immediately after the words "books of the Sadducees" states:

> This probably refers to the works of the Judeo-Christians, i.e., the **New Testament**. There were no Sadducees after the destruction of the Temple, and so **'Sadducees' is probably a censor's emendation for sectarians or Gentiles** (Herford, Christianity in the Talmud, p. 333.) [MS.M. reads, Minim.][941]

This altering of the Talmud to deceive the *goyim* is done regularly. One recent example is the Oscar-winning movie, Schindler's List, by Steven Spielberg. The movie has a motto attributed to the Talmud: "Whoever saves one life, saves the entire world." The motto was printed in banners to promote the movie and posted in schools and associations. The motto is in fact an altered quote from the Talmud. The actual quote from the Talmud, *Sanhedrin Folio 37a*, states:

> Whosoever destroys a **single soul of Israel**, scripture imputes guilt to him as though he had destroyed a complete world; and whosoever preserves a **single soul of Israel**, scripture ascribes merit to him as though he had preserved a complete world.[942]

The actual passage from the Talmud is not the universal humanitarian quote as portrayed by Spielberg. The true meaning of the passage is revealed by reference to the orthodox Jewish view toward all those who are not souls of Israel. Rabbi ben Yohai, who authored the Zohar, and is so revered in Judaism that his grave is a shrine in Israel, authoritatively held that "even the best of gentiles should all be killed."[943] In the Talmud at Sanhedrin 58b it states: "If a heathen smites a Jew, he is worthy of death."[944] Why is there such severe penalty for striking a Jew? Because that same section of the Talmud explains: "He who smites an Israelite on the jaw, is as though he had thus assaulted the Divine Presence; for it is written, one who smiteth man (i.e. an Israelite) attacketh the Holy One."[945]

Rabbi Avraham Yitzchak HaCohen Kook, who was a renowned Jewish scholar, the first

Ashkenazi Chief Rabbi of the British Mandate for Palestine, the founder of the Religious Zionist Yeshiva Merkaz HaRav, stated:

> The difference between the Jewish soul, in all its independence, inner desires, longings, character and standing, **and the soul of all the Gentiles**, on all of their levels, **is greater** and deeper **than the difference between the soul of a man and the soul of an animal**, for the difference in the latter case is one of quantity, while the difference in the first case is one of essential quality.[946]

Jewish Scholar Professor Israel Shahak explains the Jewish methods used to conceal from the *goyim* the contempt and hatred for gentiles in general and Christians in particular contained in Orthodox Jewish teachings.

> In 1962, a part of the Maimonidean Code referred to above, the so-called Book of Knowledge, which contains the most basic rules of Jewish faith and practice, was published in Jerusalem in a bilingual edition, with the English translation facing the Hebrew text. [Maimonides, who died in 1204 A.D., is considered among the Jews to be one of their greatest and most revered religious scholars]. The latter has been restored to its original purity, and the command to exterminate Jewish infidels appears in it in full: 'It is a duty to exterminate them with one's own hands.' In the English translation this is somewhat softened to: 'It is a duty to take active measures to destroy them.' But then the Hebrew text goes on to specify the prime examples of 'infidels' who must be exterminated: 'Such as Jesus of Nazareth and his pupils, and Tzadoq and Baitos 21 and their pupils, may the name of the wicked rot'. Not one 'word of this appears in the English text on the facing page (78a). And, even more significant, in spite of the wide circulation of this book among scholars in the English-speaking countries, not one of them has, as far as I know, protested against this glaring deception.

> The second example comes from the USA, again from an English translation of a book by Maimonides. Apart from his work on the codification of the Talmud, he was also a philosopher and his Guide to the Perplexed is justly considered to be the greatest work of Jewish religious philosophy and is widely read and used even today. Unfortunately, in addition to his attitude towards non-Jews generally and Christians in particular, Maimonides was also an anti-Black racist. Towards the end of the Guide, in a crucial chapter (book III, chapter 51) he discusses how various sections of humanity can attain the supreme religious value, the true worship of God. Among those who are incapable of even approaching this are:

> "Some of the Turks [i.e., the Mongol race] and the nomads in the North, and the Blacks and the nomads in the South, and those who resemble them in our climates. And their nature is like the nature of mute animals, and according to my opinion they are not on the level of human beings, and their level among existing

things is below that of a man and above that of a monkey, because they have the image and the resemblance of a man more than a monkey does."

Now, what does one do with such a passage in a most important and necessary work of Judaism? Face the truth and its consequences? God forbid! Admit (as so many Christian scholars, for example, have done in similar circumstances) that a very important Jewish authority held also rabid anti-Black views, and by this admission make an attempt at self-education in real humanity? Perish the thought. I can almost imagine Jewish scholars in the USA consulting among themselves, 'What is to be done?' - for the book had to be translated, due to the decline in the knowledge of Hebrew among American Jews. Whether by consultation or by individual inspiration, a happy solution was found: in the popular American translation of the Guide by one Friedlander, first published as far back as 1925 and since then reprinted in many editions, including several in paperback, the Hebrew word Kushi, which means Blacks, was simply transliterated and appears as 'Kushites', a word which means nothing to those who have no knowledge of Hebrew, or to whom an obliging rabbi will not give an oral explanation. During all these years, not a word has been said to point out the initial deception or the social facts underlying its continuation - and this throughout the excitement of Martin Luther King's campaigns, which were supported by so many rabbis, not to mention other Jewish figures, some of whom must have been aware of the anti-Black racist attitude which forms part of their Jewish heritage.

Surely one is driven to the hypothesis that quite a few of Martin Luther King's rabbinical supporters were either anti-Black racists who supported him for tactical reasons of 'Jewish interest' (wishing to win Black support for American Jewry and for Israel's policies) or were accomplished hypocrites, to the point of schizophrenia, capable of passing very rapidly from a hidden enjoyment of rabid racism to a proclaimed attachment to an anti-racist struggle - and back - and back again.

The third example comes from a work which has far less serious scholarly intent - but is all the more popular for that: The Joys of Yiddish by Leo Rosten. This light-hearted work - first published in the USA in 1968, and reprinted in many editions, including several times as a Penguin paperback - is a kind of glossary of Yiddish words often used by Jews or even non-Jews in English-speaking countries. For each entry, in addition to a detailed definition and more or less amusing anecdotes illustrating its use, there is also an etymology stating (quite accurately, on the whole) the language from which the word came into Yiddish and its meaning in that language. The entry Shaygets - whose main meaning is 'a Gentile boy or young man - is an exception: there the etymology cryptically states 'Hebrew Origin', without giving the form or meaning of the original Hebrew word. However, under the entry Shiksa - the feminine form of Shaygets - the author does give the original Hebrew word, sheqetz (or, in his transliteration, sheques) and defines its Hebrew meaning as 'blemish'. This is a bare-faced lie, as every speaker of Hebrew knows. The Megiddo Modern Hebrew-English Dictionary, published in Israel, correctly defines shegetz as follows: 'unclean animal; loathsome creature, abomination (colloquial - pronounced shaygets) wretch, unruly youngster; Gentile youngster'.

My final, more general example is, if possible, even more shocking than the others. It concerns the attitude of the Hassidic movement towards non-Jews. Hassidism - a continuation (and debasement!) of Jewish mysticism - is still a living movement, with hundreds of thousands of active adherents who are fanatically devoted to their 'holy rabbis', some of whom have acquired a very considerable political influence in Israel, among the leaders of most parties and even more so in the higher echelons of the army.

What, then, are the views of this movement concerning non-Jews? As an example, let us take the famous Hatanya, fundamental book of the Habbad movement, one of the most important branches of Hassidism. According to this book, all non-Jews are totally satanic creatures 'in whom there is absolutely nothing good'. Even a non-Jewish embryo is qualitatively different from a Jewish one. The very existence of a non-Jew is 'non-essential', whereas all of creation was created solely for the sake of the Jews.[947]

The Catholic Church has its own secret code that it uses to beguile unwary Protestant Christians. It uses words that have double meanings in order to deceive the uninitiated. One example of this is an agreement by highly respected leaders among Protestants with representatives of the Roman Catholic Church.

This group met and hammered out an agreement, which was announced in May 1994. The agreement was titled *Evangelicals and Catholics Together* (Hereinafter referred to as ECT).[948] That document is a window into the subtle art of wordsmithing used by the Roman Church. The coded language used by Rome passes unnoticed to those uninitiated into the esoteric meanings behind the words used by the ecclesiastical officials of Rome.

The foundational principle of the entire document is that both Roman Catholicism and Christianity are religions of equivalent merit, and the doctrines in both should be accorded equal legitimacy under the common label "Christian."

As is evident in the two thousand year history of the church, and in our contemporary experience, there are different ways of being Christian, and some of these ways are distinctively marked by communal patterns of worship, piety, and catechesis. That we are all to be one does not mean that we are all to be identical in our way of following the one Christ. Such distinctive patterns of discipleship,

it should be noted, are amply evident within the communion of the Catholic
Church as well as within the many worlds of Evangelical Protestantism.[949]

Rome and the so -called Evangelical Christian leaders agreed that Rome's
Jewish/Babylonian liturgy is as valid as the Christian gospel.

> Three observations are in order in connection with proselytizing. First, as much as
> we might believe one community is more fully in accord with the Gospel than
> another, we as Evangelicals and Catholics affirm that opportunity and means for
> growth in Christian discipleship are available in our several communities.[950]

The purpose of the ECT is to stop the gospel from being preached. If the gospel is preached,
the Catholic Church loses members. So the ECT agreement discourages spreading the gospel
among the lost within the "Christian" [read Catholic] community. They consider such
proselytizing improper interference with the "communal allegiance" of members of the Roman
Catholic Church. They feel that Christians must assiduously respect the spiritual chains with
which Rome has bound its members.

> Second, the decision of the committed Christian with respect to his communal
> allegiance and participation must be assiduously respected.[951]

One of the rather disturbing parts of the agreement was a condemnation of proselytizing. To
Proselytize means to convert. Conversion to Christianity is a result of the working of God
through faith which is made possible by evangelism. That is, in the context of the Christian faith,
a proselyte is one who has been converted to Christ by the preaching of the gospel. The
document views successful evangelism as a bad thing. All successful efforts to spread the gospel
are viewed as "sheep stealing." Since any time a person is educated about the gospel, Rome
loses adherents, it is no wonder that they want such activity stopped. The agreement states that
evangelizing is acceptable as long as one leaves the sheep in the church in which they were
found. Under the ECT, it is okay to evangelize as long as the persons evangelized are left in
spiritual chains. In essence, they approve of ineffective evangelization. The problem for them is
that there is no such thing as ineffective evangelization when the true gospel of Jesus Christ is
preached. Preaching of the true gospel of Jesus Christ will bear spiritual fruit.

The ECT wants what is impossible for a true Christian. They want a watered down gospel
that sends the poor confused newly evangelized soul back to pagan Rome. Where would such a
gospel be found? It will be found among Arminian free will preachers. They view the Satanic
Roman Catholic Church as just "another Christian community." The document actually states:

> Third, in view of the large number of non-Christians in the world and the
> enormous challenge of our common evangelistic task, it is neither theologically
> legitimate nor a prudent use of resources for one Christian community to
> proselytize among active adherents of another Christian community.[952]

The controversy over the ECT became so heated that on January 19, 1995, four of the ersatz Protestant signers of the document (Bill Bright, Chuck Colson, Kent Hill, and J. I. Packer) found it necessary to issue a joint statement allegedly affirming that their endorsement of the ECT did "not imply acceptance of Roman Catholic doctrinal distinctive or endorsement of the Roman Catholic church system."[953]

The charlatan religious luminaries were not content with the ECT of May 1994. They came out with yet another agreement, titled *The Gift of Salvation*.[954] John Robbins explains the character of *The Gift of Salvation*:

> The 1997 manifesto from the Cassidy-Colson-Neuhaus Group begins by quoting John 3:16-17, a passage, it is safe to say, that no signatory understands, for they quote it to support their Arminian-Universalist view that Christ died for every man. They do not understand even the rudiments of the Gospel: Christ died for his people, his friends, his sheep, his church, his elect; and that Christ's death actually and completely achieved their salvation. Christ's death did not merely make salvation possible, as the ersatz-evangelicals teach; Christ's death actually saved His people. That is . . . the Gospel.[955]

John Robbins explains that *The Gift of Salvation* is based upon a bankrupt theology that contradicts both the love and sovereignty of God:

> In paragraph 4, the Group unequivocally asserts its universalist position on salvation, and they do it by cleverly misquoting Scripture: "God the Creator is also God the Redeemer, offering salvation to the world. 'God desires all to be saved and come to a knowledge of the truth.' (1 Timothy 2:4)." If one reads the context of the quotation, it is clear that Paul wrote that God desires the salvation of all His people, the sheep of His pasture, not of the goats, who are condemned to everlasting punishment. If God desires the salvation of all men without exception, as the Cassidy-Colson-Neuhaus Group asserts, then His desires are clearly frustrated, and He is not God. In fact, Roman/Arminian theology requires us to say that Hell is populated with people whom God loves. The Arminian-Universalist view contradicts both the love and the sovereignty of God, and removes all grounds of confidence in God.[956]

According to the Catholics joined by their crypto-Catholic brethren who signed *The Gift of Salvation,* Jesus is a superfluous curiosity, who is not really necessary for salvation. John Robbins explains:

> [T]he doctrine of creative justification, by regarding Christ as, at best, superfluous, focuses on the sinner, not on Jesus Christ. The sinner - the man - is central; the work of Christ is unnecessary. Oh, the life and death of Christ may be useful as a moral example, or as a device to evoke our pity, but because

justification is essentially creative, not judicial, Christ's work does not satisfy the justice of the Father, nor legally benefit his church. This is religious subjectivism with a vengeance.[957]

How can these Catholics and crypto-Catholics get away with such clear heresy? How can they claim agreement between Catholicism and Christianity when there cannot ever be agreement? They use the age old deception of the devil; they redefine the words used in the bible. For example the word justification in *The Gift of Salvation* takes on a man centered meaning. To the drafters of *The Gift of Salvation* justification means that man is actually made righteous rather than the biblical definition of the imputed righteousness of Christ. They have replaced a spiritual truth with a carnal lie. This Catholic self righteousness contradicts the biblical truth that "in me (that is, in my flesh,) dwelleth no good thing." (Romans 7:18 AV). Once again, John Robbins explains:

> [T]he word justification itself has taken on a new meaning in another sense: In the mouths of the Cassidy Group, just as in the mouths of Newman, Kung, and Barth, justification means making righteous. It is the Roman doctrine of justification. That is why the Roman Cardinals and Bishops had no problem with this statement about justification. The ersatz-evangelicals were too witless, too stupid, to understand the statement they signed. Is that too cruel? Well, it would be much crueler to say that they understood what they signed and signed it anyway. I am trying to be as charitable as possible.[958]

Richard Bennett was a Catholic Priest for 22 years and was saved by the grace of God. He read carefully *The Gift of Salvation* and reveals below how that document uses coded language to subtly support and maintains the false Catholic doctrine of Justification.

> It is to be held firmly in mind that Evangelicals throughout the centuries have maintained that justification by faith alone is the way in which sinful human beings are made right and just before the all Holy God. [1] Justification itself is a judicial declarative act on the part of God alone by which He declares that only in Christ is a man perfectly just before Himself, who is the morally perfect Being and Holy Judge over all human beings. His judicial declarative act is not made on the basis of anything within a man, but rather it is made solely and wholly upon the righteous life and sacrificial death of Jesus Christ who lived a perfect life and paid the just penalty for sins upon the cross. Historically, Evangelicals have been in agreement with the Apostle Paul, "to him that worketh not, but believeth on him that justifieth the ungodly, his faith is counted for righteousness" (Romans 4:5).
>
> The Bible teaches the manifestation of God's righteousness, not man's. "But now the righteousness of God without the law is manifested, being witnessed by the law and the prophets" (Romans 3:21). The Gospel good news is the declaration of

God that His righteousness is upon believers, i.e., credited to them. "Even the righteousness of God which is by faith of Jesus Christ unto all and upon all them that believe" (Romans 3:22). Only the Lord Christ Jesus is declared to be, and actually is the Righteousness of God. The believer has His righteousness only credited to him. This is the historical position of Evangelicals.

Historically, and conversely, the Roman Catholic Church teaches as dogma that justification is conferred through her sacraments and that it consists of inner righteousness whereby a man, it is stated, becomes just within himself. The Church of Rome condemns the Biblical doctrine of justification by faith alone. This was done at the Council of Trent. Present day dogma of the RCC not only upholds the teaching of the Council of Trent but also declares that such Councils are infallible. The Council of Trent proclaims the following curses:

> If anyone shall say that justifying faith is nothing else than confidence in the divine mercy which remits sins for Christ's sake, or that it is this confidence alone by which we are justified: let him be anathema [cursed].

> If anyone shall say that by the said sacraments of the New Law, grace is not conferred from the work which has been worked [ex opere operato] but that faith alone in the divine promise suffices to obtain grace: let him be anathema.

Rome's reason for such a curse on those who hold to "justification by faith alone" is logical because of what she refuses to concede. For her, justification is not an immediate declaration of God and received by faith alone; rather, she teaches that grace is conferred through the sacraments. Thus she is able to make a place for herself as a necessary means through which inner righteousness is given. She teaches, "Justification has been merited for us by the Passion of Christ. It is granted us through Baptism."[959]

That same teaching stated clearly 450 years ago, that physical mediation through the sacraments is necessary for salvation, is stated emphatically by Rome in the present time: "The Church affirms that for believers the sacraments of the New Covenant are necessary for salvation. . . ." "Justification is conferred in Baptism, the sacrament of faith. It conforms us to the righteousness of God, who makes us inwardly just by the power of his mercy." This is what the Roman Catholics who signed the document state that they believe. It is what the Evangelicals who signed the document should know the Catholics mean when the Catholics affirm in writing that they are "Catholics who are conscientiously faithful to the teaching of the Catholic Church."[960]

In the face of such clarity, both on the part of Scripture and on the part of the RCC, this new ecumenical document claims that now both sides agree on what had been the primary dividing point between Protestants and Roman Catholics for several hundred years. The document states:

> We agree that justification is not earned by any good works or merits of our own; it is entirely God's gift, conferred through the Father's sheer graciousness, out of the love that he bears us in his Son, who suffered on our behalf and rose from the dead for our justification. Jesus was "put to death for our trespasses and raised for our justification" (Romans 4:25). In justification, God, on the basis of Christ's righteousness alone, declares us to be no longer his rebellious enemies but his forgiven friends, and by virtue of his declaration it is so.[961]

This statement teaches traditional Roman Catholic doctrine, for by careful reading one comes to see that what the two pivotal sentences state grammatically is this:

…it [justification] is entirely God's gift, conferred [rather than imputed]…and by virtue of his [Holy God's] declaration it [justification conferred] is so.

To employ the word "conferred" instead of the Biblical word "imputed" is tantamount to putting aside Scriptural authority on the issue of justification. This is precisely because the same Romans Chapter Four that is quoted clearly teaches the concept of imputation or crediting eleven times; and what the RCC means by conferred justification is just as clearly laid out in her dogma (see above). Since medieval times, the RCC has clearly distinguished between the concept of imputation and the concept of God's grace conferred as a quality of the soul. The Roman Catholic signatories, "Catholics who are conscientiously faithful to the teachings of the Catholic Church," know this dogma.[962]

In the Bible, while there is no mention whatsoever of "conferring" justification, the theme of the imputation of the righteousness of God to the believer is constant. Yet through centuries and in the face of Scriptural clarity, the teaching of Rome tenaciously holds to justification conferred rather than imputed, the present document under consideration being a case in point. Part of the perversion by which the Biblical doctrine of justification by faith alone is accomplished in this document is by the use of the RCC terminology, "conferred". It may be Idris Cardinal Cassidy's "very active support throughout the process [of drawing up the document]" [10] which accomplished the accommodation to Catholic terminology. Through that accommodation, the Biblical teaching of the righteousness of God imputed to the believer is subsumed under Rome's traditional concept of inner or infused righteousness. Evangelicals are accustomed to the Biblical word, imputed. For them to agree to the Roman Catholic word, conferred, signifying the bringing of God's grace into the soul as a quality, is a major compromise.[963]

* * *

This teaching of justification being "conferred" is the same as that of the Pharisees or that of Rome, "For they being ignorant of God's righteousness, and going about to establish their own righteousness, have not submitted themselves unto the righteousness of God" (Romans 10:3). The statements of this document perpetrate the age-old heresy that justifying righteousness is within man, because wittingly or unwittingly, the document teaches the lie of Satan that you can be as God.[964]

John Robbins explains the implications of *The Gift of Salvation:*

If Newman's, Kung's, Barth's, Cassidy's, Colson's, and Neuhaus' doctrine of justification were correct, it would not only make sinners actually righteous, it would make Christ actually sinful, for in the same divine act in which the sinner receives the righteousness of Christ, Christ receives the sins of the sinner. The notion that justification is a moral, internal change cuts both ways: The sinner becomes morally righteous, and Christ becomes morally sinful. If justification is a moral transaction, as the Roman State-Church teaches, then Jesus Christ is a sinful man. However, if justification is a legal exchange of the righteousness of Christ for the sin of his people, then there is no theological problem - and no blasphemy. Imputation makes the sinner legally righteous, but not actually righteous; imputation makes Christ legally sinful, and so liable to punishment on behalf of those he represents, but it does not make Christ actually sinful. But if justification is an internal moral change as the Roman State-Church teaches, and if it involves Christ's work at all, then not only does the sinner become actually righteous, but Christ becomes actually sinful. That is the price one pays for errors in the doctrine of justification: blasphemy.[965]

John Robbins explains that *The Gift of Salvation* is essentially Roman Catholic doctrine very cleverly packaged with an esoteric meaning in order to deceive unwary Christians.

The doctrine of justification in "The Gift of Salvation," like the doctrine of justification in "Evangelicals and Catholics Together," is the Roman doctrine. The Roman State-Church has yielded nothing in approving this document; that is why the papal representative - Cardinal Cassidy--at the Group's meetings put his stamp of approval on it. But the Roman State-Church has gained a great deal; it has confused and persuaded many non-Catholics; and it has successfully used Charles Colson as a dupe in its plans to achieve a new Roman Empire.[966]

I believe that Robbins is being too kind to Colson to call him a "dupe." Such a description suggests that he is being deceived. The evidence, however, indicates that Colson has not been deceived; he is a willing accomplice.

Robbins reveals how *The Gift of Salvation* very stealthfully avoids certain words in order to ensure that Catholic doctrines make it through unscathed.

> In paragraph 8, on faith, "The Gift of Salvation" asserts that "the gift of justification is received through faith." Not through "faith alone," please note. That little word alone is what makes the difference between Christianity and a false gospel at this point. Its absence is one more indication that the doctrine of justification espoused by the Cassidy-Colson-Neuhaus Group is not Christian. The Roman State-Church teaches that justification is also received through baptism, penance, and other rites and sacraments of the Roman State-Church.[967]

Robbins concludes by putting *The Gift of Salvation* in historical context:

> The existence of groups like the Colson-Neuhaus Group is not new; what it demonstrates, however, is how thoroughly theologically corrupt the ersatz-evangelicals are. Christians have long known that the National Council of Churches, the World Council of Churches, the mainline denominations, and the charismatic movement are anti-Christian; now the Cassidy-Colson-Neuhaus Group is making it clear that ersatz-evangelicalism is fundamentally at one with Romanism. The Synod of Dordt condemned the Arminian theology of the ersatz-evangelicals as a doctrine from the pit of Hell. Except for a scattered remnant, the American heirs of the Reformation have repudiated the faith of their fathers, they have abandoned the Gospel, and they are falling over each other in their eagerness to fawn before the beast. In the beast they see power and influence, success, respectability, fame, and riches - and they want to enjoy the things the beast can provide.

What is most disturbing about *The Gift of Salvation* is that concealed behind the ostensible agreement is a devilish deception. When Christians read the agreement they give the biblical words their unique biblical meaning. However, the signers are accomplices in a deception. In witchcraft, words have one meaning for the outside world and another different meaning for those initiated in the black arts. The true meaning is concealed behind the artifice of ambiguous phrases designed to give the appearance of one meaning, with the actual meaning being concealed from the uninitiated. John Robbins and Richard Bennett have revealed the subtlety of the deception in a couple of areas. However, the deception goes even deeper. This is what is said at the end of the document:

> We must not allow our witness as Christians to be compromised by halfhearted discipleship or needlessly divisive disputes. While we rejoice in the unity we have

discovered and are confident of the fundamental truths about the gift of salvation we have affirmed, we recognize that there are necessarily interrelated questions that require further and urgent exploration. Among such questions are these: the meaning of baptismal regeneration, the Eucharist, and sacramental grace; the historic uses of the language of justification as it relates to imputed and transformative righteousness; the normative status of justification in relation to all Christian doctrine; the assertion that while justification is by faith alone, the faith that receives salvation is never alone; diverse understandings of merit, reward, purgatory, and indulgences; Marian devotion and the assistance of the saints in the life of salvation; and the possibility of salvation for those who have not been evangelized.[968]

The Gift of Salvation purports to be a "unity" on "fundamental truths" regarding "salvation." The manifesto states that there are a number of "interrelated questions that require further and urgent exploration." It would seem then that the listed "interrelated questions" are something other than "fundamental truths," because *The Gift of Salvation* is represented as a manifesto that presents to the world an affirmation of the unity between Catholics and Protestants on "the fundamental truths about the gift of salvation."

The following are some of the "interrelated questions" that seem to be viewed by the signers of *The Gift of Salvation* as being non-fundamental and of secondary importance.

1) Both the ECT and *The Gift of Salvation* refers to the word of God. The Catholic Church, however, has a completely different definition for "the word of God" than do Christians. The Roman Catholic Church calls the combination of their traditions and the bible together to be "the word of God," whereas Protestant Christians accept the Holy Bible alone as the word of God.

2) The official Vatican statement, *Dominus Iesus*, which was written by the Vatican's chief expert on doctrine, Cardinal Josef Ratzinger (now Pope Benedict XVI) in 2000. In *Dominus Iesus* the Catholic Church states that "ecclesial communities" that do not recognize the Eucharist mystery, (that is that Almighty God is fully present in the form of bread and wine) are not truly churches at all. The Roman Church does not view Protestant Christians as truly churches at all. So how can there be any agreement between the two?

3) The Roman Catholic priests claim that when consecrating the bread and wine during Mass they are the Lord Jesus Christ. In the bible, Jesus alerted his disciples to beware of the many who would come in his name, claiming to be Christ.

4) The Catholic Church teaches baptismal regeneration, whereas under biblical Christianity salvation is by the grace of God alone through faith in Jesus Christ alone.

5) The Catholic Church teaches salvation by works. Whereas the biblical doctrine of salvation by grace alone through faith alone is an imputed legal righteousness. Christians do not

become actually righteous once saved, rather we have the righteous of Christ imputed to us. Good works follow salvation, they do not merit salvation.

6) The Catholic Church claims that the priests have the same authority as the Lord to forgive sins. There is no biblical support for such doctrine.

7) The Romish church teaches that the sacrifice of Jesus Christ on the cross did not satisfy God. God requires additional punishment of the believer in Purgatory in order to expiate the sins. The gospel of Jesus Christ, however, is that our sins are remitted once and for all by the sacrifice of Jesus on the cross. There is no more sacrifice needed for our sins.

These matters are clearly fundamental differences between Protestant Christianity and Roman Catholicism. The two religions are irreconcilable and completely different religions. Roman Catholicism is not just un-Christian, it is anti-Christian. The signatories to the of *The Gift of Salvation* were luminaries in Protestant Christianity and must have known of these differences.

The signatories to *The Gift of Salvation* claim "unity" on "fundamental truths" regarding "salvation" with the Roman Catholic Church. They then suggest that the sacraments of the Catholic Church are a secondary issue that can be discussed later. In fact, the sacraments of the Catholic Church strike at the very heart of the gospel and the signatories know that. The very existence of the Catholic sacraments makes it impossible for any true Christian to have any theological agreement with a Catholic. How can any Christian claim unity with the Catholic Church on the issue of salvation and in the next breath state that the issue of Catholic sacraments can be worked out later, when the Catholic sacraments are the very means of Salvation under Catholic theology? This double talk is evidence of double minded men and an indication that The *Gift of Salvation* and the ECT manifestos are nothing more than subterfuges designed to spiritually seduce the unwary.

Conclusion

The solution to the mystery of Babylon the Great is that the Babylonian religion flowed through the Jews to the Roman Catholic Church. The Roman Church was established by crypto-Jews as a false "Christian" front for a Judaic/Babylonian religion.

An occult society of Jews replaced God's commands with Babylonian dogma. Jesus said to them: "Ye are of your father the devil, and the lusts of your father ye will do." John 8:44. This corrupted religion, known as Judaism, was later cloaked in Christian language, while keeping its Babylonian substance, and became an apostate church. Paul warned that after he departed grievous wolves would enter in among the disciples and that "of your own selves shall men arise, speaking perverse things, to draw away disciples after them." Acts 20:29-31. Furthermore, God prophesied that "some shall depart from the faith, giving heed to seducing spirits, and doctrines of devils." 1 Tim 4:1. The attempt to corrupt the gospel to comport with this Judaic/Babylonian mysticism was immediately detected by the early Christian disciples.

> For there are certain men crept in unawares, who were before of old ordained to
> this condemnation, ungodly men, turning the grace of our God into lasciviousness,
> and denying the only Lord God, and our Lord Jesus Christ. Jude 1:4.

The Devil's disciples succeeded in perverting the gospel and creating a Judaic/Babylonian form of ersatz "Christianity," which grew to become the Roman Catholic Church. That church has a facade of piety, but it is the habitation of devils, and its doom is sealed by God.

> And he cried mightily with a strong voice, saying, Babylon the great is fallen, is
> fallen, and is become the habitation of devils, and the hold of every foul spirit, and
> a cage of every unclean and hateful bird. (Re 18:2 AV)

There are many other corrupt children of Babylon the Great; she is "the mother of harlots and abominations of the earth." Revelation 17:5. Those that are in any of her Babylonian offspring religions are partakers of her ritual foul sins, and God warns them to come out of her to avoid the judgement of God:

> And I heard another voice from heaven, saying, **Come out of her, my people**, that

ye be not partakers of her sins, and that ye receive not of her plagues. For her sins have reached unto heaven, and God hath remembered her iniquities. Reward her even as she rewarded you, and double unto her double according to her works: in the cup which she hath filled fill to her double. (Re 18:4-6 AV)

God's warning to come out of Babylon the Great is to "my people." The consequences of not being one of God's people are dire. "The Son of man shall send forth his angels, and they shall gather out of his kingdom all things that offend, and them which do iniquity; And shall cast them into a furnace of fire: there shall be wailing and gnashing of teeth." Matthew 13:41-42. Jesus will say to them: "Depart from me, ye cursed, into everlasting fire, prepared for the devil and his angels . . . And these shall go away into everlasting punishment: but the righteous into life eternal." Matthew 25:41,46.

There are only two types of religion in the world. They are diametrically opposed to each other, as though separated by a great gulf. On the one side of that gulf are the many varieties of the religion of salvation by works. The works religions require an adherent to exercise his free will to gain the blessings of God. Such religions, like Judaism and Catholicism, are premised upon the adherent either working to gain the blessings of their god or working to keep the blessings of their god.

In fact, the Catholic Church curses anyone who states that salvation is not attained by works. "If anyone say that the justice received is not preserved and also increased before God through good works; but that the said works are merely the fruits and signs of justification obtained, but not a cause of the increase thereof, let him be anathema." COUNCIL OF TRENT, SESSION VI, DECREE ON JUSTIFICATION, Canon XXIV, January 13, 1547.

A salvation based upon works requires its adherents to be righteous enough to earn their salvation. That was the religion of Babylon, which was adopted by the Pharisees and inculcated into the Roman Catholic Church. The salvation by works rejects the theme of the Christian gospel that man is fallen and is in a corrupted state unable to turn toward God without God's sovereign intervention. If man can lose his salvation by the exercise of his free will, under the Catholic theology, then he needs also to ensure that he is righteous enough not to do something that will cause him to lose his salvation. Essentially, the Catholic must be actually righteous.

On the other side of the great gulf is the one and only religion of the free grace of God, found in the Holy Bible. The premise of the bible is that man is spiritually dead in sins and trespasses and his will is enslaved to sin. Man must be made spiritually alive again by a new birth that can only come from God through his sovereign election. The religion of God's grace boldly proclaims that the sovereign God planned salvation for helpless sinners and that he furnishes them with the ability and the desire to receive it. God states in his Holy Bible: "But God, who is rich in mercy, for his great love wherewith he loved us, Even when we were dead in sins, hath quickened us together with Christ, (by grace ye are saved;) And hath raised us up together, and made us sit together in heavenly places in Christ Jesus: That in the ages to come he might shew the exceeding riches of his grace in his kindness toward us through Christ Jesus. For by grace are ye saved through faith; and that not of yourselves: it is the gift of God: Not of works, lest any man should boast. For we are his workmanship, created in Christ Jesus unto good works, which God hath before ordained that we should walk in them." Ephesians 2:4-10.

God has provided salvation for his elect. There are no works that can earn that salvation. It is a free gift from God. The Catholic Church, however, replaces the sovereign grace of God and instead requires works to be done to attain and maintain salvation. That Catholic doctrine is directly contrary to God's plan for salvation. Salvation is by God's grace alone through faith alone. The Roman Church curses anyone who states that salvation is solely by the grace of God through faith in Jesus Christ. The curses of the Roman church are aimed directly at God.

Under the true gospel God saves his elect by God's grace through faith in Jesus Christ. Good works are the evidence of faith. Hebrews 11:1-40. Faith without works is dead. James 2:14-20. Good works are done as a consequence of salvation, they do not earn salvation. God has done all the work. If you believe in Jesus, then you can please God with your good works, which he has foreordained for you to do.

The Catholic doctrine that one can attain actual righteousness is the very error of the Jews. Catholics have a zeal for God, but it is not according to knowledge. Catholics try to establish their own righteousness, rather than rest in the imputed righteousness of Christ. "For I bear them record that they have a zeal of God, but not according to knowledge. For they being ignorant of God's righteousness, and going about to establish their own righteousness, have not submitted themselves unto the righteousness of God. For Christ is the end of the law for righteousness to every one that believeth." Romans 10:2-4.

The error of the Catholic impartation of actual righteousness is apparent when one considers the fact that the atonement of Christ was a legal exchange. That means that the sins of the elect were imputed to Christ, and the righteousness of Christ was imputed to God's elect. 2 Corinthians 5:18-21. If, as required by the Catholic theology, there is an actual exchange (and not a forensic exchange), that would mean that the sinner becomes actually righteous, and it would also mean that Christ became actually sinful. That is blasphemy!

Without the imputation of the righteousness of Christ to the sinner, justification of the sinner would be impossible. That is why Jesus had to atone for the sins of his elect. It is only through the grace of God by faith in Jesus Christ that man can be justified. The sacrifice of Jesus facilitated the justification of the wicked, because God only sees the righteousness of Christ when he sees a believer. The believer is thus justified in God's eyes. The believer only needs to believe in Jesus. His faith in Jesus will justify him before God. Notice in the parallel passages below that justification is by grace and also by faith. Faith and grace go hand in hand, which indicates that faith is provided by God, through his sovereign grace.

"Being **justified freely by his grace** through the redemption that is in Christ Jesus:"

Romans 3:24

"Therefore being **justified by faith**, we have peace with God through our Lord Jesus Christ." Romans 5:1.

"That being **justified by his grace**, we should be made heirs according to the hope of eternal life." Titus 3:7.

The gospel of Jesus Christ is that our sins are remitted once and for all by the sacrifice of Jesus on the cross. There is no more sacrifice needed for our sins. Hebrews 10:10-18. Catholic doctrine, however, curses anyone who states that Christ's one sacrifice on the cross is sufficient atonement to remit all of the sins of God's elect. *See* COUNCIL OF TRENT, SESSION VI, DECREE ON JUSTIFICATION, Canon XXX, January 13, 1547.

The theme of the Holy Bible is that sins are remitted for all time by the grace of God, not by any works that we perform. Salvation by the grace of God is mutually exclusive of salvations by the works of man. Neither can there be a mixture of grace and works. Romans 4:18; 11:6. All who preach the false gospel of works are under a curse from God (Galatians 1:8-9), which is effectual, unlike the Catholic curses. Read *The Anti-Gospel: The Perversion of Christ's Grace Gospel,* for more information on the false gospel.

If you are one of God's people, and you are presently a Catholic or a Jew or practice a religion that is based upon Babylonian dogma and liturgy, you are commanded by God to come out of that religion. How do you know if you are one of God's people? First, you will be born again. "Except a man be born again, he cannot see the kingdom of God." John 3:3.

How is one born again? One is spiritually born again by the grace of God alone, through faith in Jesus Christ alone. You cannot work your way to heaven. Salvation is a gift of God, by his grace through faith in Jesus Christ.

> For by grace are ye saved through faith; and that not of yourselves: it is the gift of God: Not of works, lest any man should boast. For us are his workmanship, created in Christ Jesus unto good works, which God hath before ordained that we should walk in them. (Ephesians. 2:8-10 AV)

What about the commandments of God? They were intended to act as a schoolmaster, the purpose of which was to bring men to faith in Christ. Galatians 3:24-25. Jesus makes clear that all the law and the prophets are summarized in just two commandments. "Thou shalt love the Lord thy God with all thy heart, and with all thy soul, and with all thy mind." and "Thou shalt love thy neighbour as thyself." Matthew 22:35-40. God states that in order to gain entrance into heaven one must obey and keep all of God's law. *See* Leviticus 18:5; Luke 10:25-28. "For whosoever shall keep the whole law, and yet offend in one point, he is guilty of all." James 2:10.

All who do not keep every one of God's commands are under a curse. "Cursed is every one that continueth not in all things which are written in the book of the law to do them." Galatians 3:10. If we sin by transgressing God's law, we must be punished, because God is just. The cursed punishment for violating God's law is eternal darkness where there is weeping and gnashing of teeth. *See* John 5:29; Matthew 25:1-46, 13:41-43; Romans 2:5-8; 2 Thessalonians 1:7-9.

One cannot enter heaven with any sin. "Know ye not that the unrighteous shall not inherit the kingdom of God?" 1 Corinthians 6:9. "For thou art not a God that hath pleasure in wickedness: neither shall evil dwell with thee. The foolish shall not stand in thy sight: thou hatest all workers of iniquity." Psalms 5:4-5. *See also* Galatians 5:19-21. The punishment for one's sins is to be cast into the lake of fire and brimstone. Revelation 21:7-8. No one is capable of keeping God's law through their own effort; none is righteous, not one single person.

> As it is written, There is **none** righteous, **no, not one**: There is **none** that understandeth, there is **none** that seeketh after God. They are all gone out of the way, they are together become unprofitable; there is **none** that doeth good, **no, not one**. Romans 3:10-12.

How can anyone inherit the kingdom of God, if no one is righteous or does any good, but God requires perfect righteousness? God's very character holds the answer.

> The LORD, The LORD God, merciful and gracious, longsuffering, and abundant in goodness and truth, Keeping mercy for thousands, forgiving iniquity and transgression and sin, and that will by no means clear the guilty. Exodus 34:6-7.

God is perfectly righteous. He is both perfectly just and perfectly merciful. If God is perfectly just and must therefore punish sin, how can he allow his children into heaven without them being punished for their sins? If God punished the sinner, then no one could enter heaven, since the due punishment for sin is eternal torment in fire. If God simply forgives the sin, without punishment, that would be unjust.

God resolved the dilemma of punishing sin and at the same time forgiving the sinner by coming to earth and living a perfect life and allowing himself to be punished in our place for our sins. "For he hath made him to be sin for us, who knew no sin; that we might be made the righteousness of God in him." 2 Corinthians 5:21. The Jesus of the Holy Scriptures is the sovereign potentate over all of creation; he is Lord of Lords and King of Kings who created heaven and earth. 1 Titus 6:15; Revelation 17:4; 19:6. He came to earth and paid the price for sin, so that if you believe in him, all of your sins will be forgiven. He punished himself for our sins (being perfectly just) and forgives us who committed the sins (showing perfect mercy).

If you believe in the Lord Jesus Christ, his perfect life will be imputed to you, and in the eyes of God you are sinless and righteous. Galatians 3:6-9. You are justified not because you are good, but because Christ is good and paid the price for your sins. He took the complete punishment for your sin, which was required by God's perfect justice, so that he could forgive you completely, according to his perfect mercy. "Come now, and let us reason together, saith the LORD: though your sins be as scarlet, they shall be as white as snow; though they be red like crimson, they shall be as wool." (Isa 1:18 AV)

Jesus is the only way to heaven. "Jesus saith unto him, I am the way, the truth, and the life: no man cometh unto the Father, but by me." John 14:6. Jesus makes it clear that it is all or nothing: "He that is not with me is against me." Matthew 12:30. If you do not believe in Jesus, then you will have to pay the eternal price for your own sin in the lake of fire, because the perfect justice of God requires that sin be punished. Revelation 20:11-15. The only way to avoid being punished for your sins is by having Jesus pay the price in your stead. It is through faith in the work of Jesus Christ and not by one's own works that one is saved. Romans 3:21-28, 4:1-8. Jesus has redeemed us from the curse of the law by being cursed in our stead. He, who knew no sin was punished for our sins. Galatians 3:11-14.

None seek after God. Romans 3:10-18. The bible makes it clear that all men are born dead in trespasses and sin and must be spiritually reborn to be saved from their sins. "And you hath he quickened, who were dead in trespasses and sins." Ephesians 2:1. Salvation can only be by the spiritual faith that is a gift from Jesus. Romans 5:15-18. A man who is spiritually dead cannot make himself spiritually alive again; that is a rebirth that only God can accomplish. God must supply the faith, because man in his fallen state is incapable of believing in Jesus.

Jesus is "the author and finisher of our faith." Hebrews 12:2. That means that Jesus is the source of saving faith, and Jesus sees that faith to its completion. One cannot have faith <u>in</u> Jesus Christ without God <u>giving</u> one the faith <u>of</u> Jesus Christ. "[T]he scripture hath concluded all under sin, that the promise by **faith <u>of</u> Jesus Christ** might be **<u>given</u> to them that believe**." Galatians 3:22. *See also* Romans 3:22; Galatians 2:16; Revelation 14:12; Ephesians 3:12; Philippians 3:9.

If one tries to add works to faith as a means of salvation, that is evidence that one does not have saving faith. Galatians 2:16. Certainly, true faith will bring repentance and bear the fruit of good works. James 2:17; Acts 3:19; Matthew 3:8. However, that does not mean that salvation is merited by good works. In fact, all of your self-righteous works are as filthy rags to God. Isaiah 64:6. Salvation is a free gift, given by a loving Jesus, not a reward earned by the sinner. Once we are freed from the bondage of sin, we can bear the fruit of righteousness. "But now being made free from sin, and become servants to God, ye have your fruit unto holiness, and the end everlasting life." (Romans 6:22 AV) *See also* Romans 5:16-19; 7:1-8:17.

Salvation cannot be obtained by one's lineage, works, or even the force of one's own will; salvation is a gift by the sovereign will of God.

But as many as received him, to them gave he power to become the sons of God, even to them that believe on his name: Which were born, not of blood, nor of the will of the flesh, nor of the will of man, but of God. (John 1:12-13 AV)

The bible explains that God the Father must draw one to believe in Jesus. "No man can come to me, except the Father which hath sent me draw him: and I will raise him up at the last day." (John 6:44 AV) No one can come to Jesus unless the Father draws him. "All" those that are chosen for salvation "shall" come to Jesus. Jesus stated: **"All that the Father giveth me shall come to me; and him that cometh to me I will in no wise cast out."** John 6:37. Furthermore, Jesus assures us that he will lose none of those whom God the Father has given him. **"[O]f all which he hath given me I should lose nothing, but should raise it up again at the last day."** John 6:39.

Learn from the example of the man who knew he lacked saving faith. "Lord, I believe; help thou mine unbelief." (Mark 9:24 AV) One needs to pray to Jesus to "help thou mine unbelief." Praying to Jesus for saving faith is the best evidence that one is being drawn by the Father to Jesus. Jesus guarantees the pull of the father will be effectual. All who are drawn to Jesus by the Father will believe in Jesus and be saved, and Jesus will raise them up on the last day.

We who believe in Jesus are adopted children of God. We were chosen by God for adoption before the world was created.

> **According as he hath chosen us in him before the foundation of the world, that we should be holy and without blame before him in love: Having predestinated us unto the adoption of children by Jesus Christ to himself, according to the good pleasure of his will.** (Ephesians 1:4-5 AV)

To be glorified with Christ as an adopted son of God is too wonderful a thought to even comprehend. "But as it is written, Eye hath not seen, nor ear heard, neither have entered into the heart of man, the things which God hath prepared for them that love him." 1 Corinthians 2:9.

Endnotes

1.Edward Hendrie, *Antichrist Conspiracy, Inside the Devil's Lair* (2010), *available at* www.antichristconspiracy.com and www.lulu.com.

2.Edward Hendrie, *Antichrist Conspiracy, Inside the Devil's Lair*, at Chapter 74 (2010), *available at* www.antichristconspiracy.com and www.lulu.com.

3.Israel Shahak, Jewish History, Jewish Religion: The Weight of Two Thousand Years (1994), available at http://www.biblebelievers.org.au/jewhis3.htm#Orthodoxy%20and%20Interpretation.

4.Israel Shahak, Jewish History, Jewish Religion: The Weight of Two Thousand Years (1994), available at http://www.biblebelievers.org.au/jewhis3.htm#Orthodoxy%20and%20Interpretation.

5.*Id.* at § 2051, p.552.

6.CATECHISM OF THE CATHOLIC CHURCH § 2051, p. 551 (1994).

7.*Id.* at § 2175.

8.CATECHISM OF THE CATHOLIC CHURCH, § 2185 (1994).

9.CATECHISM OF THE CATHOLIC CHURCH, § 963 (1994).

10.NOAH WEBSTER, AMERICAN DICTIONARY OF THE ENGLISH LANGUAGE (1st ed. 1828) republished by Foundation for American Christian Education, San Francisco, California.

11.COLLIER'S ENCYCLOPEDIA, volume 20, p. 169 (1991).

12.Alexander Hislop, *The Two Babylons*, at 2 (1959).

13.Alexander Hislop, *The Two Babylons*, at 2 (1959).

14.Alexander Hislop, *The Two Babylons*, at 2 (1959).

15.Alexander Hislop, *The Two Babylons*, at 2 (1959).

16.Alexander Hislop, *The Two Babylons*, at 2 (1959).

17.G.A. RIPLINGER, NEW AGE BIBLE VERSIONS, p. 133 (1993).

18.Philip Schaff, History of the Christian Church, Volume II: Ante-Nicene Christianity. A.D. 100-325, available at http://www.ccel.org/ccel/schaff/hcc2.v.xiii.i.html.

19.Maurice Pinay, *The Plot Against the Church*, http://www.catholicvoice.co.uk/pinay/ (last visited February 10, 2010).

20. Maurice Pinay, *The Plot Against the Church, Part 4, The Jewish "Fifth Column" in the Clergy, Chapter 4, Jewry - The Father of the Gnostics,* http://www.catholicvoice.co.uk/pinay/part4a.htm (last visited on February 10, 2010).

21. Stephan A. Hoeller, *Valentinus- A Gnostic For All Seasons,* http://www.gnosis.org/valentinus.htm (last visited on February 10, 2010).

22. Edward Hendrie, *The Anti-Gospel, The Perversion of Christ's Grace Gospel, available at* www.antichristconspiracy.com and www.lulu.com.

23. Philip Schaff, *History of the Christian Church, Volume II, Ante Nicene Christianity, A.D. 100-325,* http://www.ccel.org/ccel/schaff/hcc2.v.xi.ii.html (last visited on February 10, 2010).

24. Barbara Aho, *Mystery, Babylon the Great - Catholic or Jewish?*, Watch Unto Prayer, *at* http://watch.pair.com/mystery-babylon.html (last visited on February 8, 2010).

25. Edith Starr Miller, Occult Theocrasy, p. 107 (1933).

26. Edith Starr Miller, Occult Theocrasy, p. 89 (1933).

27. Irenaeus, Against Heresies, Book I, Ch. XXIV.

28. Irenaeus, *Against Heresies*, Book III, Chapter XXI, *available at* http://www.ccel.org/ccel/schaff/anf01.ix.iv.xxii.html (last visited March 24, 2010).

29. Rabbi Tovia Singer, Does the Hebrew Word Alma Really Mean "Virgin"?, *available at* http://www.outreachjudaism.org/alma.htm (last visited on April 17, 2010). See also Rabbi Shraga Simmons, Ask Rabbi Simmons, Jesus as the Messiah, *at* http://judaism.about.com/library/3_askrabbi_o/bl_simmons_messiah3.htm (last visited on April 17, 2010).

30. G.A. RIPLINGER, BLIND GUIDES, p. 19.

31. G.A. RIPLINGER, BLIND GUIDES, p. 19.

32. G.A. RIPLINGER, BLIND GUIDES, p. 19.

33. Edward Hendrie, *Antichrist Conspiracy Inside the Devil's Lair*, at Chapter 7 (2010), *available at* www.antichristconspiracy.com and www.lulu.com.

34. Irenaeus, *Against Heresies*, Book III, Chapter XXI, *available at* http://www.ccel.org/ccel/schaff/anf01.ix.iv.xxii.html (last visited March 24, 2010).

35. Irenaeus, *Against Heresies*, Book I, Chapter XXVI, *available at* http://www.ccel.org/ccel/schaff/anf01.ix.ii.xxvii.html (last visited March 24, 2010).

36.Irenaeus, *Against Heresies*, Book I, Chapter XXV, *available at* http://www.ccel.org/ccel/schaff/anf01.ix.ii.xxvi.html. (last visited March 24, 2010).

37.Irenaeus, *Against Heresies*, Book I, Chapter XXV, *available at* http://www.ccel.org/ccel/schaff/anf01.ix.ii.xxvi.html. (last visited March 24, 2010).

38.Medieval Sourcebook: John Chrysostom (circa 347-407): Eight Homilies Against the Jews, *available at* http://www.fordham.edu/halsall/source/chrysostom-jews6.html (last visited on April 11, 2010).

39.Medieval Sourcebook: John Chrysostom (circa 347-407): Eight Homilies Against the Jews, *available at* http://www.fordham.edu/halsall/source/chrysostom-jews6.html (last visited on April 11, 2010).

40. Eusebius Pamphilius, Church History, Life of Constantine, Oration in Praise of Constantine, *available at* http://www.ccel.org/ccel/schaff/npnf201.iv.vi.iii.x.html (last visited on April 13, 2010).

41. Eusebius Pamphilius, Church History, Life of Constantine, Oration in Praise of Constantine, *available at* http://www.ccel.org/ccel/schaff/npnf201.iv.vi.iii.x.html (last visited on April 13, 2010).

42.ALEXANDER HISLOP, THE TWO BABYLONS, pp. 103-113 (1916).

43.ALEXANDER HISLOP, THE TWO BABYLONS (1916), *available at* http://www.biblebelievers.com/babylon/sect32.htm.

44.*Id.*

45.ALEXANDER HISLOP, THE TWO BABYLONS (1916), *available at* http://www.biblebelievers.com/babylon/sect32.htm.

46.ALEXANDER HISLOP, THE TWO BABYLONS (1916), *available at* http://www.biblebelievers.com/babylon/sect32.htm.

47.The Rosary, Roses of Prayer for The Queen of Heaven, Daniel A. Lord, S.J., Nihil Obstat Athur J. Scanlan S.T.D: Censor Liborum, Imprimatur + Francis J. Spellman, D.D. Archbishop, New York, http://www.truecatholic.org/rosary.htm (web address current as of March 20, 2005).

48.ALEXANDER HISLOP, THE TWO BABYLONS (1916), *available at* http://www.biblebelievers.com/babylon/sect32.htm.

49.*Id.* at § 2177.

50.*Id.* at § 2181.

51.CATECHISM OF THE CATHOLIC CHURCH, § 2174 (1994).

52.Emperor Constantine Was the First Pope, *at* http://www.reformation.org/pope-constantine.html (last visited on April 13, 2010).

53.Jewish History Sourcebook: Jews and the Later Roman Law 315-531 CE (1998) (source: Jacob Marcus, The Jew in the Medieval World: A Sourcebook, 315-1791, (New York: JPS, 1938), 3-7), *at* http://www.fordham.edu/halsall/jewish/jews-romanlaw.html.

54.The Jewish Question in Europe: The Causes, The Effects, The Remedies, from La Civilta Cattolica, vol. VII, no. XIV. 1890 (Oct, Nov, Dec) (English Translation, 1998), http://www.catholicapologetics.info/apologetics/judaism/jewrope.htm (last visited on February 11, 2010).

55.The Jewish Question in Europe: The Causes, The Effects, The Remedies, from La Civilta Cattolica, vol. VII, no. XIV. 1890 (Oct, Nov, Dec) (English Translation, 1998), *at* http://www.catholicapologetics.info/apologetics/judaism/jewrope.htm (last visited on February 11, 2010).

56.The Jewish Question in Europe: The Causes, The Effects, The Remedies, from La Civilta Cattolica, vol. VII, no. XIV. 1890 (Oct, Nov, Dec) (English Translation, 1998), *at* http://www.catholicapologetics.info/apologetics/judaism/jewrope.htm (last visited on February 11, 2010).

57.Barbara Aho, *Mystery, Babylon the Great - Catholic or Jewish?*, Watch Unto Prayer, *at* http://watch.pair.com/mystery-babylon.html (last visited on February 8, 2010).

58.DONN DE GRAND PRE, BARBARIANS INSIDE THE GATES, THE BLACK BOOK OF BOLSHEVISM, p. 250 (2000) (quoting Representative Louis McFadden, radio address, May 2, 1934).

59.75 Congressional Record 12595-12603.

60.See EDWARD GRIFFIN, THE CREATURE FROM JEKYLL ISLAND: A SECOND LOOK AT THE FEDERAL RESERVE (3RD Edition 1998).

61.CONG. REC. 12595-96 (1932) (speech of Rep. McFadden), *at* http://iresist.com/cbg/mcfadden_speech_1932.html (current as of September 30, 2001).

62.CONG. REC. 12595-96 (1932) (speech of Rep. McFadden), *at* http://iresist.com/cbg/mcfadden_speech_1932.html (current as of September 30, 2001).

63.Israel Shahak, Jewish History, Jewish Religion: The Weight of Three Thousand Years (1994), *available at* http//www.biblebelievers.org.au/jewhis3.htm#Orthodoxy%20and%20Interpretation.

64.Israel Shahak, Jewish History, Jewish Religion: The Weight of Three Thousand Years (1994), *available at* http//www.biblebelievers.org.au/jewhis3.htm#Orthodoxy%20and%20Interpretation.

65.Israel Shahak, Jewish History, Jewish Religion: The Weight of Three Thousand Years (1994), *available at* http//www.biblebelievers.org.au/jewhis3.htm#Orthodoxy%20and%20Interpretation.

66.Israel Shamir, Seven Lean Kine, November 28, 2008, *available at* http://www.thetruthseeker.co.uk/article.asp?ID=9743.

67.*Judaism: The Atheist Rabbi*, TIME, January 29, 1965, *available at* http://www.time.com/time/magazine/article/0,9171,839200,00.html.

68.*Judaism: The Atheist Rabbi*, TIME, January 29, 1965, *available at* http://www.time.com/time/magazine/article/0,9171,839200,00.html.

69.Amiram Barkat, *Rabbi Sherwin Wine, Founder of Humanistic Judaism, Dies at 79*, Haaretz, July 24, 2007, *available at* http://www.haaretz.com/hasen/spages/885330.html.

70.Amiram Barkat, *Rabbi Sherwin Wine, Founder of Humanistic Judaism, Dies at 79*, Haaretz, July 24, 2007, *available at* http://www.haaretz.com/hasen/spages/885330.html.

71.Michael Hoffman, *Judaism Revealed*, at 775 (2008) (quoting Yesaiah Tishbi, *Torat ha-Rave-Kelippah b-Kabbalat ha-Ari* ("The Theory of Evil and the Satanic Sphere in Kabbalah"), pp. 139-142 [1942; reprinted 1982]).

72.Michael Hoffman, *Judaism Revealed*, at 775 (2008) (quoting Yesaiah Tishbi, *Torat ha-Rave-Kelippah b-Kabbalat ha-Ari* ("The Theory of Evil and the Satanic Sphere in Kabbalah"), [1942; reprinted 1982]).

73.HEEDING BIBLE PROPHECY, Understanding Satan's Plan To Counterfeit the Second Coming of Christ & the Restoration of All Things, *at* http://watch.pair.com/new-israel.html, quoting Pinay, Maurice. THE PLOT AGAINST THE CHURCH, LA: St. Anthony Press, 1967, (last visited on February 11, 2010).

74.Rebecca Weiner, *The Virtual Jewish History Tour Rome, The Christian Empire*, Jewish Virtual Library, *at* http://www.jewishvirtuallibrary.org/jsource/vjw/Rome.html (last visited on February 11, 2010).

75.NESTA WEBSTER, SECRET SOCIETIES AND SUBVERSIVE MOVEMENTS, http://web.archive.org/web/20021005055527/http://www.plausiblefutures.com/text/SS.html (website address current as of 2-28-05) (citing Lexicon of Freemasonry, p. 323).

76.Edith Starr Miller, Occult Theocrasy, pp. 77 (1933) (quoting Flavien Brenier. Source: Lt. Gen. A. Netchvolodow, Nicolas II et les Juifs, p. 139.).

77.Edith Starr Miller, Occult Theocrasy, pp. 78-79 (1933) (quoting Flavien Brenier. Source: Lt. Gen. A. Netchvolodow, Nicolas II et les Juifs, p. 139.).

78.Edith Starr Miller, Occult Theocrasy, p. 80 (1933).

79.Edith Starr Miller, Occult Theocrasy, p. 81 (1933).

80.Michael Hoffman, *Judaism Discovered*, at 785 (2008).

81.Lawrence Fine, Chapter on Kabbalistic Texts, From: *Back to the Sources: Reading the Classic Jewish Texts* ("The First Complete Modern Guide to the Great Books of the Jewish Tradition: What They Are and How to Read Them"), at p. 337 (2006) (bold emphasis added, italics in original).

82.Lawrence Fine, Chapter on Kabbalistic Texts, From: *Back to the Sources: Reading the Classic Jewish Texts* ("The First Complete Modern Guide to the Great Books of the Jewish Tradition: What They Are and How to Read Them"), at p. 337 (2006) (quoting Zohar III, 152a).

83.Blavatsky, Theosophical Glossary, p. 168 (quoted by Barbara Aho, Mystery, Babylon the Great Catholic or Jewish?, at http://watch.pair.com/mystery-babylon.html#cabala (last visited on April 17, 2010)).

84.Jewish Encyclopedia, Cabala, at http://www.jewishencyclopedia.com/view.jsp?artid=1&letter=C#4 (last visited on April 18, 2010).

85.MICHAEL A. HOFFMAN, JUDAISM'S STRANGE GODS, at p. 88, (2000).

86.MICHAEL A. HOFFMAN, JUDAISM'S STRANGE GODS, at p. 88, (2000). See also Michael Hoffman, *Judaism Discovered*, at 779 (2008) (quoting Gershom Scholem, *Kabbalah* pp.183-84).

87.MICHAEL A. HOFFMAN, JUDAISM'S STRANGE GODS, at p. 91, (2000).

88.Michael Hoffman, *Judaism Discovered*, at 780 (2008) (quoting Helen Jacaobus, *Eye Jinx*, Jewish Chronicle, May 7, 1999).

89.MICHAEL A. HOFFMAN, JUDAISM'S STRANGE GODS, at p. 92, (2000).

90.Michael Hoffman, *The Truth About the Talmud, at* http://www.revisionisthistory.org/talmudtruth.html (last visited on March 10, 2010) (excerpted from MICHAEL A. HOFFMAN, JUDAISM'S STRANGE GODS (2000)).

91.Robert Goldberg, *Talmud, Back to the Sources: Reading the Classic Jewish Texts* (New York: Simon and Schuster, 1984), p. 130 (quoted by Michael Hoffman, *Judaism Discovered*, at 187 (2008)).

92. Michael Hoffman, *Judaism Discovered*, at 189 (2008).

93. Rabbi Ben Zion Bokser, *Judaism and the Christian Predicament* (1966), pp. 59 and 159 (quoted by Michael Hoffman, *Judaism Discovered*, at 190 (2008)).

94. Michael Hoffman, *The Truth About the Talmud*, at http://www.revisionisthistory.org/talmudtruth.html (excerpted from MICHAEL A. HOFFMAN, JUDAISM'S STRANGE GODS (2000)).

95. Michael Hoffman, *The Truth About the Talmud*, at http://www.revisionisthistory.org/talmudtruth.html (excerpted from MICHAEL A. HOFFMAN, JUDAISM'S STRANGE GODS (2000)) (quoting Ari Goldman, New York Times, April 10, 1993, p. 38).

96. Michael Hoffman, *The Truth About the Talmud*, at http://www.revisionisthistory.org/talmudtruth.html (excerpted from MICHAEL A. HOFFMAN, JUDAISM'S STRANGE GODS (2000)).

97. Michael Hoffman, *The Truth About the Talmud*, at http://www.revisionisthistory.org/talmudtruth.html (excerpted from MICHAEL A. HOFFMAN, JUDAISM'S STRANGE GODS (2000)).

98. See generally Athol Bloomer, *The Eucharist and The Jewish Mystical Tradition • Part 1*, Association of Hebrew Catholics, *at* http://hebrewcatholic.org/PrayerandSpirituality/eucharistjewishm.html, (last visited on February 12, 2010) (originally published in The Hebrew Catholic #77, pp 15-18.).

99. Fortescue, A. (1910). Liturgy. In The Catholic Encyclopedia. New York: Robert Appleton Company. Retrieved February 19, 2010 from New Advent: http://www.newadvent.org/cathen/09306a.htm.

100. Barbara Aho, *Mystery, Babylon the Great - Catholic or Jewish?*, Watch Unto Prayer, *at* http://watch.pair.com/mystery-babylon.html (last visited on February 8, 2010).

101. Barbara Aho, *Mystery, Babylon the Great - Catholic or Jewish?*, Watch Unto Prayer, *at* http://watch.pair.com/mystery-babylon.html (last visited on February 8, 2010).

102. Maurice Pinay, *The Plot Against the Church, Part Four, The "Jewish Fifth Column" in the Clergy, Chapter One, the Octopus Strangling Christianity*, *at* http://www.catholicvoice.co.uk/pinay/part4a.htm (last visited on February 12, 2010).

103. Anti-Zion, Jews on the Jewish Question, http://www.diac.com/~bkennedy/az/A-E.html (current as of September 10, 2001).

104. Edith Starr Miller (Lady Queenborough), Occult Theocrasy, p. 319 (1933).

105.Ivan Fraser, Protocols of the Learned Elders of Zion, Proofs of an Ancient Conspiracy, http://www.vegan.swinternet.co.uk/articles/conspiracies/protocols_proof.html (current as of September 10, 2001).

106.Barbara Aho, *Mystery, Babylon the Great - Catholic or Jewish?, Part III, The Jesuits*, Watch Unto Prayer, *at* http://watch.pair.com/mystery-babylon.html (last visited on February 8, 2010).

107.John S. Torell, European-American Evangelical Association, July 1999, http://www.eaec.org/NL99jul.htm (current as of October 2, 2001).

108.John S. Torell, European-American Evangelical Association, July 1999, http://www.eaec.org/NL99jul.htm (current as of October 2, 2001).

109.John S. Torell, European-American Evangelical Association, July 1999, http://www.eaec.org/NL99jul.htm (current as of October 2, 2001).

110.MANFRED BARTHEL, THE JESUITS, HISTORY AND LEGEND OF THE SOCIETY OF JESUS, p. 16 (1984).

111.COLLIER'S ENCYCLOPEDIA, vol. 13, p. 550 (1992).

112.Melinda Henneberger, *Vatican Says Jews' Wait for Messiah Is Validated by the Old Testament, New York Times,* January 18, 2002, http://www.hughhewitt.com/past_news_links_01.02/01.18.02.Vatican_Says_Wait_for_Messiah. html (Current as of February 10, 2002).

113.Michael Hoffman II, Secret Societies and Psychological Warfare, at p. 75 (2001).

114.Michael Hoffman II, Secret Societies and Psychological Warfare, at p. 75 (2001).

115.ALBERTO RIVERA, DOUBLE CROSS, Chick Publications, p. 12, 1981. *See also,* EDWIN A. SHERMAN, THE ENGINEER CORPS OF HELL, Library of Congress catalog card # 66-43354, p. 118 (1883); Congressional Record, House Bill 1523, contested election case of Eugene C. Bonniwell against Thos. S. Butler, February 15, 1913, at pp. 3215-16; BURKE MCCARTY, THE SUPPRESSED TRUTH ABOUT THE ASSASSINATION OF ABRAHAM LINCOLN, at pp. 14-16.

116.EDMOND PARIS, THE SECRET HISTORY OF THE JESUITS, p. 29 (1975).

117.*Id.*

118.*Id.*

119.EDMOND PARIS, THE SECRET HISTORY OF THE JESUITS, p. 26 (1975).

120.Barbara Aho, *Mystery, Babylon the Great - Catholic or Jewish?, Part III, The Jesuits*, Watch Unto Prayer, *at* http://watch.pair.com/mystery-babylon.html (last visited on February 8, 2010) (quoting Maurice Pinay, *The Plot Against the Church, Chapter Thirty-Nine, Jewish-Freemasonic Infiltration into the Jesuit Order*, http://www.catholicvoice.co.uk/pinay/part4d.htm (last visited February 10, 2010)).

121.THE PROTOCOLS OF THE LEARNED ELDERS OF ZION, Paragraph 3, Protocol 17, http://www.thewinds.org/library/protocols_of_zion.html (current as of September 9, 2001).

122.THE PROTOCOLS OF THE LEARNED ELDERS OF ZION, Paragraph 4, Protocol 17, http://www.thewinds.org/library/protocols_of_zion.html (current as of September 9, 2001).

123.ALBERTO RIVERA, DOUBLE CROSS, Chick Publications, p. 12, 1981. *See also,* EDWIN A. SHERMAN, THE ENGINEER CORPS OF HELL, Library of Congress catalog card # 66-43354, p. 118 (1883); Congressional Record, House Bill 1523, contested election case of Eugene C. Bonniwell against Thos. S. Butler, February 15, 1913, at pp. 3215-16; BURKE MCCARTY, THE SUPPRESSED TRUTH ABOUT THE ASSASSINATION OF ABRAHAM LINCOLN, at pp. 14-16.

124.EDMOND PARIS, THE SECRET HISTORY OF THE JESUITS, p. 70 (1975).

125.COLLIER'S ENCYCLOPEDIA, volume 13, p. 550 (1991); *see also,* EDMOND PARIS, THE SECRET HISTORY OF THE JESUITS, p. 70 (1975).

126.EDMOND PARIS, THE SECRET HISTORY OF THE JESUITS, p. 73 (1975).

127.EDMOND PARIS, THE SECRET HISTORY OF THE JESUITS, p. 70 (1975).

128.*Id.* at 70-71.

129.*Id.* at 71.

130.COLLIER'S ENCYCLOPEDIA, volume 12, p. 516 (1991).

131.SIDNEY HUNTER, IS ALBERTO FOR REAL?, p. 21 (1991); *see also,* EDMOND PARIS, THE SECRET HISTORY OF THE JESUITS, p. 35 (1975).

132.SIDNEY HUNTER, IS ALBERTO FOR REAL?, Chick Publications, p. 21-23 (1988).

133.ERIC JON PHELPS, VATICAN ASSASSINS: "WOUNDED IN THE HOUSE OF MY FRIENDS," P. 206 (2001).

134.WILLIAM STILL, NEW WORLD ORDER, The Ancient Plan of Secret Societies, p. 79 (1990).

135.ERIC JON PHELPS, VATICAN ASSASSINS: "WOUNDED IN THE HOUSE OF MY FRIENDS," p. 205 (2001).

136.ERIC JON PHELPS, VATICAN ASSASSINS: "WOUNDED IN THE HOUSE OF MY FRIENDS," p. 205 (2001).

137.WILLIAM STILL, NEW WORLD ORDER, The Ancient Plan of Secret Societies, pp. 81-91 (1990).

138.COLLIER'S ENCYCLOPEDIA, volume 13, p. 550 (1991).

139.EDMOND PARIS, THE SECRET HISTORY OF THE JESUITS, p. 75 (1975).

140.*Id.*

141.SAMUEL FINLEY BREESE MORSE, IMMINENT DANGERS TO THE FREE INSTITUTIONS OF THE UNITED STATES THROUGH FOREIGN IMMIGRATION AND THE PRESENT STATE OF THE NATURALIZATION LAWS, p. 9-10 (1835).

142.COLLIER'S ENCYCLOPEDIA, vol. 13, p. 550 (1991).

143.*Id.*

144.*Id. See also,* EDMOND PARIS, THE SECRET HISTORY OF THE JESUITS, p. 39 (1975).

145.COLLIER'S ENCYCLOPEDIA, volume 13, p. 550 (1991).

146.PARIS at p. 64.

147.PARIS at p. 65.

148.PARIS at p. 65.

149.PARIS at p. 65.

150.JOHN W. ROBBINS, ECCLESIASTICAL MEGALOMANIA, at p. 32 (1999) (quoting *Summa Theologiae,* ii-ii, 7th article).

151. JOHN W. ROBBINS, ECCLESIASTICAL MEGALOMANIA, at p. 40 (1999) (quoting The Second Vatican Council, *Gaudium et Spes, Pastoral Constitution on the Church in the Modern World,* at p. 69 (1965)).

152.Babylonian Talmud, *Tractate Baba Bathra, Folio 54b* (1961), *available at* http://www.come-and-hear.com/bababathra/bababathra_54.html.

153.Babylonian Talmud, *Tractate Baba Kamma, Folio 113b*, Translated into English with Notes, Glossary and Indices by E. W. Kirzner, M.A., Ph.D., M.Sc, under the Editorship of Rabbi Dr I. Epstein, B.A., Ph.D., D. Lit. (1961), *available at* http://www.come-and-hear.com/babakamma/babakamma_113.html.

154.J. E. C. SHEPHERD, THE BABINGTON PLOT, Wittenburg Publications, p.14, 1987.

155.EDMOND PARIS, THE SECRET HISTORY OF THE JESUITS, p. 26 (1975).

156.J. E. C. SHEPHERD, THE BABINGTON PLOT, Wittenburg Publications, p.16, 1987 (quoting Marianus de Luce, S.J., Professor Canon Law, Gregorian University of Rome, *Institutes of Public Ecclesiastical Law,* with personal commendation from Pope Leo XIII, 1901).

157.EDMOND PARIS, THE SECRET HISTORY OF THE JESUITS, Chick Publications, p. 166-167, 1975.

158.Babylonian Talmud: *Tractate Sanhedrin, Folio 57b*, Sanhedrin Translated into English with Notes, Glossary and Indices Chapters I - VI by Jacob Shachter, Chapters VII - XI by H. Freedman, B.A., Ph.D., Under the Editorship of Rabbi Dr I. Epstein B.A., Ph.D., D. Lit. (1961), *available at* http://www.come-and-hear.com/sanhedrin/sanhedrin_57.html (the section actually uses the word "Cuthean," but an endnote explains: "'Cuthean' (Samaritan) was here substituted by the censor for the original goy (heathen).").

159.Babylonian Talmud: *Tractate Sanhedrin, Folio 57b*, Sanhedrin Translated into English with Notes, Glossary and Indices Chapters I - VI by Jacob Shachter, Chapters VII - XI by H. Freedman, B.A., Ph.D., Under the Editorship of Rabbi Dr I. Epstein B.A., Ph.D., D. Lit. (1961), *available at* http://www.come-and-hear.com/sanhedrin/sanhedrin_57.html (the section actually uses the word "Cuthean," but an endnote explains: "'Cuthean' (Samaritan) was here substituted by the censor for the original goy (heathen).").

160.Michael Hoffman, *Judaism Discovered*, at 441 (2008).

161.Michael Hoffman, *Judaism Discovered*, at 441 (2008).

162.Canadian Jewish News, p. 9, August 23, 1980, quoted by Michael Hoffman in *Judaism Discovered*, at 442 (2008).

163.Israel Shahak, Jewish History, Jewish Religion: The Weight of Two Thousand Years (1994) (citing Maimonides, Mishneh Torah, 'Laws on Murderers' 2, 11; Talmudic Encyclopedia, 'Goy'), *available at* http://www.biblebelievers.org.au/jewhis5.htm#The%20Laws%20Against%20Non-Jews.

164.Shahak, Jewish History (citing R. Yo'el Sirkis, Bayit Hadash, commentary on Beyt Josef, 'Yoreh De'ah' 158. Shahak explains in an endnote: "The two rules just mentioned apply even if the Gentile victim is ger toshav, that is a 'resident alien' who has undertaken in front of three

Jewish witnesses to keep the 'seven Noahide precepts' (seven biblical laws considered by the Talmud to be addressed to Gentiles")).

165.Shahak, Jewish History (citing R. David Halevi (Poland, 17th century), Turey Zahav" on Shulhan 'Arukh, 'Yoreh De'ah' 158).

166.Shahak, Jewish History (citing Talmudic Encyclopedia, 'Ger' (= convert to Judaism)).

167.Shahak, Jewish History (citing Shulhan 'Arukh, 'Hoshen Mishpat' 426).

168.Shahak, Jewish History (Tractate 'Avodah Zarah', p. 26b).

169.Shahak, Jewish History (Maimonides, op. cit., 'Murderer' 4, 11).

170.Shahak, Jewish History (citing Leviticus, 19:16). Shahak also states in an endnote: "Concerning the rendering 'thy fellow', see note 14 to Chapter 3."

171.Shahak, Jewish History (citing Maimonides, op. cit., 'Idolatry' 10, 1-2).

172.Shahak, Jewish History (Shahak states in an endnote: "In both cases in section 'Yoreh De'ah' 158. The Shulhan 'Arukh repeats the same doctrine in 'Hoshen Mishpat' 425").

173.Shahak, Jewish History, *supra*.

174.EDMOND PARIS, THE SECRET HISTORY OF THE JESUITS, p. 21 (1975) (quoting *H. Boehmer*, professor at the University of Bonn, *Les Jesuits* (1910)).

175.J. E. C. SHEPHERD, THE BABINGTON PLOT, Wittenburg Publications, p.118, 1987.

176.J. E. C. SHEPHERD, THE BABINGTON PLOT, Wittenburg Publications, 1987.

177.*Id.* at p. 104-117. *See also* COLLIER'S ENCYCLOPEDIA, volume 9, p. 97 (1991). *See also*, LES GARRETT, WHICH BIBLE CAN WE TRUST?, p. 60 (1982).

178.COLLIER'S ENCYCLOPEDIA, volume 9, p. 620 (1991).

179.COLLIER'S ENCYCLOPEDIA, volume 11, p. 536 (1991).

180.COLLIER'S ENCYCLOPEDIA, volume 12, p. 192 (1991).

181.COLLIER'S ENCYCLOPEDIA, volume 13, p. 550 (1991).

182.COLLIER'S ENCYCLOPEDIA, volume 13, p. 550 (1991).

183.EDMOND PARIS, THE SECRET HISTORY OF THE JESUITS, p. 69 (1975).

184.FOXE'S BOOK OF MARTYRS, edited by William Byron Forbush, http://www.ccel.org/foxe/martyrs/fox117.htm.

185.*Washington Times*, August 19, 2003, http://www.washtimes.com/culture/culturebriefs.htm, (quoting Gene Edward Veith, Wandering Shepherds, World Magazine, Aug. 23, 2002).

186.*Washington Times*, August 19, 2003, http://www.washtimes.com/culture/culturebriefs.htm, (quoting Gene Edward Veith, Wandering Shepherds, World Magazine, Aug. 23, 2002).

187.Riazat Butt, *The Pope Was Jewish Says historian*, The Truth Seeker, (quoting Metronews,12 February 2006), *at* http://www.thetruthseeker.co.uk/article.asp?ID=4158 (last visited on February 15, 2010).

188. Barbara Aho, *Mystery, Babylon the Great - Catholic or Jewish?*, Watch Unto Prayer, *at* http://watch.pair.com/mystery-babylon.html (last visited on February 8, 2010).

189.John Whitley, *Seven Jewish American Control Most US Media*, Real News 24/7 (November 21, 2003), *available at* http://www.realnews247.com/seven_jewish_americans_control_media_rense.htm.

190.Id.

191.Id.

192.Id.

193.Ernesto Cienfuegos, *Senator John Kerry's Jewish Roots and Membership in Skulls and Bones*, *at* http://www.aztlan.net/kerry_jewish_roots.htm (last visited on February 16, 2010).

194.Brian Faler, A Revelation on Roots, *Washington Post*, February 4, 2003, http://www.washingtonpost.com/ac2/wp-dyn?pagename=article&node=&contentId=A20708-2003Feb3&notFound=true (website current as of March 27, 2003).

195.Ernesto Cienfuegos, *Senator John Kerry's Jewish Roots and Membership in Skulls and Bones*, *at* http://www.aztlan.net/kerry_jewish_roots.htm (last visited on February 16, 2010).

196.Brian Faler, A Revelation on Roots, *Washington Post*, February 4, 2003, http://www.washingtonpost.com/ac2/wp-dyn?pagename=article&node=&contentId=A20708-2003Feb3&notFound=true (website current as of March 27, 2003).

197.Barry Chamish, *Kerry, Gaza And The New Sabbatean Holocaust*, *at* http://www.conspiracyarchive.com/Commentary/Kerry_Gaza.htm (last visited on February 16, 2010).

198.See Ernesto Cienfuegos, *Senator John Kerry's Jewish Roots and Membership in Skulls and Bones*, *at* http://www.aztlan.net/kerry_jewish_roots.htm (last visited on February 16, 2010).

199.E.g., Kris Millegan, *The Order of Skull and Bones, Everything You Ever Wanted to Know, But Were Afraid to Ask, Skull and Bones = Illuminati?*, at http://jesus-is-savior.com/Evils%20in%20Government/War%20on%20Drugs%20Scam/Order%20of%20Skull%20&%20Bones/skull_and_bones_equal_illuminati.htm (last visited on February 16, 2010); Skull(s) and Bones, http://www.ontopofacloud.com/SkullandBones.htm (last visited on February 16, 2010).

200.*Skull and Bones, George Bush and John Kerry*, at http://www.bibliotecapleyades.net/sociopolitica/esp_sociopol_skullbones03.htm (last visited at February 16, 2010).

201.Lloyd Grove, *Yale Bones Connect Bush, Kerry*, NY Daily News (March 4, 2004), *available at* http://www.oilempire.us/skullbones.html.

202.Barry Chamish, *Kerry, Gaza And The New Sabbatean Holocaust*, at http://www.conspiracyarchive.com/Commentary/Kerry_Gaza.htm (last visited on February 16, 2010).

203.William F. Jasper, *The Power Behind the Presidency*, New American, August 13, 2001.

204.Maurice Pinay, *The Plot Against the Church, Chapter Two, The Origin of the "Fifth Column*, at http://www.catholicvoice.co.uk/pinay/ (last visited February 10, 2010).

205.Barbara Aho, *Mystery, Babylon the Great - Catholic or Jewish?*, Watch Unto Prayer, at http://watch.pair.com/mystery-babylon.html (last visited on February 8, 2010).

206.Barbara Aho, *Mystery, Babylon the Great - Catholic or Jewish?*, Watch Unto Prayer, at http://watch.pair.com/mystery-babylon.html (last visited on February 8, 2010).

207.Barbara Aho, *Mystery, Babylon the Great - Catholic or Jewish?*, Watch Unto Prayer, at http://watch.pair.com/mystery-babylon.html (last visited on February 8, 2010) (citing "The Pope of the Council, Part 19: John XXIII and Masonry," Sodalitium, October/November 1996).

208.ALBERT PIKE, MORALS AND DOGMA OF THE ANCIENT AND ACCEPTED SCOTTISH RITE OF FREEMASONRY, p. 205 (1871).

209.DES GRIFFIN, THE FOURTH REICH OF THE RICH, p. 70 (1993).

210.*Id.* at p. 567.

211.*Id.*

212.*Id.*

213.ERIC JON PHELPS, VATICAN ASSASSINS: "WOUNDED IN THE HOUSE OF MY FRIENDS," p. 180 (2001).

214. ALBERT PIKE, MORALS AND DOGMA OF THE ANCIENT AND ACCEPTED SCOTTISH RITE OF FREEMASONRY, p. 741 (1871).

215. *Id.* at p. 817.

216. *Id.* at p. 817-18.

217. GARY H. KAH, EN ROUTE TO GLOBAL OCCUPATION (http://www.biblebelievers.org.au/masonic.htm).

218. GARY H. KAH, EN ROUTE TO GLOBAL OCCUPATION (http://www.biblebelievers.org.au/masonic.htm).

219. ALBERT PIKE, MORALS AND DOGMA OF THE ANCIENT AND ACCEPTED SCOTTISH RITE OF FREEMASONRY, p. 820 (1871).

220. COLLIER'S ENCYCLOPEDIA, vol. 14, p. 122 (1992).

221. ALBERT PIKE, MORALS AND DOGMA OF THE ANCIENT AND ACCEPTED SCOTTISH RITE OF FREEMASONRY, p. 821 (1871).

222. Texe Marrs, Masonic Jews Plot to Control World, Power of Prophecy, April 2003, http://www.texemarrs.com/masonic_jews_plot_world_control.htm (website address current as of April 4, 2003).

223. Texe Marrs, Masonic Jews Plot to Control World, Power of Prophecy, April 2003, http://www.texemarrs.com/masonic_jews_plot_world_control.htm (website address current as of April 4, 2003).

224. Michael Hoffman, *Judaism Discovered,* at 768 (2008) (citing "The Place of Kabbalah in the Doctrine of Russian Freemasons," in Aries: Journal for the Study Western Esotericism, vol. 4, no. 1 (Brill Academic 2004) and Heimbichner, *Blood on the Alter*).

225. Michael Hoffman, *Judaism Discovered,* at 770 (2008).

226. Babylonian Talmud: *Tractate Sanhedrin, Folio 65b,* at n.24, Sanhedrin Translated into English with Notes, Glossary and Indices Chapters I - VI by Jacob Shachter, Chapters VII - XI by H. Freedman, B.A., Ph.D., Under the Editorship of Rabbi Dr I. Epstein B.A., Ph.D., D. Lit. (1961), *available at* http://www.come-and-hear.com/sanhedrin/sanhedrin_65.html.

227. NESTA WEBSTER, SECRET SOCIETIES AND SUBVERSIVE MOVEMENTS, http://web.archive.org/web/20021005055527/http://www.plausiblefutures.com/text/SS.html (website address current as of 2-28-05) (footnotes contained in original text omitted).

228. Barbara Aho, *Mystery, Babylon the Great - Catholic or Jewish?*, Watch Unto Prayer, *at* http://watch.pair.com/mystery-babylon.html (last visited on February 8, 2010).

229.Fritz Springmeier, *Bloodlines of Illuminati,* at 63 (1995), *available at* http://oneheartbooks.com/resources/ebooks/bloodlines_of_illuminati.pdf.

230.See, e.g., Barbara Aho, *Mystery, Babylon the Great - Catholic or Jewish?*, Watch Unto Prayer, *at* http://watch.pair.com/mystery-babylon.html (last visited on February 8, 2010).

231.See Barbara Aho, *Mystery, Babylon the Great - Catholic or Jewish?*, Watch Unto Prayer, *at* http://watch.pair.com/mystery-babylon.html (last visited on February 8, 2010).

232.*Priory of Sion*, Wikipedia *at* http://en.wikipedia.org/wiki/Priory_of_sion (last visited on February 15, 2010).

233.*Id. See also,* EDMOND PARIS, CONVERT OR DIE!, Chick Publications.

234.EDMOND PARIS, THE SECRET HISTORY OF THE JESUITS, Chick Publications, p. 167, 1975.

235.*Id.* at p. 164.

236.*Id.* at p. 168.

237.EDMOND PARIS, THE SECRET HISTORY OF THE JESUITS, Chick Publications, p. 165, 1975.

238.DONN DE GRAND PRE, BARBARIANS INSIDE THE GATES, THE BLACK BOOK OF BOLSHEVISM, p. 149 (2000) (citing DIETRICH BRONDER, BEFORE HITLER CAME; HENNEKE KARDEL, ADOLPH HITLER, FOUNDER OF ISRAEL).

239.DONN DE GRAND PRE, BARBARIANS INSIDE THE GATES, THE BLACK BOOK OF BOLSHEVISM, p. 149 (2000) (quoting HENNEKE KARDEL, ADOLPH HITLER: FOUNDER OF ISRAEL (1997)).

240.DONN DE GRAND PRE, BARBARIANS INSIDE THE GATES, THE BLACK BOOK OF BOLSHEVISM, p. 154 (2000) (quoting ISRAEL SHAHAK AND NORTON MEZVINSKY, JEWISH FUNDAMENTALISM IN ISRAEL, p. 125 (1999)).

241.ERIC JON PHELPS, VATICAN ASSASSINS: "WOUNDED IN THE HOUSE OF MY FRIENDS," p. 535-36 (2001).

242.Martin L. Lee, Their Will Be Done, *Mother Jones*, July/August 1983, http://www.motherjones.com/news/feature/1983/07/willbedone.html (web address current as of April 21, 2005).

243.DONN DE GRAND PRE, BARBARIANS INSIDE THE GATES, THE BLACK BOOK OF BOLSHEVISM, p. 90 (2000).

244. DONN DE GRAND PRE, BARBARIANS INSIDE THE GATES, THE BLACK BOOK OF BOLSHEVISM, p. 95 (2000).

245. DONN DE GRAND PRE, BARBARIANS INSIDE THE GATES, THE BLACK BOOK OF BOLSHEVISM, p. 94 (2000).

246. Des Griffin, Fourth Reich of the Rich, p. 216 (1993).

247. Texe Marrs, Masonic Jews Plot to Control World, Power of Prophecy, April 2003, http://www.texemarrs.com/masonic_jews_plot_world_control.htm (website address current as of April 4, 2003).

248. Texe Marrs, Masonic Jews Plot to Control World, Power of Prophecy, April 2003, http://www.texemarrs.com/masonic_jews_plot_world_control.htm (website address current as of April 4, 2003).

249. The International Jew, the World's Foremost Problem, Compiled from articles published by the Ford Motor Company in the Dearborn Independent from 1920-1922, available at http://www.biblebelievers.org.au/intern_jew.htm (last visited on November 29, 2010).

250. *See* Jack Mohr, *Satan's Kids*, http://www.christianbiblestudy.org/OPS/JM/JM0018c.htm (current as of September 9, 2001).

251. *The Protocols of the Learned Elders of Zion*, Wikipedia, *at* http://en.wikipedia.org/wiki/The_Protocols_of_the_Elders_of_Zion (last visited on February 15, 2010).

252. Shulamit Aloni: "It's a Trick We Always Use," http://wideeyecinema.com/?p=3804 (last visited on December 12, 2010).

253. Shulamit Aloni, Jewish Virtual Library, http://www.jewishvirtuallibrary.org/jsource/biography/aloni.html (last visited on December 12, 2010).

254. Shulamit Aloni: "It's a Trick We Always Use," http://wideeyecinema.com/?p=3804 (last visited on December 12, 2010).

255. Rose Cohen, *Bali, Australia & The Mossad* (October 17, 2002), *at* http://www.rense.com/general30/balias.htm.

256. *Zionism Promotes Anti-Semitism*, Jews Against Zionism, *at* http://www.jewsagainstzionism.com/antisemitism/zionismpromotes.cfm (last visited on March 26, 2010).

257. *Zionism and Anti-Semitism*, Jews Against Anti-Semitism, *at* http://www.jewsagainstzionism.com/zionism/zanda.cfm (last visited on March 26, 2010).

258. Leader of Nazis Has Jewish Father, Lakeland Ledger, AP, July 24, 1977, *available at* http://news.google.com/newspapers?nid=1346&dat=19770724&id=KXosAAAAIBAJ&sjid=vPo DAAAAIBAJ&pg=4602,6288087. See also R. D. Flavin, *Frank Collin: From neo-Nazi to Hyper-Diffusionist and Witch* (previously published in The Greenwich Village Gazette, Feb. 21, 1997, as "The Many Faces of Frank Collin").

259. Homo-Facism After Hitler, The Pink Swastika, at 278, *at* http://www.defendthefamily.com/pfrc/books/pinkswastika/html/Chapter8.htm (last visited on March 26, 2010).

260. Ted Pike, *ACLU Top Heavy with Jews*, October 4, 2006, *at* http://www.truthtellers.org/alerts/acluheavywithjews.html.

261. Robert Patrick, *Kosher Conflict in Missouri Prison*, St. Louis Post-Dispatch, Jan. 5, 2008, *available at* http://www.religionnewsblog.com/20276/norman-lee-toler.

262. *Zionism Promotes Anti-Semitism*, Jews Against Zionism, *at* http://www.jewsagainstzionism.com/antisemitism/zionismpromotes.cfm (last visited on March 26, 2010).

263. Adam Yahiye Gadahn, FBI Most Wanted Terrorists, http://www.fbi.gov/wanted/wanted_terrorists/adam-yahiye-gadahn (last visited on December 21, 2010).

264. Fake Al Qaeda, http://whatreallyhappened.com/WRHARTICLES/fakealqaeda.php (last visited on December 21, 2010).

265. Fake Al Qaeda, http://whatreallyhappened.com/WRHARTICLES/fakealqaeda.php (last visited on December 21, 2010).

266. The Official Website of Yousef Al Khattab, http://www.yousefalkhattab.com/ (last visited on December 21, 2010).

267. Fake Al Qaeda American Terrorist Adam Pearlman Jewish, http://www.youtube.com/watch?v=24Pdo_hA5Qs (last visited on December 21, 2010).

268. U.S. Based Revolution Muslim Website Spreading Messages of Hate, Fox News, March 26, 2008, http://www.foxnews.com/story/0,2933,341811,00.html#ixzz18mmCvuP0http://www.foxnews.com/story/0,2933,341811,00.html.

269. Harrav NissimKarelitz - the Rosh Kollel of Cahzon Ish; the Beis Din of Khal Machzikei Hadas (Belz); the Beis Din of Vixnhitz; and the Rabbonim of Ger. Michael Hoffman, *Judaism Discovered*, at 200 (2008).

270. "Gedolim Order Boycott of Hashavua," Hamodia (Orthodox Jewish newspaper) 19 Adar 5763 (Feb. 21, 2003), p. 14, quoted by Michael Hoffman in *Judaism Discovered*, at 201 (2008).

271. Michael Hoffman in *Judaism Discovered*, at 201 (2008).

272. DAVE HUNT, A WOMAN RIDES THE BEAST, p. 55 (1994), quoting J.H. IGNAZ VON DOLLINGER, THE POPE AND THE COUNCIL, p. 21 (London 1869).

273. JOHN W. ROBBINS, ECCLESIASTICAL MEGALOMANIA, p. 143 (1999).

274. DAVE HUNT, A WOMAN RIDES THE BEAST, p. 123 (1994).

275. CHARLES CHINIQUY, FIFTY YEARS IN THE CHURCH OF ROME, Chick Publications, p. 285 (1985) republished from the 1886 edition.

276. *Id.*

277. *Id.*

278. SAMUEL FINLEY BREESE MORSE, FOREIGN CONSPIRACY AGAINST THE LIBERTIES OF THE UNITED STATES: THE NUMBERS OF BRUTUS, p. 118-119 (1835).

279. CHARLES CHINIQUY, FIFTY YEARS IN THE CHURCH OF ROME, Chick Publications, p. 288 (1985) republished from the 1886 edition.

280. JOHN W. ROBBINS, ECCLESIASTICAL MEGALOMANIA, p. 143-44 (1999).

281. MICHAEL A. HOFFMAN II, JEWISH COMMUNISTS: THE DOCUMENTARY RECORD, http://www.hoffman-info.com/communist.html (website current as of March 5, 2003).

282. ROBERT WILTON, THE LAST DAYS OF THE ROMANOVS (1920).

283. Gordon "Jack" Mohr, The Talmudic Effect on Judeo-Christianity, http://www.christianbiblestudy.org/OPS/JM/jm0027c.htm (current as of September 19, 2001).

284. ROBERT WILTON, THE LAST DAYS OF THE ROMANOVS, p. 148 (1920).

285. COLONEL GORDON "JACK" MOHR, THE TALMUDIC EFFECT ON JUDEO-CHRISTIANITY, http://www.christianbiblestudy.org/OPS/JM/jm0027e.htm (current as of September 17, 2001).

286.*Izvestia,* July 27, 1918.

287.HENRY FORD, THE INTERNATIONAL JEW, vol. 1, p. 225 (1920).

288.HENRY FORD, THE INTERNATIONAL JEW, vol. 1, p. 225 (1920).

289.MICHAEL A. HOFFMAN II, JEWISH COMMUNISTS: THE DOCUMENTARY RECORD, http://www.hoffman-info.com/communist.html (website current as of March 5, 2003) (quoting The Christian News, Jan. 8, 1996, p. 2).

290.MICHAEL A. HOFFMAN II, JEWISH COMMUNISTS: THE DOCUMENTARY RECORD, http://www.hoffman-info.com/communist.html (website current as of March 5, 2003).

291.MICHAEL A. HOFFMAN II, JEWISH COMMUNISTS: THE DOCUMENTARY RECORD, http://www.hoffman-info.com/communist.html (website current as of March 5, 2003) (quoting Dmitri Volkogonov, *Lenin: A New Biography,* p. 112).

292.MICHAEL A. HOFFMAN II, JEWISH COMMUNISTS: THE DOCUMENTARY RECORD, http://www.hoffman-info.com/communist.html (website current as of March 5, 2003).

293.DES GRIFFIN, FOURTH REICH OF THE RICH, p. 62 (1976).

294.*Id.*

295.ERIC JON PHELPS, VATICAN ASSASSINS: "WOUNDED IN THE HOUSE OF MY FRIENDS," p. 167-77 (2001).

296.DONN DE GRAND PRE, BARBARIANS INSIDE THE GATES, THE BLACK BOOK OF BOLSHEVISM, p. 209 (2000) (quoting BEJAMIN FREEDMAN, FACTS ARE FACTS (1954)).

297.Baruch Levy, Letter to Karl Marx, `La Revue de Paris', p. 574, June 1, 1928. http://www4.stormfront.org/posterity/ci/tjg.html (current as of September 9, 2001). *See also* DON DE GRAND PRE, BARBARIANS INSIDE THE GATES, p. 64 (2000).

298.DONN DE GRAND PRE, BARBARIANS INSIDE THE GATES, THE BLACK BOOK OF BOLSHEVISM, p. 313-14 (2000) (citing JACK BERNSTEIN, THE LIFE OF AN AMERICAN JEW IN RACIST MARXIST ISRAEL (1984)).

299.DONN DE GRAND PRE, BARBARIANS INSIDE THE GATES, THE BLACK BOOK OF BOLSHEVISM, p. 313-14 (2000) (citing JACK BERNSTEIN, THE LIFE OF AN AMERICAN JEW IN RACIST MARXIST ISRAEL (1984)).

300.DONN DE GRAND PRE, BARBARIANS INSIDE THE GATES, THE BLACK BOOK OF BOLSHEVISM, p. 313-14 (2000) (citing JACK BERNSTEIN, THE LIFE OF AN AMERICAN

JEW IN RACIST MARXIST ISRAEL (1984)).

301.JACK BERNSTEIN, MY FAREWELL TO ISRAEL THE THORN IN THE MIDEAST.

302.Barbara Aho, *Mystery, Babylon the Great - Catholic or Jewish?*, Watch Unto Prayer, *at* http://watch.pair.com/mystery-babylon.html (last visited on February 8, 2010).

303.Barbara Aho, *The Merovingian Dynasty, Satanic Bloodline of the Antichrist & False Prophet*, Watch Unto Prayer, *at* http://watch.pair.com/priory.html#intro (last visited on February 15, 2010).

304.Mark of the Beast, Merovingians, *at* http://www.scribd.com/doc/20883345/Mark-of-the-Beast-merovingians (last visited on February 15, 2010).

305.ERIC JON PHELPS, VATICAN ASSASSINS: "WOUNDED IN THE HOUSE OF MY FRIENDS," p. 167-77 (2001).

306.AVRO MANHATTAN, THE VATICAN BILLIONS, p. 124-125 (1983).

307.ALBERTO RIVERA, THE GODFATHERS, p. 13 (1982) (citing SALISBURY, BLACK NIGHT WHITE SNOW, p. 405-407 (1977).

308.ALBERTO RIVERA, THE GODFATHERS, p. 13 (1982) (citing R. PAYNE, LIFE AND DEATH OF LENIN, p. 285-300 (1964)).

309.ALBERTO RIVERA, THE GODFATHERS, p. 13 (1982) (citing GERMANY AND THE REVOLUTION IN RUSSIA 1915-1918; DOCUMENTS FROM THE GERMAN FOREIGN MINISTRY, edited by Z.A.B. ZEMAN, p. IX (1958)).

310.AVRO MANHATTAN, THE VATICAN BILLIONS, p. 124-125 (1983).

311.*Id.*

312.*Id.*

313.AVRO MANHATTAN, THE VATICAN MOSCOW WASHINGTON ALLIANCE, p. 281-82 (1986).

314.ALBERTO RIVERA, ALBERTO, Chick Publications, p. 28 (1979).

315.*Id.* at p. 38, 281-82.

316.ARMANDO VALLADARES, AGAINST ALL HOPE, p. 281 (1986).

317.ARMANDO VALLADARES, AGAINST ALL HOPE, p. 282 (1986).

318.JOHN W. ROBBINS, ECCLESIASTICAL MEGALOMANIA, at p. 41 (1999) (quoting Pius XI, *Quadragesimo Anno, On Social Reconstruction,* p. 25 (1931).

319.JOHN W. ROBBINS, ECCLESIASTICAL MEGALOMANIA, at p. 67 (1999).

320.Jerry Seper, *Colombia Rebels Met With Dozen IRA Chiefs, The Washington Times*, May 6, 2002.

321.Jerry Seper, *Colombia Rebels Met With Dozen IRA Chiefs, The Washington Times*, May 6, 2002.

322.Pohle, J. (1911). Priesthood. In The Catholic Encyclopedia. New York: Robert Appleton Company. Retrieved February 19, 2010 from New Advent: http://www.newadvent.org/cathen/12409a.htm.

323.Kusala Bhikshu, *Do Buddhists Believe in God?, at* http://www.urbandharma.org/udharma3/budgod.html (last visited on February 21, 2010).

324.Id.

325.Id.

326.Id.

327.Link Between Ancient Babylon and Buddhism Believed Found, Gettysburg Times, Jan 21, 1935, http://news.google.com/newspapers?nid=2202&dat=19350121&id=uwcmAAAAIBAJ&sjid=Ef0FAAAAIBAJ&pg=4353,685294.

328.George Ripley & Charles A. Dana, The American Cyclopaedia (1873), *available at* http://chestofbooks.com/reference/American-Cyclopaedia-2/Cabala.html.

329.Sara Yohoved Rigler, *Difference Between Judaism and Buddhism*, Judaism Online, *at* http://www.simpletoremember.com/articles/a/buddhismjudaism/ (lat visited on February 21, 2010).

330.Sara Yohoved Rigler, *Difference Between Judaism and Buddhism*, Judaism Online, *at* http://www.simpletoremember.com/articles/a/buddhismjudaism/ (lat visited on February 21, 2010).

331.Peter Myers, *Israel Shahak on Jewish Fundamentalism and Militarism* (September 12, 2001), at http://www.mailstar.net/shahak2.html.

332.Michael A. Hoffman II, *Judaism's Strange God's*, at 79 (2000).

333. Babylonian Talmud: *Tractate 'Abodah Zarah, Folio 43b*, Abodah Zarah Translated into English with Notes, Glossary and Indices Folios 1-35b by A. Mishcon Folios 35b to the End By A. Cohen, M.A., Ph.D., Under the Editorship of Rabbi Dr I. Epstein B.A., Ph.D., D. Lit. (1961), *available at* http://www.come-and-hear.com/zarah/zarah_43.html.

334. Answers.com, *Talmud, at* http://www.answers.com/topic/talmud (last visited on February 21, 2010).

335. Answers.com, *Talmud, at* http://www.answers.com/topic/talmud (last visited on February 21, 2010).

336. Michael A. Hoffman II, *Judaism's Strange God's*, at 80 (2000).

337. Michael A. Hoffman II, *Judaism's Strange God's*, at 80 (2000).

338. Heng Sure, *Cleansing the Heart: Buddhist Bowing As Contemplation, at* http://www.urbandharma.org/udharma7/bowing.html (last visited on February 21, 2010).

339. Heng Sure, *Cleansing the Heart: Buddhist Bowing As Contemplation, at* http://www.urbandharma.org/udharma7/bowing.html (last visited on February 21, 2010).

340. Michael Hoffman & Alan R. Critchley, The Truth About the Talmud, http://www.hoffman-info.com/talmudtruth.html (current as of September 12, 2001).

341. Michael Hoffman & Alan R. Critchley, The Truth About the Talmud, http://www.hoffman-info.com/talmudtruth.html (current as of September 12, 2001).

342. Michael Hoffman & Alan R. Critchley, The Truth About the Talmud, http://www.hoffman-info.com/talmudtruth.html (current as of September 12, 2001).

343. Michael Hoffman & Alan R. Critchley, The Truth About the Talmud, http://www.hoffman-info.com/talmudtruth.html (current as of September 12, 2001).

344. Benjamin Freedman, Facts are Facts, http://www.biblebelievers.org.au/facts.htm#FACTS%20ARE%20FACTS%20-%20I (website address current as of April 2, 2003).

345. Michael L. Rodkinson: The History of the Talmud; http://www.come-and-hear.com/talmud/rodkin_ii3.html#E27 (web address current as of February 8, 2004).

346. Judaism vs. Christianity: The War The Lamb Wins, http://www.fixedearth.com/talmud.html (current as of September 11, 2001).

347. Michael Hoffman, *Judaism Discovered*, at 441 (2008).

348.*Yediot Ahronot*, February 28, 1994, cited by Michael Hoffman in *Judaism Discovered*, at 443 (2008).

349.Michael Hoffman, *Judaism Discovered*, at 443 (2008).

350.*Yediot Ahronot*, February 28, 1994, cited by Michael Hoffman in *Judaism Discovered*, at 443 (2008).

351.New York Times, February 28, 1994, quoted by Michael Hoffman in *Judaism Discovered*, at 443 (2008).

352.Yuval Katz, *Yerushalaim*, March 4, 1994, quoted by Michael Hoffman in *Judaism Discovered*, at 445 (2008).

353.Washington Report on Middle East Affairs, p. 102, January-February 1997, quoted by Michael Hoffman in *Judaism Discovered*, at 445 (2008).

354.Graveside Party Celebrates Hebron Massacre, Radio Islam, March 21, 2000, at http://www.radioislam.org/historia/zionism/goldstein_celebrate.html.

355.THE JEWISH ENCYCLOPEDIA, vol. V, p. 619 (1901-1906).

356.Elizabeth Dilling, THE JEWISH RELIGION: Its Influence Today, chapter IV, p. 41 (1964).

357.Israel Shahak, Jewish History, Jewish Religion: The Weight of Two Thousand Years (1994), *available at* http://www.biblebelievers.org.au/jewhis2.htm#Prejudice%20and%20Prevarication.

358.Moses Maiminodes, The Guide of the Perplexed [*Moreh Nevuk'him*], translated by Schlomo Pines [Chicago: University of Chicago Press, 1963], vol. 2, pp 618-19 (quoted by Michael Hoffman in Judaism's Strange Gods, at 65 (2002).

359.Bobby O'Connor, *The Racism of Evolution Theory,* CHARLESTON GAZETTE, June 25, 1998 at P18. (Quoting CHARLES DARWIN, THE DESCENT OF MAN (1874)). *See also* Benno C. Schmidt, *Principle and Prejudice: The Supreme Court and Race in the Progressive Era. Part 1: The Heyday of Jim Crow,* 82 COLUM. L. REV. 444, 453 (1982).

360.Rabbi Shraga Simmons, Ask Rabbi Simmons, Evolution vs. Creation, *at* http://judaism.about.com/library/3_askrabbi_o/bl_simmons_evolution.htm.

361.*See* Noah Webster, THE AMERICAN DICTIONARY OF THE ENGLISH LANGUAGE (1828); THE COMPACT EDITION OF THE OXFORD ENGLISH DICTIONARY, Oxford University Press, at 2400 (1979). *See also,* THE AMERICAN HERITAGE ILLUSTRATED ENCYCLOPEDIC DICTIONARY (1987).

362.CREATION, June-Aug. 1999, Vol. 21, No. 3, at 22.

363.*Id.*

364.Raj Bhopal, *Is Research Into Ethnicity and Health Racist, Unsound, or Important to Science?*, BRITISH MEDICAL JOURNAL, June 14, 1997.

365.Jim Dawson, *'Race' is Social Notion With No Base in Biology, Genetics, Scientists Say*, STAR TRIBUNE (Minneapolis, MN), February 20, 1995, at 6A.

366. 481 U.S. 604 (1987).

367.*Id.* at 610 n. 4.

368.Norman Hammond, Archaeology Correspondent, Expert Views Differ on Jesuit's Role in the Piltdown Man forgery, *London Times*, July 15, 1980, http://www.clarku.edu/~piltdown/map_prim_suspects/Teilhard_de_Chardin/Chardin_Prosecutio n/expertsdiffer.html (website address current as of February 28, 2005).

369.Ken Ham, The Lie: Evolution (1987), *available at* http://www.creationists.org/evolutionism-is-a-religion.html.

370.Jewish Encyclopedia, Evolution, at http://www.jewishencyclopedia.com/view.jsp?artid=534&letter=E (last visited on April 17, 2010).

371.Judaism vs. Christianity: The War The Lamb Wins, http://www.fixedearth.com/talmud.html (current as of September 11, 2001).

372.DONN DE GRAND PRE, BARBARIANS INSIDE THE GATES, THE BLACK BOOK OF BOLSHEVISM, p. 209 (2000) (quoting BEJAMIN FREEDMAN, FACTS ARE FACTS (1954)).

373.Company History: Zondervan Corporation, http://www.answers.com/topic/zondervan (last visited on April 5, 2010).

374.G. A. RIPLINGER, THE LANGUAGE OF THE KING JAMES BIBLE, p. 114 (1998).

375.G.A. RIPLINGER, NEW AGE BIBLE VERSIONS, p. 2 (1993).

376.G. A. RIPLINGER, THE LANGUAGE OF THE KING JAMES BIBLE, p. 128 (1998).

377.Company History: Zondervan Corporation, http://www.answers.com/topic/zondervan (last visited on April 5, 2010).

378.Anton La Vey, Satanic Bible, Harper Collins, *available at* http://www.harpercollins.com/book/index.aspx?isbn=9780380015399 (on sale 12/1/1976); NIV Bible, Harper Collins *available at* http://www.harpercollins.com/books/9780310949862/NIV_Bible/index.aspx.

379.G. A. RIPLINGER, THE LANGUAGE OF THE KING JAMES BIBLE, p. 128 (1998).

380.G. A. RIPLINGER, THE LANGUAGE OF THE KING JAMES BIBLE, p. 128 (1998).

381.Rupert Murdoch's Jewish Origins: a Matter of Controversy, *at* http://www.fpp.co.uk/online/02/05/Murdoch2.html (May 25, 2002).

382.G. A. RIPLINGER, THE LANGUAGE OF THE KING JAMES BIBLE, p. 128 (1998).

383.Edward Hendrie, *Antichrist Conspiracy Inside the Devil's Lair*, at Chapter 7 (2010), *available at* www.antichristconspiracy.com and www.lulu.com.

384.*Israeli Youths Burn New Testaments*, USA Today, May 21, 2008, *at* http://www.usatoday.com/news/religion/2008-05-21-jewish-new-testament_N.htm.

385.*Israeli Youths Burn New Testaments*, USA Today, May 21, 2008, *at* http://www.usatoday.com/news/religion/2008-05-21-jewish-new-testament_N.htm.

386.Michael Hoffman, *Judaism Discovered*, at 592 (2008).

387.Michael Hoffman, *Judaism Discovered*, at 592 (2008).

388.Encyclopedia , Yamaka, at http://www.statemaster.com/encyclopedia/Yamaka (last visited on February 21, 2010).

389.Braun, J. (1912). Zucchetto. In The Catholic Encyclopedia. New York: Robert Appleton Company. Retrieved February 21, 2010 from New Advent: http://www.newadvent.org/cathen/15765b.htm.

390.Rabbi Shear Yashuv-Cohen, Pope Arrives in Israel - Calls for Two-state Solution, San Francisco Sentinel, 10 May 2009 at http://www.sanfranciscosentinel.com/?p=26237.

391.Rabbi Barry Dov Lerner, Conservative Judaism - *Wearing of Yamaka* (March 19, 2009) (quoting The Encyclopedia Judaica), *at* http://en.allexperts.com/q/Conservative-Judaism-951/2009/3/Wearing-Yamaka.htm.

392. Babylonian Talmud: *Tractate Shabbath, Folio 156b*, Shabbath Translated into English with Notes, Glossary and Indices Chapters I - IV by Rabbi Dr. H. Freedman, B.A., Ph.D., Under the Editorship of Rabbi Dr I. Epstein B.A., Ph.D., D. Lit. (1961), *available at* http://www.come-and-hear.com/shabbath/shabbath_156.html.

393.Rabbi Barry Dov Lerner, Conservative Judaism - *Wearing of Yamaka* (March 19, 2009), *at* http://en.allexperts.com/q/Conservative-Judaism-951/2009/3/Wearing-Yamaka.htm.

394.Alexander Hislop, *The Two Babylons*, at 221 (1959).

395.Alexander Hislop, *The Two Babylons*, at 221 (1959).

396.Alexander Hislop, *The Two Babylons*, at 221-23 (1959).

397.Alexander Hislop, *The Two Babylons*, at 222 (1959).

398.Fanning, W. (1912). Tonsure. In The Catholic Encyclopedia. New York: Robert Appleton Company. Retrieved February 26, 2010 from New Advent: http://www.newadvent.org/cathen/14779a.htm.

399.Alexander Hislop, *The Two Babylons*, at 215 (1959).

400.Babylonian Talmud: *Tractate Sanhedrin, Folio 58b*, Sanhedrin Translated into English with Notes, Glossary and Indices Chapters I - VI by Jacob Shachter, Chapters VII - XI by H. Freedman, B.A., Ph.D., Under the Editorship of Rabbi Dr I. Epstein B.A., Ph.D., D. Lit. (1961), *available at* http://www.come-and-hear.com/sanhedrin/sahedrin_58.html.

401.*Sanhedrin, Folio 58b.*

402.Babylonian Talmud: *Tractate Yebamoth, Folio 98a,* Yebamoth Translated into English with Notes Glossary and Indices by Rev. Dr. Israel W. Slotki, M.A., Litt.D., Under the Editorship of Rabbi Dr I. Epstein B.A., Ph.D., D. Lit. (1961), *available at* http://www.come-and-hear.com/yebamoth/yebamoth_98.html .

403.Michael A. Hoffman II, *Judaism's Strange God's*, at 364 (2000) (quoting *Romemut Yisrael Ufarashat Hagalut*).

404.Michael A. Hoffman II, *Judaism's Strange God's*, at 364 (2000) (quoting *Romemut Yisrael Ufarashat Hagalut*).

405.Babylonian Talmud: Tractate 'Abodah Zarah, Folio 17a.

406.Babylonian Talmud: Tractate Sanhedrin Folio 106a.

407.Babylonian Talmud: Tractate Gittin Folio 57a.

408.Michael Hoffman, *Judaism Discovered*, at 357 (2008).

409.Chagigah 27a (a/k/a Hagigah 27a), *A Translation of the Treatise Chagigah from the Babylonian Talmud*, With Introduction, Notes, Glossary, and Indices by the Rev. A. W. Strean, M.A. Fellow, and Divinity and Hebrew Lecturer, of Corpus Christi College, Cambridge, and Formerly Tyrwhitt's Hebrew Scholar, at 145 (1891), *available at* http://www.archive.org/details/chagigahbabyloni00unknuoft.

410.Tractate Baba Bathra Folio 75a at footnote 15.

411. Michael Hoffman, *Judaism Discovered*, at 196 (2008) (quoting *Zohar Hadash, Bereshit* 18d-19a).

412. Michael Hoffman, *Judaism Discovered*, at 529 (2008) (quoting Roman A. Foxbrunner, *Habad: The Hasidism of Shneur of Lyady*, at 108-09 (1993) (quoting Rabbi Shneur Zalman)).

413. Michael Hoffman, *Judaism Discovered*, at 196 (2008).

414. Michael Hoffman, *Judaism Discovered*, at 203 (2008).

415. William Wotton, *Miscellaneous Discourses Relating to the Traditions and Usages of the Scribes and Pharisees in Our Blessed Saviour Jesus Christ's Time* (London 1718) (quoted by Michael Hoffman, *Judaism Discovered*, at 193 (2008)).

416. Michael Hoffman, *Judaism Discovered*, at 192 n.156 (2008).

417. Michael Hoffman, *Judaism Discovered*, at 534 (2008).

418. Michael Hoffman, *Judaism Discovered*, at 591 (2008).

419. Michael Hoffman, *Judaism Discovered*, at 592 (2008).

420. Michael Hoffman, *Judaism Discovered*, at 591-92 (2008).

421. Michael Hoffman, *Judaism Discovered*, at 382 (2008).

422. Babylonian Talmud: *Tractate Sanhedrin, Folio 90a*, Sanhedrin Translated into English with Notes, Glossary and Indices Chapters I - VI by Jacob Shachter, Chapters VII - XI by H. Freedman, B.A., Ph.D., Under the Editorship of Rabbi Dr I. Epstein B.A., Ph.D., D. Lit. (1961), *available at* http://www.come-and-hear.com/sanhedrin/sanhedrin_90.html.

423. Babylonian Talmud: *Tractate Sanhedrin, Folio 90a*, Sanhedrin Translated into English with Notes, Glossary and Indices Chapters I - VI by Jacob Shachter, Chapters VII - XI by H. Freedman, B.A., Ph.D., Under the Editorship of Rabbi Dr I. Epstein B.A., Ph.D., D. Lit. (1961), *available at* http://www.come-and-hear.com/sanhedrin/sanhedrin_90.html.

424. Elizabeth Dilling, *The Jewish Religion, Its Influence Today* (1963), *at* http://www.come-and-hear.com/dilling/chapt03.html#The_18_Benedictions.

425. Nathan Abrams, *Triple Ethics, Jews in the American Porn Industry*, Jewish Quarterly (Winter 2004), *available at* http://www.fpp.co.uk/BoD/origins/porn_industry.html.

426. Ted Pike, Jews Behind *'The Ten'*, August 8, 2007, at http://www.truthtellers.org/alerts/jewsbehindtheten.htm.

427. CATECHISM OF THE CATHOLIC CHURCH § 846 (1994) (emphasis added).

428.CATECHISM OF THE CATHOLIC CHURCH § 841 (1994).

429.See Michael Hoffman, *Judaism Discovered*, at 184 (2008).

430.CATECHISM OF THE CATHOLIC CHURCH § 839 (1994) (footnotes omitted, emphasis added).

431.CATECHISM OF THE CATHOLIC CHURCH § 839 (1994) (footnotes omitted, internal quotation marks omitted).

432.CATECHISM OF THE CATHOLIC CHURCH § 842 (1994) (footnote omitted, emphasis added).

433.CATECHISM OF THE CATHOLIC CHURCH § 846 (1994).

434.James Lainez, Catholic Encyclopedia (1913), *at* http://en.wikisource.org/wiki/Catholic_Encyclopedia_%281913%29/James_Lainez.

435.Robert Maryks, *Jesuits of Jewish Ancestry. A Biographical Dictionary* (2008), at http://sites.google.com/a/jewishjesuits.com/www/.

436.Edith Starr Miller (Lady Queenborough), Occult Theocrasy, p. 319 (1933).

437.Robert Maryks, *Jesuits of Jewish Ancestry. A Biographical Dictionary* (2008), at http://sites.google.com/a/jewishjesuits.com/www/.

438. COUNCIL OF TRENT, DOCTRINE ON THE SACRAMENT OF PENANCE, Canon XII, November 25, 1551.

439.COUNCIL OF TRENT, SESSION VI, DECREE ON JUSTIFICATION, Canon XXIV, January 13, 1547.

440.COUNCIL OF TRENT, SESSION VI, DECREE ON JUSTIFICATION, Canon XXX, January 13, 1547.

441.ALBERTO RIVERA, THE FOUR HORSEMEN, Chick publications, p. 7, 1985 (quoting JESSIE CORRIGAN PEGIS, A PRACTICAL CATHOLIC DICTIONARY, p. 67 (1957)).

442.CATECHISM OF THE COUNCIL OF TRENT, ORDERED BY THE COUNCIL OF TRENT, EDITED UNDER ST. CHARLES BORROMEO, PUBLISHED BY DECREE OF POPE ST. PIUS V, 1566, TAN Books, 1982 at p. 208.

443.*Id.* at p. 211.

444.*Id.* at p. 212.

445.U.S. CONST. article VI.

446.EDWARD PETERS, INQUISITION, p. 48, 1989.

447.*Id.* at p. 56.

448.CHARLES CHINIQUY, FIFTY YEARS IN THE CHURCH OF ROME, Chick Publications, p. 295 (1985) republished from the 1886 edition.

449.CHARLES CHINIQUY, FIFTY YEARS IN THE CHURCH OF ROME, Chick Publications, p. 298 (1985) republished from the 1886 edition.

450.CHARLES CHINIQUY, FIFTY YEARS IN THE CHURCH OF ROME , Chick Publications, p. 298 (1985), republished from the 1886 edition.

451.Jonathan Cook, *Why There Are No 'Israelis' in the Jewish State - Citizens Classed as Jewish or Arab Nationals*, Media Monitors, April 6, 2010, *at* http://usa.mediamonitors.net/content/view/full/73038.

452.Jonathan Cook, *Why There Are No 'Israelis' in the Jewish State - Citizens Classed as Jewish or Arab Nationals*, Media Monitors, April 6, 2010, *at* http://usa.mediamonitors.net/content/view/full/73038.

453.Jonathan Cook, *Why There Are No 'Israelis' in the Jewish State - Citizens Classed as Jewish or Arab Nationals*, Media Monitors, April 6, 2010, *at* http://usa.mediamonitors.net/content/view/full/73038.

454.Jonathan Cook, *Why There Are No 'Israelis' in the Jewish State - Citizens Classed as Jewish or Arab Nationals*, Media Monitors, April 6, 2010, *at* http://usa.mediamonitors.net/content/view/full/73038.

455.Jonathan Cook, *Why There Are No 'Israelis' in the Jewish State - Citizens Classed as Jewish or Arab Nationals*, Media Monitors, April 6, 2010, *at* http://usa.mediamonitors.net/content/view/full/73038.

456.Citing Moses Hadas, Hellenistic Culture, Fusion and Diffusion, Columbia University Press, New York, 1959, especially chapters VII and XX.

457.Israel Shahak, Jewish History, Jewish Religion: The Weight of Three Thousand Years (1997), *available at* http://www.biblebelievers.org.au/jewhis1.htm.

458.Israel Shahak, Jewish History, Jewish Religion: The Weight of Two Thousand Years (1994) http://www.biblebelievers.org.au/jewhis2.htm.

459.Hassane Zerouky, Hamas is a Creation of Mossad (23 March 2004) (the article originally appeared in French in L'Humanité), *available at* http://www.globalresearch.ca/articles/ZER403A.html.

460. Michael Hoffman, *Judaism Discovered* (2008) at 907.

461. COLLIER'S ENCYCLOPEDIA, volume 13, p. 38 (1991).

462. ENCYCLOPEDIA AMERICANA, volume 15, p. 193 (1998).

463. *Id.*

464. COLLIER'S ENCYCLOPEDIA, volume 13, p. 38 (1991).

465. COLLIER'S ENCYCLOPEDIA, volume 3, p. 644 (1991).

466. EDMOND PARIS, CONVERT OR DIE!, Chick Publications, p. 5.

467. RALPH E. WOODROW, BABYLON MYSTERY RELIGION, p. 100, 1966.

468. CORRADO PALLRNBERG, INSIDE THE VATICAN, p. 180-81, 1960.

469. ENCYCLOPEDIA BRITANNICA, volume 6, p. 329, 1998.

470. ENCYCLOPEDIA AMERICANA, volume 15, p.194 (1998).

471. DAVE HUNT, A WOMAN RIDES THE BEAST, p. 261, 1994.

472. COLLIER'S ENCYCLOPEDIA, volume 13, p. 40 (1991).

473. DAVE HUNT, A WOMAN RIDES THE BEAST, p. 261, 1994.

474. *Id.*

475. *Id.*

476. JOHN W. ROBBINS, ECCLESIASTICAL MEGALOMANIA, p. 113 (1999).

477. DAVE HUNT, A WOMAN RIDES THE BEAST, Harvest House Publishers, p. 89 (1994) (quoting Austin Flannery, O.P., gen. ed., *Vatican II, The Conciliar and Post Conciliar Documents*, rev. ed. (Costello Publishing 1988), vol. 1, p. 412).

478. CATECHISM OF THE CATHOLIC CHURCH § 846 (1994) (emphasis added).

479. DECLARATION "DOMINUS IESUS" ON THE UNICITY AND SALVIFIC UNIVERSALITY OF JESUS CHRIST AND THE CHURCH, *Rome, from the Offices of the Congregation for the Doctrine of the Faith, August 6, 2000.*

480. Jewish Encyclopedia, *Atonement*, Kaufmann Kohler, Rabbi Emeritus of Temple Beth-El, New York; President of the Hebrew Union College, Cincinnati, Ohio, *available at* http://www.jewishencyclopedia.com/view.jsp?artid=2092&letter=A&search=forgive%20sin (last visited on February 27, 2010).

481. Babylonian Talmud: *Tractate Berakoth, Folio 60a,* Translated into English with Notes, Glossary and Indices by Maurice Simon, M.A., Under the Editorship of Rabbi Dr I. Epstein B.A., Ph.D., D. Lit. (1961), *available at* http://www.come-and-hear.com/berakoth/berakoth_60.html.

482. Jewish Encyclopedia, *Atonement*, Kaufmann Kohler, Rabbi Emeritus of Temple Beth-El, New York; President of the Hebrew Union College, Cincinnati, Ohio, *available at* http://www.jewishencyclopedia.com/view.jsp?artid=2092&letter=A&search=forgive%20sin (last visited on February 27, 2010).

483. Michael A. Hoffman II, *Judaism's Strange God's*, at 80 (2000).

484. Michael A. Hoffman II, *Judaism's Strange God's*, at 80 (2000).

485. Babylonian Talmud: *Tractate 'Abodah Zarah, Folio 43b*, Abodah Zarah Translated into English with Notes, Glossary and Indices Folios 1-35b by A. Mishcon Folios 35b to the End By A. Cohen, M.A., Ph.D., Under the Editorship of Rabbi Dr I. Epstein B.A., Ph.D., D. Lit. (1961), *available at* http://www.come-and-hear.com/zarah/zarah_43.html.

486. Babylonian Talmud: *Tractate Berakoth, Folio 4b,* Translated into English with Notes, Glossary and Indices by Maurice Simon, M.A., Under the Editorship of Rabbi Dr I. Epstein B.A., Ph.D., D. Lit. (1961), *available at* http://www.come-and-hear.com/berakoth/berakoth_4.html.

487. ORDERED BY THE COUNCIL OF TRENT, EDITED UNDER ST. CHARLES BORROMEO, PUBLISHED BY DECREE OF POPE ST. PIUS V, 1566, TAN Books, p. 258, 1982.

488. *See* CHINIQUY, THE PRIEST, THE WOMAN, AND THE CONFESSIONAL, Chick Publications.

489. Michael A. Hoffman II, *Judaism's Strange God's*, at 80 (2000).

490. *Do We Need a Mediator?*, Jews for Jesus (March 1, 1989), *at* http://jewsforjesus.org/publications/issues/6_4/mediator (quoting Steinberg, Milton, *Basic Judaism*, Harvest Book, Harcourt, Brace & World, Inc., NY, 1947, p. 57-58.).

491. *Do We Need a Mediator?*, Jews for Jesus (March 1, 1989), *at* http://jewsforjesus.org/publications/issues/6_4/mediator (quoting Hertz, Dr. Joseph H., The Authorized Daily Prayer Book, 1975, p. 882.).

492.*NO MEDIATOR, SAYS THE RABBI.; A Protest Against the President's Thanksgiving Proclamation*, New York Times, November 19, 1896, *available at* http://query.nytimes.com/gst/abstract.html?res=9A02E5DD1331E033A2575AC1A9679D94679 ED7CF.

493.ORDERED BY THE COUNCIL OF TRENT, EDITED UNDER ST. CHARLES BORROMEO, PUBLISHED BY DECREE OF POPE ST. PIUS V, 1566, TAN Books, p. 331, 1982.

494.Michael Hoffman, *Judaism Discovered*, at 678 (2008).

495.Metzitzah B'peh: to Suck or Not to Suck, December 22, 2006, at http://simplyappalling.blogspot.com/2006/12/metzitzah-bpeh-to-suck-or-not-to-suck.html.

496.Michael Hoffman, *Judaism Discovered*, at 681 (2008).

497.Wayne R. Dynes, Holy fellatio, Homolexis, October 21, 2009, *at* http://homolexis.blogspot.com/2009/10/holy-fellatio.html.

498.Wayne R. Dynes, Holy fellatio, Homolexis, October 21, 2009, *at* http://homolexis.blogspot.com/2009/10/holy-fellatio.html.

499.Jim Rutenberg and Andy Newman, NY Times, January 6,2006 (quoted by Michael Hoffman in *Judaism Discovered*, at 682-83).

500.Robert Kolker, Rabbi Avi Shafran And Agudath Israel Exposed And Rebuked, June 29, 2006, at http://failedmessiah.typepad.com/failed_messiahcom/2006/06/rabbi_avi_shafr.html.

501.Kolker, Rabbi Avi Shafran And Agudath Israel Exposed And Rebuked, supra.

502.Eugene L. Meyer, Is Molestation Being Swept Underneath the Eruv?, Hidden Horrors in the Haredi Community, Jewish Journal, January 11, 2007, *at* http://www.jewishjournal.com/articles/page2/is_molestation_being_swept_underneath_the_eruv _20070112/.

503.Meyer, Hidden Horrors in the Haredi Community, Jewish Journal, supra.

504.Michael Hoffman, *Judaism Discovered*, at 705 (2008).

505.Michael Hoffman, *Judaism Discovered*, at 688 (2008).

506.Michael Hoffman, *Judaism Discovered*, at 689 (2008).

507.Michael Hoffman, *Judaism Discovered*, at 689-90 (2008).

508.Michael Hoffman, *Judaism Discovered*, at 694-95 (2008).

509.Michael Hoffman, *Judaism Discovered*, at 694-95 (2008).

510.Michael Hoffman, *Judaism Discovered*, at 694-95 (2008).

511.Michael Hoffman, *Judaism Discovered*, at 687-700 (2008).

512.Hella Winston, *So Many Rules, So Little Protection, Sex and Suppression Among Ultra-Orthodox Jews*, Lilith, at 10, Winter 2006-07, *available at* http://www.lilith.org/pdfs/LilithWinter2006_Hella1.pdf.

513.Ha'aretz, Shevat 25, 5760 (Feb. 1, 2000), *available at* http://abbc.net/islam/english/toread/talmud2.htm.

514.Ha'aretz, Shevat 25, 5760 (Feb. 1, 2000), *available at* http://abbc.net/islam/english/toread/talmud2.htm.

515.Ha'aretz, Shevat 25, 5760 (Feb. 1, 2000), *available at* http://abbc.net/islam/english/toread/talmud2.htm.

516.Ha'aretz, Shevat 25, 5760 (Feb. 1, 2000), *available at* http://abbc.net/islam/english/toread/talmud2.htm.

517.Ha'aretz, Shevat 25, 5760 (Feb. 1, 2000), *available at* http://abbc.net/islam/english/toread/talmud2.htm.

518.Ha'aretz, Shevat 25, 5760 (Feb. 1, 2000), *available at* http://abbc.net/islam/english/toread/talmud2.htm.

519.Ha'aretz, Shevat 25, 5760 (Feb. 1, 2000), *available at* http://abbc.net/islam/english/toread/talmud2.htm.

520.Tom Leonard and Nick Squires, Pope Benedict Accused of Delaying Unfrocking of Sex Abuse Priest, Telegraph, April 9, 2010, *at* http://www.telegraph.co.uk/news/worldnews/europe/vaticancityandholysee.

521.Leonard and Squires, Pope Benedict, Telegraph, April 9, 2010, supra.

522.DAVE HUNT, A WOMAN RIDES THE BEAST, Harvest House Publishers, p. 168 (1994).

523.DAVE HUNT, A WOMAN RIDES THE BEAST, Harvest House Publishers, p. 164 (1994).

524.*Id.* at p. 172.

525.*Id.* at pp. 172-173 (quoting National Catholic Reporter, p. 9, January 7, 1994).

526.*Id.* at p. 173.

527.*Diocese OKs $23 Million Payout in Abuse Case, Chicago Tribune,* July 11, 1998.

528.*Paper Says Ex-Priest Admitted Sex Abuse to Pope, The New York Times,* October 25, 1992.

529.Declan White, *Scandal of Vatican and Pervert Priest; Church Knew for 7 Years that He was a Molester; Vatican were Aware in 1987 of Sex Crimes of Father Brendan Smith, The People,* December 4, 1994.

530.Michael McCord, *Fortier Guilty in Altar Boy Sex Assaults . . ., The Union Leader*(Manchester, N.H.), August 5, 1998.

531.Walter Robinson, *A 'Grieving' Law Apologizes for the Assignment of Geoghan, The Boston Globe,* January 10, 2002, http://www.boston.com/globe/spotlight/geoghan/011002_law.htm (current as of April 4, 2002).

532.*Ex-Sudbury Priest Accused of Abuse: Local Man Claims the Cardinal Tried to Quash Allegations about 'Father B', The Metro West Daily News, AP, Boston,* April 5, 2002. http://www.metrowestdailynews.com/news/local_regional/ap_priestabuse0405002.htm (current as of April 6, 2002).

533.Elizabeth Mehren, Boston Archdiocese 'Sacrificed the Children,' *Toronto Star,* July 24 2003.

534.Elizabeth Mehren, Boston Archdiocese 'Sacrificed the Children,' *Toronto Star,* July 24 2003.

535.Elizabeth Mehren, Boston Archdiocese 'Sacrificed the Children,' *Toronto Star,* July 24 2003.

536.Don Lattin, Molestation Victim Protests Vatican Service, *San Francisco Chronicle,* April 11, 2005, http://sfgate.com/cgi-bin/article.cgi?file=/chronicle/archive/2005/04/11/rome11.TMP (web address current as of May 5, 2005).

537.Elizabeth Mehren, Boston Archdiocese 'Sacrificed the Children,' *Toronto Star,* July 24 2003.

538.Elizabeth Mehren, Boston Archdiocese 'Sacrificed the Children,' *Toronto Star,* July 24 2003.

539.U.S. House of Representatives, 8th District of Wisconsin, Press Release, U.S. House Passes Rep. Green "Two Strikes Bill," http://www.house.gov/markgreen/PRESS/2000/July00News/NR072500TwoStrikesPassage.htm (website address current as of August 16, 2003). See also http://www.geocities.com/Wellesley/2726/Molester.html (website address current as of August 16, 2003); Jon Donenberg, Keller Attacks Johnson's Vote On 1987 Bill, The Daily Illini Online,

October 3, 2000, http://www.dailyillini.com/oct00/oct03/news/printer/news01.shtml (website address current as of August 16, 2003).

540.Boston Archdiocese Offers 55 Million Dollars to Settle Lawsuits, *Boston Associated Press, Fox 23 News,* WXXA, Albany, NY, www.fox23news.com, August 11, 2003.

541.JOHN W. DECAMP, THE FRANKLIN COVER-UP, pp. 151-56 (1996).

542.JOHN W. DECAMP, THE FRANKLIN COVER-UP, pp. 283-85 (1996).

543.*The Tampa Tribune,* May 5, 1996.

544.DAVE HUNT, A WOMAN RIDES THE BEAST, Harvest House Publishers, p. 174 (1994) (quoting National Catholic Reporter, pp. 6-7, September 17, 1993).

545.*The Associated Press,* March 20, 1992.

546.DAVE HUNT, A WOMAN RIDES THE BEAST, Harvest House Publishers, p. 172 (1994).

547.*The Associated Press,* March 20, 1992.

548.Deborah Zabarenko, *Study Finds 10,600 Children Abused by U.S. Priests*, Reuters, February 27, 2004.

549.*Key Figures From a Catholic Abuse Survey*, Guardian Unlimited, Associated Press, February 27, 2004.

550.Deborah Zabarenko, *Study Finds 10,600 Children Abused by U.S. Priests*, Reuters, February 27, 2004.

551.*U.S. Church Reports 11,000 Abuse Complaints*, Globe and Mail, Associated Press, February 27, 2004.

552.Deborah Zabarenko, *Study Finds 10,600 Children Abused by U.S. Priests*, Reuters, February 27, 2004.

553.*U.S. Church Reports 11,000 Abuse Complaints*, Globe and Mail, Associated Press, February 27, 2004.

554.*Key Figures From a Catholic Abuse Survey*, Guardian Unlimited, Associated Press, February 27, 2004.

555.*Key Figures From a Catholic Abuse Survey*, Guardian Unlimited, Associated Press, February 27, 2004.

556.*Key Figures From a Catholic Abuse Survey*, Guardian Unlimited, Associated Press, February 27, 2004.

557.DAVE HUNT, A WOMAN RIDES THE BEAST, Harvest House Publishers, p. 172 (1994).

558.U.S. House of Representatives, 8th District of Wisconsin, Press Release, U.S. House Passes Rep. Green "Two Strikes Bill," http://www.house.gov/markgreen/PRESS/2000/July00News/NR072500TwoStrikesPassage.htm (website address current as of August 16, 2003). See also http://www.geocities.com/Wellesley/2726/Molester.html (website address current as of August 16, 2003); Jon Donenberg, Keller Attacks Johnson's Vote On 1987 Bill, The Daily Illini Online, October 3, 2000, http://www.dailyillini.com/oct00/oct03/news/printer/news01.shtml (website address current as of August 16, 2003).

559.Jason Berry, Vatican a Conflicted Attitude Toward Gays, Los Angeles Times, August 1, 1999, http://www.soulforce.org/catholics.html (web address current as of April 27, 2002). Notice: soulforce.org is a pro-sodomite website.

560.Cardinal in Vatican Accused of Sexual Abuse Cover-Up, ABC News, April 26, 2002, http://www.abcnews.go.com/sections/2020/DailyNews/2020_Vatican_coverup_020426.html (web address current as of April 27, 2002).

561.Jason Berry, Clergy Sex Abuse - the Trail Leads to Rome, http://www.peak.org/~snapper/News_Vatican/VATICAN_BackPage_3.htm (web address current as of April 27, 2002).

562.Jason Berry, Vatican a Conflicted Attitude Toward Gays, Los Angeles Times, August 1, 1999, http://www.soulforce.org/catholics.html (web address current as of April 27, 2002). Notice: soulforce.org is a pro-sodomite website.

563.Brian Ross, Priestly Sin, Cover-Up, Powerful Cardinal in Vatican Accused of Sexual Abuse Cover-Up, ABC News, April 26, 2002, http://www.abcnews.go.com/sections/2020/DailyNews/2020_Vatican_coverup_020426.html (web address current as of April 27, 2002).

564.Jason Berry, Vatican a Conflicted Attitude Toward Gays, Los Angeles Times, August 1, 1999, http://www.soulforce.org/catholics.html (web address current as of April 27, 2002). Notice: soulforce.org is a pro-sodomite website.

565.Ann Rodgers-melnick, Pedophile Priest Problem Blamed on Church Leadership, Pittsburgh Post-Gazette, http://www.post-gazette.com/world/20020324priests0324p1.asp (web address current as of April 27, 2002).

566.Brian Ross, Priestly Sin, Cover-Up, Powerful Cardinal in Vatican Accused of Sexual Abuse Cover-Up, ABC News, April 26, 2002, http://www.abcnews.go.com/sections/2020/DailyNews/2020_Vatican_coverup_020426.html (web address current as of April 27, 2002).

567.Brian Ross, Priestly Sin, Cover-Up, Powerful Cardinal in Vatican Accused of Sexual Abuse Cover-Up, ABC News, April 26, 2002, http://www.abcnews.go.com/sections/2020/DailyNews/2020_Vatican_coverup_020426.html (web address current as of April 27, 2002).

568.Sex Crimes Cover-Up By Vatican?, *CBS Evening News*, August 6, 2003, http://www.cbsnews.com/stories/2003/08/06/eveningnews/main566978.shtml (website address current as of August 10, 2003).

569.FROM THE SUPREME AND HOLY CONGREGATION FOR THE HOLY OFFICE FOR ALL PATRIARCHS, ARCHBISHOPS, BISHOPS, AND OTHER DIOCESAN ORDINARIES "EVEN OF THE ORIENTAL RITE," Instruction on the Manner of Proceeding in Cases of Solicitation, ¶ 11 (1962) (marked: CONFIDENTIAL).

570.FROM THE SUPREME AND HOLY CONGREGATION FOR THE HOLY OFFICE FOR ALL PATRIARCHS, ARCHBISHOPS, BISHOPS, AND OTHER DIOCESAN ORDINARIES "EVEN OF THE ORIENTAL RITE," Instruction on the Manner of Proceeding in Cases of Solicitation, ¶ 11 (1962) (marked: CONFIDENTIAL).

571.FROM THE SUPREME AND HOLY CONGREGATION FOR THE HOLY OFFICE FOR ALL PATRIARCHS, ARCHBISHOPS, BISHOPS, AND OTHER DIOCESAN ORDINARIES "EVEN OF THE ORIENTAL RITE," Instruction on the Manner of Proceeding in Cases of Solicitation, ¶ 11 (1962) (marked: CONFIDENTIAL).

572.FROM THE SUPREME AND HOLY CONGREGATION FOR THE HOLY OFFICE FOR ALL PATRIARCHS, ARCHBISHOPS, BISHOPS, AND OTHER DIOCESAN ORDINARIES "EVEN OF THE ORIENTAL RITE," Instruction on the Manner of Proceeding in Cases of Solicitation, Title V, The Worst Crime, ¶ 71 (1962) (marked: CONFIDENTIAL).

573.FROM THE SUPREME AND HOLY CONGREGATION FOR THE HOLY OFFICE FOR ALL PATRIARCHS, ARCHBISHOPS, BISHOPS, AND OTHER DIOCESAN ORDINARIES "EVEN OF THE ORIENTAL RITE," Instruction on the Manner of Proceeding in Cases of Solicitation, Title V, The Worst Crime, ¶ 73 (1962) (marked: CONFIDENTIAL).

574.FROM THE SUPREME AND HOLY CONGREGATION FOR THE HOLY OFFICE FOR ALL PATRIARCHS, ARCHBISHOPS, BISHOPS, AND OTHER DIOCESAN ORDINARIES "EVEN OF THE ORIENTAL RITE," Instruction on the Manner of Proceeding in Cases of Solicitation, Appendix, The Formula for Taking an Oath to Exercise One's Office Faithfully and to Observe the Secret of the Holy Office, Formula A (1962) (marked: CONFIDENTIAL).

575.FROM THE SUPREME AND HOLY CONGREGATION FOR THE HOLY OFFICE FOR ALL PATRIARCHS, ARCHBISHOPS, BISHOPS, AND OTHER DIOCESAN ORDINARIES

"EVEN OF THE ORIENTAL RITE," Instruction on the Manner of Proceeding in Cases of Solicitation, ¶ 13 (1962) (marked: CONFIDENTIAL).

576.FROM THE SUPREME AND HOLY CONGREGATION FOR THE HOLY OFFICE FOR ALL PATRIARCHS, ARCHBISHOPS, BISHOPS, AND OTHER DIOCESAN ORDINARIES "EVEN OF THE ORIENTAL RITE," Instruction on the Manner of Proceeding in Cases of Solicitation, Title Number One, ¶ 16 (1962) (marked: CONFIDENTIAL).

577.FROM THE SUPREME AND HOLY CONGREGATION FOR THE HOLY OFFICE FOR ALL PATRIARCHS, ARCHBISHOPS, BISHOPS, AND OTHER DIOCESAN ORDINARIES "EVEN OF THE ORIENTAL RITE," Instruction on the Manner of Proceeding in Cases of Solicitation, Appendix, Way of Undertaking the Entire Investigation, Note 1, Formula G (1962) (marked: CONFIDENTIAL).

578.FROM THE SUPREME AND HOLY CONGREGATION FOR THE HOLY OFFICE FOR ALL PATRIARCHS, ARCHBISHOPS, BISHOPS, AND OTHER DIOCESAN ORDINARIES "EVEN OF THE ORIENTAL RITE," Instruction on the Manner of Proceeding in Cases of Solicitation, ¶ 52 (1962) (marked: CONFIDENTIAL).

579.Sex Crimes Cover-Up By Vatican?, *CBS Evening News*, August 6, 2003, http://www.cbsnews.com/stories/2003/08/06/eveningnews/main566978.shtml (website address current as of August 10, 2003).

580.Michael Powell and Lois Romano, *Roman Catholic Church Shifts Legal Strategy: Aggressive Litigation Replaces Quiet Settlements, Washington Post*, May 13, 2002, http://www.washingtonpost.com/wp-dyn/articles/A8117-2002May12.html (web page current as of May 14, 2002.

581.Michael Powell and Lois Romano, *Roman Catholic Church Shifts Legal Strategy: Aggressive Litigation Replaces Quiet Settlements, Washington Post*, May 13, 2002, http://www.washingtonpost.com/wp-dyn/articles/A8117-2002May12.html (web page current as of May 14, 2002.

582.Richard Owen, *Chief exorcist Father Gabriele Amorth says Devil is in the Vatican*, The Times, March 11, 2010, http://www.timesonline.co.uk/tol/comment/faith/article7056689.ece.

583.Richard Owen, *Chief exorcist Father Gabriele Amorth says Devil is in the Vatican*, The Times, March 11, 2010, http://www.timesonline.co.uk/tol/comment/faith/article7056689.ece.

584.quoted in SIDNEY HUNTER, IS ALBERTO FOR REAL?, p. 63 (1988).

585.Edith Starr Miller (Lady Queenborough), Occult Theocrasy, p. 316 (1933) (quoting Schaff-Herzog, *The Encyclopaedia of Religious Knowledge*. Art. Jesuits.)

586.Benjamin H. Freedman, Facts are Facts, *available at* http://www.biblebelievers.org.au/facts2.htm (last visited on April 15, 2010).

587.Noah Webster, AMERICAN DICTIONARY OF THE ENGLISH LANGUAGE, *Cardinal* (1828). See also Online Etymology Dictionary, *Cardinal, at* http://www.etymonline.com/index.php?term=cardinal (last visited on March 16, 2010).

588.Jewish Encyclopedia, High Priest, *available at* http://www.jewishencyclopedia.com/view.jsp?artid=721&letter=H&search=high%20priest (last visited on March 16, 2010).

589.Jewish Encyclopeidia, Sanhedrin, *available at* http://www.jewishencyclopedia.com/view.jsp?artid=229&letter=S&search=sanhedrin (last visited on March 16, 2010).

590.Sägmüller, J.B. (1908). Cardinal. In The Catholic Encyclopedia. New York: Robert Appleton Company. Retrieved March 16, 2010 from New Advent: http://www.newadvent.org/cathen/03333b.htm.

591.The High Priest and His Garments, http://www.domini.org/tabern/highprst.htm (last visited on March 16, 2010).

592.CATECHISM OF THE CATHOLIC CHURCH, § 830-831, 1994.

593.CATECHISM OF THE CATHOLIC CHURCH, § 2034-2035, 1994.

594.ALBERTO RIVERA, FOUR HORSEMEN, Chick Publications, p. 25, 1985 (quoting AVRO MANHATTAN, VATICAN IMPERIALISM IN THE 20th CENTURY, p. 76.). *See also*, JOHN W. ROBBINS, ECCLESIASTICAL MEGALOMANIA, at p. 132 (1999).

595.ALBERTO RIVERA, THE GODFATHERS, Chick Publications, p. 32, 1982 (quoting The Registers of Boniface VIII, The Vatican Archives, L. Fol. 387 and THE CATHOLIC ENCYCLOPEDIA, Encyclopedia Press (1913)).

596.ALBERTO RIVERA, DOUBLE CROSS, Chick publications, p. 27, 1981(quoting THE GREAT ENCYCLICAL LETTERS OF POPE LEO XIII, p. 304, Benziger Brothers (1903).

597.G.A. RIPLER, NEW AGE BIBLE VERSIONS, p. 134 (1993).

598.*Id.*

599.NOAH WEBSTER, AMERICAN DICTIONARY OF THE ENGLISH LANGUAGE (1st ed. 1828) republished by Foundation for American Christian Education, San Francisco, California.

600.Oxford University Press (1979).

601.JOHN PAUL II, CROSSING THE THRESHOLD OF HOPE, p. 12, 1994.

602.*Id.* at p. 6.

603.*E.g.,* W. GRINTON BERRY, FOXE'S BOOK OF MARTYRS, p. 357.

604.GERARDUS D. BOUW, GEOCENTRICITY, p. 153 (1992).

605.*Id.*

606.*Id.*

607.*Id.*

608.RALPH E. WOODROW, BABYLON MYSTERY RELIGION, p. 72, 1966.

609.COLLIER'S ENCYCLOPEDIA, volume 19, p. 239 (1991).

610.STEWART PEROWNE, ROMAN MYTHOLOGY, p. 125-26, 1969.

611.Alexander Hislop, *The Two Babylons* (1959), *available at* http://www.biblebelievers.com/babylon/sect23.htm.

612.Alexander Hislop, *The Two Babylons*, at 211 (1959).

613.Hyam Maccoby, *Judaism on Trial*, quoted by Michael Hoffman in *Judaism Discovered*, at 344 (2008).

614.Babylonian Talmud, *Tractate Baba Mezi'a, Folio 33a*, Baba Mezi'a Translated into English, with Notes, Glossary and Indices Folios 1 - 24b by Salis Daiches, A.M., Ph.d., Folios 25a to the End by H. Freedman, B.A., Ph.d., Under the Editorship of Rabbi Dr I. Epstein B.A., Ph.D., D. Lit. (1961), *available at* http://www.come-and-hear.com/babamezia/babamezia_33.html.

615.Alexander Hislop, *The Two Babylons*, at 211-212 (1959).

616.Michael Hoffman, *Judaism Discovered*, at 344 (2008) (citing Mishnah Aboth, 1.1).

617.J.P. Stehelin, F.R.S., editor of *The Tradition of the Jews*, at 209 (1748), based upon Johann Andreas Eisenmenger's *Entdecktes Judenthum* (Judaism Revealed), at 47 of the section titled The Traditions of the Jews with the Expositions and Doctrines of the Rabbins (1700) (citing Talmud Tractate Gittin) (Stehelin's 1748 English translation was reprinted with Introduction and Annotated Bibliography by Michael A. Hoffman II (2006)).

618.J.P. Stehelin's edition of Johann Andreas Eisenmenger's *Judaism Revealed* at 209 (1748) (citing Talmud Tractate Berachoth).

619.Michael Hoffman, *Judaism Discovered*, at 344 (2008) (citing Babylonian Talmud, Tractate Rosh Hashanah, Folio 25a).

620.CODE OF CANON LAW, Canon 333 § 3, p.119 (1983).

621.DAVE HUNT, A WOMAN RIDES THE BEAST, Harvest House Publishers, p. 113 (1994).

622.RALPH E. WOODROW, BABYLON MYSTERY RELIGION, p. 94 (1966).

623.*Id.*

624.DAVE HUNT, A WOMAN RIDES THE BEAST, Harvest House Publishers, p. 188-90 (1994).

625.RALPH E. WOODROW, BABYLON MYSTERY RELIGION, p. 93 (1966).

626.*Id.* at 92-93.

627.COLLIER'S ENCYCLOPEDIA, volume 13, p. 591 (1991). *See also* DAVE HUNT, A WOMAN RIDES THE BEAST, Harvest House Publishers, p. 117 (1994).

628.DAVE HUNT, A WOMAN RIDES THE BEAST, Harvest House Publishers, p. 117 (1994).

629.*Our Sunday Visitor,* April 18, 1915. The publication is still being published today: 200 Noll Plaza, Huntington, Indiana, 46750, (800) 348-2440.

630.D.P. SIMPSON, CASSELL'S LATIN DICTIONARY, p. 621, 1968.

631.COLLIER'S ENCYCLOPEDIA, volume 1, p. 592-96 (1991).

632.TEXE MARRS, PROJECT L.U.C.I.D., Living Truth Publishers (1996) (citing Antony Sutton, "Why Clinton Wants Universal Health Care," Phoenix Letter, Vol. 13, No. 10, October 1994).

633.*Id.* at p. 88.

634.Fortescue, A. (1910). Liturgy. In The Catholic Encyclopedia. New York: Robert Appleton Company. Retrieved February 19, 2010 from New Advent: http://www.newadvent.org/cathen/09306a.htm.

635.Fortescue, A. (1910). Liturgy. In The Catholic Encyclopedia. New York: Robert Appleton Company. Retrieved February 19, 2010 from New Advent: http://www.newadvent.org/cathen/09306a.htm.

636."Jews and Christians Share Much Together," L'Osservatore Romano, English ed., May 5, 1999, quoted by Michael Hoffman, *Judaism Discovered*, at 846 (2008).

637. ORDERED BY THE COUNCIL OF TRENT, EDITED UNDER ST. CHARLES BORROMEO, PUBLISHED BY DECREE OF POPE ST. PIUS V, 1566, TAN Books, 1982 at p. 233.

638. WILLIAM AND SHARON SCHNOEBELEN, LUCIFER DETHRONED, p. 56-58 (1993).

639. *Id.* at p.141.

640. WILLIAM AND SHARON SCHNOEBELEN, LUCIFER DETHRONED, p. 259-66 (1993).

641. *Id.* at p. 264.

642. PETER J. ELLIOTT, CEREMONIES OF THE MODERN ROMAN RITE, Ignatius Press, § 663, p. 245 (1994).

643. PETER J. ELLIOTT, CEREMONIES OF THE MODERN ROMAN RITE, Ignatius Press, p. 264 (1994).

644. Israel Shahak, Jewish History, Jewish Religion: The Weight of Two Thousand Years (1994), available at http://www.biblebelievers.org.au/jewhis3.htm#Orthodoxy%20and%20Interpretation.

645. E.g., Aharon Yosef, A Catholic Jew Pontificates, *Miriam ha Kedosha the Lady Moon of Israel*, January 10, 2008, *at* http://aronbengilad.blogspot.com/2008/01/miriam-hakedosha-lady-moon-of-israel.html. See also Carrie Tomko, *Who Is Aharon Yosef?*, A Catholic Perspective on the World (July 30, 2007).

646. Athol Bloomer, *The Eucharist and The Jewish Mystical Tradition • Part 3*, Association of Hebrew Catholics, *at* http://hebrewcatholic.org/HCLives/Bloomer-Athol/eucharistandjewi.html, (originally published in The Hebrew Catholic #80 (Spring/Summer 2004)).

647. Athol Bloomer, *The Eucharist and The Jewish Mystical Tradition • Part 1*, Association of Hebrew Catholics, *at* http://hebrewcatholic.org/PrayerandSpirituality/eucharistjewishm.html, (last visited on February 12, 2010) (originally published in The Hebrew Catholic #77, pp 15-18 (Summer-Fall 2002)).

648. Fortescue, A. (1910). Liturgy. In The Catholic Encyclopedia. New York: Robert Appleton Company. Retrieved February 19, 2010 from New Advent: http://www.newadvent.org/cathen/09306a.htm.

649. Fr. John Ramsay, Catholic Belief and Practice, Chapter 20 - Catholic Devotions and Practices, *at* http://www.catholicassociates.com/cbpdocs/CBP%20Ch20.pdf (emphasis in original) (last visited on April 25, 2010).

650. The Presence of God, Missionary Priests of the Blessed Sacrament, Winter/Spring 2001, at http://www.perpetualadoration.org/ws2001.htm.

651. Joseph Cardinal Ratzinger, The Reservation of the Blessed Sacrament, Institute for Sacred Architecture, Volume 12, Fall/Winter 2006, *available at* http://www.sacredarchitecture.org/articles/reservation_of_the_blessed_sacrament/.

652. Fr. Jean Danielou, S.J., The Sacraments and the History of Salvation, at http://www.catholicculture.org/culture/library/view.cfm?recnum=681 (last visited on April 25, 2010).

653. Michael Hoffman, *Judaism Discovered*, at 266-67 (2008).

654. Michael Hoffman, *Judaism Discovered*, at 268 (2008).

655. Terry Watkins, TNIV & THE LORD JESUS, Dial-The-Truth-Ministries, at http://www.av1611.org/kjv/tniv_jesus.html (last visited on April 6, 2010).

656. To Embrace Hebrew Roots: Part IV, The Talmud & Demonology, The Talmudic Myth of Lillith, Seek God, *at* http://www.seekgod.ca/embracnotal.htm (last visited at April 6, 2010).

657. Lawrence Fine, Chapter on Kabbalistic Texts, From: *Back to the Sources: Reading the Classic Jewish Texts* ("The First Complete Modern Guide to the Great Books of the Jewish Tradition: What They Are and How to Read Them"), at p. 337 (2006).

658. Lawrence Fine, Chapter on Kabbalistic Texts, From: *Back to the Sources: Reading the Classic Jewish Texts* ("The First Complete Modern Guide to the Great Books of the Jewish Tradition: What They Are and How to Read Them"), at p. 337 (2006).

659. Lawrence Fine, Chapter on Kabbalistic Texts, From: *Back to the Sources: Reading the Classic Jewish Texts* ("The First Complete Modern Guide to the Great Books of the Jewish Tradition: What They Are and How to Read Them"), at p. 337 (2006).

660. Athol Bloomer, *The Eucharist and The Jewish Mystical Tradition • Part 1*, Association of Hebrew Catholics, *at* http://hebrewcatholic.org/PrayerandSpirituality/eucharistjewishm.html (originally published in The Hebrew Catholic #77, pp 15-18 (Summer-Fall 2002)).

661. Athol Bloomer, *The Eucharist and The Jewish Mystical Tradition • Part 1*, Association of Hebrew Catholics, *at* http://hebrewcatholic.org/PrayerandSpirituality/eucharistjewishm.html (originally published in The Hebrew Catholic #77, pp 15-18 (Summer-Fall 2002)).

662. Athol Bloomer, *The Eucharist and The Jewish Mystical Tradition • Part 1*, Association of Hebrew Catholics, *at* http://hebrewcatholic.org/PrayerandSpirituality/eucharistjewishm.html (originally published in The Hebrew Catholic #77, pp 15-18 (Summer-Fall 2002)).

663. Rabbi Geoffrey W. Dennis, *The Encyclopedia of Jewish Myth, Magic, and Mysticism*, at 199 (2007), quoted by Michael Hoffman in *Judaism Discovered*, at 239-40 (2008).

664.Dennis, at 199.

665.Michael Hoffman, *Judaism Discovered*, at 239 (2008).

666.Michael Hoffman, *Judaism Discovered*, at 240 (2008).

667.Michael Hoffman, *Judaism Discovered*, at 240 (2008).

668.Moshe Idel, *Hasidism Between Ecstacy and Magic*, at 103.

669.Ithmar Gruenwald, *Israel Oriental Studies* 1 (1971); pp. 132-177 and *Temerin*, vol. 7 (Jerusalem, 1972) pp. 101-139. Gershom Scholem, *Jewish Gnosticism, Merkabah Mysticism and Talmudic Tradition* (Jewish Theological Seminary of America, 1965) cited by Michael Hoffman in *Judaism Discovered*, at 241 (2008).

670.Michael Hoffman, *Judaism Discovered*, at 241 (2008).

671.Tiferet, Jewish Virtual Library, *at* http://www.jewishvirtuallibrary.org/jsource/Judaism/Tiferet.html (last visited on March 2, 2010).

672.Tree of Life created by Friedhelm Wessel (25 October 2008), at http://commons.wikimedia.org/wiki/File:Tree_of_Life_%28Sephiroth%29.svg.

673. Laura Ellen Shulman, Judaism, Jewish *Mysticism Kabbalah and the Sefirot* (March 13, 2007), *at* http://www.nvcc.edu/home/lshulman/Rel232/resource/sefirot.htm.

674.Athol Bloomer, *The Eucharist and The Jewish Mystical Tradition • Part 1*, Association of Hebrew Catholics, *at* http://hebrewcatholic.org/PrayerandSpirituality/eucharistjewishm.html (originally published in The Hebrew Catholic #77, pp 15-18 (Summer-Fall 2002)).

675.Athol Bloomer, *The Eucharist and The Jewish Mystical Tradition • Part 1*, Association of Hebrew Catholics, *at* http://hebrewcatholic.org/PrayerandSpirituality/eucharistjewishm.html (originally published in The Hebrew Catholic #77, pp 15-18 (Summer-Fall 2002)).

676.Yesod, Jewish Virtual Library, *at* http://www.jewishvirtuallibrary.org/jsource/Judaism/Yesod.html (last visited on March 2, 2010).

677.Dan Cohn-Sherbok and Lavinia Cohn-Sherbok, Jewish and Christian Mysticism: An Introduction, at 167 (1994).

678.Athol Bloomer, *The Eucharist and The Jewish Mystical Tradition • Part 3*, Association of Hebrew Catholics, *at* http://hebrewcatholic.org/HCLives/Bloomer-Athol/eucharistandjewi.html, (originally published in The Hebrew Catholic #80 (Spring/Summer 2004)).

679.Acharya S, *Osiris The Lord: Out of Egypt, at* http://www.truthbeknown.com/osiris.htm (last visited on March 4, 2010) (excerpt from Acharya S, *Suns of God: Krishna, Buddha and Christ*

Unveiled).

680. Athol Bloomer, *The Eucharist and The Jewish Mystical Tradition • Part 3*, Association of Hebrew Catholics, *at* http://hebrewcatholic.org/HCLives/Bloomer-Athol/eucharistandjewi.html, (originally published in The Hebrew Catholic #80 (Spring/Summer 2004)).

681. Athol Bloomer, *The Eucharist and The Jewish Mystical Tradition • Part 2*, Association of Hebrew Catholics, *at* http://hebrewcatholic.org/PrayerandSpirituality/eucharistjewisht.html (originally published in The Hebrew Catholic #78 (Winter-Spring 2003)).

682. Athol Bloomer, *The Eucharist and The Jewish Mystical Tradition • Part 3*, Association of Hebrew Catholics, *at* http://hebrewcatholic.org/HCLives/Bloomer-Athol/eucharistandjewi.html, (originally published in The Hebrew Catholic #80 (Spring/Summer 2004)). See also Tiferet, Jewish Virtual Library, at http://www.jewishvirtuallibrary.org/jsource/Judaism/Tiferet.html (last visited on March 3, 2010).

683. Athol Bloomer, *The Eucharist and The Jewish Mystical Tradition • Part 3*, Association of Hebrew Catholics, *at* http://hebrewcatholic.org/HCLives/Bloomer-Athol/eucharistandjewi.html, (originally published in The Hebrew Catholic #80 (Spring/Summer 2004)).

684. Alexander Hislop, *The Two Babylons*, at 160 (1959).

685. Acharya S, *Osiris The Lord: Out of Egypt*, *at* http://www.truthbeknown.com/osiris.htm (last visited on March 4, 2010) (excerpt from Acharya S, *Suns of God: Krishna, Buddha and Christ Unveiled*).

686. George A. Barton, *Tammuz and Osiris*, Journal of the American Oriental Society, Vol. 35, (1915), pp. 213-223, available at http://www.jstor.org/stable/592647.

687. Acharya S, *Osiris The Lord: Out of Egypt*, *at* http://www.truthbeknown.com/osiris.htm (last visited on March 4, 2010) (excerpt from Acharya S, *Suns of God: Krishna, Buddha and Christ Unveiled*).

688. Acharya S, *Osiris The Lord: Out of Egypt*, *at* http://www.truthbeknown.com/osiris.htm (last visited on March 4, 2010) (excerpt from Acharya S, *Suns of God: Krishna, Buddha and Christ Unveiled*).

689. Images of the Nile and Egypt, *at* http://www.thenileandegypt.com/deities.html (last visited on March 3, 2010).

690. Images of the Nile and Egypt, *at* http://www.thenileandegypt.com/deities.html (last visited on March 3, 2010).

691. Athol Bloomer, *The Eucharist and The Jewish Mystical Tradition • Part 2*, Association of Hebrew Catholics, *at* http://hebrewcatholic.org/PrayerandSpirituality/eucharistjewisht.html

(originally published in The Hebrew Catholic #78 (Winter-Spring 2003)).

692.Aharon Yosef, A Catholic Jew Pontificates, *Miriam ha Kedosha the Lady Moon of Israel*, January 10, 2008, *at* http://aronbengilad.blogspot.com/2008/01/miriam-hakedosha-lady-moon-of-israel.html.

693.Michael Hoffman, *Judaism Discovered*, at 269 (2008).

694.Athol Bloomer, *The Eucharist and The Jewish Mystical Tradition • Part 2*, Association of Hebrew Catholics, *at* http://hebrewcatholic.org/PrayerandSpirituality/eucharistjewisht.html (originally published in The Hebrew Catholic #78 (Winter-Spring 2003)).

695.Sketch of Chalice and Eucharistic host from SymbolDictionary.net, Religious Symbols, A Visual Glossary, *at* http://symboldictionary.net/?p=2090 (last visited on March 3, 2010).

696.Alexander Hislop, *The Two Babylons*, at 164 (1959).

697.Alexander Hislop, *The Two Babylons*, at 160 (1959).

698.Alexander Hislop, *The Two Babylons*, at 163 (1959).

699.From http://mayyoufindstrength.wordpress.com/2009/07/03/eucharistic-adoration/ (last visited on March 6, 2010).

700.Athol Bloomer, *The Eucharist and The Jewish Mystical Tradition • Part 3*, Association of Hebrew Catholics, *at* http://hebrewcatholic.org/HCLives/Bloomer-Athol/eucharistandjewi.html, (originally published in The Hebrew Catholic #80 (Spring/Summer 2004)). See also Tiferet, Jewish Virtual Library, at http://www.jewishvirtuallibrary.org/jsource/Judaism/Tiferet.html (last visited on March 3, 2010).

701.Alexander Hislop, *The Two Babylons*, at 232 (1959).

702.Alexander Hislop, *The Two Babylons*, at 232 (1959).

703.Alexander Hislop, *The Two Babylons*, at 232 (1959).

704.Michael Hoffman, *Judaism Discovered*, at 791 (2008) (citing The Zohar III, 282a).

705.Alexander Hislop, *The Two Babylons*, at 156-57 (1959).

706.Alexander Hislop, *The Two Babylons*, at 156-57 (1959).

707.Alexander Hislop, *The Two Babylons*, at 156-57 (1959).

708.J.NEUNER, S.J & J. DUPUIS, S.J., THE CHRISTIAN FAITH IN THE DOCTRINAL DOCUMENTS OF THE CATHOLIC CHURCH, PIUS X, ENCYCLICAL LETTER *AD DIEM*

§ 712 (6th ed. 1996).

709.E.g., CATECHISM OF THE CATHOLIC CHURCH, Second Edition, § 1141, *at* http://www.scborromeo.org/ccc/p2s1c2a1.htm (last visited on March 6, 2010).

710.THE CATECHISM OF THE CATHOLIC CHURCH, § 1367, 1994.

711.THE CATECHISM OF THE CATHOLIC CHURCH, § 1364, 1994.

712.THE CATECHISM OF THE COUNCIL OF TRENT, *Ordered By the Council of Trent, Edited Under St. Charles Borromeo, Published by Decree of Pope St. Pius V* (emphasis added), p. 258 (1982).

713.THE CATECHISM OF THE COUNCIL OF TRENT, *Ordered By the Council of Trent, Edited Under St. Charles Borromeo, Published by Decree of Pope St. Pius V* (emphasis added), p. 258 (1982).

714.Ariel Toaff, *Blood Passover, The Jews of Europe and Ritual Murder*, translated into English by Gian Marco Lucchese and Pietro Gianetti, 24 August 2007, English version available in HTML at http://www.bloodpassover.com/, English version available in PDF at http://www.israelshamir.net/BLOODPASSOVER.pdf, original Italian version available in PDF at http://www.laboratorio99.com/upload/Pasque%20di%20Sangue.pdf.

715.Bar Ilan University, Ramat-Gan, 52900 Israel, *at* http://www1.biu.ac.il/indexE.php (last visited on April 7, 2010).

716.Ariel Toaff, *Blood Passover, The Jews of Europe and Ritual Murder*, at http://www.bloodpassover.com/ (last visited on April 7, 2010).

717.Adi Schwartz, *The Wayward Son*, Haaretz, February 22, 2007, cited by Michael Hoffman in *Judaism Discovered*, at 581 (2008).

718.Ariel Toaff, *Blood Passover*, at 10-11.

719.Ofri Hani, Haaretz, February 12, 2007, cited by Michael Hoffman in *Judaism Discovered*, at 561 (2008).

720.Ariel Toaff, *Blood Passover, The Jews of Europe and Ritual Murder*, translated into English by Gian Marco Lucchese and Pietro Gianetti, 24 August 2007, English version available in HTML at http://www.bloodpassover.com/, English version available in PDF at http://www.israelshamir.net/BLOODPASSOVER.pdf, original Italian version available in PDF at http://www.laboratorio99.com/upload/Pasque%20di%20Sangue.pdf.

721.Ariel Toaff, *Blood Passover*, at 167.

722.Ariel Toaff, *Blood Passover*, at 167.

723. Ariel Toaff, *Blood Passover*, at 170.

724. Ariel Toaff, *Blood Passover*, at 146-47.

725. Ariel Toaff, *Blood Passover*, at 178 (Citing Israel Wolfgang's long and detailed report, which is reproduced in Divina, *Storia del beato Simone da Trento,* cit., voI. II, pp. 16-19).

726. Ariel Toaff, *Blood Passover*, at 178 (Citing Israel Wolfgang's long and detailed report, which is reproduced in Divina, *Storia del beato Simone da Trento,* cit., voI. II, pp. 16-19).

727. Ariel Toaff, *Blood Passover*, at 176.

728. Zionism and Israel - Encyclopedic Dictionary Blood Libel, at http://www.zionism-israel.com/dic/blood_libel.htm (last visited on April 7, 2010).

729. Medieval Sourcebook: John Chrysostom (circa 347-407): Eight Homilics Against the Jews, *available at* http://www.fordham.edu/halsall/source/chrysostom-jews6.html (last visited on April 11, 2010).

730. Medieval Sourcebook: John Chrysostom (circa 347-407): Eight Homilies Against the Jews, *available at* http://www.fordham.edu/halsall/source/chrysostom-jews6.html (last visited on April 11, 2010).

731. Ariel Toaff, *Blood Passover*, at 180-81 ("*Sanguis pueri Cristiani est summe necessarius ipsis Iudeis, videlicet patribusfamilias ipsorum Iudeorum.Et si esset aliquis pauper Iudeus, qui non possit haberi de sanguine, excusaretur.*" (cfr. Esposito and Quaglioni, Processi, cit., voI. I, p.356)).

732. Ariel Toaff, *Blood Passover*, at 178.

733. Ariel Toaff, *Blood Passover*, at 182-83.

734. Ariel Toaff, *Blood Passover*, at 182-83.

735. Ariel Toaff, *Blood Passover*, at 186.

736. Ariel Toaff, *Blood Passover*, at 187.

737. Ariel Toaff, *Blood Passover, The Jews of Europe and Ritual Murder*, translated into English by Gian Marco Lucchese and Pietro Gianetti, 24 August 2007, at 70, available at http://www.israelshamir.net/BLOODPASSOVER.pdf.

738. Ariel Toaff, *Blood Passover, The Jews of Europe and Ritual Murder*, translated into English by Gian Marco Lucchese and Pietro Gianetti, 24 August 2007, at 70, available at http://www.israelshamir.net/BLOODPASSOVER.pdf.

739.Israel Shamir, "The Bloody Passovers of Dr. Toaff," February, 2007, www.israelshamir.net, quoted by Michael Hoffman in *Judaism Discovered*, at 575 (2008).

740.Israel Shamir, "The Bloody Passovers of Dr. Toaff," February, 2007, www.israelshamir.net, quoted by Michael Hoffman in *Judaism Discovered*, at 575 (2008).

741.Israel Shamir, "The Bloody Passovers of Dr. Toaff," February, 2007, www.israelshamir.net, quoted by Michael Hoffman in *Judaism Discovered*, at 575 (2008).

742.Ariel Toaff, *Blood Passover*, at 128 (Citing Ch. Verlinden, *L'esclavage dans l'Europe medievale*, Brugge, 1955, vol. I, pp. 702-716; B. Blumenkranz, *Juifs et Chretiens dans le monde occidental (430-1096),* Paris 1960, pp. 18-19, 184-211).

743.Ariel Toaff, *Blood Passover*, at 129 (citing Blumenkrantz, Juifs et Chrétiens dans le monde occidental, cit., pp. 194-195, no. 142; Id., Les auteurs chrétiens , cit., p. 163, no. 53).

744.Toaff provides the following authority in an endnote: "On the rabbinical responses relating to the trade in castrated young slaves and on the role of Lucena (outside Córdoba) as a center for the castrations, see A. Assaf, Slavery and the Slave-Trade among the Jews during the Middle Ages (from the Jewish Sources), in "Zion", IV (1939), pp. 91-125 (in Hebrew); E. Ashtor, A History of the Jews in Moslem Spain, Jerusalem, 1977, vol. I, pp. 186-189 (in Hebrew)."

745. Ariel Toaff, *Blood Passover*, at 130 (citing Assaf, Slavery and the Slave-Trade, cit., pp. 100-101).

746.Ariel Toaff, *Blood Passover*, at 128-130.

747.JOHN W. ROBBINS, ECCLESIASTICAL MEGALOMANIA, p. 137 (1999).

748.*Id*. at p. 139.

749.*Id.*

750.*Id*. at p. 140-41.

751.Israel Shahak, Jewish History, Jewish Religion: The Weight of Two Thousand Years (1994), available at http://www.biblebelievers.org.au/jewhis3.htm#Orthodoxy%20and%20Interpretation.

752.Israel Shahak, Jewish History, Jewish Religion: The Weight of Two Thousand Years (1994), available at http://www.biblebelievers.org.au/jewhis3.htm#Orthodoxy%20and%20Interpretation.

753.Shahak, Jewish History (citing a 1712 book on Jewish moral custom, written by Shn'et Musar).

754.Athol Bloomer, *The Eucharist and The Jewish Mystical Tradition • Part 3*, Association of Hebrew Catholics, *at* http://hebrewcatholic.org/HCLives/Bloomer-Athol/eucharistandjewi.html, (originally published in The Hebrew Catholic #80 (Spring/Summer 2004)).

755. Kabbalah, Jewish Virtual Library, http://www.jewishvirtuallibrary.org/jsource/judaica/ejud_0002_0011_0_10514.html (last visited on March 3, 2010).

756. Athol Bloomer, *The Eucharist and The Jewish Mystical Tradition • Part 3*, Association of Hebrew Catholics, *at* http://hebrewcatholic.org/HCLives/Bloomer-Athol/eucharistandjewi.html, (originally published in The Hebrew Catholic #80 (Spring/Summer 2004)).

757. Daniel Chanan Matt, *Zohar, The Book of Enlightenment*, at 132 (1983), *at* http://books.google.com/.

758. J.P. Stehelin, F.R.S., editor of *The Tradition of the Jews*, at 301 (1748), based upon Johann Andreas Eisenmenger's *Entdecktes Judenthum* (Judaism Revealed), at 137 of the section titled The Traditions of the Jews with the Expositions and Doctrines of the Rabbins (1700) (Stehelin's 1748 English translation was reprinted with Introduction and Annotated Bibliography by Michael A. Hoffman II (2006)).

759. THE RANDOM HOUSE DICTIONARY OF THE ENGLISH LANGUAGE, unabridged edition, 1973.

760. Salvation is Obtained From . . . Mary?, http://www.aloha.net/~mikesch/mary.htm (web address current as of April 3, 2005), quoting Arthur Burton Calkins, TOTUS TUUS, pp.21, 27, Academy of the Immaculate, New Bedford, Massachusetts, ISBN 0-9635345-0-5, Nihil Obstat and Imprimatur of the Catholic Church.

761. Salvation is Obtained From . . . Mary?, http://www.aloha.net/~mikesch/mary.htm (web address current as of April 3, 2005), quoting Arthur Burton Calkins, TOTUS TUUS, pp.21, 27, Academy of the Immaculate, New Bedford, Massachusetts, ISBN 0-9635345-0-5, Nihil Obstat and Imprimatur of the Catholic Church.

762. The Rosary, Roses of Prayer for The Queen of Heaven, Daniel A. Lord, S.J., Nihil Obstat Athur J. Scanlan S.T.D: Censor Liborum, Imprimatur + Francis J. Spellman, D.D. Archbishop, New York, http://www.truecatholic.org/rosary.htm (web address current as of March 20, 2005).

763. COLLIER'S ENCYCLOPEDIA, volume 20, p. 169 (1991).

764. *E.g., CATECHISM OF THE CATHOLIC CHURCH*, §§ 105, 1141,1163, 1203, 1249, 1667 (1997), http://www.scborromeo.org/index2.htm (web address current as of March 22, 2005).

765. The Rosary, Roses of Prayer for The Queen of Heaven, Daniel A. Lord, S.J., Nihil Obstat Athur J. Scanlan S.T.D: Censor Liborum, Imprimatur + Francis J. Spellman, D.D. Archbishop, New York, http://www.truecatholic.org/rosary.htm (web address current as of March 20, 2005).

766.Rosary Meditations, http://www.cfalive.org/ReadRosary.htm (web address current as of March 20, 2005).

767.Prayer to Mary, Queen of Heaven, http://www.catholic-forum.com/saints/pray0421.htm (web address current as of March 20, 2005).

768.J.NEUNER, S.J & J. DUPUIS, S.J., THE CHRISTIAN FAITH IN THE DOCTRINAL DOCUMENTS OF THE CATHOLIC CHURCH, PIUS X, ENCYCLICAL LETTER *AD DIEM* § 712 (6th ed. 1996).

769.J.NEUNER, S.J & J. DUPUIS, S.J., THE CHRISTIAN FAITH IN THE DOCTRINAL DOCUMENTS OF THE CATHOLIC CHURCH, THE SECOND VATICAL COUNCIL, DOGMATIC CONSTITUTION *LUMEN GENTIUM,* § 716a (6th ed. 1996).

770.CATECHISM OF THE CATHOLIC CHURCH, § 2679, 1994.

771.J.NEUNER, S.J & J. DUPUIS, S.J., THE CHRISTIAN FAITH IN THE DOCTRINAL DOCUMENTS OF THE CATHOLIC CHURCH, THE SECOND VATICAL COUNCIL, DOGMATIC CONSTITUTION *LUMEN GENTIUM,* § 718a (6th ed. 1996).

772.*Id.* at § 718b.

773.CATECHISM OF THE CATHOLIC CHURCH, § 2677, 1994.

774.J.NEUNER, S.J & J. DUPUIS, S.J., THE CHRISTIAN FAITH IN THE DOCTRINAL DOCUMENTS OF THE CATHOLIC CHURCH, THE SECOND VATICAL COUNCIL, DOGMATIC CONSTITUTION *LUMEN GENTIUM,* § 716a (6th ed. 1996).

775.J.NEUNER, S.J & J. DUPUIS, S.J., THE CHRISTIAN FAITH IN THE DOCTRINAL DOCUMENTS OF THE CATHOLIC CHURCH, § 713, PIUS XII, APOSTOLIC CONSTITUTION, *MUNIFICENTISSIMUS DEUS* (6th ed. 1996).

776.J.NEUNER, S.J & J. DUPUIS, S.J., THE CHRISTIAN FAITH IN THE DOCTRINAL DOCUMENTS OF THE CATHOLIC CHURCH, § 716a (6th ed. 1996).

777.CATECHISM OF THE CATHOLIC CHURCH, § 2131, 1994.

778.Michael Hoffman, *Judaism Discovered*, at 780 (2008) (quoting Helen Jacaobus, *Eye Jinx*, Jewish Chronicle, May 7, 1999).

779.Michael Hoffman, *Judaism Discovered*, at 780 (2008) (quoting Helen Jacaobus, *Eye Jinx*, Jewish Chronicle, May 7, 1999).

780.Michael Hoffman, *Judaism Discovered*, at 780 (2008) (quoting Helen Jacaobus, *Eye Jinx*, Jewish Chronicle, May 7, 1999).

781.Michael Hoffman, *Judaism Discovered*, at 784 (2008) (quoting Gershom Scholem, *Kabbalah*, p. 184).

782.Michael Hoffman, *Judaism Discovered*, at 780 (2008).

783.Hexagram (Shatkona, Seal of Solomon), Religious Symbols: A Visual Glossary, *at* http://symboldictionary.net/?p=1533 (last visited on March 8, 2010).

784.Michael Hoffman, *Judaism Discovered*, at 784 (2008).

785.Michael Hoffman, *Judaism Discovered*, at 540 (2008).

786.Western Wall Rabbi Says Pope Should Not Wear Cross at Site, Jerusalem Post, March 17, 2009, available at http://www.jpost.com/Israel/Article.aspx?id=136169.

787.The Inverted Cross, http://www.jesus-is-lord.com/anti5.htm (last visited on May 31. 2008).

788.CATECHISM OF THE CATHOLIC CHURCH, § 881-882 (1994).

789.Michael Hoffman, *Judaism Discovered*, at 539-40 (2008) (quoting Amiram Barkat, *Haaretz*, October 11, 2004).

790.Michael Hoffman, *Judaism Discovered*, at 538-39 (2008) (quoting *Forward*, October 22, 2004).

791.Michael Hoffman, *Judaism Discovered*, at 539-40 (2008) (quoting Amiram Barkat, *Haaretz*, October 11, 2004).

792.*Israeli Youths Burn New Testaments*, USA Today, May 21, 2008, *at* http://www.usatoday.com/news/religion/2008-05-21-jewish-new-testament_N.htm.

793.*Israeli Youths Burn New Testaments*, USA Today, May 21, 2008, *at* http://www.usatoday.com/news/religion/2008-05-21-jewish-new-testament_N.htm.

794.Michael Hoffman, *Judaism Discovered*, at 534 (2008) (quoting Israel Shahak, *Jewish History, Jewish Religion*, p. 93).

795.Michael Hoffman, *Judaism Discovered*, at 534 (2008).

796.CATECHISM OF THE CATHOLIC CHURCH § 2051, p. 551 (1994).

797.*Id.* at § 2051, p.552.

798.The New American, Dark Dealings in the Vatican?, at p. 24, March 3, 1997.

799.Satanism in the Vatican,
http://www.jesus-is-savior.com/False%20Religions/Roman%20Catholicism/SS/anti3.htm (last visited on December 12, 2010).

800.The New American, The Catholic Church in Crisis, p. 39, June 9, 1997.

801.The New American, Dark Dealings in the Vatican?, at p. 24, March 3, 1997.

802.*Id.*

803.JAMES R. WHITE, THE ROMAN CATHOLIC CONTROVERSY, p. 187, 1996 (quoting *Indulgentiarum Doctrina,* January 1, 1967).

804.CATECHISM OF THE CATHOLIC CHURCH, §§ 1030-1031 (1994).

805.COUNCIL OF TRENT, SESSION VI, DECREE ON JUSTIFICATION, Canon XXX, January 13, 1547 (emphasis added).

806. J.P. Stehelin, F.R.S., editor of *The Tradition of the Jews*, at 148 (1748), based upon Johann Andreas Eisenmenger's *Entdecktes Judenthum* (Judaism Revealed), at 50 to the Preliminary Preface (1700) (Stehelin's 1748 English translation was reprinted with Introduction and Annotated Bibliography by Michael A. Hoffman II (2006) (repaginated to page 148).

807.Id. at 149.

808.Michael A. Hoffman II, Introduction to the 2006 reprint of *The Tradition of the Jews*, (1748), based upon Johann Andreas Eisenmenger's *Entdecktes Judenthum* (Judaism Revealed) (1700), at page 8.

809.Id. at page 7.

810.Alexander Hislop, *The Two Babylons*, at 170 (1959).

811.Alexander Hislop, *The Two Babylons*, at 167 (1959).

812.Alexander Hislop, *The Two Babylons*, at 168 (1959).

813.CATECHISM OF THE CATHOLIC CHURCH, § 1032 (1994).

814.*Id.* at p. 57-65.

815.PETER J. ELLIOTT, CEREMONIES OF THE MODERN ROMAN RITE, Ignatius Press, § 369, p. 135 (1994).

816.RALPH E. WOODROW, BABYLON MYSTERY RELIGION, p. 61 (1966).

817. The Left Behind Series, *at* http://www.rapidnet.com/~jbeard/bdm/BookReviews/left.htm (last visited on March 14, 2010).

818. WILLIAM R. KIMBALL, THE RAPTURE, A Question of Timing, p. 31 (1985) (quoting LEROY E. FROOM, THE PROPHETIC FAITH OF OUR FATHERS, vol. 2, pp. 243-44).

819. JOHN L. BRAY, THE MAN OF SIN OF II THESSALONIANS 2, p. 8 (1997) (Incidentally, Bray does not believe that the pope of Rome is the man of sin mentioned in II Thessalonians 2. He quotes from some of the traditional Protestant confessions of faith only to explain the historical Protestant view. While his survey of the historical confessions of faith is accurate, he is wrong regarding his conclusion about the pope.).

820. JOHN L. BRAY, MILLENNIUM - THE BIG QUESTION, P. 59 (1984) (quoting ERNEST R. SANDEEN, THE ROOTS OF FUNDAMENTALISM, p. 37 (1970)).

821. JOHN L. BRAY, MILLENNIUM - THE BIG QUESTION, P. 59 (1984) (quoting ERNEST R. SANDEEN, THE ROOTS OF FUNDAMENTALISM, p. 37 (1970)); WILLIAM R. KIMBALL, THE RAPTURE, A Question of Timing, p. 31 (1985) (OSWALD T. ALLIS, PROPHECY AND THE CHURCH, p. 297).

822. WILLIAM R. KIMBALL, THE RAPTURE, A Question of Timing, p. 31 (1985).

823. *Id.*

824. WILLIAM R. KIMBALL, THE RAPTURE, A Question of Timing, p. 31 (1985) (quoting LEROY E. FROOM, THE PROPHETIC FAITH OF OUR FATHERS, vol. 2, p. 495).

825. WILLIAM R. KIMBALL, THE RAPTURE, A Question of Timing, p. 32 (1985).

826. *Id.*

827. *Id.*

828. Anti-Zion, Jews on the Jewish Question, http://www.diac.com/~bkennedy/az/A-E.html (current as of September 10, 2001).

829. Ivan Fraser, Protocols of the Learned Elders of Zion, Proofs of an Ancient Conspiracy, http://www.vegan.swinternet.co.uk/articles/conspiracies/protocols_proof.html (current as of September 10, 2001).

830. Robert Maryks, *Jesuits of Jewish Ancestry. A Biographical Dictionary* (2008), at http://sites.google.com/a/jewishjesuits.com/www/.

831. JOHN L. BRAY, MILLENNIUM - THE BIG QUESTION, P. 34 (1984).

832.The Temple Mount and Fort Antonia, http://askelm.com/temple/t980504.htm (web address current as of October 30, 2003).

833.The Secret Key to the Dome of the Rock, http://askelm.com/temple/t991001.htm (web address current as of October 30, 2003).

834.ALBERTO RIVERA, THE GODFATHERS, Chick Publications, p. 32, 1982 (quoting The Registers of Boniface VIII, The Vatican Archives, L. Fol. 387 and THE CATHOLIC ENCYCLOPEDIA, Encyclopedia Press (1913)).

835.ALBERTO RIVERA, DOUBLE CROSS, Chick publications, p. 27, 1981(quoting THE GREAT ENCYCLICAL LETTERS OF POPE LEO XIII, p. 304, Benziger Brothers (1903).

836.WILLIAM R. KIMBALL, THE RAPTURE, A Question of Timing, p. 35 (1985); JOHN L. BRAY, MILLENNIUM - THE BIG QUESTION, P. 34 (1984).

837.JOHN L. BRAY, THE ORIGIN OF THE PRETRIBULATION RAPTURE TEACHING, p. 17, 24 (1982); JOHN L. BRAY, MILLENNIUM - THE BIG QUESTION, P. 34 (1984).

838.TIM WARNER, HISTORY OF THE PRE-TRIB DEVELOPMENT (2000), http://www.geocities.com/lasttrumpet_2000/timeline/ (current as of April 5, 2002).

839.WILLIAM R. KIMBALL, THE RAPTURE, A Question of Timing, p. 38 (1985).

840.*Id.* at 38.

841.*Id.* at 38.

842.*Id.* at 38.

843.JOHN L. BRAY, ROBERT BAXTER AND THE MID-TRIBULATION RAPTURE TEACHING (1994) (citing ROBERT BAXTER, NARRATIVE FACTS CONCERNING THE UNKNOWN TONGUES AND SPIRITUAL MANIFESTATIONS IN MEMBERS OF THE REV. EDWARD IRVING'S CONGREGATION, AND OTHER INDIVIDUALS, AND FORMERLY IN THE WRITER HIMSELF (1833)).

844.JOHN L. BRAY, ROBERT BAXTER AND THE MID-TRIBULATION RAPTURE TEACHING, p. 3 (1994)

845.*Id.* at p. 1, 3, 4.

846.*Id.* at 36.

847.PAUL ENNS, THE MOODY HANDBOOK OF THEOLOGY, p. 389-94 (1989).

848.Clifton A. Emahiser, *Old Jerusalem Shall Never Rise Again*, at 3, at http://www.israelect.com/reference/CliftonAEmahiser/studies/Old%20Jerusalem%20Shall%20Never%20Rise%20Again.pdf (last visited on March 15, 2010) (quoting John Bray, *Israel in Bible Prophecy*, at 30).

849.THE COMPACT EDITION OF THE OXFORD ENGLISH DICTIONARY, COMPLETE TEXT REDUCED MICROGRAPHICALLY, OXFORD UNIVERSITY PRESS (1979). *See also,* NOAH WEBSTER, AMERICAN DICTIONARY OF THE ENGLISH LANGUAGE (1828).

850.THE COMPACT EDITION OF THE OXFORD ENGLISH DICTIONARY, COMPLETE TEXT REDUCED MICROGRAPHICALLY, OXFORD UNIVERSITY PRESS (1979).

851.NOAH WEBSTER, AMERICAN DICTIONARY OF THE ENGLISH LANGUAGE (1828).

852.NOAH WEBSTER, AMERICAN DICTIONARY OF THE ENGLISH LANGUAGE (1828). *See also,* D.P. SIMPSON, CASSELL'S LATIN DICTIONARY p. 500-01 (1982).

853.D.P. SIMPSON, CASSELL'S LATIN DICTIONARY p. 501 (1982).

854.Dave MacPherson, *Deceiving and Being Deceived, at* http://www.moresureword.com/MacPherson.htm (last visited on March 9, 2010).

855.Dave MacPherson, *Frank Marotta's View of Morgan Edwards, Etc., available at* http://poweredbychrist.com/weighed.html.

856.Juan Josafat Ben-Ezra, *The Coming of Messiah in Glory and Majesty*, at iv-v, (1827), *available at* http://www.birthpangs.org/articles/prophetic/Lacunza_vol1.pdf.

857.Juan Josafat Ben-Ezra, *The Coming of Messiah in Glory and Majesty*, at iv-v, (1827), *available at* http://www.birthpangs.org/articles/prophetic/Lacunza_vol1.pdf.

858.Juan Josafat Ben-Ezra, *The Coming of Messiah in Glory and Majesty*, at 1, (1827), *available at* http://www.birthpangs.org/articles/prophetic/Lacunza_vol1.pdf.

859.Juan Josafat Ben-Ezra, *The Coming of Messiah in Glory and Majesty*, at 199, (1827), *available at* http://www.birthpangs.org/articles/prophetic/Lacunza_vol1.pdf.

860.Juan Josafat Ben-Ezra, *The Coming of Messiah in Glory and Majesty*, at 200, (1827), *available at* http://www.birthpangs.org/articles/prophetic/Lacunza_vol1.pdf.

861.Juan Josafat Ben-Ezra, *The Coming of Messiah in Glory and Majesty*, at 204, (1827), *available at* http://www.birthpangs.org/articles/prophetic/Lacunza_vol1.pdf.

862.Juan Josafat Ben-Ezra, *The Coming of Messiah in Glory and Majesty*, at 205, (1827), *available at* http://www.birthpangs.org/articles/prophetic/Lacunza_vol1.pdf.

863.Juan Josafat Ben-Ezra, *The Coming of Messiah in Glory and Majesty*, at 208, (1827), *available at* http://www.birthpangs.org/articles/prophetic/Lacunza_vol1.pdf.

864.Michael Hoffman, *Judaism Discovered*, at 662 (2008).

865.WILLIAM R. KIMBALL, THE RAPTURE, A Question of Timing, p. 43 (1985).

866.JOHN L. BRAY, THE ORIGIN OF THE PRETRIBULATION RAPTURE TEACHING, p. 24 (1982).

867.JOHN L. BRAY, THE ORIGIN OF THE PRETRIBULATION RAPTURE TEACHING, p. 26 (1982); *see also,* JOHN L. BRAY, ISRAEL IN BIBLE PROPHECY, p. 30 (1983) (citing *The Collected Writings of John Darby*).

868.WILLIAM R. KIMBALL, THE RAPTURE, A Question of Timing, p. 38 (1985).

869.*Id.* at p. 50.

870.JOHN L. BRAY, MILLENNIUM - THE BIG QUESTION, P. 58 (1984).

871.WILLIAM R. KIMBALL, THE RAPTURE, A Question of Timing, p. 51 (1985).

872.C.E. Carlson, The Zionist Created Scofield "bible," http://christianparty.net/scofield.htm (website address current as of August 9, 2003).

873.C.E. Carlson, The Zionist Created Scofield "bible," http://christianparty.net/scofield.htm (website address current as of August 9, 2003).

874.C.E. Carlson, The Zionist Created Scofield "bible," http://christianparty.net/scofield.htm (website address current as of August 9, 2003).

875.C.E. Carlson, The Zionist Created Scofield "bible," http://christianparty.net/scofield.htm (website address current as of August 9, 2003).

876.CYRUS SCOFIELD -- WHO WAS HE? Excerpt from "The Unified Conspiracy Theory," http://www.sweetliberty.org/issues/hoax/scofield.htm (website address current as of August 9, 2003).

877.CYRUS SCOFIELD -- WHO WAS HE? Excerpt from "The Unified Conspiracy Theory," http://www.sweetliberty.org/issues/hoax/scofield.htm (website address current as of August 9, 2003).

878.C.E. Carlson, The Zionist Created Scofield "bible," http://christianparty.net/scofield.htm (website address current as of August 9, 2003).

879.CYRUS SCOFIELD -- WHO WAS HE? Excerpt from "The Unified Conspiracy Theory," http://www.sweetliberty.org/issues/hoax/scofield.htm (website address current as of August 9, 2003).

880.CYRUS SCOFIELD -- WHO WAS HE? Excerpt from "The Unified Conspiracy Theory," http://www.sweetliberty.org/issues/hoax/scofield.htm (website address current as of August 9, 2003).

881.CYRUS SCOFIELD -- WHO WAS HE? Excerpt from "The Unified Conspiracy Theory," http://www.sweetliberty.org/issues/hoax/scofield.htm (website address current as of August 9, 2003). Scofield: The Christian Leader With Feet of Clay, http://www.virginiawater.co.uk/christchurch/articles/scofield1.html (website address current as of August 9, 2003).

882.CYRUS SCOFIELD -- WHO WAS HE? Excerpt from "The Unified Conspiracy Theory," http://www.sweetliberty.org/issues/hoax/scofield.htm (website address current as of August 9, 2003).

883.CYRUS SCOFIELD -- WHO WAS HE? Excerpt from "The Unified Conspiracy Theory," http://www.sweetliberty.org/issues/hoax/scofield.htm (website address current as of August 9, 2003).

884.Scofield: The Christian Leader With Feet of Clay, http://www.virginiawater.co.uk/christchurch/articles/scofield1.html (website address current as of August 9, 2003).

885.Scofield: The Christian Leader With Feet of Clay, http://www.virginiawater.co.uk/christchurch/articles/scofield1.html (website address current as of August 9, 2003).

886.G.A. RIPLINGER, NEW AGE BIBLE VERSIONS, p. 405 (1993).

887.Luisa Kroll, Megachurches, Megabusinesses, Forbes, September 17, 2003.

888.Luisa Kroll, Megachurches, Megabusinesses, Forbes, September 17, 2003.

889.Rick Meisel, Chuck Smith, General Teachings/Activities, *Biblical Discernment Ministries*, January 2002, http://www.rapidnet.com/~jbeard/bdm/exposes/smith/general.htm (web address current as of September 24, 2005), quoting Chuck Smith, Answers for Today, p. 157 (1993).

890.Luisa Kroll, Megachurches, Megabusinesses, Forbes, September 17, 2003.

891.Edward Hendrie, *The Anti-Gospel, Perverting Christ's Gospel of Grace*, at 63-68 (2010), available at http://www.antichristconspiracy.com/PDFDocs/Antigospel.pdf.

892. Temple Mount Fanatics Foment a New Thirty Years' War, *Executive Intelligence Review,* November 3, 2000, http://www.larouchepub.com/other/2000/temple_mount_2743.html (web address current as of November 11, 2005).

893. Temple Mount Fanatics Foment a New Thirty Years' War, *Executive Intelligence Review,* November 3, 2000, http://www.larouchepub.com/other/2000/temple_mount_2743.html (web address current as of November 11, 2005).

894. Temple Mount Fanatics Foment a New Thirty Years' War, *Executive Intelligence Review,* November 3, 2000, http://www.larouchepub.com/other/2000/temple_mount_2743.html (web address current as of November 11, 2005).

895. Temple Mount Fanatics Foment a New Thirty Years' War, *Executive Intelligence Review,* November 3, 2000, http://www.larouchepub.com/other/2000/temple_mount_2743.html (web address current as of November 11, 2005).

896. Arno Weinstein, In the Shadow of Stern: The Inside Story of a LEHI Intelligence Officer, B'tzedek, http://www.btzedek.com/focus/focus01.html (web address current as of November 11, 2005).

897. Arno Weinstein, In the Shadow of Stern: The Inside Story of a LEHI Intelligence Officer, B'tzedek, http://www.btzedek.com/focus/focus01.html (web address current as of November 11, 2005).

898. Evangelical Christians and the Building of the Temple, The Hebrew University of Jerusalem, http://sicsa.huji.ac.il/20Ariel.html (web address current as of November 11, 2005).

899. Evangelical Christians and the Building of the Temple, The Hebrew University of Jerusalem, http://sicsa.huji.ac.il/20Ariel.html (web address current as of November 11, 2005).

900. Evangelical Christians and the Building of the Temple, The Hebrew University of Jerusalem, http://sicsa.huji.ac.il/20Ariel.html (web address current as of November 11, 2005).

901. Christian Zionism, http://www.theocracywatch.org/christian_zionism.htm (last visited on January 2, 2011).

902. Christian Zionism, http://www.theocracywatch.org/christian_zionism.htm (last visited on January 2, 2011).

903. Sean McBride, *On a Learjet to Hell*, 16 May 2007, http://www.mail-archive.com/political-research@yahoogroups.com/msg07361.html.

904. Thomas L. McFadden, *PASTOR JOHN HAGEE: Is the Devil in Him?*, American Free Press May 7, 2010, http://www.americanfreepress.net/html/john_hagee_devil_221.html.

905.PAUL ENNS, THE MOODY HANDBOOK OF THEOLOGY, p. 113, 333-34, 391-92 (1989).

906.*Id.* at 389-94.

907.*Id.* at 392.

908.*Id.* at 392.

909.*Id.* at 390.

910.Edith Starr Miller, Occult Theocrasy, p. 86 (1933).

911.Edith Starr Miller, Occult Theocrasy, p. 87 (1933).

912.Edith Starr Miller, Occult Theocrasy, p. 86 (1933).

913.Edith Starr Miller, Occult Theocrasy, p. 87 (1933).

914.LES GARETT, WHICH BIBLE CAN WE TRUST?, p. 16 (1982); *See also,* COLLIER'S ENCYCLOPEDIA, volume 22, p. 563.

915.*Id.*

916.Michael Hoffman, *Judaism Discovered*, at 656 (2008).

917.Michael Hoffman, *Judaism Discovered*, at 663 (2008).

918.Michael Hoffman, *Judaism Discovered*, at 660 (2008).

919.Michael Hoffman, *Judaism Discovered*, at 660 (2008).

920.Michael Hoffman, *Judaism Discovered*, at 660 (2008).

921.Michael Hoffman, *Judaism Discovered*, at 664 (2008) (quoting Israel Shahak, Jewish History, Jewish Religion, pp. 22-23).

922.Michael Hoffman, *Judaism Discovered*, at 663 (2008).

923.Jewish Encyclopedia, *Balaam, available at* http://www.jewishencyclopedia.com/view.jsp?artid=161&letter=B (last visited on March 10, 2010).

924.Babylonian Talmud: *Tractate Sanhedrin, Folio 106b*, Sanhedrin Translated into English with Notes, Glossary and Indices Chapters I - VI by Jacob Shachter, Chapters VII - XI by H. Freedman, B.A., Ph.D., Under the Editorship of Rabbi Dr I. Epstein B.A., Ph.D., D. Lit.

(1961), *available at* http://www.come-and-hear.com/sanhedrin/sanhedrin_106.html.

925.Babylonian Talmud: *Tractate Sanhedrin, Folio 106b, at n.6,* Sanhedrin Translated into English with Notes, Glossary and Indices Chapters I - VI by Jacob Shachter, Chapters VII - XI by H. Freedman, B.A., Ph.D., Under the Editorship of Rabbi Dr I. Epstein B.A., Ph.D., D. Lit. (1961), *available at* http://www.come-and-hear.com/sanhedrin/sanhedrin_106.html.

926.Elizabeth Dilling, *The Jewish Religion, Its Influence Today* (1963), *at* http://www.come-and-hear.com/dilling/chapt03.html#T159.

927.The scholars listed as contributing to the Jewish Encyclopedia entry for *Balaam* are: Morris Jastrow, Jr., Ph.D., Professor of Semitic Languages, University of Pennsylvania; Ira Maurice Price, Ph.D., LL.D., Professor of Semitic Languages and Literature, University of Chicago; Marcus Jastrow, Ph.D., Rabbi Emeritus of the Congregation Rodef Shalom, Philadelphia; H. M. Speaker, Gratz College; John Dyneley Prince, Ph.D., Professor of Semitic Languages, New York University; Dr. S. Mühsam, Chief Rabbi of Gratz, Austria; Kaufmann Kohler, Ph.D., Rabbi Emeritus of Temple Beth-El, New York, President of the Hebrew Union College.

928.Jewish Encyclopedia, *Jesus of Nazareth,* *available at* http://www.jewishencyclopedia.com/view.jsp?artid=254&letter=J&search=jesus (last visited on March 10, 2010).

929.Babylonian Talmud: *Tractate Sanhedrin, Folio 106a*, Sanhedrin Translated into English with Notes, Glossary and Indices Chapters I - VI by Jacob Shachter, Chapters VII - XI by H. Freedman, B.A., Ph.D., Under the Editorship of Rabbi Dr I. Epstein B.A., Ph.D., D. Lit. (1961), *available at* http://www.come-and-hear.com/sanhedrin/sanhedrin_106.html.

930.Babylonian Talmud: *Tractate Sanhedrin, Folio 106a, at n.42*, Sanhedrin Translated into English with Notes, Glossary and Indices Chapters I - VI by Jacob Shachter, Chapters VII - XI by H. Freedman, B.A., Ph.D., Under the Editorship of Rabbi Dr I. Epstein B.A., Ph.D., D. Lit. (1961), *available at* http://www.come-and-hear.com/sanhedrin/sanhedrin_106.html.

931.Babylonian Talmud: *Tractate Gittin, Folio 57a*, Gittin Translated into English with Notes, Glossary and Indices By Maurice Simon, M.A. Under the Editorship of Rabbi Dr. I. Epstein B.A., Ph.D., D. Lit. (1961), *available at* http://www.come-and-hear.com/gittin/gittin_57.html.

932.Jewish Encyclopedia, *Balaam,* *available at* http://www.jewishencyclopedia.com/view.jsp?artid=161&letter=B (last visited on March 10, 2010).

933.Babylonian Talmud: *Tractate Gittin, Folio 57a*, Gittin Translated into English with Notes, Glossary and Indices By Maurice Simon, M.A. Under the Editorship of Rabbi Dr. I. Epstein B.A., Ph.D., D. Lit. (1961), *available at* http://www.come-and-hear.com/gittin/gittin_57.html.

934. Babylonian Talmud: *Tractate Gittin, Folio 57a, at n.3,* Gittin Translated into English with Notes, Glossary and Indices By Maurice Simon, M.A. Under the Editorship of Rabbi Dr. I. Epstein B.A., Ph.D., D. Lit. (1961), *available at* http://www.come-and-hear.com/gittin/gittin_57.html.

935. Babylonian Talmud: *Tractate Sanhedrin, Folio 106a,* Sanhedrin Translated into English with Notes, Glossary and Indices Chapters I - VI by Jacob Shachter, Chapters VII - XI by H. Freedman, B.A., Ph.D., Under the Editorship of Rabbi Dr I. Epstein B.A., Ph.D., D. Lit. (1961), *available at* http://www.come-and-hear.com/sanhedrin/sanhedrin_106.html.

936. Babylonian Talmud: *Tractate Sanhedrin, Folio 106a, at n.11,* Sanhedrin Translated into English with Notes, Glossary and Indices Chapters I - VI by Jacob Shachter, Chapters VII - XI by H. Freedman, B.A., Ph.D., Under the Editorship of Rabbi Dr I. Epstein B.A., Ph.D., D. Lit. (1961), *available at* http://www.come-and-hear.com/sanhedrin/sanhedrin_106.html.

937. The Jewish Encyclopedia, Vol. VII, *Jesus* (1901-1906), *available at* http://www.come-and-hear.com/je/je_170.html#E278.

938. Babylonian Talmud: *Tractate Sanhedrin, Folio 57b,* Sanhedrin Translated into English with Notes, Glossary and Indices Chapters I - VI by Jacob Shachter, Chapters VII - XI by H. Freedman, B.A., Ph.D., Under the Editorship of Rabbi Dr I. Epstein B.A., Ph.D., D. Lit. (1961), *available at* http://www.come-and-hear.com/sanhedrin/sanhedrin_57.html.

939. Babylonian Talmud: *Tractate Sanhedrin, Folio 57b,* Sanhedrin Translated into English with Notes, Glossary and Indices Chapters I - VI by Jacob Shachter, Chapters VII - XI by H. Freedman, B.A., Ph.D., Under the Editorship of Rabbi Dr I. Epstein B.A., Ph.D., D. Lit. (1961), *available at* http://www.come-and-hear.com/sanhedrin/sanhedrin_57.html.

940. Babylonian Talmud: *Tractate Sanhedrin, Folio 57b,* at n.33, Sanhedrin Translated into English with Notes, Glossary and Indices Chapters I - VI by Jacob Shachter, Chapters VII - XI by H. Freedman, B.A., Ph.D., Under the Editorship of Rabbi Dr I. Epstein B.A., Ph.D., D. Lit. (1961), *available at* http://www.come-and-hear.com/sanhedrin/sanhedrin_57.html.

941. Talmud, *Tractate Sanhedrin, Folio 100b,* n.6 (1961), *available at* http://www.come-and-hear.com/sanhedrin/sanhedrin_100.html (emphasis added).

942. Babylonian Talmud: *Tractate Sanhedrin, Folio 37a,* Sanhedrin Translated into English with Notes, Glossary and Indices Chapters I - VI by Jacob Shachter, Chapters VII - XI by H. Freedman, B.A., Ph.D., Under the Editorship of Rabbi Dr I. Epstein B.A., Ph.D., D. Lit. (1961), *available at* http://www.come-and-hear.com/sanhedrin/sanhedrin_37.html.

943. Michael Hoffman, *Judaism Discovered,* at 196 (2008).

944. Babylonian Talmud: *Tractate Sanhedrin, Folio 58b,* Sanhedrin Translated into English with Notes, Glossary and Indices Chapters I - VI by Jacob Shachter, Chapters VII - XI

by H. Freedman, B.A., Ph.D., Under the Editorship of Rabbi Dr I. Epstein B.A., Ph.D., D. Lit. (1961), *available at* http://www.come-and-hear.com/sanhedrin/sanhedrin_58.html.

945.Babylonian Talmud: *Tractate Sanhedrin, Folio 58b*, Sanhedrin Translated into English with Notes, Glossary and Indices Chapters I - VI by Jacob Shachter, Chapters VII - XI by H. Freedman, B.A., Ph.D., Under the Editorship of Rabbi Dr I. Epstein B.A., Ph.D., D. Lit. (1961), *available at* http://www.come-and-hear.com/sanhedrin/sanhedrin_58.html.

946.Carol A. Valentine, *What About Gentiles?*, July 14, 2003 (quoting Rabbi Bar-Chayim, Daat Emet, in turn quoting Rabbi Kook, Orot Yisrael, chapter 5, article 10 (page 156)) (emphasis in original), *at* http://www.come-and-hear.com/editor/gentile.html.

947.Israel Shahak, Jewish History, Jewish Religion: The Weight of Two Thousand Years (1994), *available at* http://www.biblebelievers.org.au/jewhis2.htm#Prejudice%20and%20Prevarication.

948.Evangelicals and Catholics Together, The Christian Mission in the Third Millennium, http://www.leaderu.com/ftissues/ft9405/articles/mission.html (web address current as of October 27, 2005).

949.Evangelicals and Catholics Together, The Christian Mission in the Third Millennium, http://www.leaderu.com/ftissues/ft9405/articles/mission.html (web address current as of October 27, 2005).

950.Evangelicals and Catholics Together, The Christian Mission in the Third Millennium, http://www.leaderu.com/ftissues/ft9405/articles/mission.html (web address current as of October 27, 2005).

951.Evangelicals and Catholics Together, The Christian Mission in the Third Millennium, http://www.leaderu.com/ftissues/ft9405/articles/mission.html (web address current as of October 27, 2005).

952.Evangelicals and Catholics Together, The Christian Mission in the Third Millennium, http://www.leaderu.com/ftissues/ft9405/articles/mission.html (web address current as of October 27, 2005).

953.Statement by Protestant Signers to ECT, January 19, 1995, http://www.leaderu.com/ect/ect2.html (web address current as of November 11, 2005).

954.The Gift of Salvation, http://www.firstthings.com/ftissues/ft9801/articles/gift.html (web address current as of November 7, 2005).

955.John Robbins, The Gift of Salvation Show, Healing the Wound, http://www.the-highway.com/robbins_show.html (web address current as of October 27, 2005).

956.John Robbins, The Gift of Salvation Show, Healing the Wound, http://www.the-highway.com/robbins_show.html (web address current as of October 27, 2005).

957.John Robbins, The Gift of Salvation Show, Healing the Wound, http://www.the-highway.com/robbins_show.html (web address current as of October 27, 2005).

958.John Robbins, The Gift of Salvation Show, Healing the Wound, http://www.the-highway.com/robbins_show.html (web address current as of October 27, 2005).

959.Richard Bennett, The Gift of Salvation: (ECT 11) - The Lie Documented, http://www.bereanbeacon.org/articles/gift_of_salvation.htm (web address current as of November 5, 2005).

960.Richard Bennett, The Gift of Salvation: (ECT 11) - The Lie Documented, http://www.bereanbeacon.org/articles/gift_of_salvation.htm (web address current as of November 5, 2005).

961.Richard Bennett, The Gift of Salvation: (ECT 11) - The Lie Documented, http://www.bereanbeacon.org/articles/gift_of_salvation.htm (web address current as of November 5, 2005).

962.Richard Bennett, The Gift of Salvation: (ECT 11) - The Lie Documented, http://www.bereanbeacon.org/articles/gift_of_salvation.htm (web address current as of November 5, 2005).

963.Richard Bennett, The Gift of Salvation: (ECT 11) - The Lie Documented, http://www.bereanbeacon.org/articles/gift_of_salvation.htm (web address current as of November 5, 2005).

964.Richard Bennett, The Gift of Salvation: (ECT 11) - The Lie Documented, http://www.bereanbeacon.org/articles/gift_of_salvation.htm (web address current as of November 5, 2005).

965.John Robbins, The Gift of Salvation Show, Healing the Wound, http://www.the-highway.com/robbins_show.html (web address current as of October 27, 2005).

966.John Robbins, The Gift of Salvation Show, Healing the Wound, http://www.the-highway.com/robbins_show.html (web address current as of October 27, 2005).

967.John Robbins, The Gift of Salvation Show, Healing the Wound, http://www.the-highway.com/robbins_show.html (web address current as of October 27, 2005).

968.The Gift of Salvation, http://www.firstthings.com/ftissues/ft9801/articles/gift.html (web address current as of November 7, 2005).

CPSIA information can be obtained at www.ICGtesting.com
Printed in the USA
BVOW05s1937081213

338521BV00005B/170/P